Brief Contents

LIST OF APPLIC...

PLANNING FOR OBJECTS

Dedicated to Rochelle, Matthew,
Jeremy, and David Bronson.

PROGRAM DEVELOPMENT and DESIGN USING C++

Third Edition

Gary J. Bronson
Fairleigh Dickinson University

Contributing Editor: R. Kenneth Walter
Weber State University

THOMSON

COURSE TECHNOLOGY

Australia • Canada • Mexico • Singapore • Spain • United Kingdom • United States

THOMSON
COURSE TECHNOLOGY

Program Development and Design Using C++
Third Edition

by Gary J. Bronson

Senior Product Manager:
Alyssa Pratt

Associate Product Manager:
Mirella Misiaszek

Compositor:
Pre-Press Company

Executive Editor:
Mac Mendelsohn

Editorial Assistant:
Jennifer Smith

Proofreader:
John Bosco

Production Editor:
Kelly Robinson

Senior Manufacturing
Coordinator:
Trevor Kallop

Copyeditor:
Jane Pedicini

Senior Marketing Manager:
Karen Seitz

Cover Designer
Steve Deschesne

Indexer:
Alexandra Nickerson

For more information, contact
Thomson Course Technology
25 Thomson Place, Boston,
Massachusetts, 02210.
Or find us on the World Wide Web at: www.course.com

Disclaimer
Thomson Course Technology reserves the right to revise this publication and make changes from time
to time in its content without notice.

ISBN 0-619-21677-8

Contents

Chapter 3   Assignment, Formatting, and Interactive Input   114

Chapter 13 C-Strings   713

Chapter 14 Addresses, Pointers, and Arrays   742

Preface

As with the earlier editions of this text, this new edition is designed for a first course in computer science (CS1), with an introduction to CS2. The major objectives of this book are to introduce, develop, and reinforce well-organized problem-solving and programming skills, and to present the C++ language as a powerful problem-solving tool. Students should be familiar with fundamental algebra, but no other prerequisites are assumed.

For many people, employing the full potential of a hybrid language such as C++, which contains both procedural and object-oriented features, requires a gradual refinement of programming skills from a procedural to an object orientation. This basic approach continues to form the fundamental structure of this new third edition. It was, as were its predecessors, written with the intention of making the adjustment to a complete, object-oriented approach as rapidly as possible within the confines of a pedagogically sound and achievable progression.[1]

The changes, however, from the prior edition are significant. First, all programs now make use of the ANSI/ISO C++ `iostream` library and `namespace` mechanism. Additionally, due to the increasing importance of generic programming and the Standard Template Library (STL), a complete chapter (16) is devoted to the STL. In addition, STL classes and algorithms are discussed wherever these topics are appropriate. Thus, STL algorithms for searching and sorting are presented in Section 12.4; the STL vector class is presented in Section 12.6.

In a similar manner, exception handling is now presented in its own section (Section 7.1), and practical applications of exception handling are presented throughout the text. Thus, exception handling is first presented in Section 7.1 as an alternative to the conventional error handling technique using functions, and then is used in both Sections 11.3 (File Checking) and 17.4 (Data Validation).

Although this text employs the standard progression from a procedural to full object-oriented implementation, there is still a widely varying opinion within the C++ community as to how much procedural programming should be learned before serious object-oriented programming is attempted. As a practical matter, this question is phrased as, "Should object-oriented programming be presented towards the middle or towards the end of an introductory course?"

---

[1] For those who wish to start immediately with an objects first orientation, please see my textbook *Object-Oriented Design and Development Using C++*, 0-619-15966-9, published by Thomson Course Technology.

My personal answer to this question, which is a unique feature of this textbook, is based on my fundamental belief that ultimately college level textbooks do not teach students—professors teach students. As such, all of my textbooks have been written with the intent of making them a "supporting actor" to the "leading role" belonging to the professor. In practical terms, this means that the textbook must be sufficiently flexible so that those professors who subscribe to my basic approach can still mold the text to their individual preference of topic presentation. This is achieved in the following way.

Chapter 1 presents computer literacy material for those who require this background. And then Part I of the text presents the basic procedural syntax, flow control, and modularity topics that are needed for an effective presentation of C++'s object features. Included within each procedural chapter are optional Planning for Objects sections, which can be used to help students begin the mental shift to object-oriented development and design techniques.

Once Part I is completed, Parts II and III on object-oriented programming and data structures, respectively, are *interchangeable*. Thus, if you want to present object-oriented programming early, you would follow a Part I–Part II–Part III progression. On the other hand, if you want to continue with additional procedural programming reinforcement and present object-oriented programming toward the end of the course, you would use the sequence Part I–Part III–Part II. In either case, the material on files presented in Chapter 11 can be introduced at any time after Part I.

The flexibility of introducing topics (within the overall context of procedural programming) abstract data types, and inheritance is illustrated by the following topic dependency chart on the next page.

In the process of teaching the C++ programming language, this book presents a variety of essential computer science topics, including:

- An extensive introduction to Unified Modeling Language (UML), with UML diagrams used throughout the text to present programming solutions.

- A thorough introduction to the Standard Template Library, with STL applications integrated throughout the text.

- An introduction to exception handling, with exception handling applications also presented within various sections, where appropriate.

- Focus on Problem Solving sections that introduce and reinforce sound design and development principles.

- A thorough explanation of input data validation techniques.

Every C++ program in this text has been successfully compiled, run, and tested using Microsoft® Visual C++ .NET. These programs are drawn from everyday experience, and business and technical fields. As such, the instructor may choose applications that match students' experience or for a particular course emphasis. Students can use the source code provided with the text (available online at *www.course.com*) to experiment with and extend the chapter programs. They will also use this source code in the end-of-section exercises.

Finally, an expanded set of appendices is provided. These include appendices on operator precedence, ASCII codes, program entry and compilation, I/O redirection, floating-point number storage, and additional C++ features.

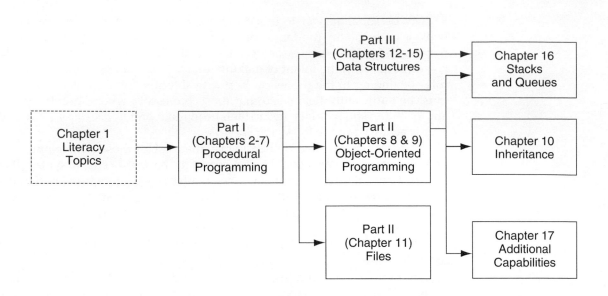

DISTINCTIVE FEATURES OF THIS BOOK

Writing Style. The one thing that I have found most important in my own teaching is that *regardless of what is written about, it must be written so that students can read it*. Once the professor sets the stage, the selected textbook must encourage, nurture, and assist the student in acquiring and "owning" the material presented in class. My primary purpose, and one of the distinctive features of this book, was to write this book for the student. Thus, first and foremost, I feel the writing style used to convey the presented concepts is an important and distinctive aspect of the text.

Modularity. To produce readable and maintainable code, modularity is essential. C++ by its nature is a modular language. Thus, the connection between C++ functions and modules is made early in the text, in Section 2.1, and sustained throughout the book. The idea of parameters passing into modules is also covered early using C++'s function library in Section 3.3. In this manner, students are introduced to functions and arguments passing as a natural technique of programming. This modular emphasis is both continued and strengthened by the object-oriented programming techniques introduced in Chapter 8.

Software Engineering. Rather than simply introduce students to programming in C++, this text introduces students to the fundamentals of software engineering, from both a procedural and object-oriented viewpoint. This begins in Section 1.3 with the introduction of the software development cycle. This is immediately followed by an introduction to algorithms and the first Planning for Objects section. The main theme of the text, which is a more formal emphasis on problem-solving techniques, is presented in Chapter 2. Here the importance of understanding a problem and selecting and refining the solution is highlighted, and the relationship between analysis, design, coding, and testing is introduced. Additionally, the Planning for Objects sections both introduce and reinforce the concepts and techniques needed for an object-oriented design solution.

PEDAGOGICAL FEATURES

To facilitate the goal of making C++ accessible as a first-level course, the following pedagogical features have been incorporated into the text.

Planning for Objects. These are a set of six sections that provide a self-contained and brief "mini-course" introduction to object-oriented concepts and design techniques. These sections can be included within the phase of a course or used as enrichment material during the object-oriented phase of your course.

End of Section Exercises. Every section in the book contains numerous and diverse skill-builder and programming exercises. Additionally, solutions to selected odd-numbered exercises are provided in an appendix.

Focus on Problem Solving. Starting with Chapter 2, each chapter contains a Focus on Problem Solving section with an average of two complete problems per chapter. Each application is used to demonstrate effective problem solving within the context of a complete program solution. This is done for both procedural and object-oriented designs.

Pseudocode Descriptions. Pseudocode is stressed throughout the text. Flowchart symbols are described, but are only used when visually presenting flow-of-control constructs.

Common Programming Errors and Chapter Review. Each chapter ends with a section on common programming errors, a glossary of key terms introduced in the chapter, a review of the main topics covered in the chapter, and a set of chapter exercises.

Closer Look Sections. Given the many different emphases that can be applied when teaching C++, a number of enrichment sections have been included. These allow you to provide different emphases with different students or in different C++ classes.

Point of Information Boxes. These are a set of shaded boxes that provide additional brief clarification of commonly used and/or difficult concepts, such as abstraction, lvalues and rvalues, values versus identities, flags, deques, and stream formatting.

Programming Notes. These are a set of shaded boxes that highlight alternative and advanced programming techniques.

Bit of Background Boxes. To make the study of computer science even more rewarding and to provide breadth material, these notes are carefully placed throughout the book. They supplement the technical material with historical, biographical, and other interesting factual asides.

SUPPLEMENTAL MATERIALS

The following supplemental materials are available when this book is used in a classroom setting.

Electronic Instructor's Manual. The Instructor's Manual that accompanies this textbook includes:

- Additional instructional material to assist in class preparation, including suggestions for lecture topics.
- Solutions to all the end-of-chapter materials, including the Programming Exercises.

ExamView®. This textbook is accompanied by ExamView, a powerful testing software package that allows instructors to create and administer printed, computer (LAN-based), and Internet exams. ExamView includes hundreds of questions that correspond to the topics covered in this text, enabling students to generate detailed study guides that include page references for further review. These computer-based and Internet-testing components allow students to take exams at their computers and save the instructor time, because each exam is graded automatically.

PowerPoint Presentations. This book comes with Microsoft PowerPoint® slides for each chapter. These are included as a teaching aid for classroom presentations, either to make available to students on the network for chapter review, or to be printed for classroom distribution. Instructors can add their own slides for additional topics that they introduce to the class.

Distance Learning. Thomson Course Technology is proud to present online courses in WebCT and Blackboard to provide the most complete and dynamic learning experience possible. When you add online content to one of your courses, you're adding a lot: Topic Reviews, Practice Tests, Review Questions, Assignments, PowerPoint presentations, and most of all, a gateway to the 21st century's most important information resource. For more information on how to bring distance learning to your course, contact your local Thomson Course Technology sales representative.

Source Code. The source code for this text is available at *www.course.com* and is also available on the Teaching Tools CD-ROM.

Solution Files. The solution files for all programming exercises are available at *www.course.com*, and are also available on the Teaching Tools CD-ROM.

Acknowledgments

The writing of this third edition is a direct result of the success (and limitations) of the first two editions. In this regard, my most heartfelt acknowledgment and appreciation is to the instructors and students who found these editions to be of service to them in their respective quests to teach and learn C++.

Once a third edition was planned, its completion depended on the encouragement, skills, and efforts of many other people. For this I especially want to thank the staff of Thomson Course Technology for their many contributions. First and foremost, these include my Executive Editor, Mac Mendelsohn, and Senior Product Manager, Alyssa Pratt. I would also like to thank Nicole Ashton for providing the solution files for the text.

Finally, the task of turning the final manuscript into a textbook again required a dedicated production staff. For this I especially want to thank Kelly Robinson, Production Editor; John Bosco, proofreader; and the compositor, Pre-Press Company. Their dedication, attention to detail, and high standards have helped immensely to improve the quality of this edition. Almost from the moment the book moved to the production stage these individuals seemed to take personal ownership of the text, and I am very grateful to them.

Special thanks also goes to Janie Schwark, Academic Product Manager of Developer Tools at Microsoft, for providing invaluable support and product information, and to Dick Grant at Seminole Community College for his thoughtful review of the text. I also gratefully acknowledge the direct encouragement and support provided by my Dean, Dr. David Steele, and my Chairperson, Dr. Paul Yoon. Without their support, this text could not have been written.

Finally, I deeply appreciate the patience, understanding, and love provided by my wife, friend, and partner, Rochelle.

Gary Bronson
2005

1

Introduction to Computers and Programming

1.1 COMPUTER SCIENCE

Our world is now almost totally dependent on and driven by the technology of gathering, processing, communicating, and using data. This technology has become a central element of our endeavors in art, science, literature, business, and engineering. It pervades our daily life, affecting transportation, medical care, grocery purchases, and almost every other aspect of our daily activities. In more formal terms, this technology both constitutes and defines what is now called the **Information Age**. The engines that drive this vast, technology-centered culture are computers. The study of these machines, including their theoretical and practical development and application, in both direct and related areas, is referred to as **computer science**.

Because computer science is a scientific discipline, it has much in common with other areas of natural and physical science and can be approached at many different levels. The simplest level is **computer literacy**. People who are computer literate have some knowledge of computers, including their history and their possible applications (such as word processors, spreadsheet programs, the Internet, and e-mail). Being computer literate, however, does not make you a computer scientist.

Rather than being merely a user of computer programs, a computer scientist is a problem solver who develops solutions to computer-related problems, both theoretical and practical, in the areas of:

- Algorithm development
- Class development and design
- Programming languages
- Data structures
- Data collection, storage, and retrieval

1

- Operating systems
- Computer architecture
- Computer applications
- Social, ethical, and professional conduct and considerations

Computer scientists solve problems using the scientific method, which is common to all sciences. The **scientific method** is a research approach in which a problem is identified, relevant data are obtained, and a hypothesis is formulated from the data and then tested in a controlled and repeatable manner. Additionally, computer science requires a foundation in mathematics, model development, designing and developing theoretical and workable systems, and human communication. It also may require knowledge of other disciplines for which applications are to be developed. These additional disciplines include biology, medicine, physics, business, law, economics, geology, education, communications, psychology, robotics, image recognition, artificial intelligence, and all areas of engineering and scientific interest.

Although this all might sound daunting at first, every journey must start with the first step. It is the intention of this text to start you on your journey into computer science by focusing on fundamental concepts in the following five areas:

- Introduction to computer architecture
- The C++ programming language
- Algorithm development
- Class development and design
- Introduction to data structures

We begin this journey by considering the evolution of computers in this section, and programming languages and the development of C++ in Section 1.2.

A Brief History of Computers

The process of using a machine to add and subtract is almost as old as recorded history. The earliest such device was the abacus—a device as common in China today as handheld calculators are in the United States. Both of these machines, however, require direct human involvement to be used. To add two numbers with an abacus requires the movement of beads on the device, while adding two numbers with a calculator requires that the operator push both the numbers and the addition operator keys.

The first recorded attempt at creating a programmable computing machine was by Charles Babbage in England in 1822 (see Figure 1.1). Ada Byron, the daughter of the poet Lord Byron, developed a set of instructions that could, if the machine were ever built, be used to operate the machine. Although this mechanical machine, which Babbage called an analytical engine, was not successfully built in his lifetime, the concept of a programmable machine remained. It was partly realized in 1937 at Iowa State University by Dr. John V. Atanasoff and a graduate student named Clifford Berry, using electronic components. The machine was known as the ABC, which stood for Atanasoff-Berry Computer. This computer manipulated binary numbers, but required a human operator to manipulate external wiring in order to perform the desired operations. Thus, the goal of internally storing a replaceable set of instructions had still not been achieved.

The outbreak of World War II led to a more concentrated development of the computer, beginning in late 1939. One of the pioneers of this work was Dr. John W. Mauchly of the Moore School of Engineering at the University of Pennsylvania.

A BIT OF BACKGROUND

Binary ABC

In the 1930s, Dr. John V. Atanasoff struggled for several years over the design of a computing machine to help his Iowa State University graduate students solve complex equations. He considered building a machine based on binary numbers—the most natural system to use with electromechanical equipment that had one of two easily recognizable states, on and off—but feared people would not use a machine that was not based upon the familiar and comfortable decimal system. Finally, on a cold evening at a roadhouse in Illinois in 1937, he determined that it had to be done the simplest and least expensive way, with binary digits (bits). Over the next two years he and graduate student Clifford Berry built the first electronic digital computer, called the *ABC* (for Atanasoff-Berry Computer). Since that time the vast majority of computers have been binary machines.

FIGURE 1.1   Charles Babbage's Analytical Engine

A BIT OF BACKGROUND

The "Turing Machine"

In the 1930s and 1940s, Alan Mathison Turing (1912–1954) and others developed a theory that described what a computing machine should be able to do. Turing's theoretical machine, known as the Turing Machine, contains the minimum set of operations for solving programming problems. Turing had hoped to prove that all problems could be solved by a set of instructions given to such a hypothetical computer.

What he succeeded in proving was that some problems cannot be solved by *any* machine, just as some problems cannot be solved by any person.

Alan Turing's work formed the foundation of computer theory before the first electronic computer was built. His contributions to the team that developed the critical code-breaking computers during World War II led directly to the practical implementation of his theories.

Dr. Mauchly, who had visited Dr. Atanasoff and seen his ABC machine, began working with J. Presper Eckert in 1939 on a computer called ENIAC (for Electrical Numerical Integrator and Computer). Funding for this project was provided by the U.S. government. One of the early functions performed by this machine was the calculation of trajectories for ammunition fired from large guns. When completed in 1946, ENIAC contained 18,000 vacuum tubes, weighed approximately 30 tons, and could perform 5,000 additions or 360 multiplications in one second (see Figure 1.2).

FIGURE 1.2   ENIAC (Courtesy IBM Archives)

While work was progressing on ENIAC using vacuum tubes, work on a computer named the Mark I was being done at Harvard University using mechanical relay switches (see Figure 1.3). The Mark I was completed in 1944, but could only perform six multiplications in one second. Both of these machines, however, like the Atanasoff-Berry computer, required external wiring to perform the desired operations.

The final goal of a stored program computer, where instructions as well as data are stored internally on the machine, was achieved at Cambridge University in England on May 6, 1949, with the successful operation of the EDSAC (Electronic Delayed Storage Automatic Computer). In addition to performing calculations, the EDSAC could store both data and the instructions that directed the computer's operation. The EDSAC incorporated a form of memory, developed by John Von Neumann, that allowed it to retrieve an instruction and then retrieve the data needed to carry out the instruction. This same design and operating principle is still used by the majority of computers manufactured today. The only things that have significantly changed are the sizes and speeds of the components used to make a computer, and the type of programs that are stored in it. Collectively, the components used to make a computer are referred to as hardware, while the programs are known as software.

FIGURE 1.3   Mark I

Computer Hardware

Computers are constructed from physical components referred to as **hardware**. The purpose of this hardware is to facilitate the storage and processing of data under the direction of a stored program. If computer hardware could store data using the same symbols that humans do, the number 126, for example, would be stored using the symbols 1, 2, and 6. Similarly, the letter that we recognize as "A" would be stored using this same symbol. Unfortunately, a computer's internal components require a different number and letter representation. It is worthwhile to understand why computers cannot use our symbols and then see how numbers are represented within the machine. This will make it easier to understand the actual parts of a computer used to store and process this data.

Bits and Bytes

The smallest and most basic data item in a computer is a **bit**. Physically, a bit is really a switch that can be either open or closed. The convention we will follow is that the open position is represented by 0 and the closed position by 1.[1]

A single bit that can represent the values 0 and 1, by itself, has limited usefulness. All computers, therefore, group a set number of bits together both for storage and transmission. The grouping of eight bits to form a larger unit is an almost universal computer standard, and is referred to as a **byte**. A single byte, where each of the eight bits is either 0 or 1, can represent any one of 256 distinct patterns. These consist of the pattern 00000000 (all eight switches open) to the pattern 11111111 (all eight switches closed) and all possible combinations of 0s and 1s in between. Each of these patterns can be used to represent a letter of the alphabet, other single characters (a dollar sign, comma, etc.), a single digit, or numbers containing more than one digit. The collections of patterns consisting of 0s and 1s used to represent letters, single digits, and other single characters are called **character codes** (two such codes, ASCII and Unicode, are presented in Section 2.1).

Character codes are extremely useful for such items as names and addresses, and any text that must be processed. They are almost never used, however, for arithmetic data. There are two reasons for this. First, converting a decimal number into a character code requires an individual code for each digit. For large numbers, this can waste a computer's memory space. The more basic reason, however, is that the decimal numbering system, which is based on the number 10, is inherently not supported by a computer's internal hardware. Recall that a bit, which is a computer's basic memory component, can take on only one of two possible states, open and closed, which is represented as a 0 and a 1. This would indicate that a numbering system based on these two states makes more sense, and in fact, this is the case. Section 1.6 presents the most commonly used base two numbering system.

The idea of a computer's internal numbering system differing from our decimal system should not come as a surprise. For example, you are probably already familiar with two other numbering systems, and can easily recognize the following:

Roman numeral: XIV

hash mark system: //// //// ////

Components

All computers, from large super computers costing millions of dollars to smaller desktop personal computers costing hundreds of dollars, must perform a minimum set of tasks and provide the capability to:

1. Accept input, both data and instructions
2. Display output, both textual and numerical
3. Store data and instructions
4. Perform arithmetic and logic operations on either the input or stored data
5. Monitor, control, and direct the overall operation and sequencing of the system

Figure 1.4 illustrates the computer components that support these capabilities and that collectively form a computer's hardware.

FIGURE 1.4 Basic Hardware Units of a Computer

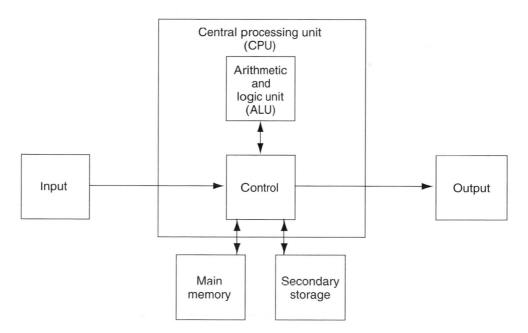

Main Memory Unit This unit stores both data and instructions as a sequence of bytes. A program must reside in main memory if it is to operate the computer. Main memories combine one or more bytes into a single unit, referred to as a word. Although larger word sizes facilitate an increase in overall speed and capacity, this increase is achieved by an increase in the computer's complexity.

Early personal computers (PCs), such as the Apple IIe and Commodore machines, internally stored and transmitted words consisting of single bytes. The first IBM PCs used word sizes consisting of two bytes, while more current Pentium-based PCs store and process words consisting of four bytes each.

The arrangement of words in a computer's memory can be compared to the arrangement of suites in a large hotel, where each suite is made up of rooms of the same size. Just as each suite has a unique room number that allow patrons to locate and identify it, each word in a computer's memory has a unique numerical address. Like room numbers, memory addresses are always positive unsigned whole numbers that are used for location and identification purposes. Also, like hotel rooms with connecting doors that form larger suites, memory locations can be combined to form larger units to accommodate different-sized data types.

As a physical device, main memories are constructed as **RAM**, which is an acronym for "Random Access Memory." This means that every section of memory can be accessed randomly as quickly as any other section. Main memory is also **volatile**, which means that whatever is stored in it is lost when the computer's power is turned off. Your programs and data are always stored in RAM when your program is being executed. The size of the computer's RAM is usually specified in terms of how many bytes of RAM are available to the user. PC memories currently start at 512 million bytes (denoted as Megabytes or MB).

A second type of memory is **ROM**, which is an acronym for "Read Only Memory." ROM is **nonvolatile**; its contents are not lost when the power goes off. As such, ROM always contains fundamental instructions that cannot be lost or changed by the casual computer user. These instructions include those necessary for starting the computer's operation when the power is first turned on, and for holding any other instructions the manufacturer requires to be permanently accessible when the computer is operating.

Central Processing Unit (CPU)   This unit consists of two essential sub-units, the **control unit** and the **arithmetic and logic unit (ALU)**. The control unit directs and monitors the overall operation of the computer. It keeps track of where in memory the next instruction resides, issues the signals needed to both read data from and write data to other units in the system, and executes all instructions. The ALU performs all of the computations, such as addition, subtraction, comparisons, and so on, that a computer provides.

The CPU is the central element of a computer and its most expensive part. Currently CPUs are constructed as a single microchip, which is referred to as a **microprocessor**. Figure 1.5 illustrates the approximate size and internal structure of a state-of-the-art microprocessor chip used in current notebook computers. Also shown are the pins on the outside of the package that is used to house the chip.

Input/Output (I/O) Unit   This unit provides access to the computer, allowing it to input and output data. It is the interface to which peripheral devices such as keyboards, console screens, and printers are attached.

FIGURE 1.5   Internal Picture of a Pentium Microprocessor Chip

Secondary Storage   Because main RAM memory in large quantities is still relatively expensive and volatile, it is not practical as a permanent storage area for programs and data. Secondary or auxiliary storage devices are used for this purpose. Although data have been stored on punched cards, paper tape, and other media in the past, virtually all secondary storage is now done on magnetic tape, magnetic disks, and CD-ROMS.

The surfaces of magnetic tapes and disks are coated with a material that can be magnetized to store data. Current tapes are capable of storing thousands of characters per inch of tape, and a single tape may store up to hundreds of megabytes. Tapes, by nature, are a sequential storage media, which means that they allow data to be written or read in one sequential stream from beginning to end. Should you want to access a block of data in the middle of the tape, all preceding data on the tape must be scanned to find the block. Because of this, tapes are primarily used for mass backup of historical data.

A more convenient method of rapidly accessing stored data is provided by a **direct access storage device (DASD)**, which allows a computer to read or write any one file or program independent of its position on the storage medium. Until the recent advent of the CD, the most popular DASD has been the magnetic disk. A **magnetic hard disk** consists of either a single rigid platter or several platters that spin together on a common spindle. A movable access arm positions the read and write mechanisms over, but not quite touching, the recordable surfaces. Such a configuration is shown in Figure 1.6.

| **FIGURE 1.6** | Internal Structure of a Hard Disk Drive |

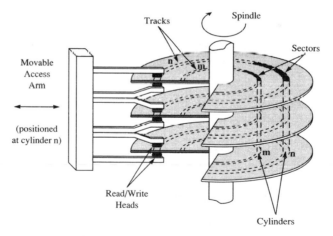

Initially, the most common magnetic disk storage device was the removable **floppy disk**. The most popular size for these is 3.5 inches in diameter, with a capacity of 1.44 megabytes. More recent removable disks, known as Zip disks, have capacities of 250 megabytes, with gigabyte compact discs (**CDs**) currently being the auxiliary storage devices of choice (one gigabyte equals 1000 megabytes).

Concurrent with the vast increase in storage capacity has been an equally significant increase in processing speed and a dramatic decrease in computer size and cost. Computer hardware capabilities that cost over a million dollars in 1950 can now be purchased for less than five hundred dollars. If the same reductions occurred in the automobile industry, for example, a Rolls-Royce could now be purchased for ten dollars! The processing speeds of current computers have also increased by a factor of thousands over their 1950s predecessors, with the computational speeds of current computers being measured in both millions of instructions per second (MIPS) and billions of instructions per second (BIPS). For comparison, Figure 1.7 shows an early desktop IBM PC of the 1980s, while Figure 1.8 illustrates a current IBM notebook computer.

FIGURE 1.7   An Original (1980s) IBM Personal Computer

FIGURE 1.8   A Current IBM Notebook Computer

Exercises 1.1

1. Define the term bit. What values can a bit assume?
2. Define the term byte. How many distinct bit patterns can a byte assume?
3. How is a byte used to represent characters in a computer?
4. Define the term *word*. Give the word sizes for some common computers.
5. What are the two principal parts of the CPU? What is the function of each part?
6. a. What is the difference between RAM and ROM? What do they have in common?
   b. Why is a ROM a random access device?
7. a. What is the input/output unit?
   b. Name three devices that would be connected to the input/output unit.
8. Define secondary storage. Give three examples of secondary storage.
9. What is the difference between sequential storage and direct access storage? What is the advantage of direct access storage?
10. Define a microprocessor. Name three ways microprocessors are used in everyday life.

1.2 PROGRAMMING LANGUAGES

A computer is the same as any other machine constructed of physical components, such as an airplane, automobile, or lawn mower. Like these other machines, a computer must be turned on and then piloted, driven, or controlled to perform its intended task. How this is accomplished is what distinguishes a computer from other types of machinery.

In an automobile, for example, control is provided by the driver, who sits inside and directs the car. In a computer, the controller is a set of instructions, called a program. Formally, a **computer program** is a self-contained set of instructions and data used to operate a computer to produce a specific result. Another term for a program or set of programs is **software**, and we will use both terms interchangeably throughout the text.

The process of developing and writing a program, or software, is called **programming**, and the set of instructions that can be used to construct a program is called a **programming language**. Available programming languages come in a variety of forms and types. Each of these different forms and types was designed to make the programming process easier, to capitalize on a special feature of the hardware, or to meet a special requirement of an application. At a fundamental level, however, all programs must ultimately be converted into a machine language program, which is the only type of program that can actually operate a computer.

Machine Language

An **executable program** is a program that can operate a computer. Such programs are always written as a sequence of binary numbers, which is a computer's internal language, and are also referred to as **machine language programs**. An example of a simple machine language program containing two instructions is:

```
11000000000000000001000000000010
11110000000000000010000000000011
```

Ada Augusta Byron, Countess of Lovelace

Ada Byron, the daughter of the Romantic poet Lord Byron, was a colleague of Charles Babbage, who during the mid-1800s attempted to build a computing machine that he called an analytical engine. It was Ada's task to develop the algorithms—solutions to problems in the form of step-by-step instructions—that would allow the engine to compute the values of mathematical functions. Babbage's machine was not built successfully in his lifetime, primarily because the technology of the time did not allow mechanical parts to be constructed with necessary tolerances. Nonetheless, Ada is recognized as the first computer programmer. She published a collection of notes that established the basis for computer programming; the Ada programming language was named in her honor.

Each sequence of binary numbers that constitutes a machine language instruction consists of, at a minimum, two parts: an instruction part and a data part. The instruction part, which is referred to as the **opcode** (short for operation code) is usually at the beginning of each binary number and tells the computer the operation to be performed, such as add, subtract, multiply, and so on. The remaining part of the number provides information about the data.

Assembly Language

Because each class of computer, such as IBM PCs, Apple Macintoshes, and Hewlett-Packard computers, has its own particular machine language, it is very tedious and time consuming to write machine language programs. One of the first advances in programming was the substitution of word-like symbols, such as ADD, SUB, MUL, for the binary opcodes, and both decimal numbers and labels for memory addresses. For example, in the following set of instructions, word-like symbols are used to add two numbers (referred to as first and second), multiply the result by a third number known as factor, and store the result as answer:

```
LOAD    first
ADD     second
MUL     factor
STORE   answer
```

Programming languages that use this type of symbolic notation are referred to as **assembly languages**. Since computers can only execute machine language programs, this set of assembly language instructions has to be translated into a machine language program before it can be executed by a computer. Programs that convert, or translate, assembly language programs into machine language are known as **assemblers**.

Low- and High-Level Languages

Both machine-level and assembly languages are classified as **low-level languages**. This is because both of these language types use instructions that are directly tied to one type of computer. As such, an assembly language program is limited in that it can only be used with the specific computer type for which the program is written. Such programs do, however, permit using special features of a particular computer type, such as IBM, Apple, or Hewlett-Packard, and generally execute at the fastest speed possible.

In contrast to low-level languages, a **high-level language** uses instructions that resemble human languages, such as English, and can be run on all computers, regardless of manufacturer. Pascal, Visual Basic, C, C++, and Java are all high-level languages. Using C++, the assembly language instructions used in the preceding section to add two numbers and multiply by a third number can be written as:

```
answer = (first + second) * factor;
```

Programs written in a computer language (high or low level) are referred to interchangeably as both **source programs** and **source code**. Once a program is written in a high-level language, it must also, like a low-level assembly program, be translated into the machine language of the computer on which it will be run (see Figure 1.9). This translation can be accomplished in two ways.

FIGURE 1.9 Assembly Programs Must Be Translated

When each statement in a high-level source program is translated individually and executed immediately upon translation, the programming language is called an **interpreted language**, and the program doing the translation is called an **interpreter**.

When all of the statements in a high-level source program are translated as a complete unit before any individual statement is executed, the programming language is called a **compiled language**. In this case, the program doing the translation is called a **compiler**. Both compiled and interpreted versions of a single language can exist, although typically one predominates. For example, although interpreted versions of C++ exist, C++ is predominantly a compiled language.

Figure 1.10 illustrates the relationship between a C++ source code program and its compilation into a machine language executable program. As shown, the source program is entered using an editor program. This is really a word processing program that is part of the development environment supplied by the compiler. It should be understood, however, that entering the code is only begun after an application has been thoroughly analyzed and understood, and the design of the program has been carefully planned. How this is accomplished is explained in the next section.

Translation of the C++ source program into a machine language program begins with the compiler. The output produced by the compiler is called an **object program**, which is a machine language version of the source code. Almost always, your source code will make use of existing preprogrammed code, either code you have written previously or code provided by the compiler. This could include mathematical code for finding a square root, for example, or code that is being reused from another application. Additionally, a large C++ program may be stored in two or more separate program files. In all of these cases, this additional code must be combined with the object program before the program can be executed. It is the task of the **linker** to accomplish this step. The result of the linking process is a completed machine language program, containing all of the code required by your program, which is now ready for execution. The last step in the process is to load this machine language program into the computer's main memory for actual execution.

FIGURE 1.10   Creating an Executable C++ Program

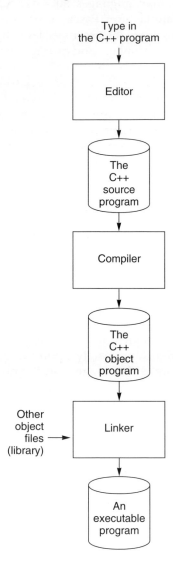

Procedural and Object Orientations

High-level languages are further classified as either procedural or object-oriented. In a **procedural language**, the available instructions are only used to create self-contained units referred to as **procedures**. The purpose of a procedure is to accept data as input and transform the data in some manner to produce a specific result as an output. Each computer language tends to refer to its procedures by a different name. For example, in FORTRAN, the term subprogram is used to denote a procedure; in C, a procedure is referred to as a function; in Java, a procedure is referred to as a method; while in C++, the terms method and function are both used. Until the mid-1990s, the majority of high-level languages were procedural.

Currently, a second approach, object orientation, has taken center stage. One of the motivations for **object-oriented languages** was the development of graphical screens and support for graphical user interfaces (GUIs) capable of displaying multiple windows containing both graphical shapes and text. In such an environment, each window on the screen can conveniently be considered an object with associated characteristics, such as color, position, and size. Using an object-oriented approach, a program must first define the objects it will be manipulating, which includes describing both the general characteristics of the objects themselves and specific units to manipulate them, such as changing size and position and transferring data between objects. Equally important is the fact that object-oriented languages tend to more easily support reusing existing code, which removes the necessity for revalidating and retesting new or modified code. C++, which is classified as an object-oriented language, contains features found in both procedural and object-oriented languages. In this text we will primarily design, develop, and present object-oriented code, which is how the majority of current C++ programs are written. Because object-oriented C++ code always contains some procedural code, and many extremely simple C++ programs are written using only procedural code, this type of code is also extensively presented.

Application and System Software

Two logical categories of computer programs are application software and system software. **Application software** consists of programs written to perform particular tasks required by the users. Most of the examples in this book would be considered application software.

System software is the collection of programs that must be readily available to any computer system to enable the computer to operate. In the early computer environments of the 1950s and 1960s, a user had to initially load the system software by hand to prepare the computer to do anything. This was done with rows of switches on a front panel. Those initial hand-entered commands were said to **boot** the computer, a term derived from the expression "pulling oneself up by the boot-straps." Today, the so-called **bootstrap loader** is internally contained in read-only memory (ROM) and is a permanent, automatically executed component of the computer's system software.

Collectively, the set of system programs used to operate and control a computer are called the **operating system**. Tasks handled by modern operating systems include memory management; allocation of CPU time; control of input and output units such as the keyboard, screen, and printers; and the management of all secondary storage devices. Many operating systems handle very large programs, as well as multiple users concurrently, by dividing programs into segments that are moved between the disk and memory as needed. Such operating systems permit more than one user to run a program on the computer, which gives each user the impression that the computer and peripherals are his or hers alone. This is referred to as a **multiuser** system. Additionally, many operating systems, including most windowed environments, permit each user to run multiple programs. Such operating systems are referred to as both **multiprogrammed** and **multitasking** systems.

The Development of C++

At a very basic level, the purpose of almost all application programs is to process data to produce one or more specific results. In a procedural language, a program is constructed from sets of instructions, with each set referred to as a procedure, as noted previously. Effectively, each procedure moves the data one step closer to the final desired output along the path shown in Figure 1.11.

It is interesting to note that the programming process illustrated in Figure 1.11 directly mirrors the input, processing, and output hardware units that are used to construct a computer (see previous section). This was not accidental, because early programming languages were specifically designed to match and, as optimally as possible, directly control corresponding hardware units.

FIGURE 1.11   Basic Procedural Operations

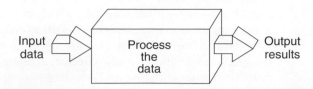

The first procedural language, named FORTRAN, whose name is derived from *For*mula *trans*lation, was introduced in 1957, and remained popular throughout the 1960s and early 1970s. (Another high-level programming language that was developed almost concurrently with FORTRAN, but that never achieved FORTRAN's overwhelming acceptance, was named Algol). FORTRAN has algebra-like instructions that concentrate on the processing phase shown in Figure 1.11, and was developed for scientific and engineering applications that required high-precision numerical outputs, accurate to many decimal places. For example, calculating the bacterial concentration level in a polluted pond, as illustrated in Figure 1.12, requires evaluating a mathematical equation to a high degree of numerical accuracy, and is typical of FORTRAN-based applications.

▲ P O I N T   O F   I N F O R M A T I O N ▲

What Is Syntax?

A programming language's **syntax** is the set of rules for formulating grammatically correct language statements. In practice this means that a C++ statement with correct syntax has the proper form specified for the compiler. As such, the compiler accepts the statement and does not generate an error message.

It should be noted that an individual statement or program can be syntactically correct and still be logically incorrect. Such a statement or program is correctly structured but produces an incorrect result. This is similar to an English statement that is grammatically correct but makes no sense. For example, although the sentence, "The tree is a ragged cat" is grammatically correct, it makes no sense.

FIGURE 1.12   FORTRAN Was Developed for Scientific and Engineering Applications

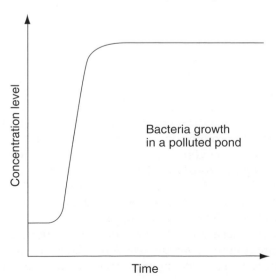

The next significant high-level application language was COBOL, which was introduced in the 1960s and remained a major procedural language through the 1980s (see Figure 1.13). COBOL is an acronym for COmmon Business-Oriented Language. This language had features geared toward business applications that required simpler mathematical calculations than those needed for scientific applications. One of COBOL's main benefits is that it provided multiple output formats that made it easy to create reports containing multiple columns of neatly formatted dollars and cents numbers and totals. It also forced programmers to carefully construct well-defined, structured procedures that followed a more consistent pattern than was required in FORTRAN.

FIGURE 1.13   COBOL Was Developed for Business Applications

```
                        INVENTORY REPORT

    Item                                In      On    Unit
    No.          Description         Stock   Order    Cost

    10365    #4  Nails, Common         20       0     1.09
    10382    #6  Nails, Common         10      50     1.14
    10420    #8  Nails, Common          2      60     1.19
    10436    #10 Nails, Common          6
    10449    #12 Nails, Common
    10486    #16 Nails, Common
```

Another language, BASIC (or Beginners All-purpose Symbolic Instruction Code), was developed at Dartmouth College about the same time as COBOL. BASIC was essentially a slightly scaled down version of FORTRAN that was intended as an introductory language for college students. It was a relatively straightforward, easy-to-understand language that did not require detailed knowledge of a specific application. Its main drawback was that it neither required nor enforced a consistent or structured approach to creating programs. It often occurred that even a programmer could not easily figure out what her or his BASIC program did after a short lapse of time.

To remedy this and put programming on a more scientific and rational basis that made understanding and reusing code easier, the Pascal language was developed. (Pascal is not an acronym, but is named after the 17th century mathematician Blaise Pascal.) Introduced in 1971, it provided students with a firmer foundation in structured programming design than that provided by early versions of BASIC.

Structured programs are created using a set of well-defined structures that are organized into individual programming sections, each of which performs a specific task that can be tested and modified without disturbing other sections of the program. The Pascal language was so rigidly structured, however, that there were no escapes from the structured sections when such escapes would be useful. This was unacceptable for many real-world projects and is one of the reasons why Pascal did not become widely accepted in the scientific, engineering, and business fields. Instead, the C language, which is a structured procedural language developed in the 1970s at AT&T Bell Laboratories by Ken Thompson, Dennis Ritchie, and Brian Kernighan, became the dominant applications language of the 1980s.

This language has an extensive set of capabilities that permits it to be written as a high-level language, while retaining the ability to directly access the machine-level features of a computer.

C++ was developed in the early 1980s, when Bjarne Stroustrup (also at AT&T) used his simulation language background to create an object-oriented programming language. A central feature of simulation languages is that they model real-life situations as objects. This object orientation, which was ideal for graphical screen objects, such as rectangles and circles, was combined with existing C features to form the C++ language. Thus, C++ retained the extensive set of structured procedural capabilities provided by C, but added its own object orientation to become a true general-purpose programming language. As such, it can be used for everything from simple, interactive programs to highly sophisticated and complex engineering and scientific programs, within the context of a truly object-oriented structure.

Exercises 1.2

1. Define the following terms:

   a. computer program

   b. programming

   c. programming language

   d. high-level language

   e. low-level language

   f. machine language

   g. assembly language

   h. procedural language

   i. object-oriented language

   j. source program

   k. compiler

   l. assembler

2. a. Describe the difference between high- and low-level languages.

   b. Describe the difference between procedural and object-oriented languages.

3. Describe the difference between assemblers, interpreters, and compilers.

4. a. Assuming the following operation codes:

   ```
   11000000    means add the 1st operand to the 2nd operand
   10100000    means subtract the 1st operand from the 2nd operand
   11110000    means multiply the 2nd operand by the 1st operand
   11010000    means divide the 2nd operation by the 1st operand
   ```

   translate the following instructions into English:

Opcode	Address of 1st Operand	Address of 2nd Operand
11000000	000000000001	0000000000010
11110000	000000000010	0000000000011
10100000	000000000100	0000000000011
11010000	000000000101	0000000000011

   b. Assuming the following locations contain the following data, determine the result produced by the instructions listed in Exercise 4a.

Address	Initial Value (in Decimal) Stored at This Address
00000000001	5
00000000010	3
00000000011	6
00000000100	14
00000000101	4

5. Rewrite the machine level instructions listed in Exercise 4a using assembly language notation. Use the symbolic names ADD, SUB, MUL, and DIV for addition, subtraction, multiplication, and division operations, respectively. In writing the instructions, use decimal values for the addresses.

6. Assuming that A = 10, B = 20, and C = .6, determine the numerical result of the following set of assembly language-type statements. For this exercise, assume that the LOAD instruction is equivalent to entering a value into the display of a calculator, and that ADD means add and MUL means multiply by.

```
LOAD    A
ADD     B
MUL     C
```

1.3 PROBLEM SOLUTION AND SOFTWARE DEVELOPMENT

No matter what field of work you choose or what your lifestyle may be, you have to solve problems. Many of these, such as adding up the change in your pocket, can be solved quickly and easily. Others, such as riding a bicycle, require some practice but soon become automatic. Still others require considerable planning and forethought if the solution is to be appropriate and efficient. For example, constructing a cellular telephone network or creating a Web-based order-entry system for a business are problems for which trial-and-error solutions could prove expensive and disastrous.

Creating a program is no different because a program is a solution developed to solve a particular problem. As such, writing a program is almost the last step in a process of first determining what the problem is and the method that will be used to solve the problem. Each field of study has its own name for the systematic method used to solve problems by designing suitable solutions. In science and engineering, the approach is referred to as the **scientific method,** while in quantitative analysis, the approach is referred to as the **systems approach.**

One technique used by professional software developers for understanding the problem that is being solved and for creating an effective and appropriate software solution is called the **software development procedure.** This procedure, as illustrated in Figure 1.14, consists of three overlapping phases:

- Development and design
- Documentation
- Maintenance

As a discipline, **software engineering** is concerned with creating readable, efficient, reliable, and maintainable programs and systems and uses the software development procedure to achieve this goal.

Phase I: Development and Design

Phase I begins with either a statement of a problem or a specific request for a program, which is referred to as a **program requirement.** Once a problem has been

| FIGURE 1.14 | The Three Phases of Program Development |

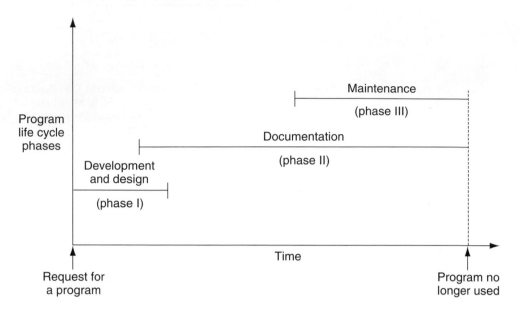

stated or a specific request for a program solution has been made, the development and design phase begins. This phase consists of the four well-defined steps illustrated in Figure 1.15 and summarized next:

1. Analyze the Problem This step is required to ensure that the problem is clearly defined and understood. The determination that the problem is clearly defined is made only after the person doing the analysis understands what outputs are required and what inputs are needed. To accomplish this, the analyst must have an understanding of how the inputs can be used to produce the desired output. For example, assume that you receive the following assignment:

> *Write a program that gives the information about circles that*
> *we need. Complete it by tomorrow.*
> —Management

A simple analysis of this program requirement reveals that it is not a well-defined problem at all because we do not know exactly what output information is required. As such, it is a major mistake to begin immediately writing a program to solve it. To clarify and define the problem statement, your first step should be to contact Management to define exactly what the program is to produce (its outputs).

Suppose you do this and learn that what is really desired is a program to calculate and display the circumference of a circle when given the radius. Because a formula exists for converting the input to the output, you may proceed to the next step. If we are not sure of how to obtain the required output or exactly what inputs are needed, a more in-depth background analysis may be called for. This typically means obtaining more background information about the problem or application. It also frequently entails doing one or more hand calculations to ensure that you understand what inputs are needed and how they can be combined to achieve the desired output.

FIGURE 1.15 The Development and Design Steps

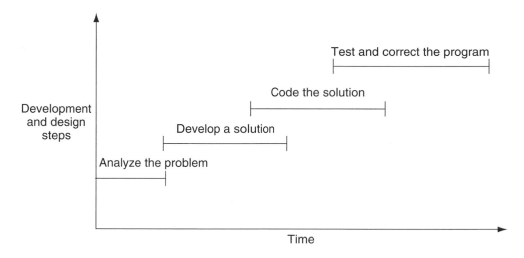

2. Develop a Solution In this step, we select the exact set of steps, called an **algorithm,** that we will use to solve the problem. The solution is typically obtained by a series of refinements, starting with the initial algorithm found in the analysis step, until an acceptable and complete algorithm is obtained. This algorithm must be checked, if this was not already done in the analysis step, to ensure that it correctly produces the desired outputs. The check is typically made by performing one or more hand calculations.

Sometimes the selected solution is quite easy, and sometimes it is quite complex. For example, the solution to determine the dollar value of the change in one's pocket or to determine the circumference of a circle is quite simple and consists of a simple calculation. The construction of an inventory tracking and control system for a computer store, however, is more complex. Techniques for solving these more complex problems are presented in Chapter 2.

3. Code the Solution This step, which is also referred to as *writing the program* and *implementing the solution,* consists of translating the solution into a computer program.

4. Test and Correct the Program As its name suggests, this step requires testing of the completed computer program to ensure that it does, in fact, provide a solution to the problem. Any errors that are found during the tests must be corrected.

Table 1.1 lists the relative amount of effort that is typically expended on each of these four development and design steps in large commercial programming projects. As this listing demonstrates, coding is not the major effort in this phase. Many new programmers have trouble because they spend the majority of their time writing the program without spending sufficient time understanding the problem or designing an appropriate solution. In this regard, it is worthwhile to remember this programming proverb: "It is impossible to write a successful program for a problem or application that is not fully understood." A somewhat equivalent and equally valuable proverb is: "The sooner you start coding a program the longer it usually takes to complete."

TABLE 1.1 Effort Expended in Phase I

Step	Effort
Analyze the problem	10%
Develop a solution	20%
Code the solution	20%
Test and correct the program	50%

Phase II: Documentation

So much work becomes useless or lost and so many tasks must be repeated because of inadequate documentation that it could be argued that documenting your work is the most important step in problem solving. Actually, many of the critical documents are created during the analysis, design, coding, and testing steps. Completing the documentation requires collecting these documents, adding user-operating material, and presenting it in a form that is most useful to you and your organization.

Although not everybody classifies them in the same way, there are essentially five documents for every problem solution:

1. Program description
2. Algorithm development and changes
3. Well-commented program listing
4. Sample test runs
5. Users' manual

"Putting yourself in the shoes" of a member of a large organization's team that might use your work—anyone from the secretary to the programmer/analysts and management—should help you to make the content and design of the important documentation clear. The documentation phase formally begins in the development and design phase and continues into the maintenance phase.

Phase III: Maintenance

The **software maintenance** phase is concerned with the ongoing correction of problems, revisions to meet changing needs, and the addition of new features. Maintenance is often the major effort, the primary source of revenue, and the longest lasting of the three phases. While development may take days or months, maintenance may continue for years or decades. An example of this was the massive maintenance effort to ensure that existing programs correctly handled dates after the turn of the century. This was referred to as the Y2K (for year 2000) problem.[2] The better the documentation is, the more efficiently maintenance can be performed.

---

[2] The source of this problem was that many commercial and engineering programs stored years as a two-digit number, such as 99. The solution was either to ensure that the program determined which specific range of years were to be assigned to a given century or to store all years as four-digit numbers.

A Closer Look at Phase I

Because the majority of this text is concerned with phase I of the software development procedure, we elaborate further on the four steps required for this phase. The use of these steps forms the central focus of our work in creating useful programming solutions.

Step 1: Analyze the Problem   Countless hours have been spent writing computer programs that either have never been used or have caused considerable animosity between programmer and user because the programmer did not produce what the user needed or expected. Successful programmers understand and avoid this by ensuring that the problem's requirements are understood. This is the first step in creating a program and the most important, because in it the specifications for the final program solution are determined. If the requirements are not fully and completely understood before programming begins, the results are almost always disastrous.

Imagine designing and building a house without fully understanding the architect's specifications. After the house is completed, the architect tells you that a bathroom is required on the first floor, where you have built a wall between the kitchen and the dining room. In addition, that particular wall is one of the main support walls for the house and contains numerous pipes and electrical cables. In this case, adding one bathroom requires a rather major modification to the basic structure of the house.

Experienced programmers know the importance of analyzing and understanding a program's requirements before coding, if for no other reason than that they too have constructed programs that later had to be entirely dismantled and redone. The following exercise should give you a sense of this experience.

Figure 1.16 illustrates the outlines of six individual shapes from a classic children's puzzle. Assume that as one or more shapes are given, starting with shapes A and B, an easy-to-describe figure must be constructed. Typically, shapes A and B are initially arranged to obtain a square, as illustrated in Figure 1.17. Next, when shape C is considered, it is usually combined with the existing square to form a rectangle, as illustrated in Figure 1.18. Then, when pieces D and E are added, they are usually arranged to form another rectangle, which is placed alongside the existing rectangle to form a square, as shown in Figure 1.19.

The process of adding new pieces onto the existing structure is identical to constructing a program and then adding to it as each subsequent requirement is understood, rather than completely analyzing the problem before a solution is undertaken. The problem arises when the program is almost finished and a requirement is added that does not fit easily into the established pattern. For example, assume that the last shape (shape F; see Figure 1.20) is now to be added. This last piece does not fit into the existing pattern that has been constructed. To include this piece with the others, the pattern must be completely dismantled and restructured.

FIGURE 1.16   Six Individual Shapes

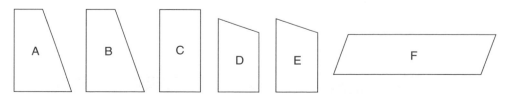

FIGURE 1.17 Typical First Figure

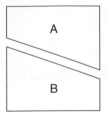

FIGURE 1.18 Typical Second Figure

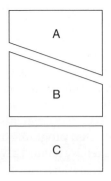

FIGURE 1.19 Typical Third Figure

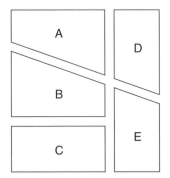

FIGURE 1.20 The Last Piece

Unfortunately, many programmers structure their programs in the same sequential manner used to construct Figure 1.19. Rather than taking the time to understand the complete set of requirements, new programmers frequently start coding based on the understanding of only a small subset of the total requirements. Then, when a subsequent requirement does not fit the existing program structure, the programmer is forced to dismantle and restructure either parts or all of the program.

Now, let's approach the problem of creating a figure from another view. If we started by arranging the first set of pieces as a parallelogram, all the pieces could be included in the final figure, as illustrated in Figure 1.21. It is worthwhile observing that the piece that caused us to dismantle the first figure (Figure 1.19) actually sets the pattern for the final figure illustrated in Figure 1.21. This is often the case with programming requirements. The requirement that seems to be the least clear is frequently the one that determines the main interrelationships of the program. It is worthwhile to include and understand all known requirements before beginning coding. Thus, before any solution is attempted, the analysis step must be completed.

FIGURE 1.21   Including All the Pieces

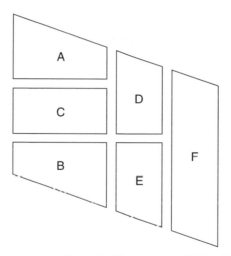

The person performing the analysis must initially take a broad perspective, see all of the pieces, and understand the main purpose of what the program or system is meant to achieve. The key to success here, which ultimately determines the success of the final program, is to determine the main purpose of the system as seen by the person making the request. For large systems, the analysis is usually conducted by a systems analyst. For smaller systems or individual programs, the analysis is typically performed directly by the programmer.

Regardless of how the analysis is done, or by whom, at its conclusion you should have a clear understanding of:

- What the system or program must do
- What outputs must be produced
- What inputs are required to create the desired outputs

Step 2: Develop (Design) a Solution   Once the problem is clearly understood, a solution can be developed. In this regard, the programmer is in a position similar to that of an architect who must draw up the plans for a house: The house must conform to certain specifications and meet the needs of its owner, but it can be designed and built in many possible ways. The same is true of a program.

For small programs, the selected algorithm may be extremely simple and consist of only one or more calculations that must be performed. More typically, the initial solution must be refined and organized into smaller subsystems, with specifications for how the subsystems interface with each other. To achieve this goal, the description of the solution starts from the highest level (topmost) requirement and proceeds downward to the parts that must be constructed to achieve this requirement. To make this more meaningful, consider a computer program that is required to track the number of parts in inventory. The required output for this program is a description of all parts carried in inventory and the number of units of each item in stock; the given inputs are the initial inventory quantity of each part, the number of items sold, the number of items returned, and the number of items purchased.

For these specifications, a designer could initially organize the requirements for the program into the three sections illustrated in Figure 1.22. This is called a **top-level structure diagram** because it represents the first overall structure of the program selected by the designer.

FIGURE 1.22   First-Level Structure Diagram

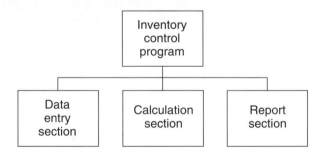

Once an initial structure is developed, it is refined until the tasks indicated in the boxes are completely defined. For example, both the data entry and report subsections shown in Figure 1.22 can be further refined as follows: The data entry section certainly must include provisions for entering the data. Since it is the system designer's responsibility to plan for contingencies and human error, provisions must also be made for changing incorrect data after an entry has been made and for deleting a previously entered value altogether. Similar subdivisions for the report section can also be constructed. Figure 1.23 illustrates a second-level structure diagram for an inventory tracking system that includes these further refinements.

The process of refining a solution continues until the smallest requirement is included within the solution. Notice that the design produces a treelike structure where the levels branch out as we move from the top of the structure to the bottom. When the design is complete, each task designated in a box is typically coded with separate sets of instructions that are executed as they are called on by tasks higher up in the structure.

Step 3: Code the Solution   Coding involves translating the chosen design solution into a computer program. If the analysis and solution steps have been correctly performed, the coding step becomes rather mechanical in nature. In a well-designed program, the statements making up the program do, however, conform to certain well-defined patterns, or structures, that have been defined in the solution step. These structures control how the program executes and consist of the following types:

1. Sequence
2. Selection
3. Iteration
4. Invocation

Sequence defines the order in which instructions are executed by the program. The specification of which instruction comes first, which comes second, and so on is essential if the program is to achieve a well-defined purpose.

Selection provides the capability to make a choice between different operations, depending on the result of some condition. For example, the value of a number can be checked before a division is performed. If the number is not zero, it can be used as the denominator of a division operation; otherwise, the division is not performed and the user is issued a warning message.

FIGURE 1.23   Second-Level Refinement Structure Diagram

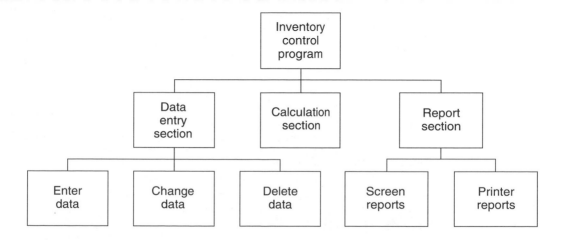

Al-Khowarizmi

One of the first great mathematicians was Mohammed ibn Musa al-Khowarizmi, who wrote a treatise in about 825 A.D. called *Ilm al-jabr wa'l muqabalah* ("The Science of Reduction and Calculation").

The word *algorism* or *algorithm* is derived from al-Khowarizmi's name, and our word *algebra* is derived from the word *al-jabr* in the title of his work.

Iteration, which is also referred to as **looping** and **repetition,** provides the ability for the same operation to be repeated based on the value of a condition. For example, grades might be repeatedly entered and added until a negative grade is entered. In this case, the entry of a negative grade is the condition that signifies the end of the repetitive input and addition of grades. At that point, a calculation of an average for all the grades entered could be performed.

Invocation involves invoking, or summoning, a set of statements as needed. For example, the computation of a person's net pay involves the tasks of obtaining pay rates and hours worked, calculating the net pay, and providing a report or check for the required amount. These individual tasks are typically coded as separate units that are called into execution, or *invoked*, as they are needed.

Step 4: Test and Correct the Solution   The purpose of testing is to verify that a program works correctly and actually fulfills its requirements. In theory, testing would reveal all existing program errors (in computer terminology, a program error is called a bug[3]). In practice, this requires checking all possible combinations of statement execution. Because of the time and effort required, this is usually an impossible goal except for extremely simple programs. (We illustrate why this is generally an impossible goal in Section 4.7.)

Because exhaustive testing is not feasible for most programs, different philosophies and methods of testing have evolved. At its most basic level, however, testing requires a conscious effort to ensure that a program works correctly and produces meaningful results. This means that careful thought must be given to what the test is meant to achieve and the data that will be used in the test. If testing reveals an error (bug), the process of debugging, which includes locating, correcting, and verifying the correction, can be initiated. It is important to realize that although testing may reveal the presence of an error, it does not necessarily indicate the absence of one. Thus, the fact that a test revealed one bug does not indicate that another one is not lurking somewhere else in the program.

---

[3] The derivation of this term is rather interesting. When a program stopped running on the Mark I at Harvard University in September 1945, Grace Hopper traced the malfunction to a dead insect that had gotten into the electrical circuits. She recorded the incident in her logbook at 15:45 hours as "Relay #70. . . . [moth] in relay. First actual case of bug being found."

A BIT OF BACKGROUND

The Young Gauss

German mathematical genius Johann Carl Fredrich Gauss (1777–1855) professed that he could "reckon" before he could talk. When only 2 years old, he discovered an error in his father's business records.

One day in school, young Johann's teacher asked his class to add up the numbers between 1 and 100. To the chagrin of the teacher, who had thought the task would keep the class busy for a while, Gauss almost instantly wrote the number on his slate and exclaimed, "There it is!" He had reasoned that the series of numbers could be written forward and backward and added term-by-term to get 101 one hundred times. Thus, the sum was 100(101)/2, and Gauss, at the age of 10, had discovered that

$$1 + 2 + \ldots + n = n\,(n + 1)\,/\,2.$$

To catch and correct errors in a program, it is important to develop a set of test data that can be used to determine whether the program gives correct answers. In fact, an accepted step in formal software development is to plan the test procedures and create meaningful test data before writing the code. This tends to help the person be more objective about what the program must do because it essentially circumvents any subconscious temptation after coding to choose test data that do not work. The procedures for testing a program should examine every possible situation under which the program will be used. The program should be tested with data in a reasonable range as well as at the limits and in areas where the program should tell the user that the data are invalid. Developing good test procedures and data for sophisticated problems can be more difficult than writing the program code itself.

Backup

Although not part of the formal design process, it is critical to make and keep **backup copies** of the program at each step of the programming and debugging process. It is easy to delete or change the current working version of a program beyond recognition. Backup copies allow the recovery of the last stage of work with a minimum of effort. The final working version of a useful program should be backed up at least twice. In this regard, another useful programming proverb is: "Backup is unimportant if you don't mind starting all over again." The three most fundamental rules of maintaining program and data integrity are:

1. backup!
2. Backup!
3. BACKUP!

Many organizations keep at least one backup on site, where it can be easily retrieved, and another backup copy either in a fireproof safe or at a remote location.

Exercises 1.3

1. a. List and describe the four steps required in the design and development stage of a program.

   b. In addition to the design and development phase, what are the other two phases required in producing a program and why are they required?

2. A note from your supervisor, Ms. J. Williams, says:

   Solve our payroll deduction problems.
   —J. Williams

   a. What should be your first task?

   b. How do you accomplish this task?

   c. How long do you expect this to take, assuming everyone cooperates?

3. Program development is only one phase in the overall software development procedure. Assuming that documentation and maintenance require 60% of the total software effort in designing a system, use Table 1.1 to determine the amount of effort required for initial program coding as a percentage of total software effort.

4. Many people requesting a program or system for the first time consider coding to be the most important aspect of program development. They feel that they know what they need and think that the programmer can begin coding with minimal time spent in analysis. As a programmer, what pitfalls can you envision in working with such people?

5. Many first-time computer users try to contract with programmers to provide programming for a fixed fee (total amount to be paid is fixed in advance). What is the advantage to the user in having this arrangement? What is the advantage to the programmer in having this arrangement? What are some disadvantages to both user and programmer?

6. Many programmers prefer to work on an hourly rate basis. Why do you think this is so? Under what conditions is it advantageous for a programmer to give a client a fixed price for the programming effort?

7. Experienced users generally want a clearly written statement of programming work to be done, including a complete description of what the program will do, delivery dates, payment schedules, and testing requirements. What is the advantage to the user in requiring this? What is the advantage to a programmer in working under this arrangement? What disadvantages does this arrangement have for both user and programmer?

1.4 ALGORITHMS

Before a program is written, the programmer must clearly understand what data are to be used, the desired result, and the procedure to be used to produce this result. The procedure, or solution, selected is referred to as an algorithm. More precisely, an **algorithm** is defined as a step-by-step sequence of instructions that describes how the data are to be processed to produce the desired outputs. In essence, an algorithm answers the question: "What method will you use to solve this problem?"

Only after we clearly understand the data that we will be using and select an algorithm (the specific steps required to produce the desired result) can we code the program. Seen in this light, programming is the translation of a selected algorithm into a language that the computer can use.

FIGURE 1.24 Summing the Numbers 1 Through 100

Method 1 — Columns: Arrange the numbers from 1 to 100 in a column and add them

$$
\begin{array}{r}
1 \\
2 \\
3 \\
4 \\
\bullet \\
\bullet \\
\bullet \\
98 \\
99 \\
+\ 100 \\
\hline
5050
\end{array}
$$

Method 2 — Groups: Arrange the numbers in groups that sum to 101. Multiply the number of groups by 101.

$$
\begin{array}{rcl}
1 + & 100 & = 101 \\
2 + & 99 & = 101 \\
3 + & 98 & = 101 \\
4 + & 97 & = 101 \\
\bullet & \bullet & \\
\bullet & \bullet & \\
\bullet & \bullet & \\
49 + & 52 & = 101 \\
50 + & 51 & = 101
\end{array}
$$

50 groups

$(50 \times 101) = 5050$

Method 3 — Formula: Use the formula

$$
\text{Sum} = \frac{n(a + b)}{2}
$$

where

$n =$ number of terms to be added (100)
$a =$ first number to be added (1)
$b =$ last number to be added (100)

$$
\text{Sum} = \frac{100(1 + 100)}{2} = 5050
$$

To illustrate an algorithm, we consider a simple problem. Assume that a program must calculate the sum of all whole numbers from 1 through 100. Figure 1.24 illustrates three methods we could use to find the required sum. Each method constitutes an algorithm.

Clearly, most people do not bother to list the possible alternatives in a detailed step-by-step manner, as we have done here, and then select one of the algorithms to solve the problem. But then, most people do not think algorithmically; they tend to think heuristically. For example, if you had to change a flat tire on your car, you would not think of all the steps required—you would simply change the tire or call someone else to do the job. This is an example of heuristic thinking.

Unfortunately, computers do not respond to heuristic commands. A general statement such as "add the numbers from 1 to 100" means nothing to a computer because the computer can only respond to algorithmic commands written in an acceptable language such as C++. To program a computer successfully, you must clearly understand this difference between algorithmic and intuitive commands. A computer is an "algorithm-responding" machine; it is not an "intuitive-responding" machine. You cannot tell a computer to change a tire or to add the numbers from 1 through 100. Instead, you must give the computer a detailed step-by-step set of instructions that, collectively, forms an algorithm. For example, the following set of instructions forms a detailed method, or algorithm, for determining the sum of the numbers from 1 through 100:

Set n equal to 100.
Set a = 1.
Set b equal to 100.

Calculate sum $= \dfrac{n(a + b)}{2}$.

Print the sum.

Notice that these instructions are not a computer program. Unlike a program, which must be written in a language the computer can respond to, an algorithm can be written or described in various ways. When English-like phrases are used to describe the algorithm (the processing steps), as in this example, the description is called **pseudocode.** When mathematical equations are used, the description is called a **formula.** When diagrams that employ the symbols shown in Figure 1.25 are used, the description is referred to as a **flowchart.** Figure 1.26 illustrates the use of these symbols in depicting an algorithm for determining the average of three numbers.

Because flowcharts are cumbersome to revise and can easily support unstructured programming practices, they have fallen out of favor by professional programmers, whereas the use of pseudocode to express the logic of algorithms has gained increasing acceptance. In describing an algorithm using pseudocode, short English phrases are used. For example, acceptable pseudocode for describing the steps needed to compute the average of three numbers is:

Input the three numbers into the computer's memory.
Calculate the average by adding the numbers and dividing the sum by 3.
Display the average.

Only after an algorithm has been selected and the programmer understands the steps required can the algorithm be written using computer-language statements. The writing of an algorithm using computer-language statements is called **coding** the algorithm, which is the third step in our program development procedure (see Figure 1.27). Most of Part I of this text is devoted to showing you how to develop and code algorithms into C++.

FIGURE 1.25 Flowchart Symbols

SYMBOL	NAME	DESCRIPTION
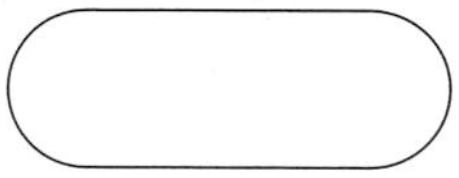	Terminal	Indicates the beginning or end of an algorithm
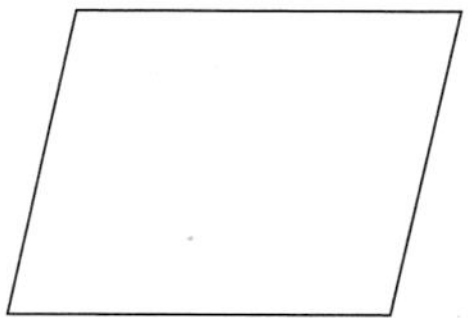	Input/Output	Indicates an input or output operation
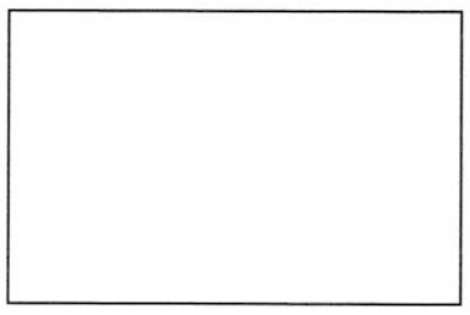	Process	Indicates computation or data manipulation
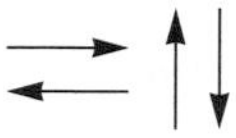	Flow lines	Connects the flowchart symbols and indicates the logic flow
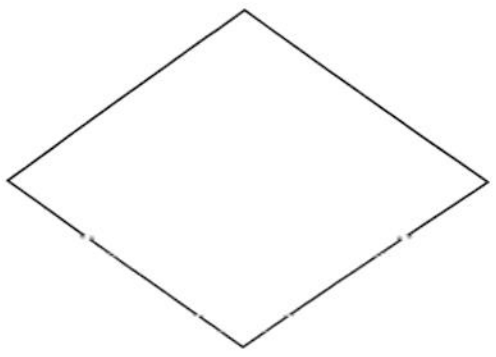	Decision	Indicates a program branch point
	Loop	Indicates the initial, limit, and increment values of a loop
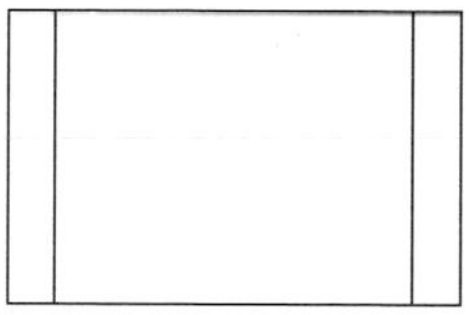	Predefined process	Indicates a predefined process, as in calling a function
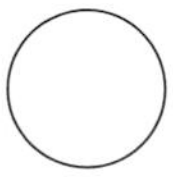	Connector	Indicates an entry to, or exit from, another part of the flowchart or a connection point
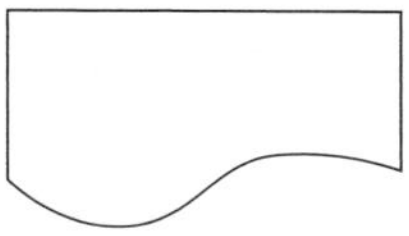	Report	Indicates a written output report

FIGURE 1.26   Flowchart for Calculating the Average of Three Numbers

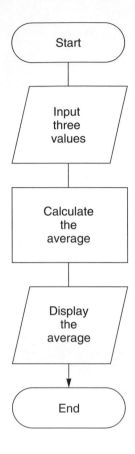

FIGURE 1.27   Coding an Algorithm

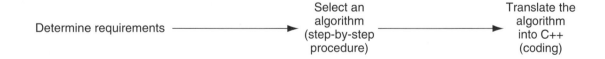

Determine requirements ⟶ Select an algorithm (step-by-step procedure) ⟶ Translate the algorithm into C++ (coding)

Exercises 1.4

1. Determine a step-by-step procedure (list the steps) to do the following tasks (*Note:* There is no single correct answer for each of these tasks. The exercise is designed to give you practice in converting heuristic-type commands into equivalent algorithms and making the shift between the thought processes involved in the two types of responses.)

   a. Fix a flat tire.
   b. Make a telephone call.
   c. Go to the store and purchase a loaf of bread.
   d. Roast a turkey.

2. a. Determine the six possible step-by-step procedures (list the steps) to paint the flower shown in Figure 1.28, with the restriction that each color must be completed before a new color can be started. (*Hint:* One of the algorithms is: Use yellow first, green second, black last.)

FIGURE 1.28 A Simple Paint-by-Number Figure

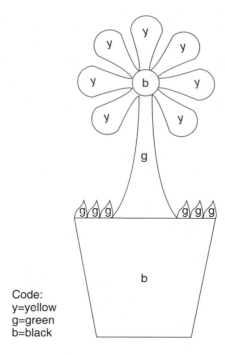

Code:
y=yellow
g=green
b=black

b. Which of the six painting algorithms (series of steps) is best if we are limited to using one paintbrush and there is no way to clean the brush?

3. Determine and write an algorithm (list the steps) to interchange the contents of two cups of liquid. Assume that a third cup is available to hold the contents of either cup temporarily. Each cup should be rinsed before any new liquid is poured into it.

4. Write a detailed set of instructions, in English, to calculate the dollar amount of money in a piggybank that contains h half-dollars, q quarters, n nickels, d dimes, and p pennies.

5. Write a set of detailed, step-by-step instructions, in English, to find the smallest number in a group of three integer numbers.

6. a. Write a set of detailed, step-by-step instructions, in English, to calculate the change remaining from a dollar after a purchase is made. Assume that the cost of the goods purchased is less than a dollar. The change received should consist of the smallest number of coins possible.

   b. Repeat Exercise 6a, but assume the change is to be given only in pennies.

7. a. Write an algorithm to locate the first occurrence of the name WESTBY in a list of names arranged in random order.

   b. Discuss how you could improve your algorithm for Exercise 7a if the list of names was arranged in alphabetical order.

8. Write an algorithm to determine the total occurrences of the letter e in any sentence.

9. Determine and write an algorithm to sort four numbers into ascending (from lowest to highest) order.

1.5 PLANNING FOR OBJECTS: OBJECT-ORIENTED PROGRAMMING

We live in a world full of objects—planes, trains, cars, telephones, books, computers, etc. Until the late 1980s, however, programming techniques did not reflect this. The primary programming paradigm[4] had been procedural, where a program is defined as an algorithm written in a machine-readable language. The reasons for this emphasis on procedural programming are primarily historical.

When computers were developed in the 1940s, they were initially used by mathematicians for military purposes, such as computing bomb trajectories, decoding enemy orders, and sending diplomatic transmissions. After World War II, computers were still used primarily by mathematicians for computations. This reality was reflected in the name of the first commercially available high-level language introduced in 1957, FORTRAN, an acronym for FORmula TRANslation. Further reflecting this predominant mathematical/engineering use was the fact that in the 1960s almost all computer courses were taught in either engineering or mathematics departments. The term *computer science* was not yet in common use, and computer science departments were just being formed.

This situation has changed dramatically, primarily for two reasons. One of the reasons for disenchantment with strictly procedural programs has been their failure in containing software costs. Software costs include all costs associated with initial program development and subsequent program maintenance. As illustrated in Figure 1.29, the major cost of most computer projects today, whether technical or commercial, is for software.

Software costs contribute so heavily to total project costs because they are directly related to human productivity, which is labor intensive, whereas the equipment associated with hardware costs is related to manufacturing technologies. For example, microchips that cost more than $500 only ten years ago can now be purchased for less than $1.

It is far easier, however, to dramatically increase manufacturing productivity a thousand-fold, with the consequent decrease in hardware costs, than it is for programmers to double either the quantity or quality of the code they produce. So as hardware costs have plummeted, software productivity and its associated costs have remained relatively constant. Thus, the ratio of software costs to total system costs (hardware plus software) has increased dramatically.

One way to significantly increase programmer productivity is to create code that can be reused without extensive revision, retesting, and revalidation. The inability of procedurally structured code to provide this type of reusability led to the search for other software approaches.

The second reason for disenchantment with strictly procedural-based programming was the emergence of graphic screens and the subsequent interest in window applications. Programming multiple windows on the same graphic screen is virtually impossible using standard procedural programming techniques.

The solution to producing programs that efficiently manipulate graphic screens and provide reusable windowing code was found in artificial intelligence-based and simulation programming techniques. Artificial intelligence contained extensive research on geometric object specification and recognition. Simulation contained considerable background on simulating items as objects with well-defined interactions between them. This object-based paradigm fit well in a graphic windows environment, in which each window can be specified as a self-contained object.

---

[4]A **paradigm** is a standard way of thinking about or doing something.

FIGURE 1.29   Software Is the Major Cost of Most Computer Projects

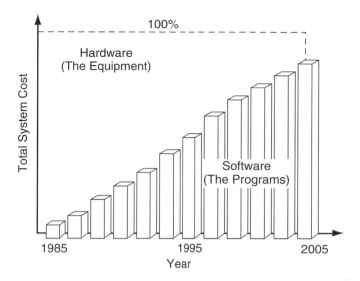

An object is also well suited to a programming representation because it can be specified by two basic characteristics: a current **state**, which defines how the object appears at the moment, and a **behavior**, which defines how the object reacts to external inputs.

To make this more tangible, consider a geometric object, such as a rectangle. A rectangle's current state is defined by its shape and location. The shape is traditionally specified by its length and width, while its location can be specified in a number of ways. One simple way is to list the values of two opposite corner positions. The behavior we provide a rectangle depends on what we are willing to have our rectangle do. For example, if we intend to display the rectangle on a screen, we might provide it with the ability to move its position and change either its length or width.

It is worthwhile distinguishing here between an actual rectangle, which might exist on a piece of paper or a computer screen, and our description of it. Our description is more accurately termed a model. By definition, a **model** is merely a representation of a real object; it is not the object itself. Very few models are ever complete; that is, a model typically does not reveal every aspect of the object it represents. Each model is defined for a particular purpose that usually only requires representing the part of an object's state or behavior that is of interest to us.

To clarify this point further, consider another common object, an elevator. Like all objects, an elevator can be modeled in terms of a state and a behavior. Its state might be given in terms of its size, location, interior decoration, or any number of other attributes. Likewise, its behavior might be specified in terms of its reaction when one of its buttons is pushed. Constructing a model of an elevator, however, requires that we select those attributes and behavior that are of interest to us. For purposes of a simulation, for example, we may only be concerned with the current floor position of the elevator and how to simulate its movement to another floor location.

Other attributes and behavior of the elevator may be left out of the model because they do not affect the aspects of the elevator that we want to study.

It is also important to distinguish between the attributes we choose to include in our model and the values that these attributes can have. The attributes and behavior together define a category or type of object out of which many individual objects can be designated. In object-oriented programming, the category of objects defined by a given set of attributes and behavior is called a **class.** Only when specific values have been assigned to the attributes is a particular object defined.

For example, the attributes of length and width can be used to define a general type of shape called a rectangle. Only when specific values have been assigned to these attributes have we represented a particular rectangle. This distinction carries over into C++: The attributes and behavior we select are said to define a general class, or type, of object. An object itself only comes into existence when we assign specific values to the attributes.

Before we can become fluent with C++'s object-oriented capabilities, however, we first need to understand C++'s procedure-oriented side. The procedural aspects of C++ are the focus of Part I. The object-oriented aspects of C++ are then presented in Part II.

Exercises 1.5

1. Define the following terms:

   a. attribute

   b. behavior

   c. state

   d. model

   e. class

   f. object

   g. interface

2. Define an appropriate class for each of the following specific objects:

   a. the number 5

   b. a square that is 4" by 4"

   c. this textbook

   d. a 1955 Ford Thunderbird

   e. the last ballpoint pen that you used

3. a. For each of the following, determine what attributes might be of interest to some-one considering buying the item:

      a book
      a can of soda
      a pen
      a CD
      a CD player
      an elevator
      a car

   b. Do the attributes you used in Exercise 3a model an object or a class of objects?

4. a. What operations should the following objects be capable of doing?

   a Ford Thunderbird
   the last ballpoint pen that you used

   b. Do the operations determined for Exercise 4a apply only to the particular object listed or are they more general and thus applicable to all objects of the type listed?

5. a. Besides the attributes of length and width that are necessary to describe a rectangle, what other characteristics of a rectangle are useful if the rectangle is to be drawn on a color monitor?

   b. Determine how a rectangle's position on a screen might be specified.

6. a. What characteristics are necessary to specify the position and size of a circle that is to be placed on a monitor's screen?

   b. What additional characteristics could be specified for a circle if it is to be drawn on a color monitor?

7. All of the examples of classes considered in this section have consisted of inanimate objects. Do you think classes of animate objects could be constructed? Why or why not?

8. a. Consider a class of dates, in which each date is of the form month/day/year. For such a class, is it appropriate to consider the date 12/25/1998 as an object?

   b. Determine what operations might be appropriate for a date class.

   c. Determine what operations are not appropriate for a date class.

9. Consider a class of strings, where each string consists of a sequence of alphanumeric characters (letters, digits, and special characters, such as $, ?, !, ., *).

   a. Determine what operations are appropriate for this class.

   b. Determine what operations are not appropriate for this class.

10. a. The attributes of a class represent how objects of the class appear to the outside world. The behavior represents how an object of a class reacts to an external stimulus. Given this information, what do you think is the mechanism by which one object "triggers" the designated behavior in another object? (*Hint:* Consider how one person typically gets another person to do something.)

    b. If behavior in C++ is constructed by defining an appropriate function, how do you think the behavior is activated in C++?

Improving Communication

11. Respond to the following request as if it was sent to you:
    MEMORANDUM

    To: U. R. A programmer

    From: Head of Programming Dept.

    Subject: Preliminary Analysis Phase

    Per our prior discussion, you will be interviewing a number of people in the company. Your goal, as we discussed, is to determine how many projects they have been involved in that have been completely specified at the start of the project. Please give me a list of questions you intend to ask and how you intend to approach the interviewees for their permission to conduct the interview.

12. Respond to the following request as if it was sent to you:

MEMORANDUM

To: U. R. It

From: Head of Programming Dept.

Subject: Sampling Project

We spent a large part of the last meeting with the marketing department discussing how the input screen should look for the new Sampling Project. Jan Programmer complained to me after the meeting that she had no interest in the input screen, that it was a boring and professionally unexciting topic, and that we should just give her the required specifications for the screen and let her do her job. Later in the day, Joan Muchsuccess, head of marketing, contacted me and said she was not impressed with Jan, did not think Jan really understood or cared about the project, and would like another programmer assigned to the task. I know Jan is one of our cracker-jack programmers and that the analysis of the data is extremely complicated and requires someone as capable as Jan. How should we handle this?

Working in Teams

13. One of the major phases of any programming project is determining what must be accomplished. Most students never get a real understanding of this phase because assignments, both programming and nonprogramming, are usually well defined, either by the professor or as written exercises in a textbook.

   a. Discuss with each of your team members how homework has been assigned throughout their educational careers. See if there is some consensus on the percentage of problems assigned for which there was sufficient information to solve the problem.

   b. How might you quantify the results of your discussions with your team members?

   c. Take a moment and review how you initially react (your thoughts and feelings) when an assignment is not totally specified; that is, when some piece of information is missing from the problem. Do you get annoyed or angry? Do you feel relieved? Determine with your team members what their reactions have been. Can you determine a pattern in reactions? Which reactions do you think are most likely to yield negative results in the working world?

   d. Take a moment and review what you typically do (actions taken) when an assignment is not totally specified; that is, when some piece of information is missing from the problem. For example, do you:

   Use it as an excuse not to do the assignment at all?
   Attempt to solve the problem and stop when you reach the point where the missing information is needed?
   Make assumptions about what the missing information is and solve the problem using your assumed data?
   Use it as a means of making the instructor wrong for not giving you all the information required?

   e. Determine what your team members typically do when an assignment is not totally specified and see if the team can determine a pattern.

   f. Summarize the findings of your team in a memorandum to your professor.

14. a. Decide with your team members what might be some useful questions to ask people in the working world to find out their experience with assigned projects. Specifically, you want to determine the percentage of projects that are completely specified at the start of a project. Include in your discussions ways you can approach people to encourage them to speak with you, both for this project and for future projects.

    b. Ask the questions developed in Exercise 14a to as many people in the working world as you can. Compare your results with those obtained by your team members and see if there is a pattern to your results.

    c. Summarize the finding of your team members in a memorandum to your professor.

15. Computer science professionals work in a number of different environments that include academia, scientific research labs, new-venture computer companies, and commercial corporations. To be successful in each environment, a different mixture of skills is frequently needed.

    a. Decide with your team members what might be some useful questions to ask people in these working environments to determine what skills they think are required for success. Include in your discussions ways you might approach people to encourage them to speak with you, both for this project and for future projects.

    b. Ask the questions developed in Exercise 15a to as many computer professionals as you can.

    c. Ask the questions developed in Exercise 15a to supervisors of computer professionals. If possible, contact the supervisors of the people you interviewed in Exercise 15b. (*Hint:* Use both the academic departments in your college as well as the nonacademic departments, such as admissions and registration.)

    d. Compare your results with those of your team members and prepare a summary of your findings in a memorandum to your professor.

16. Two interesting statements are the following: "If you think something is true, it is true" and "Just because you think something is true does not make it so." Discuss these statements with your team members and see if you can come to some consensus as to their validity. Are these statements necessarily contradictory? How might these statements be of value to you in interviewing people and determining the requirements for a new computer system?

17. Suppose you interview ten people in an organization and all of them agree on exactly what is needed and what you must do to produce a desired computer system. As a programmer, can you proceed with complete confidence to the design phase? Discuss this with your team members and come up with a few examples that confirm your position. Determine if there are any situations in which your conclusions might not be 100% correct.

18. Some programmers take the position that they, as programmers, should produce whatever their client or supervisor requests without question. Discuss the pros and cons of taking this approach with your team members, assuming you are all programmers. Then discuss the pros and cons of this approach assuming you are all supervisors of programmers.

1.6 A CLOSER LOOK AT DIGITAL STORAGE CONCEPTS

The most common number code for storing integer values inside a computer is called the **two's complement** representation. Using this code, the integer equivalent of any bit pattern, such as 10001101, is easy to determine and can be found for either positive or negative integers with no change in the conversion method. For convenience, we assume byte-size bit patterns consisting of a set of eight bits each, although the procedure carries directly over to large-size bit patterns.

The easiest way to determine the integer represented by each bit pattern is to first construct a simple device called a *value box*. Figure 1.30 illustrates such a box for a single byte. Mathematically, each value in the box represents an increasing power of 2. Because two's complement numbers must be capable of representing both positive and negative integers, the leftmost position, in addition to having the largest absolute magnitude, also has a negative sign.

Conversion of any binary number, for example, 10001101, simply requires inserting the bit pattern in the value box and adding the values having 1s under them. Thus, as illustrated in Figure 1.31, the bit pattern 10001101 represents the integer number −115.

The value box can also be used in reverse to convert a base-10 integer number into its equivalent binary bit pattern. Some conversions, in fact, can be made by inspection. For example, the base 10 number −125 is obtained by adding 3 to −128. Thus, the binary representation of −125 is 10000011, which equals −128 + 2 + 1. Similarly, the two's complement representation of the number 40 is 00101000, which is 32 + 8.

FIGURE 1.30 An Eight-Bit Value Box

−128	64	32	16	8	4	2	1

FIGURE 1.31 Converting 10001101 to a Base-10 Number

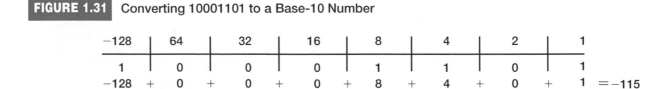

−128	64	32	16	8	4	2	1
1	0	0	0	1	1	0	1
−128 +	0 +	0 +	0 +	8 +	4 +	0 +	1	= −115

Although the value box conversion method is deceptively simple, it is directly related to the underlying mathematical basis of two's complement binary numbers. The original name of the two's complement code was the weighted-sign code, which correlates directly to the value box. As the name *weighted sign* implies, each bit position has a weight, or value, of 2 raised to a power and a sign. The signs of all bits except the leftmost bit are positive and the sign of the leftmost bit is negative.

In reviewing the value box, it is evident that any two's complement binary number with a leading 1 represents a negative number, and any bit pattern with a leading 0 represents a positive number. Using the value box, it is easy to determine the most positive and negative values capable of being stored. The most negative value that can be stored in a single byte is the decimal number −128, which has the bit pattern 10000000. Any other nonzero bit simply adds a positive amount to the number. Additionally, it is clear that a positive number must have a 0 as its leftmost bit. From this, you can see that the largest positive eight-bit two's complement number is 01111111 or 127.

1.7 COMMON PROGRAMMING ERRORS

The most common errors associated with the material presented in this chapter are as follows:

1. A major programming error made by most beginning programmers is the rush to write and run a program before fully understanding what is required, including the algorithms that will be used to produce the desired result. A symptom of this haste to get a program entered into the computer is the lack of any documentation or even a program outline or a written program itself. Many problems can be caught just by checking a copy of the program or even a description of the algorithm written in pseudocode.

2. Another major error is not backing up a program. Almost all new programmers make this mistake until they lose a program that has taken considerable time to code.

3. Many new programmers do not understand that computers respond only to explicitly defined algorithms. Telling a computer to add a group of numbers is quite different than telling a friend to add the numbers. The computer must be given the precise instructions for doing the addition in a programming language.

1.8 CHAPTER REVIEW

Key Terms

algorithm	low-level language
ALU	machine language
assembler	object-oriented language
assembly language	operating system
bit	procedural language
byte	programming
central processing unit (CPU)	programming language
compiled language	pseudocode
compiler	software
computer program	software development procedure
control unit	source code
high-level language	source program
interpreted language	syntax
interpreter	

Summary

1. The first attempt at creating a self-operating computational machine was made by Charles Babbage in 1822. The concept became a reality with the Atanasoff-Berry computer built in 1937 at Iowa State University, which was the first computer to use a binary numbering scheme to store and manipulate data. Two of the earliest large-scale digital computers were the ENIAC, built in 1946 at the Moore School of Engineering at the University of Pennsylvania, and the Mark I, built at Harvard University in 1944. All of these machines, however, required external wiring to perform the desired operations. The first computer to employ the concept of a stored program was the EDSAC, built at Cambridge University in England. The design and operating principles used in the design of this machine, developed by the mathematician John Von Neumann, are still used by most of the computers manufactured today.

2. The physical components used in constructing a computer are called its hardware. These components include input, processing, output, memory, and storage units.

3. The programs used to operate a computer are referred to as software.

4. Programming languages come in a variety of forms and types. Machine language programs, also known as executable programs, contain the binary codes that can be executed by a computer. Assembly languages permit the use of symbolic names for mathematical operations and memory addresses. Programs written in assembly languages must be converted to machine language, using translator programs called assemblers, before the programs can be executed. Assembly and machine languages are referred to as low-level languages.

    Compiler and interpreter languages are referred to as high-level languages. This means that they are written using instructions that resemble a written language, such as English, and can be run on a variety of computer types. Compiler languages require a compiler to translate the program into a binary language form, whereas interpreter languages require an interpreter to do the translation.

5. As a discipline, software engineering is concerned with creating readable, efficient, reliable, and maintainable programs and systems.

6. The software development procedure consists of three phases:

- Program development and design
- Documentation
- Maintenance

7. The program development and design phase consists of four well-defined steps:

- Analyze the problem
- Develop a solution
- Code the solution
- Test and correct the solution

8. An algorithm is a step-by-step procedure that describes how a computation or task is to be performed.

9. A computer program is a self-contained unit of instructions and data used to operate a computer to produce a specific result. In its simplest form, a computer program is a description of an algorithm written in a language that can be processed by a computer.

10. The four fundamental control structures used in a program are:

- Sequence
- Selection
- Iteration
- Invocation

Exercises

1. a. What are the phases required in the software development procedure?

   b. List the steps required in the first phase of the software development procedure.

2. Define the term *algorithm*.

3. Define the term *syntax*.

4. Determine the input(s) and output(s) for the following:

   a. Given the radius of a circle, find the circumference.

   b. Given two real numbers, A and B, calculate a sum (A + B), a difference (A − B), a product (A * B), and the quotients A / B and B / A.

   c. The final grades for your four courses last semester were B+ (3.3), A (4.0), B (3.0), and A− (3.6). What was your average grade point (on a 4.0 scale) for the term, assuming each course was worth three credits?

5. Assume that a computer store averages 15 sales per day. Assuming that the store is open six days a week and that each sale requires an average of 100 characters, determine the minimum storage that the system must have to keep all sales records for a two-year period.

6. Assume that you are creating a sales recording system for a client. Each sale input to the system requires that the operator type in a description of the item sold, the name and address of the firm buying the item, the value of the item, and a code for the person making the trade. This information consists of a maximum of 300 characters. Estimate the time it takes for an average typist to input 200 sales. (*Hint:* To solve this problem, you must make an assumption about the number of words per minute that an average typist can type and the average number of characters per word.)

7. Many dot matrix printers can print at a speed of 165 characters per second. Using such a printer, determine the time it takes to print a complete list of 10,000 records. Assume that each record consists of 300 characters.

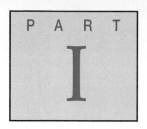

P A R T

I

Procedure-Oriented Programming in C++

Although C++ is an object-oriented language, it was developed as an extension to C, which is a procedural language. As such, C++ is a hybrid language having both procedural and object features. Because of this hybrid nature, it is not only possible to write a complete C++ program using only procedural code, but it is impossible to write an object-oriented program in C++ that does not include procedural elements. Thus, a proper start to learning C++ requires familiarity with its procedural aspects.

In addition to presenting the procedural basics of C++, Part I also introduces C++'s object side. This is done by presenting the `cin` and `cout` objects, which have immediate use in providing interactive input and output capabilities, respectively, and by the Planning for Objects sections included within each chapter. These Planning sections provide an understanding of the thought processes needed for developing and creating object-based programs. They can either be read along with the material in their respective chapters or postponed and read concurrently with the material in Part II.

Problem Solving Using C++

2.1 INTRODUCTION TO C++

A well-designed program is constructed using a design philosophy similar to that used in constructing a well-designed building: It doesn't just happen; it depends on careful planning and execution if the final design is to accomplish its intended purpose. Just as an integral part of the design of a building is its structure, the same is true for a program.

Programs whose structure consists of interrelated segments, arranged in a logical and easily understandable order to form an integrated and complete unit, are referred to as **modular programs** (Figure 2.1). Modular programs are noticeably easier to develop, correct, and modify than programs constructed in some other manner. In programming terminology, the smaller segments used to construct a modular program are referred to as **modules.**

| FIGURE 2.1 | A Well-Designed Program Is Built Using Modules |

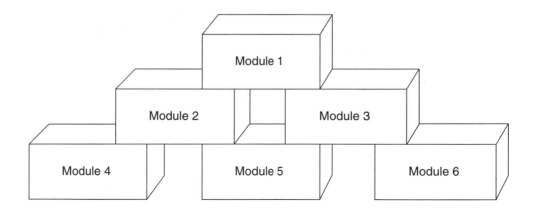

Each module is designed and developed to perform a specific task and is really a small subprogram all by itself. A complete C++ program is constructed by combining as many modules as necessary to produce the desired result. The advantage of modular construction is that the overall design of the program can be developed before any single module is written. Once the requirements for each module are finalized, the modules can be programmed and integrated within the overall program as they are completed.

In C++, modules can be either classes or functions. It helps to think of a **function** as a small machine that transforms the data it receives into a finished product. For example, Figure 2.2 illustrates a function that accepts two numbers as inputs and multiplies the numbers to produce one output. As shown, the interface of the function to the outside world is its inputs and results. The process of converting the inputs to results is both encapsulated and hidden within the function. In this regard, the function can be thought of as a single unit providing a special-purpose operation. A similar analogy is appropriate for a class.

A **class** is a more complicated unit than a function because it contains both data and specific functions appropriate for manipulating the data. Thus, unlike a function, which is used to encapsulate a set of operations, a class encapsulates both data and one or more sets of operations. The concept of a class is the subject of Part II, and for now, we will be predominantly concerned with the more basic function module.

One important requirement for designing a good function (and class) is to give it a name that conveys to the reader some idea about what the function or class does. The names permissible for functions and classes are also used to name other elements of the C++ language and are collectively referred to as identifiers. **Identifiers** can be made up of any combination of letters, digits, or underscores (_) selected according to the following rules:

1. The first character of the name must be a letter or underscore (_).
2. Only letters, digits, or underscores may follow the initial letter. Blank spaces are not allowed; separate words in a name consisting of multiple words by capitalizing the first letter of one or more of the words. (Although underscores may also be used for this purpose, they are increasingly being used only for compiler-dependent identifiers.)

FIGURE 2.2   A Multiplying Function

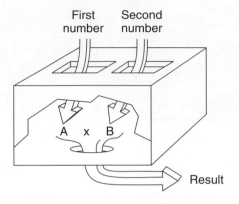

3. An identifier cannot be one of the keywords listed in Table 2.1. (A **keyword** is a word that is set aside by the language for a special purpose and can only be used in a specified manner.[1])

4. The maximum number of characters in an identifier is limited to 255 characters (this is compiler-dependent).

Examples of valid C++ identifiers are:

```
DegToRad        intersect        addNums        slope
bessel1         multTwo          FindMax        density
```

Examples of invalid identifiers are:

```
1AB3     ←————————    (Begins with a number, which violates rule 1)
E*6      ←————————    (Contains a special character, which violates rule 2)
while    ←————————    (Is a keyword, which violates rule 3)
```

TABLE 2.1 Keywords

auto	delete	goto	public	template
break	do	if	register	this
case	double	inline	return	typedef
catch	else	int	short	union
char	enum	long	signed	unsigned
class	extern	new	sizeof	virtual
const	float	operator	static	void
continue	for	private	struct	volatile
default	friend	protected	switch	while

---

[1] Keywords in C++ are also reserved words, which means they must be used only for their specified purpose. If you attempt to use them for any other purpose, C++ generates an error message.

In addition to conforming to C++'s identifier rules, a C++ function name must always be followed by parentheses (the reason for this is explained shortly). Also, a good function name should be a mnemonic. A **mnemonic** is a word or name designed as a memory aid. For example, the function name `DegToRad()` (note that we have included the required parentheses after the identifier, which clearly marks this as a function name) is a mnemonic if it is the name of a function that converts degrees to radians. Here, the name itself helps to identify what the function does.

Examples of valid function names that are not mnemonics are:

```
easy()        c3po()        r2d2()        TheForce()        mike()
```

Function names that are not mnemonic should not be used because they convey no information about what the function does.

Notice that function names can be typed in mixed uppercase and lowercase letters. This is becoming increasingly common in C++, although it is not absolutely necessary. All uppercase identifiers are usually reserved for symbolic constants, a topic covered in Section 3.5.

Note also that C++ is a **case-sensitive** language. This means that the compiler distinguishes between uppercase and lowercase letters. Thus, in C++, the names TOTAL, total, and TotaL represent three distinct and different names.

The `main()` Function

A distinct advantage of using functions and classes in C++ is that the overall structure of the program, in general, and individual modules, in particular, can be planned in advance, including provisions for testing and verifying each module's operation. Each function and class can then be written to meet its intended objective.

To provide for the orderly placement and execution of modules, each C++ program must have one and only one function named `main()`. The `main()` function is referred to as a **driver function** because it drives or tells the other modules the sequence in which they are to execute (see Figure 2.3).[2]

Figure 2.4 illustrates a structure for the `main()` function. The first line of the function, in this case `int main()`, is referred to as a **function header line.** A function header line, which is always the first line of a function, contains three pieces of information:[3]

1. What type of data, if any, is returned from the function
2. The name of the function
3. What type of data, if any, is sent into the function

The keyword before the function name defines the type of value the function returns when it has completed operating. When placed before the function's name the keyword `int` (see Table 2.1) designates that the function returns an integer value. Similarly, empty parentheses following the function name signify that no data are transmitted into the function when it is run. (Data transmitted into a function at run time are referred to as **arguments** of the function.) Braces, `{` and `}`, determine the beginning, and end, respectively, of the function body and enclose the statements making up the function. The statements inside the braces determine what the function does. Each statement inside the function must end with a semicolon (`;`).

---

[2] Modules executed from `main()` may, in turn, execute other modules. Each module, however, always returns to the module that initiated its execution. This is true even for `main()`, which returns control to the operating system.

[3] A class method must also begin with a header line that adheres to these same rules.

FIGURE 2.3   The `main()` Function Directs all Other Functions

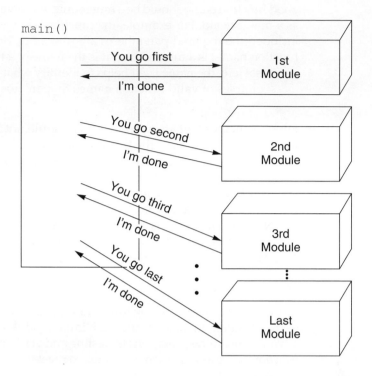

You will be naming and writing many of your own C++ functions. In fact, the rest of this book is primarily about the statements required to construct useful functions and how to combine functions and data into useful classes and programs. Each program, however, must have one and only one `main()` function. Until we learn how to pass data into a function and return data from a function (the topics of Chapter 6), the header line illustrated in Figure 2.4 will serve us for all the programs we need to write. For simple programs, the first two lines

```
int main()
{
```

designate that "the program begins here," while the last two lines

```
    return 0;
}
```

FIGURE 2.4   The Structure of a `main()` Function

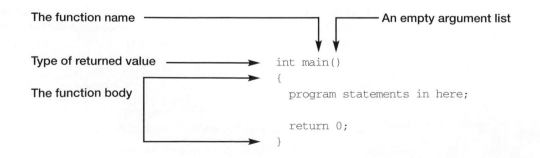

designate the end of the program. Fortunately, many useful functions and classes have already been written for us. We will now see how to use an object created from one of these classes to create our first working C++ program.

The cout Object

One of the most versatile and commonly used objects provided in C++ is named cout (pronounced "see out"). This object, whose name is derived from Console OUTput, is an output object that sends data given to it to the standard output display device.[4] For most systems, this display device is a video screen. The cout object displays on the monitor whatever is passed to it. For example, if the data Hello world! are passed to cout, these data are printed (or displayed) on your terminal screen. The data Hello world! are passed to the cout object by enclosing the text within quotation marks and putting the insertion ("put to") symbol, <<, before the message and after the object's name, as shown in Figure 2.5.

FIGURE 2.5   Passing a Message to cout

```
cout << "Hello world!";
```

Now let's put all this together into a working C++ program that can be run on your computer. Consider Program 2.1.

PROGRAM 2.1

```
// File: Pgm2-1.cpp
// Description: Displays Hello world!
// Programmer: G. Bronson
// Date: 1/15/2006

#include <iostream>
using namespace std;

int main()
{
   cout << "Hello world!";

   return 0;
}
```

The first four lines of program code, each of which begins with two slash symbols, //, are comments. We will have much more to say about comments in the next section, but for now it is important to understand that each source code program should begin with comments similar to those used here. These initial comment lines, at a minimum, should provide the file name under which the source code is saved, a short program description, the name of the programmer, and the date that the program was last modified. For all of the programs contained in this text, the file name refers to the name of the file as it exists on the source code provided with this text.

---

[4] The cout object is formally created from the ostream class, which is described in detail in Chapter 10.

The sixth line (counting blank lines) of the program:

```
#include <iostream>
```

is a preprocessor command that uses the reserved word include. Preprocessor commands begin with a pound sign (#) and perform some action before the compiler translates the source program into machine code. Specifically, the #include preprocessor command causes the contents of the named file, in this case the iostream file, to be inserted wherever the #include command appears in the program. The iostream file is a part of the standard library that contains, among other code, two classes named istream and ostream. These two classes provide the data declarations and methods used for data input and output, respectively. The iostream file is referred to as a **header file** because a reference to it is always placed at the top, or head, of a C++ program using the #include command. You may be wondering what the ostream file has to do with this simple program. The answer is that the cout object is created from the iostream class. Thus, the iostream header file must be included in all programs that use cout. As indicated in Program 2.1, preprocessor commands do not end with a semicolon.

Following the preprocessor #include command is a statement containing the reserved word using. The statement

```
using namespace std;
```

tells the compiler where to look to find the header files in the absence of any further explicit designation. You can think of a namespace as a specific named section of code within a file directory or folder that is accessed by the compiler when it is looking for prewritten classes or functions. Because the iostream header file is contained within the section of code named std, the compiler will automatically locate it using the iostream's cout object from this namespace whenever cout is referenced. Using namespaces effectively permits you to create your own classes and functions with the same names as those provided by the standard library, and place them in differently named namespaces. We can then tell the program which class or function to use by indicating the namespace where we want the compiler to look for the class or function.

The using statement is followed by the start of the program's main() function. This function begins with the header line developed at the beginning of this section. The body of the function, enclosed in braces, consists of only two statements. The first statement in main() passes one message to the cout object. The message is the string "Hello world!".

Because cout is an object of a prewritten class, we do not have to write it; it is available for use just by activating it correctly. Like all C++ objects, cout can only perform certain well-defined actions. For cout, the action is to assemble data for output display. When a string of characters is passed to cout, the object sees to it that the string is correctly displayed on the monitor, as shown in Figure 2.6.

Strings in C++ are any combination of letters, numbers, and special characters enclosed in double quotes "string in here". The double quotes are used to delimit (mark) the beginning and ending of the string and are not considered part of the string. Thus, the string of characters making up the message sent to cout must be enclosed in double quotes, as we have done in Program 2.1.

FIGURE 2.6   The Output from Program 2.1

```
Hello world!
```

Let us write another program to illustrate cout's versatility. Read Program 2.2 to determine what it does.

PROGRAM 2.2

```cpp
// File: Pgm2-2.cpp
// Description: Test program
// Programmer: G. Bronson
// Date: 1/15/2006
#include <iostream>
using namespace std;

int main()
{
 cout << "Computers, computers everywhere";
 cout << "\n as far as I can C";

 return 0;
}
```

When Program 2.2 is run, the following is displayed:

```
Computers, computers everywhere
     as far as I can C
```

You might be wondering why the \n did not appear in the output. The two characters \ and n, when used together, are called a *newline escape sequence.* They tell cout to send instructions to the display device to move to a new line. In C++, the backslash (\) character provides an "escape" from the normal interpretation of the character following it by altering the meaning of the next character. If the backslash is omitted from the second cout statement in Program 2.2, the n is printed as the letter n and the program prints:

```
Computers, computers everywheren as far as I can C
```

Newline escape sequences can be placed anywhere within the message passed to cout. See if you can determine the display produced by Program 2.3.

PROGRAM 2.3

```cpp
// File: Pgm2-3.cpp
// Description: Test program
// Programmer: G. Bronson
// Date: 2/15/2006
#include <iostream>
using namespace std;

int main()
{
  cout << "Computers everywhere\n as far as\n\n I can see";

  return 0;
}
```

The output for Program 2.3 is:

```
Computers everywhere
    as far as

I can see
```

Exercises 2.1

1. State whether the following are valid function names. If they are valid, state whether they are mnemonic names. (Recall that a mnemonic function name conveys some idea about the function's purpose.) If they are invalid names, state why.

m1234()	newBal()	abcd()	A12345()	1A2345()
power()	absVal()	mass()	do()	while()
add_5()	taxes()	netPay()	12345()	int()
cosine()	a2b3c4d5()	net$Pay()	amount()	$sine()
oldBalance()	newValue()	salestax()	1stApprox()	float()

2. Assume that the following functions have been written:

   getLength()   getWidth()   calcArea()   displayArea()

   a. From the functions' names, what do you think each function might do?

   b. In what order do you think a main() function might execute these functions (based on their names)?

3. Assume that the following functions have been written:

   inputPrice()   calcSalestax()   calcTotal()

   a. From the functions' names, what do you think each function might do?

   b. In what order do you think a main() function might execute these functions (based on their names)?

4. Determine names for functions that do the following:

   a. Find the average of a set of numbers.

   b. Find the area of a rectangle.

   c. Find the minimum value in a set of numbers.

   d. Convert a lowercase letter to an uppercase letter.

   e. Convert an uppercase letter to a lowercase letter.

   f. Sort a set of numbers from lowest to highest.

   g. Alphabetize a set of names.

5. Just as the keyword int can be used to signify that a function will return an integer, the keywords void, char, float, and double can be used to signify that a function will return no value, a character, a floating-point number, and a double-precision number, respectively. Using this information, write header lines for a main() function that will receive no arguments but will return:

   a. no value

   b. a character

   c. a floating-point number

   d. a double-precision number

6. a. Using cout, write a C++ program that displays your name on one line, your street address on a second line, and your city, state, and zip code on the third line.

   b. Run the program you have written for Exercise 6a on a computer. (*Note:* You must understand the procedures for entering and running a C++ program on the particular computer installation you are using.)

7. a. Write a C++ program to display the following verse:

```
Computers, computers everywhere
 as far as I can see
I really, really like these things,
 Oh joy, Oh joy for me!
```

   b. Run the program you have written for Exercise 7a on a computer.

8. a. How many cout statements would you use to display the following output?

PART NO.	PRICE
T1267	$6.34
T1300	$8.92
T2401	$65.40
T4482	$36.99

   b. What is the minimum number of cout statements that could be used to print the table in Exercise 8a?

   c. Write a complete C++ program to produce the output illustrated in Exercise 8a.

   d. Run the program you have written for Exercise 8c on a computer.

9. In response to a newline escape sequence, cout positions the next displayed character at the beginning of a new line. This positioning of the next character represents two distinct operations. What are they?

10. a. Many computer operating systems can redirect the output produced by cout either to a printer or directly to a floppy or hard disk file. Read the first part of Appendix D for a description of this redirection capability.

   b. If your computer supports output redirection, run the program written for Exercise 7a using this feature. Have your program's display redirected to a file named poem.

   c. If your computer supports output redirection to a printer, run the program written for Exercise 7a using this feature.

   Note for Exercises 11 through 16: Most projects, both programming and nonprogramming, can be structured into smaller subtasks or units of activity. These smaller subtasks can often be delegated to different people so that when all the tasks are finished and integrated, the project or program is completed. For Exercises 11 through 16, determine a set of subtasks that, taken together, complete the required task. (The purpose of these exercises is to have you consider the different ways that complex tasks can be structured. Although there is no one correct solution to these exercises, there are incorrect solutions and solutions that are better than others. An incorrect solution is one that does not complete the assigned task. One solution is better than another if it more clearly or easily identifies what must be done or does it more efficiently.)

11. You are given the task of wiring and installing lights in the attic of your house. Determine a set of subtasks that, taken together, accomplish this. (*Hint:* The first subtask is to determine the placement of the light fixtures.)

12. You are given the job of preparing a complete meal for five people next weekend. Determine a set of subtasks that, taken together, accomplish this. (*Hint:* One subtask, not necessarily the first one, is to buy the food.)

13. You are a sophomore in college and are planning to go to law school after graduation. List a set of major objectives that you must fulfill to meet this goal. (*Hint:* One objective is to take the right courses.)

14. You are given the job of planting a vegetable garden. Determine a set of subtasks that accomplish this. (*Hint:* One such subtask is to plan the layout of the garden.)

15. You are responsible for planning and arranging the family camping trip this summer. List a set of subtasks that, taken together, accomplish this objective successfully. (*Hint:* One subtask is to select the campsite.)

16. a. A national electrical supply distribution company wants a computer system that can prepare its customer invoices. The system must, of course, be capable of creating each day's invoices. Additionally, the company wants to be able to retrieve and output a printed report of all invoices that meet certain criteria; for example, all invoices sent in a particular month with a net value of more than a given dollar amount, all invoices sent in a year to a particular client, or all invoices sent to firms in a particular state. For this system, determine three or four major program units into which the system could be separated. (*Hint:* One program unit is "Prepare Invoices" to create each day's invoices.)

   b. Suppose someone enters incorrect data for a particular invoice. This error is discovered after the data have been entered and stored by the system. What program unit is needed to take care of correcting this problem? Discuss why such a program unit might or might not be required by most business systems.

   c. Assume a program unit exists that allows a user to alter or change data that have been incorrectly entered and stored. Discuss the need for including an "audit trail" that allows for reconstruction of the changes made, when they were made, and who made them.

2.2 PROGRAMMING STYLE

C++ programs start execution at the beginning of the main() function. Because a program can have only one starting point, every C++ language program must contain one and only one main() function. As we have seen, all of the statements that make up the main() function are then included within the braces { } following the function name. Although the main() function must be present in every C++ program, C++ does not require that the word main, the parentheses ( ), or the braces { } be placed in any particular form. The form used in the last section:

```
int main()
{
  program statements in here;

  return 0;
}
```

was chosen strictly for clarity and ease in reading the program. (If one of the program statements uses the cout object, the iostream header file must be included, as well as the statement using namespace std;.) For example, the following general form of a main() function also works:

```
int main
(
) { first statement;second statement;
        third statement;fourth
statement;

return 0;
}
```

Notice that more than one statement can be put on a line, or one statement can be written across lines. Except for strings, double quotes, identifiers, and keywords, C++ ignores all white space (white space refers to any combination of one or more blank spaces, tabs, or new lines). For example, changing the white space in Program 2.1 while making sure not to split the string Hello world! across two lines, and omitting all comments, results in the following valid program:

```
#include <iostream>
using namespace std;
int main
(){
cout <<
"Hello world!";

return 0;
}
```

Although this version of `main()` does work, it is an example of extremely poor programming style. It is difficult to read and understand. For readability, the `main()` function should always be written in standard form as:[6]

```
int main()
{
  program statements in here;

  return 0;
}
```

In this standard form, the function name starts in column 1 and is placed with the required parentheses on a line by itself. The opening brace of the function body follows on the next line and is placed under the first letter of the line containing the function name. Similarly, the closing function brace is placed by itself in column 1 as the last line of the function. This structure serves to highlight the function as a single unit.

Within the function itself, all program statements are indented at least two spaces. Indentation is another sign of good programming practice, especially if the same indentation is used for similar groups of statements. Review Program 2.2 to see that the same indentation was used for both `cout` object calls.

As you progress in your understanding and mastery of C++, you will develop your own indentation standards. Just keep in mind that the final form of your programs should be consistent and should always serve as an aid to the reading and understanding of your programs.

Comments

Comments are explanatory remarks made within a program. When used carefully, comments can be very helpful in clarifying what the complete program is about, what a specific group of statements is meant to accomplish, or what one line is intended to do. C++ supports two types of comments: line and block. Both types of comments can be placed anywhere within a program and have no effect on program execution. The computer ignores all comments; they are there strictly for the convenience of anyone reading the program.

A line comment begins with two slashes (`//`) and continues to the end of the line. For example, each of the following is a line comment:

```
// this is a comment
// this program prints out a message
// this program calculates a square root
```

---

[6] If the `main()` function did not return any value to the operating system, the appropriate first line would be `void main()`.

The symbols //, with no white space between them, designate the start of the line comment. The end of the line on which the comment is written designates the end of the comment.

A line comment can be written either on a line by itself or at the end of the same line containing a program statement. Program 2.4 illustrates the use of line comments within a program.

PROGRAM 2.4

```
// this program displays a message
#include <iostream>
using namespace std;

int main()
{
  cout << "Hello world"; // display the message

  return 0;
}
```

The first comment appears on a line by itself at the top of the program and describes what the program does. This is generally a good location to include a short comment describing the program's purpose. If more comments are required, they can be added, one per line. Thus, when a comment is too long to be contained on one line, it can be separated into two or more line comments, with each separate comment preceded by the double slash symbol set, //. The comment

```
// this comment is invalid because it
   extends over two lines
```

results in a C++ error message on your computer. This comment is correct when written as:

```
// this comment is used to illustrate a
// comment that extends across two lines
```

Comments that span two or more lines are, however, more conveniently written as block comments rather than as multiple-line comments. Such comments begin with the symbols /* and end with the symbols */. For example:

```
/* This is a block comment
   that spans
   across three lines */
```

In C++, a program's structure is intended to make the program readable and understandable, making the use of extensive comments unnecessary. This is reinforced if function, class, and variable names, described in the next chapter, are carefully selected to convey their meaning to anyone reading the program. However, if the purpose of a function, class, or statement is still not clear from its structure, name, or context, include comments where clarification is needed. Obscure code with no comments is a sure sign of bad programming when the program must be maintained or read by others. Excessive comments are also a sign of bad programming because they imply that insufficient thought was given to making the code self-explanatory.

Typically, any program that you write should begin with a set of initial program comments that include a short program description, your name, and the date that the program was last modified. For space considerations, and because all programs in this text were written by the author, initial comments will be used only for short program descriptions when they are not provided as part of the accompanying descriptive text.

---

1. a. Does the following program work?

   ```
   #include <iostream>
   using namespace std;
   int main(){cout << "Hello there world!"; return 0;}
   ```

   b. Why is the program given in Exercise 1a not a good program?

2. Rewrite the following programs to conform to good programming practice:

   a.
   ```
   #include <iostream>
   using namespace std;
   int main(
   ){
   cout             <<
   "The time has come"
   ; return 0;}
   ```

   b.
   ```
   #include <iostream>
   using namespace std;
   int main
   (){cout << "Newark is a city\n"cout <<
   "In New Jersey\n"; cout <<
   "It is also a city\n"
   ; cout << "In Delaware\n"
   ; return 0;}
   ```

   c.
   ```
   #include <iostream>
   using namespace std;
   int main(){cout << Reading a program\n"cout <<
   "is much easier\n"
   ;cout << "if a standard form for main is used\n")
   ;cout
   <<"and each statement is written\n"cout
   <<            "on a line by itself\n")
   ; return 0;}
   ```

   d.
   ```
   #include <iostream>
   using namespace std;
   int main
   (){cout << "Every C++ program"
   ;cout
   <<"\nmust have one and only one"
   ;
   cout << "main function"
   ;
   cout <<
   "\n the escape sequence of characters")
   ;cout <<
    "\nfor a newline can be placed anywhere"
   ;cout
   <<"\n within the data placed on the cout stream"
   ; return 0;}
   ```

3. a. When used in a message, the backslash character alters the meaning of the character immediately following it. If we want to print the backslash character, we have to tell cout to escape from the way it normally interprets the backslash. What character do you think is used to alter the way a single backslash character is interpreted?

   b. Using your answer to Exercise 3a, write the escape sequence for printing a backslash.

4. a. A token of a computer language is any sequence of characters that, as a unit with no intervening characters or white space, has a unique meaning. Using this definition of a token, determine whether escape sequences, function names, and the keywords listed in Table 2.1 are tokens of the C++ language.

   b. Discuss whether adding white space to a message alters the message. Discuss whether messages can be considered tokens of C++.

   c. Using the definition of a token given in Exercise 4a, determine whether the following statement is true: "Except for tokens of the language, C++ ignores all white space."

2.3 DATA TYPES

The objective of all programs is ultimately to process data, be it numerical, alphabetical, audio, or video. Central to this objective is the classification of data into specific types. For example, calculating the interest due on a bank balance requires mathematical operations on numerical data, while alphabetizing a list of names requires comparison operations on character-based data. Additionally, some operations are not applicable to certain types of data. For example, it makes no sense to add names together. To prevent the programmer from attempting to perform an inappropriate operation, C++ allows only certain operations to be performed on certain data types.

The types of data permitted and the appropriate operations defined for each type are referred to as a data type. Formally, a **data type** is defined as a set of values *and* a set of operations that can be applied to these values. For example, the set of all integer (whole) numbers constitutes a set of values, as does the set of all real numbers (numbers that contain a decimal point). These two sets of numbers, however, do not constitute a data type until a set of operations is also included. These operations, of course, are the familiar mathematical and comparison operations. The combination of a set of values plus operations becomes a true data type.

C++ categorizes data types into one of two fundamental groupings: built-in data types and class data types. A **class data type**, which is referred to as a class, for short, is a programmer-created data type. This means that the set of acceptable values and operations is defined by a programmer, using C++ code.

A **built-in data type** is one that is provided as an integral part of the C++ compiler and requires no external C++ code. Thus, a built-in data type can be used without recourse to supplementary language additions, such as that provided by the iostream header file needed for the cout object. Built-in data types, which are also referred to as **primitive** types, consist of the basic numerical types shown in Figure 2.7 and the operations listed in Table 2.2. As seen in this table, the majority of operations for built-in types are provided as symbols. This is in contrast to class types, where the majority of operations are provided as methods.

In introducing C++'s built-in data types, we will make use of literals. A **literal** is an acceptable value for a data type. The term "literal" reflects the fact that such a value explicitly identifies itself. (Another name for a literal is a **literal value**, or constant.) For example, all numbers, such as 2, 3.6, and −8.2, are referred to as literal values because they literally display their values. Text such as `"Hello world!"` is also referred to as a literal value because the text itself is displayed. You have been using literal values throughout your life and have commonly referred to them as numbers and words. In Section 2.2 you will see some examples of non-literal values—that is, values that do not display themselves but are stored and accessed using identifiers.

FIGURE 2.7 Built-In Data Types

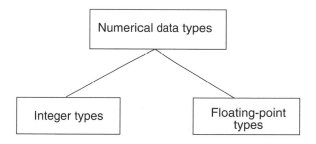

TABLE 2.2 Built-In Data Type Operations

Built-in Data Types	Operations
Integer	+, −, *, /, %, =, ==, !=, <=, >=, `sizeof()`, and bit operations (see Sec. 17.?)
Floating point	+, −, *, /, =, =−, !−, <=, >=, `sizeof()`

Integer Data Types

C++ provides nine built-in integer data types, as shown in Figure 2.8. The essential difference among the various integer data types is the amount of storage used for each type, which directly affects the range of values that each type is capable of representing. The three most important types that are used almost exclusively in the majority of applications are the `int`, `char`, and `bool` data types. The reason for the remaining types is essentially historical, as they were originally provided to accommodate special situations (a very small or a very large range of numbers). This permitted a programmer to maximize memory usage by selecting a data type that used the smallest amount of memory consistent with an application's requirements. When computer memories were both very small relative to today's computers and extremely expensive, this was a major concern. Although no longer a concern for the vast majority of programs, it still provides a programmer the ability to optimize memory usage when necessary. Typically these situations occur in engineering applications, such as control systems used in home appliances and automobiles.

FIGURE 2.8 C++ Integer Data Types

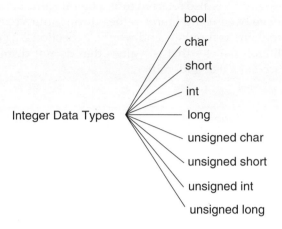

The int **Data Type**

The set of values supported by the int data type are whole numbers, which are mathematically known as integers. An integer value consists of digits only and can optionally be preceded by either a plus (+) or minus (−) sign. Thus, an integer value can be the number zero or any positive or negative numerical value without a decimal point. Examples of valid integers are:

      0   5   −10   +25   1000   253   −26351   +36

As these examples illustrate, integers may contain an explicit sign. No commas, decimal points, or special symbols, such as the dollar sign, are allowed. Examples of invalid integers are:

      $255.62   2,523   3.   6,243,892   1,492.89   +6.0

Different compilers have their own internal limit on the largest (most positive) and smallest (most negative) integer values that can be stored in each data type.[7] The most common storage allocation is four bytes for the int data type, which restricts the set of values permitted in this data type to represent integers in the range of −2,147,483,648 to 2,147,483,647.[8]

The char **Data Type**

The char data type is used to store individual characters. Characters include the letters of the alphabet (both uppercase and lowercase), the ten digits 0 through 9, and special symbols such as + $. , −!. A single character value is any one letter, digit, or special symbol enclosed by single quotes. Examples of valid character values are:

      'A'   '$'   'b'   '7'   'y'   '!'   'M'   'q'

Character values are typically stored in a computer using either the ASCII or Unicode codes. ASCII, pronounced AS-KEY, is an acronym for American Standard

---

[7] The limits imposed by the compiler can also be found in the limits header file and are defined as the hexadecimal constants int_max and int_min.

[8] It is interesting to note that in all cases the magnitude of the most negative integer number is always one more than the magnitude of the most positive integer. This is due to the two's complement method of integer storage, which is described in Section 1.6.

PROGRAMMING NOTE

Atomic Data

An **atomic data value** is a value that is considered a complete entity by itself and cannot be decomposed into a smaller data type. For example, although an integer can be decomposed into individual digits, C++ does not have a numerical digit type. Rather, each integer is regarded as a complete value by itself and, as such, is considered atomic data. Similarly, because the `int` data type supports only atomic data values, it is said to be an **atomic data type**. As you might expect, all of the built-in data types are atomic data types.

Code for Information Interchange. The ASCII code provides codes for an English-language-based character set plus codes for printer and display control, such as new line and printer paper-eject codes. Each character code is contained within a single byte, which provides for 256 distinct codes. Table 2.3 lists the ASCII byte codes for uppercase letters.

Additionally, C++ provides for the newer Unicode character set that uses two bytes per character and can represent 65,536 characters. This code is used for international applications by providing other language character sets in addition to English. Since the first 256 Unicode codes have the same numerical value as the 256 ASCII codes (the additional byte is simply coded with all 0s), you need not concern yourself with which storage code is used when using English language characters.

TABLE 2.3 The ASCII Uppercase Letter Codes

Letter	ASCII Code	Letter	ASCII Code
A	01000001	N	01001110
B	01000010	O	01001111
C	01000011	P	01010000
D	01000100	Q	01010001
E	01000101	R	01010010
F	01000110	S	01010011
G	01000111	T	01010100
H	01001000	U	01010101
I	01001001	V	01010110
J	01001010	W	01010111
K	01001011	X	01011000
L	01001100	Y	01011001
M	01001101	Z	01011010

Using Table 2.3, we can determine how the characters 'W', 'E', 'S', 'T', 'B', and 'Y', for example, are stored inside a computer that uses the ASCII character code. This sequence of six characters requires six bytes of storage (one byte for each letter) and would be stored as illustrated in Figure 2.9.

The Escape Character

One character that has a special meaning in C++ is the backslash, \, which is referred to as the **escape character**. When this character is placed directly in front of a select group of characters, it tells the compiler to escape from the way these characters would normally be interpreted. The combination of a backslash and these specific characters is called an **escape sequence**. We have already encountered an example of this in the newline escape sequence, \n, in Chapter 1. Table 2.4 lists C++'s most common escape sequences.

FIGURE 2.9   The Letters WESTBY Stored Inside a Computer

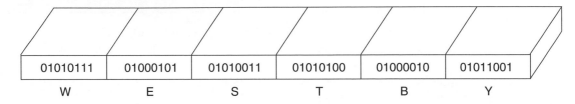

6 bytes of storage

01010111	01000101	01010011	01010100	01000010	01011001
W	E	S	T	B	Y

Although each escape sequence listed in Table 2.4 is made up of two distinct characters, the combination of the two characters, with no intervening white space, causes the compiler to create the single code listed in the ASCII Code column of Table 2.4.

TABLE 2.4 Escape Sequences

Escape Sequence	Character Represented	Meaning	ASCII Code
\n	Newline	Move to a new line	00001010
\t	Horizontal tab	Move to next horizontal tab setting	00001001
\v	Vertical tab	Move to next vertical tab setting	00001011
\b	Backspace	Move back one space	00001000
\r	Carriage return	Carriage return (moves the cursor to the start of the current line— used for overprinting)	00001101
\f	Form Feed	Issue a form feed	00001100
\a	Alert	Issue an alert (usually a bell sound)	00000111
\\	Backslash	Insert a backslash character (this is used to place an actual backslash character within a string)	01011100
\?	Question mark	Insert a question mark character	00111111
\'	Single quotation	Insert a single quote character (this is used to place an inner single quote within a set of outer single quotes)	00100111
\"	Double quotation mark	Insert a double quote character (this is used to place an inner double quote within a set of outer double quotes)	00100010
\nnn	Octal number	The number nnn (n is a digit) is to be considered an octal number	–
\xhhhh	Hexadecimal number	The number hhhh (h is a digit) is to be considered a hexadecimal number	–
\0	Null character	Insert the Null character, which is defined as having the value 0	00000000

The bool Data Type

In C++, the bool data type is used to represent Boolean (logical) data. As such, this data type is restricted to one of two values: true or false. This data type is most useful when a program must examine a specific condition and, as a result of the condition being either true or false, take a prescribed course of action. For example, in a sales application, the condition being examined might be "is the total purchase for $100 or more?" Only when this condition is true is a discount applied. The fact that the Boolean data type uses an integer storage code, however, has very useful implications that are exploited by almost all professional C++ programmers. The practical uses of Boolean conditions is considered in Chapter 4, so we defer further discussion of Boolean data until then.

Determining Storage Size

A unique feature of C++ is that it permits you to see where and how values are stored. As an example, C++ offers an operator named sizeof() that provides the number of bytes used to store values for any data type name included within the operator's parentheses. (Review Section 1.6 if you are unfamiliar with the concept of a byte.) Notice that this is a built-in operator that does not use an arithmetic symbol to perform its operation. Program 2.5 uses this operator to determine the amount of storage reserved for the int, char, and bool data types.

PROGRAM 2.5

```
#include <iostream>
using namespace std;

int main()
{
  cout < "\nData Type  Bytes"
       < "\n——-  —-"
       < "\nint          " < sizeof(int)
       < "\nchar         " < sizeof(char)
       < "\nbool         " < sizeof(bool)
       < '\n';

  return 0;
}
```

In reviewing Program 2.5 notice that a single character value is inserted into cout by enclosing it within single quotes, as is the escape sequence '\n' insertion at the end of the cout statement. Within the first five displayed lines this character is simply included within each output string. Each time the compiler encounters the newline escape sequence, either as a single character or as part of a string, it is translated as a single character that forces the display to start on a new line. Although double quotes can be used for the final newline insertion, as "\n", this would designate a string. Because only a single character is being transmitted, and to emphasize that single characters are designated using single quotes, we have used '\n' in place of "\n". From a practical standpoint, however, both notations will force a new line in the display.

PROGRAMMING NOTE

The Character '\n' and the String "\n"

Both '\n' and "\n" are recognized by the compiler as containing the newline character. The difference is in the data types being used. Formally, '\n' is a character literal, while "\n" is a string literal. From a practical standpoint both cause the same thing to happen: a new line is forced on the output display. In encountering the character value '\n', however, the compiler translates it using the single byte code 00001010 (see Table 2.4). In encountering the string value "\n", the compiler translates this string using the correct character code, but also adds an additional character to denote the end of the string.

Good programming practice requires that you end the last output display with a newline escape sequence. This ensures that the first line of output from one program does not end up on the last line displayed by the previously executed program.

The output of Program 2.5 is compiler dependent. That is to say, each compiler will correctly report the amount of storage that it provides for the data type under consideration. When run on the author's computer, which uses Microsoft's current Visual C++.net compiler, the following output was produced:

Data Type	Bytes
int	4
char	1
bool	1

For this output, which is the typical storage provided by almost all current C++ compilers, we can determine the range of values that can be stored in each of these int data types. To do so, however, requires understanding the difference between a signed and unsigned data type.

Signed and Unsigned Data Types

A **signed data type** is defined as one that permits storing negative values in addition to zero and positive values. As such, the int data type is a signed data type. An **unsigned data type** is one that provides only for non-negative (that is, zero and positive) values. Both the char and bool data types are unsigned data types, which means that they have no codes for storing negative values.

There are cases in which an application might only require unsigned numerical values. For example, many date applications store dates in the numerical form *yearmonthday* (thus, the date 12/25/2007 would be stored as 20071225) and are only concerned with dates after 0 CE. For such applications, which will never require a negative value, an unsigned data type can be used.

All unsigned integer types, such as unsigned int, provide a range of positive values that is, for all practical purposes, double the range provided for their signed counterparts. This extra positive range is made available by using the negative range of the signed version for additional positive numbers.

With the understanding of the difference between a signed and unsigned data type, Table 2.5 can be used to determine the range of integer values supported by current C++ compilers.

One item to notice in Table 2.5 is that a long int uses the same amount of storage (four bytes) as an int. The only requirement of the ANSI C++ standard is that an int must provide at least as much storage as a short int, and that a long

PROGRAMMING NOTE

Object-Oriented and Procedural Programs

Except for the Boolean type, all of C++'s built-in data types are direct carryovers from the C procedural language. It should not be surprising, therefore, that programs using only individual built-in types will not be object-oriented programs. Rather, as in Program 2.5, they become procedural programs; that is, a program primarily based on procedures, such as `main()`.

It is only when built-in types are bundled together to form a packet of data, which becomes an object, can an object-oriented program come into existence. This packaging together of individual data types takes place in a class's data declaration section.

int must provide at least as much storage as an `int`. On the first desktop computer systems (1980s), which were limited in their memory capacity to thousands of bytes, a `short int` typically used one byte of storage, an `int` two bytes, and a `long int` four bytes. Because this storage limited the range of `int` values from −32,768 to +32,767, while the use of an `unsigned int` provided a range of values from 0 to 65,535, the doubling of possible positive values was significant. With the current range of `int` values in the −2 to +2 billion range, the doubling of positive values is rarely a consideration. Additionally, using a `long int` becomes unnecessary, because it now uses the same storage capacity as an `int`.

TABLE 2.5 Integer Data Type Storage

Name of Data Type	Storage Size (in bytes)	Range of Values
char	1	256 characters
bool	1	true (which is considered as any positive value) and false (which is a zero)
short int	2	−32,768 to +32,767
unsigned short int	2	0 to 65,535
int	4	−2,147,483,648 to +2,147,483,647
unsigned int	4	0 to 4,294,967,295
long int	4	−2,147,483,648 to +2,147,483,647
unsigned long int	4	0 to 4,294,967,295

Floating-Point Types

A **floating-point number**, which is also called a **real number**, can be the number zero or any positive or negative number that contains a decimal point. Examples of floating-point numbers are:

```
+10.625   5.   −6.2   3251.92   0.0   0.33   −6.67   +2.
```

Notice that the numbers 5., 0.0, and +2. are classified as floating-point values, but the same numbers written without a decimal point (5, 0, +2) would be integer values. As with integer values, special symbols such as the dollar sign and the comma are not permitted in real numbers. Examples of invalid real numbers are:

```
5,326.25   24   6,459   $10.29   7.007.645
```

TABLE 2.6 Floating-Point Data Types

Type	Storage	Absolute Range of Values (+ and −)
float	4 bytes	1.40129846432481707e−45 to 3.40282346638528860e+38
double and long double	8 bytes	4.94065645841246544e−324 to 1.79769313486231570e+308

C++ supports three floating-point data types: float, double, and long double. The difference between these data types is the amount of storage that a compiler uses for each type. Most compilers use twice the amount of storage for doubles as for floats, which allows a double to have approximately twice the precision of a float. For this reason, a float value is sometimes referred to as a **single-precision** number and a double value as a **double-precision** number. The actual storage allocation for each data type, however, depends on the particular compiler. The ANSI C++ standard only requires that a double has at least the same amount of precision as a float and that a long double has at least the same amount of storage as a double. Currently, most C++ compilers allocate four bytes for the float data type and eight bytes for both double and long double data types. This produces the range of numbers listed in Table 2.6.

In compilers that use the same amount of storage for double and long double numbers, these two data types become identical. (The sizeof() operator that was used in Program 2.5 can always be used to determine the amount of storage reserved by your compiler for these data types.) A float literal is indicated by appending either an f or F after the number and a long double literal is created by appending either an l or L to the number. In the absence of these suffixes, a floating-point number defaults to a double. For example:

9.234   indicates a double literal
9.234f indicates a float literal
9.234L indicates a long double literal

The only difference in these numbers is the amount of storage the computer may use to store them. If you require numbers having more than six significant digits to the right of the decimal point, this storage becomes important, and you should use double-precision values. Appendix E describes the binary storage format used for floating-point numbers and its impact on number precision.

Exponential Notation

Floating-point numbers can also be written in exponential notation (see Table 2.6), which is similar to scientific notation and is commonly used to express both very large and very small values in compact form. The following examples illustrate how numbers with decimals can be expressed in exponential and scientific notation.

Decimal Notation	Exponential Notation	Scientific Notation
1625.	1.625e3	1.625×10^3
63421.	6.3421e4	6.3421×10^4
.00731	7.31e−3	7.31×10^{-3}
.000625	6.25e−4	6.25×10^{-4}

PROGRAMMING NOTE

What Is Precision?

In numerical theory, the term **precision** typically refers to numerical accuracy. In this context, a statement such as "this computation is accurate, or precise, to the fifth decimal place" is used. This means that the fifth digit after the decimal point has been rounded, and the number is accurate to within ±0.00005.

In computer programming, precision can refer either to the accuracy of a number or the amount of significant digits in the number, where significant digits are defined as the number of clearly correct digits plus 1. For example, if the number 12.6874 has been rounded to the fourth decimal place, it is correct to say that this number is precise (that is, accurate) to the fourth decimal place. In other words, all of the digits in the number are accurate except the fourth decimal digit, which has been rounded. Similarly, it can be said that this same number has a precision of six digits, which means that the first five digits are correct and the sixth digit has been rounded. Another way of saying this is that the number 12.6874 has six significant digits.

Notice that the significant digits in a number need not have any relation to the number of displayed digits. For example, if the number 687.45678921 has five significant digits, it is only accurate to the value 687.46, where the last digit is assumed to be rounded. In a similar manner, dollar values in many very large financial applications are frequently rounded to the nearest hundred-thousand dollars. In such applications, a displayed dollar value of $12,400,000, for example, is not accurate to the closest dollar. If this value is specified as having three significant digits, it is only accurate to the hundred-thousands digit.

In exponential notation, the letter e stands for exponent. The number following the e represents a power of 10 and indicates the number of places the decimal point should be moved to obtain the standard decimal value. The decimal point is moved to the right if the number after the e is positive or moved to the left if the number after the e is negative. For example, the e3 in 1.625e3 means move the decimal place three places to the right so that the number becomes 1625. The e−3 in 7.31e−3 means move the decimal point three places to the left so that 7.31e−3 becomes .00731.

Exercises 2.3

1. Determine data types appropriate for the following data:
   a. the average of four grades
   b. the number of days in a month
   c. the length of the Golden Gate Bridge
   d. the numbers in a state lottery
   e. the distance from Brooklyn, N.Y. to Newark, N.J.
   f. the single-character prefix that specifies a component type

2. Convert the following numbers into standard decimal form:

   6.34e5   1.95162e2   8.395e1   2.95e−3   4.623e−4

3. Write the following decimal numbers using exponential notation:

   126.   656.23   3426.95   4893.2   .321   .0123   .006789

4. Compile and execute Program 2-1 on your computer.

5. Modify Program 2-5 to determine the storage used by your compiler for all of C++'s integer data types.

6. Using the system reference manuals for your computer, determine the character code used by your computer.

7. Show how the name KINGSLEY would be stored inside a computer that uses the ASCII code. That is, draw a figure similar to Figure 2-9 for the name KINGSLEY.

8. Repeat Exercise 7 using the letters of your own last name.

9. Modify Program 2-5 to determine how many bytes your compiler assigns to the `float`, `double`, and `long double` data types.

10. Since computers use different representations for storing integer, floating-point, double-precision, and character values, discuss how a program might alert the computer to the data types of the various values it will be using.

11. Although we have concentrated on operations involving integer and floating-point numbers, C++ allows characters and integers to be added or subtracted. This can be done because a character is stored using an integer code (it is an integer data type). Thus, characters and integers can be freely mixed in arithmetic expressions. For example, if your computer uses the ASCII code, the expression `'a'` + 1 equals `'b'`, and `'z'` − 1 equals `'y'`. Similarly, `'A'` + 1 is `'B'`, and `'Z'` − 1 is `'Y'`. With this as background, determine the character results of the following expressions (assume that all characters are stored using the ASCII code).

    a. `'m'` − 5

    b. `'m'` + 5

    c. `'G'` + 6

    d. `'G'` − 6

    e. `'b'` − `'a'`

    f. `'g'` − `'a'` + 1

    g. `'G'` − `'A'` + 1

    Note: To complete the following exercise, you need an understanding of basic computer storage concepts. Specifically, if you are unfamiliar with the concept of a byte, refer to Section 1.6 before doing the next exercise.

12. Although the total number of bytes varies from computer to computer, memory sizes of 65,536 to more than several million bytes are not uncommon. In computer language, the letter K represents the number 1,024, which is 2 raised to the 10th power, and M represents the number 1,048,576, which is 2 raised to the 20th power. Thus, a memory size of 640 K is really 640 times 1024, or 655,360 bytes, and a memory size of 4 M is really 4 times 1,048,576, which is 4,194,304 bytes. Using this information, calculate the actual number of bytes in:

    a. a memory containing 32 M bytes

    b. a memory containing 64 M bytes

    c. a memory containing 128 M bytes

    d. a memory containing 256 M bytes

    e. a memory consisting of 256 M words, where each word consists of 2 bytes

    f. a memory consisting of 256 M words, where each word consists of 4 bytes

    g. a disk that specifies 1.44 M bytes

2.4 ARITHMETIC OPERATIONS

The last section presented the data values corresponding to each of C++'s built-in data types. In this section, the set of arithmetic operations that can be applied to these values is provided.

Integers and real numbers can be added, subtracted, multiplied, and divided. Although it is usually better not to mix integers and real numbers when performing arithmetic operations, predictable results are obtained when using different data types in the same arithmetic expression. Surprisingly, you can also add character data to, or subtract it from, both character and integer data to produce useful results (for example, 'A' + 1 results in the character 'B'). This is possible because characters are stored using integer storage codes.

The operators used for arithmetic operations are called **arithmetic operators**, and are as follows:

Operation	Operator
Addition	+
Subtraction	−
Multiplication	*
Division	/
Modulus division	%

Don't be concerned at this stage if you don't understand the term "modulus division." You'll learn more about this operator later in this section.

These operators are referred to as **binary operators**. This term reflects the fact that the operator requires two operands to produce a result. An **operand** can be either a literal value or an identifier that has a value associated with it. A **simple binary arithmetic expression** consists of a binary arithmetic operator connecting two literal values in the form:

```
literalValue operator literalValue
```

Examples of simple binary arithmetic expressions are:

```
3 + 7
18 − 3
12.62 + 9.8
.08 * 12.2
12.6 / 2.
```

The spaces around the arithmetic operators in these examples are inserted strictly for clarity and can be omitted without affecting the value of the expression. Notice that an expression in C++ must be entered in a straight-line form. Thus, for example, the C++ expression equivalent to 12.6 divided by 2 must be entered as 12.6/2 and not as the algebraic expression:

$$\frac{12.6}{2}$$

You can use cout to display the value of any arithmetic expression on the console screen. To do this, the desired value must be passed to the object. For example, the statement

```
cout << (6 + 15);
```

yields the display 21. Strictly speaking, the parentheses surrounding the expression 6 + 15 are required to indicate that the value of the expression (that is, 21) is being displayed. In practice, most compilers will accept and correctly process this statement without the parentheses.

In addition to displaying a numerical value, cout can display a string identifying the output, as was done in Section 1.3. For example, the statement

```
cout << "The sum of 6 and 15 is " << (6 + 15);
```

causes two pieces of data to be sent to cout, a string and a value. Individually, each set of data sent to cout must be preceded by its own insertion operator symbol (<<). Here, the first data sent for display is the string "The sum of 6 and 15 is", and the second item sent is the value of the expression 6 + 15. The display produced by this statement is:

The sum of 6 and 15 is 21

Notice that the space between the word "is" and the number 21 is caused by the space placed within the string passed to cout. As far as cout is concerned, its input is simply a set of characters that are then sent on to be displayed in the order they are received. Characters from the input are queued, one behind the other, and sent to the console for display. Placing a space in the input causes this space to be part of the stream of characters that is ultimately displayed. For example, the statement

```
    cout << "The sum of 12.2 and 15.754 is " <<  (12.2 + 15.754);
```

yields the display:

The sum of 12.2 and 15.754 is 27.954

Note that when multiple insertions are made to cout the code can be spread across multiple lines. Only one semicolon, however, must be used, which is placed after the last insertion and terminates the complete statement. Thus, the prior display is also produced by the statement:

```
        cout << "The sum of 12.2 and 15.754 is "
             <<  (12.2 + 15.754);
```

However, when you allow such a statement to span multiple lines, a few rules must be followed: (1) a string contained within double quotes cannot be split across lines; and (2) the terminating semicolon should appear only on the last line. Multiple insertion symbols can always be placed within a line.

Floating-point numbers are displayed with sufficient decimal places to the right of the decimal place to accommodate the fractional part of the number. This is true if the number has six or fewer digits. If the number has more than six digits, the fractional part is rounded and only six digits are displayed. If the number has no decimal digits, neither a decimal point nor any digits are displayed.[9]

Program 2.6 illustrates using cout to display the results of arithmetic expressions within the statements of a complete program.

PROGRAM 2.6

```
#include <iostream>
using namespace std;

int main()
{
  cout << "15.0 plus 2.0 equals "    << (15.0 + 2.0) << endl
       << "15.0 minus 2.0 equals "   << (15.0 - 2.0) << endl
       << "15.0 times 2.0 equals "   << (15.0 * 2.0) << endl
       << "15.0 divided by 2.0 equals " << (15.0 / 2.0) << endl;

  return 0;
}
```

---

[9] It should be noted that none of this output is defined as part of the C++ language. Rather, it is defined by a set of classes and routines provided with each C++ compiler.

The output of Program 2.6 is:

```
15.0 plus 2.0 equals 17
15.0 minus 2.0 equals 13
15.0 times 2.0 equals 30
15.0 divided by 2.0 equals 7.5
```

The only really new item presented in Program 2.6 is the term `endl`, which is an example of a C++ manipulator. A **manipulator** is an item used to manipulate how the output stream of characters is displayed. In particular, the `endl` manipulator first causes a newline character (`'\n'`) to be inserted into the display and then forces all of the current insertions to be displayed immediately, rather than waiting for more data. (Section 3.2 contains a list of the more commonly used manipulators.)

Expression Types

An **expression** is any combination of operators and operands that can be evaluated to yield a value. An expression that contains only integer values as operands is called an **integer expression**, and the result of the expression is an integer value. Similarly, an expression containing only floating-point values (single- and double-precision) as operands is called a **floating-point expression**, and the result of such an expression is a floating-point value (the term **real expression** is also used). An expression containing both integer and floating-point values is called a **mixed-mode expression**. Although it is usually better not to mix integer and floating-point values in an arithmetic operation, the data type of each operation is determined by the following rules:

1. If both operands are integers, the result of the operation is an integer.
2. If one operand is a real value, the result of the operation is a double-precision value.

Notice that the result of an arithmetic expression is never a single-precision (float) number. This is because during execution a C++ program temporarily converts all single-precision numbers to double-precision numbers when an arithmetic expression is being evaluated.

Integer Division

The division of two integer values can produce rather strange results for the unwary. For example, the expression 15/2 yields the integer result 7. Because integers cannot contain a fractional part, a value of 7.5 cannot be obtained. The fractional part obtained when two integers are divided, that is, the remainder, is always dropped (truncated). Thus, the value of 9/4 is 2, and 18/3 is 5.

Often, however, we may need to retain the remainder of an integer division. To do this, C++ provides an arithmetic operator having the symbol %. This operator, called both the **modulus** and **remainder operator**, captures the remainder when an integer number is divided by an integer (using a noninteger value with the modulus operator results in a compiler error). For example:

```
9 % 4 is 1    (that is, the remainder when 9 is divided by 4 is 1)
17 % 3 is 2   (that is, the remainder when 17 is divided by 3 is 2)
15 % 4 is 3   (that is, the remainder when 15 is divided by the 4 is 3)
14 % 2 is 0   (that is, the remainder when 14 is divided by 2 is 0)
```

More precisely, the modulus operator first determines the integer number of times that the dividend, which is the number following the % operator, can be

> **PROGRAMMING NOTE**

The `endl` manipulator

On most systems, the `endl` manipulator, which is never enclosed in quotes, and the `\n` escape sequence, which must always be enclosed in quotes, are processed in the same way and produce the same effect. The one exception is on those systems where the output is accumulated internally until there are sufficient characters to make it advantageous to display them all, in one burst, on the screen. In such systems, which are referred to as "buffered," the `endl` manipulator forces all accumulated output to be displayed immediately, without waiting for any additional characters to fill the buffer area before being printed. As a practical matter, you would not notice a difference in the final display. Thus, as a general rule, you should use the `\n` escape sequence whenever it can be included within an existing string, and use the `endl` manipulator whenever a `\n` would appear by itself or to formally signify the end of a specific group of output display.

divided into the divisor, which is the number before the `%` operator. It then returns the remainder.

Negation

In addition to the binary arithmetic operators, C++ also provides unary operators. A **unary operator** is one that operates on a single operand. One of these unary operators uses the same symbol as binary subtraction ($-$). The minus sign in front of a single numerical value negates (reverses the sign of) the number.

Table 2.7 summarizes the six arithmetic operations we have described so far and lists the data type for the result produced by each operator, based on the data type of the operands involved.

TABLE 2.7 Summary of Arithmetic Operators

Operation	Operator	Type	Operand	Result
Addition	+	Binary	Both are integers One operand is not an integer	Integer Double-precision
Subtraction	−	Binary	Both are integers One operand is not an integer	Integer Double-precision
Multiplication	*	Binary	Both are integers One operand is not an integer	Integer Double-precision
Division	/	Binary	Both are integers One operand is not an integer	Integer Double-precision
Modulus	%	Binary	Both are integers One operand is not an integer	Integer Double-precision
Negation	−	Unary	Integer or floating point	Same as operand

Operator Precedence and Associativity

In addition to such simple expressions as `5 + 12` and `.08 * 26.2`, more complex arithmetic expressions can be created. C++, like most other programming languages, requires you to follow certain rules when writing expressions containing more than one arithmetic operator. These rules are:

1. Two binary arithmetic operator symbols must never be placed side by side. For example, `5 * %6` is invalid because the two operators, `*` and `%`, are placed next to each other.

2. Parentheses may be used to form groupings, and all expressions enclosed within parentheses are evaluated first. This permits parentheses to alter the evaluation to any desired order. For example, in the expression `(6 + 4)/ (2 + 3)`, the `6 + 4` and `2 + 3` are evaluated first to yield `10/5`. The `10/5` is then evaluated to yield `2`.

3. Sets of parentheses may also be enclosed by other parentheses. For example, the expression `(2 * (3 + 7) )/5` is valid and evaluates to `4`. When parentheses are included within parentheses, the expressions in the innermost parentheses are always evaluated first. The evaluation continues from innermost to outermost parentheses until the expressions in all parentheses have been evaluated. The number of closing parentheses [`)`] must always equal the number of opening parentheses [`(`] so that there are no unpaired sets.

4. Parentheses cannot be used to indicate multiplication; rather, the multiplication operator, `*`, must be used. For example, the expression `(3 + 4) (5 + 1)` is invalid. The correct expression is `(3 + 4) * (5 + 1)`.

Parentheses should specify logical groupings of operands and indicate clearly, to both the compiler and programmers, the intended order of arithmetic operations. Although expressions within parentheses are always evaluated first, expressions containing multiple operators, both within and without parentheses, are evaluated by the priority, or **precedence**, of the operators. There are three levels of precedence:

- P1—All negations are done first.
- P2—Multiplication, division, and modulus operations are computed next. Expressions containing more than one multiplication, division, or modulus operator are evaluated from left to right as each operator is encountered. For example, in the expression `35 / 7 % 3 * 4`, the operations are all of the same priority, so the operations will be performed from left to right as each operator is encountered. Thus, the division is done first, yielding the expression `5 % 3 * 4`. The modulus operation is performed next, yielding a result of `2`. And finally, the value of `2 * 4` is computed to yield `8`.
- P3—Addition and subtraction are computed last. Expressions containing more than one addition or subtraction are evaluated from left to right as each operator is encountered.

In addition to precedence, operators have an **associativity**, which is the order in which operators of the same precedence are evaluated, as described in rule P2. For example, does the expression `6.0 * 6/4` yield `9.0`, which is `(6.0 * 6)/4`, or `6`, which is `6.0 * (6/4)`? The answer is `9.0`, because C++'s operators use the same associativity as in general mathematics, which evaluates multiplication from left to right, as rule P2 indicates. Table 2.8 lists both the precedence and associativity of the operators considered in this section. As we have seen, the precedence of an operator establishes its priority relative to all other operators. Operators at the top of Table 2.8 have a higher priority than operators at the bottom of the table. In expressions with multiple operators of different precedence, the operator with the higher precedence is used before an operator with lower precedence. For example, in the expression `6 + 4/2 + 3`, since the division operator has a higher precedence (P2) than addition, the division is done first, yielding an intermediate result of `6 + 2 + 3`. The additions are then performed, left to right, to yield a final result of `11`.

TABLE 2.8 Operator Precedence and Associativity

Operator	Associativity
unary −	right to left
* / %	left to right
+ −	left to right

Finally, let us use either Table 2.8 or the precedence rules to evaluate an expression containing operators of different precedence, such as $8 + 5 * 7 \% 2 * 4$. Because the multiplication and modulus operators have a higher precedence than the addition operator, these two operations are evaluated first (P2), using their left-to-right associativity, before the addition is evaluated (P3). Thus, the complete expression is evaluated as:

$$8 + 5 * 7 \% 2 * 4 =$$
$$8 + 35 \% 2 * 4 =$$
$$8 + 1 * 4 =$$
$$8 + 4 = 12$$

Exercises 2.2

1. Listed below are correct algebraic expressions and incorrect C++ expressions corresponding to them. Find the errors and write corrected C++ expressions.

Algebra	*C++ Expression*
a. $(2)(3) + (4)(5)$	`(2)(3)  +  (4)(5)`
b. $\dfrac{6 + 18}{2}$	`6 + 18 / 2`
c. $\dfrac{4.5}{12.2 - 3.1}$	`4.5 / 12.2 - 3.1`
d. $4.6(3.0 + 14.9)$	`4.6(3.0 + 14.9)`
e. $(12.1 + 18.9)(15.3 - 3.8)$	`(12.1 + 18.9)(15.3 - 3.8)`

2. Determine the value of the following integer expressions:

   a. `3 + 4 * 6`
   b. `3 * 4 / 6 + 6`
   c. `2 * 3 / 12 * 8 / 4`
   d. `10 * (1 + 7 * 3)`
   e. `20 - 2 / 6 + 3`
   f. `20 - 2 / (6 + 3)`
   g. `(20 - 2) / 6 + 3`
   h. `(20 - 2) / (6 + 3)`
   i. `50 % 20`
   j. `(10 + 3) % 4`

3. Determine the value of the following floating-point expressions:

   a. `3.0 + 4.0 * 6.0`
   b. `3.0 * 4.0 / 6.0 + 6.0`
   c. `2.0 * 3.0 / 12.0 * 8.0 / 4.0`
   d. `10.0 * (1.0 + 7.0 * 3.0)`
   e. `20.0 - 2.0 / 6.0 + 3.0`
   f. `20.0 - 2.0 / (6.0 + 3.0)`
   g. `(20.0 - 2.0) / 6.0 + 3.0`
   h. `(20.0 - 2.0) / (6.0 + 3.0)`

4. Evaluate the following mixed-mode expressions and list the data type of the result. In evaluating the expressions, be aware of the data types of all intermediate calculations.

   a. 10.0 + 15 / 2 + 4.3

   b. 10.0 + 15.0 / 2 + 4.3

   c. 3.0 * 4 / 6 + 6

   d. 3 * 4.0 / 6 + 6

   e. 20.0 − 2 / 6 + 3

   f. 10 + 17 * 3 + 4

   g. 10 + 17 / 3. + 4

   h. 3.0 * 4 % 6 + 6

   i. 10 + 17 % 3 + 4.

5. Assume that amount stores the integer value 1, m stores the integer value 50, n stores the integer value 10, and p stores the integer value 5. Evaluate the following expressions:

   a. n / p + 3

   b. m / p + n − 10 * amount

   c. m − 3 * n + 4 * amount

   d. amount / 5

   e. 18 / p

   f. −p * n

   g. −m / 20

   h. (m + n) / (p + amount)

   i. m + n / p + amount

6. Repeat Exercise 5 assuming that amount stores the value 1.0, m stores the value 50.0, n stores the value 10.0, and p stores the value 5.0.

7. Enter, compile, and run Program 2.2 on your computer system.

8. Determine the output of the following program:

```
#include <iostream>
using namespace std;

int main()   // a program illustrating integer truncation
{
  cout << "answer1 is the integer " << 9/4;
  cout << "\nanswer2 is the integer " << 17/3;

  return 0;
}
```

9. Determine the output of the following program:

```
#include <iostream>
using namespace std;

int main()   // a program illustrating the % operator
{
  cout << "The remainder of 9 divided by 4 is " << 9 % 4;
  cout << "\nThe remainder of 17 divided by 3 is " << 17 % 3;

  return 0;
}
```

10. Write a C++ program that displays the results of the expressions `3.0 * 5.0`, `7.1 * 8.3 - 2.2`, and `3.2/(6.1 * 5)`. Calculate the value of these expressions manually to verify that the displayed values are correct.

11. Write a C++ program that displays the results of the expressions `15/4`, `15 % 4`, and `5 * 3 - (6 * 4)`. Calculate the value of these expressions manually to verify that the displayed values are correct.

2.5 VARIABLES AND DECLARATION STATEMENTS

All integer, floating-point, and other values used in a computer program are stored and retrieved from the computer's memory unit. Conceptually, individual memory locations in the memory unit are arranged like the rooms in a large hotel. Like hotel rooms, each memory location has a unique address ("room number"). Before high-level languages such as C++ existed, memory locations were referenced by their addresses. For example, the storage of integer values 45 and 12 in the memory locations 1652 and 2548 (see Figure 2.10), respectively, required instructions equivalent to:

Put a 45 in location 1652.
Put a 12 in location 2548.

To add the two numbers just stored and save the result in another memory location, for example, at location 3000, we would need a statement comparable to:

Add the contents of location 1652
to the contents of location 2548
and store the result into location 3000.

Clearly, this method of storage and retrieval is a cumbersome process. In high-level languages such as C++, symbolic names are used in place of actual memory addresses. These symbolic names are called **variables.** A variable is simply a name chosen by the programmer that is used to refer to computer storage locations. The term **variable** is used because the value stored in the variable can change, or vary. For each name the programmer uses, the computer keeps track of the memory address corresponding to that name. In our hotel room analogy, this is equivalent to putting a name on the door of a room and referring to the room by this name, such as the "Blue" room, rather than using the actual room number.

FIGURE 2.10	Enough Storage for Two Integers

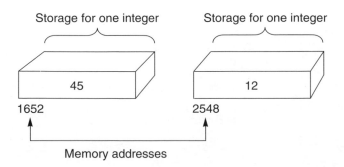

Memory addresses

In C++, the selection of variable names is left to the programmer, as long as the following rules are observed:

1. The variable name must begin with a letter or underscore (_) and may contain only letters, underscores, or digits. It cannot contain any blanks, commas, or special symbols, such as ( ) & , $ # . ! \ ?. Use capital letters to separate names consisting of multiple words.

2. A variable name cannot be a keyword (see Table 2.1).

3. The variable name cannot consist of more than 255 characters (this is compiler-dependent).

These rules are identical to those for selecting function names. As with function names, variable names should be mnemonics that give some indication of the variable's use. For example, a good name for a variable used to store a value that is the total of some other values is sum or total. Variable names that give no indication of the value stored, such as r2d2, linda, bill, and getum should not be selected. As with function names, variable names can be typed in uppercase and lowercase letters.

Now assume that the first memory location illustrated in Figure 2.11, which has address 1652, is given the variable name num1. Also assume that memory location 2548 is given the name num2, and memory location 3000 is given the name total, as illustrated in Figure 2.11.

Using these variable names, the operation of storing 45 in location 1652, storing 12 in location 2548, and adding the contents of these two locations is accomplished by the C++ statements:

```
num1 = 45;
num2 = 12;
total = num1 + num2;
```

Each of these three statements is called an **assignment statement** because it tells the computer to assign (store) a value into a variable. Assignment statements always have an equal (=) sign and one variable name immediately to the left of this sign. The value on the right of the equal sign is determined first, and this value is assigned to the variable on the left of the equal sign. The blank spaces in the assignment statements are inserted for readability. We will have much more to say about assignment statements in the next chapter, but for now we can use them to store values in variables.

FIGURE 2.11 Naming Storage Locations

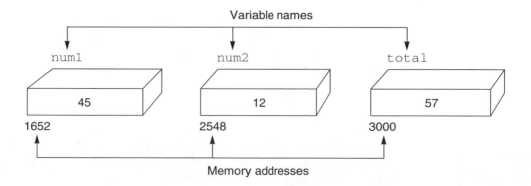

A variable name is useful because it frees the programmer from concern over where data are physically stored inside the computer. We simply use the variable name and let the compiler worry about where in memory the data are actually stored. Before storing a value into a variable, however, C++ requires that we clearly declare the type of data to be stored in it. We must tell the compiler, in advance, the names of the variables used for characters, the names used for integers, and the names used to store the other C++ data types.

Declaration Statements

Naming a variable and specifying the data type that can be stored in it is accomplished using a **declaration statement.** A declaration statement has the general form:

```
datatype variableName;
```

where `dataType` designates a valid C++ data type and `variableName` is a user-selected variable name. For example, variables used to hold integer values are declared using the keyword **int** to specify the data type and have the form:

```
int variableName;
```

Thus, the declaration statement

```
int sum;
```

declares `sum` as the name of a variable capable of storing an integer value.

In addition to the reserved word `int`, which is used to specify an integer, the reserved word **long** is used to specify a long integer.[10] For example, the statement

```
long datenum;
```

declares `datenum` as a variable used to store a long integer. When using the `long` qualifier, the keyword `int` can be included. Thus, the previous declaration can also be written as:

```
long int datenum;
```

Variables used to hold single-precision floating-point values are declared using the keyword **float**, whereas variables used to hold double-precision values are declared using the keyword **double**. For example, the statement

```
float firstnum;
```

declares `firstnum` as a variable used to store a floating-point number. Similarly, the statement

```
double secnum;
```

declares that the variable `secnum` will be used to store a double-precision number.

Although declaration statements may be placed anywhere within a function, most declarations are typically grouped together and placed immediately after the function's opening brace. In all cases, however, a variable must be declared before it can be used, and like all C++ statements, declaration statements must end with a semicolon. If the declaration statements are placed after the opening function

---

[10]Additionally, the reserved words `unsigned int` are used to specify an integer that can only store nonnegative numbers and the reserved words `short int` are used to specify a short integer.

brace, a simple `main()` function containing declaration statements has the following general form:

```
#include <iostream>
using namespace std;

int main()
{
    declaration statements;

    other statements;

    return 0;
}
```

Program 2.7 illustrates this form in declaring and using four double-precision variables, with the `cout` object used to display the contents of one of the variables.

PROGRAM 2.7

```
#include <iostream>
using namespace std;

int main()
{
  double grade1;  // declare grade1 as a double variable
  double grade2;  // declare grade2 as a double variable
  double total;   // declare total as a double variable
  double average; // declare average as a double variable

  grade1 = 85.5;
  grade2 = 97.0;
  total = grade1 + grade2;
  average = total/2.0; // divide the total by 2.0
  cout << "The average grade is " << average << endl;

  return 0;
}
```

The placement of the declaration statements in Program 2.7 is straightforward, although we will see shortly that the four individual declarations can be combined into a single declaration. When Program 2.7 is run, the following output is displayed:

```
The average grade is 91.25
```

Notice that when a variable name is sent to `cout`, the value stored in the variable is placed on the output stream and displayed.

Just as integer and real (floating-point, double-precision, and long double) variables must be declared before they can be used, a variable used to store a single character must also be declared. Character variables are declared using the reserved word `char`. For example, the declaration

```
char ch;
```

declares `ch` to be a character variable. Program 2.8 illustrates this declaration and the use of `cout` to display the value stored in a character variable.

PROGRAM 2.8

```cpp
#include <iostream>
using namespace std;

int main()
{
  char ch;      // this declares a character variable

  ch = 'a';     // store the letter a into ch
  cout << "The character stored in ch is " << ch << endl;
  ch = 'm';     // now store the letter m into ch
  cout << "The character now stored in ch is "<< ch << endl;

  return 0;
}
```

When Program 2.8 is run, the output produced is:

```
The character stored in ch is a
The character now stored in ch is m
```

Notice in Program 2.8 that the first letter stored in the variable ch is a and the second letter stored is m. Because a variable can be used to store only one value at a time, the assignment of m to the variable automatically causes a to be overwritten.

Multiple Declarations

Variables having the same data type can always be grouped together and declared using a single declaration statement. The common form of such a declaration is:

> *datatype variable List;*

For example, the four separate declarations used in Program 2.6,

```cpp
double grade1;
double grade2;
double total;
double average;
```

can be replaced by the single declaration statement:

```cpp
double grade1, grade2, total, average;
```

Similarly, the two character declarations

```cpp
char ch;
char key;
```

can be replaced with the single declaration statement:

```cpp
char ch, key;
```

Note that declaring multiple variables in a single declaration requires that the data type of the variables be given only once, that all the variable names be separated by commas, and that only one semicolon be used to terminate the declaration. (The space after each comma is inserted for readability, and is not required.)

Declaration statements can also be used to store an initial value into declared variables. For example, the declaration statement

```
int num1 = 15;
```

both declares the variable `num1` as an integer variable and sets the value of the variable to 15. When a declaration statement is used to store a value into a variable, the variable is said to be **initialized**. Thus, in this example, it is correct to say that the variable `num1` has been initialized to 15. Similarly, the declaration statements

```
double grade1 = 87.0;
double grade2 = 93.5;
double total;
```

declare three double-precision variables and initialize two of them. When initializations are used, good programming practice dictates that each initialized variable be declared on a line by itself. Constants, expressions using only constants (such as 87.0 + 12 − 2), and expressions using constants and previously initialized variables can all be used as initializers within a function. For example, Program 2.7 rewritten with a declaration initialization becomes Program 2.7a.

PROGRAM 2.7a

```
#include <iostream>
using namespace std;

int main()
{
  double grade1 = 85.5;
  double grade2 = 97.0;
  double total, average;

  total = grade1 + grade2;
  average - total/2.0; // divide the total by 2.0
  cout << "The average grade is " << average << endl;

  return 0;
}
```

Notice the blank line after the last declaration statement. Inserting a blank line after the variable declarations placed at the top of a function body is a good programming practice. It improves both a program's appearance and its readability.

An interesting feature of C++ is that variable declarations may be freely intermixed and even contained within other statements; the only requirement is that a variable must be declared prior to its use. For example, the variable `total` in Program 2.7a could have been declared at its first use by the statement `double total = grade1 + grade2`. In very restricted situations (such as debugging described in Section 4.7 or in a `for` loop described in Section 5.4), declaring a variable at its point of use can be helpful. In general, however, it is preferable not to disperse declarations but rather to group them, in as concise and clear a manner as possible, at the top of each function.

Memory Allocation

The declaration statements we have introduced have performed both software and hardware tasks. From a software perspective, declaration statements always provide a list of all variables and their data types. In this software role, variable declarations also help to control an otherwise common and troublesome error caused by the misspelling of a variable's name within a program. For example, assume that a variable named `distance` is declared and initialized using the statement:

```
int distance = 26;
```

Now assume that this variable is inadvertently misspelled in the statement:

```
mpg = distnce / gallons;
```

In languages that do not require variable declarations, the program treats `distnce` as a new variable and either assigns an initial value of zero to the variable or uses whatever value happens to be in the variable's storage area. In either case, a value is calculated and assigned to `mpg`, and finding the error or even knowing that an error occurred could be extremely troublesome. Such errors are impossible in C++ because the compiler flags `distnce` as an undeclared variable. The compiler cannot, of course, detect when one declared variable is typed in place of another declared variable.

In addition to their software role, declaration statements can also perform a distinct hardware task. Since each data type has its own storage requirements, the computer can allocate sufficient storage for a variable only after knowing the variable's data type. Because variable declarations provide this information, they can be used to force the compiler to reserve sufficient physical memory storage for each variable. Declaration statements used for this hardware purpose are also called **definition statements** because they define or tell the compiler how much memory is needed for data storage.

All of the declaration statements we have encountered so far have also been definition statements. Later, we will see cases of declaration statements that do not cause any new storage to be allocated and are used simply to declare or alert the program to the data types of variables that are created elsewhere in the program.

Figure 2.12 (parts a–d) illustrates the series of operations set in motion by declaration statements that also perform a definition role. The figure shows that definition statements (or if you prefer, declaration statements that also cause memory to be allocated) "tag" the first byte of each set of reserved bytes with a name. This name is, of course, the variable's name and is used by the computer to correctly locate the starting point of each variable's reserved memory area.

Within a program, after a variable has been declared, it is typically used by a programmer to refer to the contents of the variable (that is, the variable's value). Where in memory this value is stored is generally of little concern to the programmer. The compiler, however, must be concerned with where each value is stored and with correctly locating each variable. In this task, the computer uses the variable name to locate the first byte of storage previously allocated to the variable. Knowing the variable's data type then allows the compiler to store or retrieve the correct number of bytes.

FIGURE 2.12a   Defining the Integer Variable Named `total`

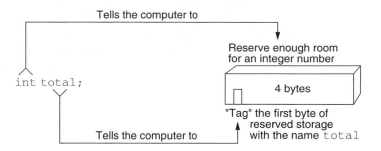

FIGURE 2.12b   Defining the Floating-Point Variable Named `firstnum`

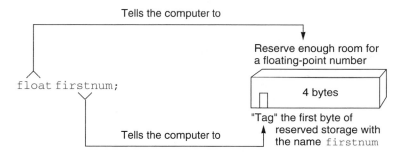

FIGURE 2.12c   Defining the Double-Precision Variable Named `secnum`

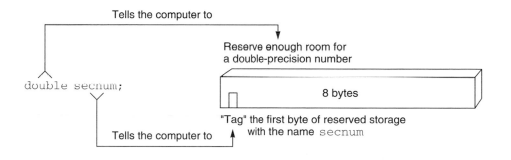

FIGURE 2.12d   Defining the Character Variable Named `ch`

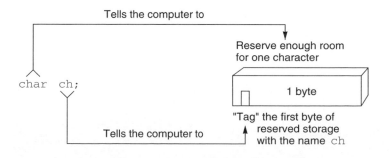

Displaying a Variable's Address

Every variable has three major items associated with it: its data type, the actual value stored in the variable, and the address of the variable. The value stored in the variable is referred to as the variable's contents, while the address of the first memory location used for the variable constitutes its address. How many locations are used for the variable, as we have just seen, depends on the variable's data type. The relationship between these three items (type, contents, location) is illustrated in Figure 2.13.

FIGURE 2.13   A Typical Variable

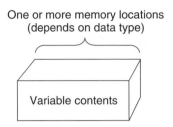

One or more memory locations
(depends on data type)

Variable contents

Variable address

Programmers are usually concerned only with the value assigned to a variable (its contents) and give little attention to where the value is stored (its address). For example, consider Program 2.9.

PROGRAM 2.9

```cpp
#include <iostream>
using namespace std;

int main()
{
  int num;

  num = 22;
  cout << "The value stored in num is " << num << endl;

  return 0;
}
```

The output displayed by Program 2.9 is:

```
The value stored in num is 22
```

FIGURE 2.14   Somewhere in Memory

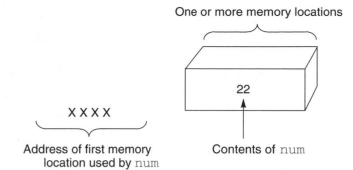

Program 2.9 merely prints the value 22, which is the contents of the variable num. We can go further, however, and ask, "Where is the number 22 actually stored?" Although the answer is "in num," this is only half of the answer. The variable name num is simply a convenient symbol for real physical locations in memory, as illustrated in Figure 2.14.

To determine the address of num, we can use C++'s address operator, &, which means "the address of." Except when used in a declaration statement, the address operator placed in front of a variable's name refers to the address of the variable.[11] For example, &num means *the address of* num, &total means *the address of* total, and &price means *the address of* price. Program 2.10 uses the address operator to display the address of the variable num. For convenience, this address, which is always a hexadecimal number, has been cast into an integer value.

PROGRAM 2.10

```
#include <iostream>
using namespace std;

int main()
{
  int num;

  num = 22;
  cout << "The value stored in num is " << num << endl;
  cout << "The address of num = " << int(&num) << endl;

  return 0;
}
```

The output of Program 2.10 is:

```
The value stored in num is 22
The address of num = 1244884
```

---

[11] When used in declaring reference variables and parameters, which is presented in Chapter 6, the ampersand (&) refers to the data type *preceding* it. Thus, the declaration double num is read as "num is the address of a double-precision variable" or more commonly as "num is a reference to a double."

FIGURE 2.15   A More Complete Picture of the Variable num

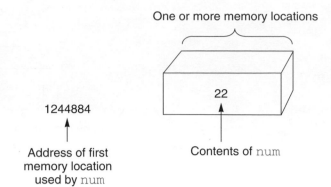

One or more memory locations

22

1244884

Address of first
memory location
used by num

Contents of num

Figure 2.15 illustrates the additional address information provided by the output of Program 2.10.

Clearly, the address output by Program 2.10 depends on the computer used to run the program. Every time Program 2.10 is executed, however, it displays the address of the first memory location used to store the variable num. This display has no effect on how addresses are used internal to the program; it merely provides us with a means of displaying addresses that is helpful in understanding them. As we shall see in Chapters 6 and 14, using addresses as opposed to only displaying them is an extremely important and powerful programming tool.

Exercises 2.5

1. State whether the following variable names are valid or invalid. If they are invalid, state the reason.

prodA	c1234	abcd	_c3	12345
newbal	while	$total	new bal	a1b2c3d4
9ab6	sum.of	average	grade1	finGrad

2. State whether the following variable names are valid or invalid. If they are invalid, state the reason why. Also indicate which of the valid variable names should not be used because they convey no information about the variable.

salestax	a243	r2d2	first_num	ccA1
harry	sue	c3p0	average	sum
maximum	okay	a	awesome	goforit
3sum	for	tot.a1	c$five	netpay

3. a. Write a declaration statement to declare that the variable count will be used to store an integer.

   b. Write a declaration statement to declare that the variable grade will be used to store a floating-point number.

   c. Write a declaration statement to declare that the variable yield will be used to store a double-precision number.

   d. Write a declaration statement to declare that the variable initial will be used to store a character.

4. Write declaration statements for the following variables:

   a. num1, num2, and num3 used to store integer numbers

   b. grade1, grade2, grade3, and grade4 used to store floating-point numbers

   c. tempa, tempb, and tempc used to store double-precision numbers

   d. ch, let1, let2, let3, and let4 used to store character types

5. Write declaration statements for the following variables:

   a. firstnum and secnum used to store integers

   b. price, yield, and coupon used to store floating-point numbers

   c. maturity used to store a double-precision number

6. Rewrite each of the following declaration statements as three individual declarations:

   a. int month, day = 30, year;

   b. double hours, rate, otime = 15.62;

   c. float price, amount, taxes;

   d. char in_key, ch, choice = 'f';

7. a. Determine what each statement causes to happen in the following program:

```
#include <iostream>
using namespace std;
int main()
{
  int num1, num2, total;

  num1 = 25;
  num2 = 30;
  total = num1 + num2;
  cout << "The total of" << num1 << " and "
       << num2 << " is " << total << endl;
  return 0;
}
```

   b. What output is printed when the program listed in Exercise 7a is run?

8. Write a C++ program that stores the sum of the integer numbers 12 and 33 in a variable named sum. Have your program display the value stored in sum.

9. Write a C++ program that stores the integer value 16 in the variable length and the integer value 18 in the variable width. Have your program calculate the value assigned to the variable perimeter using the assignment statement

   perimeter = 2 * length + 2 * width;

   and print the value stored in the variable perimeter. Make sure you declare all the variables as integers at the beginning of the main() function.

10. Write a C++ program that stores the integer value 16 in the variable num1 and the integer value 18 in the variable num2. (Make sure you declare the variables as integers.) Have your program calculate the total of these numbers and their average. The total should be stored in an integer named total and the average in an integer named average. (Use the statement average = total/2.0; to calculate the average.) Use the cout object to display total and average.

11. Repeat Exercise 10, but store the number 15 in num1 instead of 16. With a pencil, write down the average of num1 and num2. What do you think your program will store in the integer variable that you used for the average of these two numbers? How can you ensure that the correct answer will be printed for the average?

12. Write a C++ program that stores the number 105.62 in the variable `firstnum`, 89.352 in the variable `secnum`, and 98.67 in the variable `thirdnum`. (Make sure to declare the variables first as either float or double.) Have your program calculate the total of the three numbers and their average. The total should be stored in the variable total and the average in the variable average. (Use the statement `average = total /3.0;` to calculate the average.) Use the `cout` object to display the total and average.

13. Every variable has at least two items associated with it. What are these two items?

14. a. A statement used to clarify the relationship between squares and rectangles is, "All squares are rectangles but not all rectangles are squares." Write a similar statement that describes the relationship between definition and declaration statements.

    b. Why must a variable be defined before any other C++ statement that uses the variable?

    Note for Exercises 15 through 17: Assume that a character requires one byte of storage, an integer two bytes, a floating-point number four bytes, a double-precision number eight bytes, and that variables are assigned storage in the order in which they are declared. (Review Section 1.6 if you are unfamiliar with the concept of a byte.)

15. a. Using Figure 2.16 and assuming that the variable name `rate` is assigned to the byte having memory address 159, determine the addresses corresponding to each variable declared in the following statements. Also fill in the appropriate bytes with the initialization data included in the declaration statements (use letters for the characters, not the computer codes that are stored).

    ```
    float rate;
    char ch1 = 'w', ch2 = 'o', ch3 = 'w', ch4 = '!';
    double taxes;
    int num, count = 0;
    ```

    b. Repeat Exercise 15a, but substitute the actual byte patterns that an ASCII code computer uses to store the characters in the variables `ch1`, `ch2`, `ch3`, and `ch4`. (*Hint:* Use Table 2.3.)

16. a. Using Figure 2.16 and assuming that the variable named `cn1` is assigned to the byte at memory address 159, determine the addresses corresponding to each variable declared in the following statements. Also fill in the appropriate bytes with the initialization data included in the declaration statements (use letters for the characters, not the computer codes that are stored).

    ```
    char cn1 = 'a', cn2 = ' ', cn3 = 'b', cn4 = 'u', cn5 = 'n';
    char cn6 = 'c', cn7 = 'h', key = '\\', sch = '\'', inc = 'o';
    char inc1 = 'f';
    ```

    b. Repeat Exercise 16a, but substitute the actual byte patterns that an ASCII code computer uses to store the characters in each of the declared variables. (*Hint:* Use Table 2.3.)

17. Using Figure 2.14 and assuming that the variable name `miles` is assigned to the byte at memory address 159, determine the addresses corresponding to each variable declared in the following statements:

    ```
    float miles;
    int count, num;
    double dist, temp;
    ```

FIGURE 2.16   Memory Bytes for Exercises 15, 16, and 17

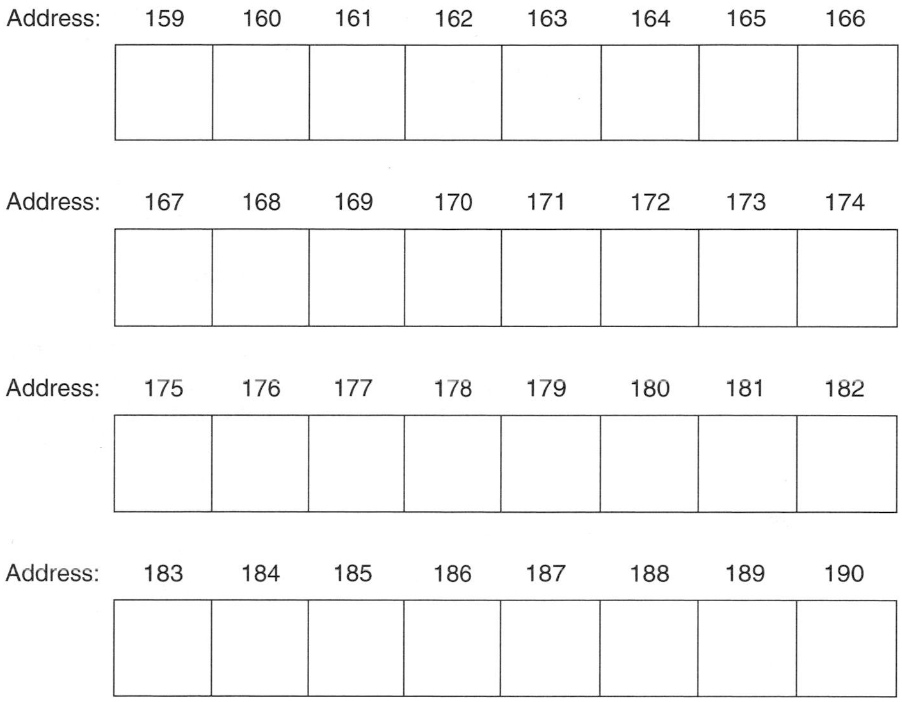

Address: 159   160   161   162   163   164   165   166

Address: 167   168   169   170   171   172   173   174

Address: 175   176   177   178   179   180   181   182

Address: 183   184   185   186   187   188   189   190

2.6 APPLYING THE SOFTWARE DEVELOPMENT PROCEDURE

Recall from Section 1.3 that writing a C++ program is the third step in the programming process. The first two steps are determining what is required and selecting the algorithm to be coded into C++. In this section, we show how the steps presented in Section 1.3 are applied in practice when converting programming problems into working C++ programs. To review, once a program requirement or problem is stated, the software development procedure consists of the following steps.

Step 1: Analyze the Problem

The analysis can consist of up to two parts. The first is a *basic analysis* that must be performed on all problems and consists of extracting the complete input and output information supplied by the problem. That is, you must (1) determine and understand the desired output items that the program must produce and (2) determine the required input items.

   Together, these two items are referred to as the problem's input/output, or I/O for short. Only after a problem's I/O has been determined is it possible to select an initial algorithm for transforming the inputs into the desired outputs. At this point, it is sometimes necessary and/or useful to perform a hand calculation to verify that the output can indeed be obtained from the inputs. Clearly, if a formula is given that relates the inputs to the output, this step can be omitted at this stage. If the required inputs are available and the desired output(s) can be produced, the problem is said to be clearly defined and can be solved.

For a variety of reasons, it may not be possible to complete a basic analysis. If this is the case, an extended analysis may be necessary. An *extended analysis* simply means that you must obtain additional information about the problem so that you thoroughly understand what is being asked for and how to achieve the result. In this text, any additional information required for an understanding of the problem is supplied along with the problem statement.

Step 2: Develop a Solution

This step is frequently referred to as the design step, and we use the terms *development* and *design* interchangeably. In this step, you must settle on an algorithm for transforming the input items into the desired outputs and refine it as necessary so that it adequately defines all of the features that you want your program to have. If you have not performed a hand calculation using the algorithm in the analysis step, you should do so here, using specific input values.

In designing a solution, the specific approach we take is often referred to as the **top-down approach.** This approach consists of starting with the most general solution and refining it in a manner such that the final program solution consists of clearly defined tasks that can be accomplished by individual program functions.

Step 3: Code the Solution

At this point, you write the C++ program that corresponds to the solution developed in Step 2.

Step 4: Test and Correct the Program

This is done by means of selected test data and is used to make corrections to the program when errors are found. One set of test data that should always be used is the data used in your previous hand calculation.

To see how each of these steps can be implemented in practice, we now apply it to a simple programming problem.

> The circumference, C, of a circle is given by the formula $C = 2\pi r$, where π is the constant 3.1416 (accurate to four decimal places) and r is the radius of the circle. Using this information, write a C++ program to calculate the circumference of a circle that has a 2-inch radius.

Step 1: Analyze the Problem   The first step in developing a program for this problem statement is to perform a basic analysis. We begin by determining the required outputs. Frequently, the statement of the problem uses such words as *calculate, print, determine, find,* or *compare,* which help determine the desired outputs.

For our sample problem statement, the key phrase is "to calculate the circumference of a circle." This clearly identifies an output item. Since there are no other such phrases in the problem, only one output item is required.

After we have clearly identified the desired output, the basic analysis step continues with the identification of all input items. It is essential at this stage to distinguish between input items and input values. An **input item** is the name of an input quantity, whereas an **input value** is a specific number or quantity for the input item. For example, in our sample problem statement, the input item is the radius of the circle (the known quantity). Although this input item has a specific numerical value in this problem (the value 2), actual input item values are generally not of importance at this stage, because the initial selection of an algorithm is typically independent of specific input values. The algorithm depends on knowing what the output and input items are and if there are any special limits. Let us see why this is so.

From the problem statement, it is clear that the algorithm for transforming the input items to the desired output is given by the formula $C = 2\pi r$. Notice that this formula can be used regardless of the specific values assigned to r. Although we cannot produce an actual numerical value for the output item (circumference) unless we have an actual numerical value for the input item, the correct relationship between inputs and outputs is expressed by the formula. Recall that this is precisely what an algorithm provides: a description of how the inputs are to be transformed into outputs that work for all inputs.

Step 2: Develop a Solution   The basic algorithm for transforming the inputs into the desired output is provided by the given formula. We must now refine it by listing, in detail, how the inputs, outputs, and algorithm are to be combined to produce a solution. This listing indicates the steps that will be taken by the program to solve the problem. As such, it constitutes an outline of the final form followed by the program code. Using pseudocode, the complete algorithm for solving this problem is:

Assign a value to r.
Calculate the circumference using the formula C $= 2\pi$r.
Display the circumference.

Notice that the structure of this algorithm conforms to the sequential control structure presented in Section 1.3.

Having selected and refined the algorithm, the next step in the design (if it was not already done in the analysis step) is to check the algorithm by hand using specific data. Performing a calculation either by hand or with a calculator helps ensure that you really do understand the problem. An added feature of a manual calculation is that the results can be used later in the testing phase to verify program operation. Then, when the final program is used with other data, you will have established a degree of confidence that a correct result is being calculated.

A manual calculation requires that we have specific input values that can be assigned and used by the algorithm to produce the desired output. For this problem, one input value is given: a radius of 2 inches. Substituting this value into the formula, we obtain a circumference = 2 (3.1416)(2) = 12.5664 inches.

Step 3: Code the Solution   Since we have carefully developed a program solution, all that remains is to code the solution algorithm in C++. This means declaring appropriate input and output variables, initializing the input variables appropriately, computing the circumference, and printing the calculated circumference value. Program 2.11 performs these steps.

PROGRAM 2.11

```cpp
#include <iostream>
using namespace std;

int main()
{
    double radius, circumference;

    radius = 2.0;
    circumference = 2.0 * 3.1416 * radius;
    cout << "The circumference of the circle is "
         << circumference << endl;

    return 0;
}
```

When program 2.11 is executed, the following output is produced:

```
The circumference of the circle is 12.5664
```

Now that we have a working program that produces a result, the final step in the development process, testing the program, can begin.

Step 4: Test and Correct the Program   The purpose of testing is to verify that a program works correctly and fulfills its requirements. Once testing has been completed, the program can be used to calculate outputs for differing input data without the need to retest. This is, of course, one of the real values in writing a program; the same program can be used over and over with new input data.

The simplest test method is to verify the program's operation for carefully selected sets of input data. One set of input data that should always be used is the data that were selected for the hand calculation made previously in Step 2 of the development procedure. In this case, the program is relatively simple and performs only one calculation. Because the output produced by the test run agrees with our hand calculation, we have a good degree of confidence that it can be used to calculate the circumference correctly for any input radius.

Exercises 2.6

Note: In each of these exercises, a programming problem is given. Read the problem statement first and then answer the questions pertaining to the problem.

1. Consider the following programming problem (*do not* program it): A C++ program is required that calculates the amount, in dollars, contained in a piggybank. The bank contains half dollars, quarters, dimes, nickels, and pennies.

    a. For this programming problem, how many outputs are required?

    b. How many inputs does this problem have?

    c. Write an algorithm for converting the input items into output items.

    d. Test the algorithm written for Exercise 1c using the following sample data: half dollars = 0, quarters = 17, dimes = 24, nickels = 16, pennies = 12.

2. Consider the following programming problem (*do not* program it): A C++ program is required to calculate the value of distance, in miles, given the relationship:

    ```
    distance = rate * elapsed time
    ```

    a. For this programming problem, how many outputs are required?

    b. How many inputs does this problem have?

    c. Write an algorithm for converting the input items into output items.

    d. Test the algorithm written for Exercise 2c using the following sample data: `rate` is 55 miles per hour and `elapsed time` is 2.5 hours.

    e. How must the algorithm you wrote in Exercise 2c be modified if the elapsed time is given in minutes instead of hours?

3. Consider the following programming problem (*do not* program it): A C++ program is required to determine the value of `Ergies`, given the relationships

    `Ergies = Fergies * ` $\sqrt{\text{Lergies}}$

    a. For this programming problem, how many outputs are required?

    b. How many inputs does this problem have?

    c. Determine an algorithm for converting the input items into output items.

    d. Test the algorithm written for Exercise 3c using the following sample data: `Fergies` = 14.65 and `Lergies` = 4.

4. Consider the following programming problem (*do not* program it): A C++ program is required to display the following name and address:

    `Mr. S. Hazlet`
    `63 Seminole Way`
    `Dumont, NJ 07030`

    a. For this programming problem, how many lines of output are required?

    b. How many inputs does this problem have?

    c. Write an algorithm for converting the input items into output items.

5. Consider the following program problem (*do not* program it): A C++ program is required to determine how far a car has traveled after 10 seconds assuming the car is initially traveling at 60 miles per hour and the driver applies the brakes to decelerate uniformly at a rate of 12 miles/sec^2. Use the fact that *distance* = $s - (1/2)dt^2$, where *s* is the initial speed of the car, *d* is the deceleration, and *t* is the elapsed time.

    a. For this programming problem, how many outputs are required?

    b. How many inputs does this problem have?

    c. Write an algorithm for converting the input items into output items.

    d. Test the algorithm written for Exercise 5c using the data given in the problem.

6. Consider the following programming problem (*do not* program it): In 1627, Manhattan Island was sold to the Dutch settlers for approximately $24. If the proceeds of that sale had been deposited in a Dutch bank paying 5% interest, compounded annually, what would the principal balance be at the end of 1999? A display is required as follows:

    `Balance as of December 31, 1999 is: xxxxxx`
    `where xxxxxx is the amount calculated by the program.`

    a. For this programming problem, how many outputs are required?

    b. How many inputs does this problem have?

    c. Write an algorithm for converting the input items into output items.

    d. Test the algorithm written for Exercise 6c using the data given in the problem statement.

7. Consider the following programming problem (*do not* program it): A C++ program is required that calculates and displays the weekly gross pay and net pay of two individuals. The first individual is paid an hourly rate of $8.43 and the second indi-

vidual is paid an hourly rate of $5.67. Both individuals have 20% of their gross pay withheld for income tax purposes and both pay 2% of their gross pay, before taxes, for medical benefits.

a. For this programming problem, how many outputs are required?

b. How many inputs does this problem have?

c. Write an algorithm for converting the input items into output items.

d. Test the algorithm written for Exercise 7c using the following sample data: The first person works 40 hours during the week and the second person works 35 hours.

8. Consider the following programming problem (*do not* program it): The formula for the standard normal deviate, z, used in statistical applications is

$$z = \frac{x - \mu}{\sigma}$$

where μ refers to a mean value and σ to a standard deviation. Using this formula, write a program that calculates and displays the value of the standard normal deviate when $x = 85.3$, $\mu = 80$, and $\sigma = 4$.

a. For this programming problem, how many outputs are required?

b. How many inputs does this problem have?

c. Write an algorithm for converting the input items into output items.

d. Test the algorithm written for Exercise 8c using the data given in the problem.

9. Consider the following programming problem (*do not* program it): The equation describing exponential growth is:

$$y = e^x$$

Using this equation, a C++ program is required to calculate the value of y.

a. For this programming problem, how many outputs are required?

b. How many inputs does this problem have?

c. Write an algorithm for converting the input items into output items.

d. Test the algorithm written for Exercise 9c assuming $e = 2.718$ and $x = 10$.

2.7 FOCUS ON PROBLEM SOLVING

In this section, the software development procedure presented in the previous section is applied to two specific programming problems. Although each problem is different, the top-down development procedure works for both situations. This procedure can be applied to any programming problem to produce a completed program and forms the foundation for all programs developed in this text.

Problem 1: Pendulum Clocks

Pendulums used in clocks, such as grandmother and grandfather clocks, keep fairly accurate time for the following reason: When the length of a pendulum is relatively large compared to the maximum arc of its swing, the time to complete one swing is independent of both the pendulum's weight and the maximum distance of the swing. When this condition is satisfied, the relationship between the time to complete one swing and the length of the pendulum is given by the formula

$$length = g[time/(2\pi)]^2$$

where π, accurate to four decimal places, is equal to 3.1416 and g is the gravitational constant equal to 32.2 ft/sec². When the time of a complete swing is given in seconds, the length of the pendulum is in feet. Using the given formula, we will write a C++ program that calculates and displays the length of a pendulum needed to produce a swing that will be completed in 1 second. The length is to be displayed in inches.

We now apply the top-down software development procedure to this problem.

Step 1: Analyze the Problem   For this problem, a single output is required by the program: the length of the pendulum. Additionally, the problem specifies that the value be displayed in units of inches. The input items required to solve for the length are the time to complete one swing, the gravitational constant, g, and π.

Step 2: Develop a Solution   The algorithm for transforming the three input items into the desired output item is given by the formula $length = g\,[time/(2\pi)]^2$. Since this formula calculates the length in feet and the problem specifies that the result be displayed in inches, we have to multiply the result of the formula by 12. Thus, the complete algorithm for our program solution is:

Assign values to g, π, and time.
Calculate the length (in inches) using the formula
length = 12g [time/(2π)]².
Display the result.

A hand calculation, using the data that $g = 32.2$, time $= 1$, and $\pi = 3.1416$, yields a length of 9.79 inches for the pendulum.

Step 3: Code the Solution   Program 2.12 provides the necessary code.

PROGRAM 2.12

```cpp
#include <iostream>
using namespace std;

int main()
{
  double time, length, pi;

  pi = 3.1416;
  g = 32.2
  time = 1.0;
  length = 12.0 * g * time/(2.0*pi) * time/(2.0*pi);
  cout << "The length is " << length << " inches\n";

  return 0;
}
```

Program 2.12 begins with an #include preprocessor command followed by a main() function. This function starts with the keyword main and ends with the closing brace, }. Additionally, Program 2.12 contains one declaration statement, three assignment statements, and one output statement. The assignment statements pi = 3.1416 and time = 1.0 are used to initialize the pi and time variables, respectively. The assignment statement

```
length = 12.0 * 32.2 * time/(2.0*pi) * time/(2.0*pi);
```

calculates a value for the variable `length`. Notice that the `12.0` is used to convert the calculated value from feet into inches. Also notice the placement of parentheses in the expression `time/(2.0*pi)`. The parentheses ensure that the value of pi is multiplied by `2.0` before the division is performed. If these parentheses were not included, the value of time would first be divided by `2.0`, and then the quantity `time/2.0` would be multiplied by pi. Finally, this same quantity is multiplied by itself to obtain the necessary squared value. (In the next chapter, we will see how to use C++'s power function to obtain the same result.) When Program 2.12 is compiled and executed, the following output is produced:

```
The length is 9.78758 inches
```

Step 4: Test and Correct the Program   The last step in the development procedure is to test the output. Because the displayed value agrees with the previous hand calculation, we have established a degree of confidence in the program. This permits us to use the program for different values of time. Note that if the parentheses were not correctly placed in the assignment statement that calculated a value for `length`, the displayed value would not agree with our previous hand calculation. This would have alerted us to the fact that the program had an error.

Problem 2: Telephone Switching Networks

A directly connected telephone network is one in which all telephones in the network are connected directly and do not require a central switching station to establish calls between two telephones. For example, financial institutions on Wall Street use such a network to maintain direct and continuously open phone lines between firms.

   The number of direct lines needed to maintain a directly connected network for n telephones is given by the formula

$$lines = n(n - 1)/2$$

For example, directly connecting four telephones requires six individual lines (see Figure 2.17). Adding a fifth telephone to the network illustrated in Figure 2.17 requires an additional four lines for a total of ten lines.

FIGURE 2.17   Directly Connecting Four Telephones

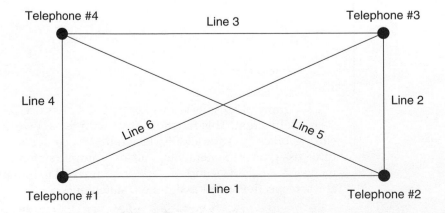

Using the given formula, write a C++ program that determines the number of direct lines required for 100 telephones and the additional lines required if 10 new telephones were added to the network. Use our top-down software development procedure.

Step 1: Analyze the Problem   For this program, two outputs are required: the number of direct lines for 100 telephones and the additional number of lines needed when 10 new telephones are added to the existing network. The input item required for this problem is the number of telephones, which is denoted as n in the formula.

Step 2: Develop a Solution   The first output is easily obtained using the formula $lines = n(n - 1)/2$. Although there is no formula given for additional lines, we can use the given formula to determine the total number of lines needed for 110 subscribers. Subtracting the number of lines for 100 subscribers from the number of lines needed for 110 subscribers then yields the number of additional lines required. Thus, the complete algorithm for our program, in pseudocode, is:

Calculate the number of direct lines for 100 subscribers.
Calculate the number of direct lines for 110 subscribers.
Calculate the additional lines needed, which is the
difference between the second and first calculation.
Display the number of lines for 100 subscribers.
Display the additional lines needed.

Checking our algorithm by hand, using the data given, yields this answer: lines = $100(100 - 1)/2 = 100(99)/2 = 4950$ for 100 telephones and lines = 5995 for 110 telephones. Thus, an additional 1045 lines are needed to directly connect the 10 additional telephones into the existing network.

Step 3: Code the Solution   Program 2.13 provides the necessary code.

PROGRAM 2.13

```cpp
#include <iostream>
using namespace std;

int main()
{
  int numin1, numin2, lines1, lines2;

  numin1 = 100;
  numin2 = 110;
  lines1 = numin1 * (numin1 - 1)/2;
  lines2 = numin2 * (numin2 - 1)/2;
  cout << "The number of initial lines is " << lines1 << ".\n";
  cout << "There are " << lines2 - lines1
       << " additional lines needed.\n";

  return 0;
}
```

As before, the C++ program includes the `iostream` header file and consists of one `main()` function. The body of this function begins with the opening brace, {, and ends with the closing brace, }. Since the number of lines between subscribers must be an integer (a fractional line is not possible), the variables `lines1` and `lines2` are specified as integer variables. The first two assignment statements initialize the variables `numin1` and `numin2`. The next assignment statement calculates the number of lines needed for 100 subscribers, and the last assignment statement calculates the number of lines for 110 subscribers. The first `cout` statement is used to display a message and the result of the first calculation. The next `cout` statement is used to display the difference between the two calculations. The following output is produced when Program 2.13 is compiled and executed:

```
The number of initial lines is 4950.
There are 1045 additional lines needed.
```

Step 4: Test and Correct the Program   Because the displayed value agrees with the previous hand calculation, we have established a degree of confidence in the program.

Exercises 2.7

1. a. Modify Program 2.12 to calculate the length of a pendulum that produces an arc that takes 2 seconds to complete.

   b. Compile and execute the program written for Exercise 1a on a computer.

2. a. Modify Program 2.12 to determine the time it takes a 3-foot pendulum to complete one swing. Your program should produce the following display:

   ```
   The time to complete one swing (in seconds) is: _____
   ```

   where the underscore is replaced by the value calculated by your program.

   b. Compile and execute the program written for Exercise 2a on a computer. Make sure you do a hand calculation so that you can verify the results produced by your program.

   c. After you have verified the results of the program written in Exercise 2a, modify the program to calculate the time it takes a 4-foot pendulum to complete one swing.

3. a. Modify Program 2.13 to calculate and display the total number of lines needed to connect 1000 individual phones directly to each other.

   b. Compile and execute the program written for Exercise 3a on a computer.

4. a. Modify Program 2.13 so that the variable `numfin` is initialized to 10, which is the additional number of subscribers to be connected to the existing network. Make any other changes in the program so that the program produces the same display as Program 2.13.

   b. Compile and execute the program written for Exercise 4a on a computer. Check that the display produced by your program matches the display shown in the text.

5. a. Design, write, compile, and execute a C++ program to convert temperature in degrees Fahrenheit to degrees Celsius. The equation for this conversion is

   $$Celsius = 5.0/9.0 \, (Fahrenheit - 32.0)$$

   Have your program convert and display the Celsius temperature corresponding to 98.6 degrees Fahrenheit. Your program should produce the display:

   ```
   For a Fahrenheit temperature of _____ degrees, the equivalent
   Celsius temperature is _____ degrees
   ```

   where appropriate values are inserted by your program in place of the underscores.

b. Check the values computed by your program by hand. After you have verified that your program is working correctly, modify it to convert 86.5 degrees Fahrenheit into its equivalent Celsius value.

6. a. Design, write, compile, and execute a C++ program to calculate the dollar amount contained in a piggy bank. The bank currently contains 12 half dollars, 20 quarters, 32 dimes, 45 nickels, and 27 pennies.

b. Check the values computed by your program by hand. After you have verified that your program is working correctly, modify it to determine the dollar value of a bank containing no half dollars, 17 quarters, 19 dimes, 10 nickels, and 42 pennies.

7. a. Design, write, compile, and execute a C++ program to calculate the elapsed time it took to make a 183.67-mile trip. The equation for computing elapsed time is

elapsed time = total distance/average speed

Assume that the average speed during the trip was 58 miles per hour.

b. Check the values computed by your program by hand. After you have verified that your program is working correctly, modify it to determine the elapsed time it takes to make a 372-mile trip at an average speed of 67 miles per hour.

8. a. Design, write, compile, and execute a C++ program to calculate the sum of the numbers from 1 to 100. The formula for calculating this sum is

$$sum = (n/2)[2*a + (n - 1)d]$$

where n = number of terms to be added, a = the first number, and d = the difference between each number.

b. Check the values computed by your program by hand. After you have verified that your program is working correctly, modify it to determine the sum of the integers from 100 to 1000.

Note: Exercises 9, 10, and 11 require raising a number to a power. This can be accomplished using C++'s power function pow(). For example, the statement pow(2.0,5.0); raises the number 2.0 to the fifth power, and the statement pow(num1,num2); raises the variable num1 to the num2 power. To use the power function, either place an #include <cmath> preprocessor command on a line by itself after the #include <iostream> command or include the declaration statement double pow(); with the variable declaration statements used in your program. The power function is explained in more detail in Section 3.3.

9. a. Newton's law of cooling states that when an object with an initial temperature T is placed in a surrounding substance of temperature A, it reaches a temperature *TFIN* in t minutes according to the formula

$$TFIN = (T - A)e^{-kt} + A$$

In this formula, e is the irrational number 2.71828 rounded to five decimal places, commonly known as Euler's number, and k is a thermal coefficient, which depends on the material being cooled. Using this formula, write, compile, and execute a C++ program that determines the temperature reached by an object after 20 minutes when it is placed in a glass of water whose temperature is 60 degrees. Assume that the object initially has a temperature of 150 degrees and a thermal constant of 0.0367.

b. Check the value computed by your program by hand. After you have verified that your program is working correctly, modify it to determine the temperature reached after 10 minutes when it is placed in a glass of water whose temperature is 50 degrees.

10. a. Given an initial deposit of money, denoted as A, in a bank that pays interest annually, the amount of money at a time N years later is given by the formula

$$Amount = A * (1 + I)^N$$

where *I* is the interest rate as a decimal number (e.g., 9.5% is .095). Using this formula, design, write, compile, and execute a C++ program that determines the amount of money that will be available in 4 years if $10,000 is deposited in a bank that pays 10% interest annually.

b. Check the value computed by your program by hand. After you have verified that your program is working correctly, modify it to determine the amount of money available if $24 is invested at 4% for 300 years.

11. a. If an initial deposit of *A* dollars is made in a bank and the interest, *I*, is compounded *M* times a year, the amount of money available after *N* years is given by the expression

$$A * (1 + I/M)^{M*N}$$

Using this expression, design, write, compile, and run a C++ program to determine the amount of money available after 10 years if $5000 is invested in a bank paying 6% interest compounded quarterly ($M = 4$).

b. Check the value computed by your program by hand. After you have verified that your program is working correctly, modify it to determine the amount of money available if $1000 are invested at 8%, compounded quarterly, for 10 years.

2.8 PLANNING FOR OBJECTS: INTRODUCTION TO ABSTRACTION

A very important programming concept, and one that is central to object-oriented programming, is the idea of abstraction. In its most general usage, an **abstraction** is simply an idea or term that identifies the general qualities or characteristics of a group of objects, independent of any one specific object in the group. For example, consider the term "car." As a term, this is an abstraction: It refers to a group of objects that individually contain the characteristics associated with a car, such as a motor, passenger compartment, wheels, steering capabilities, brakes, etc. A particular instance of a car, such as my car or your car, is not an abstraction; it is a real object that is classified as "type car" because it has the attributes associated with a car.

Although we use abstract concepts all the time, we tend not to think of them as such. For example, the words *tree, dog, cat, table,* and *chair* are all abstractions, just as *car* is. Each of these terms refers to a set of qualities that are met by a group of particular things. For each of these abstractions, there are many individual trees, dogs, and cats, each instance of which conforms to the general characteristics associated with the abstract term. Hence, a type—such as dog or cat—is considered an abstraction that defines a general type of which specific instances can be realized. Such types, then, simply identify common qualities of each group.

Having defined what we mean by a type, we can now create the definition of a data type. In programming terminology, a **data type** consists of *both* an acceptable range of values for a particular type and a set of operations that can be applied to those values. Thus, the integer data type not only defines a range of acceptable integer values but also defines what operations can be applied to those values.

Although users of programming languages such as C++ ordinarily assume that mathematical operations such as addition, subtraction, multiplication, and division are supplied for integers, the designers of C++ had to consider carefully what operations would be provided as part of the integer data type. For example, the designers of C++ did not include an exponentiation operator as part of the integer data type, whereas it is included in FORTRAN's data abstraction of integers (in C++, exponentiation is supplied as a library function).

To summarize, then, a data type is an abstraction that consists of

A set of values of a particular type

and

> A set of operations that can be applied to those values.

The set of allowed values is more formally referred to as the data type's **domain.** Table 2.9 lists the domain and the most common operations defined for the data types int, double, char, and bool.[12]

Built-In and Abstract Data Types (ADTs)

All of the data types listed in Table 2.9 are provided as part of the C++ language. They are formally referred to as **built-in** or **primitive** data types (the two terms are synonyms). In contrast to built-in data types, some programming languages permit programmers to create their own data types; that is, define a type of value with an associated domain and operations that can be performed on the acceptable values. Such user-defined data types are formally referred to as **abstract data types.**

In C++, abstract data types are called **classes,** and the ability to create classes is the major enhancement provided to C by C++. (In fact, the original name for C++ was *C with Classes.*) After we obtain a basic understanding of C++'s syntax and how to use its built-in data types, we will be ready to use C++'s class capabilities.

TABLE 2.9 C++'s Major Data Types

Data Type	Minimum Acceptable Domain	Operations
int	−2,147,483,648 to +2,147,483,647	+, −, *, /, %, =, ==, !=, <=, >=, <, and bit operations
double	$4.94065645841246544e^{-324}$ to $1.79769313486231570e^{+308}$	+, −, *, /, =, ==, !=, <=, and >=
char	All characters with an ASCII value between 0 and 127	+, −, *, /, =, ==, !=, <=, and >= bool true (1) and false (0) ==, !, <=, and >=

Improving Communication

1. Respond to the following request:

   MEMORANDUM

   To: U. R. It

   From: Head of Programming Dept.

   Subject: Moving to an Object Orientation

   The term *abstraction* keeps popping up in our discussions of object-oriented programming (OOP). I understand that abstraction is somewhat of an important concept that is central to OOP. Could you please explain what abstraction is and how it relates to OOP?

---

[12] The domain for integers can be found in the <climits> header file supplied by your compiler. Similarly, the domain for floating-point numbers can be found in the header file <cfloat>.

Working in Teams

2. Every object has a set of attributes and a set of behaviors. For example, a radio's attributes consist of its size, its color, its display (dial or digital), whether it has a tape player or not, etc. Similarly, its behaviors should include being able to respond to an on–off switch, being able to respond to a volume control, etc. Consider the following objects:

- A car

- A computer

- A house

- A computer programming class

- An elevator

a. Have the team select one object.

b. For the selected object, have the team determine a list of attributes and behaviors.

3. a. Establish criteria for names of variables and functions that will be consistently used by each member of the group in all of their programs. Some choices are:

- Always use lowercase letters.

- Always start with a lowercase or uppercase letter.

- Use uppercase letters to separate words.

- Use the underscore character, (_), to separate words.

For example, using your rules, should a variable's name be maxnumber, max_ number, maxNumber, MaxNumber, or Max_number? Make a determination for both variable and function names. Make sure your criteria are acceptable to your professor.

b. After your group has come up with its recommendation, designate a representative to list your selections on the board. Then, either have all of the groups choose one of the criteria that will be common to the class or have your professor choose one and tell you why, based on experience, he or she prefers the chosen style.

4. Now that you have had at least one team meeting, discuss among your team members the following issues:

a. How did each team member feel about your last meeting? That is, did each one participate in discussions or did one person tend to dominate? Was input solicited from each person and did each person feel that his or her input was really listened to and heard? Was it an open discussion or was the discussion more of an "I'm right, you're wrong" type?

b. Was a leader appointed or did a leader emerge? If not, first find out which members might have an interest in leading the group because effective groups always have one or two people who organize and focus the discussion. Select a leader. If more than one person wants to lead, alternate leaders on different team projects. If no one wants to lead, take time to select a leader anyway.

c. Was someone keeping track of the time spent on each issue? Effective groups allocate time before discussing an issue, and someone should be designated as the timekeeper. Find out who in the group is good at keeping time and is willing to be the timekeeper.

d. Discuss whether team members tend to ignore or even sabotage group decisions if the decision is not the one they want. Discuss the difference between agreeing on a course of action and aligning on a course of action. Aligning on a course of action refers to the willingness to support a course of action and make it successful even if it is not the one you personally wanted. Make sure each member is comfortable with aligning on a course of action before closing an issue.

e. Do you think alignment or agreement is necessary for a group of people to accomplish a given task successfully?

2.9 COMMON PROGRAMMING ERRORS

Part of learning any programming language is making the elementary mistakes commonly encountered as you begin to use the language. These mistakes tend to be quite frustrating because each language has its own set of common programming errors waiting for the unwary. The more common errors made when initially programming in C++ are:

1. Omitting the parentheses after `main`.

2. Omitting or incorrectly typing the opening brace, {, that signifies the start of a function body.

3. Omitting or incorrectly typing the closing brace, }, that signifies the end of a function.

4. Misspelling the name of an object or function; for example, typing `cot` instead of `cout`.

5. Forgetting to close a string sent to `cout` with a double quote symbol.

6. Forgetting to separate individual data streams passed to `cout` with an insertion ("put to") symbol, <<.

7. Omitting the semicolon at the end of each C++ statement.

8. Adding a semicolon at the end of the `#include` preprocessor command.

9. Forgetting the `\n` to indicate a new line.

10. Incorrectly typing the letter O for the number zero (0), or vice versa. Incorrectly typing the letter l for the number 1, or vice versa.

11. Forgetting to declare all the variables used in a program. This error is detected by the compiler, and an error message is generated for all undeclared variables.

12. Storing an inappropriate data type in a declared variable. This error is detected by the compiler, and the assigned value is converted to the data type of the variable to which it is assigned.

13. Using a variable in an expression before a value has been assigned to the variable. Here, whatever value happens to be in the variable is used when the expression is evaluated, and the result is meaningless.

14. Dividing integer values incorrectly. This error is usually disguised within a larger expression and can be very troublesome to detect. For example, the expression

$$3.425 + 2/3 + 7.9$$

yields the same result as the expression

$$3.425 + 7.9$$

because the integer division of 2/3 is 0.

15. Mixing data types in the same expression without clearly understanding the effect produced. Since C++ allows expressions with "mixed" data types, it is important to understand the order of evaluation and the data type of all intermediate calculations. As a general rule, you should never mix data types in an expression unless a specific effect is desired.

The third, fifth, seventh, eighth, and ninth errors in this list are initially the most common, while even experienced programmers occasionally make the tenth error. It is worthwhile for you to write a program and specifically introduce each of these errors, one at a time, to see what error messages are produced by your compiler. Then, when these error messages appear due to inadvertent errors, you will have experience with the messages and understand how to correct the errors.

On a more fundamental level, a major programming error made by all beginning programmers is the rush to code and run a program before the programmer fully understands what is required and the algorithms and procedures that will be used to produce the desired result. A symptom of this haste to get a program entered into the computer is the lack of either an outline of the proposed program or a written program itself. Many problems can be caught just by checking a copy of the program, either handwritten or listed from the computer, before it is ever compiled.

2.10 CHAPTER REVIEW

Key Terms

abstraction	float
argument	floating-point number
ASCII	function
arithmetic operators	identifier
assignment statement	int
associativity	integer value
char	keyword
character values	long
cout	manipulator
data type	mixed-mode expression
declaration statement	mnemonic
definition statement	precedence
double	precision
double-precision number	sizeof()
escape sequence	variable
expression	

Summary

1. A C++ program consists of one or more modules called functions. One of these functions must be named `main()`. The `main()` function identifies the starting point of a C++ program.

2. The simplest C++ program consists of the single function `main()`.

3. Following the function name, the body of a function has the general form:

```
{
    All C++ statements in here;
}
```

4. All C++ statements must be terminated by a semicolon.

5. Three types of data were introduced in this chapter: integer, floating-point, and character data. Each of these types of data is typically stored in a computer using different amounts of memory. C++ recognizes each of these data types in addition to other types yet to be presented.

6. The `cout` object can be used to display all of C++'s data types.

7. When the `cout` object is used within a program, the preprocessor command `#include <iostream>` must be placed at the top of the program. Preprocessor commands do not end with a semicolon.

8. Every variable in a C++ program must be declared as to the type of value it can store. Declarations within a function may be placed anywhere within a function, although a variable can only be used after it is declared. Variables may also be initialized when they are declared. Additionally, variables of the same type may be declared using a single declaration statement. Variable declaration statements have the general form:

```
data-type variableName(s);
```

9. A simple C++ program containing declaration statements has the typical form:

```
#include <iostream>
using namespace std;
int main()
{
    declaration statements;

    other statements;

    return 0;

}
```

Although declaration statements may be placed anywhere within the function's body, a variable may only be used after it is declared.

10. Declaration statements always play a software role of informing the compiler of a function's valid variable names. When a variable declaration also causes the computer to set aside memory locations for the variable, the declaration statement is also called a definition statement. (All the declarations we have used in this chapter have also been definition statements.)

11. The `sizeof()` operator can be used to determine the amount of storage reserved for variables.

Exercises

1. Given the following variable declarations, determine which statements and commands are valid and which are invalid. If invalid, explain why.

```
int numOfApples, numOfOranges;
int vector, digitialTemp;
float average, distance;
char letter, symbol;
```

   a. `average = 89.4;`

   b. `distyance= 130;`

   c. `numOfOranges = (54 * numOfApples) % 3;`

   d. `vector = numOfApples;`

   e. `digitalTemp = float (average);`

   f. `numOfApples = numOfOranges + letter;`

   g. `symbol = letter;`

   h. `distance = distance % average;`

   i. `vector = distance / average;`

   j. `numOfApples = float(average);`

   k. `numOfOranges = int (distance);`

   l. `average = float (vector);`

   m. `distance = float(numOfApples);`

   n. `numOfApples = numOfOranges - distance;`

   o. `numOfOragnes = -17;`

2. Evaluate the following mixed-mode expressions and list the data type of the result. In evaluating the expressions, be aware of the data types of all intermediate calculations.

   a. `10.0 + 15 / 2 + 4.3`

   b. `10.0 + 15.0 / 2 + 4.3`

   c. `3.0 * 4 / 6 + 6`

   d. `3 * 4.0 / 6 + 6`

   e. `20.0 - 2 / 6 + 3`

   f. `10 + 17 * 3 + 4`

   g. `10 + 17 / 3. + 4`

   h. `3.0 * 4 % 6 + 6`

   i. `10 + 17 % 3 + 4.`

3. Repeat Exercise 7 in Section 2.3 assuming that amount has the value 1.0, m has the value 50.0, n has the value 10.0, and p has the value 5.0.

4. Analyze the following problem statements and determine if each problem's statement is well defined. If the problem is not well defined, explain why.

   a. In a list consisting of 50 test grades, find the grade that appears most frequently.

   b. If a person can only pay $600 to $750 for house payments, find the range of houses that should be considered.

c. Determine the smallest number such that the difference of its digits is 31.

d. Find the first ten sets of integer numbers a, b, and c such that $a^2 + b^2 = c^2$.

5. Determine if the given algorithm solves the following problem:

Problem: Determine the largest value for any two given numbers.
Algorithm: Compute the difference, D, between the two numbers A and B as
$$D = A - B.$$

If D is greater than 1, the first number is larger; otherwise, the second number is larger.

6. Design and write a C++ program that determines which letter lies halfway between any two letters of the alphabet. Test your program using the following letters:

A and C
A and Z
M and Q
M and P
Z and Z

7. a. The table in Appendix B lists the integer values corresponding to each letter stored using the ASCII code. Using this table, notice that the uppercase letters consist of contiguous codes starting with an integer value of 65 for A and ending with 90 for Z. Similarly, the lowercase letters begin with the integer value of 97 for a and end with 122 for z. With this as background, determine the character value of the expressions 'A' + 32 and 'Z' + 32.

b. Using Appendix B, determine the integer value of the expression 'a' − 'A'.

c. Determine the character value of the following expression, where `uppercase letter` can be any uppercase letter from A to Z:

```
uppercase letter + 'a' - 'A'
```

8. You decide to make your company's logo—a red circle surrounded by a concentric blue ring—a well-recognized symbol. To do this, you intend to pay farmers throughout the country to paint the logo on their barns. The problem is to determine, for a given-sized barn, how much red paint and how much blue paint is required. From experience, the number of quarts of paint is equal to the area to be painted (in square feet) divided by 125. Using this information, construct a chart for determining the quarts of red and blue paint that are needed. (*Hint:* You need to determine the area of the inner circle and outer ring. Assume that the outer circle has a radius of b, and the inner circle has a radius of a.)

9. Design, write, test, and run a C++ program to do the following: Given the current time (hours and minutes) on a 24-hour clock, add a whole number of hours and determine what the new clock reading is and how many days later it is. (*Hint:* Use / 24 and % 24, and designate midnight as 0:00 hours instead of 24:00 hours. Example: 17:30 + 37 hours is 6:30, two days later).

10. In a game of Woodenbleevit, three players make up a team. At the end of each round, the team score is the total points accumulated by the team divided by 3 and truncated to the next smaller whole number. For example, if your team received 76 points in a round, the team score for that round is 25 (76/3 = 25.333 = 25 truncated). A game consists of five rounds.

Design, write, test, and run a C++ program that uses the following team scores:

Round 1: 14 points (still learning)
Round 2: 292 points (beginners' luck)
Round 3: 77 points
Round 4: 82 points
Round 5: 45 points

Your program should divide each round's score by 3 and truncate to get the team score for the round. Add the team scores for the five rounds to get the team score for the game. Determine how many points the team lost because of the truncation process. (*Hint:* Use both the division and modular operations.)

11. Hap's Hazard County Phone Company, Inc., charges for phone calls by distance (miles) and length of time (minutes). The cost of a call (in dollars) is computed as 0.30 * (time + 0.05 * distance). Design, write, test, and run a C++ program that calculates the cost for each of three phone calls and the total cost of all three calls using the following data:

Call 1: 3 miles, 20 minutes
Call 2: 2 miles, 15 minutes
Call 3: 6 miles, 4 minutes

The output of your program should include the time, distance, and cost of each call.

Note: Exercises 12 and 13 require raising a number to a power. This can be accomplished using C++'s power function `pow()`. For example, the statement `pow(2.0,5.0);` raises the number 2.0 to the fifth power, and the statement `pow(num1,num2);` raises the variable `num1` to the `num2` power. To use the power function, either place an `#include cmath` preprocessor command on a line by itself after the `#include iostream` command or include the declaration statement `double pow();` with the variable declaration statements used in your program. The power function is explained in more detail in Section 3.3.

12. a. Effective annual interest is the rate that must be compounded annually to generate the same interest as a stated rate compounded over a stipulated conversion period. For example, a stated rate of 8% compounded quarterly is equivalent to an effective annual rate of 8.24%. The relationship between the effective annual rate, E, and the stated rate, I, compounded M times a year is $E = (1 + I/M)M - 1$. Using this formula, design, write, compile, and execute a C++ program to determine the effective annual rate for a stated rate of 6% compounded four times a year (quarterly).

   b. Check the value computed by your program by hand. After you have verified that your program is working correctly, modify it to determine the effective annual rate for a stated rate of 8% compounded monthly.

13. a. The present value of a dollar amount is the amount of money that must be deposited in a bank account today to yield a specified dollar amount in the future. For example, if a bank is currently paying 8% interest annually, you need to deposit $6,947.90 in the bank today to have $15,000 in 10 years. Thus, the present value of $15,000 is $6,947.90. Using this information, design, write, compile, and execute a C++ program that calculates how much must be deposited in a bank today

to provide exactly $8,000 in 9 years at an annual interest rate of 8%. Use the formula:

present value = future amount/(1.0 + annual interest rate)^{years}

b. Check the value computed by your program by hand. After you have verified that your program is working correctly, modify it to determine the amount of money that must be invested in a bank today to yield $15,000 in 18 years at an annual rate of 6%.

14. a. The set of linear equations

$$a_{11}X_1 + a_{12}X_2 = c_1$$

$$a_{21}X_1 + a_{22}X_2 = c_2$$

can be solved using Cramer's rule as:

$$X_1 = \frac{c_1 a_{22} - a_{12} c_2}{a_{11} a_{22} - a_{12} a_{21}}$$

$$X_2 = \frac{a_{11} c_2 - c_1 a_{21}}{a_{11} a_{22} - a_{12} a_{21}}$$

Using these equations, design, write, compile, and execute a C++ program to solve for the X_1 and X_2 values that satisfy the following equations:

$$3X_1 + 4X_2 = 40$$
$$5X_1 + 2X_2 = 34$$

b. Check the values computed by your program by hand. After you have verified that your program is working correctly, modify it to solve the following set of equations:

$$3X_1 + 12.5X_2 = 22.5$$
$$4.2X_1 - 6.3X_2 = 30$$

Assignment, Formatting, and Interactive Input

In the last chapter, we explored how results are displayed using C++'s cout object and how numerical data are stored and processed using variables and assignment statements. In this chapter, we complete our introduction to C++ by presenting additional processing and input capabilities.

3.1 ASSIGNMENT OPERATIONS

We have already encountered simple assignment statements in Chapter 2. Assignment statements are the most basic C++ statements for both assigning values to variables and performing computations. This statement has the syntax:

> *variable = expression;*

The simplest expression in C++ is a single constant. In each of the following assignment statements, the operand to the right of the equal sign is a constant:

```
length = 25;
width = 17.5;
```

In each of these assignment statements, the value of the constant to the right of the equal sign is assigned to the variable on the left of the equal sign. It is important to note that the equal sign in C++ does not have the same meaning as an equal sign

A BIT OF BACKGROUND

Napier's Bones

Scottish mathematician John Napier, born near Edinburgh, Scotland, in 1550, spent most of his life creating methods and devices to make mathematical calculations easier. One of his early inventions was a set of square rods, made of bone, that were used for multiplying whole numbers.

Napier is also credited with the discovery that the weight of any object can be found by balancing the object on a scale against weights of relative size 1, 2, 4, 8, . . . His most valuable invention, however, was the natural logarithm, which replaced multiplication and division problems with the addition and subtraction of logarithms. For 25 years beginning in 1590, Napier devoted himself almost entirely to generating tables of logarithms.

The contribution of the logarithmic technique to science and technology is immeasurable. Until the advent of electronic calculators and computers, logarithms were *the* approach to lengthy calculations. The logarithmic slide rule, invented by William Oughtred early in the 17th century, was the only reasonably affordable computing tool for engineers, scientists, and students until the mid-1970s.

In most modern high-level languages, including C++, you will find a function, such as `log(x)`, for calculating logarithms.

in algebra. The equal sign in an assignment statement tells the computer first to determine the value of the operand to the right of the equal sign and then to store (or assign) that value in the location(s) associated with the variable to the left of the equal sign. In this regard, the C++ statement `length = 25;` is read "length is assigned the value 25." The blank spaces in the assignment statement are inserted for readability only.

Recall that a variable can be initialized when it is declared. If an initialization is not done within the declaration statement, the variable should be assigned a value with an assignment statement or input operation before it is used in any computation. Subsequent assignment statements can, of course, be used to change the value assigned to a variable. For example, assume the following statements are executed one after another and that `total` was not initialized when it was declared:

```
total = 3.7;
total = 6.28;
```

The first assignment statement assigns the value of 3.7 to the variable named `total`.[1] The next assignment statement causes the computer to assign a value of 6.28 to `total`. The 3.7 that was in `total` is overwritten with the new value of 6.28 because a variable can store only one value at a time. It is sometimes useful to think of the variable to the left of the equal sign as a temporary parking spot in a huge parking lot. Just as an individual parking spot can be used only by one car at a time, each variable can store only one value at a time. The "parking" of a new value in a variable automatically causes the program to remove any value previously parked there.

---

[1] Since this is the first time a value is explicitly assigned to this variable, it is frequently referred to as an *initialization*. This stems from historical usage that said a variable was initialized the first time a value was assigned to it. Under this usage, it is correct to say that "`total` is initialized to 3.7." From an implementation viewpoint, however, this later statement is incorrect. This is because the assignment operation is handled differently by the C++ compiler than an initialization performed when a variable is created by a declaration statement. This difference is only important when using C++'s class features and is explained in detail in Section 8.1.

In addition to being a constant, the operand to the right of the equal sign in an assignment statement can be a variable or any other valid C++ expression. An **expression** is any combination of constants, variables, and function calls that can be evaluated to yield a result. Thus, the expression in an assignment statement can be used to perform calculations using the arithmetic operators introduced in Section 2.3. Some assignment statements that use expressions containing these operators follow:

```
sum = 3 + 7;
diff = 15 - 6;
product = .05 * 14.6;
tally = count + 1;
newtotal = 18.3 + total;
taxes = .06 * amount;
totalWeight = factor * weight;
average = sum / items;
slope = (y2 - y1) / (x2 - x1);
```

As always in an assignment statement, the computer first calculates the value of the expression to the right of the equal sign and then stores this value in the variable to the left of the equal sign. For example, in the assignment statement `totalWeight=factor*weight;` the computer first evaluates the arithmetic expression `factor*weight` to yield a result. This result, which is a number, is then stored in the variable `totalWeight`.

In writing assignment expressions, you must be aware of two important considerations. Since the expression to the right of the equal sign is evaluated first, all variables used in the expression must previously have been given valid values if the result is to make sense. For example, the assignment statement `totalWeight = factor * weight;` causes a valid number to be stored in `totalWeight` only if the programmer first takes care to assign valid numbers to `factor` and `weight`. Thus, the sequence of statements

```
factor = 1.06;
weight = 155.0;
totalWeight = factor * weight;
```

tells us what values are used to obtain the result stored in `totalWeight`. Figure 3.1 illustrates the values stored in the variables `factor`, `weight`, and `totalWeight`.

FIGURE 3.1   Values Stored in the Variables

factor   weight   totalWeight

1.06   155.0   164.30

The second consideration to keep in mind is that because the value of an expression is stored in the variable to the left of the equal sign, only one variable can be listed in this position. For example, the assignment statement

```
amount + 1892 = 1000 + 10 * 5;
```

is invalid. The expression on the right-hand side of the equal sign evaluates to the integer 1050, which can be stored only in a variable. Because `amount + 1892` is is not a valid variable name, the compiler does not know where to store the calculated value. Program 3.1 illustrates the use of assignment statements to calculate the volume of a cylinder. As illustrated in Figure 3.2, the volume of a cylinder is determined by the formula volume $= \pi r^2 h$, where r is the radius of the cylinder, h is the height, and π is the constant 3.1416 (accurate to four decimal places).

PROGRAM 3.1

```cpp
// this program calculates the volume of a cylinder,
// given its radius and height
#include <iostream>
using namespace std;

int main()
{
    double radius, height, volume;

    radius = 2.5;
    height = 16.0;
    volume = 3.1416 * radius * radius * height;
    cout << "The volume of the cylinder is " << volume << endl;

    return 0;
}
```

When Program 3.1 is compiled and executed, the output is:

```
The volume of the cylinder is 314.16
```

Consider the flow of control that the computer uses in executing Program 3.1. Program execution begins with the first statement within the body of the `main()` function and continues sequentially, statement by statement, until the closing brace of `main` is encountered. This flow of control is true for all programs. The computer works on one statement at a time, executing that statement with no knowledge of what the next statement will be. This explains why all operands used in an expression must have values assigned to them before the expression is evaluated. When the computer executes the statement

```
volume = 3.1416 * radius * radius * height;
```

FIGURE 3.2 Determining the Volume of a Cylinder

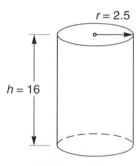

in Program 3.1, it uses whatever value is stored in the variables `radius` and `height` at the time the assignment statement is executed.[2] If no values have been specifically assigned to these variables before they are used in the assignment statement, the computer uses whatever values happen to occupy these variables when they are referenced (on some systems all variables are automatically initialized to zero). The computer does not look ahead to see if you assign values to these variables later in the program.

It is important to realize that in C++, the equal sign, =, used in assignment statements is itself an operator, *which differs from the way most other high-level languages process this symbol.* In C++ (as in C), the = symbol is called the **assignment operator,** and an expression using this operator, such as a = b * c, is an **assignment expression.** Because the assignment operator has a lower precedence than any other arithmetic operator, the value of any expression to the right of the equal sign is evaluated first, prior to assignment.

Like all expressions, assignment expressions themselves have a value. The value of the complete assignment expression is the value assigned to the variable to the left of the assignment operator. For example, the expression a = 5 assigns a value of 5 to the variable a and also results in the expression itself having a value of 5. The value of the expression can always be verified using a statement such as

```
cout << "The value of the expression is " << (a = 5);
```

Here, the value of the expression itself is displayed and not the contents of the variable a. Although both the contents of the variable and the expression have the same value, you should realize that we are dealing with two distinct entities.

From a programming perspective, it is the actual assignment of a value to a variable that is significant in an assignment expression; the final value of the assignment expression itself is of little consequence. However, the fact that assignment expressions have a value has implications that must be considered when C++'s relational operators are used.

Any expression that is terminated by a semicolon becomes a C++ statement. The most common example is the assignment statement, which is simply an assignment expression terminated with a semicolon. For example, terminating the assignment expression a = 33 with a semicolon results in the assignment statement a = 33;, which can be used in a program on a line by itself.

Because the equal sign is an operator in C++, multiple assignments are possible in the same expression or its equivalent statement. For example, in the statement a = b = c = 25;, all of the assignment operators have the same precedence. Because the assignment operator has a right-to-left associativity, the final evaluation proceeds in the sequence

```
c = 25;
b = c;
a = b;
```

In this case, this has the effect of assigning the number 25 to each of the variables individually, and can be represented as

```
a = (b = (c = 25));
```

---

[2] Since C++ does not have an exponentiation operator, the square of the radius is obtained by the term `radius * radius`. In Section 3.3, we introduce C++'s power function `pow()`, which allows us to raise a number to a power.

▲ **P O I N T   O F   I N F O R M A T I O N** ▲

lvalues and rvalues

You will encounter the terms *lvalue* and *rvalue* frequently in almost all programming languages that define assignment using an operator that permits multiple assignments in the same statement. The term lvalue refers to any quantity that is valid on the left side of an assignment operator. An rvalue refers to any quantity that is valid on the right side of an assignment operator.

For example, each variable we have encountered so far can be either an lvalue or rvalue (that is, a variable, by itself, can appear on both sides of an assignment operator), while a number can only be an rvalue. More generally, any expression that yields a value can be an rvalue. Not all variables, however, can be used as either lvalues or rvalues. For example, an array type, which is introduced in Chapter 8, cannot be either an lvalue or an rvalue, while individual array elements can be both.

Coercion

One thing to keep in mind when working with assignment statements is the data type assigned to the values on both sides of the expression, because data type conversions take place across assignment operators; that is, the value of the expression on the right side of the assignment operator will be converted to the data type of the variable to the left of the assignment operator. This type of conversion is referred to as a **coercion,** because the value assigned to the variable on the left side of the assignment operator is forced into the data type of the variable it is assigned to. An example of a coercion occurs when an integer value is assigned to a real variable; this causes the integer to be converted to a real value. Similarly, assigning a real value to an integer variable forces conversion of the real value to an integer, which always results in the loss of the fractional part of the number due to truncation. For example, if `temp` is an integer variable, the assignment `temp = 25.89` causes the integer value `25` to be stored in the integer variable `temp`.[3]

A more complete example of data type conversion, which includes both mixed-mode and assignment conversion, is the evaluation of the statement

$$a = b * d;$$

where `a` and `b` are integer variables and `d` is a single-precision variable. When the mixed-mode expression `b * d` is evaluated,[4] the value of `d` used in the expression is converted to a double-precision number for purposes of computation. (It is important to note that the value stored in `d` remains a single-precision number.) Because one of the operands is a double-precision variable, the value of the integer variable `b` is converted to a double-precision number for the computation (again, the value stored in `b` remains an integer) and the resulting value of the expression `b * d` is a double-precision number. Finally, data type conversion across the assignment operator comes into play. Because the left side of the assignment operator is an integer variable, the double-precision value of the expression `(b * d)` is truncated to an integer value and stored in the variable `a`.

Assignment Variations

Although only one variable is allowed immediately to the left of the equal sign in an assignment expression, the variable to the left of the equal sign can also be used

---

[3] The correct integer portion, clearly, is retained only when it is within the range of integers allowed by the compiler.

[4] Review the rules in Table 2.8 in Section 2.5 for the evaluation of mixed-mode expressions, if necessary.

on the right side of the equal sign. For example, the assignment expression sum = sum + 10 is valid. Clearly, as an algebra equation, sum could never be equal to itself plus 10. But in C++, the expression sum = sum + 10 is not an equation—it is an expression that is evaluated in two major steps. The first step is to calculate the value of sum + 10. The second step is to store the computed value in sum. See if you can determine the output of Program 3.2.

PROGRAM 3.2

```cpp
#include <iostream>
using namespace std;

int main()
{
   int sum;

   sum = 25;
   cout << "The number stored in sum is " << sum << endl;
   sum = sum + 10;
   cout << "The number now stored in sum is " << sum << endl;

   return 0;
}
```

The assignment statement sum = 25; tells the computer to store the number 25 in sum, as shown in Figure 3.3. The first cout statement causes the value stored in sum to be displayed by The number stored in sum is 25. The second assignment statement in Program 3.2, sum = sum + 10;, causes the computer to retrieve the 25 stored in sum and add 10 to this number, yielding 35. The number 35 is then stored in the variable on the left side of the equal sign, which is the variable sum. The 25 that was in sum is simply overwritten with the new value of 35, as shown in Figure 3.4.

Assignment expressions such as sum = sum + 25, which use the same variable on both sides of the assignment operator, can be written using the following **shortcut assignment operators**:

$$+= \quad -= \quad *= \quad /= \quad \%=$$

For example, the expression sum = sum + 10 can be written as sum += 10. Similarly, the expression price *= rate is equivalent to the expression price = price * rate.

When you use these new assignment operators, it is important to note that the variable to the left of the assignment operator is applied to the *complete* expression on the right. For example, the expression price *= rate + 1 is equivalent to the expression price = price * (rate + 1), not price = price * rate + 1.

FIGURE 3.3 The Integer 25 Is Stored in sum

sum

25

FIGURE 3.4   sum = sum + 10; **Causes a New Value to Be Stored in** sum

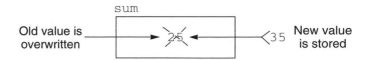

Old value is
overwritten ————→ 25 ←———— < 35   New value
                              is stored

sum

Accumulating

Assignment expressions such as sum += 10 or its equivalent, sum = sum + 10, are very common in programming. These expressions are used for accumulating subtotals when data are entered one number at a time. For example, if we want to add the numbers 96, 70, 85, and 60 in calculator fashion, the following statements could be used:

Statement	Value in sum
sum = 0;	0
sum = sum + 96;	96
sum = sum + 70;	166
sum = sum + 85;	251
sum = sum + 60;	311

The first statement initializes sum to 0. This removes any number ("garbage value") stored in sum that would invalidate the final total. As each number is added, the value stored in sum is increased accordingly. After completion of the last statement, sum contains the total of all the added numbers. Program 3.3 illustrates the effect of these statements by displaying sum's contents after each addition is made.

PROGRAM 3.3

```cpp
#include <iostream>
using namespace std;

int main()
{
  int sum;

  sum = 0;
  cout << "The value of sum is initially set to " << sum << endl;
  sum = sum + 96;
  cout << "  sum is now " << sum << endl;
  sum = sum + 70;
  cout << "  sum is now " << sum << endl;
  sum = sum + 85;
  cout << "  sum is now " << sum << endl;
  sum = sum + 60;
  cout << "  The final sum is " << sum << endl;

  return 0;
}
```

The output displayed by Program 3.3 is:

```
The value of sum is initially set to 0
  sum is now 96
  sum is now 166
  sum is now 251
The final sum is 311
```

Although Program 3.3 is not a practical program (it is easier to add the numbers by hand), it does illustrate the subtotaling effect of repeated use of statements having the form:

```
variable = variable + newValue;
```

We will find many uses for this type of a **statement** when we become more familiar with the repetition statements introduced in Chapter 5.

Counting

An assignment statement that is very similar to the accumulating statement is the **counting statement**. Counting statements have the form:

```
variable = variable + fixedNumber;
```

Examples of counting statements are:

```
i = i + 1;
n = n + 1;
count = count + 1;
j = j + 2;
m = m + 2;
kk = kk + 3;
```

In each of these examples, the same variable is used on both sides of the equal sign. After the statement is executed, the value of the respective variable is increased by a fixed amount. In the first three examples, the variables i, n, and count have all been increased by 1. In the next two examples, the respective variables have been increased by 2, and in the final example, the variable kk has been increased by 3.

For the special case in which a variable is either increased or decreased by 1, C++ provides two unary operators. Using the **increment operator**,[5] ++, the expression variable = variable + 1 can be replaced by either the expression variable++ or ++variable. Examples of the increment operator are:

Expression	Alternative
i = i + 1	i++ or ++i
n = n + 1	n++ or ++n
count = count + 1	count++ or ++count

Program 3.4 illustrates the use of the increment operator.

---

[5] As an historical note, the ++ in C++ was inspired from the increment operator symbol. It was used to indicate that C++ was the next increment to the C language.

PROGRAM 3.4

```cpp
#include <iostream>
using namespace std;

int main()
{
  int count;

  count = 0;
  cout << "The initial value of count is " << count << endl;
  count++;
  cout << "  count is now " << count << endl;
  count++;
  cout << "  count is now " << count << endl;
  count++;
  cout << "  count is now " << count << endl;
  count++;
  cout << "  count is now " << count << endl;

  return 0;
}
```

The output displayed by Program 3.4 is:

```
The initial value of count is 0
   count is now 1
   count is now 2
   count is now 3
   count is now 4
```

When the ++ operator appears before a variable, it is called a **prefix increment operator**; when it appears after a variable, it is called a **postfix increment operator**. The distinction between a prefix and postfix increment operator is important when the variable being incremented is used in an assignment expression. For example, the expression kk = ++n does two things in one expression. Initially, the value of n is incremented by 1 and then the new value of n is assigned to the variable k. Thus, the statement k = ++n; is equivalent to the following two statements:

```
n = n + 1;       // increment n first
k = n;           // assign n's value to k
```

The assignment expression k = n++, which uses a postfix increment operator, reverses this procedure. A postfix increment operates after the assignment is completed. Thus, the statement k = n++; first assigns the current value of n to k and then increments the value of n by 1. This is equivalent to the two statements

```
k = n;           // assign n's value to k
n = n + 1;       // and then increment n
```

In addition to the increment operator, C++ also provides a **decrement operator**, --. As you might expect, the expressions variable-- and --variable are both equivalent to the expression `variable = variable - 1`. Examples of the decrement operator are:

Expression	Alternative
`i = i - 1`	`i-- or --i`
`n = n - 1`	`n-- or --n`
`count = count - 1`	`count-- or --count`

When the `--` operator appears before a variable, it is called a **prefix decrement operator**; when it appears after a variable, it is called a **postfix decrement operator**. For example, both of the expressions `n--` and `--n` reduce the value of n by 1. These expressions are equivalent to the longer expression `n = n - 1`. As with the increment operator, however, the prefix and postfix decrement operators produce different results when used in assignment expressions. For example, the expression `k = --n` first decrements the value of n by 1 before assigning the value of n to k, while the expression `k = n--` first assigns the current value of n to k and then reduces the value of n by 1.

The increment and decrement operators can often be used advantageously to reduce program storage requirements and increase execution speed. For example, consider the following three statements:

```
count = count + 1;
count += 1;
count++;
```

All perform the same function; however, when these instructions were compiled for execution on an IBM personal computer, the storage requirements for the instructions were nine, four, and three bytes, respectively.[6] If we use the assignment operator, =, instead of the increment operator, we use three times the storage space for the instruction, with an accompanying decrease in execution speed.

Exercises 3.1

1. Write an assignment statement to calculate the circumference of a circle having a radius of 3.3 inches. The equation for determining the circumference, c, of a circle is $c = 2\pi r$, where r is the radius and $\pi = 3.1416$.

2. Write an assignment statement to calculate the area of a circle. The equation for determining the area, a, of a circle is $a = pr^2$, where r is the radius and $\pi = 3.1416$.

3. Write an assignment statement to convert temperature in degrees Fahrenheit to degrees Celsius. The equation for this conversion is *Celsius = 5/9 (Fahrenheit − 32)*.

4. Write an assignment statement to calculate the round-trip distance, d, in feet, of a trip that is s miles long, one way.

5. Write an assignment statement to calculate the elapsed time, in minutes, that it takes to make a trip. The equation for computing elapsed time is *elapsed time = total distance/average speed*. Assume that the distance is in miles and the average speed is in miles/hour.

6. Write an assignment statement to calculate the nth term in an arithmetic sequence. The formula for calculating the value, v, of the nth term is $v = a + (n - 1)d$, where a = the first number in the sequence and d = the difference between any two numbers in the sequence.

---

[6] This is clearly a compiler-dependent result.

7. Determine the output of the following program:

```cpp
#include <iostream>
using namespace std;
int main() // a program illustrating integer truncation
{
  int num1, num2;

  num1 = 9/2;
  num2 = 17/4;
  cout << "the first integer displayed is " << num1 << endl;
  cout << "the second integer displayed is " << num2 << endl;

  return 0;
}
```

8. Determine the output produced by the following program:

```cpp
#include <iostream>
using namespace std;
int main()
{
  double average = 26.27;

  cout << "the average is " << average << endl;
  average = 682.3;
  cout << "the average is " << average << endl;
  average = 1.968;
  cout << "the average is " << average << endl;

  return 0;
}
```

9. Determine the output produced by the following program:

```cpp
#include <iostream>
using namespace std;
int main()
{
  double sum;

  sum = 0.0;
  cout << "the sum is " << sum << endl;
  sum = sum + 26.27;
  cout << "the sum is " << sum << endl;
  sum = sum + 1.968;
  cout << "the final sum is "<< sum << endl;

  return 0;
}
```

10. a. Determine what each statement causes to happen in the following program:

```cpp
#include <iostream>
using namespace std;
int main()
{
  int num1, num2, num3, total;

  num1 = 25;
  num2 = 30;
  total = num1 + num2;
  cout << num1 << " + " << num2 << " = " << total << endl;

  return 0;
}
```

 b. What output is produced when the program in Exercise 10a is compiled and executed?

11. Determine and correct the errors in the following programs:

a.
```cpp
#include <iostream>
using namespace std;
int main()
{
  width = 15
  area = length * width;
  cout << "The area is " << area
}
```

b.
```cpp
#include <iostream>
using namespace std;
int main()
{
  int length, width, area;
  area = length * width;
  length = 20;
  width = 15;
  cout << "The area is " << area;
}
```

c.
```cpp
#include <iostream>
using namespace std;
int main()
{
  int length = 20; width = 15, area;
  length * width = area;
  cout << "The area is " , area;
}
```

12. By mistake, a programmer reordered the statements in Program 3.3 as follows:

```cpp
#include <iostream>
using namespace std;

int main()
{
  int sum;
  sum = 0;
  sum =  sum + 96;
  sum =  sum + 70;
  sum =  sum + 85;
  sum =  sum + 60;
  cout << "The value of sum is initially set to " << sum << endl;
  cout <<   " sum is now " << sum << endl;
  cout <<   " sum is now " << sum << endl;
  cout <<   " sum is now " << sum << endl;
  cout <<   " The final sum is " << sum << endl;
  return 0;
}
```

Determine the output that this program produces.

13. Using Program 3.1, determine the volume of cylinders having the following radii and heights:

Radius (in.)	Height (in.)
1.62	6.23
2.86	7.52
4.26	8.95
8.52	10.86
12.29	15.35

14. The area of an ellipse (see Figure 3.5) is given by the formula

$$area = \pi ab$$

Using this formula, write a C++ program to calculate the area of an ellipse having a minor axis, a, of 2.5 inches and a major axis, b, of 6.4 inches.

FIGURE 3.5 The Minor Axis *a* and the Major Axis *b* of an Ellipse

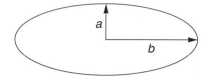

3.2 FORMATTING NUMBERS FOR PROGRAM OUTPUT

Besides displaying correct results, it is extremely important for a program to present its results attractively. Most programs are judged, in fact, on the perceived ease of data entry and the style and presentation of their output. For example, displaying a monetary result as 1.897 is not in keeping with accepted report conventions. The display should be either $1.90 or $1.89, depending on whether rounding or truncation is used.

The format of numbers displayed by cout can be controlled by field width manipulators included in each output stream. Table 3.1 lists the most commonly used manipulators available for this purpose.[7]

For example, the statement

```
cout << "The sum of 6 and 15 is" << setw(3) << 21;
```

creates this printout:

```
The sum of 6 and 15 is 21
```

The setw(3) field width manipulator included in the stream of data passed to cout is used to set the displayed field width. The 3 in this manipulator sets the default field width for the next number in the stream to be three spaces wide. This field width setting causes the 21 to be printed in a field of three spaces, which includes one blank and the number 21. As illustrated, integers are right-justified within the specified field.

Field width manipulators are useful in printing columns of numbers so that the numbers in each column align correctly. For example, Program 3.5 illustrates how a column of integers would align in the absence of field width manipulators.

---

[7] As was noted in Chapter 2, the endl manipulator inserts a newline and then flushes the stream.

TABLE 3.1 Commonly Used Stream Manipulators

Manipulator	Action
setw(*n*)	Set the field width to *n*.
setprecision(*n*)	Set the floating-point precision to *n* places. If the fixed manipulator is designated, n specifies the total number of displayed digits after the decimal point; otherwise n specifies the total number of significant digits displayed (integer plus fractional digits).
setfill('*x*')	Set the default leading fill character to *x*. (The default leading fill character is a space, which is output to fill the front of an output field whenever the width of the field is larger than the value being displayed.)
setiosflags(*flags*)	Set the format flags (see Table 3.3 for flag settings).
scientific	Set the output to display real numbers in scientific notation.
showbase	Display the base used for numbers. A leading 0 is displayed for octal numbers and a leading 0x for hexadecimal numbers.
showpoint	Always display 6 digits in total (combination of integer and fractional parts). Fill with trailing zeros, if necessary. For larger integer values revert to scientific notation.
showpos	Display all positive numbers with a leading + sign.
boolalpha	Display Boolean values as true and false, rather than as 1 and 0.
dec	Set output for decimal display (this is the default).
endl	Output a newline character and display all characters in the buffer.
fixed	Always show a decimal point and use a default of 6 digits after the decimal point. Fill with trailing zeros, if necessary.
flush	Display all the characters in the buffer.
left	Left-justify all numbers.
hex	Set output for hexadecimal display.
oct	Set output for octal display.
uppercase	Display hexadecimal digits and display the exponent in scientific notation in uppercase.
right	Right-justify all numbers (this is the default).
noboolalpha	Display Boolean values as 1 and 0, rather than as true and false.
noshowbase	Do not display octal numbers with a leading 0 and hexadecimal numbers with a leading 0x.
noshowpoint	Do not use a decimal point for real numbers with no fractional parts, do not display trailing zeros in the fractional part of a number, and display a maximum of 6 decimal digits only.
noshowpos	Do not display leading + signs (this is the default).
nouppercase	Display hexadecimal digits and the exponent in scientific notation in lowercase.

PROGRAM 3.5

```
#include <iostream>
using namespace std;

int main()
{
  cout << 6 << endl
       << 18 << endl
       << 124 << endl
       << "---\n"
       << (6+18+124) << endl;

  return 0;
}
```

The output of Program 3.5 is:

```
  6
 18
124
---
148
```

Since no field width manipulators are included in Quick Test Program 3.5, the cout object allocates enough space for each number as it is received. To force the numbers to align on the units digit requires a field width wide enough for the largest displayed number. For Program 3.5, a width of three would suffice. The use of this field width is illustrated in Program 3.6.

PROGRAM 3.6

```
#include <iostream>
#include <iomanip>
using namespace std;

int main()
{
  cout << setw(3) << 6 << endl
       << setw(3) << 18 << endl
       << setw(3) << 124 << endl
       << "---\n"
       << (6+18+124) << endl;

  return 0;
}
```

The output of Program 3.6 is:

```
  6
 18
124
---
148
```

Notice that the field width manipulator must be included for each occurrence of a number inserted into the data stream sent to cout, and that this particular manipulator only applies to the next insertion of data immediately following it. The other manipulators remain in effect until they are changed.

When a manipulator requiring an argument is used, the iomanip header file must be included as part of the program. This is accomplished by the preprocessor command #include <iomanip>, which is listed as the second line in Program 3.6.

Formatted floating-point numbers completely requires the use of three field width manipulators. The first manipulator sets the total width of the display, the second manipulator forces the display of a decimal point, and the third manipulator determines how many significant digits will be displayed to the right of the decimal point. For example, the statement

```
cout << "|" << setw(10) << fixed << setprecision(3) << 25.67 << "|";
```

causes the printout:

```
|    25.670|
```

The bar symbol, |, in the example is used to delimit (mark) the beginning and end of the display field. The `setw` manipulator tells `cout` to display the number in a total field of 10, and the `fixed` manipulator explicitly forces the display of a decimal point and designates that the `setprecision` manipulator is used to designate the number of digits to be displayed after the decimal point. In this case, a display of 3 digits after the decimal point is specified by `setprecision`. Without the explicit designation of a decimal point (which can also be designated as `setiosflags(ios::fixed)`), the `setprecision` manipulator specifies the total number of displayed digits, which includes both the integer and fractional parts of the number.

For all numbers (integers, single-precision, and double precision), `cout` ignores the `setw` manipulator specification if the total specified field width is too small, and allocates enough space for the integer part of the number to be printed. The fractional part of both single-precision and double-precision numbers is displayed up to the precision set with the `setprecision` manipulator (in the absence of a `setprecision` manipulator, the default precision is set to six decimal places). If the fractional part of the number to be displayed contains more digits than called for in the `setprecision` manipulator, the number is rounded to the indicated number of decimal places; if the fractional part contains fewer digits than specified, the number is displayed with the fewer digits. Table 3.2 illustrates the effect of various format manipulator combinations. Again, for clarity, the bar symbol, |, is used to clearly delineate the beginning and end of the output fields.

In addition to the `setw` and `setprecision` manipulators, a field justification manipulator is also available. As we have seen, numbers sent to `cout` are normally displayed right-justified in the display field, while strings are displayed left-justified. To alter the default justification for a stream of data, the `setiosflags` manipulator can be used. For example, the statement

```
cout << "|" << setw(10) << setiosflags(ios::left) << 142 << "|";
```

causes the following left-justified display:

```
|142       |
```

As we have previously seen, since data passed to `cout` may be continued across multiple lines, the previous display would also be produced by the statement:

```
cout << "|" << setw(10)
     << setiosflags(ios::left)
     << 142 << "|";
```

As always, the field width manipulator is only in effect for the next single set of data displayed by `cout`. Right-justification for strings in a stream is obtained by the manipulator `setiosflags(ios::right)`. The symbol `ios` in both the func-

▲ P O I N T   O F   I N F O R M A T I O N ▲

What Is a Flag?

In current programming usage the term **flag** refers to an item, such as a variable or argument, that sets a condition usually considered as either active or nonactive. Although the exact origin of this term in programming is not known, it probably originates from the use of real flags to signal a condition, such as the Stop, Go, Caution, and Winner flags commonly used at car races.

In a similar manner, each flag argument for the `setiosflags()` manipulator function activates a specific condition. For example, the `ios::dec` flag sets the display format to decimal, while the flag `ios::oct` activates the octal display format. Since these conditions are mutually exclusive (that is, only one condition can be active at a time), activating one such flag automatically deactivates the other flags.

Flags that are not mutually exclusive, such as `ios::dec`, `ios::showpoint`, and `ios::fixed` can all be set to on at the same time. This can be done using three individual `setiosflag()` calls or combining all arguments into one call as follows:

```
cout << setiosflags(ios::dec | ios::fixed | ios::showpoint);
```

TABLE 3.2 Effect of Format Manipulators

Manipulator(s)	Number	Display	Comments
`setw(2)`	3	|3|	Number fits in field
`setw(2)`	43	| 43|	Number fits in field
`setw(2)`	143	| 143 |	Field width ignored
`setw(2)`	2.3	| 2.3 |	Field width ignored

`setw(5)`
`fixed`
`setprecision(2)`
	2.366	| 2.37|	Field width of 5 with 2 decimal digits

`setw(5)`
`fixed`
`setprecision(2)`
	42.3	| 42.30|	Number fits in field with specified precision

`setw(5)` `setprecision(2)`	142.364	| 1.4e+002|	Field width ignored and scientific notation used with the `setprecision` manipulator specifying the total number of significant digits (integer plus fractional)

`setw(5)`
`fixed`
`setprecision(2)`
	142.364	| 142.36|	Field width ignored but precision specification used; here the `setprecison` manipulator specifies the number of fractional digits

`setw(5)`
`fixed`
`setprecision(2)`
	142.366	| 142.37|	Field width ignored but precision specification used; here the `setprecison` manipulator specifies the number of fractional digits (note the rounding of the last decimal digit)

`setw(5)`
`fixed`
`setprecision(2)`
	142	| 142 |	Field width used, `fixed` and `setprecision` manipulators irrelevant, because the number is an integer

▲ P O I N T   O F   I N F O R M A T I O N ▲

Formatting cout Stream Data

Floating-point data in a cout output stream can be formatted in precise ways. One of the most common format requirements is to display numbers in a monetary format with two digits after the decimal point, such as 123.45. This can be done with the following statement:

```
cout << setiosflags(ios::fixed)
     << setiosflags(ios::showpoint)
     << setprecision(2);
```

The first manipulator flag, ios::fixed, forces all floating-point numbers placed on the cout stream to be displayed in decimal notation. This flag also prevents the use of scientific notation. The next flag, ios::showpoint, tells the stream always to display a decimal point. Finally, the setprecision manipulator tells the stream always to display two decimal values after the decimal point. Instead of using manipulators, you can also use the cout stream methods setf() and precision(). For example, the previous formatting can also be accomplished using the code:

```
cout.setf(ios::fixed);
cout.setf(ios::showpoint);
cout.precision(2);
```

Note the syntax here: the name of the object, cout, is separated from the method with a period. This is the standard way of specifying a method and connecting it to a specific object.

Addtionally, the flags used in both the setf() method and the setiosflags() manipulator can be combined using the bitwise Or operator, | (explained in Section 16.1). Using this operator, the following two statements are equivalent:

```
cout <<  setiosflags(ios::fixed | ios::showpoint);
cout.setf(ios::fixed | ios::showpoint);
```

Which style you select is a matter of preference.

tion name and the ios::right argument comes from the first letters of the words "input output stream."

In addition to the left and right flags that can be used with the setiosflags() manipulator, other flags may also be used to affect the output. The most commonly used flags for this manipulator are listed in Table 3.3. Notice that the flags in this table effectively provide an alternate way of setting the equivalent manipulators previously listed in Table 3.1.

Because the flags in Table 3.3 are used as arguments to the setiosflags() manipulator method, and the terms argument and parameter are synonymous, another name for a manipulator method that uses arguments is a **parameterized manipulator**. The following is an example of parameterized manipulator methods:

```
cout << setiosflags(ios::showpoint) << setprecision(4);
```

This forces all subsequent floating-point numbers sent to the output stream to be displayed with a decimal point and four decimal digits. If the number has fewer than four decimal digits it will be padded with trailing zeros.

In addition to outputting integers in decimal notation, the oct and hex manipulators permit conversions to octal and hexadecimal, respectively. Program 3.7 illustrates the use of these flags. Because decimal is the default display, the dec manipulator is not required in the first output stream.

PROGRAM 3.7

```cpp
// a program that illustrates output conversions
#include <iostream>
#include <iomanip>
using namespace std;

int main()
{
  cout << "The decimal (base 10) value of 15 is " << 15 << endl;
  cout << "The octal (base 8) value of 15 is "
       << showbase << oct << 15 <<endl;
  cout << "The hexadecimal (base 16) value of 15 is "
       << showbase << hex << 15 << endl;

  return 0;
}
```

The output produced by Program 3.7 is:

```
The decimal (base 10) value of 15 is 15
The octal (base 8) value of 15 is 017
The hexadecimal (base 16) value of 15 is 0xf
```

The display of integer values in one of the three possible number systems (decimal, octal, and hexadecimal) does not affect how the number is actually stored inside a computer. All numbers are stored using the computer's own internal codes. The manipulators sent to `cout` simply tell the object how to convert the internal code for output display purposes.

Besides displaying integers in octal or hexadecimal form, integer constants can also be written in a program in these forms. To designate an octal integer constant, the number must have a leading zero. The number 023, for example, is an octal number in C++. Hexadecimal numbers are denoted using a leading 0x. The use of octal and hexadecimal integer constants is illustrated in Program 3.8.

TABLE 3.3 Format Flags for Use with `setiosflags()`

Flag	Meaning
`ios::fixed`	Always show the decimal point with 6 digits after the decimal point. Fill with trailing zeros, if necessary. This flag takes precedence if it is set with the `ios::showpoint` flag.
`ios::scientific`	Use exponential display on output.
`ios::showpoint`	Always display a decimal point and 6 significant digits in total (combination of integer and fractional parts). Fill with trailing zeros after the decimal point, if necessary. For larger integer values revert to scientific notation unless the `ios::fixed` flag is set.
`ios::showpos`	Display a leading + sign when the number is positive.
`ios::left`	Left-justify output.
`ios::right`	Right-justify output.

PROGRAM 3.8

```cpp
#include <iostream>
using namespace std;

int main()
{
  cout << "The decimal value of 025 is " << 025 << endl
       << "The decimal value of 0x37 is "<< 0x37 << endl;

  return 0;
}
```

FIGURE 3.6   Input, Storage, and Display of Integers

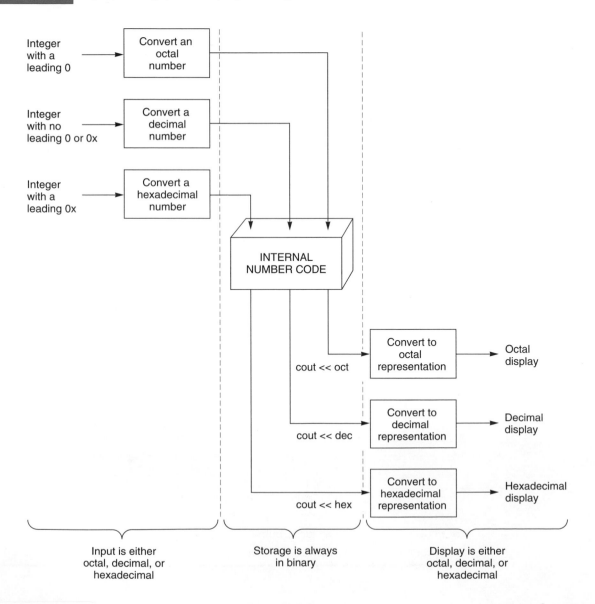

The output produced by Program 3.8 is:

```
The decimal value of 025 is 21
The decimal value of 0x37 is 55
```

The relationship between the input, storage, and display of integers is illustrated in Figure 3.6.

Finally, the manipulators specified in Tables 3.1 and 3.2 can also be set using the `ostream` class methods listed in Table 3.4.

TABLE 3.4 `ostream` **Class Methods**

Method	Comment	Example
`precision(n)`	Equivalent to `setprecision()`	`cout.precision(2)`
`fill('x')`	Equivalent to `setfill()`	`cout.fill('*')`
`setf(ios::fixed)`	Equivalent to `setiosflags(ios::fixed)`	`cout.setf(ios::fixed)`
`setf(ios::showpoint)`	Equivalent to `setiosflags(ios::showpoint)`	`cout.setf(ios::showpoint)`
`setf(iof::left)`	Equivalent to `left`	`cout.setf(ios::left)`
`setf(ios::right)`	Equivalent to `right`	`cout.setf(ios::right)`
`setf(ios::flush)`	Equivalent to `endl`	`cout.setf(ios::flush)`

Note that in the Examples column of Table 3.4 the name of the object, `cout`, is separated from the method with a period. This is the standard way of calling a class method and providing it with the object it is to operate on.

Exercises 3.2

1. Determine the output of the following program:

```
#include <iostream>
using namespace std;
int main() // a program illustrating integer truncation
{
  cout << "answer1 is the integer " << 27/5
       << "\nanswer2 is the integer " << 16/6 << endl;
  return 0;
}
```

2. Determine the output of the following program:

```
#include <iostream>
using namespace std;
int main() // a program illustrating the % operator
{
  cout << "The remainder of 9 divided by 4 is " << 9 % 4
       << "\nThe remainder of 17 divided by 3 is " << 17 % 3 << endl;
  return 0;
}
```

3. Write a C++ program that displays the results of the expressions `3.0 * 5.0`, `7.1 * 8.3 - 2.2`, and `3.2 / (6.1 * 5)`. Calculate the value of these expressions manually to verify that the displayed values are correct.

4. Write a C++ program that displays the results of the expressions `15 / 4`, `15 % 4`, and `5 * 3 - (6 * 4)`. Calculate the value of these expressions manually to verify that the display produced by your program is correct.

5. Determine the errors in each of the following statements:

   a. `cout << "\n << " 15)`

   b. `cout << "setw(4)" << 33;`

   c. `cout << "setprecision(5)" << 526.768;`

   d. `"Hello World!" >> cout;`

   e. `cout << 47 << setw(6);`

   f. `cout << set(10) <.768 << setprecision(2);`

6. Determine and write out the display produced by the following statements:

   a. `cout << "|" << 5 << "|";`

   b. `cout << "|" << setw (4) << 5 << "|";`

   c. `cout << "|" << setw (4) << 56829 << "|";`

   d. `cout << "|" << setw (5) << setprecision(2) << 5.26 << "|";`

   e. `cout << "|" << setw (5) << setprecision(2) << 5.267 << "|";`

   f. `cout << "|" << setw (5) << setprecision(2) << 53.264 << "|";`

   g. `cout << "|" << setw (5) << setprecision(2) << 534.264 << "|";`

   h. `cout << "|" << setw (5) << setprecision(2) << 534. << "|";`

7. Write out the display produced by the following statements:

   a.
   ```
   cout << "The number is " << setw(6)
        << setprecision(2) << 26.27 << endl;
   cout << "The number is " << setw(6)
        << setprecision(2) << 682.3 << endl;
   cout << "The number is " << setw(6)
        << setprecision(2) << 1.968 << endl;
   ```

   b.
   ```
   cout << setw(6) << setprecision(2) << 26.27 << endl;
   cout << setw(6) << setprecision(2) << 682.3 << endl;
   cout << setw(6) << setprecision(2) << 1.968 << endl;
   cout << "--------\n";
   cout << setw(6) << setprecision(2) << 26.27 + 682.3 + 1.968
        << endl;
   ```

   c.
   ```
   cout << setw(5) << setprecision(2) << 26.27 << endl;
   cout << setw(5) << setprecision(2) << 682.3 << endl;
   cout << setw(5) << setprecision(2) << 1.968 << endl;
   cout << "--------\n";
   cout << setw(5) << setprecision(2)
        << 26.27 + 682.3 + 1.968 << endl;
   ```

   d.
   ```
   cout << setw(5) << setprecision(2) << 36.164 << endl;
   cout << setw(5) << setprecision(2) << 10.003 << endl;
   cout << "-----" << endl;
   ```

8. The following table lists the correspondence between the decimal numbers 1 through 15 and their octal and hexadecimal representations:

Decimal:	1	2	3	4	5	6	7	8	9	10	11	12	13	14	15
Octal:	1	2	3	4	5	6	7	10	11	12	13	14	15	16	17
Hexadecimal:	1	2	3	4	5	6	7	8	9	a	b	c	d	e	f

Using this table, determine the output of the following program:

```
#include <iostream>
#include <iomanip>
using namespace std;
```

```
int main()
{
  cout << "\nThe value of 14 in octal is " << oct << 14
       << "\nThe value of 14 in hexadecimal is " << hex << 14
       << "\nThe value of 0xA in decimal is " << dec << 0xa
       << "\nThe value of 0xA in octal is " << oct << 0xa
       << endl;
  return 0;
}
```

3.3 USING MATHEMATICAL LIBRARY FUNCTIONS

As we have seen, assignment statements can be used to perform arithmetic computations. For example, the assignment statement

$$\text{totalPrice} = \text{unitPrice} * \text{amount};$$

multiplies the value in unitPrice times the value in amount and assigns the resulting value to totalPrice. Although addition, subtraction, multiplication, and division are easily accomplished using C++'s arithmetic operators, no such operators exist for raising a number to a power, finding the square root of a number, or determining trigonometric values. To facilitate such calculations, C++ provides standard preprogrammed functions that can be included in a program.

Before using one of C++'s mathematical functions, you need to know:

- the name of the desired mathematical function
- what the mathematical function does
- the type of data required by the mathematical function
- the data type of the result returned by the mathematical function
- how to include the library

To illustrate the use of C++'s mathematical functions, consider the mathematical function named sqrt, which calculates the square root of a number. The square root of a number is computed using the expression

$$\text{sqrt(number)}$$

where the function's name, in this case sqrt(), is followed by parentheses containing the number for which the square root is desired. The purpose of the parentheses following the function name is to provide a funnel through which data can be passed to the function (see Figure 3.7). The items that are passed to the function through the parentheses are called **arguments** of the function and constitute its input data. For example, the following expressions are used to compute the square root of the arguments 4, 17.0, 25, 1043.29, and 6.4516, respectively:

```
sqrt(4)
sqrt(17.0)
sqrt(25)
sqrt(1043.29)
sqrt(6.4516)
```

Notice that the argument to the sqrt() function can be either an integer or real value. This is an example of C++'s function overloading capabilities. Function

FIGURE 3.7   Passing Data to the sqrt() Function

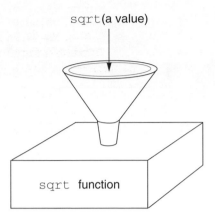

overloading permits the same function name to be defined for different argument data types. In this case, there are really three square root functions named sqrt()—one defined for float, double, and long double arguments. The correct sqrt function is called depending on the type of value given it. The sqrt() function determines the square root of its argument and returns the result as a double. The values returned by the previous expressions are:

Expression	Value Returned
sqrt(4.)	2
sqrt(17.0)	4.12311
sqrt(25.)	5
sqrt(1043.29)	32.3
sqrt(6.4516)	2.54

Table 3.5 lists the more commonly used mathematical functions provided in C++ including the sqrt() function. To access these functions in a program requires that the **mathematical header** file named cmath, which contains appropriate declarations for the mathematical function, be included with the function. This is done

TABLE 3.5 Common C++ Functions

Function Name	Description	Returned Value
abs(a)	Absolute value	Same data type as argument
pow(a1,a2)	a1 raised to the a2 power	Data type of argument a1
sqrt(a)	Square root of a	Double
sin(a)	Sine of a (a in radians)	Double
cos(a)	Cosine of a (a in radians)	Double
tan(a)	Tangent of a (a in radians)	Double
log(a)	Natural logarithm of a	Double
log10(a)	Common log (base 10) of a	Double
exp(a)	e raised to the a power	Double

by placing the following preprocessor statement at the top of any program using a mathematical function:

```
#include <cmath>
```
← ──────── no semicolon

Although some of the mathematical functions listed require more than one argument, all functions, by definition, can directly return at most one value. Additionally, all of the functions listed are overloaded; this means the same function name can be used with integer and real arguments. Table 3.6 illustrates the value returned by selected functions using example arguments.

TABLE 3.6 Selected Function Examples

Example	Returned Value
abs(-7.362)	7.362
abs(-3)	3
pow(2.0,5.0)	32
pow(10,3)	1000
log(18.697)	2.92836
log10(18.697)	1.27177
exp(-3.2)	0.0407622

When a mathematical function is used, it is called into action by giving the name of the function and passing any data to it within the parentheses following the function's name (see Figure 3.8).

The arguments that are passed to a function need not be single constants. Expressions can also be arguments provided that the expression can be computed to yield a value of the required data type. For example, the following arguments are valid for the given functions:

```
sqrt(4.0 + 5.3 * 4.0)     abs(2.3 * 4.6)
sqrt(16.0 * 2.0 - 6.7)    sin(theta - phi)
sqrt(x * y - z/3.2)       cos(2.0 * omega)
```

The expressions in parentheses are first evaluated to yield a specific value. Thus, values have to be assigned to the variables theta, phi, x, y, z, and omega before their use in the preceding expressions. After the value of the argument is calculated, it is passed to the function.

FIGURE 3.8   Using and Passing Data to a Function

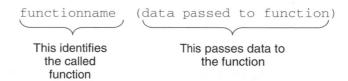

functionname (data passed to function)

This identifies the called function   This passes data to the function

Functions may be included as part of larger expressions. For example:

```
  4 * sqrt(4.5 * 10.0 - 9.0) - 2.0
= 4 * sqrt(36.0) - 2.0
= 4 * 6.0 - 2.0
= 24.0 - 2.0
= 22.0
```

The step-by-step evaluation of an expression such as

```
3.0 * sqrt(5 * 33 - 13.71) / 5
```

is:

Step	Result
1. Perform multiplication in argument.	`3.0 * sqrt(165 - 13.71) / 5`
2. Complete argument calculation.	`3.0 * sqrt(151.29) / 5`
3. Return a function value.	`3.0 * 12.3 / 5`
4. Perform the multiplication.	`36.9 / 5`
5. Perform the division.	`7.38`

Program 3.9 illustrates the use of the `sqrt` function to determine the time it takes a ball to hit the ground after it has been dropped from an 800-foot tower. The mathematical formula used to calculate the time, in seconds, that it takes to fall a given distance, in feet, is:

$$time = sqrt(2 * distance / g)$$

where g is the gravitational constant equal to 32.2 ft/sec^2.

PROGRAM 3.9

```cpp
#include <iostream> // this line may be placed second instead of first
#include <cmath> // this line may be placed first instead of second
using namespace std;

int main()
{
  int height;
  double time;

  height = 800;
  time = sqrt(2 * height / 32.2);
  cout << "It will take " << time << " seconds to fall "
       << height << " feet.\n";

  return 0;
}
```

The output produced by Program 3.9 is:

```
It will take 7.049074 seconds to fall 800 feet.
```

As used in Program 3.9, the value returned by the `sqrt` function is assigned to the variable `time`. In addition to assigning a function's returned value to a variable, the returned value may be included within a larger expression or even used as an argument to another function. For example, the expression

```
sqrt( pow( abs(num1),num2 ) )
```

is valid. The computation proceeds from the inner to the outer pairs of parentheses. Thus, the absolute value of num1 is computed first and used as an argument to the pow() function. The value returned by the pow() function is then used as an argument to the sqrt() function.

Casts

We have already seen the conversion of an operand's data type within mixed-mode arithmetic expressions and across assignment operators. In addition to these implicit data type conversions that are automatically made within mixed-mode arithmetic and assignment expressions, C++ also provides for explicit user-specified **type conversions.** The operators that are used to force the conversion of a value to another type are the **cast** operators. C++ provides both a compile-time and run-time cast operator.

The compile-time cast is a unary operator of syntax data-type (expression), where data-type is the desired data type that the expression within parentheses is converted to. For example, the expression

```
int (a * b)
```

ensures that the value of the expression a * b is converted to an integer value.[8]

With the introduction of the new C++ standard, run-time casts were introduced. In this type of cast, the requested type conversion is checked at run time and is only applied if the conversion results in a valid value. Although four types of run-time casts are available, the most commonly used cast and the one corresponding to the compile-time cast has the syntax staticCast<data=type> (expression). For example, the run-time cast staticCast<int>(a * b) is equivalent to the compile-time cast int (a * b).

Exercises 3.3

1. Write function calls to determine the following:

   a. the square root of 6.37

   b. the square root of $x - y$

   c. the sine of 30 degrees

   d. the sine of 60 degrees

   e. the absolute value of $a^2 - b^2$

   f. the value of e raised to the third power

2. For a = 10.6, b = 13.9, and c = −3.42, determine the following values:

   a. int (a)

   b. int (b)

   c. int (c)

   d. int (a + b)

---

[8] The C type cast syntax, in this case int (a * b), also works in C++.

e. `int (a) + b + c`

f. `int (a + b) + c`

g. `int (a + b + c)`

h. `float (int (a)) + b`

i. `float (int (a + b))`

j. `abs(a) + abs(b)`

k. `sqrt(abs(a - b))`

3. Write C++ statements for the following:

a. $b = \sin x - \cos x$

b. $b = \sin^2 x - \cos^2 x$

c. area $= (c * b * \sin a)/2$

d. $c = \sqrt{a^2 + b^2}$

e. $p = \sqrt{|m - n|}$

f. sum $= \dfrac{a(r^n - 1)}{r - 1}$

4. Write, compile, and execute a C++ program that calculates and returns the fourth root of the number 81.0, which is 3. When you have verified that your program works correctly, use it to determine the fourth root of 1,728.8964. Your program should make use of the `sqrt()` function.

5. Write, compile, and execute a C++ program that calculates the distance between two points whose coordinates are (7,12) and (3,9). Use the fact that the distance between two points having coordinates $(x1,y1)$ and $(x2,y2)$ is $distance = sqrt([x1 - x2]^2 + [y1 - y2]^2)$. When you have verified that your program works correctly by calculating the distance between the two points manually, use your program to determine the distance between the points (−12,−15) and (22,5).

6. If a 20-foot ladder is placed on the side of a building at an 85-degree angle, as illustrated in Figure 3.9, the height at which the ladder touches the building can be calculated as $height = 20 * \sin 85°$. Calculate this height by hand and then write, compile, and execute a C++ program that determines and displays the value of the height. When you have verified that your program works correctly, use it to determine the height of a 25-foot ladder placed at an angle of 85 degrees.

FIGURE 3.9 Illustration for Exercise 6

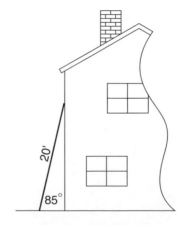

7. A model of worldwide population, in billions of people, after 2000 is given by the equation

$$population = 6.0e^{.02[year - 2000]}$$

Using this formula, write, compile, and execute a C++ program to estimate the worldwide population in the year 2005. Verify the result displayed by your program by calculating the answer manually. After you have verified your program is working correctly, use it to estimate the world's population in the year 2012.

3.4 INTERACTIVE KEYBOARD INPUT

Data for programs that are only going to be executed once may be included directly in the program. For example, if we wanted to multiply the numbers 30.0 and 0.05, we could use Program 3.10.

The output displayed by Program 3.10 is:

```
30.0 times 0.05 is 1.5
```

Program 3.10 can be shortened, as illustrated in Program 3.11. Both programs, however, suffer from the same basic problem in that they must be rewritten to multiply different numbers. Both programs lack the facility for entering different numbers on which to operate.

Except for the practice provided to the programmer of writing, entering, and running the program, programs that do the same calculation only once, on

PROGRAM 3.10

```cpp
#include <iostream>
using namespace std;

int main()
{
    double num1, num2, product;

    num1 = 30.0;
    num2 = 0.05;
    product = num1 * num2;
    cout << "30.0 times 0.05 is " << product << endl;

    return 0;
}
```

the same set of numbers, are clearly not very useful. After all, it is simpler to use a calculator to multiply two numbers than to enter and run either Program 3.10 or 3.11.

This section presents the **cin** object, which is used to enter data into a program while it is executing. Just as the cout object displays a copy of the value stored in-

PROGRAM 3.11

```cpp
#include <iostream>
using namespace std;

int main()
{
    cout << "30.0 times 0.05 is " << 30.0 * 0.05 << endl;

    return 0;
}
```

This section presents the **cin** object, which is used to enter data into a program while it is executing. Just as the cout object displays a copy of the value stored inside a variable, the cin object allows the user to enter a value at the terminal (see Figure 3.10), which is then stored directly in a variable. When a statement such as cin >> num1; is encountered, the computer stops program execution and accepts data from the keyboard. When a data item is typed, the cin object stores the item into the variable listed after the extraction ("get from") operator, >>. The program then continues execution with the next statement after the call to cin. Consider Program 3.12.

The first cout statement in Program 3.12 prints a string that tells the person at the terminal what should be typed. When an output string is used in this manner, it is called a **prompt.** In this case, the prompt tells the user to type a number. The computer then executes the next statement, which is a call to cin. The cin object puts the computer into a temporary pause (or wait) state for as long as it takes the user to type a value. Then the user signals the cin object that the data entry is finished by pressing the return key after the value has been typed. The entered value is stored in the variable to the right of the extraction symbol, and the computer leaves the paused state. Program execution then proceeds with the next statement, which in Program 3.12 is another call to cout. This call causes the next message to be displayed. The second call to cin again puts the computer into a temporary wait state while the user types a second value. This second number is stored in the variable num2.

The following sample run was made using Program 3.12:

```
Please type in a number: 30
Please type in another number: 0.05
30 times 0.05 is 1.5
```

FIGURE 3.10   cin **Is Used to Enter Data;** cout **Is Used to Display Data**

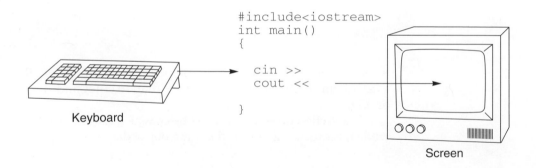

Keyboard

```
#include<iostream>
int main()
{

    cin >>
    cout <<

}
```

Screen

PROGRAM 3.12

```cpp
#include <iostream>
using namespace std;

int main()
{
  double num1, num2, product;

  cout << "Please type in a number: ";
  cin >> num1;
  cout << "Please type in another number: ";
  cin >> num2;
  product = num1 * num2;
  cout << num1 << " times " << num2 << " is " << product << endl;

  return 0;
}
```

In Program 3.12, each time `cin` is invoked, it is used to store one value into a variable. The `cin` object, however, can be used to enter and store as many values as there are extraction symbols, `>>`, and variables to hold the entered data. For example, the statement

`cin >> num1 >> num2;`

results in two values being read from the terminal and assigned to the variables `num1` and `num2`. If the following data are entered at the terminal:

`0.052 245.79`

the variables `num1` and `num2` contain the values 0.052 and 245.79, respectively. Notice that when entering numbers such as 0.052 and 245.79, there must be at least one space between the numbers. The space between the entered numbers clearly indicates where one number ends and the next begins. Inserting more than one space between numbers has no effect on `cin`.

The same spacing is also applicable to entering character data; that is, the extraction operator, `>>`, skips blank spaces and stores the next nonblank character in a character variable. For example, in response to the statements

```cpp
char ch1, ch2, ch3; // declare three character variables
cin >> ch1 >> ch2 >> ch3; // accept three characters
```

the input

`a    b    c`

causes the letter `a` to be stored in the variable `ch1`, the letter `b` to be stored in the variable `ch2`, and the letter `c` to be stored in the variable `ch3`. Because a character variable can be used to store only one character, the input

`abc`

can also be used.

Any number of statements using the `cin` object can be made in a program, and any number of values can be input using a single `cin` statement. Program 3.13 illustrates use of the `cin` object to input three numbers from the keyboard. The program then calculates and displays the average of the numbers entered.

PROGRAM 3.13

```cpp
#include <iostream>
using namespace std;

int main()
{
  int num1, num2, num3;
  double average;

  cout << "Enter three integer numbers: ";
  cin  >> num1 >> num2 >> num3;
  average = (num1 + num2 + num3) / 3.0;
  cout << "The average of the numbers is " << average << endl;

  return 0;
}
```

The following sample run was made using Program 3.13:

```
Enter three integer numbers: 22 56 73
The average of the numbers is 50.3333
```

Note that the data typed at the keyboard for this sample run consist of the input:

```
22 56 73
```

In response to this stream of input, Program 3.13 stores the value 22 in the variable num1, the value 56 in the variable num2, and the value 73 in the variable num3 (see Figure 3.11). Since the average of three integer numbers can be a floating-point number, the variable average, which is used to store the average, is declared as a floating-point variable. Note also that the parentheses are needed in the assignment statement average = (num1 + num2 + num3) / 3.0;. Without these parentheses, the only value to be divided by 3 would be the integer in num3 (because division has a higher precedence than addition).

The cin extraction operation, like the cout insertion operation, is "clever" enough to make a few data type conversions. For example, if an integer is entered in place of a floating-point or double-precision number, the integer is converted to the correct data type.[9] Similarly, if a floating-point or double-precision number is entered when an integer is expected, only the integer part of the number is used. For example, assume the following numbers are typed in response to the statement cin >> num1 >> num2 >> num3;, where num1 and num3 have been declared as floating-point variables and num2 is an integer variable:

```
56 22.879 33.923
```

The 56 is converted to 56.0 and stored in the variable num1. The extraction operation continues extracting data from the input stream sent to it, expecting an integer

---

[9] Strictly speaking, what comes in from the keyboard is not any data type, such as an int or double; instead, it is simply a sequence of characters. The extraction operation handles the conversion from the character sequence to a defined data type.

value. As far as `cin` is concerned, the decimal point after the `22` in the number `22.879` indicates the end of an integer and the start of a decimal number. Thus, `22` is assigned to `num2`. Continuing to process its input stream, `cin` takes `.879` as the next floating-point number and assigns it to `num3`. As far as `cin` is concerned, `33.923` is extra input that is ignored. If, though, you do not initially type enough data, the `cin` object continues to make the computer pause until sufficient data have been entered.

FIGURE 3.11   **Inputting Data into the Variables** num1, num2, **and** num3

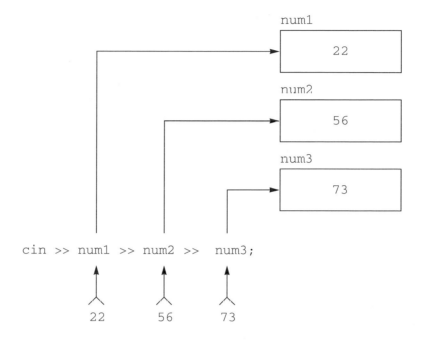

A First Look at User-Input Validation

A well-constructed program should validate user input and ensure that a program does not either crash or produce nonsensical output due to unexpected input. The term *validate* means checking that the entered value matches the data type of the variable that the value is assigned to within a `cin` statement, and that the value is within an acceptable range of values appropriate to the application. Programs that detect and respond effectively to unexpected user input are formally referred to as robust programs and informally as "bullet-proof" programs. One of your jobs as a programmer is to produce such programs. As written, both Programs 3.12 and 3.13 are not robust programs. Let's see why.

The first problem with these programs becomes evident when a user enters a non-numerical value. For example, consider the following sample run using Program 3.13.

```
Enter three integer numbers: 10 20.68 20
The average of the numbers is −2.86331e+008
```

This output occurs because the conversion of the second input number results in the integer value 20 assigned to `num2` and the value −858993460 assigned to `num3`. This last value corresponds to an invalid character, the decimal point, being assigned to an expected integer value. The average of the numbers 10, 20, and

−858993460 is then computed correctly as −286331143.3, which is displayed in scientific notation with six significant digits as −2.86331e+08. As far as the average user is concerned, this will be reported as a program error. This same problem occurs whenever a noninteger value is entered for either of the first two inputs (it does not occur for any numerical value entered as the third input, because the integer part of the last input is accepted and the remaining input ignored). As a programmer your initial response may be "The program clearly asks you to enter integer values." This, however, is the response of a very inexperienced programmer. Professional programmers understand that it is their responsibility to ensure that a program anticipates and appropriately handles any and all input that a user can possibly enter. This is accomplished by first thinking about what can go wrong with your own program as you develop it and then having another person or group thoroughly test the program.

The basic approach to handling invalid data input is referred to as **user-input validation**, which means validating the entered data either during or immediately after the data have been entered, and then providing the user with a way of re-entering any invalid data. User-input validation is an essential part of any commercially viable program, and if done correctly, it will protect a program from attempting to process data that can cause computational problems. We will see how to provide this type of validation after C++'s selection and repetition statements have been presented in Chapters 4 and 5, respectively.

Exercises 3.4

1. For the following declaration statements, write a statement using the `cin` object that causes the computer to pause while the appropriate data are typed by the user:

   a. `int firstnum;`

   b. `float grade;`

   c. `double secnum;`

   d. `char keyval;`

   e. `int month years;`
      `float average;`

   f. `char ch;`
      `int num1,num2;`
      `double grade1,grade2;`

   g. `float interest, principal, capital;`
      `double price,yield;`

   h. `char ch,letter1,letter2;`
      `int num1,num2,num3;`

   i. `float temp1,temp2,temp3;`
      `double volts1,volts2;`

2. a. Write a C++ program that first displays the following prompt:
      `Enter the temperature in degrees Celsius:`

      Have your program accept a value entered from the keyboard and convert the temperature entered to degrees Fahrenheit using the equation *Fahrenheit = (9.0 / 5.0) * Celsius + 32.0*. Your program should then display the temperature in degrees Celsius using an appropriate output message.

   b. Compile and execute the program written for Exercise 2a.

      Verify your program by calculating by hand, and then by using your program, the Fahrenheit equivalent of the following test data:

Test data set 1: 0 degrees Celsius
Test data set 2: 50 degrees Celsius
Test data set 3: 100 degrees Celsius

When you are sure your program is working correctly, use it to determine the Fahrenheit temperatures corresponding to the following Celsius values:

Celsius	Fahrenheit
45	
50	
55	
60	
65	
70	

3. Write, compile, and execute a C++ program that displays the following prompt:

```
Enter the radius of a circle:
```

After accepting a value for the radius, your program should calculate and display the circumference of the circle. (*Hint: circumference = 2 * 3.1416 * radius.*) For testing purposes, verify your program using a test input radius of 3 inches. After manually determining that the result produced by your program is correct, use your program to determine the circumferences of the following data:

Radius (in.)
1.0
1.5
2.0
2.5
3.0
3.5

4. a. Write, compile, and execute a C++ program that displays the following prompts:

```
Enter the miles driven:
Enter the gallons of gas used:
```

After each prompt is displayed, your program should use a `cin` statement to accept data from the keyboard for the displayed prompt. After the gallons of gas used number has been entered, your program should calculate and display miles per gallon obtained. This value should be included in an appropriate message and calculated using the equation *miles per gallon = miles/gallons used*. Verify your program using the following test data:

Test data set 1: miles = 276, gas = 10 gallons
Test data set 2: miles = 200, gas = 15.5 gallons

When you have completed your verification, use your program to determine the miles-per-gallon for the following data:

Miles Driven	Gallons Used
250	16.00
275	18.00
312	19.54
296	17.39

b. For the program written for Exercise 4a, determine how many verification runs are required to ensure the program is working correctly and give a reason supporting your answer.

5. a. Write, compile, and execute a C++ program that displays the following prompts:

```
Enter a number:
Enter a second number:
Enter a third number:
Enter a fourth number:
```

After each prompt is displayed, your program should use a cin statement to accept a number from the keyboard for the displayed prompt. After the fourth number has been entered, your program should calculate and display the average of the numbers. The average should be included in an appropriate message. Check the average displayed by your program using the following test data:

```
Test data set 1: 100, 100, 100, 100
Test data set 2: 100, 0, 100, 0
```

When you have completed your verification, use your program to determine the averages of the following data:

Numbers

92, 98, 79, 85

86, 84, 75, 86

63, 85, 74, 82

b. Repeat Exercise 5a, making sure that you use the same variable name, number, for each number input. Also use the variable sum for the sum of the numbers. (*Hint:* To do this, you may use the statement sum = sum + number after each number is accepted. Review the material on accumulating presented in Section 3.1.)

6. a. Write, compile, and execute a C++ program that computes and displays the value of the second-order polynomial $ax^2 = + bx + c$ for any user input values of the coefficients $a, b, c,$ and the variable x. Have your program first display a message informing the user as to what the program will do and then display suitable prompts to alert the user to enter the desired data. (*Hint:* Use a prompt such as *Enter the coefficient of the x squared term.*)

b. Check the result produced by your program written for Exercise 6a using the following test data:

Test data set 1: $a = 0, b = 0, c = 22, x = 56$
Test data set 2: $a = 0, b = 22, c = 0, x = 2$
Test data set 3: $a = 22, b = 0, c = 0, x = 2$
Test data set 4: $a = 2, b = 4, c = 5, x = 2$
Test data set 5: $a = 5, b = -3, c = 2, x = 1$

When you have completed your verification, use your program to determine the polynomial values for the following data:

a	b	c	x
2.0	17.0	−12.0	1.3
3.2	2.0	15.0	2.5
3.2	2.0	15.0	−2.5
−2.0	10.0	0.0	2.0
−2.0	10.0	0.0	4.0
−2.0	10.0	0.0	5.0
−2.0	10.0	0.0	6.0
5.0	22.0	18.0	8.3
4.2	−16	−20	−5.2

7. The number of bacteria, B, in a certain culture that is subject to refrigeration can be approximated by the equation $B = 300000 \, e^{-.032t}$, where e is the irrational number 2.71828 rounded to five decimal places, known as Euler's number, and t is the amount of time, in hours, the culture has been refrigerated. Using this equation, write, compile, and execute a single C++ program that prompts the user for a value of time, calculates the number of bacteria in the culture, and displays the result. For testing purposes, check your program using a test input of 10 hours. When you have verified the operation of your program, use it to determine the number of bacteria in the culture after 12, 18, 24, 36, 48, and 72 hours.

8. Write, compile, and execute a program that calculates and displays the square root value of a user-entered real number. Verify your program by calculating the square roots of the following data: 25, 16, 0, and 2. When you have completed your verification, use your program to determine the square root of 32.25, 42, 48, 55, 63, and 79.

9. Program 3.12 prompts the user to input two numbers, where the first value entered is stored in num1 and the second value is stored in num2. Using this program as a starting point, write a program that swaps the values stored in the two variables.

10. Write a C++ program that prompts the user to type in a number. Have your program accept the number as an integer and immediately display the integer using a cout object call. Run your program three times. The first time you run the program enter a valid integer number, the second time enter a floating-point number, and the third time enter a character. Using the output display, see what number your program actually accepted from the data you entered.

11. Repeat Exercise 10 but have your program declare the variable used to store the number as a floating-point variable. Run the program four times. The first time enter an integer, the second time enter a decimal number with fewer than six decimal places, the third time enter a number having more than six decimal places, and the fourth time enter a character. Using the output display, keep track of what number your program actually accepted from the data you typed. What happened, if anything, and why?

12. Repeat Exercise 10 but have your program declare the variable used to store the number as a double-precision variable. Run the program four times. The first time enter an integer, the second time enter a decimal number with fewer than six decimal places, the third time enter a number having more than six decimal places, and the fourth time enter a character. Using the output display, keep track of what number your program actually accepted from the data you typed. What happened, if anything, and why?

13. a. Why do you think that successful programs contain extensive data input validity checks? (*Hint:* Review Exercises 10, 11, and 12.)

    b. What do you think is the difference between a data type check and a data reasonableness check?

    c. Assume that a program requests that a month, day, and year be entered by the user. What are some checks that could be made on the entered data?

3.5 SYMBOLIC CONSTANTS

Literal data are any data within a program that explicitly identify themselves. For example, the constants 2 and 3.1416 in the assignment statement

```
circum = 2 * 3.1416 * radius;
```

are also called literals because they are literally included directly in the statement. Additional examples of literals are contained in the following C++ assignment statements. See if you can identify them.

```
perimeter = 2 * length * width;
        y = (5 * p) / 7.2;
salestax = 0.05 * purchase;
```

The literals are the numbers 2, 5 and 7.2, and 0.05 in the first, second, and third statements, respectively.

Quite frequently, literal data used within a program have a more general meaning that is recognized outside the context of the program. Examples of these types of constants include 3.1416, which is π accurate to four decimal places; 32.2 ft/sec^2, which is the gravitational constant; and 2.71828, which is Euler's number accurate to five decimal places. The meaning of certain other constants appearing in a program are defined strictly within the context of the application being programmed. For example, in a program used to determine bank interest charges, the interest rate typically appears in a number of different places throughout the program. Similarly, in a program used to calculate taxes, the tax rate might appear in many individual instructions. Numbers such as these are referred to by programmers as **magic numbers.** By themselves, the numbers are quite ordinary, but in the context of a particular application, they have a special ("magical") meaning.

When the same magic number appears repeatedly within a program it becomes a potential source of error should the constant have to be changed. For example, if either the interest rate or sales tax rate changes, as rates are prone to do, the programmer has the cumbersome task of changing the value everywhere it appears in the program. Multiple changes, however, are subject to error; if just one rate value is overlooked and not changed, the result obtained when the program is run will be incorrect and the source of the error difficult to locate.

To avoid the problem of having a magic number spread throughout a program in many places and to permit clear identification of more universal constants, such as π, C++ allows the programmer to give these constants their own symbolic name. Then, instead of using the number throughout the program, the symbolic name is used. If the number ever has to be changed, the change need only be made once at the point where the symbolic name is equated to the actual number value. Other terms for symbolic names are **symbolic constants** and **named constants**. We will use these terms interchangeably.

Equating numbers to symbolic names is accomplished using a `const` declaration qualifier. The `const` qualifier specifies that the declared identifier can be read only after it is initialized; it cannot be changed. Three examples using this qualifier are:

```
const double PI = 3.1416;
const float SALESTAX = 0.05f;
const int MAXNUM = 100;
```

The first declaration statement creates a double-precision symbolic constant named PI having the value 3.1416. The second declaration statement creates the single-precision symbolic constant named SALESTAX having a value of 0.05. Finally, the third declaration creates an integer symbolic constant named MAXNUM having the value 100.

Once a symbolic constant is created, the value stored in the constant cannot be changed. Thus, for all practical purposes, the name of the constant and its value are linked together for the duration of the program that declares them.

Although we have typed the symbolic constants in uppercase letters, lowercase letters could have been used. It is common in C++, however, to use all uppercase letters for symbolic constants to identify them easily as such. Then, whenever a programmer sees all uppercase letters in a program, he or she will know that the identifier is not a variable whose value can be changed within the program.

Once declared, a symbolic constant can be used in any C++ statement in place of the number it represents. For example, the assignment statements

```
circum = 2 * PI * radius;
amount = SALESTAX * purchase;
```

are both valid. These statements must, of course, appear after the declarations for all their variables.

Placement of Statements

At this stage, we have introduced a variety of statement types. The general rule in C++ for statement placement is simply that a variable or named constant must be declared before it can be used. Although this rule permits both preprocessor directives and declaration statements to be placed throughout a program, doing so results in a very poor program structure. As a matter of good programming form, the following statement ordering should be used:

```
Preprocessor directives

int main()
{
  symbolic constants
  variable declarations

  other executable statements

  return value
}
```

As new statement types are introduced, we will expand this placement structure to accommodate them. Notice that comment statements can be freely intermixed anywhere within this basic structure.

Program 3.14 illustrates the use of a named constant using this placement order.

PROGRAM 3.14

```cpp
#include <iostream>
#include <iomanip>
using namespace std;

int main()
{
  const double SALESTAX = 0.05;
  double amount, taxes, total;

  cout << "\nEnter the amount purchased: ";
  cin  >> amount;
  taxes = SALESTAX * amount;
  total = amount + taxes;

    // set output formats
  cout << setiosflags(ios::fixed)
       << setiosflags(ios::showpoint)
       << setprecision(2);

  cout << "The sales tax is " << setw(4) << taxes << endl;
  cout << "The total bill is " << setw(5) << total << endl;

  return 0;
}
```

The following sample run was made using Program 3.14:

```
Enter the amount purchased: 36.00
The sales tax is 1.80
The total bill is 37.80
```

Although we have used the const qualifier to construct symbolic constants, we encounter this data type once again in Chapter 6, where we show that they are useful as function arguments in ensuring that the argument is not modified within the function.

Exercises 3.5

Determine the purpose of the programs given in Exercises 1, 2, and 3. Then rewrite each program using a symbolic constant for the appropriate literals.

```
1. #include <iostream>
   using namespace std;

   int main()
   {
     float radius, circum;
     cout << "Enter a radius: ";
     cin >> radius;
     circum = 2.0 * 3.1416 * radius;
     cout << "\nThe circumference of the circle is " << circum << endl;

     return 0;
   }

2. #include <iostream>
   using namespace std;

   int main()
   {
      prime, amount, interest;
     prime = .04; // prime interest rate
     cout << // Enter the amount: ";
     cin >> amount;
     interest = prime * amount;
     cout << "\nThe interest earned is" << interest << endl;

    return 0;
   }

3. #include <iostream>
   using namespace std;

   int main()
   {
     float fahren, celsius;
     cout << "Enter a temperature in degrees Fahrenheit: ";
     cin >> fahren;
     celsius = (5.0/9.0) * (fahren - 32.0);
     cout << "\nThe equivalent Celsius temperature is "
          << celsius << endl;

     return 0;
   }
```

3.6 FOCUS ON PROBLEM SOLVING

In this section, we present two programming problems to further illustrate both the use of `cin` statements to accept user input data and the use of library functions for performing calculations.

Problem 1: Acid Rain

The use of coal as the major source of steam power began with the Industrial Revolution. Currently, coal is one of the principal sources of electrical power generation in many industrialized countries.

Since the middle of the nineteenth century, we have known that the oxygen used in the burning process combines with the carbon and sulfur in the coal to produce both carbon dioxide and sulfur dioxide. When these gases are released into the atmosphere, the sulfur dioxide combines with the water and oxygen in the air to form sulfuric acid, which itself is transformed into separate hydronium ions and sulfates (see Figure 3.12). It is the hydronium ions in the atmosphere that fall to earth, either as components of rain or as a dry deposition, and change the acidity level of lakes and forests.

The acid level of rain and lakes is measured on a pH scale using the formula

$$pH = -\log_{10}(\text{concentration of hydronium ions})$$

where the concentration of hydronium ions is measured in units of moles/liter. A pH value of 7 indicates a neutral value (neither acid nor alkaline), whereas levels below 7 indicate the presence of an acid, and levels above 7 indicate the presence of an alkaline substance. For example, sulfuric acid has a pH value of approximately 1, lye has a pH value of approximately 13, and water typically has a pH value of 7. Marine life usually cannot survive in water with a pH level below 4.

Using the formula for pH, we will write a C++ program that calculates the pH level of a substance based on a user input value for the concentration of hydronium ions. In the following subsections, we use the top-down development procedure described in Section 2.6.

FIGURE 3.12   The Formation of Acid Rain

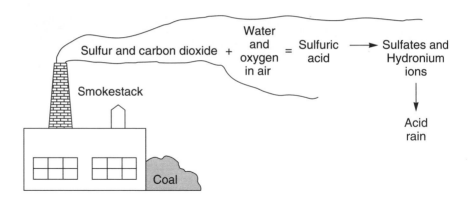

Step 1: Analyze the Problem   Although the statement of the problem provides technical information on the composition of acid rain, from a programming viewpoint this is a rather simple problem. Here, there is only one required output (a pH level) and one input (the concentration of hydronium ions).

Step 2: Develop a Solution   The algorithm required to transform the input to the required output is a rather straightforward use of the pH formula that is provided. The pseudocode representation of the complete algorithm for entering the input data, processing the data to produce the desired output, and displaying the output is:

Display a prompt to enter an ion concentration level.
Read a value for the concentration level.
Calculate a pH level using the given formula.
Display the calculated value.

To ensure that we understand the formula used in the algorithm, we will do a hand calculation. The result of this calculation can then be used to verify the result produced by the program. Assuming a hydronium concentration of 0.0001 (any value would do), the pH level is calculated as $-\log_{10} 10^{-4}$. Either by knowing that the logarithm of 10 raised to a power is the power itself or by using a log table, the value of this expression is $-(-4) = 4$.

Step 3: Code the Solution   Program 3.15 describes the selected algorithm in C++. The choice of variable names is arbitrary.

PROGRAM 3.15

```cpp
#include <iostream>
#include <cmath>
using namespace std;

int main()
{
  float hydron, pHlevel;

  cout << "Enter the hydronium ion concentration: ";
  cin  >> hydron;
  pHlevel = -log10(hydron);
  cout << "The pH level is " << pHlevel << endl;

  return 0;
}
```

Program 3.15 begins with two `#include` preprocessor statements, followed by the function `main()`. Within `main()`, a declaration statement declares two floating-point variables, `hydron` and `pHlevel`. The program then displays a prompt requesting input data from the user. After the prompt is displayed, a `cin` statement is used to store the entered data in the variable `hydron`. Finally, a value for `pHlevel` is calculated, using the logarithmic library function, and displayed. As always, the program is terminated with a closing brace.

Step 4: Test and Correct the Program   A test run using Program 3.15 produced the following:

```
Enter the hydronium ion concentration: 0.0001
The pH level is 4
```

Because the program performs a single calculation and the result of this test run agrees with our previous hand calculation, the program has been completely tested. It can now be used to calculate the pH level of other hydronium concentrations with confidence that the results being produced are accurate.

Problem 2: Approximating the Exponential Function

The exponential function e^x, where e is known as Euler's number (and has the value 2.718281828459045. . .) appears many times in descriptions of natural phenomena. For example, radioactive decay, population growth, and the normal (bell-shaped) curve used in statistical applications all can be described using this function.

The value of e^x can be approximated using the following series:[10]

---

[10] The formula from which this is derived is $e^x = \dfrac{x^0}{0!} + \dfrac{x^1}{1!} + \dfrac{x^2}{2!} + \dfrac{x^3}{3!} + \ldots + \dfrac{x^n}{n!}$

$$1 + \frac{x^1}{1} + \frac{x^2}{2} + \frac{x^3}{6} + \frac{x^4}{24} + \frac{x^5}{120} + \frac{x^6}{720} \cdots$$

Using this polynomial as a base, assume you are given the following assignment: Write a program that approximates e raised to a user input value of x using the first four terms of this series. For each approximation, display the value calculated by C++'s exponential function, `exp()`, the approximate value, and the absolute difference between the two. Make sure to verify your program using a hand calculation. Once the verification is complete, use the program to approximate e^4. Using the top-down development procedure described in Section 2.6, we perform the following steps.

Step 1: Analyze the Problem   The statement of the problem specifies that four approximations are to be made using one, two, three, and four terms of the approximating polynomial, respectively. For each approximation, three output values are required: the value of e^x produced by the exponential function, the approximate value, and the absolute difference between the two values. Figure 3.13 illustrates, in symbolic form, the structure of the required output display. The output indicated in Figure 3.13 can be used to get a "feel" for what the program must look like. Realizing that each line in the display can only be produced by executing a `cout` statement, it should be clear that four such statements must be executed. Additionally, since each output line contains three computed values, each `cout` statement will have three items in its expression list.

FIGURE 3.13   Values Stored in the Variables

e^x	Approximation	Difference
library function value	1st approximate value	1st difference
library function value	2nd approximate value	2nd difference
library function value	3rd approximate value	3rd difference
library function value	4th approximate value	4th difference

The only input to the program consists of the value of x. This will, of course, require a single prompt and a `cin` statement to input the necessary value.

Step 2: Develop a Solution   Before any output items can be calculated, the program needs to prompt the user for a value of x and then accept the entered value. The output display consists of two title lines followed by four lines of calculated data. The title lines can be produced using two `cout` statements. Now let's see how the data being displayed are produced.

The first item on the first data output line illustrated in Figure 3.13 can be obtained using the `exp()` function. The second item on this line, the approximation to e^x, can be obtained by using the first term in the polynomial that was given in the program specification. Finally, the third item on the line can be calculated by using the `abs()` function on the difference between the first two items. When all of these items are calculated, a single `cout` statement can be used to display the three results on the same line.

The second output line illustrated in Figure 3.13 displays the same type of items as the first line, except that the approximation to e^x requires the use of two terms of the approximating polynomial. Notice also that the first item on the second line, the value obtained by the `exp()` function, is the same as the first item on the first line. This means that this item does not have to be recalculated; the value calculated for the first line can simply be displayed a second time. Once the data for the second line have been calculated, a single `cout` statement can again be used to display the required values.

Finally, only the second and third items on the last two output lines shown in Figure 3.13 need to be recalculated because the first item on these lines is the same as previously calculated for the first line. Thus, for this problem, the complete algorithm described in pseudocode is:

Display a prompt for the input value of x.
Read the input value.
Display the heading lines.
Calculate the exponential value of x using the exp() function.
Calculate the first approximation.
Calculate the first difference.
Print the first output line.
Calculate the second approximation.
Calculate the second difference.
Print the second output line.
Calculate the third approximation.
Calculate the third difference.
Print the third output line.
Calculate the fourth approximation.
Calculate the fourth difference.
Print the fourth output line.

To ensure that we understand the processing used in the algorithm, we will do a hand calculation. The result of this calculation can then be used to verify the result produced by the program that we write. For test purposes, we use a value of 2 for x, which causes the following approximations:

Using the first term of the polynomial, the approximation is

$$e^2 \approx 1$$

Using the first two terms of the polynomial, the approximation is

$$e^2 \approx 1 + 2/1 = 3$$

Using the first three terms of the polynomial, the approximation is

$$e^2 \approx 3 + 2^2/2 = 5$$

Using the first four terms of the polynomial, the approximation is

$$e^2 \approx 5 + 2^3/6 = 6.3333$$

Notice that, in using four terms of the polynomial, it was not necessary to recalculate the value of the first three terms; instead, we used the previously calculated value.

Step 3: Code the Solution   Program 3.16 represents a description of the selected algorithm in C++.

PROGRAM 3.16

```cpp
// this program approximates the function e raised to the x power
// using one, two, three, and four terms of an approximating
// polynomial
#include <iostream>
#include <iomanip>
#include <cmath>
using namespace std;

int main()
{
  double x, funcValue, approx, difference;

  cout << "\nEnter a value of x: ";
  cin >> x;

    // print two title lines
  cout << " e to the x        Approximation       Difference\n";
  cout << "-------------        -------------       -------------\n";

  funcValue = exp(x);       // use the library function

    // calculate the first approximation
  approx = 1;
  difference = abs(funcValue - approx);
  cout << setw(10) << setiosflags(ios::showpoint) << funcValue
       << setw(18) << approx
       << setw(18) << difference << endl;

    // calculate the second approximation
  approx = approx + x;
  difference = abs(funcValue - approx);
  cout << setw(10) << setiosflags(ios::showpoint) << funcValue
       << setw(18) << approx
       << setw(18) << difference << endl;

    // calculate the third approximation
  approx = approx + pow(x,2)/2.0;
  difference = abs(funcValue - approx);
  cout << setw(10) << setiosflags(ios::showpoint) << funcValue
       << setw(18) << approx
       << setw(18) << difference << endl;

    // calculate the fourth approximation
  approx = approx + pow(x,3)/6.0;
  difference = abs(funcValue - approx);
  cout << setw(10) << setiosflags(ios::showpoint) << funcValue
       << setw(18) << approx
       << setw(18) << difference << endl;

  return 0;
}
```

In reviewing Program 3.16, notice that the input value of x is obtained first. The two title lines are then printed prior to any calculations being made. The value of e^x is then computed using the `exp()` library function and assigned to the variable `funcValue`. This assignment permits this value to be used in the four `difference` calculations and displayed four times without the need for recalculation.

Since the approximation to the e^x is "built up" using more and more terms of the approximating polynomial, only the new term for each approximation is calculated and added to the previous approximation. Finally, to permit the same variables to be reused, the values in them are immediately printed before the next approximation is made. The following is a sample run produced by Program 3.16:

```
Enter a value of x: 2
          e to the x      Approximation      Difference
          7.389056        1.000000           6.389056
          7.389056        3.000000           4.389056
          7.389056        5.000000           2.389056
          7.389056        6.333333           1.055723
```

Step 4: Test and Correct the Program   The first two columns of output data produced by the sample run agree with our hand calculation. A hand check of the last column verifies that it also correctly contains the difference in values between the first two columns.

Because the program only performs nine calculations and the result of the test run agrees with our hand calculations, it appears that the program has been completely tested. However, it is important to understand that this is due to our choice of test data. Selecting a value of 2 for x forced us to verify that the program was, in fact, calculating 2 raised to the required powers. A choice of 0 or 1 for our hand calculation would not have given us the verification that we need. Do you see why this is so?

Using 0 or 1 does not adequately test whether the program used the `pow()` function correctly, or even if it used it at all! That is, an incorrect program that did not use the `pow()` function could have been constructed to produce correct values for $x = 0$ and $x = 1$, but for no other values of x. Because the test data we used do adequately verify the program, however, we can use it with confidence in the results produced. Clearly, however, the output demonstrates that to achieve a fairly good level of accuracy using an approximating polynomial, more terms than four are required.

Exercises 3.6

1. Enter, compile, and run Program 3.15 on your computer system.

2. a. Enter, compile, and run Program 3.16 on your computer system.

   b. Determine how many terms of the approximating polynomial should be used to achieve an error of less than 0.0001 between the approximation and the value of e^2 as determined by the `exp()` function.

3. By mistake, a student wrote Program 3.16 as follows:

```
// this program approximates the function e raised to the x power
// using one, two, three, and four terms of an approximating
polynomial
#include <iostream>
#include <iomanip>
#include <cmath>
using namespace std;
```

```
int main()
{
    double x, funcValue, approx, difference;

    // print two title lines
    cout << " e to the x      Approximation      Difference\n";
    cout << "-------------    -------------    -------------\n";

    cout << "\nEnter a value of x: ";
    cin >> x;
    funcValue = exp(x);        // use the library function

        // calculate the first approximation
    approx = 1;
    difference = abs(funcValue - approx);
    cout << setw(10) << setiosflags(ios::showpoint) << funcValue
         << setw(18) << approx
         << setw(18) << difference << endl;
      // calculate the second approximation
    approx = approx + x;
    difference = abs(funcValue - approx);
    cout << setw(10) << setiosflags(ios::showpoint) << funcValue
         << setw(18) << approx
         << setw(18) << difference << endl;
      // calculate the third approximation
    approx = approx + pow(x,2)/2.0;
    difference = abs(funcValue - approx);
    cout << setw(10) << setiosflags(ios::showpoint) << funcValue
         << setw(18) << approx
         << setw(18) << difference << endl;
      // calculate the fourth approximation
    approx = approx + pow(x,3)/6.0;
    difference = abs(funcValue - approx);
    cout << setw(10) << setiosflags(ios::showpoint) << funcValue
         << setw(18) << approx
         << setw(18) << difference << endl;

    return 0;
}
```

Determine the output that is produced by this program.

4. The value of π can be approximated by the series

$$4\left(1 - \frac{1}{3} + \frac{1}{5} - \frac{1}{7} + \ldots\right)$$

Using this formula, write a program that calculates and displays the value of π using the first four terms of the series.

5. a. The formula for the standard normal deviate, z, used in statistical applications is

$$z = \frac{x - m}{\sigma}$$

where μ refers to a mean value and σ to a standard deviation. Using this formula, write a program that calculates and displays the value of the standard normal deviate when $x = 85.3$, $\mu = 80$, and $\sigma = 4$.

b. Rewrite the program written in Exercise 5a to accept the values of x, μ, and σ as user inputs while the program is executing.

6. a. The equation of the normal (bell-shaped) curve used in statistical applications is:

$$y = \frac{1}{\sigma\sqrt{2\pi}} e^{-(1/2)(x-\mu)/\sigma^2}$$

Using this equation, and assuming $\mu = 90$ and $\sigma = 4$, write a program that determines and displays the value of y when $x = 80$.

b. Rewrite the program written in Exercise 6a to accept the values of x, μ, and σ as user inputs while the program is executing.

7. a. Write, compile, and execute a program that calculates and displays the gross pay and net pay of two individuals. The first individual works 40 hours and is paid an hourly rate of $8.43. The second individual works 35 hours and is paid an hourly rate of $5.67. Both individuals have 20% of their pay withheld for income tax purposes and both pay 2% of their net pay, before taxes, for medical benefits.

b. Redo Exercise 7a assuming that the individuals' hours and rate are entered when the program is run.

8. The volume of oil stored in an underground 200-foot-deep cylindrical tank is determined by measuring the distance from the top of the tank to the surface of the oil. Knowing this distance and the radius of the tank, the volume of oil in the tank can be determined using the formula *volume* $= \pi$ *radius*^{2} $(200 -$ distance$)$. Using this information, write, compile, and execute a C++ program that accepts the radius and distance measurements, calculates the volume of oil in the tank, and displays the two input values and the calculated volume. Verify the results of your program by doing a hand calculation using the following test data: Radius equals 10 feet and distance equals 12 feet.

9. The perimeter, approximate surface area, and approximate volume of an in-ground pool are given by the following formulas:

perimeter = 2(length + width)
volume = length * width * average depth
underground surface area = 2(length + width) * average depth
+ length * width

Using these formulas as a basis, write a C++ program that accepts the length, width, and average depth measurements and then calculates the perimeter, volume, and underground surface area of the pool. In writing your program, make the following two calculations immediately after the input data have been entered: *length * width* and *length + width*. The results of these two calculations should then be used, as appropriate, in the assignment statements for determining the perimeter, volume, and underground surface area. Verify the results of your program by doing a hand calculation using the following test data: Length equals 25 feet, width equals 15 feet, and average depth equals 5.5 feet. When you have verified that your program is working, use it to complete the following table:

Length	Width	Depth	Perimeter	Volume	Underground Surface Area
25	10	5.0			
25	10	5.5			
25	10	6.0			
25	10	6.5			
30	12	5.0			
30	12	5.5			
30	12	6.0			
30	12	6.5			

3.7 PLANNING FOR OBJECTS: PROGRAM PERFORMANCE MEASURES AND OBJECT-ORIENTED TECHNOLOGY (OOT)

Coding a program is always an implementation process, where the word *implement* means *to put into effect according to a definite plan*. In practice, the plan being implemented was designed during the design phase. In this sense, programming is the last step of the programming process illustrated in Figure 3.14.

FIGURE 3.14 The Programming Process

Requirements Specification → Analysis → Design → Programming

Because coding a program produces something tangible, which is a working program that can be run and tested, writing a program is almost always one of the first courses presented in a computer science curriculum. Thus the sequence of learning all of the tools in the complete programming process is generally that shown in Figure 3.15.

FIGURE 3.15 The Programming Learning Sequence

Programming → Analysis → Design → Requirements Specification

The learning sequence illustrated in Figure 3.15 is used in learning almost all skills. For example, you learned to read and write English words before you learned how to compose sentences and paragraphs, or structure complete written compositions. Later, some people go on to analyze and design more intricate compositions, such as essays and novels. Similarly, you always learn how to use tools, such as a hammer and screwdriver, before actually building something simple. Later, some people go on to analyze people's requirements and actually design more complicated structures such as houses. This learning sequence, however, does have its downside, especially in programming.

To enable a student to learn basic programming techniques, simple program requirements are initially used in almost all programming texts, including this one. This permits reducing the analysis and design steps to a minimum. Thus a new programmer is somewhat like a new carpenter building a house who knows how to build it without necessarily knowing how to design it. The positive side of the traditional learning sequence, however, is that being an implementor does provide a framework for understanding what is actually possible, which is indispensable for a designer. Therefore, before we attempt to understand the design process, we should understand what constitutes a good implementation.

Clearly, at a minimum, a program should be correct. Obviously any program that works is better than any program that doesn't work. But this criteria provides little help in determining what is a good program. Besides just working, a good program should provide:

- Clarity
- Efficiency

- Robustness
- Extensibility
- Reusability
- Programming-in-the-large

Clarity has two meanings. From a programming viewpoint it means both that another programmer can read and understand your code and that you can read and understand your own code months after you have written it. From a user's viewpoint it means that the program clearly identifies what inputs are required and what outputs are being produced.

Efficiency means that a program or function produces its results in the most time efficient manner. This includes both computer run time as well as human time spent in preparing to run the program and analyzing and understanding the results of a program or function. Efficiency, although very important, is the least important of all measures and should always be sacrificed in the interest of clarity, robustness, extensibility, and the other measures.

Robustness means that a program or function will not fail even if it receives improper data. For example, if your program is expecting an integer and the user types a letter, the program should not crash. Robust programs are sometimes referred to as bullet-proof programs.

Extensibility means that a program can easily be modified and extended to handle cases and situations that the original designers did not expect. Being able to accommodate bigger tasks than originally designed for makes a program industrial-strength.

Reusability means that existing code can be reused, both within an existing project and for new projects.

Programming-in-the-large means that large, complex programs can be written using teams of programmers.

Procedure-oriented programming has always had the capability of producing clear, efficient, robust programs that could be programmed in the large. Where procedural techniques have not produced the desired result is in reusability and extensibility. Once written, procedure-oriented programs have generally proven to be very cumbersome and extremely time consuming and costly to extend or be reused for new applications.

Object-oriented technology (OOT) provides a framework for rectifying this situation by producing both extensible and reusable code. The guidelines for producing object-oriented programs include traditional procedural programming techniques with the addition of new principles that are unique to the object-oriented methodology.

Moving to OOT

A true object-oriented technology (OOT) is where one works with objects from the problem definition stage through the programming stage. It encompasses all of the following object-oriented methods:

- OORS—Object-oriented requirements specification
- OOA—Object-oriented analysis
- OOD—Object-oriented design
- OOP—Object-oriented programming

FIGURE 3.16   The Object-Oriented Technology Programming Process

Object-Oriented Requirements Specification	Object-Oriented Analysis	Object-Oriented Design	Object-Oriented Programming
OOR ⟶	OOA ⟶	OOD ⟶	OOP

Thus, from an OOT viewpoint, the programming process previously shown in Figure 3.14 appears as illustrated in Figure 3.16.

As you might expect, the actual learning of OOT proceeds in the sequence illustrated in Figure 3.17. This, of course, simply implements the standard learning sequence previously shown in Figure 3.15 as it applies to OOT.

FIGURE 3.17   The Object-Oriented Technology Learning Sequence

Object-Oriented Programming	Object-Oriented Analysis	Object-Oriented Design	Object-Oriented Requirements Specification
OOP ⟶	OOA ⟶	OOD ⟶	OOR

FIGURE 3.18   Introduction of OOT by One Development Group at AT&T

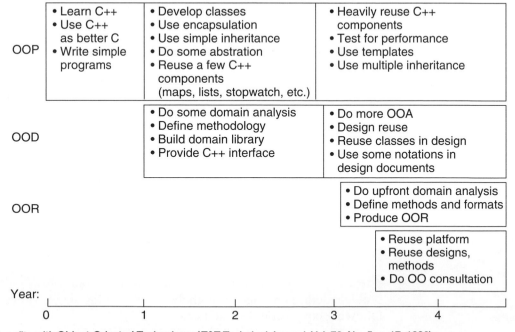

(*Source: Reaping Benefits with Object-Oriented Technology,* AT&T Technical Journal, Vol. 72, No. 5, p. 17, 1993)

As a practical application of the learning sequence shown in Figure 3.17, consider Figure 3.18. This figure represents how OOT was introduced by one development group within AT&T over a four year period. In reviewing Figure 3.18, notice that OOT began with C++ as the implementation language of choice (remember that C++ was developed at AT&T and was the preeminent object-oriented language before Java was developed) and progressed, in an incremental and systematic way, to object-oriented analysis, object-oriented design, and finally object-oriented requirements specification.

Exercises 3.7

1. Define the terms:

   a. clarity

   b. correct

   c. efficiency

   d. robustness

   e. extensibility

   f. reusability

   g. programming-in-the-large

2. a. For a demonstration or one-time use program, which measures of program performance do you think are *least* important?

   b. From a user's viewpoint, which two measures of programming performance do you think are *most* important in a program written by someone else?

3. a. In reviewing how you respond to assignments, have you ever done an assignment just to hand it in on time rather than doing the assignment right?

   b. In general, do you do assignments to just get them in on time or do you do spend the time on them to do them right? What does right mean? Do you think your answer to this question is the same answer that an amateur or professional programmer would give when referring to programming projects?

   c. Have you ever been so concerned with doing an assignment perfectly that you either fail to start it or fail to complete it? Do you think your answer to this question is the same answer that an amateur or professional programmer would give when referring to programming projects?

4. a. Review how you have approached programming assignments made in this and other programming courses you have taken. Have you tended to approach these assignments as an amateur or as a professional? Has your approach been reasonable based on the time pressures of other commitments?

   b. Based on your responses to Exercise 4a, what sacrifices or adjustments do you think professionals made in their lives, regardless of their chosen fields, to become professionals?

3.8 A CLOSER LOOK: PROGRAMMING ERRORS

The ideal in programming is to produce readable, error-free programs that work correctly and can be modified or changed with a minimum of testing. You can work toward this ideal by keeping in mind the different types of errors that can occur, when they are typically detected, and how to correct them.

An error can be detected:

1. Before a program is compiled

2. While the program is being compiled

3. While the program is being run

4. After the program has been executed and the output is being examined

In some cases, an error may not be detected at all. Errors detected by the compiler are formally referred to as **compile-time errors**, and errors that occur while the program is running are formally referred to as **run-time errors**. Other names for compile-time errors are **syntax errors** and **parse errors**, terms that emphasize the type of error being detected by the compiler.

By now, you have probably encountered numerous compile-time errors. Although beginning programmers tend to be frustrated by them, experienced programmers understand that the compiler is doing a lot of valuable checking, and that it is usually quite easy to correct any errors the compiler does detect. In addition, because these errors occur while the program is being developed, and not while a user is attempting to perform an important task, no one but the programmer ever knows they occurred; you fix them and they go away.

Run-time errors are much more troubling because they occur while a user is executing the program, and in most commercial systems the user is not the programmer. Although there are a number of error types that can cause a run-time error, such as a failure in the hardware, from a programming standpoint the majority of run-time errors are referred to as logic errors; that is faulty logic, which encompasses not fully thinking out what the program should do or not anticipating how a user can make the program fail, is at fault. For example, if a user enters data that results in an attempt to divide a number by zero, a run-time error occurs. As a programmer, the only way to protect against run-time errors is to sufficiently anticipate everything a person might do to cause errors and submit your program to rigorous testing. Although beginning programmers tend to blame a user for an error caused by entering obviously incorrect data, professionals don't. They understand that a run-time error is a flaw in the final product that additionally can cause damage to the reputation of both program and programmer.

There are ways to detect errors both before a program is compiled and after it has been executed. The method for detecting errors before a program is compiled is called **desk checking**. Desk checking, which typically is performed while sitting at a desk with the code in front of you, refers to the process of checking the actual program code for syntax and logic errors. The method for detecting errors either while a program is executing or after it has executed is called **program testing**.

The terms compile-time and run-time distinguish between errors based on when the error is detected. In terms of preventing these errors, it is more fruitful to distinguish between them based on what causes them. As we have seen, compile-time errors are also named syntax errors, which refer to errors in either the structure or spelling of a statement. For example, the statements

```
cout << "There are four syntax errors here\n
cot " Can you find tem";
```

contain four syntax errors. These errors are:

1. A closing quote is missing in line 1.

2. A terminating semicolon (;) is missing in line 1.

3. The keyword `cout` is misspelled in line 2.

4. The insertion symbol, <<, is missing in line 2.

All of these errors will be detected by the compiler when the program is compiled. This is true of all syntax errors because they violate the basic rules of C++; if they are not discovered by desk checking, the compiler detects them and displays an error message.[11] In some cases, the error message is clear and the error is obvious; in other cases, it takes a little detective work to understand the error message displayed by the compiler. Because syntax errors are the only type of error that can be detected at compile time, the terms compile-time errors and syntax errors are used interchangeably. Strictly speaking, however, compile-time refers to when the error was detected and syntax refers to the type of error detected.

Note that the misspelling of the word `them` in the second statement is not a syntax error. Although this spelling error will result in an undesirable output line being displayed, it is not a violation of C++'s syntactical rules. It is a simple case of a typographical error, commonly referred to as a "typo."

A logic error can either cause a run-time error or produce incorrect results. Such errors are characterized by erroneous, unexpected, or unintentional output that is a direct result of some flaw in the program's logic. These errors, which are never caught by the compiler, may be detected by desk checking, by program testing, by accident when a user obtains an obviously erroneous output while the program is executing, or not at all. If the error is detected while the program is executing, a run-time error can occur that results in an error message being generated or premature program termination, or both.

The most serious logic error is caused by an incorrect understanding of the full requirements that the program is expected to fulfill. This is true because the logic contained within a program is always a reflection of the logic upon which it is coded. For example, if the purpose of a program is to calculate a mortgage payment on a house or the load bearing strength of a steel beam, and the programmer does not fully understand how the calculation is to be made, what inputs are needed to perform the calculation, or what special conditions exist (such as what happens when someone makes an extra payment on a mortgage or how temperature effects the beam), a logic error will occur. Because such errors are not detected by the compiler and frequently even may go undetected at run time, they are always more difficult to detect than syntax errors. If they are detected, a logic error typically reveals itself in one of two predominant ways. In one instance, the program executes to completion but produces obviously incorrect results. Generally, logic errors of this type are revealed by:

- **No output**—This is caused either by an omission of an output statement or a sequence of statements that inadvertently bypasses an output statement.

- **Unappealing or misaligned output**—This is caused by an error in an output statement.

- **Incorrect numerical results**—This is caused by incorrect values assigned to the variables used in an expression, the use of an incorrect arithmetic expression, an omission of a statement, a round-off error, or the use of an improper sequence of statements.

A second way that logic errors reveal themselves is by causing a run-time error. Examples of this type of logic error are attempts to divide by zero or to take the square root of a negative number.

You should plan your program testing carefully to maximize the possibility of locating errors. Also, keep in mind that *although a single test can reveal the presence of an error, it does not verify the absence of another error*. That is, the fact that one error is revealed by testing does not indicate that another error is not lurking somewhere else in the program; furthermore, *the fact that one test revealed no errors does not mean there are no errors*.

---

[11] They may not, however, all be detected at the same time. Frequently, one syntax error masks another error, and the second error is only detected after the first error is corrected.

Once you discover an error, however, the programmer must locate where the error occurs and then fix it. In computer jargon, a program error is referred to as a **bug,** and the process of isolating, correcting, and verifying the correction is called **debugging**.

Although there are no hard-and-fast rules for isolating the cause of an error, some useful techniques can be applied. The first of these is a preventive technique. Frequently, many errors are introduced by the programmer in the rush to code and run a program before fully understanding what is required and how the result is to be achieved. A symptom of this haste to get a program entered into the computer is the lack of an outline of the proposed program or the lack of a detailed understanding of what is actually required. Many errors can be eliminated simply by desk checking a copy of the program before it is ever entered or compiled.

A second useful technique is to imitate the computer and execute each statement by hand, as the computer would. This means writing down each variable as it is encountered in the program and listing the value that should be stored in the variable as each input and assignment statement is encountered. Doing this also sharpens your programming skills because it requires that you fully understand what each statement in your program causes to happen. Such a check is called **program tracing**.

A third and very powerful debugging technique is to include some temporary code in your program that displays the values of selected variables. If the displayed values are incorrect, you can then determine what part of your program generated them, and make the necessary corrections.

In the same manner, you could add temporary code that displays the values of all input data. This technique is referred to as **echo printing**, and it is useful in establishing that the program is correctly receiving and correctly interpreting the input data.

The most powerful of all debugging and tracing techniques is to use a special program called a **debugger**. A debugger program controls the execution of a C++ program, can interrupt the C++ program at any point in its execution, and can display the values of all variables at the point of interruption.

Finally, no discussion of debugging is complete without mentioning the primary ingredient needed for successful isolation and correction of errors. This is the attitude and spirit you bring to the task. After you write a program, it's natural to assume it is correct. It is extremely difficult to back away and honestly test and find errors in your own software. As a programmer, you must constantly remind yourself that just because you think your program is correct does not make it so. Finding errors in your own programs is a sobering experience, but one that will help you to become a master programmer. It can also be exciting and fun if approached as a detection problem with you as the master detective.

3.9 COMMON PROGRAMMING ERRORS

In using the material presented in this chapter, be aware of the following possible errors:

1. Forgetting to assign or initialize values for all variables before the variables are used in an expression. Such values can be assigned by assignment statements, initialized within a declaration statement, or assigned interactively by entering values using the `cin` object.

2. Using a mathematical library function without including the preprocessor statement `#include <cmath>` (and on a UNIX-based system, forgetting to include the `-lm` argument to the `cc` command).

3. Using a library function without providing the correct number or arguments having the proper data type.

4. Applying either the increment or decrement operator to an expression. For example, the expression

```
(count + n)++
```

is incorrect. The increment and decrement operators can only be applied to individual variables.

5. Forgetting to separate all variables passed to `cin` with an extraction symbol, `>>`.

6. Using increment and decrement operators with variables that appear more than once in the same expression (a more exotic and less common error). This error basically occurs because C++ does not specify the order in which operands are accessed within an expression. For example, the value assigned to `result` in the statement

```
result = i + i++;
```

is compiler dependent. If your compiler accesses the first operand, `i`, first, the preceding statement is equivalent to

```
result = 2 * i;
i++;
```

However, if your compiler accesses the second operand, `i++`, first, the value of the first operand is altered before it is used the second time, and the value $2i + 1$ is assigned to `result`. As a general rule, therefore, do not use either the increment or decrement operator in an expression when the variable it operates on appears more than once in the expression.

7. Being unwilling to test a program in depth. After all, because you wrote the program, you assume it is correct or you would have changed it before it was compiled. It is extremely difficult to back away and honestly test your own software. As a programmer, you must constantly remind yourself that just because you *think* your program is correct does not make it so. Finding errors in your own program is a sobering experience, but one that helps you become a master programmer.

3.10 CHAPTER REVIEW

Key Terms

accumulating	decrement operator
arguments	desk checking
assignment operators	echo printing
cast	field width manipulators
cin	hexadecimal
compile-time errors	implement
counting	increment operator

justification	program verification and testing
logic errors	prompt
lvalues	run-time errors
magic numbers	rvalues
mathematical header	symbolic constants
mathematical library	syntax errors
named constants	tracing
octal	type conversions
parameterized manipulator	

Summary

1. An *expression* is a sequence of one or more operands separated by operators. An operand is a constant, a variable, or another expression. A value is associated with an expression.

2. Expressions are evaluated according to the precedence and associativity of the operators used in the expression.

3. The assignment symbol, =, is an operator. Expressions using this operator assign a value to a variable; additionally, the expression itself takes on a value. Since assignment is an operation in C++, multiple uses of the assignment operator are possible in the same expression.

4. The increment operator, ++, adds 1 to a variable; the decrement operator, --, subtracts 1 from a variable. Both of these operators can be used as prefixes or postfixes. In prefix operation, the variable is incremented (or decremented) before its value is used. In postfix operation, the variable is incremented (or decremented) after its value is used.

5. C++ provides library functions for calculating square root, logarithmic, and other mathematical computations. Each program using one of these mathematical functions must either include the statement #include <cmath> or have a function declaration for the mathematical function before it is called.

6. Every mathematical library function operates on its arguments to calculate a single value. To use a library function effectively, you must know what the function does, the name of the function, the number and data types of the arguments expected by the function, and the data type of the returned value.

7. Data passed to a function are called *arguments* of the function. Arguments are passed to a library function by including each argument, separated by commas, within the parentheses following the function's name. Each function has its own requirements for the number and data types of the arguments that must be provided.

8. Functions may be included within larger expressions.

9. The cin object is used for data input. This object accepts a stream of data from the keyboard and assigns the data to variables. The general form of a statement using cin is:

```
cin >> var1 >> var2 . . . >> varn;
```

The extraction symbol, >>, must be used to separate the variable names.

10. When a cin statement is encountered, the computer temporarily suspends statement execution until sufficient data have been entered for the number of variables listed in the cin statement.

11. It is good programming practice, prior to a `cin` statement, to display a message that alerts the user as to the type and number of data items to be entered. Such a message is called a *prompt*.

12. A value can be equated to a symbolic constant using the `const` qualifier. This makes the symbolic constant a read-only identifier after it is initialized within its declaration statement. This declaration has the syntax

```
const data-type symbolicName = initial value;
```

and permits the `symbolicName` to be used instead of the initial value anywhere in the program after its declaration. Generally, such declarations are placed at the top of a C++ program.

Exercises

1. a. Write a C++ program to calculate and display the value of the slope of the line connecting the two points whose coordinates are (3,7) and (8,12). Use the fact that the slope between two points having coordinates $(x1,y1)$ and $(x2,y2)$ is $(y2 - y1) / (x2 - x1)$.

   b. How do you know that the result produced by your program is correct?

   c. Once you have verified the output produced by your program, modify it to determine the slope of the line connecting the points (2,10) and (12,6).

   d. What do you think will happen if you use the points (2,3) and (2,4), which results in a division by zero? How do you think this situation can be handled?

2. a. Write a C++ program to calculate and display the coordinates of the midpoint of the line segment connecting the two end points given in Exercise 1a. Use the fact that the coordinates of the midpoint between two points having coordinates $(x1,y1)$ and $(x2,y2)$ are $((x1 + x2)/2, (y1 + y2)/2)$. Your program should produce the following display:

```
The x midpoint coordinate is _____
The y midpoint coordinate is _____
```

   where the blank spaces are replaced with the values calculated by your program.

   b. How do you know that the midpoint values calculated by your program are correct?

   c. Once you have verified the output produced by your program, modify it to determine the midpoint coordinates of the line connecting the points (2,10) and (12,6).

3. Redo Exercise 1 but change the output produced by your program to be:

```
The value of the slope is xxx.xx
```

   where xxx.xx denotes that the calculated value should be placed in a field wide enough to fit three places to the left of the decimal point and two places to the right of it.

4. Redo Exercise 2 but change the output produced by your program to be:

```
The x coordinate of the midpoint is xxx.xx
The y coordinate of the midpoint is xxx.xx
```

   where xxx.xx denotes that the calculated value should be placed in a field wide enough to fit three places to the left of the decimal point and two places to the right of it.

5. The dollar change remaining after an amount `paid` is used to pay a restaurant check of amount `check` can be calculated using the following C++ statements:

```
// determine the amount of pennies in the change
   change = (paid - check) * 100;
// determine the number of dollars in the change
   dollars = (int) (change/100);
```

   a. Using the previous statements as a starting point, write a C++ program that calculates the number of dollar bills, quarters, dimes, nickels, and pennies in the change when $10 is used to pay a bill of $6.06.

   b. Without compiling or executing your program, check the effect, by hand, of each statement in the program and determine what is stored in each variable as each statement is encountered.

   c. When you have verified that your algorithm works correctly, compile and execute your program. Verify that the result produced by your program is correct. After you have verified your program is working correctly, use it to determine the change when a check of $12.36 is paid using a $20 bill.

6. a. For display purposes, the `setprecision` manipulator allows the programmer to round all outputs to the desired number of decimal places. This can, however, yield seemingly incorrect results when used in financial programs that require all monetary values to be displayed to the nearest penny. For example, the display produced by the program:

```
#include <iostream>
#include <iomanip>
using namespace std;

int main()
{
  double a, b, c;

  a = 1.674;
  b = 1.322;
  cout << setprecision(2) << a << endl;
  cout << setprecision(2) << b << endl;
  cout << "----\n";
  c = a + b;
  cout << setiosflags(ios::showpoint)
       << setprecision(2) << c << endl;
0
  return 0;
}
```

   is:

```
                    1.67
                    1.32
                    ----
                    3.00
```

   Clearly, the sum of the displayed numbers should be 2.99 and not 3.00. The problem is that although the values in a and b have been displayed with two decimal digits, they were added internal to the program as three-digit numbers. The solution is to round the values in a and b before they are added by the statement c = a + b;. Using the int cast, devise a method to round the values in variables a and b to the nearest hundredth (penny value) before they are added.

b. Include the method you have devised for Exercise 6a into a working program that produces the following display:

```
1.67
1.32
----
2.99
```

7. Design, write, compile, and execute a program that calculates and displays the fourth root of a user-entered number. Recall from elementary algebra that the fourth root of a number can be found by raising the number to the 1/4 power. (*Hint:* Do not use integer division—do you know why?) Verify your program by calculating the fourth root of the following data: 81, 16, 1, and 0. When you have completed your verification, use your program to determine the fourth root of 42, 121, 256, 587, 1240, and 16256.

8. Using `cin` statements, write, compile, and execute a C++ program that accepts the x and y coordinates of two points. Have your program determine and display the midpoint of the line connecting the two points (use the formula given in Exercise 2). Verify your program using the following test data:

Test data set 1: Point 1 = (0,0) and Point 2 = (16,0).
Test data set 2: Point 1 = (0,0) and Point 2 = (0,16)
Test data set 3: Point 1 = (0,0) and Point 2 = (–16,0)
Test data set 4: Point 1 = (0,0) and Point 2 = (0,–16)
Test data set 5: Point 1 = (–5,–5) and Point 2 = (5,5)

When you have completed your verification, use your program to complete the following table:

Point 1	Point 2	Midpoint
(4,6)	(16,18)	
(22,3)	(8,12)	
(–10,8)	(14,4)	
(–12,2)	(14,3.1)	
(3.1,–6)	(20,16)	
(3.1,–6)	(–16,–18)	

9. Design, write, compile, and execute a C++ program that calculates and displays the amount of money, A, available in N years when an initial deposit of X dollars is deposited in a bank account paying an annual interest rate of R percent. Use the relationship that $A = X(1.0 + R/100)^N$. The program should prompt the user to enter appropriate values and use `cin` statements to accept the data. Use statements such as `Enter the amount of the initial deposit` in constructing your prompts. Verify the operation of your program by calculating, by hand and with your program, the amount of money available for the following test cases:

```
Test data set 1: $1000 invested for 10 years at 0% interest
Test data set 2: $1000 invested for 10 years at 6% interest
```

When you have completed your verification, use your program to determine the amount of money available for the following cases:

a. $1000 invested for 10 years at 8% interest

b. $1000 invested for 10 years at 10% interest

c. $1000 invested for 10 years at 12% interest

d. $5000 invested for 15 years at 8% interest

   e. $5000 invested for 15 years at 10% interest

   f. $5000 invested for 15 years at 12% interest

   g. $24 invested for 300 years at 4% interest

10. Write a C++ program that prompts the user for a cost per item, number of items purchased, and a discount rate. The program should then calculate and print the total cost, tax due, and amount due. Use the formulas:

```
total cost = number of items * cost-per-item
total cost (discounted) = total cost - (discount rate * total cost)
tax due = total cost * TAXRATE
amount due = total cost + tax due
```

   For this problem, assume that TAXRATE is 6%.

11. The roads of Kansas are laid out in a rectangular grid at exactly 1-mile intervals, as shown in Figure 3.19. Pete drives his pickup x miles east and y miles north to get to Sally's farm. Both x and y are integer numbers. Using this information, write, test, and run a C++ program that prompts the user for the values of x and y and then uses the formula

$$distance = sqrt(x * x + y * y);$$

   to find the shortest driving distance across the fields to Sally's farm. Round the answer to the nearest integer value before it is displayed.

FIGURE 3.19   Illustration for Exercise 11

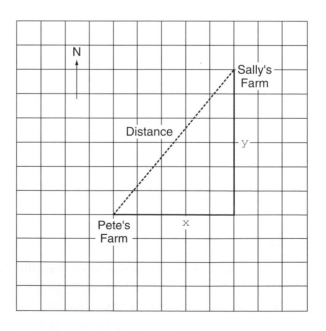

12. When a particular rubber ball is dropped from a given height (in meters), its impact speed (in meters/second) when it hits the ground is given by the formula *speed = sqrt(2 * g * height)*. The ball then rebounds to two-thirds the height from which it last fell. Using this information, write, test, and run a C++ program that calculates and displays the impact speed of the first three bounces and the rebound height of each bounce. Test your program using an initial height of 2.0 meters. Run the program twice and compare the results for dropping the ball on earth ($g = 9.81$ meters/sec^2) and on the moon ($g = 1.67$ meters/sec^2).

Improving Communication

13. Assuming you are the Lead Programmer, respond to the following memorandum:

    MEMORANDUM

    To: Lead Programmer

    From: Head of Programming Dept.

    Subject: OOP

    The Executive Committee is considering moving to an object-oriented programming environment and has asked for my recommendation. Please provide me with your thoughts and understanding as to the advantages of OOP.

14. Assuming you are the Lead Programmer, respond to the following memorandum:

    MEMORANDUM

    To: Lead Programmer

    From: Head of Programming Dept.

    Subject: Moving to an OOP Environment

    Thank you for your last memorandum to me on the advantages of OOP. At our last Executive Committee meeting, the directors asked for a timetable and brief explanation on how we should proceed to a fully implemented OOP environment. Please provide me with a schedule and backup documentation on how you see us moving to such an environment.

Working in Teams

15. a. Have each team member make a list of their objectives in taking this course.

    b. Have each team member make a list of five attributes of courses that they have enjoyed taking.

16. a. Have each team member list and rank three technical traits that they feel are most important for a successful programmer.

    b. Have each team member list and rank three personality traits that they feel are most important for a successful programmer.

c. Using each member's lists as a starting point, come up with three technical and three personality traits that the group, as a whole, considers most important.

d. Put the list constructed in Exercise 16c on the board and compare lists with the other groups in the class.

e. How could you verify that the traits you have identified are indeed valid?

17. a. Have each team member list three technical traits that they feel are detrimental to success as a programmer.

b. Have each team member list three personality traits that they feel are detrimental to success as a programmer.

c. Using each member's lists as a starting point, come up with three technical and three personality traits that the group, as a whole, agrees are detrimental.

d. Put the list constructed in Exercise 17c on the board and compare lists with the other groups in the class.

e. How could you verify that the traits you have identified are indeed detrimental?

4 | Selection Statements

Many advances have occurred in the theoretical foundations of programming since the inception of high-level languages in the late 1950s. One of the most important of these advances was the recognition in the late 1960s that any algorithm, no matter how complex, could be constructed using combinations of four standardized flow of control statements: sequential, selection, repetition, and invocation.

The term **flow of control** refers to the order in which a program's statements are executed. Unless directed otherwise, the normal flow of control for all programs is **sequential**. This means that statements are executed in sequence, one after another, in the order in which they are placed within the program.

Selection, repetition, and invocation statements permit the sequential flow of control to be altered in precisely defined ways. As you might have guessed, the selection statement is used to select which statements are to be performed next and the repetition statement is used to repeat a set of statements. In this chapter, we present C++'s selection statements. Repetition and invocation techniques are presented in Chapters 5 and 6.

4.1 SELECTION CRITERIA

In the solution of many problems, different actions must be taken depending on the value of the data. Examples of simple situations include calculating an area *only if* the measurements are positive, performing a division *only if* the divisor is not zero, printing different messages *depending on* the value of a grade received, and so on.

FIGURE 4.1   Anatomy of a Simple Relational Expression

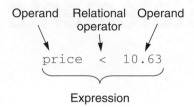

The `if-else` statement in C++ is used to implement such a decision structure in its simplest form—that of choosing between two alternatives. The most commonly used pseudocode syntax of this statement is:

```
if (condition)
   statement executed if condition is "true";
else
   statement executed if condition is "false";
```

When an executing program encounters the `if` statement, the condition is evaluated to determine its numerical value, which is then interpreted as either true or false. If the condition evaluates to any positive or negative nonzero numerical value, the condition is considered as a "true" condition and the statement following the `if` is executed. If the condition evaluates to a zero numerical value, the condition is considered as a "false" condition and the statement following the `else` is executed. The `else` part of the statement is optional and may be omitted.

The condition used in an `if` statement can be any valid C++ expression (even including, as we will see, an assignment expression). The most commonly used expressions, however, are called **relational expressions**. A **simple relational expression** consists of a relational operator that compares two operands, as shown in Figure 4.1.

While each operand in a relational expression can be either a variable or a constant, the relational operators must be one of those listed in Table 4.1. These relational operators may be used with integer, floating-point, double-precision, or character operands, but must be typed exactly as given in Table 4.1. Thus, while the following examples are all valid:

```
age > 40        length <= 50       temp > 98.6
3 < 4           flag == done       idNum == 682
day != 5        2.0 > 3.3          hours > 40
```

the following are invalid:

```
length =< 50        // operator out of order
2.0 >> 3.3          // invalid operator
flag = = done       // spaces are not allowed
```

Relational expressions are sometimes called **conditions,** for short, and we use both terms to refer to these expressions. Like all C++ expressions, relational expressions are evaluated to yield a numerical result.[1] In the case of a relational expression, the value of the expression can only be the integer value of 1 or 0, which is interpreted

---

[1]In this regard, C++ differs from other high-level languages that yield a Boolean (true, false) result.

as true or false, respectively. *A relational expression that we interpret as true evaluates to an integer value of 1, and a false relational expression results in an integer value of 0.* For example, because the relationship 3 < 4 is always true, this expression has a value of 1, and because the relationship 2.0 > 3.3 is always false, the value of the expression itself is 0. This can be verified using these statements:

```
cout << "The value of 3 < 4 is " << (3 < 4) << endl;
cout << "The value of 2.0 > 3.0 is " << (2.0 > 3.3) << endl;
cout << "The value of true is " << true << endl;
cout << "The value of false is " << false << endl;
```

which result in the displays:

```
The value of 3 < 4 is 1
The value of 2.0 > 3.0 is 0
The value of true is 1
The value of false is 0
```

TABLE 4.1 Relational Operators

Operator	Meaning	Example
<	Less than	age < 30
>	Greater than	height > 6.2
<=	Less than or equal to	taxable <= 20000
>=	Greater than or equal to	temp >= 98.6
==	Equal to	grade == 100
!=	Not equal to	number != 250

The value of a relational expression such as hours > 40 depends on the value stored in the variable hours. In a C++ program, a relational expression's value is not as important as the interpretation C++ places on the value when the expression is used as part of a selection statement. In these statements, which are presented in the next section, we see that a zero value is used by C++ to represent a false condition and any nonzero value is used to represent a true condition. The selection of which statement to execute next is then based on the value obtained.

In addition to numerical operands, character data can also be compared to using relational operators. For such comparisons, the char values are automatically coerced to int values for the comparison. For example, in the ASCII code the letter 'A' is stored using a code that has a lower numerical value than the letter 'B'; the code for 'B' has a lower value than the code for 'C'; and so on. For character sets coded in this manner, the following conditions are evaluated as follows:

Expression	Value	Interpretation
'A' > 'C'	0	false
'D' <= 'Z'	1	true
'E' == 'F'	0	false
'g' >= 'm'	0	false
'b' != 'c'	1	true
'a' == 'A'	0	false
'B' < 'a'	1	true
'b' > 'Z'	1	true

Comparing letters is essential in alphabetizing names or using characters to select a particular choice in decision-making situations. Strings of characters may also be compared. Finally, two string expressions may be compared using relational operators or the `string` class's comparison methods (Chapter 9). In the ASCII character set, a blank precedes (and is considered "less than") all letters and numbers; the letters of the alphabet are stored in order from A to Z; and the digits are stored in order from 0 to 9. In this sequence, the lowercase letters come after (are considered "greater than") the uppercase letters, and the letter codes come after (are "greater than") the digit codes (see Appendix B).

When two strings are compared, their individual characters are compared one pair at a time (both first characters, then both second characters, and so on). If no differences are found, the strings are equal; if a difference is found, the string with the first lower character is considered the smaller string. Following are examples of string comparisons:

Expression	Value	Interpretation	Comment
`"Hello" > "Good-bye"`	1	true	The first `'H'` in `Hello` is greater than the first `'G'` in `Good-bye`.
`"SMITH" > "JONES"`	1	true	The first `'S'` in `SMITH` is greater than the first `'J'` in `JONES`.
`"123" > "1227"`	1	true	The third character, the `'3'` in `123` is greater than the third character, the `'2'` in `1227`.
`"Behop" > "Beehive"`	1	true	The third character, the `'h'`, in `Behop` is greater than the third character `'e'` in `Beehive`.
`"He" == "She"`	0	false	The `'H'` in `He` is not equal to the `'S'` in `She`.
`"plant" < "planet"`	0	false	The `'t'` in `plant` is greater than the `'e'` in `planet`.

Logical Operators

In addition to using simple relational expressions as conditions, more complex conditions can be created using the logical operations AND, OR, and NOT. These operations are represented by the symbols `&&`, `||`, and `!`, respectively.

When the AND operator, `&&`, is used with two simple expressions, the condition is true only if both individual expressions are true by themselves. Thus, the compound condition

```
(age > 40) && (term < 10)
```

is true (has a value of 1) only if `age` is greater than `40` and `term` is less than `10`. Since relational operators have a higher precedence than logical operators, the parentheses in this logical expression could have been omitted.

A BIT OF BACKGROUND

De Morgan's Laws

Augustus De Morgan was born at Madura, India, in 1806 and died in London in 1871. He became a professor of mathematics in London in 1828 and spent many years performing investigations into a variety of mathematical topics. He was a revered teacher and wrote numerous textbooks that contained a wealth of information on mathematics and its history, but which generally were very difficult for his students to understand.

De Morgan's contributions to modern computing include two laws by which AND statements can be converted to OR statements, and vice versa. They are:

1. NOT(A AND B) = (NOT A) OR (NOT B)
2. NOT(A OR B) = (NOT A) AND (NOT B)

Thus, from De Morgan's first law, the statement "Either it is not raining or I am not getting wet" says the same thing as "It is not true that it is raining and I am getting wet." Similarly, from the second law, "It is not true that politicians always lie or that teachers always know the facts" becomes "Politicians do not always lie and teachers do not always know the facts."

In computer usage, De Morgan's laws are typically more useful in the following form:

1. A AND B = NOT((NOT A) OR (NOT B))
2. A OR B = NOT((NOT A) AND (NOT B))

The ability to convert from an OR statement to an AND statement, and vice versa, is extremely useful in many programming situations.

The logical OR operator, ||, is also applied between two expressions. When using the OR operator, the condition is satisfied if either one or both of the two expressions are true. Thus, the compound condition

```
(age > 40) || (term < 10)
```

is true if either age is greater than 40, term is less than 10, or both conditions are true. Again, the parentheses surrounding the relational expressions are included to make the expression easier to read. Because of the higher precedence of relational operators with respect to logical operators, the same evaluation is made even if the parentheses are omitted.

For the declarations

```
int i, j;
double a, b, complete;
```

the following represent valid conditions:

```
a > b
(i == j) || (a < b) || complete
(a/b > 5) && (i <= 20)
```

Before these conditions can be evaluated, the values of a, b, i, j, and complete must be known. Assuming a = 12.0, b = 2.0, i = 15, j = 30, and complete = 0.0, the previous expressions yield the following results:

Expression	Value	Interpretation
a > b	1	true
(i == j) || (a < b) || complete	0	false
(a/b > 5) && (i <= 20)	1	true

The NOT operator is used to change an expression to its opposite state; thus, if the expression has any nonzero value (true), !expression produces a zero value (false). If an expression is false to begin with (has a zero value), `!expression` is true and evaluates to 1. For example, assuming the number 26 is stored in the variable `age`, the expression `age > 40` has a value of 0 (it is false), while the expression `!(age > 40)` has a value of 1. Since the NOT operator is used with only one expression, it is a unary operator.

The relational and logical operators have a hierarchy of execution similar to the arithmetic operators. Table 4.2 lists the precedence of these operators in relation to the other operators we have used.

TABLE 4.2 Operator Precedence

Operator	Associativity
! unary − ++ −−	Right to left
* / %	Left to right
+ -	Left to right
< <= > >=	Left to right
== !=	Left to right
&&	Left to right
||	Left to right
= += -= *= /=	Right to left

The following example illustrates the use of an operator's precedence and associativity to evaluate relational expressions, assuming the following declarations:

```
char key = 'm';
int i = 5, j = 7, k = 12;
double x = 22.5;
```

Expression	Equivalent Expression	Value	Interpretation
i + 2 == k - 1	(i + 2) == (k - 1)	0	false
3 * i - j < 22	(3 * i) - j < 22	1	true
i + 2 * j > k	(i + (2 * j)) > k	1	true
k + 3 <= -j + 3 * i	(k + 3) <= ((-j) + (3*i))	0	false
'a' + 1 == 'b'	('a' + 1) == 'b'	1	true
key - 1 > 'p'	(key - 1) > 'p'	0	false
key + 1 == 'n'	(key + 1) == 'n'	1	true
25 >= x + 1.0	25 >= (x + 1.0)	1	true

As with all expressions, parentheses can be used to alter the assigned operator priority and improve the readability of relational expressions. By evaluating the expressions within parentheses first, the following compound condition is evaluated as:

```
(6 * 3 == 36 / 2) || (13 < 3 * 3 + 4) && !(6 - 2 < 5)
    (18 == 18) ||    (13 < 9 + 4)   && !(4 < 5)
         1     ||    (13 < 13)      && ! 1
         1     ||        0          &&   0
         1     ||        0
                    1
```

A Numerical Accuracy Problem

A problem that can occur with C++'s relational expressions is a subtle numerical accuracy problem related to floating-point and double-precision numbers. Due to the way computers store these numbers, tests for equality of floating-point and double-precision values and variables using the relational operator == should be avoided because many decimal numbers, such as 0.1, cannot be represented exactly in binary using a finite number of bits. Thus, testing for exact equality for such numbers can fail. When equality of noninteger values is desired, it is better to require that the absolute value of the difference between operands be less than some extremely small value. Thus, for floating-point and double-precision operands, the general expression

$$operand\text{-}1 \; == \; operand\text{-}2$$

should be replaced by the condition

$$abs(operand\text{-}1 \; - \; operand\text{-}2) \; < \; 0.000001$$

where the value 0.000001 can be altered to any other acceptably small value. Thus, if the difference between the two operands is less than 0.000001 (or any other user-selected amount), the two operands are considered essentially equal. For example, if x and y are floating-point variables, a condition such as

$$x/y \; == \; 0.35$$

should be programmed as

$$abs(x/y \; - \; 0.35) \; < \; EPSILON$$

where EPSILON can be a named constant set to any acceptably small value, such as 0.000001.[2] This latter condition ensures that slight inaccuracies in representing noninteger numbers in binary do not affect evaluation of the tested condition. Since all computers have an exact binary representation of zero, comparisons for exact equality to zero do not encounter this numerical accuracy problem.

Exercises 4.1

1. Determine the value of the following expressions. Assume a = 5, b = 2, c = 4, d = 6, and e = 3.

   a. a > b

   b. a != b

   c. d % b == c % b

   d. a * c != d * b

   e. d * b == c * e

   f. !(a * b)

   g. !(a % b * c)

   h. !(c % b * a)

   i. b % c * a

---

[2] Using the abs() function requires inclusion of the cmath header file. This is done by placing the preprocessor statement #include <cmath> either immediately before or after the #include <iostream> preprocessor statement. On Unix systems, it may also require specific inclusion of the math library at compile time with a -lm command line argument.

2. Using parentheses, rewrite the following expressions to correctly indicate their order of evaluation. Then evaluate each expression assuming a = 5, b = 2, and c = 4.

   a. a % b * c && c % b * a

   b. a % b * c || c % b * a

   c. b % c * a && a % c * b

   d. b % c * a || a % c * b

3. Write relational expressions to express the following conditions (use variable names of your own choosing):

   a. A person's age is equal to 30.

   b. A person's temperature is greater than 98.6.

   c. A person's height is less than 6 feet.

   d. The current month is 12 (December).

   e. The letter input is m.

   f. A person's age is equal to 30 and the person is taller than 6 feet.

   g. The current day is the 15th day of the 1st month.

   h. A person is older than 50 or has been employed at the company for at least 5 years.

   i. A person's identification number is less than 500 and the person is older than 55.

   j. A length is greater than 2 feet and less than 3 feet.

4. Determine the value of the following expressions, assuming a = 5, b = 2, c = 4, and d = 5.

   a. a == 5

   b. b * d == c * c

   c. d % b * c > 5 || c % b * d < 7

4.2 THE if-else STATEMENT

The **if-else statement** directs the computer to select a sequence of one or more instructions based on the result of a comparison. For example, the state of New Jersey has a two-level state income tax structure. If a person's taxable income is less than $20,000, the applicable state tax rate is 2%. For incomes exceeding $20,000, a different rate is applied. The if-else statement can be used in this situation to determine the actual tax based on whether the gross income is less than or equal to $20,000. The general form of the if-else statement is:

```
if (expression) statement1;
else statement2;
```

The expression is evaluated first. If the value of the expression is nonzero, *statement1* is executed. If the value is zero, the statement after the keyword else is executed. Thus, one of the two statements (either *statement1* or *statement2*, but not both) is always executed depending on the value of the expression. Notice that the tested expression must be put in parentheses and a semicolon is placed after each statement.

The Boolean Data Type

Before the current ANSI/ISO C++ standard, C++ did not have a built-in Boolean data type with its two Boolean values, true and false. Because this data type was not originally part of the language, a tested expression could not evaluate to a Boolean value. Thus, the syntax

```
if (Boolean expression is true)
```

was not a part of the C++ language. Rather, C++ used the more encompassing syntax

```
if (expression)
    execute this statement;
```

where *expression* is any expression (relational, logical, or numeric) that evaluates to a numeric value. If this value were nonzero, it was considered true, and only a zero value was considered false.

As specified by the ANSO/ISO standard, C++ has a built-in Boolean data type, `bool`, containing the two values true and false. As currently implemented, the actual values represented by the `bool` values, true and false, are the integer values 1 and 0, respectively. For example, consider the following program, which declares two Boolean variables:

```
#include <iostream>
using namespace std;

int main()
{
  bool t1, t2;

  t1 = true;
  t2 = false;

  cout << "The value of t1 is "<< t1
       << "\n and the value of t2 is "<< t2 << endl;

  return 0;
}
```

The output displayed by this method is:

```
The value of t1 is 1
 and the value of t2 is 0
```

As can be seen by this output, the Boolean values true and false are represented by the integer values 1 and 0, respectively. To see Boolean values displayed as true and false, you can insert the manipulator `boolalpha` into the `cout` stream prior to displaying Boolean values. The Boolean values have the following relationships:

```
!true = false
!false = true
```

Additionally, applying either a postfix or prefix increment (++) operator to a variable of type `bool` sets the Boolean value to true. The postfix and prefix decrement operators (−−) cannot be applied to a Boolean variable.

Boolean values can also be compared. For example, if `flag1` and `flag2` are two Boolean variables, the relational expression `flag1 == flag2` is valid. Lastly, assigning any nonzero value to a Boolean variable results in the variable being set to true (that is, a value of 1), and assigning a zero to a Boolean variable results in the variable being set to false (that is, a value of 0).

For clarity, the `if-else` statement is generally written on four lines using the form:

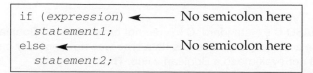

```
if (expression)  ←——— No semicolon here
    statement1;
else  ←——————— No semicolon here
    statement2;
```

The form of the `if-else` statement that is selected generally depends on the length of statements 1 and 2. However, when using the second form, do not put a semicolon after the parentheses or the keyword `else`. The semicolons go only after the ends of the statements. The flowchart for the `if-else` statement is shown in Figure 4.2.

FIGURE 4.2   The `if-else` **Flowchart**

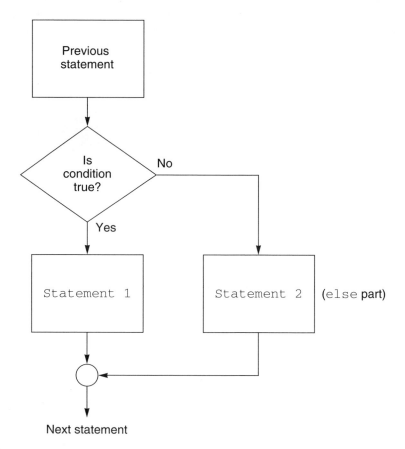

As a specific example of an `if-else` statement, we construct a C++ program for determining New Jersey income taxes. As previously described, these taxes are assessed at 2% of taxable income for incomes less than or equal to $20,000. For taxable income greater than $20,000, state taxes are 2.5% of the income that exceeds $20,000 plus a fixed amount of $400. The expression to be tested is whether taxable income is less than or equal to $20,000. An appropriate `if-else` statement for this situation is:[3]

---

[3] Note that in actual practice, the numerical values in this statement are defined as constants.

```
   if (taxable <= 20000.0)
     taxes = 0.02 * taxable;
   else
     taxes = 0.025 * (taxable - 20000.0) + 400.0;
```

Here, we have used the relational operator <= to represent the relation "less than or equal to." If the value of taxable is less than or equal to 20000, the condition is true (has a value of 1) and the statement taxes = .02 * taxable; is executed. If the condition is not true, the value of the expression is zero, and the statement after the keyword else is executed. Program 4.1 illustrates the use of this statement in a complete program.

PROGRAM 4.1

```
#include <iostream>
#include <iomanip>
using namespace std;

int main()
{
  const float LOWRATE = 0.02;    // lower tax rate
  const float HIGHRATE = 0.025;  // higher tax rate
  const float CUTOFF = 20000.0;  // cut off for low rate
  const float FIXEDAMT = 400;    // fixed dollar amount for higher rate amounts
  double taxable, taxes;

  cout << "Please type in the taxable income: ";
  cin  >> taxable;

  if (taxable <= CUTOFF)
    taxes = LOWRATE * taxable;
  else
    taxes = HIGHRATE * (taxable - CUTOFF) + FIXEDAMT;

    // set output format
  cout << setiosflags(ios::fixed)
       << setiosflags(ios::showpoint)
       << setprecision(2);

  cout << "Taxes are $ " << taxes << endl;

  return 0;
}
```

A blank line was inserted before and after the if-else statement to highlight it in the complete program. We will continue to do this throughout the text to emphasize the statement being presented.

To illustrate selection in action, Program 4.1 was run twice with different input data. The results are:

```
             Please type in the taxable income: 10000
             Taxes are $ 200.00
```

and

```
             Please type in the taxable income: 30000
             Taxes are $ 650.00
```

Observe that the taxable income input in the first run of the program was less than $20,000, and the tax was correctly calculated as 2% of the number entered. In the second run, the taxable income was more than $20,000, and the `else` part of the `if-else` statement was used to yield a correct tax computation of:

$$0.025 * (\$30,000. - \$20,000.) + \$400. = \$650.$$

Although any expression can be tested by an `if-else` statement, relational expressions are predominantly used. However, statements such as

```
             if (num)
               cout << "Bingo!";
             else
               cout << "You lose!";
```

are valid. Since `num`, by itself, is a valid expression, the message `Bingo!` is displayed if `num` has any nonzero value and the message `You lose!` is displayed if `num` has a value of zero.

Compound Statements

Although only a single statement is permitted in both the `if` and `else` parts of the `if-else` statement, this statement can be a single compound statement. A **compound statement** is a sequence of single statements contained between braces, as shown in Figure 4.3. The use of braces to enclose a set of individual statements creates a single block of statements, which may be used anywhere in a C++ program in place of a single statement. The next example illustrates the use of a compound statement within the general form of an `if-else` statement.

```
        if (expression)
        {
          statement1;      // as many statements as necessary
          statement2;      // can be put within the braces
          statement3;      // each statement must end with a ;
        }
        else
        {
          statement4;
          statement5;
                 .
                 .
          statementn;
        }
```

FIGURE 4.3 A Compound Statement Consists of Individual Statements Enclosed within Braces

```
{
    statement1;
    statement2;
    statement3;
           .
           .
           .
    last statement;
}
```

Program 4.2 illustrates the use of a compound statement in an actual program.

PROGRAM 4.2

```cpp
#include <iostream>
#include <iomanip>
using namespace std;

// a temperature conversion program
int main()
{
  char tempType;
  double temp, fahren, celsius;

  cout << "Enter the temperature to be converted: ";
  cin  >> temp;
  cout << "Enter an f if the temperature is in Fahrenheit";
  cout << "\n or a c if the temperature is in Celsius: ";
  cin  >> tempType;

    // set output formats
  cout << setiosflags(ios::fixed)
       << setiosflags(ios::showpoint)
       << setprecision(2);

  if (tempType == 'f')
  {
     celsius = (5.0 / 9.0) * (temp - 32.0);
     cout << "\nThe equivalent Celsius temperature is "
          << celsius << endl;
  }
  else
  {
    fahren = (9.0 / 5.0) * temp + 32.0;
    cout << "\nThe equivalent Fahrenheit temperature is "
         << fahren << endl;
  }

  return 0;
}
```

Program 4.2 checks whether the value in `tempType` is f. If the value is f, the compound statement corresponding to the `if` part of the `if-else` statement is executed. Any other letter results in execution of the compound statement corresponding to the `else` part. A sample run of Program 4.2 follows:

```
Enter the temperature to be converted: 212
Enter an f if the temperature is in Fahrenheit
  or a c if the temperature is in Celsius: f
The equivalent Celsius temperature is 100.00
```

PROGRAMMING NOTE

Placement of Braces in a Compound Statement

A common practice for some C++ programmers is to place the opening brace of a compound statement on the same line as the `if` and `else` statements. Using this convention, the `if` statement in Program 4.2 would appear as shown. (This placement is a matter of style only—both styles are used and both are acceptable.)

```cpp
if (tempType == 'f') {
  celsius = (5.0 / 9.0) * (temp - 32.0);
  cout << "\nThe equivalent Celsius temperature is "
       << celsius << endl;
}
else {
   fahren = (9.0 / 5.0) * temp + 32.0;
   cout << "\nThe equivalent Fahrenheit temperature is "
        << fahren << endl;
}
```

Block Scope

All statements within a compound statement constitute a single block of code, and any variable declared within such a block only has meaning between its declaration and the closing braces defining the block. For example, consider the following section of code, which consists of two blocks of code:

```cpp
{ // start of outer block
  int a = 25;
  int b = 17;

  cout << "The value of a is " << a
       <<" and b is " << b << endl;

  {     // start of inner block
    float a = 46.25;
    int c = 10;

    cout << "a is now " << a
         << " b is now " << b
         << " and c is " << c << endl;
  }     // end of inner block

  cout << "a is now " << a
       << " and b is " << b << endl;
}     // end of outer block
```

The output produced by this section of code is:

```
The value of a is 25 and b is 17
a is now 46.25 b is now 17 and c is 10
a is now 25 and b is 17
```

This output is produced as follows. The first block of code defines two variables named a and b, which may be used anywhere within this block after their declaration, including any block contained inside of it. Within the inner block, two new variables have been declared, named a and c. At this stage, then, we have created four different variables, two of which have the same name. Any referenced variable first results in an attempt to access a variable correctly declared within the block containing the reference. If no variable is defined within the block, an attempt is made to access a variable in the next immediate outside block until a valid access results.

Thus, the values of the variables a and c referenced within the inner block use the values of the variables a and c declared in that block. Since no variable named b was declared inside the inner block, the value of b displayed from within the inner block is obtained from the outer block. Finally, the last cout object, which is outside of the inner block, displays the value of the variable a declared in the outer block. If an attempt is made to display the value of c anywhere in the outer block, the compiler would issue an error message stating that c is an undefined symbol.

The location within a program where a variable can be used is formally referred to as the **scope** of the variable. We will have much more to say on this subject in Chapter 6.

One-Way Selection

A useful modification of the if-else statement involves omitting the else part of the statement altogether. In this case, the if statement takes the shortened and frequently useful form:

```
if (expression)
    statement;
```

The statement following if (expression) is only executed if the expression has a nonzero value (a true condition). As before, the statement may be a compound statement. The flowchart for this statement is shown in Figure 4.4.

This modified form of the if statement is called a **one-way if statement.** Program 4.3 uses this statement to selectively display a message for cars that have been driven more than 3000.0 miles.

As an illustration of its one-way selection criteria in action, Program 4.3 was run twice, each time with different input data. Only the input data for the first run cause the message Car 256 is over the limit. to be displayed:

```
Please type in car number and mileage: 256 3562.8
  Car 256 is over the limit.
End of program output.
```

and

```
Please type in car number and mileage: 23 2562.3
End of program output.
```

FIGURE 4.4   Flowchart for the One-Way `if` Statement

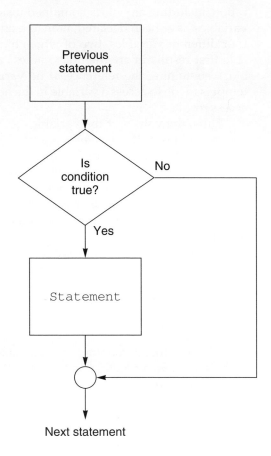

PROGRAM 4.3

```cpp
#include <iostream>
using namespace std;
int main()
{
  const float LIMIT = 3000.0;
  int idNum;
  double miles;

  cout << "Please type in car number and mileage: ";
  cin  >> idNum >> miles;

  if(miles > LIMIT)
    cout << " Car " << idNum << " is over the limit.\n";

  cout << "End of program output.\n";

  return 0;
}
```

Problems Associated with the if-else **Statement**

Two of the most common problems encountered in initially using C++'s if-else statement are:

1. misunderstanding the full implications of what an expression is
2. using the assignment operator = in place of the relational operator ==

Recall that an expression is any combination of operands and operators that yields a result. This definition is extremely broad and more encompassing than is initially apparent. For example, all of the following are valid C++ expressions:

```
age + 5
age = 30
age == 40
```

Assuming that the variables are suitably declared, each of the preceding expressions yields a result. Program 4.4 uses the cout object to display the value of these expressions when age = 18.

PROGRAM 4.4

```
#include <iostream>
using namespace std;
int main()
{
  int age = 18;

  cout << "The value of the first expression is " << (age + 5) << endl;
  cout << "The value of the second expression is " << (age = 30) << endl;
  cout << "The value of the third expression is " << (age == 40) << endl;

  return 0;
}
```

The display produced by Program 4.4 is:

```
The value of the first expression is 23
The value of the second expression is 30
The value of the third expression is 0
```

As the output of Program 4.4 illustrates, each expression, by itself, has a value associated with it. The value of the first expression is the sum of the variable age plus 5, which is 23. The value of the second expression is 30, which is also assigned to the variable age. The value of the third expression is 0, since age is not equal to 40, and a false condition is represented in C++ with a value of 0. If the value in age had been 40, the relational expression a == 40 would be true and would have a value of 1.

Now assume that the relational expression `age == 40` was intended to be used in the following `if` statement:

```
if (age == 40)
    cout << "Happy Birthday!";
```

but was mistyped as `age = 40`, resulting in:

```
if (age = 40)
    cout << "Happy Birthday!";
```

Since the mistake results in a valid C++ expression, and any C++ expression can be tested by an `if` statement, the resulting `if` statement is valid and causes the message `Happy Birthday!` to be printed regardless of what value was previously assigned to age. Can you see why?

The condition tested by the `if` statement does not compare the value in `age` to the number 40, but assigns the number 40 to age. That is, the expression `age = 40` is not a relational expression, but is an assignment expression. At the completion of the assignment, the expression itself has a value of 40. Since C++ treats any nonzero value as true, the call to `cout` is made. Another way of looking at this is to realize that the `if` statement is equivalent to the following two statements:

```
age = 40;      // assign 40 to age
if (age)       // test the value of age
cout << "Happy Birthday!";
```

Because a C++ compiler has no means of knowing that the expression being tested is not the desired one, you must be especially careful when writing conditions.

Exercises 4.2

1. Write appropriate `if` statements for each of the following conditions:

   a. If an angle is equal to 90 degrees, print the message "The angle is a right angle," else print the message "The angle is not a right angle."

   b. If the temperature is above 100 degrees, display the message "above the boiling point of water," else display the message "below the boiling point of water."

   c. If the number is positive, add the number to possum, else add the number to negsum.

   d. If the slope is less than .5, set the variable flag to zero, else set flag to one.

   e. If the difference between num1 and num2 is less than .001, set the variable approx to zero, else calculate approx as the quantity (num1 - num2) / 2.0.

   f. If the difference between temp1 and temp2 exceeds 2.3, calculate error as (temp1 - temp2) * factor.

   g. If x is greater than y and z is less than 20, read in a value for p.

   h. If distance is greater than 20 and it is less than 35, read in a value for time.

2. Write if statements corresponding to the conditions illustrated by each of the following flowcharts:

a.

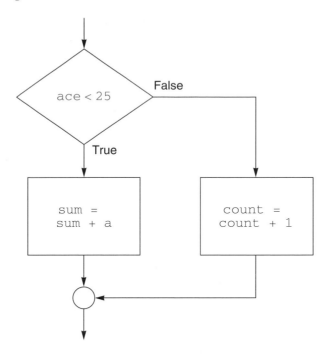

b.

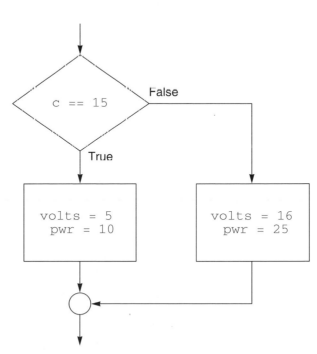

c.

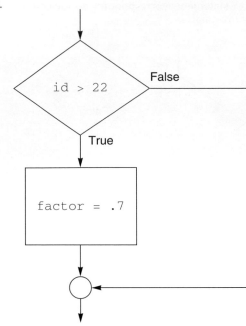

d.

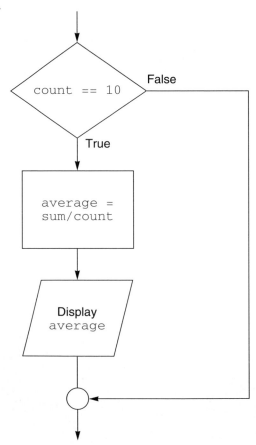

3. Write a C++ program that asks the user to input two numbers. If the first number entered is greater than the second number, the program should print the message The first number is greater, otherwise it should print the message The first number is smaller. Test your program by entering 5 and 8 and then using 11 and 2. What do you think your program will display if the two numbers entered are equal? Test this case.

4. a. If money is left in a particular bank for more than 2 years, the interest rate given by the bank is 8.5%, else the interest rate is 7%. Write a C++ program that uses the cin object to accept the number of years into the variable nyrs and display the appropriate interest rate depending on the input value.

   b. How many runs should you make for the program written in Exercise 4a to verify that it is operating correctly? What data should you input in each of the program runs?

5. a. In a pass/fail course, a student passes if the grade is greater than or equal to 70 and fails if the grade is lower. Write a C++ program that accepts a grade and prints the message A passing grade or A failing grade, as appropriate.

   b. How many runs should you make for the program written in Exercise 5a to verify that it is operating correctly? What data should you input in each of the program runs?

4.3 NESTED if STATEMENTS

As we have seen, an if-else statement can contain simple or compound statements. Any valid C++ statement can be used, including another if-else statement. Thus, one or more if-else statements can be included within either part of an if-else statement. The inclusion of one or more if statements within an existing if statement is called a **nested if** statement. For example, substituting the one way if statement

```
if (distance > 500)
    cout << "snap";
```

for statement1 in the following if statement:

```
if (hours < 9)
    statement1;
else
    cout << "pop";
```

results in the nested if statement:

```
if (hours < 9)
{
    if (distance > 500)
    cout << "snap";
}
else
    cout << "pop";
```

The braces around the inner one-way if are essential because in their absence C++ associates an else with the closest unpaired if. Thus, without the braces, the previous statement is equivalent to:

```
if (hours < 9)
    if (distance > 500)
    cout << "snap";
    else
    cout << "pop";
```

Here, the `else` is paired with the inner `if`, which destroys the meaning of the original `if-else` statement. Notice also that the indentation is irrelevant as far as the compiler is concerned. Whether the indentation exists or not, *the statement is compiled by associating the last `else` with the closest unpaired `if`, unless braces are used to alter the default pairing.*

The process of nesting `if` statements can be extended indefinitely so that the `cout << "snap";` statement could itself be replaced by either a complete `if-else` statement or another one-way `if` statement.

Figure 4.5 illustrates the general form of a nested `if-else` statement when an `if-else` statement is nested (a) within the `if` part of an `if-else` statement and (b) within the `else` part of an `if-else` statement.

The `if-else` Chain

In general, the nesting illustrated in Figure 4.5a tends to be confusing and is best avoided in practice. However, an extremely useful construction occurs for the nesting illustrated in Figure 4.5b, which has the form:

```
if (expression-1)
    statement1;
else
    if (expression-2)
        statement2;
    else
        statement3;
```

FIGURE 4.5a   The `if-else` **Nested within the** `if` **Part**

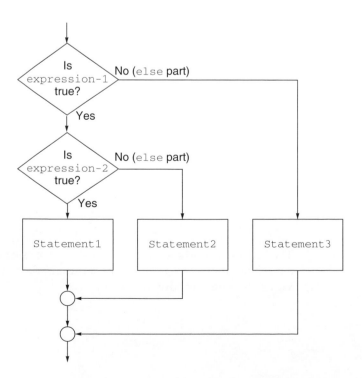

FIGURE 4.5b	The `if-else` Nested within the `else` Part

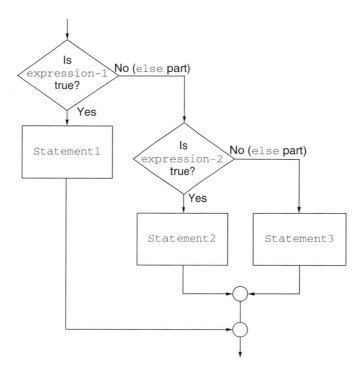

As with all C++ programs, since white space is ignored, the indentation shown is not required. More typically, the preceding construction is written using the following arrangement:

```
if (expression-1)
    statement-1;
else if (expression-2)
    statement-2;
else
    statement-3;
```

This form of a nested `if` statement is extremely useful in practice and is formally referred to as an **if-else chain.** Each condition is evaluated in order, and if any condition is true, the corresponding statement is executed and the remainder of the chain is terminated. The statement associated with the final `else` is only executed if none of the previous conditions is satisfied. This serves as a default or catchall case that is useful for detecting an impossible or error condition.

The chain can be continued indefinitely by repeatedly making the last statement another `if-else` statement. Thus, the general form of an `if-else` chain is:

```
if (expression-1)
    statement-1;
else if (expression-2)
    statement-2;
else if (expression-3)
```

(continued from the previous page)

```
    statement-3;
        .
        .
        .
    else if (expression-n)
        statement-n;
else
    last-statement;
```

Each condition is evaluated in the order in which it appears in the statement. For the first condition that is true, the corresponding statement is executed, and the remainder of the statements in the chain are not executed. Thus, if `expression-1` is true, only `statement-1` is executed; otherwise, `expression-2` is tested. If `expression-2` is then true, only `statement-2` is executed; otherwise, `expression-3` is tested, and so on. The final `else` in the chain is optional, and `last-statement` is only executed if none of the previous expressions were true. As a specific example, consider the following `if-else` chain:

```
if (marcode == 'M')
    cout << "Individual is married.\n";
else if (marcode == 'S')
    cout << "Individual is single.\n";
else if (marcode == 'D')
    cout << "Individual is divorced.\n";
else if (marcode == 'W')
    cout << "Individual is widowed.\n")
else
    cout << "An invalid code was entered.\n";
```

Execution through this chain begins by testing the expression `marcode == 'M'`. If the value in `marcode` is M, the message `Individual is married.` is displayed, no further expressions in the chain are evaluated, and execution resumes with the next statement immediately following the chain. If the value in `marcode` was not M, the expression `marcode == 'S'` is tested, and so on, until a true condition is found. If none of the conditions in the chain is true, the message `An invalid code was entered.` is displayed. In all cases, execution resumes with whatever statement immediately follows the chain. Program 4.5 uses this `if-else` chain within a complete program.

In Program 4.5, note that `Thanks for participating in the survey.` is always printed. This is the statement immediately after the `if-else` chain to which execution is transferred once the chain completes its execution. Which message is printed within the `if-else` chain depends on the value entered into `marcode`.

As a final example illustrating the `if-else` chain, let us calculate the monthly income of a computer salesperson using the following commission schedule:

Monthly Sales	Income
Greater than or equal to $50,000	$375 plus 16% of sales
Less than $50,000 but greater than or equal to $40,000	$350 plus 14% of sales
Less than $40,000 but greater than or equal to $30,000	$325 plus 12% of sales
Less than $30,000 but greater than or equal to $20,000	$300 plus 9% of sales
Less than $20,000 but greater than or equal to $10,000	$250 plus 5% of sales
Less than $10,000	$200 plus 3% of sales

PROGRAM 4.5

```cpp
#include <iostream>
using namespace std;

int main()
{
  char marcode;

  cout << "Enter a marital code: ";
  cin  >> marcode;

  if (marcode == 'M')
    cout << "Individual is married.\n";
  else if (marcode == 'S')
    cout << "Individual is single.\n";
  else if (marcode == 'D')
    cout << "Individual is divorced.\n";
  else if (marcode == 'W')
    cout << "Individual is widowed.\n";
  else
    cout << "An invalid code was entered.\n";

  cout << "Thanks for participating in the survey.\n";

  return 0;
}
```

The following if-else chain can be used to determine the correct monthly income, where the variable `monthlySales` is used to store the salesperson's current monthly sales:

```cpp
if (monthlySales >= 50000.00)
    income = 375.00 + 0.16 * monthlySales;
else if (monthlySales >= 40000.00)
    income = 350.00 + 0.14 * monthlySales;
else if (monthlySales >= 30000.00)
    income = 325.00 + 0.12 * monthlySales;
else if (monthlySales >= 20000.00)
    income = 300.00 + 0.09 * monthlySales;
else if (monthlySales >= 10000.00)
    income = 250.00 + 0.05 * monthlySales;
else
    income = 200.00 + 0.03 * monthlySales;
```

Notice that this example makes use of the fact that the chain is stopped once a true condition is found. This is accomplished by checking for the highest monthly sales first. If the salesperson's monthly sales is less than $50,000, the if-else chain continues checking for the next highest sales amount until the correct category is obtained.

Program 4.6 uses this if-else chain to calculate and display the income corresponding to the value of monthly sales input in the cin object.

PROGRAM 4.6

```cpp
#include <iostream>
#include <iomanip>
using namespace std;

int main()
{
  double monthlySales, income;

  cout << "Enter the value of monthly sales: ";
  cin  >> monthlySales;

  if (monthlySales >= 50000.00)
    income = 375.00 + 0.16 * monthlySales;
  else if (monthlySales >= 40000.00)
    income = 350.00 + 0.14 * monthlySales;
  else if (monthlySales >= 30000.00)
    income = 325.00 + 0.12 * monthlySales;
  else if (monthlySales >= 20000.00)
    income = 300.00 + 0.09 * monthlySales;
  else if (monthlySales >= 10000.00)
    income = 250.00 + 0.05 * monthlySales;
  else
    income = 200.00 + 0.03 * monthlySales;

    // set output format
  cout << setiosflags(ios::fixed)
       << setiosflags(ios::showpoint)
       << setprecision(2);

  cout << "The income is $" << income << endl;

  return 0;
}
```

A sample run of Program 4.6 is illustrated here:

```
Enter the value of monthly sales: 36243.89
The income is $4674.27
```

As with all C++ statements, each individual statement within an `if-else` chain can be replaced by a compound statement bounded by the braces { and }.

Exercises 4.3

1. Modify Program 4.5 to accept both lowercase and uppercase letters as marriage codes. For example, if a user enters either m or M, the program should display the message `Individual is married`.

2. Write nested if statements corresponding to the conditions illustrated in each of the following flowcharts:

a.   b.

3. An angle is considered acute if it is less than 90 degrees, obtuse if it is greater than 90 degrees, and a right angle if it is equal to 90 degrees. Using this information, write a C++ program that accepts an angle, in degrees, and displays the type of angle corresponding to the degrees entered.

4. The grade level of undergraduate college students is typically determined according to the following schedule:

Number of Credits Completed	Grade Level
Less than 32	Freshman
32 to 63	Sophomore
64 to 95	Junior
96 or more	Senior

Using this information, write a C++ program that accepts the number of credits a student has completed, determines the student's grade level, and displays the grade level.

5. A student's letter grade is calculated according to the following schedule:

Numerical Grade	Letter Grade
Greater than or equal to 90	A
Less than 90 but greater than or equal to 80	B
Less than 80 but greater than or equal to 70	C
Less than 70 but greater than or equal to 60	D
Less than 60	F

Using this information, write a C++ program that accepts a student's numerical grade, converts the numerical grade to an equivalent letter grade, and displays the letter grade.

6. The interest rate used on funds deposited in a bank is determined by the amount of time the money is left on deposit. For a particular bank, the following schedule is used:

Time on Deposit	Interest Rate
Greater than or equal to 5 years	0.0475
Less than 5 years but greater than or equal to 4 years	0.045
Less than 4 years but greater than or equal to 3 years	0.040
Less than 3 years but greater than or equal to 2 years	0.035
Less than 2 years but greater than or equal to 1 year	0.030
Less than 1 year	0.025

Using this information, write a C++ program that accepts the time that funds are left on deposit and displays the interest rate corresponding to the time entered.

7. Write a C++ program that accepts a number followed by one space and then a letter. If the letter following the number is f, the program is to treat the number entered as a temperature in degrees Fahrenheit, convert the number to the equivalent degrees Celsius, and print a suitable display message. If the letter following the number is c, the program is to treat the number entered as a temperature in degrees Celsius, convert the number to the equivalent degrees Fahrenheit, and print a suitable display message. If the letter is neither f nor c, the program is to print a message that the datum entered is incorrect and terminate. Use an if-else chain in your program and make use of the conversion formulas:

```
Celsius = (5.0 / 9.0) * (Fahrenheit - 32.0)
Fahrenheit = (9.0 / 5.0) * Celsius + 32.0
```

8. Using the commission schedule from Program 4.6, the following program calculates monthly income:

```cpp
#include <iostream>
#include <iomanip>
using namespace std;

int main()
{
  double monthlySales, income;

  cout << "Enter the value of monthly sales: ";
  cin  >> monthlySales;

  if (monthlySales >= 50000.00)
    income = 375.00 + .16 * monthlySales;
  if (monthlySales >= 40000.00 && monthlySales < 50000.00)
    income = 350.00 + .14 * monthlySales;
  if (monthlySales >= 30000.00 && monthlySales < 40000.00)
    income = 325.00 + .12 * monthlySales;
  if (monthlySales >= 20000.00 && monthlySales < 30000.00)
    income = 300.00 + .09 * monthlySales;
  if (monthlySales >= 10000.00 && monthlySales < 20000.00)
    income = 250.00 + .05 * monthlySales;
  if (monthlySales < 10000.00)
    income = 200.00 + .03 * monthlySales;

  cout << setiosflags(ios::showpoint)
       << setiosflags(ios:: fixed)
       << setprecision(2)
       << "The income is $" << income << endl;

  return 0;
}
```

a. Does this program produce the same output as Program 4.6?

b. Which program is better and why?

9. The following program was written to produce the same result as Program 4.6:

```cpp
#include <iostream>
#include <iomanip>
using namespace std;

int main()
{
  double monthlySales, income;

  cout << "Enter the value of monthly sales: ";
  cin >> monthlySales;

  if (monthlySales < 10000.00)
    income = 200.00 + .03 * monthlySales;
  else if (monthlySales >= 10000.00)
    income = 250.00 + .05 * monthlySales;
  else if (monthlySales >= 20000.00)
    income = 300.00 + .09 * monthlySales;
  else if (monthlySales >= 30000.00)
    income = 325.00 + .12 * monthlySales;
  else if (monthlySales >= 40000.00)
    income = 350.00 + .14 * monthlySales;
  else if (monthlySales >= 50000.00)
    income = 375.00 + .16 * monthlySales;

  cout << setiosflags(ios::showpoint)
       << setiosflags(ios:: fixed)
       << setprecision(2)
       << "The income is $" << income << endl;

  return 0;
}
```

a. Does this program run?

b. What does this program do?

c. For what values of monthly sales does this program calculate the correct income?

4.4 THE switch STATEMENT

The if-else chain is used in programming applications where one set of instructions must be selected from many possible alternatives. The **switch statement** provides an alternative to the if-else chain for cases that compare the value of an integer expression to a specific value. The switch statement syntax is:

```cpp
switch (expression)
{    // start of compound statement
  case value-1:              ◄——————————— Terminated with a colon
    statement1;
    statement2;
       .
       .
    break;
  case value-2:              ◄——————————— Terminated with a colon
```

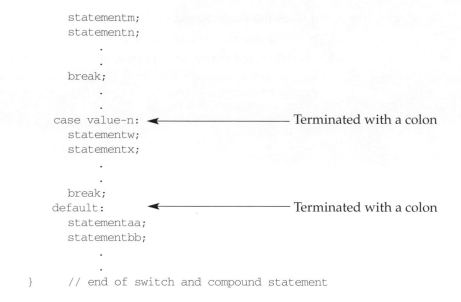

```
        statementm;
        statementn;
               .
               .
        break;
               .
               .
    case value-n:  ◄─────────────── Terminated with a colon
        statementw;
        statementx;
               .
               .
        break;
    default:       ◄─────────────── Terminated with a colon
        statementaa;
        statementbb;
               .
               .
    }      // end of switch and compound statement
```

The switch statement uses four new keywords: switch, case, default, and break. Let's see what each of these words does.

The keyword switch identifies the start of the switch statement. The expression in parentheses following this word is evaluated, and the result of the expression is compared to various alternative values contained within the compound statement. The expression in the switch statement must evaluate to an integer result or a compilation error occurs.

Internal to the switch statement, the keyword case is used to identify or label individual values that are compared to the value of the switch expression. The switch expression's value is compared to each of these case values in the order in which these values are listed until a match is found. When a match occurs, execution begins with the statement immediately following the match. Thus, as illustrated in Figure 4.6, the value of the expression determines where in the switch statement execution actually begins.

Any number of case labels may be contained within a switch statement, in any order. If the value of the expression does not match any of the case values, however, no statement is executed unless the keyword default is encountered. The word default is optional and operates just like the last else operates in an if-else chain. If the value of the expression does not match any of the case values, program execution begins with the statement following the word default.

Once an entry point has been located by the switch statement, all further case evaluations are ignored and execution continues through the end of the compound statement unless a break statement is encountered. This is the reason for the break statement, which identifies the end of a particular case and causes an immediate exit from the switch statement. Thus, just as the word case identifies possible starting points in the compound statement, the break statement determines terminating points. If the break statements are omitted, all cases following the matching case value, including the default case, are executed.

When writing a switch statement, you can use multiple case values to refer to the same set of statements; the default label is optional. For example, consider the following:

```cpp
switch (number)
{
  case 1:
    cout << "Have a Good Morning\n";
    break;
  case 2:
    cout << "Have a Happy Day\n";
    break;
  case 3:
  case 4:
  case 5:
    cout << "Have a Nice Evening\n";
}
```

FIGURE 4.6   The Expression Determines an Entry Point

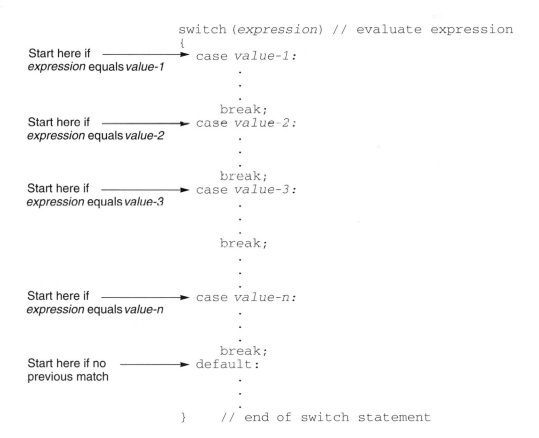

If the value stored in the variable number is 1, Have a Good Morning is the message displayed. Similarly, if the value of number is 2, the second message is displayed. Finally, if the value of number is 3 or 4 or 5, the last message is displayed. Since the statement to be executed for these last three cases is the same, the cases for these values can be "stacked together" as shown in the example. Also, since there is no default, no message is printed if the value of number is not one of the listed case values. Although it is good programming practice to list case values in increasing order, this is not required by the switch statement. A switch statement may have any number of case values, in any order; only the values being tested for need be listed.

Program 4.7 uses a switch statement to select the arithmetic operation (addition, multiplication, or division) to be performed on two numbers depending on the value of the variable opselect.

PROGRAM 4.7

```cpp
#include <iostream>
using namespace std;

int main()
{
  int opselect;
  double fnum, snum;

  cout << "Please type in two numbers: ";
  cin  >> fnum >> snum;
  cout << "Enter a select code: ";
  cout << "\n        1 for addition";
  cout << "\n        2 for multiplication";
  cout << "\n        3 for division";
  cin  >> opselect;

  switch (opselect)
  {
    case 1:
      cout << "The sum of the numbers entered is " << fnum+snum;
      break;
    case 2:
      cout << "The product of the numbers entered is " << fnum*snum;
      break;
    case 3:
      cout << "The first number divided by the second is " << fnum/snum;
      break;
  }     // end of switch

  cout << endl;

  return 0;
}
```

Program 4.7 was run twice. The resulting displays clearly identify the case selected. The results are:

```
Please type in two numbers: 12 3
Enter a select code:
        1 for addition
        2 for multiplication
        3 for division: 2
The product of the numbers entered is 36
```

and

```
Please type in two numbers: 12 3
Enter a select code:
        1 for addition
        2 for multiplication
        3 for division: 3
The first number divided by the second is 4
```

In reviewing Program 4.7, notice the break statement in the last case. Although this break is not necessary, it is a good practice to terminate the last case in a switch statement with a break. This prevents a possible program error later if an additional case is subsequently added to the switch statement. With the addition of a new case, the break between cases becomes necessary; having the break in place ensures you do not forget to include it at the time of the modification.

Because character data types are always converted to integers in an expression, a switch statement can also be used to "switch" based on the value of a character expression. For example, assuming that choice is a character variable, the following switch statement is valid:

```
switch(choice)
{
  case 'a':
  case 'e':
  case 'i':
  case 'o':
  case 'u':
    cout << "The character in choice is a vowel\n";
    break;
  default:
    cout << "The character in choice is not a vowel\n";
    break;    // this break is optional
}  // end of switch statement
```

Exercises 4.4

1. Rewrite the following if-else chain using a switch statement:

```
if (letterGrade == 'A')
  cout << "The numerical grade is between 90 and 100\n";
else if (letterGrade == 'B')
  cout << "The numerical grade is between 80 and 89.9\n";
else if (letterGrade == 'C')
  cout << "The numerical grade is between 70 and 79.9\n";
else if (letterGrade == 'D';
  cout << "How are you going to explain this one?\n";
else
{
  cout << "Of course I had nothing to do with my grade.\n";
  cout << "It must have been the professor's fault.\n";
}
```

2. Rewrite the following if-else chain using a switch statement:

```
if (resType == 1)
{
  indata();
  check();
}
else if (resType == 2)
{
  capacity();
  devtype();
}
else if (resType == 3)
{
  volume();
  mass();
}
else if (resType == 4)
{
  area();
  weight();
}
else if (resType == 5)
{
  files();
  save();
}
else if (resType == 6)
{
  retrieve();
  screen();
}
```

3. Each disk drive in a shipment of these devices is stamped with a code from 1 through 4, which indicates a drive manufacturer as follows:

Code	Disk Drive Manufacturer
1	3M Corporation
2	Maxell Corporation
3	Sony Corporation
4	Verbatim Corporation

Write a C++ program that accepts the code number as an input and, based on the value entered, displays the correct disk drive manufacturer.

4. Rewrite Program 4.5 using a switch statement.

5. Determine why the if-else chain in Program 4.6 cannot be replaced with a switch statement.

6. Rewrite Program 4.7 using a character variable for the select code.

4.5 FOCUS ON PROBLEM SOLVING

Two major uses of C++'s if statements are to select appropriate processing paths and to prevent undesirable data from being processed at all. In this section, examples of both uses are provided.

Problem 1: Data Validation

An important use of C++'s if statements is to validate data by checking for clearly invalid cases. For example, a date such as 5/33/2002 contains an obviously invalid day. Similarly, the division of any number by zero within a program, such as 14/0, should not be allowed. Both of these examples illustrate the need for a technique called **defensive programming**, in which the program includes code to check for improper data before an attempt is made to process them further. The defensive programming technique of checking user-input data for erroneous or unreasonable data is referred to as **input data validation**.

Consider the case where we are to write a C++ program to calculate the square root and the reciprocal of a user-entered number. Before calculating the square root, we should validate that the number is not negative, and before calculating the reciprocal, check that the number is not zero.

Step 1: Analyze the Problem   The statement of the problem requires that we accept a single number as an input, validate the entered number, and based on the validation, produce two possible outputs: If the number is nonnegative, we are to determine its square root, and if the input number is not zero, we are to determine its reciprocal.

Step 2: Develop a Solution   Since the square root of a negative number does not exist as a real number and the reciprocal of zero cannot be taken, our program must contain input data validation statements to screen the user-input data and avoid these two cases. The pseudocode describing the processing required is:

Display a program purpose message.
Accept a user-input number.
If the number is negative
    print a message that the square root cannot be taken.
Else
    calculate and display the square root.
Endif
If the number is zero then
    print a message that the reciprocal cannot be taken.
Else
    calculate and display the reciprocal.
Endif

Step 3: Code the Solution   The C++ code corresponding to our pseudocode solution is listed in Program 4.8. This is a rather straightforward program containing two separate (nonnested) if statements. The first if statement checks for a negative input number; if the number is negative, a message indicating that the square root of a negative number cannot be taken is displayed, else the square root is taken. The second if statement checks whether the entered number is zero; if it is zero, a message indicating that the reciprocal of zero cannot be taken is displayed, else the reciprocal is taken.

Step 4: Test and Correct the Program   Test values should include an appropriate value for the input, such as 5, and values for the limiting cases, such as a negative and zero input value. Test runs follow for two of these cases:

PROGRAM 4.8

```cpp
#include <iostream>
#include <cmath>
using namespace std;

int main()
{
  double usenum;

  cout << "This program calculates the square root and\n"
       << "reciprocal (1/number) of a number\n"
       << "\nPlease enter a number: ";
  cin  >> usenum;
  if (usenum < 0.0)
    cout << "The square root of a negative number does not exist.\n";
  else
    cout << "The square root of " << usenum
         << " is " << sqrt(usenum) << endl;
  if (usenum == 0.0)
    cout << "The reciprocal of zero does not exist.\n";
  else
    cout << "The reciprocal of " << usenum
         << " is " << (1.0/usenum) << endl;

  return 0;
}
```

```
This program calculates the square root and
reciprocal (1/number) of a number

Please enter a number: 5

The square root of 5 is 2.236068
The reciprocal of 5 is 0.2
```

and

```
This program calculates the square root and
reciprocal (1/number) of a number

Please enter a number: -6

The square root of a negative number does not exist.
The reciprocal of -6 is -0.166667
```

Problem 2: Solving Quadratic Equations

A **quadratic equation** is an equation that has the form $ax^2 + bx + c = 0$ or that can be algebraically manipulated into this form. In this equation, x is the unknown variable, and a, b, and c are known constants. Although the constants b and c can be any numbers, including 0, the value of the constant a cannot be 0 (if a is 0, the equation becomes a **linear equation** in x). Examples of quadratic equations are:

$$5x^2 + 6x + 2 = 0$$

$$x^2 - 7x + 20 = 0$$

$$34x^2 + 16 = 0$$

In the first equation, $a = 5$, $b = 6$, and $c = 2$; in the second equation, $a = 1$, $b = -7$, and $c = 20$; and in the third equation, $a = 34$, $b = 0$, and $c = 16$.

The real roots of a quadratic equation can be calculated using the quadratic formula as:

$$\text{root } 1 = \frac{-b + \sqrt{b^2 - 4ac}}{2a}$$

and

$$\text{root } 2 = \frac{-b - \sqrt{b^2 - 4ac}}{2a}$$

Using these equations, we will write a C++ program to solve for the roots of a quadratic equation.

Step 1: Analyze the Problem   The problem requires that we accept three inputs—the coefficients a, b, and c of a quadratic equation—and compute the roots of the equation using the given formulas.

Step 2: Develop a Solution   A first attempt at a solution is to use the user-entered values of a, b, and c to directly calculate a value for each of the roots. Thus, our first solution is:

Display a program purpose message.
Accept user-input values for a, b, and c.
Calculate the two roots.
Display the values of the calculated roots.

However, this solution must be refined further to account for a number of possible input conditions. For example, if a user entered a value of 0 for both a and b, the equation is neither quadratic nor linear and has no solution (this is referred to as a **degenerate case**). Another possibility is that the user supplies a nonzero value for b but makes a 0. In this case, the equation becomes a linear one with a single solution of $-c/b$. A third possibility is that the value of the term $b^2 - 4ac$, which is called the **discriminant,** is negative. Since the square root of a negative number cannot be taken, this case has no real roots. Finally, when the discriminant is 0, both roots are the same (this is referred to as the **repeated roots case**).

Taking into account all four of these limiting cases, a refined solution for correctly determining the roots of a quadratic equation is expressed by the following pseudocode:

Display a program purpose message.
Accept user-input values for a, b, and c.
If a = 0 and b = 0 then
    display a message saying that the equation has no solution.
Else if a = 0 then
      calculate the single root equal to –c/b.
      display the single root.

Else
    calculate the discriminant.
    If the discriminant > 0 then
        solve for both roots using the given formulas.
        display the two roots.
    Else if the discriminant < 0 then
        display a message that there are no real roots.
    Else
        calculate the repeated root equal to –b/(2a).
        display the repeated root.
    Endif.
Endif.

Notice in the pseudocode that we have used nested `if-else` structures. The outer `if-else` structure is used to validate the entered coefficients and determine that we have a valid quadratic equation. The inner `if-else` structure is then used to determine if the equation has two real roots (discriminant > 0), two imaginary roots (discriminant < 0), or repeated roots (discriminant = 0).

Step 3: Code the Solution   The equivalent C++ code corresponding to our pseudocode solution is listed in Program 4.9.

Step 4: Test and Correct the Program   Test values should include values for a, b, and c that result in two real roots, plus limiting values for a and b that result in linear equation ($a = 0$, $b \neq 0$), a degenerate equation ($a = 0$, $b = 0$), and a negative and 0 discriminant. Two such test runs of Program 4.9 follow:

```
This program calculates the roots of a
   quadratic equation of the form

            ax² + bx + c = 0

Please enter values for a, b, and c: 1 2 -35

The two real roots are 5 and -7
```

and

```
This program calculates the roots of a
   quadratic equation of the form

            ax² + bx + c = 0

Please enter values for a, b, and c: 0 0 16

The equation is degenerate and has no roots.
```

The first run solves the quadratic equation $x^2 + 2x - 35 = 0$, which has the real roots $x = 5$ and $x = -7$. The input data for the second run result in the equation $0x^2 + 0x + 16 = 0$. Because this degenerates into the mathematical impossibility of $16 = 0$, the program correctly identifies it as a degenerate equation. We leave it as an exercise to create test data for the other limiting cases checked for by the program.

PROGRAM 4.9

```cpp
#include <iostream>
#include <cmath>
using namespace std;

// this program solves for the roots of a quadratic equation
int main()
{
  double a, b, c, disc, root1, root2;

  cout << "This program calculates the roots of a\n";
  cout << "   quadratic equation of the form\n";
  cout << "                2\n";
  cout << "            ax + bx + c = 0\n\n";
  cout << "Please enter values for a, b, and c: ";
  cin  >> a >> b >> c;
  if ( a == 0.0 && b == 0.0)
    cout << "The equation is degenerate and has no roots.\n";
  else if (a == 0.0)
    cout << "The equation has the single root x = "
         << -c/b << endl;
  else
  {
    disc = pow(b,2.0) - 4 * a * c; // calculate discriminant
    if (disc > 0.0)
    {
      disc = sqrt(disc);
      root1 = (-b + disc) / (2 * a);
      root2 = (-b - disc) / (2 * a);
      cout << "The two real roots are "
           << root1 << " and " << root2 << endl;
    }
    else if (disc < 0.0)
      cout << "Both roots are imaginary.\n";
    else
      cout << "Both roots are equal to " << -b / (2 * a) << endl;
  }

  return 0;
}
```

Exercises 4.5

1. a. Write a program that accepts two real numbers from a user and a select code. If the entered select code is 1, have the program add the two previously entered numbers and display the result; if the select code is 2, the numbers should be multiplied; and if the select code is 3, the first number should be divided by the second number.

   b. Determine what the program written in Exercise 1a does when the entered numbers are 3 and 0, and the select code is 3.

   c. Modify the program written in Exercise 1a so that division by 0 is not allowed and an appropriate message is displayed when such a division is attempted.

2. a. Write a program to display the following two prompts:

```
Enter a month (use a 1 for Jan, etc.):
Enter a day of the month:
```

Have your program accept and store a number in the variable month in response to the first prompt and accept and store a number in the variable day in response to the second prompt. If the month entered is not between 1 and 12 inclusive, print a message informing the user that an invalid month has been entered. If the day entered is not between 1 and 31, print a message informing the user that an invalid day has been entered.

b. What will your program do if the user types a number with a decimal point for the month? How can you ensure that your if statements check for an integer number?

c. In a nonleap year, February has 28 days, the months January, March, May, July, August, October, and December have 31 days, and all other months have 30 days. Using this information, modify the program written in Exercise 2a to display a message when an invalid day is entered for a user-entered month. For this program, ignore leap years.

3. a. The quadrant in which a line drawn from the origin resides is determined by the angle that the line makes with the positive X axis as follows:

Angle from the Positive X Axis	Quadrant
Between 0 and 90 degrees	I
Between 90 and 180 degrees	II
Between 180 and 270 degrees	III
Between 270 and 360 degrees	IV

Using this information, write a C++ program that accepts the angle of the line as user input and determines and displays the quadrant appropriate to the input data. (*Note:* If the angle is exactly 0, 90, 180, or 270 degrees, the corresponding line does not reside in any quadrant but lies on an axis.)

b. Modify the program written for Exercise 3a so that a message is displayed that identifies an angle of 0 degrees as the positive X axis, an angle of 90 degrees as the positive Y axis, an angle of 180 degrees as the negative X axis, and an angle of 270 degrees as the negative Y axis.

4. All years that are evenly divisible by 400 or are evenly divisible by 4 and not evenly divisible by 100 are leap years. For example, since 2000 is evenly divisible by 400, the year 2000 is a leap year. Similarly, since 1996 is evenly divisible by 4 but not by 100, the year 1996 was also a leap year. Using this information, write a C++ program that accepts the year as user input, determines if the year is a leap year, and displays an appropriate message that tells the user if the entered year is or is not a leap year.

5. Based on an automobile's model year and weight, the state of New Jersey determines the car's weight class and registration fee using the following schedule:

Model Year	Weight	Weight Class	Registration Fee
1970 or earlier	Less than 2700 lbs	1	$16.50
	2700 to 3800 lbs	2	25.50
	More than 3800 lbs	3	46.50
1971 to 1979	Less than 2700 lbs	4	27.00
	2700 to 3800 lbs	5	30.50
	More than 3800 lbs	6	52.50
1980 or later	Less than 3500 lbs	7	19.50
	3500 or more lbs	8	52.50

Using this information, write a C++ program that accepts the year and weight of an automobile and determines and displays the weight class and registration fee for the car.

6. Modify Program 4.9 so that the imaginary roots are calculated and displayed when the discriminant is negative. For this case, the two roots of the equation are:

$$x_1 = \frac{-b}{2a} + \frac{sqrt[-(b^2 - 4ac)]}{2a} i$$

and

$$x_2 = \frac{-b}{2a} - \frac{sqrt[-(b^2 - 4ac)]}{2a} i$$

where i is the imaginary number symbol for the square root of –1. (*Hint:* Calculate the real and imaginary parts of each root separately.)

7. In the game of Blackjack, the cards 2 through 10 are counted at their face values, regardless of suit, all face cards (jack, queen, and king) are counted as 10, and an ace is counted as either 1 or 11, depending on the total count of all the cards in a player's hand. The ace counts as 11 only if the resulting total value of all cards in a player's hand does not exceed 21, else it is counted as 1. Using this information, write a C++ program that accepts three card values as inputs (1 corresponding to an ace, 2 corresponding to a two, and so on), calculates the total value of the hand appropriately, and displays the value of the three cards with a printed message.

4.6 PLANNING FOR OBJECTS: INSIDES AND OUTSIDES

The primary distinction between procedural and object-oriented programming is their treatment of data and processing. In contrast to procedural programming, where software is organized by what it does (its function) to the data, object-oriented programming organizes software as a collection of discrete objects that include both data and functional behavior.

As such, procedural programs are constructed as a sequence of processing transformations that convert input data into output data. In a well-constructed procedural program, each transformation is captured within a procedure, which in C++ is coded as a function. In this context, the overall effect of a procedural program can be illustrated as in Figure 4.7.

The method for converting inputs to outputs is described by an algorithm, which explains the importance of algorithms to procedural code. Seen in this light, procedural code is nothing more than an algorithm written in a programming language.

In object-oriented programming, the packaging of data and processing is handled in a much different manner. Both the data and the processing that can be applied to them are combined and packaged in a new unit called an *object*. Once suitable objects are defined, object-oriented programming is concerned with the interactions between objects. Notice that this way of thinking about code does not remove the necessity to understand data and the algorithms applied to them. It simply binds the data and procedures in a new package (the object) and then concerns itself with the interactions between objects. One advantage to this approach is that once objects are defined for one application, they can be used—as is and without reprogramming—in other applications. They can also be easily enhanced by adding additional code to the existing code, rather than completely rewriting all of the code.

| FIGURE 4.7 | Processing Inputs to Produce Outputs |

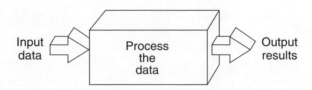

Just as the concept of an algorithm is central to procedures, the concept of encapsulation is central to objects. In this section, we present this encapsulation concept using an inside–outside analogy, which should help your understanding of what object-oriented programming is all about.

Recall from our discussion in Section 1.5 that an object is defined by two distinct aspects, its attributes and behavior. In programming terms, an object's attributes are described by data, such as the length and width of a rectangle, and the operations that can be applied to the attributes are described by functions.

As a practical example, assume that we are writing a program that can deal a hand of cards. From an object-oriented approach, one of the objects that we must model is clearly a deck of cards. For our purposes, the attributes of interest for the card deck are that it contains 52 cards, consisting of four suits (hearts, diamonds, spades, and clubs), with each suit consisting of 13 pip values (ace to 10, jack, queen, and king).

Now consider the behavior of our deck of cards, which consists of the operations that can be applied to the deck. At a minimum, we want the ability to shuffle the deck and deal single cards. Let's now see how this simple example relates to encapsulation using an inside–outside concept.

A useful visualization of the inside–outside concept is to consider an object as a boiled egg, such as that shown in Figure 4.8. Notice that the egg consists of three parts: a very inside yolk, a less inside white surrounding the yolk, and an outside shell, which is the only part of the egg visible to the outside world.

In terms of our boiled egg model, the attributes and behavior of an object correspond to the yolk and white, respectively, which are inside the egg. That is, the

| FIGURE 4.8 | The Boiled Egg Object Model |

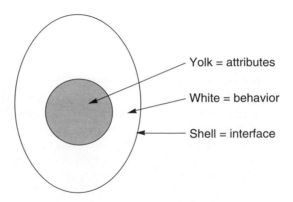

innermost protected area of an object, its data attributes, can be compared to the egg yolk.

Surrounding the data attributes, in a manner similar to the way an egg's white surrounds its yolk, are the operations that we choose to incorporate within an object. Finally, in this analogy, the interface to the outside world, which is symbolized by the shell, represents how a user gets to invoke the object's internal procedures.

The egg model, with its eggshell interface separating the inside of the egg from the outside, is useful precisely because it so clearly depicts the separation between what should be contained inside an object and what should be seen from the outside. This separation forms an essential element in object-oriented programming. Let's see why this is so.

From an inside–outside perspective, an object's data attributes, the selected algorithms for the object's operations, and how these algorithms are implemented are always inside issues that are hidden from the view of an object user. What remains—how a user or another object can actually activate an inside procedure—is an outside issue.

Now let's apply this concept to our card deck example. First, consider how we might represent cards in the deck. Any of the following attributes (and there are others) could be used to represent a card:

1. Two integer variables, one representing a suit (a number from 1 to 4) and one representing a value (a number from 1 to 13).

2. One character value and one integer value. The character represents a card's suit, and the integer represents a card's value.

3. One integer variable from 0 to 51 in value . The expression `(number % 13 + 1)` represents a card value from 1 to 13. The expression `int (number / 13 + 1)` provides a number from 1 to 4, which represents the suit.

Whichever representation we decide on, however, is not relevant to the outside. The specific way we choose to represent a card is an inside issue to be decided on by the designer of the deck object. From the outside, the sole concern is that we have access to a deck consisting of 52 cards having the necessary suits and pip values.

The same is true for the operations we decide to provide as part of our card deck object. Consider just the shuffling for now.

A number of algorithms are available for producing a shuffled deck. For example, we could use C++'s `rand()` library function or create our own random number generator using a power residue algorithm (see Section 6.7). Again, the selected algorithm is an inside issue to be determined by the designer of the deck. The specifics of which algorithm is selected and how it is applied to the attributes we have chosen for each card in the deck are not relevant from the object's outside. For purposes of illustration, assume that we decide to use C++'s `rand()` function to produce a randomly shuffled deck.

If we use the first attribute set previously given, each card in a shuffled deck is produced using `rand()` at least twice: once to create a random number from 1 to 4 for the suit and then to create a random number from 1 to 13 for the card's pip value. This sequence must be done to construct 52 different attribute sets, with no duplicates allowed.

If, on the other hand, we use the second attribute set previously given, a shuffled deck can be produced in exactly the same fashion as before, with one modification: The first random number (from 1 to 4) must be changed into a character to represent the suit.

Finally, if we use the third representation for a card, we need to use `rand()` once for each card to produce 52 random numbers from 0 to 51, with no duplicates allowed.

The important point here is that the selection of an algorithm and how it is applied to an object's attributes are implementation issues, and *implementation issues are always inside issues.* A user of the card deck, who is outside, does not need to know how the shuffling is done. All the user must know is how to produce a shuffled deck. In practice, this means that the user is supplied with sufficient information to correctly invoke a shuffle function. This corresponds to the interface, or outer shell of the egg.

Abstraction and Encapsulation

The distinction between insides and outsides relates directly to the concepts of abstraction and encapsulation. *Abstraction* means concentrating on what an object is and does before making any decisions about how the object will be implemented. Thus, abstractly, we define a deck and the operations we want to provide. (Clearly, if our abstraction is to be useful, it must capture the attributes and operations of a real-world deck.) Once we have decided on the attributes and operations, we can implement, which means code, them.

Encapsulation, which is also referred to as information hiding, means separating and hiding the implementation details of the chosen abstract attributes and behavior from outside users of the object. The external side of an object should provide only the necessary interface to users of the object for activating internal procedures. Imposing a strict inside–outside discipline when creating objects is really another way of saying that the object successfully encapsulates all implementation details. In our deck-of-cards example, encapsulation means that the user need never know how we have internally modeled the deck or how an operation, such as shuffling, is performed; the user need only know how to activate the given operations. (How the implementation is actually done is provided in Chapter 7.)

Code Reuse and Extensibility

A direct advantage of an inside–outside object approach is that it encourages both code reuse and extensibility. This is a direct result of having all interactions between objects centered on the outside interface and hiding all implementation details within the object's inside.

For example, consider the object shown in Figure 4.9. Here, either of the object's two operations can be activated by correctly stimulating either the circle or square on the outside. In practice, the stimulation is simply a function call. We have used a circle and square to emphasize that two different functions are provided for outside use. In our card deck example, activation of one function might produce a shuffled deck, while activation of the other function results in a card suit and pip value being returned from the object.

Now assume that we want to alter the implementation of an existing operation or add more functionality to our object. *As long as the existing outside interface is maintained, the internal implementation of any and all operations can be changed without the user ever being aware that a change took place.* This is a direct result of encapsulating the attribute data and operations within an object.

FIGURE 4.9 Using an Object's Interface

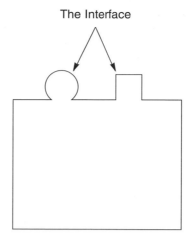

The Interface

Additionally, as long as the interface to existing operations is not changed, new operations can be added as they are needed. Essentially, from the outside world, all that is being added is another function call that accesses the inside attributes and modifies them in a new way.

Exercises 4.6

1. Define the terms:
   a. abstraction
   b. encapsulation
   c. extensibility
   d. implementation
   e. information hiding

2. a. An automobile provides a gas pedal, a brake pedal, and a gear shift. Using the boiled egg analogy presented in this section, do these correspond to the yolk, white, or eggshell?

   b. Give two different implementations for the engine, brakes, and gear shifting methods used in automobiles.

3. Defining suitable attributes for distinguishing individual objects typically depends on the universe of objects being considered. For the following set of telephone objects, list attributes that can be used to identify individual telephones within each group:
   a. all telephones within a single office
   b. all telephones within a state
   c. all telephones in the world

4. a. Describe a computer program that you developed in the past that required a user to know something about its internal operation for it to be used.

   b. Would you classify a program that required a user to know something about its internal operation as a "good" program? Why or why not?

5. For the following objects, list a set of attributes and behavior that appropriately model the object:

   a. a bicycle

   b. a book

   c. a pencil

   d. a person

   e. a date, such as 3/15/2007

   f. an employee

   g. a printer

6. For a typical programming assignment, estimate what percentage of time you spent in analysis, design, and coding, respectively.

7. In terms of the programming assignments you have had in the past, answer these questions:

   a. How much time do you spend selecting the algorithm to solve the problem?

   b. What criteria do you generally use when selecting an algorithm?

4.7 A CLOSER LOOK AT PROGRAM TESTING

In theory, a comprehensive set of test runs reveals all possible program errors and ensures that a program works correctly for any and all combinations of input and computed data. In practice, this requires checking all possible combinations of statement execution. Due to the time and effort required, this is an impossible goal except for extremely simple programs. Let us see why this is so. Consider Program 4.10.

PROGRAM 4.10

```cpp
#include <iostream>
using namespace std;

int main()
{
  int num;

  cout << "Enter a number: ";
  cin  >> num;
  if (num == 5)
    cout << "Bingo!\n";
  else
    cout << "Bongo!\n";

  return 0;
}
```

Program 4.10 has two paths that can be traversed from when the program is run to when the program reaches its closing brace. The first path, which is executed when the input number is 5, is in the sequence:

```
cout << "Enter a number";
cin  >> num;
cout << "Bingo!\n";
```

The second path, which is executed whenever any number except 5 is input, includes the sequence of instructions:

```
cout << "Enter a number";
cin  >> num;
cout << "Bongo!\n";
```

To test each possible path through Program 4.10, we must conduct two runs, with a judicious selection of test input data to ensure that both paths of the if statement are exercised. The addition of one more if statement in the program increases the number of possible execution paths by a factor of 2 and requires four (2^2) runs of the program for complete testing. Similarly, 2 additional if statements increase the number of paths by a factor of 4 and require 8 (2^3) runs for complete testing. Three additional if statements produce a program that requires sixteen (2^4) test runs.

Now consider a modestly sized application program consisting of only ten modules, each module containing five if statements. If we assume the modules are always called in the same sequence, then there are 32 possible paths through each module (2 raised to the fifth power) and more than 1 quadrillion (2 raised to the fiftieth power) possible paths through the complete program (all modules executed in sequence). The time needed to create individual test data to exercise each path and the computer run time required to check each path make the complete testing of such a program impossible.

The inability to fully test all combinations of statement execution sequences has led to the programming saying, "There is no error-free program." It has also led to the realization that any testing that is done should be well thought out to maximize the possibility of locating errors. At a minimum, test data should include appropriate values for input values, illegal input values that the program should reject, and limiting values that are checked by selection statements within the program.

4.8 COMMON PROGRAMMING ERRORS

Three programming errors are common to C++'s selection statements:

1. Using the assignment operator = in place of the relational operator ==. This can cause an enormous amount of frustration because any expression can be tested by an if-else statement. For example, the statement:

```
if (opselect = 2)
   cout << "Happy Birthday\n";
else
   cout << "Good Day\n";
```

always results in the message Happy Birthday being printed, regardless of the initial value in the variable opselect. The reason is that the assignment expression opselect = 2 has a value of 2, which is considered a true value in C++. The correct expression to determine the value in opselect is opselect == 2.

2. Letting the `if-else` statement appear to select an incorrect choice. In this typical debugging problem, the programmer mistakenly concentrates on the tested condition as the source of the problem. For example, assume that the following `if-else` statement is part of your program:

```
if (key == 'F')
{
    contemp = (5.0/9.0) * (intemp - 32.0);
    cout << "Conversion to Celsius was done";
}
else
{
    contemp = (9.0/5.0) * intemp + 32.0;
    cout << "Conversion to Fahrenheit was done";
}
```

This statement always displays `Conversion to Celsius was done` when the variable key contains an F. Therefore, if this message is displayed when you believe `key` does not contain F, investigation of `key`'s value is called for. As a general rule, whenever a selection statement does not act as you think it should, test your assumptions about the values assigned to the tested variables by displaying their values. If an unanticipated value is displayed, you have at least isolated the source of the problem to the variables themselves, rather than the structure of the `if-else` statement. From there, you need to determine where and how the incorrect value was obtained.

3. Using nested `if` statements without including braces to indicate the desired structure. Without braces, the compiler defaults to pairing `else`s with the closest unpaired `if`s, which sometimes destroys the original intent of the selection statement. To avoid this problem and to create code that is readily adaptable to change, it is useful to write all `if-else` statements as compound statements in the form:

```
if (expression)
{
    one or more statements in here
}
else
{
    one or more statements in here
}
```

By using this form, no matter how many statements are added later, the original integrity and intent of the `if` statement are maintained.

4.9 CHAPTER REVIEW

Key Terms

compound statement	nested if
condition	one-way if statement
encapsulation	scope
false condition	simple relational expression
if-else chain	switch statement
if-else statement	true condition

Summary

1. Relational expressions, which are also called *simple conditions*, are used to compare operands. If a relational expression is true, the value of the expression is the integer 1. If the relational expression is false, it has an integer value of 0. Relational expressions are created using the following relational operators:

Relational Operator	Meaning	Example
<	Less than	`age < 30`
>	Greater than	`height > 6.2`
<=	Less than or equal to	`taxable <= 20000`
>=	Greater than or equal to	`temp >= 98.6`
==	Equal to	`grade == 100`
!=	Not equal to	`number != 250`

2. More complex conditions can be constructed from relational expressions using C++'s logical operators, `&&` (AND), `||` (OR), and `!` (NOT).

3. An `if-else` statement is used to select between two alternative statements based on the value of an expression. Although relational expressions are usually used for the tested expression, any valid expression can be used. In testing an expression, `if-else` statements interpret a nonzero value as true and a zero value as false. The general form of an `if-else` statement is:

```
if (expression)
   statement1;
else
   statement2;
```

This is a two-way selection statement. If the expression has a nonzero value, it is considered as true, and `statement1` is executed; otherwise, `statement2` is executed.

4. An `if-else` statement can contain other `if-else` statements. In the absence of braces, each `else` is associated with the closest preceding unpaired `if`.

5. The `if-else` chain is a multiway selection statement having the general form:

```
if (expression-1)
   statement-1;
else if (expression-2)
   statement-2;
else if (expression-3)
   statement-3;
         .
         .
         .
else if (expression-m)
    statement-m;
else
    statement-n;
```

Each expression is evaluated in the order in which it appears in the chain. Once an expression is true (has a nonzero value), only the statement between that expression and the next `else if` or `else` is executed, and no further expressions are tested. The final `else` is optional, and the statement corresponding to the final `else` is only executed if none of the previous expressions is true.

6. A compound statement consists of any number of individual statements enclosed within the brace pair, { and }. Compound statements are treated as a single unit and can be used anywhere a single statement is used.

7. The `switch` statement is a multiway selection statement. The general form of a `switch` statement is:

```
switch (expression)
{      // start of compound statement
  case value-1:  ◄──────────── Terminated with a colon
    statement1;
    statement2;
          .
          .
    break;
  case value-2:  ◄──────────── Terminated with a colon
    statementm;
    statementn;
          .
          .
    break;
          .
  case value-n:  ◄──────────── Terminated with a colon
    statementw;
    statementx;
          .
          .
    break;
  default:       ◄──────────── Terminated with a colon
    statementaa;
    statementbb;
          .
          .
}      // end of switch and compound statement
```

For this statement, the value of an integer expression is compared to a number of integer or character constants or constant expressions. Program execution is transferred to the first matching case and continues through the end of the `switch` statement unless an optional `break` statement is encountered. The cases in a `switch` statement can appear in any order and an optional default case can be included. The default case is executed if none of the other cases is matched.

Exercises

1. Write C++ code sections to make the following decisions:

   a. Ask for two integer temperatures. If their values are equal, display the temperature; otherwise, do nothing.

   b. Ask for character values `letter1` and `letter2`, representing capital letters of the alphabet, and display them in alphabetical order.

   c. Ask for three integer values `num1`, `num2`, and `num3` and display them in decreasing order.

2. a. Write a C++ program to compute and display a person's weekly salary as determined by the following conditions:

   If the hours worked are less than or equal to 40, the person receives $8.00 per hour, else the person receives $320.00 plus $12.00 for each hour worked over 40 hours.

   The program should request the hours worked as input and should display the salary as output.

   b. How many runs should you make for the program written in Exercise 2a to verify that it is operating correctly? What data should you input in each of the program runs?

3. a. Write a program that displays either the message I FEEL GREAT TODAY! or I FEEL DOWN TODAY #$*! depending on the input. If the character u is entered in the variable code, the first message should be displayed, else the second message should be displayed.

   b. How many runs should you make for the program written in Exercise 3a to verify that it is operating correctly? What data should you input in each of the program runs?

4. a. A senior engineer is paid $1500 a week and a junior engineer $800 a week. Write a C++ program that accepts as input an engineer's status in the character variable status. If status equals 'S', the senior person's salary should be displayed, else the junior person's salary should be output.

   b. How many runs should you make for the program written in Exercise 4a to verify that it is operating correctly? What data should you input in each of the program runs?

5. Write a C++ program that accepts a character as input data and determines if the character is an uppercase letter. An uppercase letter is any character that is greater than or equal to 'A' and less than or equal to 'Z'. If the entered character is an uppercase letter, display the message The character just entered is an uppercase letter. If the entered letter is not uppercase, display the message The character just entered is not an uppercase letter.

6. Repeat Exercise 5 to determine if the character entered is a lowercase letter. A lowercase letter is any character greater than or equal to 'a' and less than or equal to 'z'.

7. The following program displays the message Hello there! regardless of the letter input. Determine where the error is.

```cpp
#include <iostream>

using namespace std;
int main()
{
  char letter;
  cout << "Enter a letter: ";
  cin  >> letter;
  if (letter = 'm')
    cout << "Hello there!\n";

  return 0;
}
```

8. a. Write, run, and test a C++ program that accepts a user-input integer number and determines whether it is even or odd. Display the entered number and the message `Even` or `Odd`.

b. Modify the program written for Exercise 8a to determine if the entered number is exactly divisible by a value specified by the user. That is, is it divisible by 3, 7, 13, or any other user-specified value?

9. As a part-time student, you took two courses last term. Write, run, and test a C++ program that calculates and displays your grade-point average (GPA) for the term. Your program should prompt the user to enter the grade and credit hours for each course. These should then be displayed with the lower grade first. The grade-point average for the term should be calculated and displayed. A warning message should be printed if the GPA is less than 2.0 and a congratulatory message if the GPA is 3.5 or above.

10. Write a program that gives the user only three choices: Convert from Fahrenheit to Celsius, convert from Celsius to Fahrenheit, or quit. If the third choice is selected, the program stops. If one of the first two choices is selected, the program should prompt the user for either a Fahrenheit or Celsius temperature, as appropriate, and then calculate and display the corresponding temperature. Use the conversion equations:

$$F = (9/5) \, C + 32$$
$$C = (5/9) \, (F - 32)$$

Improving Communication

11. Respond to the following memorandum:

MEMORANDUM

To: Lead Programmer

From: Head of Programming Dept.

Subject: OOP Course

Now that you have returned from a course in OOP, could you please explain what encapsulation means and why it is important in OOP?

12. Respond to the following memorandum:

MEMORANDUM

To: U. R. It

From: Lead Programmer

Subject: OOP Approach

Please provide me with a brief summary of the difference between procedural and object-oriented programming. Specifically, our latest project requires us to use dates extensively by comparing a beginning date to an ending date and determining the number of days between the two dates. What do you see as the main differences in the implementation if this is programmed procedurally as opposed to using object-oriented methods?

Working in Teams

13. Your team is responsible for analyzing a gas station pumping system. The pump itself consists of a gun, holster, pump display, and meter. Connected to the pump is the main gas tank. The tank supplies gas to the pump. The attributes of the tank are its capacity, current level, and grade of gas. The pump's attributes are the amount it dispenses and the cost of the pumped gas. The pump is enabled when the gun is removed from the holster and is disabled when the gun is replaced.

   For this description, have the team, as a group, identify potential objects in the problem. Typically, objects are identified by locating the nouns, such as pump, tank, etc., in the problem statement.

   Once you have identified potential objects, have each team member select one object and write a paragraph describing what the object does and how it interacts with other objects.

14. Your team is responsible for developing a software simulation program to model the operation of a single elevator. The elevator is capable of moving from the basement of the building it is housed in to the sixth floor, which is at the top of the building. The elevator responds to the external up and down buttons as follows:

   If the elevator is moving down and a down button is activated on a lower floor, the elevator stops at the designated floor.

   If the elevator is moving up and an up button is activated on a higher floor, the elevator stops at the designated floor.

   The external buttons are pushed by people who arrive randomly at any floor.

   Internally, the elevator responds to an activated floor button by turning on the button's light and then stopping at the next activated floor in the direction it is moving. When it reaches the designated floor, it opens the doors and turns off the internal floor button.

   For this description, have the team, as a group, identify potential objects in the problem. Typically, objects are identified by locating the nouns, such as people, button, etc., in the problem statement.

   Once you have identified potential objects, have each team member select one object and write a paragraph describing what the object does and how it interacts with other objects.

5 | Repetition Statements

The programs examined so far have illustrated the programming concepts involved in input, output, assignment, and selection capabilities. By this time, you should have gained enough experience to be comfortable with these concepts and the mechanics of implementing them using C++. Many problems, however, require a repetition capability, in which the same calculation or sequence of instructions is repeated, over and over, using different sets of data. Examples of such repetition include continual checking of user data entries until an acceptable entry, such as a valid password, is entered, counting and accumulating running totals, and constant acceptance of input data and recalculation of output values that only stop on entry of a sentinel value.

This chapter explores the different methods programmers use to construct repeating sections of code and how that code can be implemented in C++. More commonly, a section of code that is repeated is referred to as a **loop,** because after the last statement in the code is executed, the program branches, or loops, back to the first statement and starts another repetition through the code. Each repetition is also referred to as an **iteration** or **pass through the loop**.

5.1 BASIC LOOP STRUCTURES

The real power of a program is realized when the same type of operation must be made over and over. For example, consider Program 3.16 in Section 3.6, where the same set of instructions is repeated three times. Retyping this same set of instructions is tedious, time consuming, and subject to error. It is certainly more convenient to type such repeating instructions only once and then inform the program to repeat execution of the instructions three times, which we can do using repetitive sections of code.

Constructing a repetitive section of code requires that four elements be present. The first necessary element is a repetition statement. This **repetition statement** defines the boundaries containing the repeating section of code and also controls whether the code is executed or not. In general, there are three different forms of repetition statements, all of which are provided in C++:

1. `while`
2. `for`
3. `do-while`

Each of these statements requires a condition that must be evaluated, which is the second required element for constructing repeating sections of code. Valid conditions are identical to those used in selection statements. If the condition is true, the code is executed; otherwise, it is not.

The third required element is a statement that initially sets the condition. This statement must always be placed before the condition is first evaluated to ensure correct loop execution the first time the condition is evaluated.

Finally, there must be a statement within the repeating section of code that allows the condition to become false. This is necessary to ensure that, at some point, the repetitions stop.

Repetition statements can also be categorized based on the position of the condition being tested. They can also be categorized based on the type of condition being tested. These distinctions are covered below.

Pretest and Posttest Loops

The condition being tested can be evaluated at either the beginning or the end of the repeating section of code. Figure 5.1 illustrates the case where the test occurs at the beginning of the loop. This type of loop is referred to as a **pretest loop** because the condition is tested before any statements within the loop are executed. If the condition is true, the executable statements within the loop are executed. If the initial value of the condition is false, the executable statements within the loop are never executed at all and control transfers to the first statement after the loop. To avoid infinite repetitions, the condition must be updated within the loop. Pretest loops are also referred to as **entrance-controlled loops.** Both the `while` and `for` loop structures are examples of such loops.

A loop that evaluates a condition at the end of the repeating section of code, as illustrated in Figure 5.2, is referred to as a **posttest loop** or **exit-controlled loop.** Such loops always execute the loop statements at least once before the condition is tested. Since the executable statements within the loop are continually executed until the condition becomes false, there always must be a statement within the loop that updates the condition and permits it to become false. The `do-while` construct is an example of a posttest loop.

FIGURE 5.1   A Pretest Loop

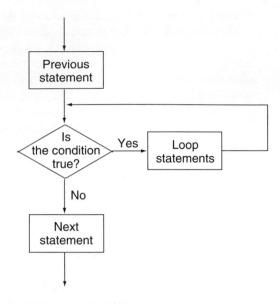

Fixed Count Versus Variable Condition Loops

In addition to where the condition is tested (pretest or posttest), repeating sections of code are also classified as to the type of condition being tested. In a **fixed count loop**, the condition is used to keep track of how many repetitions have occurred.

FIGURE 5.2   A Posttest Loop

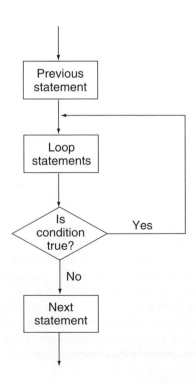

A BIT OF BACKGROUND

Comptometer Arithmetic

In the early 1900s, mechanical calculators, called *comptometers,* performed only addition. Because multiplication is simply a quick method of addition (for example, 5 times 4 is really 5 added 4 times), producing multiplication results presented no problems—the results were obtained using repeated additions. Subtraction and division, however, initially did present a problem. Clever accountants soon discovered that subtraction and division were possible. Subtraction was accomplished by writing the nine's complement on each numeric key. That is, 9 was written on the 0 key, 8 on the 1 key, 7 on the 2 key, and so on. Subtraction was then performed by adding the nine's complement numbers and then adding 1 to the result. For example, consider the subtraction problem

$$637 - 481 = 156$$

The nine's complement of 481 is 518, and

$$637 + 518 + 1 = 1,156$$

which gives the answer (156) to the problem when the leftmost carry digit is ignored.

It did not take accountants long to solve division problems using repeated subtractions—all on a machine designed to handle only additions.

Early computers, which could only perform addition, used similar algorithms for performing subtraction, multiplication, and division. They used, however, two's complement numbers rather than nine's complement. (See Section 1.6 for an introduction to two's complement numbers.)

Although many computers now come with special-purpose hardware, called floating-point processors, to perform multiplication and division directly, they still use two's complement number representation internally and perform subtraction using two's complement addition. And when a floating-point processor is not used, sophisticated software algorithms are employed that perform multiplications and divisions based on repeated additions and subtractions.

For example, we might want to produce a table of ten numbers, including their squares and cubes, or a fixed design such as:

```
**************************
**************************
**************************
**************************
```

In each of these examples, a fixed number of calculations are performed or a fixed number of lines are printed, at which point the repeating section of code is exited. All of C++'s repetition statements can be used to produce fixed count loops.

In many situations, the exact number of repetitions are not known in advance or the items are too numerous to count beforehand. For example, when entering a large amount of market research data, we might not want to take the time to count the number of actual data items to be entered. In such cases, a variable condition loop is used. In a **variable condition loop,** the tested condition does not depend on a count being achieved, but rather on a variable that can change interactively with each pass through the loop. When a specified value is encountered, regardless of how many iterations have occurred, repetitions stop. All of C++'s repetition statements can be used to create variable condition loops.[1] In this chapter, we will encounter examples of both fixed count and variable condition loops.

---

[1] In this respect, C++ differs from most other languages such as BASIC, FORTRAN, and Pascal. In those languages, the for statement (which is implemented using a DO statement in FORTRAN) can only be used to produce fixed count loops. C++'s for statement, as we will see shortly, is virtually interchangeable with its while statement.

Exercises 5.1

1. List the three repetition statements that are provided in C++.

2. List the four elements that must be present in a repetition statement.

3. a. What is an entrance-controlled loop?

    b. Which of C++'s repetition statements produce entrance-controlled loops?

4. a. What is an exit-controlled loop?

    b. Which of C++'s repetition statements produce exit-controlled loops?

5. a. What is the difference between a pretest and posttest loop?

    b. If the condition being tested in a pretest loop is false to begin with, how many times will statements internal to the loop be executed?

    c. If the condition being tested in a posttest loop is false to begin with, how many times will statements internal to the loop be executed?

6. What is the difference between a fixed count and variable-condition loop?

5.2 while LOOPS

In C++, a **while loop** is constructed using a `while` statement. The syntax of this statement is:

```
while (expression)
    statement;
```

The *expression* within parentheses is the condition tested to determine if the *statement* following the parentheses is executed. The expression is evaluated in exactly the same manner as that of an `if-else` statement; the difference is in how the expression is used. As we have seen, when the expression is true (has a nonzero value) in an `if-else` statement, the statement following the expression is executed once. In a `while` statement, the statement following the expression is executed repeatedly as long as the expression evaluates to a nonzero value. Considering just the expression and the statement following the parentheses, the process used by the computer in evaluating a `while` statement is:

1. *Test the expression*
2. *If the expression has a nonzero (true) value,*
        a. *execute the statement following the parentheses*
        b. *go back to step 1*
    else
        exit the while statement and execute the next executable statement following the while statement

Notice that step 2b forces program control to be transferred back to step 1. This transfer of control back to the start of a `while` statement to reevaluate the expression is what forms the program loop. The `while` statement literally loops back on itself to recheck the expression until it evaluates to zero (becomes false). This naturally means that somewhere in the loop provision must be made to permit the value of the tested expression to be altered. As we will see, this is indeed the case.

This looping process produced by a `while` statement is illustrated in Figure 5.3. A diamond shape is used to show the two entry and two exit points required in the decision part of the `while` statement.

FIGURE 5.3 Structure of a while Loop

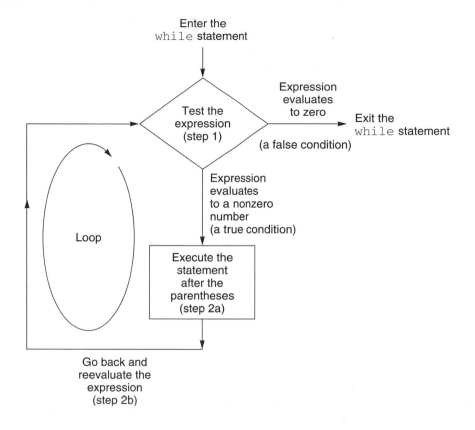

To make this more tangible, consider the relational expression count <= 10 and the statement cout << count;. Using these, we can write the following valid while statement:

```
while (count <= 10)
    cout << count;
```

Although this statement is valid, the alert reader will realize that we have created a situation in which the cout object either is called forever (or until we stop the program) or is not called at all. Let us see why this happens.

If count has a value less than or equal to 10 when the expression is first evaluated, the cout statement is executed. The while statement then automatically loops back on itself and retests the expression. Because we have not changed the value stored in count, the expression is still true and another call to cout is made. This process continues forever or until the program containing this statement is prematurely stopped by the user. However, if count starts with a value greater than 10, the expression is false to begin with and the cout object is never used.

How do we set an initial value in count to control what the while statement does the first time the expression is evaluated? The answer, of course, is to assign values to each variable in the tested expression before the while statement is encountered. For example, the following sequence of instructions is valid:

```
count = 1;
while (count <= 10)
    cout << count;
```

Using this sequence of instructions, we have ensured that count starts with a value of 1. We could assign any value to count in the assignment statement; the important thing is to assign some value. In practice, the assigned value depends on the application.

We must still change the value of count so that we can finally exit the while statement. To do this, we need an expression such as count++ to increment the value of count each time the while statement is executed. The fact that a while statement provides for the repetition of a single statement does not prevent us from including an additional statement to change the value of count. All we have to do is replace the single statement with a compound statement. For example:

```
count = 1;              // initialize count
while (count <= 10)
{
  cout << count;
  count++;              // increment count
}
```

Note that, for clarity, we have placed each statement in the compound statement on a different line. This is consistent with the convention adopted for compound statements in the last chapter. Let us now analyze the preceding sequence of instructions.

The first assignment statement sets count equal to 1. The while statement is then entered and the expression is evaluated for the first time. Since the value of count is less than or equal to 10, the expression is true and the compound statement is executed. The first statement in the compound statement uses the cout object to display the value of count. The next statement adds 1 to the value currently stored in count, making this value equal to 2. The while statement now loops back to retest the expression. Since count is still less than or equal to 10, the compound statement is again executed. This process continues until the value of count reaches 11. Program 5.1 illustrates these statements in an actual program.

PROGRAM 5.1

```
#include <iostream>
using namespace std;

int main()
{
  int count;

  count = 1;              // initialize count
  while (count <= 10)
  {
    cout << count << " ";
    count++;              // increment count
  }

  return 0;
}
```

The output for Program 5.1 is:

1 2 3 4 5 6 7 8 9 10

There is nothing special about the name count used in Program 5.1. Any valid integer variable could have been used.

Before we consider other examples of the while statement, two comments concerning Program 5.1 are in order. First, the statement count++ can be replaced with any statement that changes the value of count. A statement such as count = count + 2, for example, causes every second integer to be displayed. Second, it is the programmer's responsibility to ensure that count is changed in a way that ultimately leads to a normal exit from the while loop. For example, if we replace the expression count++ with the expression count--, the value of count never exceeds 10 and an infinite loop is created. An **infinite loop** is a loop that never ends. The computer does not reach out, touch you, and say, "Excuse me, you have created an infinite loop." It just keeps displaying numbers until you realize that the program is not working as you expected.

Now that you have some familiarity with the while statement, see if you can read and determine the output of Program 5.2.

PROGRAM 5.2

```cpp
#include <iostream>
using namespace std;

int main()
{
    int i;

    i - 10;
    while (i >= 1)
    {
        cout << i << " ";
        i--;              // subtract 1 from i
    }

    return 0;
}
```

The assignment statement in Program 5.2 initially sets the int variable i to 10. The while statement then checks to see if the value of i is greater than or equal to 1. While the expression is true, the value of i is displayed by the cout object and the value of i is decremented by 1. When i finally reaches 0, the expression is false and the program exits the while statement. Thus, the following display is obtained when Program 5.2 is run:

10 9 8 7 6 5 4 3 2 1

To illustrate the power of the while statement, consider the task of printing a table of numbers from 1 to 10 with their squares and cubes. This can be done with a simple while statement as illustrated by Program 5.3.

PROGRAM 5.3

```cpp
#include <iostream>
#include <iomanip>
using namespace std;

int main()
{
  int num;

  cout << "NUMBER    SQUARE    CUBE\n"
       << "------    ------    ----\n";

  num = 1;
  while (num < 11)
  {
    cout  << setw(3) << num << "          "
          << setw(3) << num * num        << "          "
          << setw(4) << num * num * num << endl;
    num++;   // increment num
  }

  return 0;
}
```

When Program 5.3 is run, the following display is produced:

NUMBER	SQUARE	CUBE
1	1	1
2	4	8
3	9	27
4	16	64
5	25	125
6	36	216
7	49	343
8	64	512
9	81	729
10	100	1000

Note that the expression used in Program 5.3 is num < 11. For the integer variable num, this expression is exactly equivalent to the expression num <= 10. The choice of which to use is entirely up to you.

If we want to use Program 5.3 to produce a table of 1000 numbers, all we do is change the expression in the while statement from num < 11 to num < 1001. Changing the 11 to 1001 produces a table of 1000 lines—not bad for a simple five-line while statement.

All the program examples illustrating the while statement are examples of fixed count loops because the tested condition is a counter that checks for a fixed number of repetitions. A variation on the fixed count loop can be made where the counter is not incremented by 1 each time through the loop, but by some other value. For example, consider the task of producing a Celsius-to-Fahrenheit temperature conversion table. Assume that Fahrenheit temperatures corresponding to Celsius temperatures ranging from 5 to 50 degrees are to be displayed in increments of 5 degrees. The desired display can be obtained with this series of statements:

```
celsius = 5;      // starting Celsius value
while (celsius <= 50)
{
  fahren = (9.0/5.0) * celsius + 32.0;
  cout << celsius
       << fahren;
  celsius = celsius + 5;
}
```

PROGRAM 5.4

```cpp
#include <iostream>
#include <iomanip>
using namespace std;

// a program to convert Celsius to Fahrenheit
int main()
{
  const int MAXCELSIUS = 50;
  const int STARTVAL = 5;
  const int STEPSIZE = 5;

  int celsius;
  double fahren;

  cout << "DEGREES    DEGREES\n"
       << "CELSIUS    FAHRENHEIT\n"
       << "-------    ----------\n";

  celsius = STARTVAL;

    // set output formats for floating-point numbers only
  cout << setiosflags(ios::showpoint)
       << setprecision(2);

  while (celsius <= MAXCELSIUS)
  {
    fahren = (9.0/5.0) * celsius + 32.0;
    cout << setw(4) << celsius
         << setw(13) << fahren << endl;
    celsius = celsius + STEPSIZE;
  }

  return 0;
}
```

As before, the `while` statement consists of everything from the word `while` through the closing brace of the compound statement. Prior to entering the `while` loop, we have made sure we assigned a value to the counter being evaluated, and there is a statement to alter the value of the counter within the loop (in increments of 5) to ensure an exit from the `while` loop. Program 5.4 illustrates the use of this code in a complete program. The display obtained when Program 5.4 is executed is:

```
DEGREES     DEGREES
CELSIUS    FAHRENHEIT
-------    ----------
   5          41.00
  10          50.00
  15          59.00
  20          68.00
  25          77.00
  30          86.00
  35          95.00
  40         104.00
  45         113.00
  50         122.00
```

Exercises 5.2

1. Rewrite Program 5.1 to print the numbers 2 to 10 in increments of 2. The output of your program should be:

   2   4   6   8   10

2. Rewrite Program 5.4 to produce a table that starts at a Celsius value of −10 and ends with a Celsius value of 60 in increments of 10 degrees.

3. a. For the following code, determine the total number of items displayed. Also determine the first and last numbers printed.

```
int num = 0;
while (num <= 20)
{
    num++;
    cout << num << " ";
}
```

   b. Enter and run the code from Exercise 3a within the context of a complete program to verify your answers to the exercise.

   c. How is the output affected if the two statements within the compound statement were reversed (that is, if the `cout` call were made before the `n++` statement)?

4. Write a C++ program that converts gallons to liters. The program should display gallons from 10 to 20 in 1-gallon increments and the corresponding liter equivalents. Use the relationship that 1 gallon contains 3.785 liters.

5. Write a C++ program to produce the following display:

```
0
 1
  2
   3
    4
     5
      6
       7
        8
         9
```

6. Write a C++ program to produce the following displays:

a. ****
   ****
     ****
       ****

b.   ****
  ****
  ****
  ****

7. Write a C++ program that converts feet to meters. The program should display feet from 3 to 30 in 3-foot increments and the corresponding meter equivalents. Use the relationship that there are 3.28 feet to a meter.

8. A machine purchased for $28,000 is depreciated at a rate of $4000 a year for 7 years. Write and run a C++ program that computes and displays a depreciation table for 7 years. The table should have the form:

Year	Depreciation	End-of-Year Value	Accumulated Depreciation
1	4000	24000	4000
2	4000	20000	8000
3	4000	16000	12000
4	4000	12000	16000
5	4000	8000	20000
6	4000	4000	24000
7	4000	0	28000

9. An automobile travels at an average speed of 55 miles per hour for 4 hours. Write a C++ program that displays the distance driven, in miles, that the car has traveled after .5, 1, 1.5, 2, etc., hours until the end of the trip.

10. a. An approximate conversion formula for converting Fahrenheit to Celsius temperatures is:

$$\text{Celsius} = (\text{Fahrenheit} - 30) / 2$$

Using this formula and starting with a Fahrenheit temperature of 0 degrees, write a C++ program that determines when the approximate equivalent Celsius temperature differs from the exact equivalent value by more than 4 degrees. (*Hint:* Use a while loop that terminates when the difference between approximate and exact Celsius equivalents exceeds 4 degrees.)

b. Using the approximate Celsius conversion formula given in Exercise 10a, write a C++ program that produces a table of Fahrenheit temperatures, exact Celsius equivalent temperatures, approximate Celsius equivalent temperatures, and the difference between the correct and approximate equivalent Celsius values. The table should begin at 0 degrees Fahrenheit, use 2-degree Fahrenheit increments, and terminate when the difference between exact and approximate values differs by more than 4 degrees.

11. Write a C++ program to find the sum, sum of squares, and sum of cubes of the first n integers, beginning with 1 and ending with $n = 100$. Verify that in each case:

$$1 + 2 + 3 + \ldots + n = n(n + 1)/2$$
$$1^2 + 2^2 + 3^2 + \ldots + n^2 = n(n + 1)(2n + 1)/6$$
$$1^3 + 2^3 + 3^3 + \ldots + n^3 = n^2(n + 1)^2/4$$

12. Write a C++ program to find the sum of the first 100 terms in the series:

$$1/(1 * 2) + 1/(2 * 3) + 1/(3 * 4) + \ldots + 1/[n*(n + 1)]$$

Verify that the sum equals $n/(n + 1)$. Determine the value that the sum approaches as n gets infinitely large.

5.3 INTERACTIVE while LOOPS

Combining interactive data entry with the repetition capabilities of the while statement produces very adaptable and powerful programs. To understand the concept involved, consider Program 5.5, in which a while statement is used to accept and then display four user-entered numbers, one at a time. Although it uses a very simple idea, the program highlights the flow of control concepts needed to produce more useful programs.

PROGRAM 5.5

```cpp
#include <iostream>
#include <iomanip>
using namespace std;

int main()
{
 const int MAXNUMS = 4;

 int count;
 double num;

 cout << "\nThis program will ask you to enter "
      << MAXNUMS << " numbers.\n";
 count = 1;

 cout << setiosflags(ios::fixed) << setprecision(3);

 while (count <= MAXNUMS)
 {
   cout << "\nEnter a number: ";
   cin  >> num;
   cout << "The number entered is " << num;
   count++;
 }
 cout << endl;

 return 0;
}
```

The following is a sample run of Program 5.5. The italicized items were input in response to the appropriate prompts.

```
This program will ask you to enter 4 numbers.

Enter a number: 26.2
The number entered is 26.200
Enter a number: 5
The number entered is 5.000
Enter a number: 103.456
The number entered is 103.456
Enter a number: 1267.89
The number entered is 1267.890
```

Let us review the program so we clearly understand how the output was produced. The first message displayed is caused by execution of the first cout object call. This call is outside and before the while statement, so it is executed once before any statement in the while loop.

Once the while loop is entered, the statements within the compound statement are executed while the tested condition is true. The first time through the compound statement, the message Enter a number: is displayed. The program then calls cin, which forces the computer to wait for a number to be entered at the keyboard. Once a number is typed and the return or enter key is pressed, the cout object displays the number. The variable count is then incremented by one. This continues until four passes through the loop are made and the value of count is 5. Each pass causes the message Enter a number: to be displayed, causes one call to cin to be made, and causes the message The number entered is to be displayed. Figure 5.4 illustrates this flow of control.

Rather than simply displaying the entered numbers, Program 5.5 can be made to use the entered data. For example, let us add the numbers entered and display the total. To do this, we must be very careful about how we add the numbers, since the same variable, num, is used for each number entered. Because of this, the entry of a new number in Program 5.5 automatically causes the previous number stored in num to be lost. Thus, each number entered must be added to the total before another number is entered. The required sequence is:

Enter a number
Add the number to the total

How do we add a single number to a total? A statement such as total = total + num does the job perfectly. This is the accumulating statement introduced in Section 3.1. After each number is entered, the accumulating statement adds the number into the total, as illustrated in Figure 5.5. The complete flow of control required for adding the numbers is illustrated in Figure 5.6. In reviewing Figure 5.6, note that we have made a provision for initially setting the total to zero before the while loop is entered. If we were to clear the total inside the while loop, it would be set to zero each time the loop was executed, and any value previously stored would be erased.

Program 5.6 incorporates the necessary modifications to Program 5.5 to total the numbers entered. As indicated in the flow diagram shown in Figure 5.6, the statement total = total + num; is placed immediately after the cin object call. Putting the accumulating statement at this point in the program ensures that the entered number is immediately "captured" by the total.

Let us review Program 5.6. The variable total was created to store the total of the numbers entered. Prior to entering the while statement, the value of total is set to zero. This ensures that any previous value present in the storage location(s) assigned to the variable total is erased. Within the while loop, the statement total = total + num; is used to add the value of the entered number into total. As each value is entered, it is added into the existing total to create a new total. Thus, total becomes a running subtotal of all the values entered. Only when all numbers are entered does total contain the final sum of all the numbers. After the while loop is finished, the last cout statement is used to display this sum.

PROGRAM 5.6

```cpp
#include <iostream>
#include <iomanip>
using namespace std;

int main()
{
  const int MAXNUMS = 4;

  int count;
  double num, total;

  cout << "\nThis program will ask you to enter "
       << MAXNUMS << " numbers.\n";
  count = 1;
  total = 0;

  cout << set iosflags(ios::fixed) << setprecision(3);

  while (count <= MAXNUMS)
  {
    cout << "\nEnter a number: ";
    cin  >> num;
    total = total + num;
    cout << "The total is now " << total;
    count++;
  }

  cout << "\n\nThe final total is " << total << endl;

  return 0;
}
```

Using the same data we entered in the sample run for Program 5.5, the following sample run of Program 5.6 was made:

```
This program will ask you to enter 4 numbers.

Enter a number: 26.2
The total is now 26.200
Enter a number: 5
The total is now 31.200
Enter a number: 103.456
The total is now 134.656
Enter a number: 1267.89
The total is now 1402.546

The final total is 1402.546
```

Having used an accumulating assignment statement to add the numbers entered, we can now go further and calculate the average of the numbers. Where do we calculate the average: within the `while` loop or outside of it?

FIGURE 5.4   Flow of Control for Program 5.5

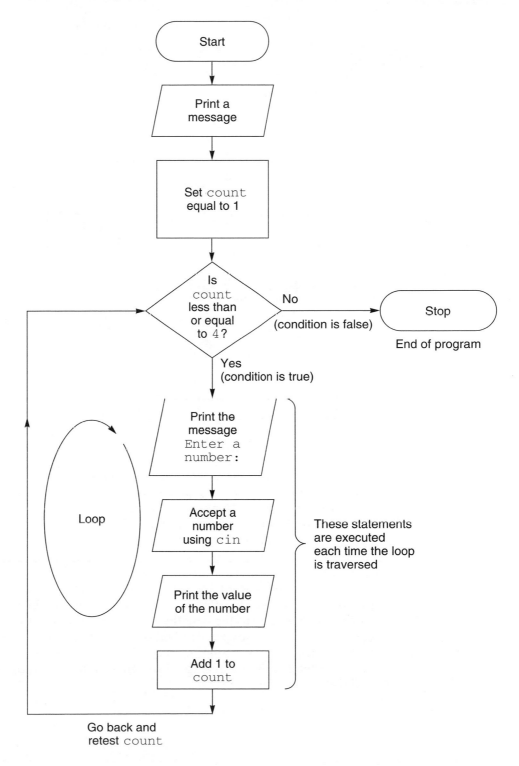

FIGURE 5.5   Accepting and Adding a Number to a Total

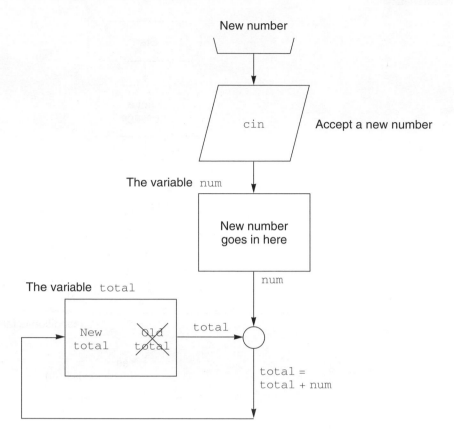

In the case at hand, calculating an average requires that both a final sum and the number of items in that sum be available. The average is then computed by dividing the final sum by the number of items. At this point, we must ask, "At what point in the program is the correct sum available, and at what point is the number of items available?" In reviewing Program 5.6, we see that the correct sum needed for calculating the average is available after the while loop is finished. In fact, the whole purpose of the while loop is to ensure that the numbers are entered and added correctly to produce a correct sum. After the loop is finished, we also have a count of the number of items used in the sum. However, due to the way the while loop was constructed, the number in count (5) when the loop is finished is 1 more than the number of items (4) used to obtain the total. Knowing this, we simply subtract 1 from count before using it to determine the average. With this as background, see if you can read and understand Program 5.7.

FIGURE 5.6 Accumulation Flow of Control

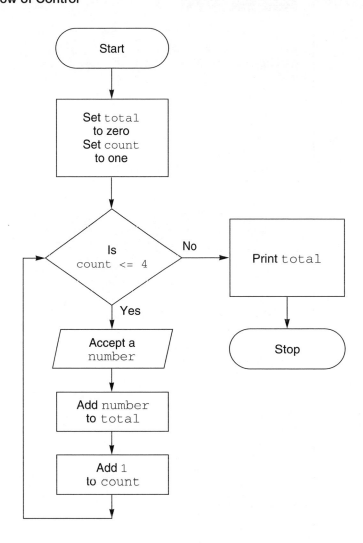

Program 5.7 is almost identical to Program 5.6, except for the calculation of the average. We have also removed the constant display of the total within and after the `while` loop. The loop in Program 5.7 is used to enter and add four numbers. Immediately after the loop is exited, the average is computed and displayed. A sample run of Program 5.7 follows:

```
This program will ask you to enter 4 numbers.

Enter a number: 26.2
Enter a number: 5
Enter a number: 103.456
Enter a number: 1267.89

The average of the numbers is 350.637
```

PROGRAM 5.7

```cpp
#include <iostream>
#include <iomanip>
using namespace std;

int main()
{
  const int MAXNUMS = 4;

  int count;
  double num, total, average;

  cout << "\nThis program will ask you to enter "
       << MAXNUMS << " numbers.\n\n";
  count = 1;
  total = 0;

  cout << setiosflags(ios::fixed) << setprecision(3);

  while (count <= MAXNUMS)
  {
    cout << "Enter a number: ";
    cin  >> num;
    total = total + num;
    count++;
  }

  count--;
  average = total / count;
  cout << "\nThe average of the numbers is " << average << endl;

  return 0;
}
```

Sentinels

All of the loops we have created thus far have been examples of fixed count loops, where a counter has been used to control the number of loop iterations. By means of a `while` statement, variable condition loops may also be constructed. For example, when entering grades, we may not want to count the number of grades that will be entered, but prefer to enter the grades continuously and, at the end, type in a special data value to signal the end of data input.

In computer programming, data values used to signal either the start or end of a data series are called **sentinels**. The sentinel values must, of course, be selected so as not to conflict with legitimate data values. For example, if we were constructing a program to process a student's grades (assume that no extra credit is given that could produce a grade higher than 100), we could use any grade higher than 100 as a sentinel value. Program 5.8 illustrates this concept. In Program 5.8, data are continuously requested and accepted until a number larger than 100 is entered. Entry of a number higher than 100 alerts the program to exit the `while` loop and display the sum of the numbers entered.

We show a sample run using Program 5.8 next. As long as grades less than or equal to 100 are entered, the program continues to request and accept additional data. When a number less than or equal to 100 is entered, the program adds this number to the total. When a number greater than 100 is entered, the while loop is exited and the sum of the grades that were entered is displayed.

```
To stop entering grades, type in any number greater than 100.

Enter a grade: 95
Enter a grade: 100
Enter a grade: 82
Enter a grade: 101

The total of the grades is 277
```

PROGRAM 5.8

```cpp
#include <iostream>
using namespace std;

const int HIGHGRADE = 100;

int main()
{
  double grade, total;

  grade = 0;
  total = 0;
  cout << "\nTo stop entering grades, type in any number";
  cout << "\n greater than 100.\n\n";

  cout << "Enter a grade: ";
  cin  >> grade;

  while (grade <= HIGHGRADE)
  {
    total = total + grade;
    cout << "Enter a grade: ";
    cin  >> grade;
  }

  cout << "\nThe total of the grades is " << total << endl;

  return 0;
}
```

break **and** continue **Statements**

Two useful statements in connection with repetition statements are the **break** and **continue statements**. We encountered the break statement when we studied the switch statement. The general form of this statement is:

```
break;
```

A break statement, as its name implies, forces an immediate break, or exit, from the switch, while, for, and do-while statements presented in the next sections.

For example, execution of the following `while` loop is immediately terminated if a number greater than 76 is entered:

```
while(count <= 10)
{
  cout << "Enter a number: ";
  cin  >> num;
  if (num > 76)
  {
    cout << "You lose!\n";
    break;         // break out of the loop
  }
  else
    cout << "Keep on trucking!\n";
  count++;
}
// break jumps to here
```

The `break` statement violates pure structured programming principles because it provides a second, nonstandard exit from a loop. Nevertheless, it is extremely useful and valuable for breaking out of loops when an unusual condition is detected. The `break` statement is also used to exit from a `switch` statement, but this is because the desired case has been detected and processed.

The `continue` statement is similar to the break statement but applies only to loops created with `while`, `do-while`, and `for` statements. The general format of a continue statement is:

```
continue;
```

When a `continue` statement is encountered in a loop, the next iteration of the loop begins immediately. For `while` loops, this means that execution is automatically transferred to the top of the loop and reevaluation of the tested expression is initiated. Although the `continue` statement has no direct effect on a `switch` statement, it can be included within a `switch` statement that itself is contained in a loop. Here, the effect of `continue` is the same: The next loop iteration begins.

As a general rule, the `continue` statement is less useful than the `break` statement, but it is convenient for skipping over data that should not be processed while remaining in a loop. For example, invalid grades are simply ignored in the following section of code, and only valid grades are added to the total:[2]

```
while (count < 30)
{
  cout << "Enter a grade: ";
  cin  >> grade;
  if(grade < 0 || grade > 100)
    continue;
  total = total + grade;
  count++;
}
```

---

[2] The `continue` is not essential, however, and the selection could have been written as:

```
if (grade >= 0 && grade <= 100)
{
  total = total + grade;
  count++;
}
```

The Null Statement

All statements must be terminated by a semicolon. A semicolon with nothing preceding it is also a valid statement, called the **null statement**. Thus, the statement

;

is a null statement. This is a do-nothing statement that is used where a statement is syntactically required, but no action is called for. Null statements typically are used either with while or for statements. An example of a for statement that uses a null statement is found in Program 5.10c in the next section.

Exercises 5.3

1. Rewrite Program 5.6 to compute the total of eight numbers.

2. Rewrite Program 5.6 to display the prompt:

   ```
   Please type in the total number of data values to be added:
   ```

   In response to this prompt, the program should accept a user-entered number and then use this number to control the number of times the while loop is executed. Thus, if the user enters 5 in response to the prompt, the program should request the input of five numbers and display the total after five numbers have been entered.

3. a. Write a C++ program to convert Celsius degrees to Fahrenheit. The program should request the starting Celsius value, the number of conversions to be made, and the increment between Celsius values. The display should have appropriate headings and list the Celsius value and the corresponding Fahrenheit value. Use the relationship *Fahrenheit = (9.0 / 5.0) * Celsius + 32.0.*

   b. Run the program written in Exercise 3a on a computer. Verify that your program begins at the correct starting Celsius value and contains the exact number of conversions specified in your input data.

4. a. Modify the program written in Exercise 3a to request the starting Celsius value, the ending Celsius value, and the increment. Thus, instead of the condition checking for a fixed count, the condition checks for the ending Celsius value.

   b. Run the program written in Exercise 4a on a computer. Verify that your output starts at the correct beginning value and ends at the correct ending value.

5. Rewrite Program 5.7 to compute the average of ten numbers.

6. Rewrite Program 5.7 to display the prompt:

   ```
   Please type in the total number of data values to be averaged:
   ```

   In response to this prompt, the program should accept a user-entered number and then use this number to control the number of times the while loop is executed. Thus, if the user enters 6 in response to the prompt, the program should request the input of six numbers and display the average of the next six numbers entered.

7. By mistake, a programmer put the statement average = total / count; within the while loop immediately after the statement total = total + num; in Program 5.7. Thus, the while loop becomes:

   ```
   while (count <= MAXNUMS)
   {
     cout << "Enter a number: ";
     cin  >> num;
     total = total + num;
     average = total / count;
     count++;
   }
   ```

Will the program yield the correct result with this `while` loop? If so, which `while` loop is better to use from a programming perspective, and why?

8. An arithmetic series is defined by

$$a + (a + d) + (a + 2d) + (a + 3d) + \ldots + (a + (n - 1)d)$$

where a is the first term, d is the "common difference," and n is the number of terms to be added. Using this information, write a C++ program that uses a `while` loop to display each term and determine the sum of the arithmetic series having $a = 1$, $d = 3$, and $n = 15$. Make sure that your program displays the value it has calculated.

9. A geometric series is defined by

$$a + ar + ar^2 + ar^3 + \ldots + ar^{n-1}$$

where a is the first term, r is the "common ratio," and n is the number of terms in the series. Using this information, write a C++ program that uses a `while` loop to display each term and determine the sum of a geometric series having $a = 1$, $r = .5$, and $n = 10$. Make sure that your program displays the value it has calculated.

10. In addition to the arithmetic average of a set of numbers, both a geometric and a harmonic mean can be calculated. The geometric mean of a set of n numbers $x_1, x_2, \ldots x_n$ is defined as

$$\sqrt[n]{x_1 \cdot x_2 \cdot \ldots \cdot x_n}$$

and the harmonic mean as:

$$\frac{n}{\dfrac{1}{x_1} + \dfrac{1}{x_2} + \ldots + \dfrac{1}{x_n}}$$

Using these formulas, write a C++ program that continues to accept numbers until the number 999 is entered and then calculates and displays both the geometric and harmonic means of the entered numbers. (*Hint:* It is necessary for your program to correctly count the number of values entered.)

11. a. The following data were collected on a recent automobile trip:

	Mileage	Gallons
Start of trip:	22495	Full tank
	22841	12.2
	23185	11.3
	23400	10.5
	23772	11.0
	24055	12.2
	24434	14.7
	24804	14.3
	25276	15.2

Write a C++ program that accepts mileage and gallons values and calculates the miles per gallon (mpg) achieved for that segment of the trip. The mpg is the difference in mileage between fill-ups divided by the number of gallons of gasoline received in the fill-up.

b. Modify the program written for Exercise 11a to additionally compute and display the cumulative mpg achieved after each fill-up. The cumulative mpg is the difference between each fill-up mileage and the mileage at the start of the trip divided by the sum of the gallons used to that point in the trip.

12. a. A bookstore summarizes its monthly transactions by keeping the following information for each book in stock:

   Book identification number
   Inventory balance at the beginning of the month
   Number of copies received during the month
   Number of copies sold during the month

   Write a C++ program that accepts these data for each book and then displays the book identification number and an updated book inventory balance using the relationship:

   new balance = inventory balance at the beginning of the month
   + number of copies received during the month
   − number of copies sold during the month

   Your program should use a while loop with a fixed count condition so that information on only three books is requested.

   b. Run the program written in Exercise 12a on a computer. Review the display produced by your program and verify that the output produced is correct.

13. Modify the program you wrote for Exercise 12a to keep requesting and displaying results until a sentinel identification value of 999 is entered. Run the program on a computer.

5.4 for **LOOPS**

In C++, a **for loop** is constructed using a for statement. This statement performs the same functions as the while statement, but it uses a different form. In many situations, especially those that use a fixed count condition, the for statement format is easier to use than its while statement equivalent.

The general form of the for statement is:

```
for (initializing list; expression; altering list)
   statement;
```

Although the for statement looks a little complicated, it is really quite simple if we consider each of its parts separately.

Within the parentheses of the for statement are three items separated by semicolons. Each of these items is optional and can be described individually, but the semicolons must be present.

In its most common form, the initializing list consists of a single statement used to set the starting (initial) value of a counter, the expression contains the maximum or minimum value the counter can have and determines when the loop is finished, and the altering list provides the increment value that is added to or subtracted from the counter each time the loop is executed. Examples of simple for statements having this form are:

```
for (count = 1; count < 10; count = count + 1)
   cout << count;
```

and

```
for (i = 5; i <= 15; i = i + 2)
   cout << i;
```

In the first `for` statement, the counter variable is named `count`, the initial value assigned to `count` is 1, the loop continues as long as the value in `count` is less than 10, and the value of `count` is incremented by 1 each time through the loop. In the next `for` statement, the counter variable is named `i`, the initial value assigned to `i` is 5, the loop continues as long as `i`'s value is less than or equal to 15, and the value of `i` is incremented by 2 each time through the loop. In both cases, a `cout` statement is used to display the value of the counter. Another example of a `for` loop is given in Program 5.9.

PROGRAM 5.9

```cpp
#include <iostream>
#include <iomanip>
#include <cmath>
using namespace std;

int main()
{
  const int MAXCOUNT = 5;

  int count;

  cout << "NUMBER    SQUARE ROOT\n";
  cout << "------    -----------\n";

  cout << setiosflags(ios::showpoint);
  for (count = 1; count <= MAXCOUNT; count++)
    cout << setw(4) << count
         << setw(15) << sqrt(double(count)) << endl;

  return 0;
}
```

When Program 5.9 is executed, the following display is produced:

```
NUMBER    SQUARE ROOT
------    -----------
    1       1.00000
    2       1.41421
    3       1.73205
    4       2.00000
    5       2.23607
```

The first two lines displayed by the program are produced by the two `cout` statements placed before the `for` statement. The remaining output is produced by the `for` loop. This loop begins with the `for` statement and is executed as follows:

The initial value assigned to the counter variable `count` is 1. Because the value in `count` does not exceed the final value of 5, the execution of the `cout` statement within the loop produces the display:

```
    1       1.00000
```

Control is then transferred back to the for statement, which then increments the value in count to 2, and the loop is repeated, producing the display:

2   1.41421

This process continues until the value in count exceeds the final value of 5, producing the complete output table. For comparison purposes, a while loop equivalent to the for loop contained in Program 5.9 is:

```
count = 1;
while (count <= MAXCOUNT)
{
  cout << setw(4) << count
       << setw(15) << setiosflags(ios::showpoint)
       << sqrt(count) << endl;
  count++;
}
```

As seen in this example, the difference between the for and while loops is the placement of the initialization, condition test, and incrementing items. The grouping of these items in the for statement is very convenient when fixed count loops must be constructed. See if you can determine the output produced by Program 5.10.

PROGRAM 5.10

```
#include <iostream>
using namespace std;

int main()
{
  int count;

  for (count = 2; count <= 20; count = count + 2)
    cout << count << " ";

  return 0;
}
```

Did you figure it out? The loop starts with count initialized to 2, stops when count exceeds 20, and increments count in steps of 2. The output of Program 5.10 is:

2 4 6 8 10 12 14 16 18 20

The for statement does not require that any of the items in parentheses be present or that they be used for initializing or altering the values in the expression statements. However, the two semicolons must be present within the for's parentheses. For example, the construction for (; count <= 20 ;) is valid.

If the initializing list is missing, the initialization step is omitted when the for statement is executed. This, of course, means that the programmer must provide the required initializations before the for statement is encountered. Similarly, if the altering list is missing, any expressions needed to alter the evaluation of the tested expression must be included directly within the statement part of the loop.

The `for` statement only ensures that all expressions in the initializing list are executed once before evaluation of the tested expression and that all expressions in the altering list are executed at the end of the loop before the tested expression is rechecked. Thus, Program 5.10 can be rewritten in any of the three ways shown in Programs 5.10a, 5.10b, and 5.10c.

PROGRAM 5.10a

```
#include <iostream>
using namespace std;

int main()
{
  int count;

  count = 2;    // initializer outside for statement
  for ( ; count <= 20; count = count + 2)
    cout << count << " ";

  return 0;
}
```

PROGRAM 5.10b

```
#include <iostream>
using namespace std;

int main()
{
  int count;

  count = 2;    // initializer outside for loop
  for( ; count <= 20; )
  {
    cout << count << " ";
    count = count + 2;      // alteration statement
  }

  return 0;
}
```

In Program 5.10a, `count` is initialized outside the `for` statement and the first list inside the parentheses is left blank. In Program 5.10b, both the initializing list and the altering list are removed from within the parentheses. Program 5.10b also uses a compound statement within the `for` loop, with the expression-altering statement included in the compound statement. Finally, Program 5.10c has included all items within the parentheses, so there is no need for any useful statement following the parentheses. Here, the null statement satisfies the syntactical requirement of one statement to follow the `for`'s parentheses.

PROGRAM 5.10c

```cpp
#include <iostream>
using namespace std;

int main()    // all expressions within the for's parentheses
{
  int count;

  for (count = 2; count <= 20; cout << count << "  ", count = count + 2);

  return 0;
}
```

Observe also in Program 5.10c that the altering list (last set of items in parentheses) consists of two items and that a comma separates these items. The use of commas to separate items in both the initializing and altering lists is required if either of these two lists contains more than one item. Finally, note the fact that Programs 5.10a, 5.10b, and 5.10c are all inferior to Program 5.10, and although you may encounter them in your programming career, you should not use them. Adding items other than loop control variables and their updating conditions within the for statement tends to confuse program readability and can introduce unwanted effects. Keeping the loop control structure "clean," as is done in Program 5.10, is an important programming practice.

Although the initializing and altering lists can be omitted from a for statement, omitting the tested expression results in an infinite loop. For example, such a loop is created by the statement:

```cpp
for (count - 2;  ; count - count + 1)
   cout << count;
```

As with the while statement, both break and continue statements can be used within a for loop. A break forces an immediate exit from the for loop, as it does in the while loop. A continue, however, forces control to be passed to the altering list in a for statement, after which the tested expression is reevaluated. This differs from the action of a continue in a while statement, where control is passed directly to the reevaluation of the tested expression.

Figure 5.7 illustrates the internal workings of a for loop. As shown, when the for loop is completed, control is transferred to the first executable statement following the loop. To avoid the necessity of always illustrating these steps, a simplified set of flowchart symbols is available for describing for loops. Using the fact that a for statement can be represented by the flowchart symbol

for statement

complete for loops can be alternatively illustrated as shown in Figure 5.8.

To understand the enormous power of for loops, consider the task of printing a table of numbers from 1 to 10, including their squares and cubes, using this statement. Such a table was previously produced using a while loop in Program 5.3. You may wish to review Program 5.3 and compare it to Program 5.11 to get a further sense of the equivalence between for and while loops.

FIGURE 5.7   for **Loop Flowchart**

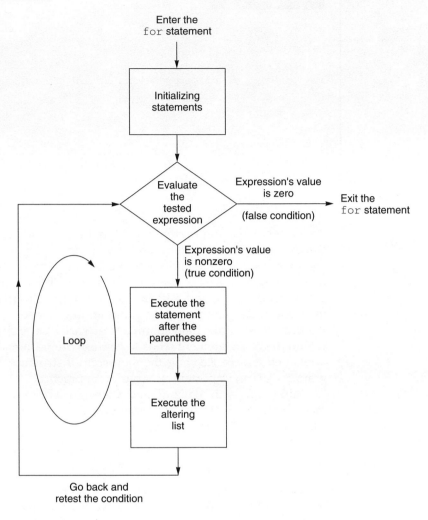

FIGURE 5.8   Simplified for **Loop Flowchart**

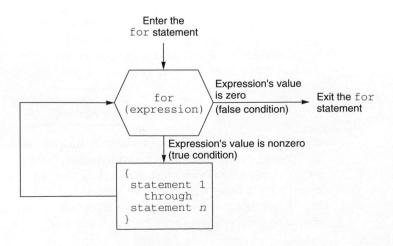

> ## PROGRAMMING NOTE
>
> **Do You Use a** for **or** while **Loop?**
> A commonly asked question by beginning programmers is which loop structure should they use: a for or while loop? This is a good question because both of these loop structures are pretest loops that, in C++, can be used to construct both fixed count and variable condition loops.
>
> In almost all other computer languages the answer is relatively straightforward because the for statement can only be used to construct fixed count loops. Thus, in most other languages, for statements are used to construct fixed count loops, and while statements are generally used only when constructing variable condition loops.
>
> In C++, this easy distinction does not hold, since each statement can be used to create each type of loop. The answer in C++, then, is really a matter of style. Since for and while loops are interchangeable in C++, either loop is appropriate. Some professional programmers always use a for statement for every pretest loop they create and almost never use a while statement; others always use a while statement and rarely use a for statement. Still a third group tends to retain the convention used in other languages: A for loop is generally used to create fixed count loops, and a while loop is used to create variable condition loops. In C++, it is all a matter of style, and you will encounter all three styles in your programming career.

PROGRAM 5.11

```cpp
#include <iostream>
#include <iomanip>
using namespace std;

int main()
{
  const int MAXNUMS = 10;
  int num;

  cout << "NUMBER    SQUARE    CUBE\n"
       << "------    ------    ----\n";

  for (num = 1; num <= MAXNUMS; num++)
    cout << setw(3) << num << "          "
         << setw(3) << num * num << "        "
         << setw(4) << num * num * num << endl;

  return 0;
}
```

PROGRAMMING NOTE

Where to Place the Opening Braces

There are two styles of writing `for` loops that are used by professional C++ programmers. These styles only come into play when the `for` loop contains a compound statement. The style illustrated and used in the text takes the form:

```
for (expression)
{
   compound statement in here
}
```

An equally acceptable style that is used by many programmers places the initial brace of the compound statement on the first line. Using this style, a `for` loop appears as:

```
for (expression) {
   compound statement in here
}
```

The advantage of the first style is that the braces line up under one another, making it easier to locate brace pairs. The advantage of the second style is that it makes the code more compact and saves a display line, permitting more code to be viewed in the same display area. Both styles are used but are almost never intermixed. Select whichever style appeals to you or is specified by your professor or place of work, and be consistent in its use. As always, the indentation you use within the compound statement (two or four spaces, or a tab) should also be consistent throughout all of your programs. The combination of styles that you select becomes a "signature" for your programming work.

When Program 5.11 is run, the display produced is:

NUMBER	SQUARE	CUBE
1	1	1
2	4	8
3	9	27
4	16	64
5	25	125
6	36	216
7	49	343
8	64	512
9	81	729
10	100	1000

Simply changing 10 to 1000 in the `for` statement of Program 5.11 creates a loop that is executed 1000 times and produces a table of numbers from 1 to 1000. As with the `while` statement, this small change produces an immense increase in the processing and output provided by the program. Notice that the expression `num++` was used in the altering list in place of the usual `num = num + 1`.

Exercises 5.4

1. Write individual for statements for the following cases:

   a. Use a counter named i that has an initial value of 1, a final value of 20, and an increment of 1.

   b. Use a counter named icount that has an initial value of 1, a final value of 20, and an increment of 2.

   c. Use a counter named j that has an initial value of 1, a final value of 100, and an increment of 5.

   d. Use a counter named icount that has an initial value of 20, a final value of 1, and an increment of −1.

   e. Use a counter named icount that has an initial value of 20, a final value of 1, and an increment of −2.

   f. Use a counter named count that has an initial value of 1.0, a final value of 16.2, and an increment of 0.2.

   g. Use a counter named xcnt that has an initial value of 20.0, a final value of 10.0, and an increment of −0.5.

2. Determine the number of times each for loop is executed for the for statements written for Exercise 1.

3. Determine the value in total after each of the following loops is executed:

   a.
   ```
   total = 0;
   for (i = 1; i <= 10; i = i + 1)
      total = total + 1;
   ```

   b.
   ```
   total = 1;
   for (count = 1; count <= 10; count = count + 1)
      total = total * 2;
   ```

   c.
   ```
   total = 0;
   for ( i = 10; i <= 15; i = i + 1)
      total = total + i;
   ```

   d.
   ```
   total = 50;
   for (i = 1; i <= 10; i = i + 1)
      total = total - i;
   ```

   e.
   ```
   total = 1;
   for (icnt = 1; icnt <= 8; icnt++)
      total = total * icnt;
   ```

   f.
   ```
   total = 1.0;
   for (j = 1; j <= 5; j++)
      total = total / 2.0;
   ```

4. Determine the output of the following program:

   ```
   #include <iostream>
   using namespace std;

   int main()
   {
     int i;

     for (i = 20; i >= 0; i = i - 4)
        cout << i << " ";

     return 0;
   }
   ```

5. Modify Program 5.11 to produce a table of the numbers 0 through 20 in increments of 2 with their squares and cubes.

6. Modify Program 5.11 to produce a table of numbers from 10 to 1, instead of 1 to 10 as it currently does.

7. Write and run a C++ program that displays a table of 20 temperature conversions from Fahrenheit to Celsius. The table should start with a Fahrenheit value of 20 degrees and be incremented in values of 4 degrees. Recall that *Celsius = (5.0/9.0) * (Fahrenheit − 32)*.

8. Modify the program written for Exercise 7 to initially request the number of conversions to be made.

9. A programmer starts with a salary of $25,000 and expects to receive a $1500 raise each year.

   a. Write a C++ program to compute and print the programmer's salary for each of the first 10 years and the total amount of money the programmer receives over the 10-year period.

   b. Write a C++ program to compute and print the programmer's salary for 10 years if the programmer begins at $25,000 and receives a 5% raise each year.

10. The probability that an individual telephone call will last less than *t* minutes can be approximated by the exponential probability function

   $$\text{probability that a call lasts less than } t \text{ minutes} = 1 - e^{-t/a}$$

   where *a* is the average call length and *e* is Euler's number (2.71828). For example, assuming that the average call length is 2 minutes, the probability that a call lasts less than 1 minute is calculated as $1 - e^{-1/2} = 0.3297$.

   Using this probability function, write a C++ program that calculates and displays a list of probabilities of a call lasting less than 1 to less than 10 minutes, in 1-minute increments.

11. a. The arrival rate of customers in a busy New York bank can be estimated using the Poisson probability function:

   $$P(x) = \frac{\lambda^x e^{-2}}{x!}$$

   where *x* = the number of customer arrivals per minute, λ = the average number of arrivals per minute, and *e* = Euler's number (2.71828). For example, if the average number of customers entering the bank is three per minute, then λ is equal to three. Thus:

   $$\text{probability of one customer arriving in any 1 minute} =$$

   $$P(x = 1) = \frac{3^1 e^{-3}}{1!} = 0.149361$$

   and

   $$\text{probability of two customers arriving in any 1 minute} =$$

   $$P(x = 2) = \frac{3^2 e^{-3}}{2!} = 0.224042$$

   Using the Poisson probability function, write a C++ program that calculates and displays the probability of 1 to 10 customer arrivals in any 1 minute when the average arrival rate is 3 customers per minute.

   b. The formula given in Exercise 11a is also applicable for estimating the arrival rate of planes at a busy airport (here, an arriving "customer" is an incoming airplane). Using this same formula, modify the program written in Exercise 11a to accept the average arrival rate as an input data item. Then run the modified program to determine the probability of 0 to 10 planes attempting to land in any 1-minute period at an airport during peak arrival times. Assume that the average rate for peak arrival times is 2 planes per minute.

12. Write and run a program that calculates and displays the amount of money available in a bank account that initially has $1000 deposited in it and earns 8% interest

A BIT OF BACKGROUND

The Blockhead

One mathematician of the Middle Ages who has had a profound influence on modern science is Leonardo of Pisa (1170–1250). In his youth, he was called *Filus Bonacci,* which means "son of (Guglielmo) Bonacci," and the name "stuck." Hence, he is commonly known today as Fibonacci. He traveled widely, met with scholars throughout the Mediterranean area, and produced four very significant works on arithmetic and geometry. One of his discoveries is the sequence of numbers that bears his name: 0,1,1,2,3,5,8,13, . . . After the first two values, 0 and 1, each number of the Fibonacci sequence is obtained from the sum of the preceding two numbers.

Fibonacci often referred to himself as Leonardo Bigollo, probably because *bigollo* is

Italian for "traveler." However, another meaning of *bigollo* in Italian is "blockhead." Some people suspect he may have adopted this name to show the professors of his time what a blockhead—a person who had not been educated in their schools—could accomplish.

Some blockhead! The Fibonacci sequence alone describes such natural phenomena as the spiraling pattern of nautilus shells, elephant tusks, sheep horns, bird's claws, pineapples, branching patterns of plants, *and* the proliferation of rabbits. The ratio of successively higher adjacent terms in the sequence also approaches the "golden section," a ratio that describes an aesthetically pleasing proportion used in the visual arts.

a year. Your program should display the amount available at the end of each year for a period of 10 years. Use the relationship that the money available at the end of each year equals the amount of money in the account at the start of the year plus 0.08 times the amount available at the start of the year.

13. The Fibonacci sequence is 0, 1, 1, 2, 3, 5, 8, 13, . . . , where the first two terms are 0 and 1, and each term thereafter is the sum of the two preceding terms; that is, $Fib[n] = Fib[n-1] + Fib[n-2]$. Using this information, write a C++ program that calculates the nth number in a Fibonacci sequence, where n is interactively entered into the program by the user. For example, if $n = 6$, the program should display the value 5.

14. A machine purchased for $28,000 is depreciated at a rate of $4000 a year for 7 years. Write and run a C++ program that computes and displays a depreciation table for 7 years. The table should have the form:

Depreciation Schedule

Year	Depreciation	End-of-Year Value	Accumulated Depreciation
1	4000	24,000	4000
2	4000	20,000	8000
3	4000	16,000	12,000
4	4000	12,000	16,000
5	4000	8000	20,000
6	4000	4000	24,000
7	4000	0	28,000

15. A well-regarded manufacturer of widgets has been losing 4% of its sales each year. The annual profit for the firm is 10% of sales. This year the firm had $10 million in sales and a profit of $1 million. Determine the expected sales and profit for the next 10 years. Your program should complete and produce a display as follows:

Sales and Profit Projection		
Year	Expected Sales	Projected Profit
1	$10,000,000	$1,000,000
2	$ 9,600,000	$ 960,000
3	.	.
.	.	.
.	.	.
.	.	.
10	.	.
Totals:	$.	$.

5.5 LOOP PROGRAMMING TECHNIQUES

In this section, we present four common programming techniques associated with pretest (for and while) loops. All of these techniques are commonly used by experienced programmers.

Technique 1: Interactive Input within a Loop

In Section 5.3, we presented the effect of including a cin statement within a while loop. Interactively entering data within a loop is a general technique that is equally applicable to for loops. For example, in Program 5.12, a cin statement is used to allow a user to input interactively a set of numbers. As each number is input, it is added to a total. When the for loop is exited, the average is calculated and displayed.

PROGRAM 5.12

```cpp
#include <iostream>
using namespace std;

// This program calculates the average of MAXCOUNT
// user-entered numbers
int main()
{
  const int MAXCOUNT = 5;

  int count;
  double num, total, average;

  total = 0.0;

  for (count = 0; count < MAXCOUNT; count++)
  {
    cout << "Enter a number: ";
    cin  >> num;
    total = total + num;
  }

  average = total / MAXCOUNT;
  cout << "The average of the data entered is "
       << average << endl;

  return 0;
}
```

The `for` statement in Program 5.12 creates a loop that is executed five times. The user is prompted to enter a number each time through the loop. After each number is entered, it is immediately added to the total. Notice that `total` is initialized to zero as part of the `for` statement's initializing list is executed. The loop in Program 5.12 executes as long as the value in `count` is less than or equal to 5 and is terminated when `count` becomes 6 (the increment to 6, in fact, is what causes the loop to end).

Technique 2: Selection within a Loop

Another common programming technique is to use either a `for` or `while` loop to cycle through a set of numbers and select those numbers that meet one or more criteria. For example, assume that we want to find both the positive and negative sum of a set of numbers. The criterion here is whether the number is positive or negative, and the logic for implementing this program is given by the following pseudocode:

While the loop condition is true
   Enter a number
   If the number is greater than zero
      add the number to the positive sum
   Else
      add the number to the negative sum
   End If
EndWhile

Program 5.13 describes this algorithm in C++ for a fixed count loop where five numbers are to be entered.

The following is a sample run of Program 5.13:

```
Enter a number (positive or negative): 10
Enter a number (positive or negative): -10
Enter a number (positive or negative): 5
Enter a number (positive or negative): -7
Enter a number (positive or negative): 11
The positive total is 26.000000
The negative total is -17.000000
```

Technique 3: Evaluating Functions of One Variable

Loops can be conveniently constructed to determine and display the values of a single-variable mathematical function for a set of values over any specified interval. For example, assume that we want to know the values of the function

$$y = 10x^2 + 3x - 2$$

for x between 2 and 6. Assuming that x has been declared as an integer variable, the following `for` loop can be used to calculate the required values:

```
for (x = 2; x <= 6; x++)
{
    y = 10 * pow(x,2) + 3 * x - 2;
    cout << setw(4) << x
         << setw(11) << y << endl;
}
```

PROGRAM 5.13

```cpp
#include <iostream>
using namespace std;

// This program computes the positive and negative sums of a set
// of MAXNUMS user-entered numbers
int main()
{
  const int MAXNUMS = 5;

  int i;
  double usenum, postot, negtot;

  postot = 0; // this initialization can be done in the declaration

  negtot = 0; // this initialization can be done in the declaration

  for (i = 1; i <= MAXNUMS; i++)
  {
    cout << "Enter a number (positive or negative): ";
    cin  >> usenum;
    if (usenum > 0)
      postot = postot + usenum;
    else
      negtot = negtot + usenum;
  }
  cout << "The positive total is " << postot << endl;
  cout << "The negative total is " << negtot << endl;

  return 0;
}
```

For this loop, we have used the variable x as both the counter variable and the unknown (independent variable) in the function. For each value of x from two to five, a new value of y is calculated and displayed. This `for` loop is contained within Program 5.14, which also displays appropriate headings for the values printed.

The following is displayed when Program 5.14 is executed:

x value	y value
2	44
3	97
4	170
5	263
6	376

Two items are of importance here. The first is that any equation with one unknown can be evaluated using a single `for` or an equivalent `while` loop. The method requires substituting the desired equation into the loop in place of the equation used in Program 5.14 and adjusting the counter values to match the desired solution range.

PROGRAM 5.14

```cpp
#include <iostream>
#include <iomanip>
#include <cmath>
using namespace std;

int main()
{
  int x, y;

  cout << "x value    y value\n";
  cout << "-------    -------\n";
  for (x = 2; x <= 6; x++)
  {
    y = 10 * pow(x,2) + 3 * x - 2;
    cout << setw(4) << x
         << setw(11) << y << endl;
  }

  return 0;
}
```

The second item to note is that we are not constrained to the use of integer values for the counter variable. For example, by specifying a noninteger increment, solutions for fractional values can be obtained. This is shown in Program 5.15, where the equation $y = 10x^2 + 3x - 2$ is evaluated in the range $x = 2$ to $x = 6$ in increments of 0.5.

PROGRAM 5.15

```cpp
#include <iostream>
#include <iomanip>
#include <cmath>
using namespace std;

int main()
{
  double x, y;

  cout << "x value      y value\n";
  cout << "-------      -------\n";
  cout << setiosflags(ios::showpoint);
  for (x = 2.0; x <= 6.0; x = x + 0.5)
  {
    y = 10.0 * pow(x,2.0) + 3.0 * x - 2.0;
    cout << setw(8) <<  x
         << setw(11) << y << endl;
  }

  return 0;
}
```

Notice that x and y have been declared as floating-point variables in Program 5.15 to allow these variables to take on fractional values. The following output is produced by this program:

x value	y value
2.00000	44.0000
2.50000	68.0000
3.00000	97.0000
3.50000	131.0000
4.00000	170.0000
4.50000	214.0000
5.00000	263.0000
5.50000	317.0000
6.00000	376.0000

Technique 4: Interactive Loop Control

Values used to control a loop may be set using variables rather than constant values. For example, the four statements

```
i = 5;
j = 10;
k = 1;
for (count = i; count <= j; count = count + k)
```

produce the same effect as the single statement:

```
for (count = 5; count <= 10; count = count + 1)
```

Similarly, the statements

```
i = 5;
j = 10;
k = 1;
count = i;
while (count <= j)
   count = count + k;
```

produce the same effect as the following while loop:

```
count = 5;
while (count <= 10)
   count = count + 1;
```

The advantage of using variables in the initialization, condition, and altering expressions is that it allows us to assign values for these expressions external to either the for or while statement. This is especially useful when a cin statement is used to set the actual values. To make this a little more tangible, consider Program 5.16.

PROGRAM 5.16

```cpp
#include <iostream>
#include <iomanip>
using namespace std;

// this program displays a table of numbers, their squares and cubes
// starting from the number 1. The final number in the table is
// input by the user

int main()
{
  int num, final;

  cout << "Enter the final number for the table: ";
  cin  >> final;

  cout << "NUMBER SQUARE CUBE\n";
  cout << "------ ------ ----\n";

  for (num = 1; num <= final; num++)
    cout << setw(3) << num
         << setw(8) << num*num
         << setw(7) << num*num*num << endl;

  return 0;
}
```

In Program 5.16, we have used a variable to control the condition (middle) expression. Here, a `cin` statement has been placed before the loop to allow the user to decide what the final value should be. Notice that this arrangement permits the user to set the size of the table at run time rather than having the programmer set the table size at compile time. This also makes the program more general because it now can be used to create a variety of tables without being reprogrammed or recompiled.

Exercises 5.5

1. *cin within a loop:* Write and run a C++ program that accepts six Fahrenheit temperatures, one at a time, and converts each value entered to its Celsius equivalent before the next value is requested. Use a `for` loop in your program. The conversion required is *Celsius = (5.0 / 9.0) * (Fahrenheit − 32)*.

2. *cin within a loop:* Write and run a C++ program that accepts ten individual values of gallons, one at a time, and converts each value entered to its liter equivalent before the next value is requested. Use a `for` loop in your program. Use the fact that there are 3.785 liters in 1 gallon.

3. *Interactive loop control:* Modify the program written for Exercise 2 to initially request the number of data items that will be entered and converted.

4. *Interactive loop control:* Modify Program 5.13 so that the number of entries to be input is specified by the user when the program is executed.

5. *Selection:* Modify Program 5.13 so that it displays the average of the positive and negative numbers. (*Hint:* Be careful not to count the number 0 as a negative number.) Test your program by entering 17, −10, 19, 0, and −4. The positive average displayed by your program should be 18 and the negative average −7.

6. a. *Selection:* Write a C++ program that selects and displays the maximum value of five numbers that are to be entered when the program is executed. (*Hint:* Use a for loop with both a cin and an if statement internal to the loop.)

   b. Modify the program written for Exercise 6a so that it displays both the maximum value and the position in the input set of numbers where the maximum occurs.

7. *Selection:* Write a C++ program that selects and displays the first 20 integer numbers that are evenly divisible by 3.

8. *Selection:* A child's parents promise to give the child $10 on her 12th birthday and double the gift on every subsequent birthday until the gift exceeds $1000. Write a C++ program to determine on which birthday the last amount is given and the total amount received.

9. *Mathematical functions:* Modify Program 5.15 to produce a table of Y values for the following:

   a. $y = 3x^5 - 2x^3 + x$

      for x between 5 and 10 in increments of 0.2

   b. $y = 1 + x + \dfrac{x^2}{2} + \dfrac{x^3}{6} + \dfrac{x^4}{24}$

      for x between 1 and 3 in increments of 0.1

   c. $y = 2e^{.8t}$

      for t between 4 and 10 in increments of 0.2

10. *Mathematical functions:* A model of worldwide population, in billions of people, is given by the equation

$$\text{population} = 6e^{0.02*t}$$

where t is the time in years ($t = 0$ represents January 2000 and $t = 1$ represents January 2001). Using this formula, write a C++ program that displays a yearly population table for the years January 2001 through January 2010.

11. *Mathematical functions:* The height, as a function of time t, of a projectile fired with an initial velocity v straight into the air is given by

$$\text{height} = vt - \tfrac{1}{2}gt^2$$

where g is the gravitational constant equal to 32.2 ft/sec^2. Using these formulas, write a C++ program that displays a table of heights for a projectile fired with an initial velocity of 500 ft/sec. The table should contain values corresponding to the time interval 0 to 10 seconds in increments of 0.5 seconds.

12. *Interactive loop control:* Modify Program 5.16 to accept the starting and increment values of the table produced by the program.

13. *Interactive loop control:* Write a C++ program that converts Fahrenheit to Celsius temperature in increments of 5 degrees. The initial value of the Fahrenheit temperature and the total conversions to be made are to be requested as user input during program execution. Recall that *Celsius = (5.0/9.0) * (Fahrenheit − 32.0)*.

14. a. *Interactive loop control:* Modify the program written for Exercise 12 of Section 5.4 to initially prompt the user for the amount of money deposited in the account.

   b. Modify the program written for Exercise 14a to additionally prompt the user for the number of years that should be used.

   c. Modify the program written for Exercise 14a to additionally prompt the user for both the interest rate and the number of years to be used.

5.6 NESTED LOOPS

In many situations, it is convenient to use a loop contained within another loop. Such loops are called **nested loops**. A simple example of a nested loop is:

```
for(i = 1; i <= 5; i++)          // start of outer loop   ←─────┐
{                                //                              │
   cout << "\ni is now " << i << endl;   //                     │
                                 //                              │
   for(j = 1; j <= 4; j++)          // start of inner loop      │
     cout << "  j = " << j;         // end of inner loop   ←─────┘
}                                   // end of outer loop
```

The first loop, controlled by the value of i, is called the **outer loop**. The second loop, controlled by the value of j, is called the **inner loop**. Notice that all statements in the inner loop are contained within the boundaries of the outer loop and that we have used a different variable to control each loop. For each single trip through the outer loop, the inner loop runs through its entire sequence. Thus, each time the i counter increases by 1, the inner for loop executes completely. This situation is illustrated in Figure 5.9. Program 5.17 includes this type of code in a working program.

PROGRAM 5.17

```cpp
#include <iostream>
using namespace std;

int main()
{
  const int MAXI = 5;
  const int MAXJ = 4;

  int i, j;

  for(i = 1; i <= MAXT; i++)      // start of outer loop   ←─────┐
  {                               //                              │
    cout << "\ni is now " << i <<  endl; //                       │
                                  //                               │
    for(j = 1; j <= MAXJ; j++)    // start of inner loop           │
      cout << "  j = " << j;      // end of inner loop   ←─────────┘
  }                               // end of outer loop

  cout << endl;

  return 0;
}
```

The output of a sample run of Program 5.17 is:

```
i is now 1
    j = 1  j = 2  j = 3  j = 4
```

```
i is now 2
    j = 1  j = 2  j = 3  j = 4
i is now 3
    j = 1  j = 2  j = 3  j = 4
i is now 4
    j = 1  j = 2  j = 3  j = 4
i is now 5
    j = 1  j = 2  j = 3  j = 4
```

    To illustrate the usefulness of a nested loop, we use one to compute the average grade for each student in a class of 20. Each student has taken four exams during the course of the semester. The final grade is calculated as the average of these

---

FIGURE 5.9   For Each `i`, `j` Loop

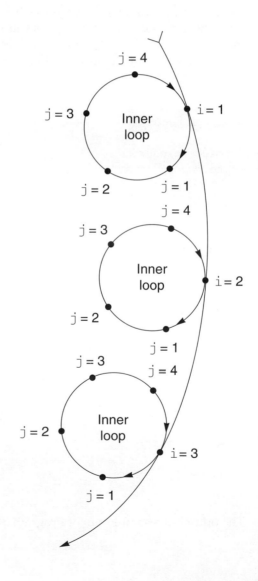

examination grades. The following pseudocode describes how this computation can be done:

For 20 times
    Set the student grade total to zero
    For 4 times
        Input a grade
        Add the grade to the total
    EndFor   // end of inner for loop
    Calculate student's average grade
    Print the student's average grade
EndFor   // end of outer for loop

As described by the pseudocode, an outer loop consisting of 20 passes is used to compute the average grade for each student. The inner loop consists of 4 passes. One examination grade is entered in each inner loop pass. As each grade is entered, it is added to the total for the student, and at the end of the loop, the average is calculated and displayed. Since both outer and inner loops are fixed count loops of 20 and 4, respectively, we use `for` statements to create these loops (see Programming Note on p. 261). Program 5.18 provides the C++ code corresponding to the pseudocode.

PROGRAM 5.18

```cpp
#include <iostream>
using namespace std;

int main()
{
  const int NUMGRADES = 4;
  const int NUMSTUDENTS = 20;

  int i,j;
  double grade, total, average;

  for (i = 1; i <= NUMSTUDENTS; i++) // start of outer loop
  {
    total = 0;                        // clear the total for this student
    for (j = 1; j <= NUMGRADES; j++) // start of inner loop
    {
      cout << "Enter an examination grade for this student: ";
      cin  >> grade;
      total = total + grade;         // add the grade into the total
    }                                 // end of the inner for loop
    average = total / NUMGRADES;     // calculate the average
    cout << "\nThe average for student " << i
         << " is " << average << "\n\n";
  }                                   // end of the outer for loop

  return 0;
}
```

In reviewing Program 5.18, pay particular attention to the initialization of `total` within the outer loop before the inner loop is entered. The variable `total` is initialized 20 times, once for each student. Also notice that the average is calculated and displayed immediately after the inner loop is finished. Since the statements that compute and print the average are also contained within the outer loop, 20 averages are calculated and displayed. The entry and addition of each grade-within the inner loop use techniques we have seen before, which should now be familiar to you.

Exercises 5.6

1. Four experiments are performed, each consisting of six test results. The results for each experiment are given in the following list. Write a program using a nested loop to compute and display the average of the test results for each experiment.

1st experiment results:	23.2	31	16.9	27	25.4	28.6
2nd experiment results:	34.8	45.2	27.9	36.8	33.4	39.4
3rd experiment results:	19.4	16.8	10.2	20.8	18.9	13.4
4th experiment results:	36.9	39	49.2	45.1	42.7	50.6

2. Modify the program written for Exercise 1 so that the number of test results for each experiment is entered by the user. Write your program so that a different number of test results can be entered for each experiment.

3. a. A bowling team consists of five players. Each player bowls three games. Write a C++ program that uses a nested loop to enter each player's individual scores and then computes and displays the average score for each bowler. Assume that each bowler has the following scores:

1st bowler:	286	252	265
2nd bowler:	212	186	215
3rd bowler:	252	232	216
4th bowler:	192	201	235
5th bowler:	186	236	272

   b. Modify the program written for Exercise 3a to calculate and display the average team score. (*Hint:* Use a second variable to store the total of all the players' scores.)

4. Rewrite the program written for Exercise 3a to eliminate the inner loop. To do this, you have to input three scores for each bowler rather than one at a time.

5. Write a program that calculates and displays values for y when:

$$y = xz/(x - z)$$

   Your program should calculate y for values of x ranging between 1 and 5 and values of z ranging between 2 and 6. x should control the outer loop and be incremented in steps of 1, and z should also be incremented in steps of 1. Your program should also display the message `"Function Undefined"` when the x and z values are equal.

6. Write a program that calculates and displays the yearly amount available if $1000 is invested in a bank account for 10 years. Your program should display the amounts available for interest rates from 6% to 12% inclusively, in 1% increments. Use a nested loop, with the outer loop controlling the interest rate and the inner loop controlling the years. Use the relationship that the money available at the end of each year equals the amount of money in the account at the start of the year plus the interest rate times the amount available at the start of the year.

7. In the Duchy of Upenchuck, the fundamental unit of currency is the Upenchuck dragon (UD). Income tax deductions are based on salary in units of 10,000 UD and on the number of dependents the individual has. The formula, designed to favor low-income families, is:

$$\text{deduction (UD)} = \text{dependents} \times 500 + 0.05 \times (50{,}000 - \text{salary})$$

Beyond five dependents and beyond 50,000 UD, the deduction does not change. There is no tax, hence no deduction, on incomes of less than 10,000 UD. Based on this information, create a table of Upenchuck income tax deductions, with dependents 0 to 5 as the column headings and salary 10000, 20000, 30000, 40000, and 50000 as the rows.

5.7 do-while **LOOPS**

Both the `while` and `for` statements evaluate an expression at the start of the repetition loop; hence, they are always used to create pretest loops. Posttest loops, which are also referred to as exit-controlled loops, can also be constructed in C++. The basic structure of such a loop, which is referred to as a **do-while loop**, is illustrated in Figure 5.10. Notice that a `do-while` loop continues to iterate through the loop while the condition is true and exits the loop when the condition is false.

FIGURE 5.10 do-while **Loop Structure**

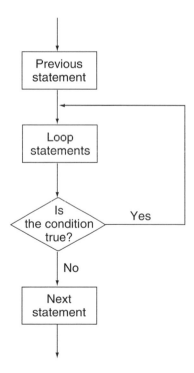

In C++, a posttest loop is created using a `do` statement. As its name implies, this statement allows us to do some statements before an expression is evaluated at the end of the loop. The general form of C++'s do statement is:

```
do
    statement;
while (expression);                    do not forget the final ;
```

As with all C++ programs, the single statement in the do loop may be replaced with a compound statement. A flow control diagram illustrating the operation of the do statement is shown in Figure 5.11.

As illustrated, all statements within the do statement are executed at least once before the expression is evaluated. Then, if the expression has a nonzero value, the statements are executed again. This process continues until the expression evaluates to zero (becomes false). For example, consider the following do statement:

```
do
{
    cout << "\nEnter a price: ";
    cin >> price;
    if (fabs(price - SENTINEL) < 0.0001)
        break;
    salestax = RATE * price;
    cout << setiosflags(ios::showpoint)
         << setprecision(2)
         << "The sales tax is $ " << salestax;
}
while (price != SENTINEL);
```

FIGURE 5.11 The do Statement's Flow of Control

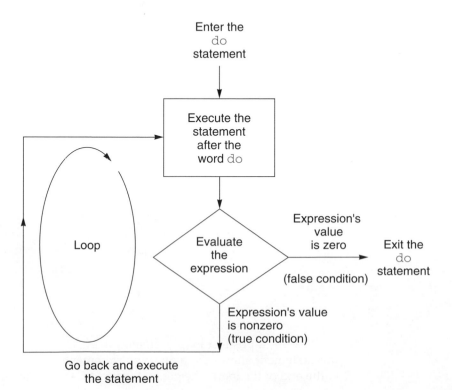

Observe that only one prompt and one cin statement are used here because the tested expression is evaluated at the end of the loop.

As with all repetition statements, the do statement can always replace or be replaced by an equivalent while or for statement. The choice of which statement to use depends on the application and the style preferred by the programmer. In general, the while and for statements are preferred because they clearly let anyone reading the program know what is being tested "right up front" at the top of the program loop.

Validity Checks

The do statement is particularly useful in filtering user-entered input and providing data validation checks. For example, assume that an operator is required to enter a valid customer identification number between the numbers 1000 and 1999. A number outside this range is to be rejected and a new request for a valid number made. The following section of code provides the necessary data filter to verify the entry of a valid identification number:

```
do
{
  cout << "\nEnter an identification number: ";
  cin  >> idNum;
}
while (idNum < 1000 ||  idNum > 1999);
```

Here, a request for an identification number is repeated until a valid number is entered. This section of code is "bare bones" in that it neither alerts the operator to the cause of the new request for data nor allows premature exit from the loop if a valid identification number cannot be found. An alternative removing the first drawback is:

```
do
{
  cout << "\nEnter an identification number: ";
  cin  >> idNum;
  if (idNum < 1000 || idNum > 1999)
  {
    cout << "An invalid number was just entered\n";
    cout << "Please check the ID number and re-enter\n";
  }
  else
    break;  // break if a valid id num was entered
} while(1); // this expression is always true
```

Here, we have used a break statement to exit the loop. Because the expression being evaluated by the do statement is always 1 (true), an infinite loop has been created that is only exited when the break statement is encountered.

Exercises 5.7

1. a. Using a do statement, write a program to accept a grade. The program should request a grade continuously as long as an invalid grade is entered. An invalid grade is any grade less than 0 or greater than 100. After a valid grade has been entered, your program should display its value.

b. Modify the program written for Exercise 1a so that the user is alerted when an invalid grade has been entered.

c. Modify the program written for Exercise 1b so that it allows the user to exit the program by entering the number 999.

d. Modify the program written for Exercise 1b so that it automatically terminates after five invalid grades have been entered.

2. a. Write a program that continuously requests a grade to be entered. If the grade is less than 0 or greater than 100, your program should print an appropriate message informing the user that an invalid grade has been entered, else the grade should be added to a total. When a grade of 999 is entered, the program should exit the repetition loop and compute and display the average of the valid grades entered.

b. Run the program written in Exercise 2a on a computer and verify the program using appropriate test data.

3. a. Write a program to reverse the digits of a positive integer number. For example, if the number 8735 is entered, the number displayed should be 5378. [*Hint:* Use a do statement and continuously strip off and display the units digit of the number. If the variable num initially contains the number entered, the units digit is obtained as (num % 10). After a units digit is displayed, dividing the number by 10 sets up the number for the next iteration. Thus, (8735 % 10) is 5 and (8735/10) is 873. The do statement should continue as long as the remaining number is not 0.]

b. Run the program written in Exercise 3a on a computer and verify the program using appropriate test data.

4. Repeat Exercise 5 in Section 5.4 using a do statement rather than a for statement.

5. Given a number n and an approximation for its square root, a closer approximation to its actual square root can be obtained using the formula:

$$\text{new approximation} = \frac{(n/\text{previous approximation}) + \text{previous approximation}}{2}$$

Using this information, write a C++ program that prompts the user for a number and an initial guess at its square root. Using this input data, your program should calculate an approximation to the square root that is accurate to 0.00001. (*Hint:* Stop the loop when the difference between the two approximations is less than 0.00001.)

6. Here is a challenging problem for those who know a little calculus. The Newton-Raphson method can be used to find the roots of any equation $y(x) = 0$. In this method, the $(i + 1)$st approximation, x_{i+1}, to a root of $y(x) = 0$ is given in terms of the ith approximation, x_i, by the formula

$$x_{i+1} = x_i - y(x_i) / y'(x_i)$$

For example, if $y(x) = 3x^2 + 2x - 2$, then $y'(x) = 6x + 2$, and the roots are found by making a reasonable guess for a first approximation x_1 and iterating using the equation

$$x_{i+1} = x_i - (3x_i^2 + 2x_i - 2) / (6x_i + 2)$$

a. Using the Newton-Raphson method, find the two roots of the equation $3x^2 + 2x - 2 = 0$. (*Hint:* There is one positive root and one negative root.)

b. Extend the program written for Exercise 6a so that it finds the roots of any function $y(x) = 0$, when the function for $y(x)$ and the derivative of $y(x)$ are placed in the code.

5.8 PLANNING FOR OBJECTS: INTRODUCTION TO UML

When solving any problem, it's often helpful to start by creating a diagram or map, or devising some kind of theoretical analogy for the problem you are trying to solve. In other words, you need to create some kind of model. Creating a model helps you see all the parts of the problem and helps you understand what you need to do in order to solve it. For procedural programs the preferred model is the structure chart introduced in Section 2.6. Formally, procedural programs are defined as algorithms that have been written in a computer language. Because acceptable algorithms are based on structured concepts, procedural programs are also known as structured programs.

As we move to object-oriented programs, a different model is required. In this section, we introduce both the general ideas underlying object-based modeling and introduce the basics of an object-modeling language known as the Unified Modeling Language (UML).

Representing Problems with Models

Formally, a **model** is a representation of a problem. The first step in creating an object-based model is to begin "thinking in objects." As a specific example, if the result of tossing a coin 100 times is desired, it certainly can be done by tossing a real coin. However, if a coin could be accurately modeled, the result could also be obtained by writing a program to simulate a coin toss. Similarly, a game of solitaire could be simulated if a realistic model of a deck of cards could be created, and if methods such as shuffling the deck could be coded.

Objects, such as coins, cards, and more complicated graphical objects, are well suited to a programming representation because they can all be modeled by two basic characteristics: attributes and behaviors. **Attributes** define the properties of interest, while **behaviors** define how the object reacts to its environment. When designing and developing an object-oriented program, you will need to follow these two steps:

1. Identify the required objects.
2. For each object:
   a. Identify the attributes of interest.
   b. Identify the behaviors (operations) of interest.

To make this more tangible, let us reconsider a coin-tossing experiment. Step 1 tells us to identify the required objects. For this experiment, the object under consideration is a coin. Step 2 tells us to identify the relevant attributes and behaviors. In terms of attributes, a coin has a denomination, size, weight, color, condition (tarnished, worn, proof), country of origin, and a side (head or tail). If we were purchasing a coin for collectable purposes, we would be interested in all but the last of these attributes. For the purpose of a coin-toss, however, the only attribute that is of interest is the side; whether the coin is a penny or a quarter, copper or silver colored, tarnished or not, is of no concern to us. Thus, in terms of modeling a coin for performing a coin toss, the only attribute that need initially be considered is what side is visible when the coin is tossed. It is important to understand the underlying significance of our choice of attributes—very few models are ever complete. A model typically does not reveal every aspect of the object it represents and should only include those attributes that are of relevance to the problem under consideration.

Having determined the attributes to be used in modeling a coin, the next step requires identifying the behavior that this object should exhibit. In this case, we must have a means of simulating a toss and determining the side that faces up when the toss is completed.

Just as in the structured design approach presented in Section 2.6, as you expand your design for an object-oriented program, you will frequently have to refine and expand the number of attributes and behaviors in your initial object description. Refinement, or improving and modifying a model, is generally always required for all but extremely simple situations.

For example, suppose we want to display a geometric object, such as a rectangle, on a screen. In its simplest representation a rectangle has a shape and location. Let us now refine this model to more accurately define what is meant by shape and location. A rectangle's shape attribute can actually be broken down into two more specific attributes: length and width. As for its location, you can also break that down into something more specific. For example, one approach might be to list the position of the upper-left corner of the rectangle relative to the upper-left corner of the screen, and then do the same for the upper-right corner of the rectangle. Those two positions, along with the length and width of the rectangle, would be enough information to allow the program to generate a rectangle. However, simply specifying one location for the rectangle may not be enough. For example, you may want to give the rectangle the ability to move its position and change either its length or width.

As was presented in Section 1.5, in object-based programming the category of objects defined by a given set of attributes and behavior is called a class. For example, the length and width attributes can define a general type of shape, or class, called a rectangle. Only when specific values have been assigned to these attributes have we represented a specific and particular rectangle, which is referred to as an object. The term **state** is then used to refer to how the created object appears at any one moment.

Following is an introduction to the Unified Modeling Language (UML), which is a program-modeling language, with its own set of rules and notations, that has become the predominate modeling language for describing the attributes and behaviors required of a class and the initial state provided to all objects created from a class.

Introduction to UML

The Unified Modeling Language (UML) has achieved wide acceptance as a primary technique for developing object-oriented programs. UML is not a part of the C++ language, but a separate language with its own set of rules and diagrams for creating an object-oriented design. If used correctly, a UML design can significantly help in understanding and clarifying a program's requirements. The finished design can serve as both a set of detailed specifications (which can easily be coded in an object-oriented programming language such as C++) and documentation for the final program.

UML uses a set of diagrams and techniques that are reasonably easy to understand and that support all of the features required for implementing an object-oriented design. At its most fundamental level, designing an object-oriented application requires understanding and specifying:

- The objects in the system
- What can happen to these objects
- When something can happen to these objects

In a UML analysis, each of these three items is addressed by a number of individual and separate views and diagrams. This situation is very similar to the plan for a house, which contains a number of diagrams, all required for the final construction. For example, there must be blueprints for the physical outlay; electrical, plumbing, heating, and cooling duct diagrams; and landscape and elevation diagrams. Each of these diagrams presents a different view of the completed house, and each presents different information, all of which is required for the finished product. The same is true for the diagrams specified in a UML analysis. Specifically, UML provides nine diagram types known as class, object, state, sequence, activity, use-case, component, deployment, and collaboration diagrams.

Not all of these diagram types are required for every analysis, as some provide specific details that are only needed in more advanced situations. In this text, we present the four basic UML diagram types that you should be familiar with and the rules needed to create them. Once these rules are understood, it is relatively easy to read almost any UML diagram that you will encounter. The diagrams covered in this text are the class, object, state, and sequence types.

Class and object diagrams are similar in structure, with class diagrams used to model classes and object diagrams used to model objects. As such, both diagrams include the attributes and operations for classes and objects, respectively, and the relationship between either classes or objects. A sequence diagram is used to describe the interactions between objects. Finally, a state diagram is used to describe when things happen to the objects. Although each of these diagrams may contain information present in the other three diagrams, each diagram type is intended to model and emphasize a different aspect of a system. As such, each diagram type simply views the same system from a different angle and highlights a particular characteristic of the system. Of these four diagrams, the most important and initially useful are class and object diagrams, which are described in this section. (State and sequence diagrams are described in Section 6.8). For many systems, the description provided by class and object diagrams are more than sufficient for design and implementation purposes.

Class and Object Diagrams

Class diagrams are used to describe classes and their relationships, while **object diagrams** are used to describe specific objects and their relationships. As you already know, a class refers to a type of object, out of which many specific objects can be created, while an object always refers to a specific, single item created from a class. For example, a class of books might be described as either fiction or nonfiction, of which many specific instances, or objects, exist. The book *A History of England* is a specific object of the class nonfiction, while *Pride and Prejudice* is a specific object of the class fiction. Thus, it is always the class that is the basic plan, or recipe, from which real objects are created. It is the class that describes the properties and operations that each object must have to be a member of the class.

An **attribute**, as we have seen, is simply a characteristic that each object in the class must have. For example, title and author are attributes of Book objects, while name, age, sex, weight, and height are attributes of Person objects. Once data values are assigned to attributes, a unique object is created. It should be noted that each and every object created from a class must also have an identity, in that one object can be distinguished from another object of the same class. This is not true of a pure data value, such as the number 5, where all occurrences of this number are indistinguishable from one another.

FIGURE 5.12   A Class and Object Representation

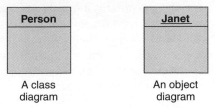

A class
diagram

An object
diagram

Both classes and objects are represented using a diagram consisting of a box. For class diagrams, the class name is centered at the top of the box and is written in bold face. For object diagrams, the class name is optional, but when it is included it is simply underlined at the top of the diagram. When the class name is provided, an optional object name can precede the class name, with a mandatory colon separating the two names. Alternatively, an object diagram may contain only the object's name, underlined, with no class name provided. For example, Figure 5.12 illustrates the representation of a Person class, along with one Person object named Janet.

The basic symbols and notations used in constructing class and object diagrams are presented in Figure 5.13.

Once the attributes of a class have been identified, they are listed in a class diagram box below the class name, separated by a line. Specific objects are shown in a similar manner, with data values provided for all attributes. For example, Figure 5.14 shows the attributes and values associated with the class Country. As you might expect, the attributes listed in a class diagram will become, in C++, the variables declared in a class's data declaration section.

Attributes have two qualities, *type* and *visibility*. An attribute's **type** is either a primitive data type, such as integer, real, boolean, or character, or a class type, such as a string. Type is required in a class diagram and is indicated by following an attribute name with a mandatory colon and the data type.

Visibility defines where an attribute can be seen—that is, whether the attribute can be used in other classes or is restricted to the class defining it. If an attribute has a private visibility, it can only be used within its defining class and cannot be directly accessed by other classes. An attribute with public visibility can be used directly in any other class. In UML, public visibility is expressed by placing a plus sign (+) in front of the attribute's name within the class diagram. A minus sign (−) in front of the attribute's name designates the attribute as private. Protected visibility means that an attribute can be passed along to a derived class and is indicated by including neither a plus nor minus sign. In a class diagram, an attribute's name and type are required; all other information is optional. Figure 5.15 illustrates the class diagram for a class named RoomType that contains two private attributes, name length and width. Notice that we have also included default values that the class is expected to provide to its attributes.

FIGURE 5.13 Basic UML Symbols and Notation

Class:

```
ClassName
```

```
            ClassName
attribute
attribute:data-type
attribute:data-type=init-value
 ...
operation
operation (arg-list):return-type
 ...
```

Association:

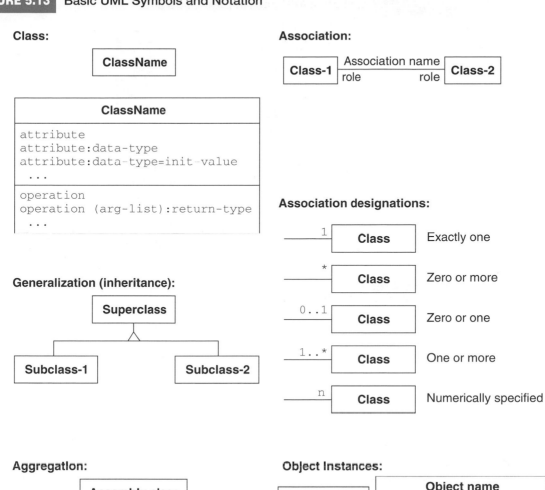

Class-1 — Association name / role — role — Class-2

Association designations:

1	Class	Exactly one
*	Class	Zero or more
0..1	Class	Zero or one
1..*	Class	One or more
n	Class	Numerically specified

Generalization (inheritance):

Superclass

Subclass-1   Subclass-2

Aggregation:

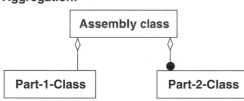

Assembly class

Part-1-Class   Part-2-Class

Object Instances:

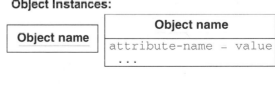

Object name

```
          Object name
attribute-name — value
 ...
```

Aggregation (alternate form):

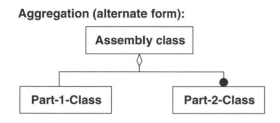

Assembly class

Part-1-Class   Part-2-Class

Instantiation relationship:

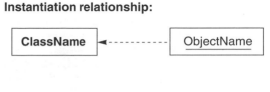

ClassName ◄- - - - - - - - ObjectName

FIGURE 5.14 Including Attributes in UML Class and Object Diagrams

U.S.A
North
America
381 million
Object Diagram
Country
Continent
population
Class diagram
Spain
Europe
34 million
Object diagram

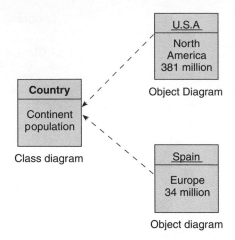

FIGURE 5.15 A Class with Attributes

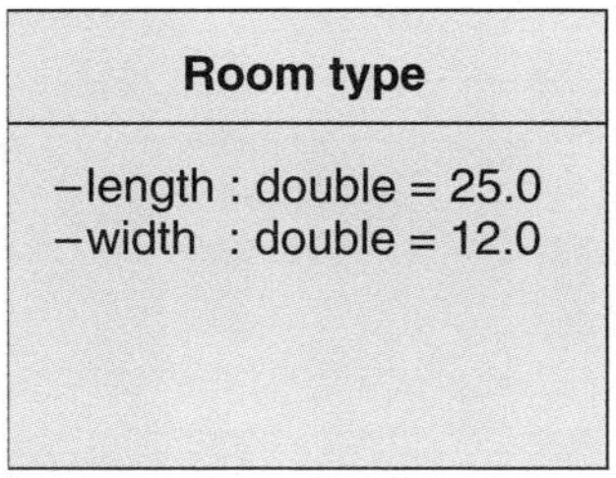

Room type
–length : double = 25.0
–width : double = 12.0

FIGURE 5.16 Including Operations in Class Diagrams

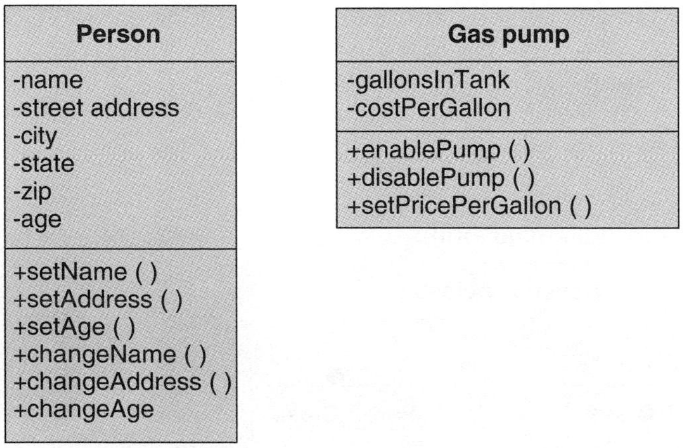

Person
-name
-street address
-city
-state
-zip
-age
+setName ( )
+setAddress ( )
+setAge ( )
+changeName ( )
+changeAddress ( )
+changeAge
Gas pump
-gallonsInTank
-costPerGallon
+enablePump ( )
+disablePump ( )
+setPricePerGallon ( )

Just as attributes are designated within a class diagram, so are operations. **Operations** are transformations that can be applied to attributes, and it is the operations that will ultimately be coded as C++ methods. Operation names are listed in a class box below the attributes and separated from them by a line. Figure 5.16 illustrates two class diagrams that include operations.

Relationships

In addition to graphically describing classes and objects, UML class and object diagrams present the relationships existing between classes and objects. The three basic relationships are association, aggregation, and generalization.

Associations between classes are typically signified by phrases such as "is related to," "is associated with," "has a," "is employed by," "works for," etc. This type of association is indicated by a straight line connecting two classes or two objects, where the type of association is listed above or below the line. For example, Figure 5.17 shows an association between a Person and a Company. As indicated, a Person is "employed by" a Company, and a Company "employs" zero or more Persons. The designation of "zero or more," which is referred to as the multiplicity of the relationship, is indicated by the notation * in the diagram. Table 5.1 lists the symbols used to indicate an association's multiplicity. These symbols can be placed either above or below the line connecting two classes or objects.

TABLE 5.1 UML Association Notation

Symbol	Relationship
1	One and only one
n	Exactly the specified number (n an integer)
0..1	Zero or one
m..n	From m to n (m and n integers)
* or 0..*	From zero to any positive integer
1..*	From one to any positive integer

FIGURE 5.17 An Association

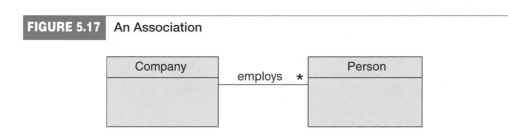

An **aggregation** is a particular type of an association where one class or object, referred to as the whole element, "consists of" or, alternatively, "is composed of," other classes or objects, which are referred to as parts. For example, a sentence consists of words, which consists of characters. Thus, characters are parts of words, which are themselves parts of sentences. This type of association is indicated by a diamond symbol. Figures 5.18, 5.19, and 5.20 illustrate three aggregation associations. Reading each of these object diagrams is much easier if you replace the diamond with either the words "consists of" or "is composed of." When the diamond symbol is hollow, as it is in Figure 5.18, it indicates that the parts can still exist independent of the whole to which they belong. Thus, even if a team is broken up or destroyed, its individual members can still exist. When the diamond symbol is solid, as it is in Figures 5.19 and 5.20, it indicates that the component parts are intrinsic members of the whole. As such, if the central, or whole, class or object is removed, its aggregated parts will also be destroyed. Therefore, as indicated in Figure 5.19, if a sentence is removed, all of its associated words are removed. Similarly, erasing a word causes the erasure of the characters within the word. As indicated in all three figures, the diamond symbol always attaches to the whole, or central, class or object.

FIGURE 5.18 Single-Level Aggregation

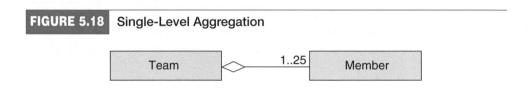

FIGURE 5.19 Another Single-Level Aggregation

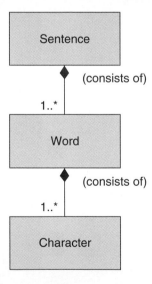

The last type of relationship that we will consider is generalization, which is more commonly referred to as inheritance. **Generalization** is a relationship between a class and a refined version of the class.

For example, a refinement of the object type Vehicle can be either a Land, Space, or Water version. In this case, Vehicle would be the base class, and Land, Space, and Water are the refined classes. Figure 5.21 shows how this generalization relationship is illustrated using a class diagram.

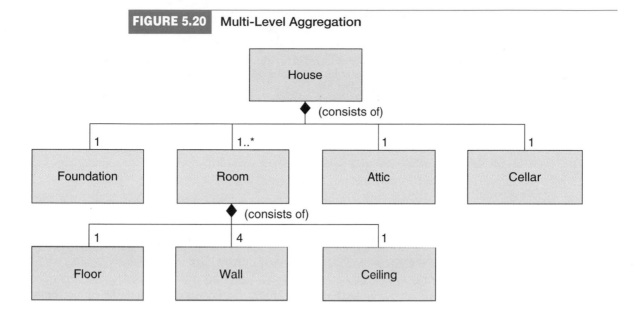

FIGURE 5.20 Multi-Level Aggregation

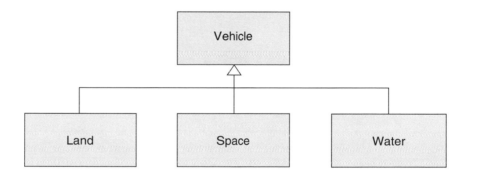

FIGURE 5.21 A Generalization Relationship

Exercises 5.8

1. Define the following terms:

    a. attribute

    b. aggregation

    c. association

    d. class

    e. class diagram

    f. generalization

    g. multiplicity

    h. program model

    i. object

    j. object diagram

    k. operation

2. Construct a class diagram for a Country class. Each Country has a capital city. The attributes of interest for each country are its population, size, main agricultural product, and main manufactured product.

3. a. Construct a class diagram for a single gas tank that is connected to one or more gas pumps. The attributes of interest for the tank are its capacity, current level, and grade of gas. The attributes of interest for a pump are the amount of gallons dispensed and the cost per gallon. Additionally, the pump responds to being enabled and disabled.

   b. Modify the class diagram constructed in Exercise 3a to account for the fact that a gas pump may be associated with more than one gas tank.

4. Construct a class diagram for a book consisting of one or more chapters, each of which consists of one or more sections.

5. a. Construct a class diagram for a computer that consists of a monitor, keyboard, mouse, printer, and system box.

   b. Modify the class diagram constructed in Exercise 5a to account for the fact that one or more monitors and keyboards may be attached to the system box and that the system may have no mouse or may have multiple mice.

   c. Extend the class diagram constructed for Exercise 5b to denote that the system box is composed of a CPU chip, a memory board containing zero or more RAM chips, and one case.

6. Construct a class diagram for a class of circles that is the base class to a class of spheres and a class of cylinders.

7. Construct a class diagram for a collection of cards that consists of zero or more individual cards. The collection of cards forms a base class for both a deck of cards and an individual hand of cards.

5.9 COMMON PROGRAMMING ERRORS

Five errors are commonly made by beginning C++ programmers when using repetition statements. Two of these pertain to the tested expression and have already been encountered with the `if` and `switch` statements.

1. Inadvertently using the assignment operator = instead of the equality operator == in the tested expression. An example of this error is typing the assignment expression a = 5 instead of the desired relational expression a == 5. Since the tested expression can be any valid C++ expression, including arithmetic and assignment expressions, this error is not detected by the compiler.

2. As with the `if` statement, repetition statements should not use the equality operator == when testing floating-point or double-precision operands. For example, the expression fnum == 0.01 should be replaced by a test requiring that the absolute value of fnum − 0.01 be less than an acceptable amount. The reason is that all numbers are stored in binary form. Using a finite number of bits, decimal numbers such as .01 have no exact binary equivalent so that tests requiring equality with such numbers can fail.

3. Placing a semicolon at the end of the `for`'s parentheses, which frequently produces a do-nothing loop. For example, consider these statements:

```
for(count = 0; count < 10; count++);
    total = total + num;
```

Here, the semicolon at the end of the first line of code is a null statement. This has the effect of creating a loop that is executed ten times with nothing done except the incrementing and testing of count. This error tends to occur because C++ programmers are used to ending most lines with a semicolon.

4. Using commas to separate the items in a for statement instead of the required semicolons. An example of this is the statement:

```
for (count = 1, count < 10, count++)
```

Commas are used to separate items within the initializing and altering lists, but semicolons *must be used* to separate these lists from the tested expression.

5. Omitting the final semicolon from the do statement. This error is usually made by programmers who have learned to omit the semicolon after the parentheses of a while statement and carry over this habit when the reserved word while is encountered at the end of a do statement.

5.10 CHAPTER REVIEW

Key Terms

break statement	null statement
continue statement	posttest loop
do-while loop	pretest loop
fixed count loop	repetition statement
for loop	sentinel
infinite loop	variable condition loop
nested loop	while loop

Summary

1. A section of repeating code is referred to as a *loop*. The loop is controlled by a repetition statement that tests a condition to determine whether the code will be executed. Each pass through the loop is referred to as a *repetition* or *iteration*. The tested condition must always be explicitly set prior to its first evaluation by the repetition statement. Within the loop, there must always be a statement that permits altering of the condition so that the loop, once entered, can be exited.

2. There are three basic type of loops: while, for, and do-while.

   The while and for loops are *pretest* or *entrance-controlled loops*. In this type of loop, the tested condition is evaluated at the beginning of the loop, which requires that the tested condition be explicitly set prior to loop entry. If the condition is true, loop repetitions begin; otherwise, the loop is not entered. Iterations continue as long as the condition remains true. In C++, while and for loops are constructed using while and for statements, respectively.

   The do-while loop is a *posttest* or *exit-controlled loop*, where the tested condition is evaluated at the end of the loop. This type of loop is always executed at least once. `do-while` loops continue to execute as long as the tested condition remains true.

3. Loops are also classified as to the type of tested condition. In a *fixed count loop*, the condition is used to keep track of how many repetitions have occurred. In a *variable condition loop*, the tested condition is based on a variable that can change interactively with each pass through the loop.

4. In C++, a `while` loop is constructed using a `while` statement. The most commonly used form of this statement is:

```
while (expression)
{
    statements;
}
```

The expression contained within parentheses is the condition tested to determine if the statement following the parentheses, which is generally a compound statement, is executed. The expression is evaluated in exactly the same manner as that contained in an `if-else` statement; the difference is how the expression is used. In a `while` statement, the statement following the expression is executed repeatedly as long as the expression retains a nonzero value, rather than just once, as in an `if-else` statement. An example of a `while` loop is:

```
count = 1;                    // initialize count
while (count <= 10)
{
    cout << count << "  ";
    count++;                  // increment count
}
```

The first assignment statement sets `count` equal to 1. The `while` statement is then entered and the expression is evaluated for the first time. Since the value of `count` is less than or equal to 10, the expression is true and the compound statement is executed. The first statement in the compound statement uses the `cout` object to display the value of `count`. The next statement adds 1 to the value currently stored in `count`, making this value equal to 2. The `while` statement now loops back to retest the expression. Because `count` is still less than or equal to 10, the compound statement is again executed. This process continues until the value of `count` reaches 11.

The `while` statement always checks its expression at the top of the loop. This requires that any variables in the tested expression must have values assigned before the `while` statement is encountered. Within the `while` loop, there must be a statement that alters the tested expression's value.

5. In C++, a `for` loop is constructed using a `for` statement. This statement performs the same functions as the `while` statement but uses a different form. In many situations, especially those that use a fixed count condition, the `for` statement format is easier to use than its `while` statement equivalent. The most commonly used form of the `for` statement is:

```
for (initializing list; expression; altering list)
{
   statements;
}
```

Within the parentheses of the `for` statement are three items separated by semi-colons. Each of these items is optional but the semicolons must be present.

The initializing list is used to set any initial values before the loop is entered; generally it is used to initialize a counter. Statements within the initializing list are only executed once. The expression in the `for` statement is the condition being tested: It is tested at the start of the loop and prior to each iteration. The altering list contains loop statements that are not contained within the compound statement; generally it is used to increment or decrement a counter each time the loop is executed. Multiple statements within a list are separated by commas. An example of a `for` loop is:

```
for (total = 0, count = 1; count < 10; count++)
{
   cout << "Enter a grade: ";
   cin  >> grade;
   total = total + grade;
}
```

In this `for` statement, the initializing list is used to initialize both `total` and `count`. The expression determines that the loop will execute as long as the value in `count` is less than 10, and the value of `count` is incremented by 1 each time through the loop.

6. The `for` statement is extremely useful in creating fixed count loops. This is because the initializing statements, the tested expression, and statements affecting the tested expression can all be included in parentheses at the top of a `for` loop for easy inspection and modification.

7. The `do` statement is used to create posttest loops because it checks its expression at the end of the loop. This ensures that the body of a `do` loop is executed at least once. Within a `do` loop, there must be at least one statement that alters the tested expression's value.

Exercises

1. Write sections of C++ code to do the following:

   a. Display the multiples of 3 backward from 33 to 3, inclusive.

   b. Display the capital letters of the alphabet backward from Z to A.

2. Write, run, and test a C++ program to find the value of 2^n using a `for` loop where n is an integer value entered by the user at the keyboard. (*Hint:* Initialize `result = 1` and then let `result = 2 * result`.)

3. The value of Euler's number, e, can be approximated using the formula:

$$e = 1 + 1/1! + 1/2! + 1/3! + 1/4! + 1/5! + \ldots.$$

Using this formula, write a C++ program that approximates the value of *e* using a `while` loop that terminates when the difference between two successive approximations differs by less than 1.0E−6.

4. Using the formula provided in Exercise 3, determine how many terms are needed to approximate the value returned by the intrinsic `exp()` function with an error less than 1.0E−6. [*Hint:* Use a `while` loop that terminates when the difference between the value returned by the `exp()` function and the approximation is less than 1.0E−6.]

5. a. The outstanding balance on Rhona Karp's car loan is $5000. Each month, Rhona is required to make a payment of $300, which includes both interest and principal repayment of the car loan. The monthly interest is calculated as 0.09/12 of the outstanding balance of the loan. After the interest is deducted, the remaining part of the payment is used to pay off the loan. Using this information, write a C++ program that produces a table indicating the beginning monthly balance, the interest payment, the principal payment, and the remaining loan balance after each payment is made. Your output should resemble and complete the entries in the following table until the outstanding loan balance is 0:

Beginning Balance	Interest Payment	Principal Payment	Ending Loan Balance
5000.00	37.50	121.50	4878.50
4874.50	36.59	122.41	4756.09
4756.09	.	.	.
.	.	.	.
.	.	.	.
.	.	.	0.00

b. Modify the program written in Exercise 5a to display the total of the interest and principal paid at the end of the table produced by your program.

6. The monthly payment due on an outstanding car loan is typically calculated using the formula:

$$\text{Monthly payment} = \frac{(\text{loan amount})\,(\text{monthly interest rate})}{1.0 - (1.0 + \text{Monthly interest rate})^{-(\text{number of months})}}$$

where:

Monthly interest rate = Annual percentage rate/(12.0 * 100)

Using these formulas, write, run, and test a C++ program that prompts the user for the amount of the loan, the annual percentage rate, and the number of years of the loan. From this input data, produce a loan amortization table similar to the one shown below:

What is the amount of the loan? $ 1500.00
What is the annual percentage rate? 14.0
How many years will you take to pay back the loan? 1.0

Amount	Annual % Interest	Years	Monthly Payment
1500.00	14.00	1	134.68

Payment Number	Interest Paid	Principal Paid	Cumulative Interest	Total Paid to Date	New Balance Due
1	17.50	117.18	17.50	134.68	1382.82
2	16.13	118.55	33.63	269.36	1264.27
3	14.75	119.93	48.38	404.04	1144.34
4	13.35	121.33	61.73	538.72	1023.01
5	11.94	122.75	73.67	673.40	900.27
6	10.50	124.18	84.17	808.08	776.09
7	9.05	125.63	93.23	942.76	650.46
8	7.59	127.09	100.81	1077.45	523.37
9	6.11	128.57	106.92	1212.13	394.79
10	4.61	130.07	111.53	1346.81	264.72
11	3.09	131.59	114.61	1481.49	133.13
12	1.55	133.13	116.17	1616.17	0.00

In constructing the loop necessary to produce the body of the table, the following initializations must be made:

    New balance due = original loan amount
    Cumulative interest = 0.0
    Paid to date = 0.0
    Payment number = 0

Within the loop, the following calculations and accumulations should be used:

    Payment number = payment number + 1
    Interest paid = new balance due * monthly interest rate
    Principal paid = monthly payment − interest paid
    Cumulative interest = cumulative interest + interest paid
    Paid to date = paid to date + monthly payment
    New balance due = new balance due − principal paid

7. Modify the program written for Exercise 6 to prevent the user from entering an illegal value for the interest rate. That is, write a loop that asks the user repeatedly for the annual interest rate until a value between 1.0 and 20.0 is entered.

8. In the hypothetical Republic of Dwump, the basic unit of currency is the dwork, and the exchange rate at present is 27 dworks per U.S. dollar. Develop, run, and test a C++ program to create a table of dollars versus dworks in steps of $0.25 from `MinDollars` to `MaxDollars`, where values for these two variables are entered by the user at the keyboard. The exchange rate (27 dworks per dollar) and the step value (0.25) should be declared as named constants so that they can be found and changed easily. The exchange rate should be displayed at the head of the output table, and the columns `Dollars` and `Dworks` should be labeled.

9. Develop, test, and execute a C++ program that uses a `while` loop to determine the smallest integer power of 3 that exceeds 30,000. That is, find the smallest value of n such that $3^n > 30,000$. (*Hint*: Initialize `PowerOfThree = 1` and then let `PowerOfThree = 3 * PowerOfThree`.)

10. A prime integer number is one that has exactly two different divisors, namely, 1 and the number itself. Write, run, and test a C++ program that finds and prints all the prime numbers less than 100. [*Hint:* 1 is a prime number. For each number from 2 to 100, find `remainder = number % n`, where n ranges from 2 to

sqrt(number). If n is greater than sqrt(number), then the number is not equally divisible by n. (Why?) If any remainder equals 0, then the number is not a prime number.]

11. Print the decimal, octal, and hexadecimal values of all characters between the start and stop characters entered by a user. For example, if the user enters a and z, the program should print all the characters between a and z and their respective numerical values. Make sure that the second character entered by the user occurs later in the alphabet than the first character. If it does not, write a loop that repeatedly asks the user for a valid second character, until one is entered.

12. Create a table of selling price versus purchase price. Have the user enter the range of purchase prices (from lowest to highest), the percent markup, and the increment between purchase prices. Display the table of purchase prices and selling prices on the screen with appropriate headings. The formulas for calculating the selling price from the purchase price are:

```
Markup fraction = Percent markup / 100.0
Selling price = (1.0 + Markup fraction) * Purchase price
```

13. The quotient in long division is the number of times the divisor can be subtracted from the dividend. The remainder is what is left over after the last subtraction. Write a C++ program that performs division using this method.

14. Write a C++ program that uses iteration to accumulate the sum $1 + 2 + 3 + \ldots + N$, where N is a user-entered integer number. Then evaluate the expression $N(N + 1)/2$ to verify that this expression yields the same result as the iteration.

15. a. An old Arabian legend has it that a fabulously wealthy but unthinking king agreed to give a beggar one cent and double the amount for 64 days. Using this information, write, run, and test a C++ program that displays how much the king must pay the beggar on each day. The output of your program should appear as follows:

```
Day              Amount Owed
---              -----------
 1                  0.01
 2                  0.02
 3                  0.04
 .                   .
 .                   .
 .                   .
64                   .
```

b. Modify the program you wrote for Exercise 15a to determine on which day the king will have paid a total of at least $1 million to the beggar.

16. According to legend, the island of Manhattan was purchased from the Native American population in 1626 for $24. Assuming that this money was invested in a Dutch bank paying 5% simple interest per year, construct a table showing how much money the Native Americans would have at the end of each 20-year period starting in 1626 and ending in 2006.

Improving Communication

17. Assuming you are the Lead Programmer, respond to the following memorandum:

    MEMORANDUM

    To: Lead Programmer

    From: Head of Programming Dept.

    Subject: Object-Oriented Analysis

    Please explain to me why the structured top-down analysis and design approach that we have been using cannot be used after we switch to an OOP environment.

18. Assuming you are the Lead Programmer, respond to the following memorandum:

    MEMORANDUM

    To: Lead Programmer

    From: Head of Programming Dept.

    Subject: Objects and Values

    Please explain to me the difference between the values we have been using in our programs and objects. For example, is the string "England" an object or a value?

Working in Teams

19. Have the team, as a group, determine a car's major subsystems, such as brakes, steering, etc. Then, considering these subsystems as classes, construct an object diagram for a Car class that simply shows the associations between classes (no attributes or operations). Assign each subsystem to individual team members. Have them determine a set of attributes and operations appropriate to the assigned subsystem. When each member has completed the task, modify the original object diagram to include the additional information.

20. Have the team, as a group, determine a cellular telephone's major subsystems, such as keypad, antenna, etc. Then, considering these subsystems as classes, construct an object diagram for a Cellular class that simply shows the associations between classes (no attributes or operations). Assign each subsystem to individual team members. Have them determine a set of attributes and operations appropriate to the assigned subsystem. When each member has completed the task, modify the original object diagram to include the additional information.

6 Modularity Using Functions

Professional programs are designed, coded, and tested very much like hardware, as a set of modules that are integrated to perform a completed whole. A good analogy of this is an automobile in which one major module is the engine, another is the transmission, a third the braking system, a fourth the body, and so on. Each of these modules is linked and ultimately placed under the control of the driver, which can be compared to a supervisor or main program module. The whole now operates as a complete unit that is able to do useful work, such as driving to the store. During the assembly process, each module is individually constructed, tested, and found to be free of defects (bugs) before it is installed in the final product.

Now think of what you might do if you wanted to improve your car's performance. You might alter the existing engine or remove it altogether and bolt in a new engine. Similarly, you might change the transmission or tires or shock absorbers, making each modification individually as your time and budget allowed. In each case, the majority of the other modules can stay the same, but the car now operates differently.

A BIT OF BACKGROUND

Subprograms

Although the concepts are similar, user-defined program units are generically referred to as *subprograms*, but are called by different names in different programming languages. In C++ subprograms are all referred to as both *functions* and *methods*.

In Pascal, they are *procedures* and *functions*. Modula-2 names them *PROCEDURES* (even though some of them are actually functions). COBOL refers to them as *paragraphs*, and FORTRAN and BASIC refer to them as *subroutines* and *functions*.

In this analogy, each of the major components of a car can be compared to a function. For example, the driver calls on the engine when the gas pedal is pressed. The engine accepts inputs of fuel, air, and electricity to turn the driver's request into a useful product—power—and then sends this output to the transmission for further processing. The transmission receives the output of the engine and converts it to a form that can be used by the drive axle. An additional input to the transmission is the driver's selection of gears (drive, reverse, neutral, etc.).

In each case, the engine, transmission, and other modules only "know" the universe bounded by their inputs and outputs. The driver need know nothing of the internal operation of the engine, transmission, air conditioning, or other modules that are being controlled. All that is required is an understanding of *what* each unit does and *how* to use it. The driver simply "calls" on a module, such as the engine, brakes, air conditioning, or steering, when that module's output is required. Communication between modules is restricted to passing needed inputs to each module as it is called on to perform its task, and each module operates internally in a relatively independent manner. This same modular approach is used by programmers to create and maintain reliable C++ programs using functions.

As we have seen, each C++ program must contain a `main()` function. In addition to this required function, C++ programs can also contain any number of additional functions. In this chapter, we learn how to write these functions, pass data to them, process the passed data, and return a result.

6.1 FUNCTION AND PARAMETER DECLARATIONS

In creating C++ functions, we must be concerned with both the function itself and how it interacts with other functions, such as `main()`. These concerns include correctly passing data into a function when it is called and returning values from a function. In this section, we describe the first part of the interface, passing data to a function and having the function correctly receive, store, and process the transmitted data.

As we have already seen with mathematical functions, a function is called, or used, by giving the function's name and passing any data to it, as arguments, within the parentheses following the function name (see Figure 6.1).

The called function must be able to accept the data passed to it by the function doing the calling. Only after the called function successfully receives the data can the data be manipulated to produce a useful result.

FIGURE 6.1   Calling and Passing Data to a Function

$$\underbrace{\text{functionName}}_{\substack{\text{This identifies} \\ \text{the called} \\ \text{function}}}\underbrace{(\text{data passed to function})}_{\substack{\text{This passes data to} \\ \text{the function}}};$$

To clarify the process of sending and receiving data, consider Program 6.1, which calls a function named findMax(). The program, as shown, is not yet complete. Once the function findMax() is written and included in Program 6.1, the completed program, consisting of the functions main() and findMax(), can be compiled and executed.

PROGRAM 6.1

```
#include <iostream>
using namespace std;

void findMax(int, int);  // the function declaration (prototype)

int main()
{
  int firstnum, secnum;

  cout << "\nEnter a number: ";
  cin  >> firstnum;
  cout << "Great! Please enter a second number: ";
  cin  >> secnum;

  findMax(firstnum, secnum); // the function is called here

  return 0;
}
```

Let us examine the declaration and calling of the function findMax() from main(). We will then write findMax() to accept the data passed to it and determine the largest or maximum value of the two passed values.

The function findMax() is referred to as the **called function**, since it is called or summoned into action by its reference in main(). The function that does the calling, in this case main(), is referred to as the **calling function**. The terms *called* and *calling* come from standard telephone usage, where one party calls the other on a telephone.

The called function, findMax() in this case, is declared as a function that expects to receive two integer numbers and to return no value (a void) to main(). This declaration is formally referred to as a function prototype. The function is then called by the last statement in the program.

Function Prototypes

Before a function can be called, it must be declared to the function that will do the calling. The declaration statement for a function is referred to as a **function proto-type**. The function prototype tells the calling function the type of value that will be formally returned, if any, and the data type and order of the values that the calling function should transmit to the called function. For example, the function proto-type previously used in Program 6.1

```
void findMax(int, int);
```

declares that the function `findMax()` expects two integer values to be sent to it and that this particular function formally returns no value `(void)`. Function pro-totypes may be placed with the variable declaration statements of the calling func-tion, above the calling function name, as in Program 6.1, or in a separate header file that is included using an `#include` preprocessor statement. Thus, the function prototype for `findMax()` could have been placed either before or after the state-ment `#include <iostream>`, `prior to main()`, or within `main()`. Placing the prototype before `main()` permits the `findMax()` function to be called by any and all functions in the file; placing the prototype within `main()` restricts the call to within `main()`, unless the `findMax()` function is itself placed at the top of the file. (The reasons for the choice of placement are presented in Section 6.2.) The syn-tax of function prototype statements is:

```
returnDataType functionName(list of argument data types);
```

where *returnDataType* refers to the data type of the value that will be formally returned by the function. An **argument** is a value that is passed into a function when the function is actually called.

Examples of function prototypes are:

```
int fmax(int, int);
double swap(int, char, char, double);
void display(double, double);
```

In the first example, the function prototype for `fmax()` declares that this function ex-pects to receive two integer arguments and will formally return an integer value. The function prototype for `swap()` declares that this function requires four arguments consisting of an integer, two characters, and a double-precision argument, in that or-der, and will formally return a double-precision number. Finally, the function proto-type for `display()` declares that this function requires two double-precision argu-ments and does not return any value. Such a function might be used to display the results of a computation directly without returning any value to the called function.

The use of function prototypes permits error checking of data types by the com-piler. If the function prototype does not agree with the function's header line when the function is written, an error message occurs.

Calling a Function

Calling a function is a rather easy operation. The only requirements are that the name of the function be used and that any data passed to the function be enclosed within the parentheses following the function name using the same order and type as declared in the function prototype. The items enclosed within the paren-theses in the call statement are called **arguments** of the called function (see Figure 6.2). Other terms used as synonyms for arguments are **actual arguments** and **actual**

parameters. All of these terms refer to the data values supplied to a function within the calling statement when the call is made.

FIGURE 6.2   Calling and Passing Two Values to `findMax()`

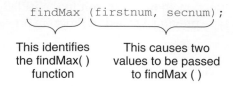

If a variable is one of the actual arguments in a function call, the called function receives a copy of the value stored in the variable. For example, the statement `findMax(firstnum, secnum);` calls the function `findMax()` and causes the values currently residing in the variables `firstnum` and `secnum` to be passed to `findMax()`. The variable names in parentheses are actual arguments that provide values to the called function. After the values are passed, control is transferred to the called function.

FIGURE 6.3   `findMax()` **Receives Actual Values**

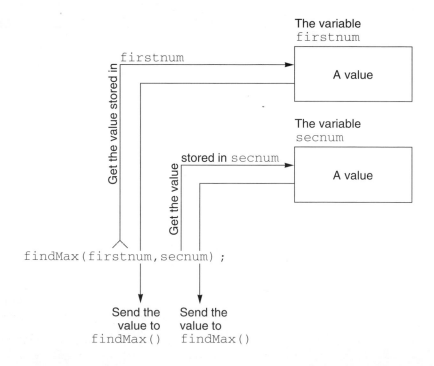

As illustrated in Figure 6.3, *the function* `findMax()` *does not receive the variables named* `firstnum` *and* `secnum` *and has no knowledge of these variable names.*[1] The

---

[1] This is significantly different from computer languages such as FORTRAN, where functions and subroutines receive access to the variables and can pass data back through them. In Section 6.5, we will see how, using reference variables, C++ can also permit direct access to the calling function's parameters.

function simply receives the values in these variables and must itself determine where to store these values before it does anything else. Although this procedure for passing data to a function may seem surprising, it is really a safety procedure for ensuring that a called function does not inadvertently change data stored in a variable. The function gets a copy of the data to use. It may change its copy and, of course, change any variables declared inside itself. However, unless specific steps are taken to do so, a function is not allowed to change the contents of variables declared in other functions.

Now we will begin writing the function `findMax()` to process the values passed to it.

Defining a Function

A function is defined when it is written. Each function is defined once (that is, written once) in a program and can then be used by any other function in the program that suitably declares it.

Like the `main()` function, every C++ function consists of two parts, a **function header** and a **function body**, as illustrated in Figure 6.4. The purpose of the function header is to identify the data type of the value returned by the function, provide the function with a name, and specify the number, order, and type of arguments expected by the function. The purpose of the function body is to operate on the passed data and directly return, at most, one value to the calling function. (We will see, in Section 6.5, how a function can be made to return multiple values through the parameter list.)

FIGURE 6.4   General Format of a Function

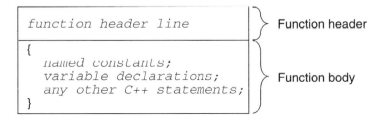

The function header is always the first line of a function and contains the function's returned value type, its name, and the names and data types of its arguments. Since `findMax()` does not formally return any value and is to receive two integer arguments, the following header line can be used:

        void findMax(int x, int y) ◄——————————— No semicolon

The identifier names in the header line are referred to as **formal parameters**, **formal arguments**, and **parameters**; we use these terms interchangeably.[2] Thus, the parameter x is used to store the first value passed to `findMax()` and the parameter y is used to store the second value passed at the time of the function call. The function does not know where the values come from when the call is made from `main()`. The first part of the call procedure executed by the program involves going

---

[2] The portion of the function header that contains the function name and parameters is formally referred to as a *function declarator*.

to the variables `firstnum` and `secnum` and retrieving the stored values. These values are then passed to `findMax()` and ultimately stored in the parameters `x` and `y` (see Figure 6.5).

FIGURE 6.5   Storing Values into Parameters

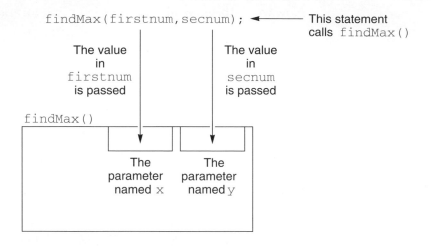

The function name and all parameter names in the header line, in this case `findMax`, `x`, and `y`, are chosen by the programmer. Any names selected according to the rules for choosing variable names can be used. All parameters listed in the function header line must be separated by commas and must have their individual data types declared separately.

Now that we have written the function header for the `findMax()` function, we can construct its body. Let us assume that the `findMax()` function selects and displays the larger of the two numbers passed to it.

As illustrated in Figure 6.6, a function body begins with an opening brace, {, contains any necessary named constants, variable declarations, and other C++ statements, and ends with a closing brace, }. This structure should be familiar to you because it is the same structure used in all the `main()` functions we have written. This fact should not be a surprise because `main()` is itself a function and must adhere to the rules required for constructing all legitimate functions.

FIGURE 6.6   Structure of a Function Body

```
{
    named constants
    variable declarations
    other C++ statements
}
```

In the body of the function `findMax()`, we declare one variable to store the maximum of the two numbers passed to it. We then use an `if-else` statement to

▲ P O I N T   O F   I N F O R M A T I O N ▲

Function Definitions and Function Prototypes

When you write a function, you are formally creating a **function definition**. A function definition begins with a header line that includes a formal parameter list, if any, enclosed in parentheses and ends with the closing brace that terminates the function's body. The parentheses are required whether or not the function uses any parameters. The syntax for a function definition is:

```
returnDataType functionName(parameter list)
{
  named constants
  variable declarations

  other C++ statements

  return value
}
```

A **function prototype** declares a function. The syntax for a function prototype, which provides the return data type of the function, the function's name, and a list of argument data types (argument names are optional), is:

```
returnDataType functionName(list of argument data types);
```

Thus, the prototype along with pre- and postcondition comments (see Point of Information box on p. 308) should provide a user with all the programming information needed to successfully call the function.

Generally, all function prototypes are placed at the top of the program, and all definitions are placed after the `main()` function. However, this placement can be changed. The only requirement in C++ is that a function cannot be called before it has been either declared or defined.

find the maximum of the two numbers. Finally, a `cout` object stream is used to display the maximum. Thus, the complete function definition for the `findMax()` function is:

```
void findMax(int x, int y)
{                       // start of function body
  int maxnum;           // variable declaration

  if (x >= y)           // find the maximum number
    maxnum = x;
  else
    maxnum = y;

  cout << "\nThe maximum of the two numbers is "
       << maxnum << endl;

  return;

} // end of function body and end of function
```

Notice that the parameter declarations are made within the header line and the variable declaration is made immediately after the opening brace of the function's body. This is in keeping with the concept that parameter values are passed to a function from outside the function and that variables are declared and assigned values from within the function body.

Program 6.2 includes the findMax() function within the program code previously listed in Program 6.1.

PROGRAM 6.2

```cpp
#include <iostream>
using namespace std;

void findMax(int, int);    // the function prototype

int main()
{
  int firstnum, secnum;

  cout << "\nEnter a number: ";
  cin  >> firstnum;
  cout << "Great! Please enter a second number: ";
  cin  >> secnum;

  findMax(firstnum, secnum);   // the function is called here

  return 0;
}

// following is the function findMax()

void findMax(int x, int y)
{                     // start of function body
  int maxnum;       // variable declaration

  if (x >= y)      // find the maximum number
     maxnum = x;
  else
     maxnum = y;

  cout << "\nThe maximum of the two numbers is "
       << maxnum << endl;

  return;
} // end of function body and end of function
```

Program 6.2 can be used to select and print the maximum of any two integer numbers entered by the user. A sample run of Program 6.2 follows:

```
Enter a number: 25
Great! Please enter a second number: 5

The maximum of the two numbers is 25
```

A BIT OF BACKGROUND

Procedural Abstraction

Assigning a name to a function or procedure in such a way that the function is invoked by simply using a name with appropriate arguments is formally referred to as *procedural abstraction*. In writing your own user-named functions, you are actually creating procedural abstractions.

Notice that procedural abstraction effectively hides the implementation details of how a function performs its task. This hiding of the details is one of the hallmarks and strengths of abstraction. By thinking of tasks on an abstract procedural level, programmers can solve problems at a higher level without immediately being concerned with the nitty-gritty details of the actual solution implementation.

The placement of the `findMax()` function after the `main()` function in Program 6.2 is a matter of choice. Some programmers prefer to put all called functions at the top of a program and make `main()` the last function listed. We prefer to list `main()` first because it is the driver function that should give anyone reading the program an idea of what the complete program is about before encountering the details of each function. Either placement approach is acceptable, and you will encounter both styles in your programming work. In no case, however, can the definition of `findMax()` be placed inside `main()`. This is true for all C++ functions: *Each function must be defined by itself outside any other function.* Each C++ function is a separate and independent entity with its own parameters and variables; nesting of functions is never permitted.

Placement of Statements

C++ does not impose a rigid statement ordering structure on the programmer. The general rule for placing statements in a C++ program is simply that all preprocessor directives, variables, named constants, and functions must be either declared or defined *before* they can be used. As we have noted previously, although this rule permits both preprocessor directives and declaration statements to be placed throughout a program, doing so results in a very poor program structure.

As a matter of good programming form, the following statement ordering should form the basic structure around which all of your C++ programs are constructed:

```
preprocessor directives
function prototypes
int main()
{
  symbolic constants
  variable declarations

  other executable statements
  return value
}
function definitions
```

As always, comment statements can be freely intermixed anywhere within this basic structure.

Preconditions and Postconditions

Preconditions are any set of conditions required by a function to be true if it is to operate correctly. For example, if a function uses the named constant MAXCHARS, which must have a positive value, a precondition is that MAXCHARS be declared with a positive value before the function is called.

Similarly, a postcondition is a condition that is true after the function is executed, assuming that the preconditions are met.

Pre- and postconditions are typically documented by user comments. For example, consider the following function header line and comments:

```
bool leapyr(int year)
// Preconditions: the parameter year must represent a year in a four
//              : digit form, such as 2006
// Postconditions: a value of true is returned if the year is a leap year;
//                : otherwise false will be returned
```

Pre- and postcondition comments should be included with both function prototypes and function definitions whenever clarification is needed.

Variations[3]

There are a number of useful variations to defining and declaring functions. One of these, overloading, we have met before in multiple versions of the math methods `sqrt()` and `abs()`. Following is an introduction to construction of a number of useful variations, including overloaded functions.

Function Stubs

An alternative to completing each function required in a complete program is to write the `main()` function first and then add the functions later, as they are developed. The problem that arises with this approach, however, is the same problem that occurred with Program 6.1; that is, the program cannot be run until all of the functions are included. For convenience, we have reproduced the code for Program 6.1:

```
#include <iostream>
using namespace std;
void findMax(int, int);  // the function declaration (prototype)

int main()
{
  int firstnum, secnum;

  cout << "\nEnter a number: ";
  cin  >> firstnum;
  cout << "Great! Please enter a second number: ";
  cin  >> secnum;

  findMax(firstnum, secnum); // the function is called here

  return 0;
}
```

---

[3] All of these variations may be omitted on first reading without loss of subject continuity.

▲ P R O G R A M M I N G   N O T E ▲

Isolation Testing

One of the most successful software testing methods known is always to embed the code being tested within an environment of working code. For example, assume you have two untested functions that are called in the order shown below, and the result returned by the second function is incorrect:

From the information shown in this figure, one or possibly both of the functions could be operating incorrectly. The first order of business is to isolate the problem to a specific function.

One of the most powerful methods of performing this code isolation is to decouple the functions. This is done either by testing each function individually or by testing one function first, and only when you know it is operating correctly, reconnecting it to the second function. Then, if an error occurs, you have isolated the error to either the transfer of data between functions or the internal operation of the second function.

This specific procedure is an example of the **basic rule of testing,** which states that each function should only be tested in a program in which all other functions are known to be correct. This means that one function must first be tested by itself, using stubs if necessary for any called functions, then a second tested function should be tested either by itself or with a previously tested function, and so on. This ensures that each new function is isolated within a test bed of correct functions, with the final program effectively built up of tested function code.

This program would be complete if there were a function definition for `findMax()`. But we really don't need a *correct* `findMax()` function to test and run what has been written, we just need a function that *acts* like it is correct: A "fake" `findMax()` that accepts the proper number and types of parameters and returns values of the proper form for the function call is all we need to allow initial testing. This fake function is called a stub. A **stub** is the beginning of a final function that serves as a placeholder until the function is completed. A stub for `findMax()` follows:

```
void findMax(int x, int y)
{
  cout << "In findMax()\n";
  cout << "The value of x is " << x << endl;
  cout << "The value of y is " << y << endl;

  return;

}
```

This stub function can now be compiled and linked with the previously completed code to obtain an executable program. The code for the function can then be further developed, and when it is completed, it replaces the stub portion. As illustrated, a stub should always display the name of the function that it represents.

The minimum requirement of a stub function is that it compile and link with its calling module. In practice, it is a good idea to have a stub display both a message that it has been entered successfully along with the value(s) of its received arguments, as in the stub for findMax.

As the function is refined, you let it do more and more, perhaps allowing it to return intermediate or incomplete results. This incremental, or stepwise, refinement is an important concept in efficient program development that provides you with the means to run a program that does not yet meet all of its final requirements.

Functions with Empty Parameter Lists

Although useful functions having an empty parameter list are extremely limited (one such function is provided in Exercise 10 at the end of this section), they can occur. The function prototype for such a function requires either the keyword void or nothing at all between the parentheses following the function name. For example, both prototypes

```
int display();
```

and

```
int display(void);
```

indicate that the display() function takes no arguments and returns an integer value. A function with an empty parameter list is called by its name with nothing written inside the required parentheses following the function's name. For example, the statement display(); correctly calls the display() function whose prototype was just given.

Default Arguments

A convenient feature of C++ is its flexibility for providing default arguments in a function call. The primary use of default arguments is to extend the parameter list of existing functions without requiring any change in the calling argument lists already in place within a program.

Default argument values are listed in the function prototype and are automatically transmitted to the called function when the corresponding arguments are omitted from the function call. For example, the function prototype

```
void example(int, int = 5, double = 6.78);
```

provides default values for the last two arguments. If any of these arguments are omitted when the function is actually called, the C++ compiler supplies these default values. Thus, all of the following function calls are valid:

```
example(7, 2, 9.3);   // no defaults used
example(7, 2);        // same as example(7, 2, 6.78);
example(7);           // same as example(7, 5, 6.78);
```

Four rules must be followed when using default parameters. The first is that default values can only be assigned in the function prototype. The second is that if any parameter is given a default value in the function prototype, all parameters following it must also be supplied with default values. The third rule is that if one argument is omitted in the actual function call, then all arguments to its right must also be omitted. These latter two rules make it clear to the C++

compiler which arguments are being omitted and permits the compiler to supply correct default values for the missing arguments, starting with the rightmost argument and working toward the left. The last rule specifies that the default value used in the function prototype may be an expression consisting of both constants and previously declared variables. If such an expression is used, it must pass the compiler's check for validly declared variables, even though the actual value of the expression is evaluated and assigned at run time.

Default arguments are extremely useful when extending an existing function to include more features that require additional arguments. Adding the new arguments to the right of the existing arguments and providing each new argument with a default value permit all existing function calls to remain as they are. Thus, the effect of the new changes is conveniently isolated from existing code in the program.

Reusing Function Names (Overloading)

C++ provides the capability of using the same function name for more than one function, which is referred to as **function overloading**. The only requirement in creating more than one function with the same name is that the compiler must be able to determine which function to use based on the data types of the parameters (not the data type of the return value, if any). For example, consider the three following functions, all named `showabs()`.

```
void showabs(int x)   // display the absolute value of an integer
{
  if ( x < 0 )
    x = -x;
  cout << "The absolute value of the integer is  " << x << endl;
}

void showabs(long x)   // display the absolute value of a long integer
{
  if ( x < 0 )
    x = -x;
  cout << "The absolute value of the long integer is  " << x << endl;
}

void showabs(double x)   // display the absolute value of a double
{
  if ( x < 0 )
    x = -x;
  cout << "The absolute value of the double is  " << x << endl;
}
```

Which of the three functions named `showabs()` is actually called depends on the argument types supplied at the time of the call. Thus, the function call `showabs(10);` causes the compiler to use the function named `showabs()` that expects an integer argument, and the function call `showabs(6.28);` causes the compiler to use the function named `showabs()` that expects a double-valued argument.[4]

Notice that overloading a function's name simply means using the same name for more than one function. Each function that uses the name must still be written and

---

[4] This is accomplished by a process referred to as *name mangling*. Using this process, the function name generated by the C++ compiler differs from the function name used in the source code. The compiler appends information to the source code function name depending on the type of data being passed, and the resulting name is said to be a mangled version of the source code name.

exists as a separate entity. The use of the same function name does not require that the code within the functions be similar, although good programming practice dictates that functions with the same name should perform essentially the same operations. The only formal requirement when using the same function name is that the compiler must be able to distinguish which function to select based on the data types of the arguments when the function is called. Clearly, however, if all that is different about the overloaded functions is the argument types, a better programming solution is simply to create a function template. The use of overloaded functions, however, is extremely useful with constructor functions, a topic that is presented in Section 7.2.

Function Templates

In most high-level languages, including C++'s immediate predecessor, C, each function requires its own unique name. In theory, this makes sense, but in practice it can lead to a profusion of function names, even for functions that perform essentially the same operations. For example, consider determining and displaying the absolute value of a number. If the number passed into the function can be either an integer, a floating-point, or a double-precision value, three distinct functions must be written to handle each case correctly. Certainly, we could give each of these functions a unique name, such as abs (), fabs (), and dabs (), respectively, having the function prototypes:

```
void abs(int);
void fabs(float);
void dabs(double);
```

Clearly, each of these three functions performs essentially the same operation but on different parameter data types. A much cleaner and more elegant solution is to write a general function that handles all cases, but whose parameters, variables, and even return type can be set by the compiler based on the actual function call. This is possible in C++ using function templates.

A **function template** is a single, complete function that serves as a model for a family of functions. Which function from the family that is actually created depends on subsequent function calls. To make this more concrete, consider a function template that computes and displays the absolute value of a passed argument. An appropriate function template is:

```
template <class T>
void showabs(T number)
{
  if (number < 0)
    number = -number;
  cout << "The absolute value of the number "
       << " is " << number << endl;

  return
}
```

For the moment, ignore the first line template <class T>, and look at the second line, which consists of the function header void showabs (T number). Notice that this header line has the same syntax that we have been using for all of our function definitions, except for the T where a data type is usually placed. For example, if the header line were void showabs(int number), you should recognize this as a function named `showabs` that expects one integer argument to be passed to it and that returns no value. Similarly, if the header line were `void showabs(float number)`, you should recognize it as a function that expects one floating-point argument to be passed when the function is called.

The advantage in using the T within the function template header line is that it represents a general data type that is replaced by an actual data type, such as `int`, `float`, `double`, etc., when the compiler encounters an actual function call. For example, if a function call with an integer argument is encountered, the compiler uses the function template to construct the code for a function that expects an integer parameter. Similarly, if a call is made with a floating-point argument, the compiler constructs a function that expects a floating-point parameter. As a specific example of this, consider Program 6.3.

PROGRAM 6.3

```cpp
#include <iostream>
using namespace std;

template <class T>
void showabs (T number)
{

  if (number < 0)
    number = -number;
  cout << "The absolute value of the number is "
       << number << endl;

  return;
}

int main()
{
  int num1 = -4;
  float num2 - -4.23f;
  double num3 = -4.23456;
  showabs(num1);
  showabs(num2);
  showabs(num3);

 return 0;
}
```

First notice the three function calls made in the `main()` function shown in Program 6.3, which call the function `showabs()` with an integer, floating-point, and double-precision value, respectively. Now review the function template for `showabs()` and let us consider the first line, `template<classT>`. This line, which is called a **template prefix**, is used to inform the compiler that the function immediately following is a template that uses a data type named T. Within the function template, T is used in the same manner as any other data type, such as `int`, `float`, `double`, etc. Then, when the compiler encounters an actual function call for `showabs()`, the data type of the argument passed in the call is substituted for T throughout the function. In effect, the compiler creates a specific function, using the template, that expects the argument type in the call. Since Program 6.3 makes three calls to showabs, each with a different argument data type, the compiler creates three separate showabs() functions. The compiler knows which function to use based on the arguments passed at the time of the call. The output displayed when Program 6.3 is executed is:

```
The absolute value of the number is 4
The absolute value of the number is 4.23
The absolute value of the number is 4.23456
```

The letter T used in the template prefix template <class T> is simply a placeholder for a data type that is defined when the function is invoked. Any letter or nonkeyword identifier can be used instead. Thus, the showabs() function template could have been defined as:

```
template <class DTYPE>
void showabs (DTYPE number)
{
  if (number < 0)
    number = -number;
  cout << "The absolute value of the number is "
       << number << endl;
  return;
}
```

In this regard, it is sometimes simpler and clearer to read the word *class* in the template prefix as *data type*. Thus, the template prefix template <class T> can be read as "we are defining a function template that has a data type named T." Then, within both the header line and body of the defined function, the data type T (or any other letter or identifier defined in the prefix) is used in the same manner as any built-in data type, such as int, float, double, etc.

Now suppose we want to create a function template to include both a return type and an internally declared variable. For example, consider the following function template:

```
template <class T> // template prefix
T abs (T value)         // header line
{
  T absnum;  // variable declaration

  if (value < 0)
    absnum = -value;
  else
    absnum = value;

  return absnum;
}
```

In this template definition, we have used the data type T to declare three items: the return type of the function, the data type of a single function parameter named value, and one variable declared within the function. Program 6.4 illustrates how this function template could be used within the context of a complete program.

PROGRAM 6.4

```cpp
#include <iostream>
using namespace std;

template <class T> // template prefix
T abs (T value)    // header line
{
  T absnum;  // variable declaration

  if (value < 0)
    absnum = -value;
  else
    absnum = value;

  return absnum;
}
int main()
{
  int num1 = -4;
  float num2 = -4.23f;
  double num3 = -4.23456;

cout << "The absolute value of " << num1
     << " is '' << abs(num1) << endl;
cout << "The absolute value of " << num2
     << " is " << abs(num2) << endl;
cout << "The absolute value of " << num3
     << " is " << abs(num3) << endl;
    return 0;
}
```

In the first call to abs() made within main(), an integer value is passed as an argument. In this case, the compiler substitutes an int data type for the T data type in the function template and creates the following function:

```cpp
int abs(int value) // header line
{
  int absnum;  // variable declaration

  if (value < 0)
    absnum = -value;
  else
    absnum = value;

  return (absnum);
}
```

Similarly, in the second and third function calls, the compiler creates two more functions, one in which the data type T is replaced by the keyword float and one in which the data type T is replaced by the keyword double. The output produced by Program 6.4 is:

```
The absolute value of -4 is 4
The absolute value of -4.23 is 4.23
The absolute value of -4.23456 is 4.23456
```

The value of using the function template is that one function definition has been used to create three different functions, each of which uses the same logic and operations but operates on different data types.

Finally, although both Programs 6.3 and 6.4 define a function template that uses a single placeholder data type, function templates with more than one data type can be defined. For example, the template prefix

```
template <class DTYPE1, class DTYPE2, class DTYPE3>
```

can be used to create a function template that requires three different data types. As before, within the header and body of the function template, the data types DTYPE1, DTYPE2, and DTYPE3 are used in the same manner as any built-in data type, such as int, float, double, etc. Additionally, as noted previously, the names DTYPE1, DTYPE2, and DTYPE3 can be any nonkeyword identifier. Conventionally, the letter T followed by zero or more digits would be used, such as T, T1, T2, T3, etc.

Exercises 6.1

1. For the following function headers, determine the number, type, and order (sequence) of the values that must be passed to the function:

   a. void factorial(int n)

   b. void price(int type, double yield, double maturity)

   c. void yield(int type, double price, double maturity)

   d. void interest(char flag, float price, float time)

   e. void total(float amount, float rate)

   f. void roi(int a, int b, char c, char d, float e, float f)

   g. void getVal(int item, int iter, char decflag, char delim)

2. a. Write a function named check() that has three parameters. The first parameter should accept an integer number, the second parameter a floating-point number, and the third parameter a double-precision number. The body of the function should just display the values of the data passed to the function when it is called. (*Note:* When tracing errors in functions, it is very helpful to have the function display the values it has been passed. Quite frequently, the error is not in the function but in the data received and stored.)

   b. Include the function written in Exercise 2a in a working program. Make sure your function is called from main(). Test the function by passing various data to it.

3. a. Write a function named findAbs() that accepts a double-precision number passed to it, computes its absolute value, and displays the absolute value. The absolute value of a number is the number itself if the number is positive and the negative of the number if the number is negative.

   b. Include the function written in Exercise 3a in a working program. Make sure your function is called from main(). Test the function by passing various data to it.

4. a. Write a function called mult() that accepts two floating-point numbers as parameters, multiplies these two numbers, and displays the result.

   b. Include the function written in Exercise 4a in a working program. Make sure your function is called from main(). Test the function by passing various data to it.

5. a. Write a function named `sqrIt()` that computes the square of the value passed to it and displays the result. The function should be capable of squaring numbers with decimal points.

   b. Include the function written in Exercise 5a in a working program. Make sure your function is called from `main()`. Test the function by passing various data to it.

6. a. Write a function named `powFun()` that raises an integer number passed to it to a positive integer power and displays the result. The positive integer should be the second value passed to the function. Declare the variable used to store the result as a long integer data type to ensure sufficient storage for the result.

   b. Include the function written in Exercise 6a in a working program. Make sure your function is called from `main()`. Test the function by passing various data to it.

7. a. Write a function that produces a table of the numbers from 1 to 10, their squares, and cubes. The function should produce the same display as that produced by Program 5.11.

   b. Include the function written in Exercise 7a in a working program. Make sure your function is called from `main()`. Test the function by passing various data to it.

8. a. Modify the function written for Exercise 7 to accept the starting value of the table, the number of values to be displayed, and the increment between values. If the increment is not explicitly sent, the function should use a default value of 1. Name your function `selTab()`. A call to `selTab(6,5,2);` should produce a table of five lines, the first line starting with the number 6 and each succeeding number increasing by 2.

   b. Include the function written in Exercise 8a in a working program. Make sure your function is called from `main()`. Test the function by passing various data to it.

9. a. Write a C++ program that accepts an integer argument and determines whether the passed integer is even or odd.

      (*Hint:* Use the % operator.)

   b. Enter, compile, and execute the program written for Exercise 9a.

10. A useful function with an empty parameter list can be constructed to return a value for π that is accurate to the maximum number of decimal places allowed by your computer. This value is obtained by taking the arcsine of 1.0, which is $\pi/2$, and multiplying the result by 2. In C++, the required expression is *2.0 * asin(1.0)*, where the `asin()` function is provided in the standard C++ mathematics library (remember to include `cmath`). Using this expression, write a C++ function named `Pi()` that calculates and displays the value of π.

11. a. Write a function template named `display()` that displays the value of the single argument passed to it when the function is called.

    b. Include the function template created in Exercise 11a within a complete C++ program that calls the function four times: once with a character argument, once with an integer argument, once with a floating-point argument, and once with a double-precision argument.

12. a. Write a function template named `whole()` that returns the integer value of any argument passed to it when the function is called.

    b. Include the function template created in Exercise 12a within a complete C++ program that calls the function four times: once with a character argument, once with an integer argument, once with a floating-point argument, and once with a double-precision argument.

13. a. Write a function template named `maximum()` that returns the maximum value of three arguments passed to the function when it is called. Assume that all three arguments are of the same data type.

    b. Include the function template created for Exercise 13a within a complete C++ program that calls the function with three integers and then with three floating-point numbers.

14. a. Write a function template named `square()` that computes and returns the square of the single argument passed to the function when it is called.

    b. Include the function template created for Exercise 14a within a complete C++ program.

6.2 RETURNING VALUES

Using the method of passing data into a function presented in the previous section, the called function only receives copies of the values contained in the arguments at the time of the call (review Figure 6.3 if this is unclear). This method of passing values to a called function is referred to as a function **pass by value** and is a distinct advantage of C++. Since the called function does not have direct access to any of the calling function's variables, it cannot inadvertently alter the value stored in one of these variables.

The function receiving the passed by value arguments may process the data sent to it in any fashion desired and directly return at most one, and only one, "legitimate" value to the calling function (see Figure 6.7). In this section, we see how such a value is returned to the calling function. As you might expect, given C++'s flexibility, there is a way of returning more than a single value, but that is the topic of Section 6.5.

FIGURE 6.7   A Function Directly Returns at Most One Value When It Is Called by Value

A function can receive many values

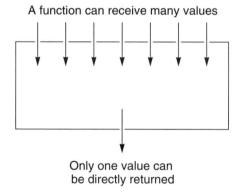

Only one value can
be directly returned

As with the calling of a function, directly returning a single value requires that the interface between the called and calling functions be handled correctly. From its side of the return transaction, the called function must provide the following items:

- the data type of the returned value
- the actual value being returned

A function returning a value must specify, in its header line, the data type of the value that will be returned. Recall that the function header line is the first line of the function, which includes both the function's name and a list of parameter names. As an example, consider the `findMax()` function written in the last section. It determined the maximum value of two numbers passed to the function. For convenience, the `findMax()` code is listed here again:

```
void findMax(int x, int y)
{                       // start of function body
  int maxnum;           // variable declaration

  if (x >= y)           // find the maximum number
    maxnum = x;
  else
    maxnum = y;

  cout << "\nThe maximum of the two numbers is "
       << maxnum << endl;

  return;

} // end of function body and end of function
```

As written, the function's header line is

```
void findMax(int x, int y)
```

where x and y are the names chosen for the function's formal parameters.

If findMax() is now to return a value, the function's header line must be amended to include the data type of the value being returned. For example, if an integer value is to be returned, the proper function header line is:[5]

```
int findMax(int x, int y)
```

Similarly, if the function is to receive two floating-point values and return a floating-point value, the correct function header line is:

```
float findMax(float x, float y)
```

And if the function is to receive two double-precision values and return a double-precision value, the header line is:

```
double findMax(double x, double y)
```

Let us now modify the function findMax() to return the maximum value of the two numbers passed to it. To do this, we must first determine the data type of the value that is to be returned and include this data type in the function's header line.

Since the maximum value determined by findMax() is stored in the integer variable maxnum, it is the value of this variable that the function should return. Returning an integer value from findMax() requires that the function header line be:

```
int findMax(int x, int y)
```

Observe that this is the same as findMax()'s original function header line with the substitution of the keyword int for the keyword void.

Having declared the data type that findMax() will return, all that remains is to include a statement within the function to cause the return of the correct value. To return a value, a function must use a **return statement**, which has the form:[6]

```
return expression;
```

_____

[5] The return data type is only related to the parameter data types inasmuch as the returned value is computed from parameter values. In this case, since the function is used to return the maximum value of its parameters, it makes little sense to return a data type that does not match the function's parameter types.

[6] Many programmers place the expression within parentheses, yielding the statement return (expression);. Either syntax can be used.

When the return statement is encountered, the expression is evaluated first. The value of the expression is then automatically converted to the data type declared in the function header before being sent back to the calling function. After the value is returned, program control reverts to the calling function. Thus, to return the value stored in `maxnum`, all we need to do is add the statement `return maxnum;` before the closing brace of the `findMax()` function. The complete function code is:

```
            int findMax(int x, int y)   // function header line
            {                           // start of function body
               int maxnum;              // variable declaration

               if (x >= y)
                  maxnum = x;
               else
                  maxnum = y;

               return maxnum;           // return statement
            }
```

These should be the same data type.

In this new code for the function `findMax()`, note that the data type of the expression contained within the parentheses of the return statement correctly matches the data type in the function's header line. It is up to the programmer to ensure that this is true for every function returning a value. Failure to match the return value exactly with the function's declared data type may not result in an error when your program is compiled, but it may lead to undesired results since the return value is always converted to the data type declared in the function declaration. Usually, this is a problem only when the fractional part of a returned floating-point or double-precision number is truncated because the function was declared to return an integer value.

Having taken care of the sending side of the return transaction, we must now prepare the calling function to receive the value sent by the called function. On the calling (receiving) side, the calling function must:

- be alerted to the type of value to expect
- properly use the returned value

Alerting the calling function as to the type of return value to expect is properly taken care of by the function prototype. For example, including the function prototype

```
            int findMax(int, int);
```

before `main()` is sufficient to alert `main()` that `findMax()` is a function that returns an integer value.

To use a returned value, we must either provide a variable in which to store the value or use the value directly in an expression. Storing the returned value in a variable is accomplished using a standard assignment statement. For example, the assignment statement

```
            max = findMax(firstnum, secnum);
```

can be used to store the value returned by `findMax()` in the variable named `max`. This assignment statement does two things. First, the right-hand side of the assignment statement calls `findMax()`; then the result returned by `findMax` is stored in the variable `max`. Since the value returned by `findMax()` is an integer, the variable `max` must also be declared as an integer variable within the calling function's variable declarations.

The value returned by a function need not be stored directly in a variable, but it can be used wherever an expression is valid. For example, the expression 2 * findMax(firstnum,secnum) multiplies the value returned by 2, and the statement

```
cout << findMax(firstnum,secnum);
```

displays the returned value.

Program 6.5 illustrates the inclusion of prototype and assignment statements for main() to correctly call and store a returned value from findMax(). As before and in keeping with our convention of placing the main() function first, we have placed the findMax() function after main().

PROGRAM 6.5

```cpp
#include <iostream>
using namespace std;

int findMax(int, int); // the function prototype

int main()
{
  int firstnum, secnum, max;

  cout << "\nEnter a number: ";
  cin  >> firstnum;
  cout << "Great! Please enter a second number: ";
  cin  >> secnum;

  max = findMax(firstnum, secnum); // the function is called here

  cout << "\nThe maximum of the two numbers is " << max << endl;

  return 0;
}

int findMax(int x, int y)
{                       // start of function body
  int maxnum;           // variable declaration

  if (x >= y)           // find the maximum number
    maxnum = x;
  else
    maxnum = y;

  return maxnum;        // return statement
}
```

In reviewing Program 6.5, it is important to note the four items we have introduced in this section. The first item is the prototype for findMax(). This statement, which ends with a semicolon as all declaration statements do, alerts main() and any subsequent function definitions to the data type that findMax() will be returning. The second item to notice in `main()` is the use of an assignment statement to store the returned value from the `findMax()` call into the variable `max`. We have also made sure to correctly declare `max` as an integer within `main()`'s variable declarations so that it matches the data type of the returned value.

The last two items to note concern the coding of the `findMax()` function. The first line of `findMax()` declares that the function returns an integer value, and the expression in the return statement evaluates to a matching data type. `findMax()`, thus, is internally consistent in sending an integer value back to `main()`, and `main()` has been correctly alerted to receive and use the returned integer.

In writing your own functions, you must always keep these four items in mind. For another example, see if you can identify these four items in Program 6.6.

PROGRAM 6.6

```cpp
#include <iostream>
using namespace std;

double tempvert(double);   // function prototype

int main()
{
  const int CONVERTS = 4;   // number of conversions to be made

  int count;                // start of declarations
  double fahren;

  for(count = 1; count <= CONVERTS; count++)
  {
    cout << "\nEnter a Fahrenheit temperature: ";
    cin  >> fahren;
    cout << "The Celsius equivalent is "
         << tempvert(fahren) << endl;
  }

  return 0;
}

// convert fahrenheit to celsius
double tempvert(double inTemp)
{
  return (5.0/9.0) * (inTemp - 32.0);
}
```

In reviewing Program 6.6, let us first analyze the function `tempvert()`. The complete definition of the function begins with the function's header line and ends with the closing brace after the return statement. The function is declared as a `double`; this means the expression in the function's return statement must evaluate to a double-precision number, which it does. Since a function header line is not a statement but the start of the code defining the function, the function header line does not end with a semicolon.

For the receiving side, there is a prototype for the function `tempvert()` that agrees with `tempvert()`'s function definition. No variable is declared in `main()`

to store the returned value from `tempvert()` because the returned value is immediately passed to `cout` for display.

One further point is worth mentioning here. One of the purposes of declarations, as we learned in Chapter 2, is to alert the compiler to the amount of internal storage reserved for the data. The prototype for `tempvert()` performs this task and tells the computer how much storage area must be accessed by `main()` when the returned value is retrieved. Had we placed the `tempvert()` function before `main()`, however, the function header line for `tempvert()` would suffice to alert the computer to the type of storage needed for the returned value. In this case, the function prototype for `tempvert()` could be eliminated. Since we have chosen always to list `main()` as the first function in a file, we must include function prototypes for all functions called by `main()`.

Inline Functions[7]

Calling a function places a certain amount of overhead on a computer: This consists of placing argument values in a reserved memory region that the function has access to (this memory region is referred to as the **stack**), passing control to the function, providing a reserved memory location for any returned value (again, the stack region of memory is used for this purpose), and finally returning to the proper point in the calling program. Use of this overhead is well justified when a function is called many times because it can significantly reduce the size of a program. Rather than repeating the same code each time it is needed, the code is written once, as a function, and called whenever it is needed.

For small functions that are not called many times, however, paying the overhead for passing and returning values may not be warranted. It is still convenient, though, to group repeating lines of code together under a common function name and have the compiler place this code directly into the program wherever the function is called. This capability is provided by inline functions.

Telling the C++ compiler that a function is *inline* causes a copy of the function code to be placed in the program at the point the function is called. For example, consider the function `tempvert()` defined in Program 6.6. Since this is a relatively short function, it is an ideal candidate to be an inline function. To make this, or any other function, an inline one, we simply place the reserved word `inline` before the function name and define the function before any calls are made to it. This is done for the `tempvert()` function in Program 6.7.

Observe in Program 6.7 that the inline function is placed ahead of any calls to it. This is a requirement of all inline functions and obviates the need for a function prototype. Since the function is now an inline one, its code is expanded directly into the program wherever it is called.

The advantage of using an inline function is increased execution speed. Since the inline function is directly expanded and included in every expression or statement calling it, there is no execution time loss due to the call and return overhead required by a noninline function. The disadvantage is the increase in program size when an inline function is called repeatedly. Each time an inline function is referenced, the complete function code is reproduced and stored as an integral part of the program. A noninline function, however, is stored in memory only once. No matter how many times the function is called, the same code is used. Therefore, inline functions should only be used for small functions that are not extensively called in the program.

---

[7] This topic is optional and may be omitted on first reading without loss of subject continuity.

PROGRAM 6.7

```cpp
#include <iostream>
using namespace std;

inline double tempvert(double inTemp)  // an inline function
{
  return (5.0/9.0) * (inTemp - 32.0);
}

int main()
{
  const int CONVERTS = 4;    // number of conversions
  int count;                 // start of declarations
  double fahren;

  for(count = 1; count <= CONVERTS; count++)
  {
    cout << "\nEnter a Fahrenheit temperature: ";
    cin  >> fahren;
    cout << "The Celsius equivalent is "
         << tempvert(fahren) << endl;
  }

  return 0;
}
```

Exercises 6.2

1. Rewrite Program 6.5 so that the function findMax() accepts two floating-point arguments and returns a floating-point value to main(). Make sure you modify main() to pass two floating-point values to findMax() and accept and store the floating-point value returned by findMax().

2. For the following function headers, determine the number, type, and order (sequence) of values that should be passed to the function when it is called and the data type of the value returned by the function:

   a. int factorial(int n)

   b. double price(int type, double yield, double maturity)

   c. double yield(int type, double price, maturity)

   d. char interest(char flag, float price, float time)

   e. int total(float amount, float rate)

   f. float roi(int a, int b, char c, char d, float e, float f)

   g. void getVal(int item, int iter, char decflag)

3. Write function headers for the following:

   a. A function named check that has three parameters. The first parameter should accept an integer number, the second parameter a floating-point number, and the third parameter a double-precision number. The function returns no value.

   b. A function named findAbs() that accepts a double-precision number and returns its absolute value.

   c. A function named mult() that accepts two floating-point numbers as parameters, multiplies these two numbers, and returns the result.

d. A function named `sqrIt()` that computes and returns the square of the integer value passed to it.

e. A function named `powFun()` that raises an integer number passed to it to a positive integer power (also passed as an argument) and returns the result.

f. A function that produces a table of the numbers from 1 to 10, their squares, and cubes. No arguments are to be passed to the function and the function returns no value.

4. a. Write a C++ function named `findAbs()` that accepts a double-precision number passed to it, computes its absolute value, and returns the absolute value to the calling function. The absolute value of a number is the number itself if the number is positive and the negative of the number if the number is negative.

   b. Include the function written in Exercise 4a in a working program. Make sure your function is called from `main()` and correctly returns a value to `main()`. Have `main()` display the value returned. Test the function by passing various data to it.

5. a. Write a C++ function called `mult()` that uses two double-precision numbers as parameters, multiplies these two numbers, and returns the result to the calling function.

   b. Include the function written in Exercise 5a in a working program. Make sure your function is called from `main()` and correctly returns a value to `main()`. Have `main()` display the value returned. Test the function by passing various data to it.

6. a. Write a function named `hypotenuse()` that accepts the lengths of two sides of a right triangle as the parameters a and b, respectively. This function should determine and return the hypotenuse, c, of the triangle (*Hint:* use Pythagoras' theorem that $c^2 = a^2 + b^2$).

   b. Include the function written in Exercise 6a in a working program. Make sure your function is called from `main()` and correctly returns a value to `main()`. Have `main()` display the value returned. Test the function by passing various data to it.

7. A second-degree polynomial in x is given by the expression $ax2 + bx + c$, where *a*, *b*, and *c* are known numbers and *a* is not equal to zero. Write a C++ function named `polyTwo(a,b,c,x)` that computes and returns the value of a second-degree polynomial for any passed values of a, b, c, and x.

8. a. Rewrite the function `tempvert()` in Program 6.6 to accept a temperature and a character as arguments. If the character passed to the function is the letter f, the function should convert the passed temperature from Fahrenheit to Celsius, else the function should convert the passed temperature from Celsius to Fahrenheit.

   b. Modify the `main()` function in Program 6.6 to call the function written for Exercise 8a. Your `main()` function should ask the user for the type of temperature being entered and pass the type (f or c) into `tempvert()`.

9. a. An extremely useful programming algorithm for rounding a real number to *n* decimal places is:

   Step 1: Multiply the number by 10^n.
   Step 2: Add 0.5.
   Step 3: Delete the fractional part of the result.
   Step 4: Divide by 10^n.

   For example, using this algorithm to round the number 78.374625 to three decimal places yields:

   Step 1: $78.374625 \times 10^3 = 78374.625$
   Step 2: $78374.625 + 0.5 = 78375.125$
   Step 3: Retaining the integer part = 78375
   Step 4: 78375 divided by $10^3 = 78.375$

   Use this information to write a C++ function named `round()` that rounds the value of its first parameter to the number of decimal places specified by its second parameter. Incorporate the round() function into a program that accepts a user-entered value of money, multiplies the entered amount by an 8.675% interest rate, and displays the result rounded to two decimal places.

b. Enter, compile, and execute the program written for Exercise 9a.

10. a. Write a C++ function named whole() that returns the integer part of any number passed to the function. (*Hint:* Assign the passed argument to an integer variable.)

b. Include the function written in Exercise 10a in a working program. Make sure your function is called from main() and correctly returns a value to main(). Have main() use a cout statement to display the value returned. Test the function by passing various data to it.

11. a. Write a C++ function named fracpart() that returns the fractional part of any number passed to the function. For example, if the number 256.879 is passed to fracpart(), the number .879 should be returned. Have the function fracpart() call the function whole() that you wrote in Exercise 10. The number returned can then be determined as the number passed to fracpart() less the returned value when the same argument is passed to whole(). The completed program should consist of main() followed by fracpart() followed by whole().

b. Include the function written in Exercise 11a in a working program. Make sure your function is called from main() and correctly returns a value to main(). Have main() use a cout statement to display the value returned. Test the function by passing various data to it.

12. a. Write a function named totamt() that accepts four actual integer arguments named quarters, dimes, nickels, and pennies, which represent the number of quarters, dimes, nickels, and pennies in a piggy bank. The function should determine the dollar value of the number of quarters, dimes, nickels, and pennies passed to it and display the calculated value.

b. Include the totamt() function written for Exercise 12a in a working program. The main() function should correctly call and pass the values of 26 quarters, 80 dimes, 100 nickels, and 216 pennies to totamt(). Make sure you do a hand calculation to verify the result displayed by your program.

6.3 VARIABLE SCOPE

Now that we have begun to write programs containing more than one function, we can look more closely at the variables declared within each function and their relationship to variables in other functions.

By their very nature, C++ functions are independent modules. As we have seen, values are passed to a function using the function's parameter list and a value is returned from a function using a return statement. Seen in this light, a function can be thought of as a closed box, with slots at the top to receive values and a single slot at the bottom to return a value (see Figure 6.8). The metaphor of a closed box is useful because it emphasizes the fact that what goes on inside the function, including all variable declarations within the function's body, are hidden from the view of all other functions.

Since the variables created inside a function are conventionally available only to the function itself, they are said to be local to the function, or **local variables**. This term refers to the **scope** of a variable, where scope is defined as the section of the program where the variable is valid or "known." This section of the program is also referred to as the part in which the variable is visible. A variable can have either a local scope or a global scope. A variable with a **local scope** is simply one that has had storage locations set aside for it by a declaration statement made within a function body. Local variables are only meaningful when used in expressions or statements inside the function that declared them. This means that the same variable name can be declared and used in more than one function. For each function that declares the variable, a separate and distinct variable is created.

FIGURE 6.8   A Function Can Be Thought of as a Closed Box

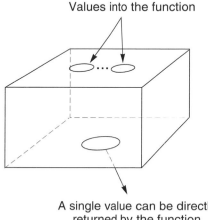

Values into the function

A single value can be directly
returned by the function

All the variables we have used until now have been local variables. This is a direct result of placing our declaration statements inside functions and using them as definition statements that cause the compiler to reserve storage for the declared variable. As we shall see, declaration statements can be placed outside functions and need not act as definitions that cause new storage areas to be reserved for the declared variable.

A variable with **global scope**, more commonly termed a **global variable**, is one whose storage has been created for it by a declaration statement located outside any function. These variables can be used by all functions that are physically placed after the global variable declaration. This is shown in Program 6.8, where we have purposely used the same variable name inside both functions contained in the program.

The variable `firstnum` in Program 6.8 is a global variable because its storage is created by a definition statement located outside a function. Because both functions, `main()` and `valfun()`, follow the definition of `firstnum`, both of these functions can use this global variable with no further declaration needed.

Program 6.8 also contains two separate local variables, both named `secnum`. Storage for the `secnum` variable named in `main()` is created by the definition statement located in `main()`. A different storage area for the `secnum` variable in `valfun()` is created by the definition statement located in the `valfun()` function. Figure 6.9 illustrates the three distinct storage areas reserved by the three definition statements in Program 6.8.

Each of the variables named `secnum` is local to the function in which their storage is created, and each of these variables can only be used from within the appropriate function. Thus, when `secnum` is used in `main()`, the storage area reserved by `main()` for its `secnum` variable is accessed, and when `secnum` is used in valfun(), the storage area reserved by valfun() for its secnum variable is accessed. The following output is produced when Program 6.8 is run:

```
From main(): firstnum = 10
From main(): secnum = 20

From valfun(): firstnum = 10
From valfun(): secnum = 30

From main() again: firstnum = 40
From main() again: secnum = 20
```

PROGRAM 6.8

```cpp
#include <iostream>
using namespace std;

int firstnum;        // create a global variable named firstnum

void valfun();   // function prototype (declaration)

int main()
{
  int secnum;       // create a local variable named secnum

  firstnum = 10;  // store a value into the global variable
  secnum = 20;    // store a value into the local variable

  cout << "From main(): firstnum = " << firstnum << endl;
  cout << "From main(): secnum = " << secnum << endl;

  valfun();  // call the function valfun

  cout << "\nFrom main() again: firstnum = " << firstnum << endl;
  cout << "From main() again: secnum = " << secnum << endl;

  return 0;
}

void valfun() // no values are passed to this function
{
  int secnum;    // create a second local variable named secnum

  secnum = 30;   // this only affects this local variable's value

  cout << "\nFrom valfun(): firstnum = " << firstnum << endl;
  cout << "From valfun(): secnum = " << secnum << endl;

  firstnum = 40; // this changes firstnum for both functions

  return;
}
```

FIGURE 6.9 The Three Storage Areas Created by Program 6.8

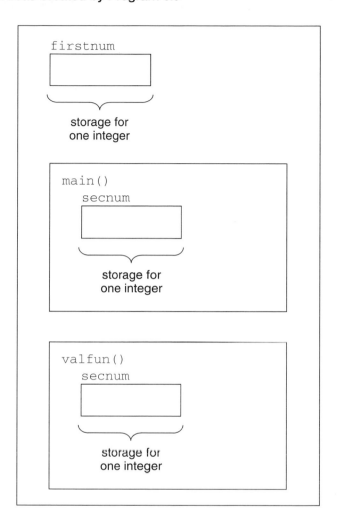

Let's analyze this output. Because `firstnum` is a global variable, both the `main()` and `valfun()` functions can use and change its value. Initially, both functions print the value of 10 that `main()` stored in `firstnum`. Before returning, `valfun()` changes the value of `firstnum` to 40, which is the value displayed when the variable `firstnum` is next displayed from within `main()`.

Because each function only "knows" its own local variables, `main()` can only send the value of its `secnum` to the `cout` object, and `valfun()` can only send the value of its `secnum` to the `cout` object. Thus, whenever `secnum` is obtained from `main()`, the value 20 is displayed, and whenever `secnum` is obtained from `valfun()`, the value 30 is displayed.

C++ does not confuse the two `secnum` variables because only one function can execute at a given moment. While a function is executing, only those variables and parameters that are "in scope" for that function (global and local) can be accessed.

The scope of a variable in no way influences or restricts the data type of the variable. Just as a local variable can be a character, integer, floating-point, double-precision, or any of the other data types (long/short) we have introduced, so can global variables be of these data types, as illustrated in Figure 6.10. The scope of a variable is determined by the placement of the definition statement that reserves storage for it and optionally by a declaration statement that makes it visible, whereas the data type of the variable is determined by using the appropriate keyword (char, int, bool, double, etc.) before the variable's name in a declaration statement.

FIGURE 6.10   Relating the Scope and Type of a Variable

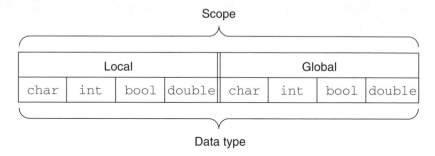

Scope Resolution Operator

When a local variable has the same name as a global variable, all uses of the variable's name made within the scope of the local variable refer to the local variable. This situation is illustrated in Program 6.9, where the variable name number is defined as both a global and local variable.

PROGRAM 6.9

```
#include <iostream>
using namespace std;

double number = 42.8;       // a global variable named number

int main()
{
  double number = 26.4;     // a local variable named number

  cout << "The value of number is " << number << endl;

  return 0;
}
```

When Program 6.9 is executed, the following output is displayed:

                    The value of number is 26.4

As shown by this output, the local variable name takes precedence over the global variable. In such cases, we can still access the global variable by using C++'s scope resolution operator. This operator, which is the symbol : :, must be placed immediately before the variable name, as in : :number. When used in this manner, : : tells the compiler to use the global variable. As an example, the scope resolution operator is used in Program 6.9a.

```
#include <iostream>
using namespace std;

double number = 42.5;       // a global variable named number

int main()
{
  double number = 26.4;     // a local variable named number

  cout << "The value of number is " << ::number << endl;

  return 0;
}
```

The output produced by Program 6.9a is:

```
The value of number is 42.5
```

As indicated by this output, the scope resolution operator causes the global, rather than the local, variable to be accessed.

Misuse of Globals

Global variables allow the programmer to "jump around" the normal safeguards provided by functions. Rather than passing variables to a function, it is possible to make all variables global ones. **Do not do this.** By indiscriminately making all variables global, you instantly destroy the safeguards C++ provides to make functions independent and insulated from each other, including the necessity of carefully designating the type of parameters needed by a function, the variables used in the function, and the value returned.

Using only global variables can be especially disastrous in larger programs that have many user-created functions. Because all variables in a function must be declared, creating functions that use global variables requires that you remember to write the appropriate global declarations at the top of each program using the function—they no longer come along with the function. More devastating than this, however, is the horror of trying to track down an error in a large program that uses global variables. Because a global variable can be accessed and changed by any function following the global declaration, it is a time-consuming and frustrating task to locate the origin of an erroneous value.

Globals, however, are sometimes useful in creating variables and named constants that must be shared among many functions. Rather than passing the same value to each function, it is easier to define a variable or constant once as a global. Doing so also alerts anyone reading the program that many functions use the variable. Most large programs almost always make use of a few global variables. Smaller programs containing a few functions, however, should almost never contain globals.

1. a. For the following section of code, determine the data type and scope of all declared variables. To do this, use a separate sheet of paper and list the three column headings that follow (we have filled in the entries for the first variable):

Variable Name	Data Type	Scope
price	int	Global to main, roi, and step

```cpp
#include <iostream>
using namespace std;
int price;
long int years;
double yield;

int main()
{
  int bondtype;
  double interest, coupon;
      .
      .
      .
  return 0;
}

double roi(int mat1, int mat2)
{
  int count;
  double effectiveInt;
      .
      .
  return effectiveInt;
}
int step(float first, float last)
{
  int numofyrs;
  float fracpart;
      .
      .
  return (10*numofyrs);
}
```

b. Draw boxes around the appropriate section of the Exercise 1a code to enclose the scope of each variable.

c. Determine the data type of the parameters for the functions roi() and step() and the data type of the value returned by these functions.

2. a. For the following section of code, determine the data type and scope of all declared variables. To do this, use a separate sheet of paper and list the three column headings that follow (we have filled in the entries for the first variable):

Variable Name	Data Type	Scope
key	char	Global to main, func1, and func2

```cpp
#include <iostream>
using namespace std;
char key;
long int number;

int main()
{
  int a,b,c;
  double x,y;
      .
      .
  return 0;
}

double secnum;

int func1(int num1, int num2)
{
```

```
      int o,p;
      double q;
         .
         .
      return p;
    }
   double func2(double first, double last)
   {
      int a,b,c,o,p;
      double r;
      double s,t,x;
         .
         .
      return (s * t);
   }
```

b. Draw a box around the appropriate section of the Exercise 2a code to enclose the scope of the variables key, secnum, y, and r.

c. Determine the data type of the parameters for functions func1 and func2 and the data type of the value returned by these functions.

3. Besides speaking about the scope of a variable, we can also apply the term to a function's parameters. What do you think is the scope of all function parameters?

4. Consider the following program structure:

```
      #include <iostream>
      using namespace std;
      int a, b;
      double One(double);
      void Two();

      int main()
      {
        int c, d;
        float e, f;
           .
           .
      return 0;
      }

      double One(double p2)
      {
        char m, n;
           .
           .
      }

      void Two()
      {
        int p, d;
        float q, r;
           .
           .
      }
```

Define the scope of the parameter p2 and the variables a, b, c, d, e, f, m, n, p, d, q, and r.

5. Determine the values displayed by each cout statement in the following program:

```
      #include <iostream>
      using namespace std;
      int firstnum = 10;  // declare and initialize a global variable
      void display();  // function prototype

      int main()
```

(continued from previous page)

```
    {
      int firstnum = 20;    // declare and initialize a local variable

      cout << "\nThe value of firstnum is " << firstnum << endl;
      display();
      return 0;
    }
    void display(void)
    {
      cout << "The value of firstnum is now " << firstnum << endl;
      return;
    }
```

6.4 VARIABLE STORAGE CLASS

The scope of a variable defines the location within a program where that variable can be used. Given a program, you could take a pencil and draw a box around the section of the program where each variable is valid. The space inside the box represents the scope of a variable. From this viewpoint, the scope of a variable can be thought of as the space within the program where the variable is valid.

In addition to the space dimension represented by its scope, variables also have a time dimension. The time dimension refers to the length of time that storage locations are reserved for a variable. This time dimension is referred to as the variable's "lifetime." For example, all variable storage locations are released back to the operating system when a program is finished running. However, while a program is still executing, interim variable storage areas are also reserved and subsequently released back to the operating system. Where and how long a variable's storage locations are kept before they are released can be determined by the **storage class** of the variable.

The four available storage classes are called **auto**, **static**, **extern**, and **register**. If one of these class names is used, it must be placed before the variable's data type in a declaration statement. Examples of declaration statements that include a storage class designation are:

```
auto int num;       // auto storage class and int data type
static int miles;   // static storage class and int data type
register int dist;  // register storage class and int data type
extern int price;   // extern storage class and int data type
auto float coupon;  // auto storage class and float data type
static double yrs;  // static storage class and double data type
extern float yld;   // extern storage class and float data type
auto char in_key;   // auto storage class and char variable
```

To understand what the storage class of a variable means, we first consider local variables (those variables created inside a function) and then global variables (those variables created outside a function).

Local Variable Storage Classes

Local variables can only be members of the auto, static, or register storage classes. If no class description is included in the declaration statement, the variable is automatically assigned to the auto class. Thus, auto is the default class used by C++. All the local variables we have used, since the storage class designation was omitted, have been auto variables.

PROGRAM 6.10

```cpp
#include <iostream>
using namespace std;

void testauto();        // function prototype

int main()
{
  int count;                 // count is a local auto variable

  for(count = 1; count <= 3; count++)
    testauto();

  return 0;
}

void testauto()
{
  int num = 0;  // num is a local auto variable
                // that is initialized to zero
  cout << "The value of the automatic variable num is "
      << num << endl;
  num++;

  return;
}
```

The term `auto` is short for **automatic**. Storage for automatic local variables is automatically reserved (that is, created) each time a function declaring automatic variables is called. As long as the function has not returned control to its calling function, all automatic variables local to the function are "alive"—that is, storage for the variables is available. When the function returns control to its calling function, its local automatic variables "die"—that is, the storage for the variables is released back to the operating system. This process repeats itself each time a function is called. For example, consider Program 6.10, where the function `testauto()` is called three times from `main()`.

The output produced by Program 6.10 is:

```
The value of the automatic variable num is 0
The value of the automatic variable num is 0
The value of the automatic variable num is 0
```

Each time `testauto()` is called, the automatic variable `num` is created and initialized to zero. When the function returns control to `main()`, the variable `num` is destroyed along with any value stored in `num`. Thus, the effect of incrementing `num` in `testauto()`, before the function's return statement, is lost when control is returned to `main()`.

For most applications, the use of automatic variables works just fine. Sometimes, however, we want a function to remember values between function calls. This is the purpose of the static storage class. A local variable that is declared as `static` causes the program to keep the variable and its latest value even when the function that declared it is through executing. Examples of static variable declarations are:

```
static int rate;
static float taxes;
static double amount;
static char in_key;
static long years;
```

A local static variable is not created and destroyed each time the function declaring the static variable is called. Once created, local static variables remain in existence for the life of the program. This means that the last value stored in the variable when the function is finished executing is available to the function the next time it is called.

Because local static variables retain their values, they are not initialized within a declaration statement in the same way as automatic variables. To understand why, consider the automatic declaration int num = 0;, which causes the automatic variable num to be created and set to zero each time the declaration is encountered. This is called a **run-time initialization** because initialization occurs each time the declaration statement is encountered. This type of initialization is disastrous for a static variable because resetting the variable's value to zero each time the function is called destroys the very value we are trying to save.

The initialization of static variables (both local and global) is done only once, when the program is first compiled. At compilation time, the variable is created and any initialization value is placed in it.[8] Thereafter, the value in the variable is kept without further initialization each time the function is called. To see how this works, consider Program 6.11.

PROGRAM 6.11

```
#include <iostream>
using namespace std;

void teststat();        // function prototype

int main()
{
  int count;                    // count is a local auto variable

  for(count = 1; count <= 3; count++)
      teststat();

  return 0;
}

void teststat()
{
  static int num = 0;      // num is a local static variable
  cout << "The value of the static variable num is now "
       << num << endl;
  num++;

  return;
}
```

---

[8] Some compilers initialize static local variables the first time the definition statement is executed rather than when the program is compiled.

The output produced by Program 6.11 is:

```
The value of the static variable num is now 0
The value of the static variable num is now 1
The value of the static variable num is now 2
```

As illustrated by this output, the static variable num is set to zero only once. The function teststat() then increments this variable just before returning control to main(). The value that num has when leaving the function teststat() is retained and displayed when the function is next called.

Unlike automatic variables that can be initialized by either constants or expressions using both constants and previously initialized variables, static variables can only be initialized using constants or constant expressions, such as 3.2 + 8.0. Also, unlike automatic variables, all static variables are set to zero when no explicit initialization is given. Thus, the specific initialization of num to zero in Program 6.11 is not required.

The remaining storage class available to local variables, the register class, is not used as extensively as either automatic or static variables. Examples of register variable declarations are:

```
register int time;
register double diffren;
register float coupon;
```

Register variables have the same time duration as automatic variables; that is, a local register variable is created when the function declaring it is entered and is destroyed when the function completes execution. The only difference between register and automatic variables is where the storage for the variable is located.

Storage for all variables (local and global), except register variables, is reserved in the computer's memory area. Most computers have a few additional high-speed storage areas located directly in the computer's processing unit that can also be used for variable storage. These special high-speed storage areas are called registers. Since registers are physically located in the computer's processing unit, they can be accessed faster than the normal memory storage areas located in the computer's memory unit. Also, computer instructions that access registers typically require less space than instructions that access memory locations because there are fewer registers than there are memory locations.

For example, the UNIX operating system, written in C and C++, makes use of registers. Besides decreasing the size of a compiled C++ program, using register variables can also increase the execution speed of a C++ program, if the computer you are using supports this data type. Applications programs that are intended to be executed on a variety of computers should not use registers. Attempts to do so will generally be foiled by the compiler by automatically switching variables declared with the register storage category to the auto storage category.

The only restriction in using the register storage class is that the address of a register variable, using the address operator &, cannot be taken. This is easily understood when you realize that registers do not have standard memory addresses.

Global Variable Storage Classes

Global variables are created by definition statements external to a function. By their nature, these externally defined variables do not come and go with the calling of any function. Once a global variable is created, it exists until the program in which it is declared is finished executing. Thus, global variables cannot be declared as either auto or register variables that are created and destroyed as the program is executing. Global variables may additionally be declared as members of the static or extern storage classes (but not both). Examples of declaration statements including these two class descriptions are:

```
extern int sum;
extern double price;
static double yield;
```

The global static and extern classes affect both the scope and the time duration, of these variables. As with static local variables, all static global variables are initialized to zero at compile time.

The purpose of the extern storage class is to extend the scope of a global variable beyond its normal boundaries. To understand this, we must first note that the programs we have written so far have always been contained together in one file. Thus, when you have saved or retrieved programs, you have only needed to give the computer a single name for your program. This is not required by C++.

FIGURE 6.11   A Program May Extend Beyond One File

file1
```
int price;
double yield;
static double coupon;

     .
     .
     .
int main( )
{
    func1( );
    func2( );
    func3( );
    func4( );
}
int func1( )
{

     .
     .
     .

}
int func2( )
{

     .
     .
     .

}
```

file2
```
double interest;
int func3( )
{

     .
     .
     .

}
int func4( )

     .
     .
     .

}
```

Larger programs typically consist of many functions stored in multiple files. An example of this is shown in Figure 6.11, where the three functions main(), func1(), and func2() are stored in one file and the two functions func3() and func4() are stored in a second file. For the files illustrated in Figure 6.11, the global variables price, yield, and coupon declared in file1 can only be used by the functions main(), func1(), and func2() in this file. The single global variable, interest, declared in file2 can only be used by the functions func3() and func4() in file2.

Although the variable price has been created in file1, we may want to use it in file2. Placing the declaration statement extern int price; in file2, as shown in Figure 6.12, allows us to do this. Putting this statement at the top of file2 extends the scope of the variable price into file2 so that it may be used by both func3() and func4(). Thus, the extern designation simply declares a global variable that is defined in another file. So placing the statement extern double yield; in func4() extends the scope of this global variable, created in file1, into func4(), and the scope of the global variable interest, created in file2, is extended into func1() and func2() by the declaration statement extern double interest; placed before func1(). Notice that interest is not available to main().

FIGURE 6.12   Extending the Scope of a Global Variable

```
file1                                   file2

int price;                              double interest;
double yield;                           extern int price;
static double coupon;                   int func3( )
        .                               {
        .                                       .
        .                                       .
int main( )                                     .
{                                       }
    func1( );                           int func4( )
    func2( );                           {
    func3( );                                   extern double yield;
    func4( );                                   .
}                                               .
extern double interest;                         .
int func1( )                            }
{

        .
        .
        .

}
int func2( )
{

        .
        .
        .

}
```

A declaration statement that specifically contains the word extern is different from every other declaration statement in that it does not cause the creation of a new variable by reserving new storage for the variable. An extern declaration statement simply informs the compiler that a global variable already exists and can now be used. The actual storage for the variable must be created somewhere else in the program using one, and only one, global declaration statement in which the word extern has not been used. Initialization of the global variable can, of course, be

▲ **P O I N T   O F   I N F O R M A T I O N** ▲

Storage Classes

Variables of type auto and register are always local variables. Only non-static global variables may be declared using the `extern` keyword. Doing so extends the variable's scope into another file or function.

Making a global variable `static` makes the variable private to the file in which it is declared. Thus, `static` variables *cannot* use the `extern` keyword. Except for `static` variables, all variables are initialized each time they come into scope. `static` variables are only initialized once, when they are defined.

made with the original declaration of the global variable. Initialization within an `extern` declaration statement is not allowed and causes a compilation error.

The existence of the `extern` storage class is the reason we have been so careful to distinguish between the creation and declaration of a variable. Declaration statements containing the word `extern` do not create new storage areas; they only extend the scope of existing global variables.

The last global class, static global variables, is used to prevent the extension of a global variable into a second file. Global static variables are declared in the same way as local static variables, except that the declaration statement is placed outside any function.

The scope of a global static variable cannot be extended beyond the file in which it is declared. This provides a degree of privacy for static global variables. Since they are only "known" and can only be used in the file in which they are declared, other files cannot access or change their values. Static global variables cannot be subsequently extended to a second file using an `extern` declaration statement. Trying to do so results in a compilation error.

Exercises 6.4

1. a. List the storage classes available to local variables.

   b. List the storage classes available to global variables.

2. Describe the difference between a local `auto` variable and a local `static` variable.

3. What is the difference between the following functions?

```
void init1()
{
    static int yrs = 1;
    cout << "The value of yrs is " << yrs << endl;
    yrs = yrs + 2;
}

void init2()
{
    static int yrs;
    yrs = 1;
    cout << "The value of yrs is " << yrs << endl;
    yrs = yrs + 2;
}
```

4. a. Describe the difference between a `static` global variable and an `extern` global variable.

   b. If a variable is declared with an `extern` storage class, what other declaration statement must be present somewhere in the program?

5. The declaration statement `static double years;` can be used to create either a local or global static variable. What determines the scope of the variable `years`?

6. For the function and variable declarations illustrated in Figure 6.13, place an `extern` declaration to individually accomplish the following:

   a. Extend the scope of the global variable `choice` into all of `file2`.

   b. Extend the scope of the global variable `flag` into function `pduction()` only.

   c. Extend the scope of the global variable `date` into `pduction()` and `bid()`.

   d. Extend the scope of the global variable `date` into `roi()` only.

   e. Extend the scope of the global variable `coupon` into `roi()` only.

   f. Extend the scope of the global variable `bondType` into all of `file1`.

   g. Extend the scope of the global variable `maturity` into both `price()` and `yield()`.

FIGURE 6.13 Files for Exercise 6.4, #6

```
file1                           file2

char choice;                    char bondType;
int flag;                       double maturity;
long date, time;                double roi( )
int main( )                     {
{                                   .
    .                               .
    .                               .
    .                           }
}                               double pduction( )
double coupon;                  {
double price( )                     .
{                                   .
    .                               .
    .                           }
    .                           double bid( )
}                               {
double yield( )                     .
{                                   .
    .                               .
    .                           }
    .
}
```

6.5 PASS BY REFERENCE USING REFERENCE PARAMETERS

In a typical function invocation, the called function receives values from its calling function, stores and manipulates the passed values, and directly returns at most one single value. As we have seen, this method of calling a function and passing values to it is referred to as a **pass by value**.

Calling a function and passing parameters by value are a distinct advantage of C++. They allow functions to be written as independent entities that can use any variable or parameter name without concern that other functions may also be using the same name. They also alleviate any concern that altering a parameter or local variable in one function may inadvertently alter the value of a variable in another function. Under this approach, formal (receiving) parameters can be considered as either initialized variables or variables that are assigned values when the function is executed. At no time, however, does the called function have direct access to any local variable contained in the calling function.

There are times, however, when it is necessary to alter this approach by giving a called function direct access to the local variables of its calling function. This allows one function, which is the called function, to use and change the value of another function's local variable. To do this, the address of the variable must be passed to the called function. Once the called function has the variable's address, it "knows where the variable lives," so to speak, and can access and change the value stored there directly.

Passing addresses is referred to as a function **pass by reference**,[9] since the called function can reference, or access, the variable using the passed address. C++ provides two types of address parameters, references and pointers. In this section, we describe reference arguments.

Passing and Using Reference Paremeters

As always, in exchanging data between two functions, we must be concerned with both the sending and receiving sides of the data exchange. From the sending side, however, calling a function and passing an address as an actual argument that is accepted as a reference parameter on the receiving side is exactly the same as calling a function and passing a value: The called function is summoned into action by giving its name and a list of arguments. For example, the `newval(firstnum, secnum);` statement calls the function named `newval()` and passes two arguments to it. Whether a value or an address is actually passed depends on the parameter types declared for `newval()`. Let us now write the `newval` function and prototype so that the function receives the addresses of the variables `firstnum` and `secnum`, which we assume to be double-precision variables, rather than their values.

One of the first requirements for writing `newval()` is to declare two reference parameters for accepting passed addresses. In C++, a reference parameter is declared using the following syntax:

> *dataType& referenceName*

For example, the reference declaration

```
double& num1;
```

declares that `num1` is a reference parameter that is used to store the address of a double-precision variable. Similarly, `int& secnum` declares that `secnum` is a reference to an integer, and `char& key` declares that `key` is a reference to a character.

Recall from Section 2.3 that the ampersand, `&`, in C++ means "the address of." Additionally, an `&` symbol used within a declaration refers to "the address of" the preceding data type. Using this information, declarations such as `double& num1` and `int& secnum` are sometimes more clearly understood if they are read backward. Reading the declaration `double& num1` in this manner yields the information that "`num1` is the address of a double-precision value."

Since we need to accept two addresses in the parameter list for `newval()`, the declarations `double& num1`, `double& num2` can be used. Including these declarations within the parameter list for `newval()`, and assuming that the function returns no value (`void`), the function header for `newval()` becomes:

```
void newval(double& num1, double& num2)
```

---

[9] It can also be referred to as a *call by reference* when it is clearly understood that the term applies only to those arguments whose address have been passed.

For this function header line, an appropriate function prototype is:

```
void newval(double&, double&);
```

This prototype and header line are included in Program 6.12, which includes a completed `newval()` function body that both displays and directly alters the values stored in these reference parameters from within the called function.

PROGRAM 6.12

```
#include <iostream>
using namespace std;

void newval(double&, double&);  // prototype with two reference
                                // parameters

int main()
{
  double firstnum, secnum;


  cout << "Enter two numbers: ";
  cin  >> firstnum >> secnum;
  cout << "\nThe value in firstnum is: " << firstnum << endl;
  cout << "The value in secnum is: " << secnum << "\n\n";

  newval(firstnum, secnum);   // call the function

  cout << "The value in firstnum is now: " << firstnum << endl;
  cout << "The value in secnum is now: " << secnum << endl;

  return 0;
}

void newval(double& xnum, double& ynum)
{
  cout << "The value in xnum is: " << xnum << endl;
  cout << "The value in ynum is: " << ynum << "\n\n";
  xnum = 89.5;
  ynum = 99.5;

return;
}
```

In calling the `newval()` function within Program 6.12, it is important to understand the connection between the arguments, `firstnum` and `secnum`, used in the function call and the parameters, `xnum` and `ynum`, used in the function header. *Both access the same data items.* This is significant because the values in the arguments (`firstnum` and `secnum`) can now be altered from within `newval()` by using the parameter names (`xnum` and `ynum`). Thus, the parameters xnum and ynum do not store copies of the values in firstnum and secnum, but directly access the locations in memory set aside for these two arguments. The equivalence of argument and parameter names in Program 6.12, which is the essence of a pass by reference, is illustrated in Figure 6.14, where both argument names and their matching parameter names are simply different names referring to the same memory storage areas. In main() these memory locations are referenced by the names firstnum and secnum, respectively, while in newval() the same locations are referenced by the formal parameter names xnum and ynum, respectively.

The following sample run was obtained from Program 6.12:

```
Enter two numbers: 22.5 33.0

The value in firstnum is: 22.5
The value in secnum is: 33

The value in xnum is: 22.5
The value in ynum is: 33

The value in firstnum is now: 89.5
The value in secnum is now: 99.5
```

In reviewing this output, note that the values initially displayed for the parameters xnum and ynum are the same as those displayed for the arguments firstnum and secnum. Since xnum and ynum are reference parameters, so, newval() now has direct access to the arguments firstnum and secnum. Thus, any change to xnum within newval() directly alters the value of firstnum in main() and any change to ynum directly changes secnum's value. As illustrated by the final displayed values, the assignment of values to xnum and ynum within newval() is reflected in main() as the altering of firstnum's and secnum's values.

FIGURE 6.14   The Equivalence of Arguments and Parameters in Program 6.12

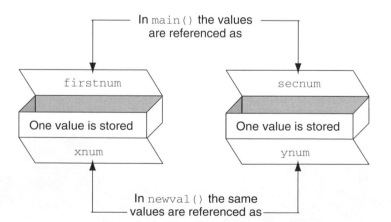

The equivalence between calling arguments and function parameters illustrated in Program 6.12 provides the basis for returning multiple values from within a function. For example, assume that a function is required to accept three values, compute the sum and product of these values, and return these computed results to the calling routine. Naming the function calc() and providing five parameters (three for the input data and two references for the returned values), the following function can be used:

```
void calc(double num1, double num2, double num3, double& total, double& product)
{
  total = num1 + num2 + num3;
  product = num1 * num2 * num3;
  return;
}
```

This function has five parameters, num1, num2, num3, total, and product, of which only the last two are declared as references. Within the function, only the last two parameters are altered. The value of the fourth parameter, total, is calculated as the sum of the first three parameters; the last parameter, product, is computed as the product of the parameters num1, num2, and num3. Program 6.13 includes this function in a complete program.

PROGRAM 6.13

```
#include <iostream>
using namespace std;

void calc(double, double, double, double&, double&);  // function prototype

int main()
{
  double firstnum, secnum, thirdnum, sum, product;

  cout << "Enter three numbers: ";
  cin >> firstnum >> secnum >> thirdnum;

  calc(firstnum, secnum, thirdnum, sum, product);  // function call

  cout << "\nThe sum of the numbers is: " << sum << endl;
  cout << "The product of the numbers is: " << product << endl;

  return 0;
}

void calc(double num1, double num2, double num3, double& total, double& product)
{
  total = num1 + num2 + num3;
  product = num1 * num2 * num3;
  return;
}
```

Within main(), the function calc() is called using the five arguments firstnum, secnum, thirdnum, sum, and product. As required, these arguments agree in number and data type with the parameters declared by calc(). Of the five arguments passed, only firstnum, secnum, and thirdnum have been assigned values when the call to calc() is made. The remaining two arguments have not been initialized and are used to receive values back from calc().

Depending on the compiler used in compiling the program, these arguments initially contain either zeros or "garbage" values. Figure 6.15 illustrates the relationship between argument and parameter names and the values they contain after the return from `calc()`.

FIGURE 6.15 Relationship between Arguments and Parameters

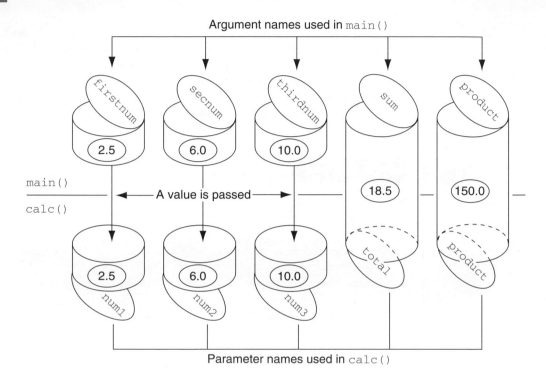

Once `calc()` is called, it uses its first three parameters to calculate values for `total` and `product` and then returns control to `main()`. Because of the order of its actual calling arguments, `main()` knows the values calculated by `calc()` as `sum` and `product`, which are then displayed. A sample run of Program 6.13 follows:

```
Enter three numbers: 2.5 6.0 10.0
The sum of the numbers is: 18.5
The product of the numbers is: 150
```

As a final example illustrating the usefulness of passing references to a called function, we construct a function named `swap()` that exchanges the values of two of `main()`'s double-precision variables. Such a function is useful when sorting a list of numbers and is used in Chapter 11 for just such an application.

Since the value of more than a single variable is affected, `swap()` cannot be written as a pass by value function that returns a single value. The desired exchange of `main()`'s variables by `swap()` can only be obtained by giving `swap()` access to `main()`'s variables. One way to do this is to use reference variables.

We have already seen how to pass two references in Program 6.13. We now construct a function to exchange the values in the passed reference parameters.

Exchanging values in two parameters is accomplished using the three-step exchange algorithm:

1. Save the first parameter's value in a temporary location (see Figure 6.16a).
2. Store the second parameter's value in the first parameter (see Figure 6.16b).
3. Store the temporary value in the second parameter (see Figure 6.16c).

FIGURE 6.16a   Save the First Value

FIGURE 6.16b   Replace the First Value with the Second Value

FIGURE 6.16c   Change the Second Value

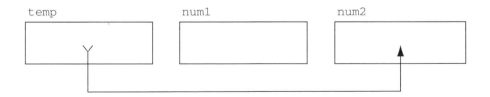

The function `swap()`, written according to these specifications, follows:

```
void swap(double& num1, double& num2)
{
  double temp;

  temp = num1;        // save num1's value
  num1 = num2;        // store num2's value in num1
  num2 = temp;        // change num2's value

  return;
}
```

Notice that the use of references in `swap()`'s header line gives `swap()` access to the equivalent arguments in the calling function. Thus, any changes to the two reference parameters in `swap()` automatically change the values in the calling function's arguments. Program 6.14 contains `swap()` in a complete program.

PROGRAM 6.14

```cpp
#include <iostream>
using namespace std;

void swap(double&, double&);      // function receives 2 references

int main()
{
  double firstnum = 20.5, secnum = 6.25;

  cout << "The value stored in firstnum is: " << firstnum << endl;
  cout << "The value stored in secnum is: "<< secnum << "\n\n";

  swap(firstnum, secnum);    // call the function with references

  cout << "The value stored in firstnum is now: "
       << firstnum << endl;
  cout << "The value stored in secnum is now: "
       << secnum << endl;

  return 0;
}

void swap(double& num1, double& num2)
{
  double temp;

  temp = num1;      // save num1's value
  num1 = num2;      // store num2's value in num1
  num2 = temp;      // change num2's value

  return;
}
```

The following sample run was obtained using Program 6.14:

```
The value stored in firstnum is: 20.5
The value stored in secnum is: 6.25

The value stored in firstnum is now: 6.25
The value stored in secnum is now: 20.5
```

As illustrated by this output, the values stored in main()'s variables have been modified from within swap(), which was made possible by the use of reference parameters. If a pass by value had been used instead, the exchange within swap() affects only swap()'s parameters and accomplishes nothing with respect to main()'s variables. Thus, a function such as swap() can only be written using references or some other means that provide access to main()'s variables. (This other means is by the use of pointers, the topic of Chapter 14.)

In using reference parameters, two cautions need to be mentioned. The first is that reference parameters *cannot* be used to change constants. For example, calling

A   B I T   O F   B A C K G R O U N D

The "Universal Algorithm Machine"
In the 1930s and 1940s, Alan Mathison Turing (1912–1954) and others studied in considerable depth the theory of what a computing machine should be able to do. Turing invented a theoretical, pencil-and-paper computer—now appropriately called a Turing machine—that he hoped would be a "universal algorithm machine." That is, he hoped to prove theoretically that all problems could be solved by a set of instructions to a hypothetical computer. What he succeeded in proving was that some problems cannot be solved by *any* machine, just as some problems cannot be solved by any person. However, he did show that recursively defined algorithms can indeed be solved by machine, though it may not be possible to predict how long it will take the machine to find the solution.

Alan Turing's work formed the foundation of computer theory before the first electronic computer was built. His contribution to the team that developed the critical code-breaking computers during World War II led directly to the practical implementation of his theories.

swap() with two constants, such as in the call swap(20.5, 6.5), passes two constants to the function. Although swap() may execute, it does not change the values of these constants.[10]

The second caution to note is that a function call itself gives no indication that the called function will be using reference parameters. The default in C++ is to make passes by value rather than passes by reference precisely to limit a called function's ability to alter variables in the calling function. This calling procedure should be adhered to whenever possible, which means that reference parameters should only be used in very restricted situations that require multiple return values, such as in the swap() function illustrated in Program 6.14. The calc() function included in Program 6.13, while useful for illustrative purposes, can also be written as two separate functions, each returning a single value.

Exercises 6.5

1. Write parameter declarations for the following:

   a. A parameter named amount that is a reference to a floating-point value.

   b. A parameter named price that is a reference to a double-precision number.

   c. A parameter named minutes that is a reference to an integer number.

   d. A parameter named key that is a reference to a character.

   e. A parameter named yield that is a reference to a double-precision number.

2. Three integer arguments are to be used in a call to a function named time(). Write a suitable function header for time(), assuming that time() accepts sec, min, and hours as reference parameters and returns no value to its calling function.

3. Rewrite the findMax() function in Program 6.5 so that the variable max, declared in main(), is used to store the maximum value of the two passed numbers. The value of max should be set directly from within findMax(). [*Hint:* A reference to max will have to be accepted by findMax().]

4. Write a function named change() that has a floating-point parameter and four integer reference parameters named quarters, dimes, nickels, and pennies. The function is to consider the floating-point passed value as a dollar amount and convert the value into an equivalent number of quarters, dimes, nickels, and

---

[10] Most compilers catch this error.

pennies. Using the references, the function should directly alter the respective arguments in the calling function.

5. Write a function named `time()` that has an integer parameter named `seconds` and three integer reference parameters named `hours`, `min`, and `sec`. The function is to convert the passed number of seconds into an equivalent number of hours, minutes, and seconds. Using the references, the function should directly alter the respective arguments in the calling function.

6. Write a function named `yrCalc()` that has a long integer parameter representing the total number of days from the date 1/1/1900 and reference parameters named `year`, `month`, and `day`. The function is to calculate the current year, month, and day for the given number of days passed to it. Using the references, the function should directly alter the respective arguments in the calling function. For this problem, assume that each year has 365 days and each month has 30 days.

7. Write a function named `liquid()` that has an integer number parameter named `totCups` and reference parameters named `gallons`, `quarts`, `pints`, and `cups`. The passed integer represents the total number of cups, and the function is to determine the number of gallons, quarts, pints, and cups in the passed value. Using the references, the function should directly alter the respective arguments in the calling function. Use the relationships of 2 cups to a pint, 4 cups to a quart, and 16 cups to a gallon.

8. The following program uses the same argument and parameter names in both the calling and called function. Determine if this causes any problem for the computer.

```cpp
#include <iostream>
using namespace std;
void time(int&, int&);     // function prototype
int main()
{
  int min, hour;

  cout << "Enter two numbers :";
  cin  >> min >> hour;
  time(min, hour);
  return 0;
}

void time(int& min, int& hour) // accept two references
{
  int sec;

  sec = (hour * 60 + min) * 60;
  cout << "The total number of seconds is " << sec << endl;
}
```

6.6 RECURSION[11]

Mathematical Recursion

In 1936, Alan Turing showed that although not every possible problem can be solved by computer, those problems that have recursive solutions also have computer solutions, at least in theory. The basic concept at work here is that the solution to a problem can be stated in terms of recurring versions of the same algorithm. Some problems can be solved using an algebraic formula that shows recursion explicitly. For example, consider finding the factorial of a number n, denoted as $n!$, where n is non-negative. This is defined as:

$$0! = 1$$
$$1! = 1 * 1 = 1 * 0!$$

---

[11] This topic may be omitted on first reading with no loss of subject continuity.

$$2! = 2 * 1 = 2 * 1!$$
$$3! = 3 * 2 * 1 = 3 * 2!$$
$$4! = 4 * 3 * 2 * 1 = 4 * 3!$$

and, so on.

For consistency the definition for n! can be summarized by the following statements:

```
0! = 1
n! = n * (n − 1)!     for n >= 0
```

This definition illustrates the two questions you must ask when constructing a recursive algorithm:

1. What is the first case?

2. How is the nth case related to the $(n − 1)$st case?

Although the definition seems to define a factorial in terms of a factorial, the definition is valid, because it can always be computed. For example, using the definition, 3! is first computed as:

$$3! = 3 * 2!$$

The value of 2! is determined from the definition as:

$$2! = 2 * 1!$$

Substituting this expression for 2! in the determination of 3! yields:

$$3! = 3 * 2 * 1!$$

Finally, substituting the expression 1* 0! for 1!, yields:

$$3! = 3 * 2 * 1 * 0!$$

0! is not defined in terms of the recursive formula, but is simply defined as being equal to 1. Substituting this value into the expression for 3! gives us:

$$3! = 3 * 2 * 1 * 1 = 6$$

To see how a recursive function is defined in C++, we construct the function `factorial`. In pseudocode, the processing required of this function is:

If n = 0
  factorial = 1
Else
  *factorial = n * factorial(n – 1)*

Notice that this algorithm is simply a restatement of the recursive definition previously given. In C++, this can be written as:

```cpp
int factorial(int n)
{
  if (n == 0)
    return (1);
  else
    return (n * factorial(n–1));
}
```

Program 6.15 illustrates this code in a complete program.

PROGRAM 6.15

```cpp
#include <iostream>
using namespace std;

int main()
{
  int factorial(int);    // function prototype
  int n, result;

  cout << "Enter a number: ";
  cin >> n;
  result = factorial(n);
  cout << "\nThe factorial of " << n << " is " << result << endl;

  return 0;
}

int factorial(int n)
{
  if (n == 0)
    return (1);
  else
    return (n * factorial(n-1));
}
```

Following is a sample run of Program 6.15.

```
Enter a number: 3

The factorial of 3 is 6
```

How the Computation Is Performed

The sample run of Program 6.15 invoked factorial from `main()` with a value of 3 using the call

```
result = factorial(n);
```

Let's see how the program performs the computation. The mechanism that makes it possible for a C++ function to call itself is that C++ allocates new memory locations for all function parameters and local variables as each function is called. This allocation is made dynamically, as a program is executed, in a memory area referred to as the stack.

A **memory stack** is simply an area of memory used for rapidly storing and retrieving data. It is conceptually similar to a stack of trays in a cafeteria, where the last tray placed on top of the stack is the first tray removed. This last-in/first-out mechanism provides the means for storing information in order of occurrence. Each function call simply reserves memory locations on the stack for its parameters, its local variables, a return value, and the address where execution is to resume in the calling program when the function has completed execution. Thus, when the function call `factorial(n)` is made, the stack is initially used to store the argument value for n (which is 3), a space for the value to be returned by

FIGURE 6.17   The Stack for the First Call to `factorial`

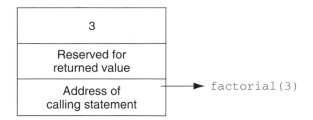

factorial(3)

the `factorial()` function, and the address of the instruction being executed (`result = factorial(n);`). At this stage, the stack can be envisioned as shown in Figure 6.17. From a program execution standpoint, the function that made the call to `factorial()`, in this case `main()`, is suspended and the compiled code for the `factorial()` function starts executing.

Within the `factorial()` function itself, another function call is made. That this call is to `factorial()` is irrelevant as far as C++ is concerned. The call simply is another request for stack space. In this case, the stack stores the number 2, a space for the value to be returned by the function, and the address of the instruction being executed in `factorial()`. The stack can now be envisioned as shown in Figure 6.18. At this point, a second version of the compiled code for `factorial()` begins execution, while the first version is temporarily suspended.

Once again, the currently executing code, the second invocation of `factorial`, makes a function call. That this call is to itself is irrelevant in C++. The call is once again handled in the same manner as any function call and begins with allocation of the stack's memory space. Here, the stack stores the number 1, a space for the value to be returned by the function, and the address of the instruction being executed in the calling funcion, which happens to be `factorial(1)`. The stack can now be envisioned as shown in Figure 6.19. At this point, the third version of the compiled code for `factorial` begins execution, while the second version is temporarily suspended.

FIGURE 6.18   The Stack for the Second Call to `factorial`

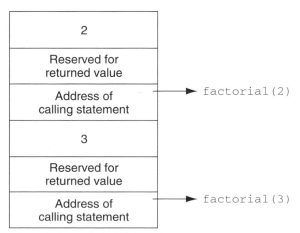

factorial(2)

factorial(3)

The next and final call (also the fourth call) to factorial continues in the same fashion, except, rather than resulting in another call, it results in a returned value of 1 being placed on the stack. This completes the set of recursive calls and permits the suspended calling functions to resume execution and be completed in reverse order. The value of 1 is used by the third invocation of `factorial()` to complete its operation and place a return value of 1 on the stack. This value is then used by the second invocation of `factorial()` to place a return value of .2 on the stack. Finally, this value is then used by the first invocation of `factorial()` to complete its operation and place a return value of 6 on the stack, with execution now returning to `main()`. The original calling statement within `main()` stores the return value of its invocation of `factorial()` into the variable result.

FIGURE 6.19 **The Stack for the Third Call to** `factorial`

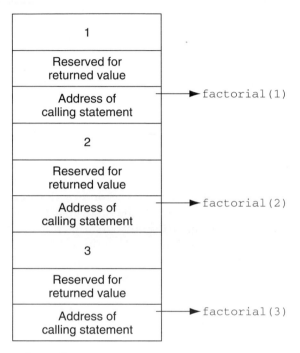

Recursion Versus Iteration

The recursive method can be applied to any problem in which the solution is represented in terms of solutions to simpler versions of the same problem. The most difficult tasks when implementing recursion are deciding how to create the process and visualizing what happens at each successive invocation.

Any recursive function can always be written in a nonrecursive manner using an iterative solution. For example, the `factorial` function can be written using an iteration algorithm such as:

```
int factorial(int n)
{
    int fact;

    for(fact = 1; n > 0; n--)
        fact = fact * n;
    return fact;
}
```

Since recursion is usually a difficult concept for beginning programmers, under what conditions do you use it in preference to a repetitive solution? The answer is rather simple.

If a problem solution can be expressed iteratively or recursively with equal ease, the iterative solution is preferable because it executes faster (there are no additional function calls, which consume processing time) and uses less memory (the stack is not used for the multiple function calls needed in recursion). There are times, however, when recursive solutions are preferable.

First, some problems are simply easier to visualize using a recursive algorithm than a repetitive one. The Towers of Hanoi problem, which is a classic recursion problem, is an example of this (see Exercise 28 at the end of this chapter).

A second reason for using recursion is that it sometimes provides a much simpler solution. In these situations, obtaining the same result using repetition requires extremely complicated coding that can be avoided by using recursion. An example of this is the quicksort sorting algorithm presented in Section 11.6.

Related to both of these reasons is a third. In many advanced applications, recursion is both simpler to visualize and the only practical means of implementing a solution. Examples of these applications are the implementation of a quicksort algorithm (see Section 11.6) and the creation of dynamically allocated data structures (see Section 14.5).

Exercises 6.6

1. The Fibonacci sequence is 0, 1, 1, 2, 3, 5, 8, 13, . . . , such that the first two terms are 0 and 1, and each term thereafter is defined recursively as the sum of the two preceding terms; that is:

$$\text{Fib}(n) = \text{Fib}(n - 1) + \text{Fib}(n - 2)$$

Write a recursive function that returns the nth number in a Fibonacci sequence when n is passed to the function as an argument. For example, when $n = 8$, the function returns the eighth number in the sequence, which is 13.

2. The sum of a series of consecutive numbers from 1 to n can be defined recursively as:

```
sum(1) = 1;
sum(n) = n + sum(n - 1)
```

Write a recursive C++ function that accepts n as an argument and calculates the sum of the numbers from 1 to n.

3. a. The value of x^n can be defined recursively as:

$$x^0 = 1$$
$$x^n = x * x^{n-1}$$

Write a recursive function that computes and returns the value of x^n.

   b. Rewrite the function written for Exercise 3a so that it uses a repetitive algorithm for calculating the value of x^n.

4. a. Write a function that recursively determines the value of the nth term of a geometric sequence defined by the terms:

$$a, ar, ar^2, ar^3, \ldots, ar^{n-1}$$

The argument to the function should be the first term, a, the common ratio, r, and the value of n.

   b. Modify the function written for Exercise 4a so that the sum of the first n terms of the sequence is returned.

5. a. Write a function that recursively determines the value of the nth term of an arithmetic sequence defined by the terms:

$$a, a + d, a + 2d, a + 3d, \ldots, a + (n-1)d$$

The argument to the function should be the first term, a, the common difference, d, and the value of n.

   b. Modify the function written for Exercise 5a so that the sum of the first n terms of the sequence is returned. (*Note:* This is a more general form of Exercise 2.)

6.7 FOCUS ON PROBLEM SOLVING

There are many mathematical and simulation problems in which probability must be considered or statistical sampling techniques must be used. For example, in simulating automobile traffic flow or telephone usage patterns, statistical models are required. Additionally, applications such as simple computer games and more involved "strategy games" in business and science can only be described statistically. All of these statistical models require the generation of **random numbers**, that is, a series of numbers whose order cannot be predicted.

In practice, there are no truly random numbers. Dice never are perfect; cards are never shuffled completely randomly; the supposedly random motions of molecules are influenced by the environment; and digital computers can handle numbers only within a finite range and with limited precision. The best one can do is generate **pseudorandom numbers**, which are sufficiently random for the task at hand.

Some computer languages contain a library function that produces random numbers; others do not. The functions provided by C++ are named `rand()` for generating random numbers and `srand()` for setting initial random "seed" values. We present these two functions and then use them in three applications: The first simulates tossing a coin to determine the number of resulting heads and tails; the second creates a game of HiLo; and the third finds an approximation to the area under a curve using Monte Carlo simulation.

Generating Pseudorandom Numbers

Two functions are provided by C++ compilers for creating random numbers: `rand()` and `srand()`. The `rand()` function produces a series of random numbers in the range $0 \leq$ `rand()` $\leq$ `RAND_MAX`, where the constant `RAND_MAX` is defined in the `cmath` header file. The `srand()` function provides a starting "seed" value for `rand()`. If `srand()` or some other equivalent "seeding" technique is not used, `rand()` always produces the same series of random numbers.

The general procedure for creating a series of N random numbers using C++'s library functions is illustrated by the following code:

```
srand(time(NULL));  // this generates the first "seed" value

for (int i = 1; i <= N; i++)  // this generates N random numbers
{
  rvalue - rand();
  cout << rvalue << endl;
}
```

Here, the argument to the `srand()` function is a call to the `time()` function with a `NULL` argument. With this argument, the `time()` function reads the computer's internal clock time in seconds. The `srand()` function then uses this time, converted to an unsigned `int`, to initialize the random number generator function `rand()`.[12] Program 6.16 uses this code to generate a series of ten random numbers.

---

[12]Alternatively, many C++ compilers have a `randomize()` routine that is defined using the `srand()` function. If this routine is available, the call `randomize()` can be used in place of the call `srand(time(NULL))`.

PROGRAM 6.16

```cpp
#include <iostream>
#include <cmath>
#include <ctime>
using namespace std;

// this program generates ten pseudorandom numbers
// using C++'s rand() function

int main()
{
  const int NUMBERS = 10;

  double randvalue;
  int i;

  srand(time(NULL));
  for (i = 1; i <= NUMBERS; i++)
  {
    randvalue = rand();
    cout << randvalue << endl;
  }

  return 0;
}
```

The following is the output produced by one run of Program 6.16:

```
20203
21400
15265
26935
 8369
10907
31299
15400
 5074
20663
```

Because the `srand()` function was used in Program 6.16, the series of ten random numbers differs each time the program is executed. Without the randomizing "seeding" effect of this function, the same series of random numbers is always produced. Note also the inclusion of the `cmath` and `ctime` header files. The `cmath` file contains the function prototypes for the `srand()` and `rand()` functions, while the `ctime` header file contains the function prototype for the `time()` function.

Scaling   One modification to the random numbers produced by the `rand()` function typically must be made in practice. In most applications, either the random numbers are required to be floating-point values within the range 0.0 to 1.0 or integers within a specified range, such as 1 to 100. The method for adjusting the random numbers produced by a random number generator to reside within such ranges is called **scaling**.

Scaling random numbers to reside within the range 0.0 to 1.0 is easily accomplished by dividing the returned value of `rand()` by `RAND_MAX`. Thus, the expression `double(rand())/RAND_MAX` produces a floating-point random number between 0.0 and 1.0.

Scaling a random number as an integer value between 0 and $N - 1$ is accomplished using the either of the expressions `int(double(rand())/RAND_MAX * N)` or `rand() % N`. For example, the expression `int(double(rand())/RAND_MAX * 100)` produces a random integer between 0 and 99, as does the expression `rand() % 100`.

To produce an integer random number between 1 and `N`, you can use the expression `1 + int(double(rand())/RAND_MAX * N)` or the expression `1 + rand() % N`.

For example, in simulating the roll of a die, the expression `1 + int(double(rand())/RAND_MAX * 6)` produces a random integer between 1 and 6, as does the expression `1 + rand() % 6`. In general, to produce a random integer between the numbers `a` and `b`, you can use the expression `a + int(rand()) % (b-a + 1)`.

Having presented the basics of C++'s random number functions, we now use them to solve three different problems.

Problem 1: Create a Coin Toss Simulation

A common use of random numbers is to simulate events using a program rather than going through the time and expense of constructing a real-life experiment. For example, statistical theory tells us that the probability of having a single tossed coin turn up heads is one-half. Similarly, there is a 50 percent probability of having a single tossed coin turn up tails.

Using these probabilities, we would expect a single coin that is tossed 1000 times to turn up heads 500 times and tails 500 times. In practice, however, this is seldom exactly realized for a single experiment consisting of 1000 tosses. Instead of tossing a coin 1000 times, we can use a random number generator to simulate these tosses. In particular, we use the random number function developed in the previous application.

Analyze the Problem for Input/Output Requirements   For this problem, two outputs are required: the percentage of heads and the percentage of tails that result when a simulated coin is tossed 1000 times. No input item is required for the random number generator function.

Develop a Solution   The percentage of heads and tails is determined as:

$$\text{percentage of heads} = \frac{\text{number of heads}}{1000} \times 100\%$$

$$\text{percentage of tails} = \frac{\text{number of tails}}{1000} \times 100\%$$

To determine the number of heads and tails, we need to simulate 1000 random numbers in such a manner that we can define a result of "heads" or "tails" from each generated number. There are numerous ways to do this.

One way is to use the `rand()` function to generate integers between 0 and `RAND_MAX`. Knowing that any single toss has a 50% chance of being either a head or a tail, we could designate a "head" as an even random number and a "tail" as an odd random number. A second method is to scale the return value from `rand()` to reside between 0.0 and 1.0 as described earlier. Then we could define a "head" as any number greater than 0.5 and any other result as a "tail." This is the algorithm we will adopt.

Having defined how we will create a single toss that has a 50% chance of turning up heads or tails, the generation of 1000 tosses is rather simple: We use a fixed count loop that generates 1000 random numbers. For each generation, we identify the result as either a head or tail and accumulate the results in a heads and tails counter. Thus, the complete simulation algorithm is given by the pseudocode:

Initialize a heads count to 0
Initialize a tails count to 0
For 1000 times
　　generate a random number between 0 and 1
　　If the random number is greater than 0.5
　　　consider this as a head and
　　　add 1 to the heads' count
　Else
　　　consider this as a tail and
　　　add 1 to the tails' count
　Endif
Endfor
Calculate the percentage of heads as
　　the number of heads divided by 1000 × 100%
Calculate the percentage of tails as
　　the number of tails divided by 1000 × 100%
Print the percentage of heads and tails obtained

Code the Solution　Program 6.17 shows the C++ algorithm. Two sample runs of Program 6.17 follow:

```
Heads came up 51.5 percent of the time
Tails came up 48.5 percent of the time
```

and

```
Heads came up 49.3 percent of the time
Tails came up 50.7 percent of the time
```

Writing and executing Program 6.17 is certainly easier than manually tossing a coin 1000 times. Note, however, that the validity of the results produced by the program depends on how random the numbers produced by `rand()` actually are.

Test and Correct the Program　Program 6.17 must pass two tests. The more important test concerns the randomness of each generated number. This, of course, is really a test of the random number function. For our purposes, we have used a previously written function supplied by the compiler. So at this point, we accept the "randomness" of the generator. (See Exercise 4 for Section 6.7 for a method of verifying the function's randomness.)

Once the question of the random number generator has been settled, the second test requires that we correctly generate 1000 numbers and accumulate a head and tail count. That this is correctly accomplished is adequately verified by a simple desk check of the `for` loop within Program 6.17. Also, we do know that the result of the simulation must be close to 50% heads and 50% tails. The results of the simulation verify this to be the case.

PROGRAM 6.17

```cpp
#include <iostream>
#include <cmath>
#include <ctime>
using namespace std;

// a program to simulate the tossing of a coin NUMTOSSES times
int main()
{
  const int NUMTOSSES = 1000;

  int heads = 0;  // initialize heads count
  int tails = 0;  // initialize tails count
  int i;
  double flip, perheads, pertails;

    // simulate NUMTOSSES tosses of a coin
  srand(time(NULL));
  for (i = 1; i <= NUMTOSSES; i++)
  {
    flip = double (rand())/RAND_MAX;   // scale the number between 0 and 1
    if (flip > 0.5)
      heads = heads + 1;
    else
      tails = tails + 1;
  }
  perheads = (heads / double (NUMTOSSES)) * 100.0;  // calculate heads percentage
  pertails = (tails / double (NUMTOSSES)) * 100.0;  // calculate tails percentage
  cout << "\nHeads came up " << perheads << " percent of the time";
  cout << "\nTails came up " << pertails << " percent of the time" << endl;

  return 0;
}
```

Problem 2: Write a HiLo Computer Game

For this problem, a computer game named HiLo is required. In this game, the computer chooses an integer number between 1 and 100 and asks the user/player to guess its value. Guesses are counted and the player is told after each incorrect guess whether the guess was too high or too low and is asked for another guess. When the player has found the number, he or she is told how many guesses it took.

Analyze the Problem for Input/Output Requirements   The generation of a random number requires using the srand() and rand() functions. Additionally, the user repeatedly is asked to input a guess until the randomly generated number is

A   BIT   OF   BACKGROUND

Monte Carlo

Monte Carlo is a community within the principality of Monaco on the Mediterranean coast of France. Monte Carlo's fame as a gambling resort is responsible for its name being adopted for mathematical methods involving random numbers.

Monte Carlo techniques involve creating random numbers within given limits and determining what percentage of those numbers meet certain criteria. They can be used to calculate the area between curves (as on page 363), to estimate the arrival of airplanes at an airport, to predict the percentage of manufac-

tured parts that will be defective, to project the growth and decline of populations with fixed resources, to specify the needed thickness of nuclear reactor shielding, and so forth.

Monte Carlo calculations were hardly feasible before the development of high-speed computers. However, new parallel-processing machines, which can handle many operations concurrently, are reducing the time required for Monte Carlo calculations using large data samples.

found. When the correct guess is made, the program is required to display the number of guesses.

Develop a Solution   On entry of the program, a random number between 0 and 100 must be generated. This is easily accomplished using the scaling algorithm:

$$\text{number} = 1 + \text{int (rand ( )) \% 100}$$

A loop, beginning with a count of 0, can then be used to ask for the guess, increment count, compare the guess with the number, and repeat until the guess equals the number. A repeat-until structure ensures that the player gets to guess at least once. The pseudocode describing this procedure is:

Generate a random number
Initialize count = 0
REPEAT
  Ask for guess
  Increment count
  If guess < random number,
   Print "Too Low."
  Else if guess > random number,
   Print "Too High."
UNTIL guess equals random number
Write count

Code the Solution   Program 6.18 presents the algorithm written as C++ code.

PROGRAM 6.18

```cpp
#include <iostream>
#include <cmath>
#include <ctime>
using namespace std;

int main()
{
  const int DEBUG = 0;

  int guess, count, val;
  double rnum;

  srand(time(NULL));

  rnum = rand();
    // scale the number to be between 0 and 100
  val = 1 + int(rnum)%100;
  if (DEBUG)
    cout << "rnum = " << rnum << " val = " << val;
  count = 0;

  do
  {
    cout << "\nEnter your guess: ";
    cin  >> guess;
    count++;
    if (guess < val)
      cout << "\nYour guess was too low - guess again!";
    else if (guess > val)
      cout << "\nYour guess was too high - guess again!";
  } while (guess != val);

  cout << "\nCongratulations!  You did it in " << count << " guesses\n";

  return 0;
}
```

Test and Correct the Program   Included within Program 6.18 is the named constant DEBUG. When this constant is set to 1, the program displays its randomly generated number. Using this display, we can run the program and select guesses that are known to be too high and too low to see that the program reacts correctly. Once this testing is done, the DEBUG constant should be set to 0. Here is a sample run:

```
Enter your guess: 50

Your guess was too high - guess again!
Enter your guess: 25
```

```
Your guess was too low - guess again!
Enter your guess: 37

Your guess was too low - guess again!
Enter your guess: 41

Congratulations! You did it in 4 guesses
```

Problem 3: Use Monte Carlo Simulation to Estimate the Area Under a Curve

Here is a more serious application of random numbers. It uses a technique called a *Monte Carlo* method, by which large numbers of experiments involving random outcomes are performed to find an approximate solution to a problem.

The area under a curve can be approximated by using Monte Carlo simulation. To understand how this simulation works, consider that we wish to determine the area under the curve $y = f(x)$, shown in Figure 6.20, between the limits $x = a$ and $x = b$. On top of this curve, we build a rectangular box bounded by the x axis, the lines $x = a$, $x = b$, and the line defined by the curve at its highest y value.

FIGURE 6.20   A General Curve $y = f(x)$

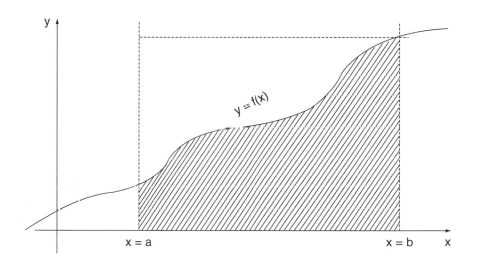

Now assume that we toss N darts at random into the rectangular box and that M of these darts land between the curve and the x axis. Calculate the ratio M/N as:

$$\frac{M}{N} \approx \frac{\text{number of darts between the curve and the } x \text{ axis}}{\text{total number of darts in the box}}$$

The ratio M/N is approximately equal to the ratio of the shaded area under the curve to the total area of the box; that is:

$$\frac{M}{N} \approx \frac{\text{area under the curve (shaded area)}}{\text{total area of the box}}$$

From this, we can calculate the area under the curve as

$$\text{Area under the curve (shaded area)} \approx \text{total area of the box} \, \frac{M}{N}$$

where the total area of the box is found by multiplying the length by the width. The problem is to write a computer program that effectively tosses darts and determines the area under any curve $y = f(x)$ between the limits $x = a$ and $x = b$.

Analyze the Problem for Input/Output Requirements   The inputs required for this problem are:

1. the equation of the curve we want the area for
2. the lower x limit, a, between which the area is to be calculated
3. the upper x limit, b, between which the area is to be calculated

The output is the approximate area under the curve.

Develop a Solution   We restrict ourselves to functions and ranges in which the curve is generally increasing or decreasing within the desired range and in which the curve lies entirely above the x axis. These restrictions are not necessary to find the area, but they help simplify the solution. The increasing/decreasing restriction makes it easy to locate the maximum y value because for increasing curves the maximum y value occurs at $x = b$ and has the value $f(b)$. For decreasing curves the maximum y value occurs at $x = a$ and has the value $f(a)$. Requiring that the curve lie above the x axis removes the problem of assessing which parts of the curve are above and below the x axis.

The equation $y = f(x)$ for the curve is written in a function that finds y for a given argument value of x. For example, if the function is $y = 3x^2 + 2x + 1$, the function is simply:

```
double fcn(double x)
{
   return (3.0 * pow(x,2) + 2.0 * x + 1.0);
}
```

For any other function $y = f(x)$, just replace the content of the return statement with the expression defining $f(x)$.

The formula for determining the total area of the box is

$$width * length = (b - a) * \text{ymax}$$

where $\text{ymax} = f(b)$ for an increasing curve and $f(a)$ for a decreasing curve.

Now choose a pair of random numbers `xrnd` and `yrnd` such that $a \leq \text{xrnd} < b$ and $0 \leq \text{yrnd} \leq \text{ymax}$ to simulate the coordinates where a dart lands in the box. A random number between a and b can be found using the equation $(b - a) * random number + a$, where *random number* is between 0.0 and 1.0. Using `xrnd`, determine `ycalc` = `f(xrnd)` and then determine if `yrnd` lies under the curve; that is, whether `yrnd` $\leq$ `ycalc`. If so, increment the count of numbers under the curve. Increment the count of total number of points selected. Repeat this process for a large number of randomly selected points. Then calculate and display the area under the curve.

A structure chart for the solution is shown in Figure 6.21. The pseudocode for this solution is:

Define the function fcn(x)
Define whether the function is increasing or decreasing
Define the number of iterations as MAXREPS
Ask for the limits a and b
If the function is increasing
  ymax = f(b)
Else
  ymax = f(a)

Calculate the total area as (b − a)(ymax)
Initialize undercount and totalcount to zero
While totalcount # MAXREPS
  Generate an xrnd and yrnd random number
  Calculate ycalc = f(xrnd)
    If yrnd = ycalc
      increment undercount
  increment totalcount
End While
Calculate area = (total area)(undercount / totalcount)
Print the area

FIGURE 6.21   Structure Chart for Monte Carlo Simulation

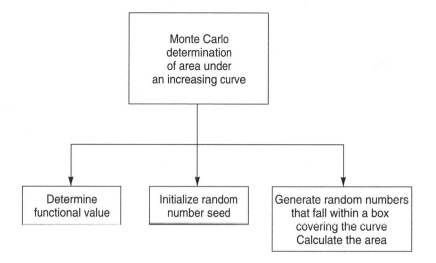

Code the Solution   Program 6.19 presents the algorithm written as C++ code.

PROGRAM 6.19

```
#include <iostream>
#include <ctime>
#include <cmath>
using namespace std;

const int INCREASE = 1;   // this is an increasing curve

double fcn(double x)
{
  return (3.0*pow(x,2) + 2.0*x + 1.0);
}

int main()
{
```

(continued from previous page)

```cpp
    const int MAXCOUNT  = 1000;

    int undercount = 0;
    int totalcount = 0;
    double rnumx, rnumy;
    double x, val, xrnd, yrnd, ymax, ycalc, a, b, boxarea, area;

    srand(time(NULL));
    cout << "What is the lower limit on x? ";
    cin  >> a;
    cout << "What is the upper limit on x? ";
    cin  >> b;

    if (INCREASE)
      ymax = fcn(b);
    else
      ymax = fcn(a);

    boxarea = (b - a) * ymax;

    while (totalcount < MAXCOUNT)
    {
      rnumx = rand(); // get a random x value
      val = rnumx / RAND_MAX; // creates a number between 0 and 1
      xrnd = (b - a) * val + a;
      rnumy = rand(); // get a random y value
      val = rnumy / RAND_MAX;
      yrnd = ymax * val;
      if (yrnd <= fcn(xrnd))
        undercount++;
      totalcount++;
    }

    area = boxarea * (float)undercount/(float)totalcount;

    cout << "\nFor the curve defined in the function fcn(x),\n";
    cout << "between x = " << a << " and x = " << b << endl;
    cout << "The area is approximately " << area << endl;

    return 0;
}
```

Notice that we have placed the `fcn()` function, which defines the curve, at the top of the program. This alerts us that this function must be changed for each curve $y = f(x)$.

Test and Correct the Program During the testing phase, statements could be inserted into the code to display the values of `xrnd`, `yrnd`, `ycalc`, `undercount`, and `totalcount` during each iteration. If you assign a very large value to `MAXREPS`, you may want to print a message during each iteration that tells the user that the program is executing. Test the program for various values of *a* and *b*. Increase

MAXREPS for greater accuracy. Alter the function $fcn(x)$ to find the area under a different curve. If you are comfortable with calculus, compare your answers with the integral of the function; otherwise, sketch the curve on graph paper and estimate the area to see if you are getting reasonable results. A sample run looks like:

```
What is the lower limit on x? 2.0
What is the upper limit on x? 4.0

For the curve defined in the function fcn(x),
between x = 2.00 and x = 4.00
The area is approximately 69.084
```

For this curve, using calculus, the true area under the curve between $x = 2.0$ and $x = 4.0$ is 70.0.

Exercises 6.7

1. Modify Program 6.17 so that it requests the number of tosses from the user. (*Hint:* Make sure the program correctly determines the percentages of heads and tails obtained.)

2. *Central Limit Theorem Simulation:* Modify Program 6.17 so that it automatically generates 20 simulations, with each simulation having 1000 tosses. Print out the percentage for each run and the percentages for the 20 runs combined.

3. Modify Program 6.18 to allow the user to run the game again after a game has been completed. The program should display the message "WOULD YOU LIKE TO PLAY AGAIN - 'Y'/'N'?: " and restart if the user enters either Y or y.

4. Write a program that tests the effectiveness of the rand() library function. Start by initializing ten counters such as zerocount, onecount, twocount, . . . , ninecount to 0. Then generate a large number of pseudorandom integers between 0 and 9. Each time 0 occurs, increment zerocount, when 1 occurs, increment onecount, etc. Finally, print out the number of 0s, 1s, 2s, etc. that occurred and the percentage of the time they occurred.

5. Many algorithms have been developed for generating pseudorandom numbers. Some of these algorithms utilize a counting scheme, such as counting bits beginning at some arbitrary location in a changing memory. Another scheme, which creates pseudorandom numbers by performing a calculation, is the *power residue method*. The power residue method begins with an odd n-digit integer, which is referred to as the "seed" number. The seed is multiplied by the value $(10^{n/2}-3)$. Use of the lowest n digits of the result (the "residue") produces a new seed. Continuing this procedure produces a series of random numbers, with each new number used as the seed for the next number. If the original seed has four or more digits (n equal to or greater than 4) and is not divisible by either 2 or 5, this procedure yields $5 \times 10^{(n-2)}$ random numbers before a sequence of numbers repeats itself. For example, starting with a six-digit seed ($n = 6$), such as 654321, a series of $5 \times 10^4 = 50,000$ random numbers can be generated.

    As an algorithm, the specific steps in generating pseudorandom numbers using a power residue procedure consists of the following steps:

    Step 1: Have a user enter a six-digit integer seed that is not divisible by 2 or 5; this means the number should be an odd number not ending in 5.

    Step 2: Multiply the seed number by 997, which is 10^3-3.

    Step 3: Extract the lower six digits of the result produced by step 2. Use this random number as the next seed.

    Step 4: Repeat steps 2 and 3 for as many random numbers as needed.

    Thus, if the user-entered seed number is 654321 (step 1), the first random number generated is calculated as follows:

Step 2: 654321 * 997 = 652358037

Step 3: Extract the lower six digits of the number obtained in step 2. This is accomplished using a standard programming "trick."

The trick involves:

Step 3a: Dividing the number by 10^6 = 1000000. For example, 652358037/1000000 = 652.358037.

Step 3b: Taking the integer part of the result of step 3a. For example, the integer part of 652.358037 = 652.

Step 3c: Multiplying the previous result by 10^6. For example, 652 × 10^6 = 652000000.

Step 3d: Subtracting this result from the original number. For example, 652358037 − 652000000 = 358037.

The integer part of a double-precision number can either be taken by assigning the double-precision number to an integer variable or by a C++ cast (see Section 3.3). In our procedure, we use the cast mechanism. Thus, the algorithm for producing a random number can be accomplished using the following code:

```
i = int(997.0 * x / 1.e6);    // take the integer part
x = 997.0 * x - i * 1.e6;
```

Using this information:

a. Create a function named `randnum()` that accepts a double-precision "seed" as a parameter and returns a double-precision random number between 0 and 1.e6.

b. Incorporate the `randnum()` function created in Exercise 5a into a working C++ program that produces ten random numbers between 0 and 1.e6.

c. Test the randomness of the `randnum()` function created in Exercise 5a using the method described in Exercise 4. Try some even seed values and some odd seed values that end in 5 to determine whether these affect the randomness of the numbers.

6. In the game of Blackjack, the cards 2 through 10 are counted at their face values, regardless of suit, all picture cards (jack, queen, and king) are counted as 10, and an ace is counted as either 1 or 11, depending on the total count of all the cards in a player's hand. The ace is counted as 11 only if the total value of all cards in a player's hand does not exceed 10, else it is counted as 1. Using this information, write a C++ program that uses a random number generator to select three cards (1 initially corresponding to an ace, 2 corresponding to a face card of two, and so on), calculate the total value of the hand appropriately, and display the value of the three cards with a printed message.

7. Write a C++ function that determines the quadrant in which a line drawn from the origin resides. The determination of the quadrant is made using the angle that the line makes with the positive X as follows:

Angle from the Positive X Axis	Quadrant
Between 0 and 90 degrees	1
Between 90 and 180 degrees	2
Between 180 and 270 degrees	3
Between 270 and 360 degrees	4

Note: If the angle is exactly 0, 90, 180, or 270 degrees, the corresponding line does not reside in any quadrant but lies on an axis. For this case, your function should return a zero.

8. All years that are evenly divisible by 400 or are evenly divisible by 4 and not evenly divisible by 100 are leap years. For example, since 1600 is evenly divisible by 400, the year 1600 was a leap year. Similarly, since 1988 is evenly divisible by four but not by 100, the year 1988 was also a leap year. Using this information, write a C++ function that accepts the year as a user input and returns 1 if the passed year is a leap year or 0 if it is not.

9. Based on an automobile's model year and weight, the state of New Jersey determines the car's weight class and registration fee using the following schedule:

Model Year	Weight	Registration Fee
1970 or earlier	Less than 2,700 lbs	$16.50
	2,700 to 3,800 lbs	25.50
	More than 3,800 lbs	46.50
1971 to 1979	Less than 2,700 lbs	27.00
	2,700 to 3,800 lbs	30.50
	More than 3,800 lbs	52.50
1980 or later	Less than 3,500 lbs	19.50
	3,500 or more lbs	52.50

Using this information, write a C++ function that accepts the year and weight of an automobile and returns the registration fee for the car.

10. Deal and display a hand of four different cards that can come from four different suits (hearts, clubs, diamonds, spades) of 13 cards each named ace = 1, 2, 3, 4, 5, 6, 7, 8, 9, 10, jack = 11, queen = 12, king = 13.
[*Hint:* Use the expressions `suit = (int)(4.0 * random number + 1.0)` and `card = (int)(13.0 * random number + 1)`, where the random number is between 0 and 1.]

11. It has been said that a monkey pushing keys at random on a typewriter could produce the works of Shakespeare, given sufficient time. Simulate this by having a program select and display letters at random. Count the number of letters typed until the program produces one of these two-letter words: *at, is, he, we, up,* or *on.* When one of these words is produced, stop the program and display the total number of letters typed. (*Hint:* Choose a letter by selecting a random integer number between 1 and 26.)

12. Write a program to simulate the rolling of two dice. If the total of the two dice is 7 or 11, you win; otherwise, you lose. Embellish this program as much as you like, with betting, different odds, different combinations for win or lose, stopping play when you have no money left or reach the house limit, displaying the dice, etc.
[*Hint:* Calculate the dots showing on each die by the expression `dots = (int)(6.0 * random number + 1)`, where the random number is between 0 and 1.]

13. Modify the value of the named constant MAXCOUNT to 10, 100, 1000, and 10000, respectively, and rerun Program 6.19 to see how these values affect the accuracy of the result. Fill in the following table with the area reported by each run of the program. Comment on what did occur and what you think should have occurred. If there were any differences between what did occur and what you expected, comment on what you think caused the differences.

MAXCOUNT			
10	100	1000	10000

14. Use the Monte Carlo algorithm developed in Program 6.19 to find an approximate value for π, which is 3.14159 accurate to five decimal places. In Figure 6.22, the shaded area represents one-quarter of a circle having a radius r of 1 unit. The area of the box bounded by the axes and the lines $x = 1$ and $y = 1$ is 1 square unit. The area of the quarter-circle is $1/4\pi r^2$, but since $r = 1$, this area equals $\pi/4$ square units. Therefore

$$\frac{\pi}{4} = \frac{\text{area of quarter circle}}{\text{area of the box}} \approx \frac{M}{N}$$

where M is the number of random numbers that fall under the curve and N is the total number of random numbers selected within the box. Generate random points inside the box (xrnd, yrnd) such that $0 \le \text{xrnd} \le 1$ and $0 \le \text{yrnd} \le 1$, and test to see if yrnd $\le$ ycalc, where ycalc = f(xrnd), and *f(x)* is the curve defined by the circle:

$$y = f(x) = sqrt(1 - x^2)$$

FIGURE 6.22 Calculation of π

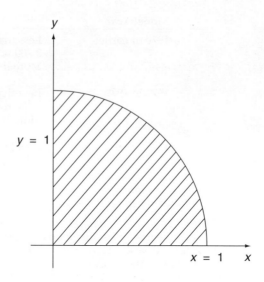

15. Here is a version of a problem called "the random walk." It can be extended to two or three dimensions and used to simulate molecular motion, to determine the effectiveness of reactor shielding, or to calculate a variety of other probabilities.

    Assume that your very tired and sleepy pet dog leaves his favorite lamppost on warm summer evenings and staggers randomly either two steps in the direction toward home or one step in the opposite direction. After the first step, the dog again staggers randomly two steps toward home or one step backward, and does this again and again. If the pet reaches a total distance of ten steps from the lamppost in the direction toward home, you find him and take him home. If the dog arrives back at the lamppost before reaching ten steps in the direction toward home, he lies down and spends the night at the foot of the lamppost.

    Write a C++ program that simulates 500 summer evenings and calculate and print the percentage of the time your pet sleeps at home for these evenings. [*Hint*: In a loop, determine forward or backward based on the value of a random number. Accumulate the distance the dog has reached toward your home. If the distance reaches ten, stop the loop and increment the home count. If the distance reaches zero before it reaches ten, stop the loop but do not increment the home count. Repeat this loop 500 times and find the ratio of (home count)/500.]

6.8 PLANNING FOR OBJECTS: UML STATE DIAGRAMS

The UML object diagrams presented in Section 5.8 are considered static models because they portray objects and classes at a fixed point in time, in the same manner that a photograph captures a scene in a single moment. State diagrams present the transition of an object's state over time, and are therefore considered dynamic models. A state diagram shows the different states that an object can have and the events that cause these states to appear. In effect, a state diagram describes how an objects' attributes change over time.

The most important part of creating state diagrams is clearly specifying the events that can cause a change in an object's state. Each event then becomes associated with a method that is included in the class model. Figure 6.23 illustrates that an event becomes coded as a class method. It is a method that permits a change in an object's state to occur.

FIGURE 6.23   **The State Model Identifies Operations to Be Included in the Class Diagram**

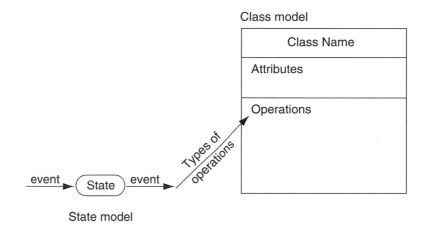

A state diagram consists of events and states. An **event** is defined as an individual signal (sometimes called a stimulus) from one object to another. For example, turning the key in a car's ignition is a signal to the electrical system to turn on or off. In object terms, turning the key is an event. Similarly, pushing the button on an elevator is considered an event. The press of the button is a signal to the elevator to move to another floor.

In contrast to events are states. An object's **state**, in its simplest form, is defined by the values of an object's attributes. For example, a switch that can be either on or off has two states—on and off. Similarly, if a rectangle is described by three attributes, its length, width, and position, giving values to these attributes defines a single state for a rectangle object.

In a state diagram each object has a clearly defined set of states. For example, if the system being programmed has three objects, then you will typically have three state diagrams, one for each object, each with its own set of states. Each state diagram, then, is a structured network of events and states. Figure 6.24 illustrates the basic symbols and notation used in a state diagram. As shown, the two primary symbols are a flow line, which denote an event, and a rectangle with rounded corners, which denotes a state. Each event shown in a state diagram can be augmented by a guard, attribute, or action, which are all explained later in this section. Similarly, each state can have an optional state name listed in the state rectangle plus activity information.

Notice in Figure 6.24 that events separate states. A state has duration in that it exists over an interval of time and only changes in response to an event, which is assumed to occur in zero time. For example, turning a car's ignition key to start the engine is an event. Once the car's engine is started the state of the engine, which is running, is assumed to continue until an event occurs that turn's the engine off. Figure 6.25 illustrates a state diagram for a car's ignition system.

FIGURE 6.24   State Diagram Symbols

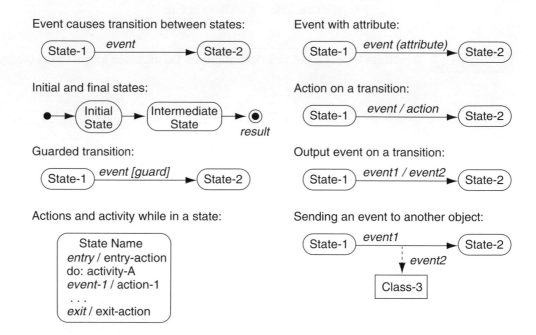

Event causes transition between states:

State-1 — *event* → State-2

Event with attribute:

State-1 — *event (attribute)* → State-2

Initial and final states:

● → Initial State → Intermediate State → ◉ *result*

Action on a transition:

State-1 — *event / action* → State-2

Guarded transition:

State-1 — *event [guard]* → State-2

Output event on a transition:

State-1 — *event1 / event2* → State-2

Actions and activity while in a state:

> State Name
> *entry* / entry-action
> do: activity-A
> *event-1* / action-1
> . . .
> *exit* / exit-action

Sending an event to another object:

State-1 — *event1* → State-2
↓ *event2*
Class-3

FIGURE 6.25   A Car's Ignition System State Diagram

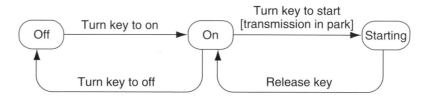

Off — Turn key to on → On — Turn key to start [transmission in park] → Starting

On — Release key → On

Off ← Turn key to off ← On

As shown, the ignition system consists of three states On, Off, and Starting. The events associated with these states are "Turn key to on," "Turn key to start," "Release key," and "Turn key to off." Notice that the event "Turn key to start," has the precondition "transmission in park." Preconditions, which are also referred to as guards, are listed within square brackets after the event's name. A precondition specifies that the event cannot take place unless the precondition is satisfied. In this case, the "Turn key to start" event will not force a change in state unless the transmission is in Park.

Events are always one-way signals from one object to another. If the signal also provides data values to an object, the data values are listed in parentheses following the event name. As we have seen, these data values are referred to as an event's attributes. Since each event eventually defines an operation, which in C++ is coded as a method, an event's attributes become the method's arguments. As one-way signals, however, events never receive a return value from the implemented method. Any reply from the receiving object is considered a separate event to the sending object, which must be realized using another method.

FIGURE 6.26   An Example of an Event Activity

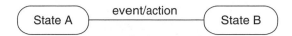

In addition to conditions and attributes, an event may also be associated with some instantaneous action. For example, pressing the right button on a mouse may cause a pop-up menu to appear, while the state of the original menu item becomes highlighted. Such actions are listed after the event and are separated by a forward slash (/) from the event description, as shown in Figure 6.26. These actions form the basis for events that interact with other objects.

Just as events may have actions associated with them, states may have activities. The difference between an action and an activity is the time needed to accomplish them. Actions, as we have noted, are assumed to be accomplished in zero-time (instantaneously), while activities take time to complete. As such, activities are associated with states. The notation *do: activity* within a state rectangle denotes that the activity begins when the state is entered and terminates when the state is left. For example, as illustrated in Figure 6.27, if the state of a house bell-chime system is ringing in response to the event "Push bell-button," the action is "ring the chimes."

FIGURE 6.27   A State with an Activity

A state diagram can either represent a continuously operating system or a finite, one-time, life-cycle. For example, making one phone call, or filling a car with a tank of gas can be modeled as a finite, one-time, activity. The operation of the phone itself or the gas pump, however, where the system goes from idle to active is a continuous operation. One-time activities are typically modeled by a state diagram where the initial state, which represents the creation of an object, is shown by a solid circle. The final state, which represents the end of the cycle and the destruction of an object, is shown by a bull's eye circle, as illustrated in Figure 6.28.

Although state diagrams almost always have an initial state, they may have one or more final states, or no final state. For example, Figure 6.29 illustrates a state diagram for an elevator. As shown, the elevator initially begins at the first floor, but once in operation it can be positioned at any other floor. Its activity is restricted to moving either up or down between floors, and it remains at its last destination until a new activity takes place. In the next section we will create a C++ class that implements these activities and states.

FIGURE 6.28 A State Diagram of a Water Sprinkler

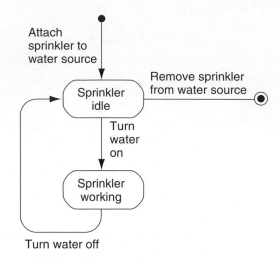

FIGURE 6.29 A State Diagram for an Elevator

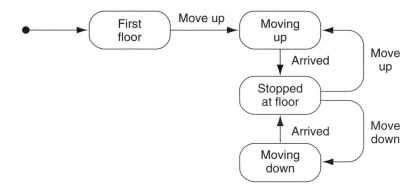

Exercises 6.8

1. Describe the differences between a class and state diagram.

2. Why are state diagrams referred to as dynamic models?

3. Construct a state diagram for a game of checkers.

4. Construct a state diagram for using the brakes on a car.

5. Construct a state diagram for shifting a car's transmission. Assume that there are six gears: Park, Reverse, Neutral, Drive, Drive-1, and Drive-2.

6. The control switch on a thermostat has three positions: Cool, Off, and Heat. Construct a state diagram for the switch.

7. Draw a state diagram for a traffic light that can be in one of three states: green, yellow, or red.

6.9 COMMON PROGRAMMING ERRORS

1. Passing incorrect data types. This is an extremely common programming error related to functions. The values passed to a function must correspond to the data types of the parameters declared for the function. One way to verify that correct values have been received is to display all passed values within a function's body before any calculations are made. Once this verification has taken place, you can dispense with the display.[13]
2. Giving a local variable the same name as a global variable. Within the function declaring it, the use of the variable's name only affects the local variable's contents unless the scope resolution operator, : :, is used.
3. Omitting the called function's prototype either within or before the calling function. The called function must be alerted to the type of value that will be returned, and this information is provided by the function prototype. The prototype can be omitted if the called function is physically placed in a program before its calling function. The actual value returned by a function can be verified by displaying it both before and after it is returned.
4. Terminating a function's header line with a semicolon.
5. Forgetting to include the data type of a function's parameters within the header line.

6.10 CHAPTER REVIEW

Key Terms

actual arguments	global scope
actual parameter	global variable
argument	local scope
auto	local variable
basic rule of testing	memory stack
called function	parameter
calling function	pass by reference
dynamic model	pass by value
extern	recursive functions
formal arguments	register
formal parameters	return statement
function body	scaling
function definition	scope
function header	static
function overloading	storage class
function prototype	stub
function template	template prefix
functional model	variable scope

---

[13] In practice, a good debugger program should be used.

Summary

1. A function is called by giving its name and passing any data to it in the parentheses following the name. If a variable is one of the arguments in a function call, the called function receives a copy of the variable's value.

2. The common form of a user-written function is:

```
returnType functionName(parameter list)
{
    declarations and other C++ statements;
    return expression;
}
```

The first line of the function is called the function header. The opening and closing braces of the function and all statements in between these braces constitute the function's body. The returned data type is, by default, an integer when no returned data type is specified. The parameter list is a comma-separated list of parameter declarations.

3. A function's return type is the data type of the value returned by the function. If no type is declared, the function is assumed to return an integer value. If the function does not return a value, it should be declared as a `void` type.

4. Functions can directly return at most a single data type value to their calling functions. This value is the value of the expression in the return statement.

5. Using reference parameters, a function can be passed the address of a variable. If a called function is passed an address, it has the ability to access directly the respective calling function's variable. Using passed addresses permits a called function effectively to return multiple values.

6. Functions can be declared to all calling functions by means of a *function prototype*. The function prototype provides a declaration for a function that specifies the data type returned by the function, its name, and the data types of the arguments expected by the function. As with all declarations, a function prototype is terminated with a semicolon and may be included within local variable declarations or as a global declaration. The most common form of a function prototype is:

```
dataType functionName(argument data type list);
```

If the called function is placed physically above the calling function, no further declaration is required, because the function's definition serves as a global declaration to all following functions.

7. Every variable used in a program has a *scope*, which determines where in the program the variable can be used. The scope of a variable is either local or global and is determined by where the variable's definition statement is placed. A local variable is defined within a function and can be used only within its defining function or block. A global variable is defined outside a function and can be used in any function following the variable's definition. All global variables that are not specifically initialized by the user are initialized to zero by the compiler and can be shared between files using the keyword `extern`.

8. Every variable has a *class*. The class of a variable determines how long the value in the variable is retained: `auto` variables are local variables that exist only while their defining function is executing; `register` variables are similar to automatic variables but are stored in a computer's internal registers rather than in memory; `static` variables can be either global or local and

retain their values for the duration of a program's execution. The `static` variables are also set to zero when they are defined, if they are not explicitly initialized by the user.

9. A *recursive solution* is one in which the solution can be expressed in terms of a "simpler" version of itself. A recursive algorithm must always specify the first case or cases and how the *n*th case is related to the (*n* − 1) case.

10. If a problem solution can be expressed repetitively or recursively with equal ease, the repetitive solution is preferable because it executes faster and uses less memory. In many advanced applications, recursion is simpler to visualize and the only practical means of implementing a solution.

Exercises

1. A function is defined by the following code:

```
double FractionToDecimal(double numerator, double denominator)
{
    return (numerator/denominator);
}
```

   Write the shortest driver program module you can to test this function and check the passing of parameters.

2. A formula to raise a real number *a* to the real power *b* is given by the formula

$$a^b = e^{[b * \ln(a)]}$$

   where *a* must be positive and *b* must be positive or zero. Using this formula, write a function named `power()` that accepts *a* and *b* as real values and returns a^b.

3. A fraction handling program contains this menu:

```
A. Add two fractions
B. Convert a fraction to decimal
C. Multiply two fractions
Q. Quit
```

   a. Write C++ code for the program with stub functions for the choices.

   b. Insert the function `FractionToDecimal()` from Exercise 1 into the code with appropriate commands to pass and display the parameters.

   c. Complete the program by replacing the stub functions with functions that perform appropriate operations.

4. a. The time in hours, minutes, and seconds is to be passed to a function named `totsec()`. Write `totsec()` to accept these values, determine the total number of seconds in the passed data, and display the calculated value.

   b. Include the `totsec()` function written for Exercise 4a in a working program. The `main()` function should correctly call `totsec` and display the value returned by the function. Use the following test data to verify your program's operation: hours = 10, minutes = 36, and seconds = 54. Make sure you do a hand calculation to verify the result displayed by your program.

5. A value that is sometimes useful is the greatest common divisor (gcd) of two integers *n*1 and *n*2. A famous mathematician, Euclid, discovered an efficient method to do this more than 2000 years ago. Right now, however, we'll settle for

a stub. Write the integer function stub `gcd(n1, n2)`. Simply have it return a value that suggests it received its arguments correctly. (*Hint:* `n1 + n2` is a good choice of return values. Why isn't `n1 / n2` a good choice?)

6. Euclid's method for finding the greatest common divisor of two positive integers consists of the following steps:

> *Step 1:* Divide the larger number by the smaller and retain the remainder.
> *Step 2:* Divide the smaller number by the remainder, again retaining the remainder.
> *Step 3:* Continue dividing the prior remainder by the current remainder until the remainder is zero, at which point the last nonzero remainder is the greatest common divisor.

For example, assuming the two positive integers are 84 and 49, we have:

> *Step 1:* 84/49 yields a remainder of 35.
> *Step 2:* 49/35 yields a remainder of 14.
> *Step 3:* 35/14 yields a remainder of 7.
>   14/7 yields a remainder of 0.

Thus, the last nonzero remainder, which is 7, is the greatest common divisor of 84 and 49.

Using Euclid's algorithm, replace the stub function written for Exercise 5 with an actual function that determines and returns the gcd of its two integer arguments.

7. a. Write a function named `tax()` that accepts a dollar amount and a tax rate as formal arguments and returns the tax due on the dollar amount. For example, if the numbers 100.00 and .06 are passed to the function, the value returned should be 6.00, which is 100.00 X .06.

   b. Include the `tax()` function written for Exercise 7a in a working program. The `main()` function should correctly call `tax()` and display the value returned by the function.

8. a. Write a function named `daycount()` that accepts a month, day, and year as its input parameters, calculates an integer representing the total number of days from 1/1/1900, inclusive, corresponding to the passed date, and returns the calculated integer to the calling function. For this problem, assume that each year has 365 days and each month has 30 days. Test your function by verifying that the date 1/1/1900 returns a day count of 1.

   b. Include the `daycount()` function written for Exercise 8a in a working program. The `main()` function should correctly call `daycount()` and display the integer returned by the function.

9. a. A clever and simple method of preparing to sort dates into either ascending (increasing) or descending (decreasing) order is to first convert a date having the form month/day/year into an integer number using the formula *date = year * 10000 + month * 100 + day*. For example, using this formula, the date 12/6/1999 converts to the integer 19991206 and the date 2/28/2000 converts to the integer 20000228. Sorting the resulting integer numbers automatically puts the dates into the correct order. Using this formula, write a function named `convertdays()` that accepts a month, day, and year, converts the passed data into a single date integer, and returns the integer to the calling function.

   b. Include the `convertdays()` function written for Exercise 9a in a working program. The `main()` function should correctly call `convertdays()` and display the integer returned by the function.

10. The following program uses the same variable names in both the calling and called function. Determine if this causes any problem for the compiler.

```
#include <iostream>
void main(void)
{
    int min, hour, sec;
    int time(int, int); // function prototype

    cout << "Enter two numbers: ";
    cin >> min, hour;
    sec = time(min, hour);
    cout << "The total number of seconds is " << sec << endl;
}

int time(int min, int hour)
{
    int sec;

    sec = (hour * 60 + min) * 60;
    return (sec);
}
```

11. Write a program that reads a key pressed on the keyboard and displays its code on the screen. Use the program to determine the code for the enter key. Then write a function named `readOneChar()` that reads a character and ignores any succeeding characters until the enter key is pressed. The entered character should be returned by the function.

12. Write a function named `pass()` that returns a reject or accept code depending on whether the mean tolerance of a group of parts is less than or greater than 1%. If the average is less than 1.0%, the function should return A for accept, else it should return R for reject.

13. a. Write and test a C++ function `makeMilesKmTable()` to display a table of miles converted to kilometers. The arguments to the function should be the starting and stopping values of miles and the increment. The output should be a table of miles and their equivalent kilometer values. Use the relationship that 1 mile equals 1.61 kilometers.

    b. Modify the function written for Exercise 13a so that two columns are printed. For example, if the starting value is 1 mile, the ending value 20 miles, and the increment is 1, the display should look like:

Miles	Kilometers	Miles	Kilometers
1	1.61	11	17.70
2	3.22	12	19.31
.	.	.	.
.	.	.	.
10	16.09	20	32.18

    [*Hint:* Find `split = (start + stop)/2`. Let a loop execute from miles = start to split, and calculate and print across one line the values of miles and kilometers for both miles and `(miles - start + split + 1)`.]

14. Heron's formula for the area A of a triangle with sides of length a, b, and c is $A = sqrt[s(s - a)(s - b)(s - c)]$, where $s = (a + b + c)/2$. Write, test, and execute a function that accepts the values of a, b, and c as parameters from a calling function and then calculates the values of s and $s(s - a)(s - b)(s - c)$. If this quantity

is positive, the function calculates *A*. If the quantity is negative, *a*, *b*, and *c* do not form a triangle, and the function should set *A* = −1. The value of *A* should be returned by the function.

15. Write and test two functions `enterData()` and `printCheck()` to produce the sample paycheck illustrated in Figure 6.30 on the screen. The items in parentheses should be accepted by `enterData()` and passed to `printCheck()` for display.

FIGURE 6.30   Sample Check Form

Zzyz Corp.   Date: (today's date)
1164 Sunrise Avenue
Kalispell, Montana

Pay to the order of: (first and last name) $ (amount)

UnderSecurity Bank
Missoula, MT
                                                     _____
                                                        Authorized Signature

16. Your company will soon open a new office in France. To help them do business there, they have asked you to prepare a comprehensive package that performs the following conversions on demand:

Measure	American	to	Metric	by	Formula
Distance	Inch		Centimeter		2.54 cm/in
	Foot		Meter		0.305 m/ft
	Yard		Meter		0.9144 m/yd
	Mile		Kilometer		1.6909 km/mi
Temperature	Fahrenheit		Celsius		$C = (5/9)(F - 32)$
Weight	Pound		Kilogram		0.454 kg/lb
	Ounce		Gram		28.35 gm/oz
Currency	Dollar		Franc		Entered by the user
					About 5 Franc/$
Capacity	Quart		Liter		0.946 liter/qt
	Teaspoon		Milliliter		4.9 ml/tsp
Math	Degree		Radian		$rad = (\pi/180)(degree)$
	Degree		Grad		$Grad = (200/180)(degree)$

17. Write a function named `time()` that has an integer parameter named `seconds` and three integer reference parameters named `hours`, `min`, and `sec`. The function is to convert the passed number of seconds into an equivalent number of hours, minutes, and seconds. Using the references, the function should directly alter the respective actual arguments in the calling function.

18. a. Write a function named `date()` that accepts a long integer of the form yyyymmdd, such as 20060412L, determines the corresponding month, day, and year, and returns these three values to the calling function. For example, if `date()` is called using the statement:

        date(20060412L, &month, &day, &year)

the number 4 should be returned in `month`, the number 12 in `day`, and the number 2006 in `year`.

b. Include the `date()` subroutine written for Exercise 18a in a working program. The `main()` function should correctly call `date()` and display the three values returned by the function.

19. Write a function named `payment()` that has three parameters: `principal`, which is the amount financed; `int`, which is the monthly interest rate; and `months`, which is length of the loan in the number of months. The function should return the monthly payment according to the following formula:

$$payment = \frac{principal}{\left[\dfrac{1 - (1 + interest)^{-months}}{interest}\right]}$$

Note that the interest value used in this formula is a monthly rate, as a decimal. Thus, if the yearly rate were 10%, the monthly rate is (.10/12). Test your function. What argument values cause it to malfunction (and should not be input)?

20. The volume of a right circular cylinder is given by its radius squared times its height times π. Write a function that accepts two floating-point arguments—the cylinder's radius and the cylinder's height—and returns the cylinder's volume.

21. Write a function named `distance()` that accepts the rectangular coordinates of two points (x_1, y_1) and (x_2, y_2) and calculates and returns the distance between the points. The distance, d, between two points is given by the formula:

$$d = \sqrt{(x_2 - x_1)^2 + (y_2 - y_1)^2}$$

Include your function in a complete working C++ program.

22. a. Write a function that calculates the area a of a circle when its circumference c is given. This function should call a second function that returns the radius r of the circle, given c. The relevant formulas are $r = c/2\pi$ and $a - \pi r^2$.

b. Write a structure chart for a program that accepts the value of the circumference from the user, calculates the radius and area, and displays the calculated values.

c. Write and run a C++ program for the structure chart developed in Exercise 22b.

23. a. A recipe for making enough acorn squash for four people requires the following ingredients:

2 acorn squashes
2 teaspoons of lemon juice
1/4 cup of raisins
1 1/2 cups of applesauce
1/4 cup of brown sugar
3 tablespoons of chopped walnuts

Using this information, write and test six functions that each accepts the number of people that must be served and returns the amount of each ingredient, respectively, that is required.

b. Write a structure chart for a program that accepts the number of people to be served, calculates the quantity of each ingredient needed, and displays the calculated values.

c. Write and run a C++ program for the structure chart developed in Exercise 23b.

24. The owner of a strawberry farm has made the following arrangement with a group of students: They may pick all the strawberries they want. When they are through picking, the strawberries will be weighed. The farm will retain 50% of the strawberries and the students will divide the remainder evenly between them. Using this information, write and test a C++ function named `straw()` that accepts the number of students and the total pounds picked as input arguments and returns the approximate number of strawberries each receives. Assume that a strawberry weighs approximately 1 ounce. There are 16 ounces to a pound. Include the `straw()` function in a working C++ program.

25. a. The determinant of a 2 × 2 matrix

$$\begin{vmatrix} a_{11} & a_{12} \\ a_{21} & a_{22} \end{vmatrix}$$

is $a_{11}a_{22} - a_{21}a_{12}$. Similarly, the determinant of a 3 × 3 matrix

$$\begin{vmatrix} a_{11} & a_{12} & a_{13} \\ a_{21} & a_{22} & a_{23} \\ a_{31} & a_{32} & a_{33} \end{vmatrix} =$$

$$a_{11}\begin{vmatrix} a_{22} & a_{23} \\ a_{32} & a_{33} \end{vmatrix} - a_{21}\begin{vmatrix} a_{12} & a_{13} \\ a_{32} & a_{33} \end{vmatrix} + a_{31}\begin{vmatrix} a_{12} & a_{13} \\ a_{22} & a_{23} \end{vmatrix}$$

Using this information, write and test two functions, named `det2()` and `det3()`. The `det2()` function should accept the four coefficients of a 2 × 2 matrix and return its determinant. The `det3()` function should accept the nine coefficients of a 3 × 3 matrix and return its determinant by calling `det2()` to calculate the required 2 × 2 determinants.

b. Write a structure chart for a program that accepts the nine coefficients of a 3 × 3 matrix in one function, passes these coefficients to `det3()`, and uses a third function to display the calculated determinant.

c. Write and run a C++ program for the structure chart developed in Exercise 25b.

FIGURE 6.31   Correspondence between Polar (Distance and Angle) and Cartesian (x,y) Coordinates

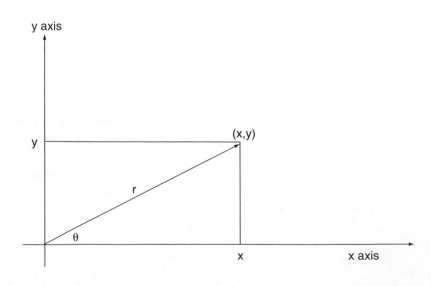

26. Assume that we must write a C++ program to convert the rectangular (x,y) coordinates of a point into polar form. That is, given an x and y position on a Cartesian coordinate system, as illustrated in Figure 6.31, we must calculate the distance from the origin, r, and the angle from the x axis, θ, specified by the point. The values of r and θ are referred to as the point's **polar coordinates.**

When the x and y coordinates of a point are known, the equivalent r and θ coordinates can be calculated using the following formulas:

$$r = \sqrt{x^2 + y^2}$$

$$\theta = \operatorname{atan}(y/x) \quad \text{for} \quad x \neq 0$$

Using these formulas, write a function named `polar()` that returns the r and θ values, respectively, for a point having rectangular coordinates x and y.

27. In the Fibonacci series 1, 1, 2, 3, 5, each element after the first two elements is simply the sum of the prior two values. In Exercise 1 of Section 6.6, you were asked to write a function that recursively computed the nth term of this series. For this exercise, write a function that uses repetition to calculate the nth term.

28. A classic recursion problem is represented by the Towers of Hanoi puzzle, which consists of three pegs and a set of disks initially set up as shown in Figure 6.32. The object of the puzzle is to move all the disks from peg A to peg C, using peg B as needed, with the following constraints:

1. Only one disk may be moved at a time.

2. A larger disk can never be placed on a smaller disk. The legend associated with this problem is that it was initially given, with 64 disks, to ancient monks in a monastery with the understanding that, when the task was completed and all 64 disks reached peg C in the correct order, the world would end.

The solution to this puzzle is easily expressed as a recursive procedure where each n disk solution is defined in terms of an $n - 1$ disk solution. To see how this works, first consider a one-disk puzzle. Clearly, this has a simple solution, where we move the disk from peg A to peg C.

Now consider the two-disk problem. The solution to this puzzle is:

1. Use a one-disk solution to move the first disk to peg B.

2. Move the second disk to peg C.

3. Use a one-disk solution to move the disk on peg B to peg C.

FIGURE 6.32 The Towers of Hanoi Puzzle

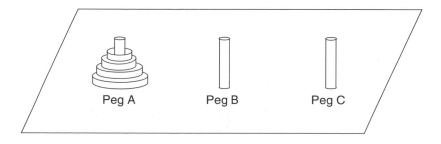

Peg A   Peg B   Peg C

The three-disk problem is slightly more complicated, but can be solved in terms of the two- and one-disk puzzles. The solution is:

1. Use a two-disk solution to get the first two disks in the right order on peg B.
2. Move the third disk to peg C.
3. Use a two-disk solution to correctly move the two disks from peg B to peg C.

Notice how the three-disk solution uses the two-disk solution and the two-disk solution uses the one-disk solution. Let's see if this same recursive reference holds for a four-disk puzzle.

The solution to the four-disk puzzle is:

1. Use a three-disk solution to get the first three disks in the right order on peg B.
2. Move the fourth disk to peg C.
3. Use a three-disk solution to move the three disks from peg B to peg C.

At this stage, we are ready to generalize the solution to n disks, which is:

1. Use an $n - 1$ disk solution to get the first $n - 1$ disks in the right order on peg B.
2. Move the nth disk to peg C.
3. Use the $n - 1$ solution to move the $n - 1$ disks from peg B to peg C.

Using this information, write a C++ program that asks the user how many disks to use and then prints the individual moves that must be made to solve the puzzle. For example, if the user responded with three for the number of disks, the program should display the following:

```
Move a disk from Peg A to Peg C
Move a disk from Peg A to Peg B
Move a disk from Peg C to Peg B
Move a disk from Peg A to Peg C
Move a disk from Peg B to Peg A
Move a disk from Peg B to Peg C
Move a disk from Peg A to Peg C
```

Improving Communication

29. Assuming you are the Lead Programmer, respond to the following memorandum:

MEMORANDUM

To: Lead Programmer

From: Head of Programming Dept.

Subject: Object Models

Please explain to me why we need three models to do an object-oriented analysis when a single functional model was sufficient in our procedure-oriented projects.

Working in Teams

30. Have your team list the sequence of events that occurs when selecting an item from a soda vending machine. The sequence should start when a customer puts money in the machine and end when the customer removes a can of soda. From this list, complete the event trace diagram shown in Figure 6.33.

FIGURE 6.33

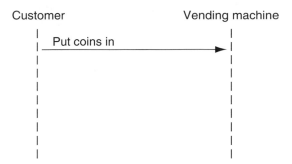

Each vertical line on the event trace diagram corresponds to an object, and the horizontal lines correspond to events. The arrowhead on the event line corresponds to the event receiver, while the line's tail corresponds to the event sender. Although time is assumed to increase from the top of the diagram to the bottom, the spacing between events is not drawn to time scale. The sequence of events from first to last, however, is indicated on the diagram, starting with the first event shown and ending with the last event.

Once your team has completed the event trace diagram, use it to create a state diagram for the vending machine.

31. Have your team list the sequence of events that occurs when using an ATM machine. The sequence should start when the customer inserts his or her card and end when the card is returned. From this list, complete the event trace diagram shown in Figure 6.34.

FIGURE 6.34

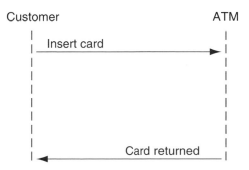

Each vertical line on the event trace diagram corresponds to an object, and the horizontal lines correspond to events. The arrowhead on the event line corresponds to the event receiver, while the line's tail corresponds to the event sender. Although time is assumed to increase from the top of the diagram to the bottom, the spacing between events is not drawn to time scale. The sequence of events from first to last, however, is indicated on the diagram starting with the first event shown and ending with the last event.

Once your team has completed the event trace diagram, use it to create a state diagram for the ATM machine.

32. Have your team list the sequence of events that occurs when making a phone call. The sequence should start when the caller picks up the phone and end when the caller hangs up. From this list, complete the event trace diagram shown in Figure 6.35.

FIGURE 6.35

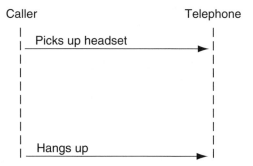

Each vertical line on the event trace diagram corresponds to an object, and the horizontal lines correspond to events. The arrowhead on the event line corresponds to the event receiver, while the line's tail corresponds to the event sender. Although time is assumed to increase from the top of the diagram to the bottom, the spacing between events is not drawn to time scale. The sequence of events from first to last, however, is indicated on the diagram starting with the first event shown and ending with the last event.

Once your team has completed the event trace diagram, use it to create a state diagram for the phone system.

CHAPTER

7 | Completing the Basics

The current ANSI/ISO standard for C++ introduced two new features that were not part of the original C++ specification: exception handling and a string class. Both of these new features are presented in this chapter.

Exception handling is a means of error detection and processing, which has gained increasing acceptance in programming technology. It permits detecting an error at the point in the code at which the error has occurred and provides a means of processing the error and returning control to the line that generated the error. Although such error detecting and code correcting was always possible using if statements and functions, exception handling provides one more extremely useful programming tool specifically targeted at error detection and processing.

With the new ANSI/ISO C++ standard, a class named string is now part of the standard C++ library. This class provides a greatly expanded set of class methods that includes easy insertion and removal of characters from a string, automatic string expansion whenever its original capacity is exceeded, automatic string contraction when characters are removed from the string, and range checking to detect invalid character positions.

In addition to presenting these two new C++ features, this chapter shows how exception handling, when applied to strings, provides a very useful means of validating user input. Finally, the strong connection between the string class and the Standard Template Library (STL) is described and illustrated with a practical example.

7.1 EXCEPTION HANDLING

The traditional C++ approach to error handing uses a function, such as `main()`, to return a specific value to indicate specific operations. Typically, a return value of 0 or 1 is used to indicate a successful completion of the function's task, whereas a negative value is used to indicate an error condition. For example, if a function were used to divide two numbers, a return value of -1 could be used to indicate that the denominator was zero and that the division could not be performed. When multiple error conditions can occur, different return values are used to indicate specific errors.

Although this approach is still available and used often, there are a number of problems that can occur with this method. First, it requires that the programmer actually checks the return value to detect if an error did occur. Next, the error handling code that checks the return value frequently becomes intermixed with normal processing code, making it sometimes difficult to clearly determine which part of the code is handling errors as opposed to normal program processing. And finally, returning an error condition from a method means that the condition must be the same data type as a valid returned value; hence, the error code must be a specific value that can be identified as an error alert. Thus, the error code is effectively imbedded as one of the possible non-error values that may be required from the function and is only available at the point where the method returns a value. Finally, a function that returns a Boolean value has no additional values that can be used to report an error condition.

None of this is insurmountable, and many times this approach is simple and effective. However, in the latest versions, all C++ compilers have added a technique specifically designed for error detection and handling referred to as exception handling.

In **exception handling**, when an error occurs while a method is executing, the method creates a value, variable, or object, which is referred to as an **exception** that contains information about the error at the point the error occurs. This exception is then immediately passed, again at the point it was generated, to code that is referred to as the **exception handler**, which is designed to correctly deal with the exception. The process of generating and passing the exception at the point the error was detected is referred to as **throwing an exception**. Notice that the exception is thrown from within the method while it is still executing. This process allows the error to be handled and control to be returned to the method, so that it can complete its assigned task correctly.

In general, there are two fundamental types of errors that can cause C++ exceptions: those that result from an inability of the program to obtain a required resource and those that result from flawed data. Examples of the first error type are attempts to obtain a system resource, such as locating and finding a file for input. These types of errors are the result of external resources over which the programmer has no control.

Examples of the second type of error can occur when a program prompts the user to enter an integer, and the user enters a string, such as e234, that cannot be converted to a numerical value. Another example is the attempt to divide two numbers when the denominator has a value of 0. This latter condition is referred to as a division by zero error. Each of these errors can always be checked and handled in a manner that does not result in a program crash. Before seeing how this is accomplished using exception handling, review Table 7.1 to familiarize yourself with the terminology that is used in relation to the processing of exceptions.

TABLE 7.1 Exception Handling Terminology

Terminology	Description
Exception	A value, variable, or object that identifies a specific error that has occurred while a program is executing.
Throw an exception	Sends the exception to a section of code that processes the detected error.
Catch or handle an exception	Receives a thrown exception and processes it.
Catch clause	The section of code that processes the error.
Exception handler	The code that throws and catches an exception.

The general syntax of the code required to throw and catch an exception is:

```
try
{
   // one or more statements,
   // at least one of which should
   // be capable of throwing an exception;
}
catch(exceptionDataType parameterName)
{
   // one or more statements
}
```

The example here uses two keywords not yet discussed: `try` and `catch`.

The keyword `try` identifies the start of an exception handling block of code. At least one of the statements within the braces defining this block of code must be capable of throwing an exception if the exception handling is to be activated. For example, the `try` block in the following section of code:

```
try
{
   cout << "Enter the numerator (whole numbers only): ";
   cin  >> numerator;
   cout << "Enter the denominator (whole numbers only): ";
   cin  >> denominator;
   result = numerator/denominator;
}
```

contains five statements, three of which may result in an error that you want to catch. In particular, a professionally written program would ensure that valid integers are entered in response to both prompts and that the second entered value is not a zero. For this example, you will only check that the second value entered is not zero (in Section 17.4 you will find the exception handling code that can be used to validate both inputs to ensure that the entered data are integers).

From the standpoint of the `try` block, only the value of the second number is of concern. Essentially, the `try` block will be altered to say "try all of the statements within me to see if an exception, which in this particular case is a zero second value, occurs." To check that the second value is not a zero, you add a `throw` statement within the `try` block, as follows:

```
try
{
   cout << "Enter the numerator: (whole numbers only) ";
   cin  >> numerator;
   cout << "Enter the denominator: (whole numbers only) ";
   cin  >> denominator;
   if (denominator == 0)
     throw denominator
   else
     result = numerator/denominator;
}
```

There are two points worth noting with respect to this `try` block. First, the item that is thrown is an integer literal. A string literal, a variable, or an object could have been used, but then only one of these items could be thrown by any single `throw` statement. Second, the first three statements in the `try` block do not have to be included in the code; however, doing so keeps all of the relevant statements together. Keeping related statements together can facilitate adding `throw` statements within the same `try` block to ensure that the two input values are integer values, making it is more convenient to have all the relevant code available within the same `try` block.

A `try` block must be followed by one or more `catch` blocks, which serve as exception handlers for any exceptions thrown by the statements in the `try` block. Here is a `catch` block that handles the thrown exception, which is an integer:

```
catch(int e)
  {
    cout << "A denominator value of " << e << " is invalid." << endl;
    exit (1);
  }
```

The exception handling provided by this `catch` block is simply an output statement that identifies the particular exception that has been caught and terminates program execution. Notice the parentheses following the `catch` keyword. Listed within the parentheses is the data type of the exception that is thrown and a parameter name (which is `e`) used to receive it. This identifier, which is programmer-selected, but conventionally uses the letter `e` for exception, holds the exception value generated when an exception is thrown.

Multiple `catch` blocks can be used as long as each block catches a unique data type. The only requirement is that at least one `catch` block be provided for each `try` block. The more exceptions that can be caught with the same `try` block, the better. Program 7.1 provides a complete program that includes a `try` block and a `catch` block to detect a division by zero error.

PROGRAM 7.1

```cpp
#include <iostream>
using namespace std;

int main()
{
 int numerator, denominator;

  try
  {
    cout << "Enter the numerator (whole number only): ";
    cin  >> numerator;
    cout << "Enter the denominator (whole number only): ";
    cin  >> denominator;
    if (denominator == 0)
      throw denominator;  // an integer value is thrown
    else
      cout << numerator <<'/' << denominator
           << " = " << double(numerator)/ double(denominator) << endl;
  }
  catch(int e)
  {
    cout << "A denominator value of " << e << " is invalid." << endl;
    exit (1);
  }

  return 0;
}
```

Following are two sample runs using Program 7.1. Note that the second output indicates that an attempt to divide by a zero denominator has been successfully detected before the operation is performed.

```
Enter the numerator (whole number only): 12
Enter the denominator (whole number only): 3
12/3 = 4
```

and

```
Enter the numerator (whole number only): 12
Enter the denominator (whole number only): 0
A denominator value of 0 is invalid.
```

Having detected a zero denominator, rather than terminating program execution, a more robust program now can provide the user with the opportunity to re-enter a nonzero value. This can be accomplished by including the try block within a while statement and then having the catch block return program control to the while statement after informing the user that a zero value has been entered. The code in Program 7.2 accomplishes this.

PROGRAM 7.2

```cpp
#include <iostream>
using namespace std;

int main()
{
  int numerator, denominator;
  bool needDenominator = true;

  cout << "Enter a numerator (whole numbers only): ";
  cin  >> numerator;

  cout << "Enter a denominator (whole numbers only): ";
  while(needDenominator)
  {
    cin  >> denominator;
    try
    {
      if (denominator == 0)
      throw denominator;  // an integer value is thrown
    }
    catch(int e)
    {
      cout << "A denominator value of " << e << " is invalid." << endl;
      cout << "Please re-enter the denominator (whole number only): ";
      continue;  // this sends control back to the while statement
    }
    cout << numerator <<'/' << denominator
         << " = " << double(numerator)/ double(denominator) << endl;
    needDenominator = false;
  }

  return 0;
}
```

In this code, notice that it is the `continue` statement within the `catch` block that returns control to the top of the `while` statement (see Section 6.3 for a review of the `continue` statement). Following is a sample run using Program 7.2:

```
Enter a numerator (whole number only): 12
Enter a denominator (whole number only): 0
A denominator value of 0 is invalid.
Please re-enter the denominator (whole number only): 5
12/5 = 2.4
```

One caution should be mentioned when throwing string literals as opposed to numeric values. Whenever a string literal is thrown, it is a C-string, not a `string` class object that is thrown. This means that the `catch` statement must declare the received argument as a C-string, which is a character array, rather than as a string. As an example, consider that rather than throwing the value of the denominator variable in Programs 7.1 and 7.2, the following statement was used:

```
throw "***Invalid input - A denominator value of zero is not permitted***";
```

A correct catch statement for the preceding throw statement is:

```
catch(char e[])
```

An attempt to declare the exception as a string class variable will result in a compiler error.

Exercises 7.1

1. Define the following terms:

   exception

   try block

   catch block

   exception handler

   throw an exception

   catch an exception

2. Enter and execute Program 7.1.

3. Replace the statement

   ```
   cout << numerator <<'/' << denominator
        << " - " << double (numerator)/ double (denominator) << endl;
   ```

   in Program 7.1 with the statement:

   ```
   cout << numerator <<'/' << denominator
        << " - " << numerator/denominator << endl;
   ```

   and execute the modified program. Enter the values 12 and 5, and explain why the result is incorrect from the user's viewpoint.

4. a. Modify Program 7.2 to throw an exception when a negative number is entered. The exception handler should provide the user with the number entered and then display a message that the factorial of a negative number is not defined.

   b. Modify the program written for Exercise 4a to have the program continuously request a non-negative number until a valid value is entered. Also, if the user enters either an upper- or lowercase q, for quit, in place of a number, the program should terminate. Use an if statement to detect the input of this letter.

5. Modify Program 6.15 so that it throws and correctly catches the message ***Invalid input - A denominator value of zero is not permitted***. (*Hint:* Review the caution presented at the end of this section.)

6. Enter and execute Program 7.2.

7. Modify Program 7.2 so that it continues to divide two numbers until the user enters the character q (either as a numerator or denominator) to terminate program execution.

8. Include the exception handling code provided in Section 16.5 within Program 7.1 to ensure that the user enters a valid integer value for both the numerator and denominator.

7.2 THE string CLASS

The programs in this text have used the istream class' cout object extensively without having investigated this class or how the cout object is created. This is one of the advantages of object-oriented program design; thoroughly tested classes can be used without knowing the internals of how the class is constructed. In this section we will use another class provided by C++'s standard library, the string class. However, in this case, we will actually create objects from the class before using them, rather than just use an existing object, such as cout.

A class is a user-created data type. Like the built-in data types, a class defines both a valid set of data values and a set of operations that can be used on them. The difference between a user-created class and a built-in type is simply how the class is constructed. A built-in data type is provided as an integral part of the compiler, and a class is constructed by a programmer using C++ code. Other than that and the terminology used, the two types are used in much the same manner. The key difference in terminology is that storage areas for built-in types are referred to as variables, whereas storage areas declared for a class are referred to as objects.

The values permitted by the string class are referred to as string literals. A string literal is any sequence of characters enclosed in double quotation marks. A string literal is also referred to as a string value, a string constant, and more conventionally, simply as a string. Examples of strings are "This is a string", "Hello World!", and "xyz 123 *!#@&". The double quotation marks indicate the beginning and ending points of the string and are never stored with the string.

Figure 7.1 shows the programming representation of the string Hello whenever this string is created as an object of the string class. By convention, the first character in a string is always designated as position 0. This position value is also referred to as both the character's index value and its offset value.

FIGURE 7.1   The Storage of a String as a Sequence of Characters

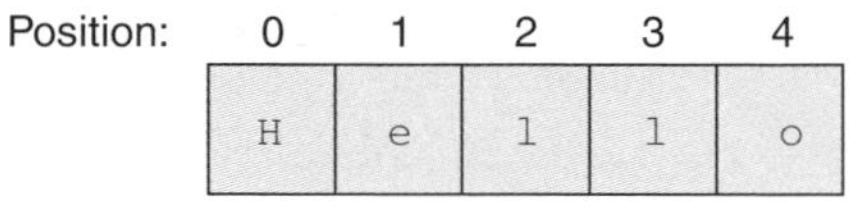

string **Class Methods**

The string class provides a number of methods for declaring, creating, and initializing a string. In the earlier versions of C++, the process of creating a new object is referred to as instantiating an object, which in terms of a string class becomes instantiating a string object, or creating a string, for short. Table 7.2 lists the methods provided by the string class for creating and initializing a string object. In class terminology, methods that perform this task are referred to as constructor methods, or constructors, for short.

TABLE 7.2 string **Class Constructors (Required Header File Is** string**)**

Constructor	Description	Examples

string objectName = value	Creates and initializes a string object to value that can be a string literal, a previously declared string object, or an expression containing both string literals and string objects	string str1 = "Good Morning";
		string str2 = str1;
		string str3 = str1 1+ str2;

string objectName (stringValue)	Produces the same initialization as above	string str1("Hot"); string str1(str1 + "Dog");
string objectName(str, n)	Creates and initializes a string object with a substring of string object str, starting at index position n of str	string str1(str2, 5) If str2 contains the string Good Morning, then str1 becomes the string Morning
string objectName(str, n, p)	Creates and initializes a string object with a substring of string object str, starting at index position n of str and containing p characters	string str1(str2, 5,2) If str2 contains the string Good Morning, then str1 becomes the string Mo
string objectName(n, char)	Creates and initializes a string object with n copies of char	string str1(5,'*') This makes str1 = "*****"
string objectName;	Creates and initializes a string object to represent an empty character sequence (same as string objectName = ""; the length of the string is 0)	string message;

Program 7.3 illustrates examples of each of the constructor methods provided by the string class.

PROGRAM 7.3

```cpp
#include <iostream>
#include <string>
using namespace std;

int main()
{
    string str1; // an empty string
    string str2("Good Morning");
    string str3 = "Hot Dog";
    string str4(str3);
    string str5(str4, 4);
    string str6 = "linear";
    string str7(str6, 3, 3);

    cout << "str1 is: " << str1 << endl;
    cout << "str2 is: " << str2 << endl;
    cout << "str3 is: " << str3 << endl;
    cout << "str4 is: " << str4 << endl;
    cout << "str5 is: " << str5 << endl;
    cout << "str6 is: " << str6 << endl;
    cout << "str7 is: " << str7 << endl;

    return 0;
}
```

The output created by Program 7.3 is:

```
str1 is:
str2 is: Good Morning
str3 is: Hot Dog
str4 is: Hot Dog
str5 is: Dog
str6 is: linear
str7 is: ear
```

Although this output is straightforward, two comments are in order. First, notice that str1 is an empty string consisting of no characters. Second, because the first character in a string is designated as position zero, not one, the character position of the D in the string Hot Dog is located at position four, which is shown in Figure 7.2.

FIGURE 7.2   **The Character Positions of the String** Hot Dog

Character Position: 0   1   2   3   4   5   6

| H | o | t | | D | o | g |

String Input and Output

In addition to a string being initialized using the constructor methods listed in Table 7.2, strings can be input from the keyboard and displayed on the screen. Table 7.3 lists the basic methods and objects that can be used to input and output string values.

In addition to the standard cout and cin streams, the string class provides the getline() method for string input. For example, the expression getline(cin, message) will continuously accept and store characters typed at the terminal—until the Enter key is pressed. Pressing the Enter key at the terminal generates a newline character, '\n', which is interpreted by getline() as the end-of-line entry. All the characters encountered by getline(), except the newline character, are stored in the string named message, as illustrated in Figure 7.3.

TABLE 7.3 string **Class Input and Output Routines**

C++ Routine	Description
cout	General purpose screen output
cin	General purpose terminal input that stops reading when a white space is encountered
getline(cin, strObj)	General purpose terminal input that inputs all characters entered into the string named strObj and stops accepting characters when it receives a newline character (\n)

| FIGURE 7.3 | Inputting a String with getline() |

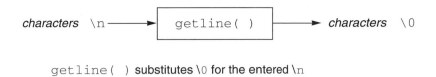

characters \n ⟶ getline( ) ⟶ *characters* \0

getline( ) substitutes \0 for the entered \n

Program 7.4 illustrates using the getline() method and cout stream to input and output a string, respectively, that is entered at the user's terminal.

| PROGRAM 7.4 |

```cpp
#include <iostream>
#include <string>
using namespace std;

int main()
{
  string message;       // declare a string object

  cout << "Enter a string:\n";
  getline(cin, message);
  cout << "The string just entered is:\n"
       << message << endl;

  return 0;
}
```

The following is a sample run of Program 7.4:

```
Enter a string:
This is a test input of a string of characters.
The string just entered is:
This is a test input of a string of characters.
```

Although the cout stream object is used in Program 7.4 for string output, the cin stream input object generally cannot be used in place of getline() for string input. This is because the cin object reads a set of characters up to either a blank space or a newline character. Thus, attempting to enter the characters This is a string using the statement cin >> message; only results in the word This being assigned to message.

The fact that a blank terminates a `cin` extraction operation restricts the usefulness of the `cin` object for entering string data and is the reason for using `getline()`.

In its most general form, the `getline()` method has the syntax

```
getline(cin, strObj, terminatingChar)
```

where *strObj* is a string variable name, and *terminatingChar* is an optional character constant, or variable, specifying the terminating character. For example, the expression `getline(cin, message, '!')` will accept all characters entered at the keyboard , including a newline character, until an exclamation point is entered. The exclamation point will not be stored as part of the string.

If the optional third argument is omitted when `getline()` is called, the default terminating character is the newline (`'\n'`) character. Thus, the statement `getline(cin, message,'\n');` can be used in place of the statement `getline(cin, message);`. Both of these statements stop reading characters when the Enter key is pressed. For all the programs used from this point forward, you can assume that input is terminated by pressing the Enter key, which generates a newline character. As such, the optional third argument passed to `getline()`, which is the terminating character, will be omitted.

Caution: The Phantom newline Character

Seemingly strange results can be obtained when either the `cin` input stream and `getline()` method are used together to accept data or when the `cin` input stream is used to accept individual characters. To see how this can occur, consider Program 7.5, which uses `cin` to accept an integer entered at the keyboard, storing it in the variable named `value`, followed by a `getline()` method call.

PROGRAM 7.5

```cpp
#include <iostream>
#include <string>
using namespace std;

int main()
{ int value;
  string message;
  cout << "Enter a number: ";
  cin  >> value;
  cout << "The number entered is:\n"
       << value << endl;
  cout << "Enter text:\n";
  getline(cin, message);
  cout << "The string entered is:\n"
       << message << endl;
  cout << message.length();

  return 0;
}
```

> # PROGRAMMING NOTE

The `string` **and** `char` **Data Types**

A string can consist of zero, one, or more characters. When the string has no characters, it is said to be an empty string with a length of zero. A string with a single character, such as `"a"`, is a string of length one and is stored differently than a `char` data type, such as `'a'`. However, for many practical purposes, a string of length one and a `char` respond in the same manner; for example, `cout >> "\n"` and `cout >> '\n'` both produce a new line on the screen. It is important to understand that they are different data types; for example, both declarations

```
string s1 = 'a';  // INVALID INITIALIZATION
char key = "\n"; // INVALID INITIALIZATION
```

produce a compiler error because they attempt to initialize one data type with literal values of another type.

When Program 7.5 is run, the number entered in response to the prompt `Enter a number:` is stored in the variable named `value`. At this point, everything seems to be working fine. Notice, however, that in entering a number, you actually enter a number and press the Enter key. On almost all computer systems this entered data is stored in a temporary holding area called a buffer immediately after the characters are entered, as illustrated in Figure 7.4.

The `cin` input stream in Program 7.5 first accepts the number entered, but leaves the `'\n'` in the buffer. The next input statement, which is a call to `getline()` then automatically picks up the code for the Enter key as the next character and immediately terminates any further input. Following is a sample run for Program 7.5:

```
Enter a number: 26
The number entered is 26
Enter text:
The text entered is
```

Notice that in this output no text is accepted in response to the prompt `Enter text:` . No text occurs because, after the number 26 has been accepted by the program, the code for the Enter key, which is a newline escape sequence, remains in the buffer and is picked up and interpreted by the `getline()` method as the end of its input. This will occur whether an integer, as in Program 7.5, a string, or any other input is accepted by `cin` and then followed by a `getline()` method call.

FIGURE 7.4   Typed Keyboard Characters are First Stored in a Buffer

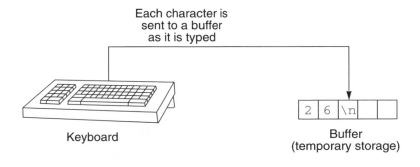

There are three separate solutions to this "phantom" Enter key problem:

- Do not mix `cin` with `getline()` inputs in the same program.
- Follow the `cin` input with the call to `cin.ignore()`.
- Accept the Enter key into a character variable and then ignore it.

The preferred solution is the first one. All solutions, however, center on the fact that the Enter key is a legitimate character input and must be recognized as such. You will encounter this problem once again when you consider accepting `char` data types in the next section.

String Processing

Strings can be manipulated using either `string` class methods or the character-at-a-time methods described in the next section. Table 7.4 lists the most commonly used `string` class methods. These include `accessor` and `mutator` methods, plus methods and operator functions that use the standard arithmetic and comparison operators.

The most commonly used method in Table 7.4 is the `length()` method. This returns the number of characters in the string, which is referred to as the string's length. For example, the value returned by the method call `"Hello World!".length()` is 12. As always, the double quotation marks surrounding a string value are not considered part of the string. Similarly, if the string referenced by `string1` contains the value `"Have a good day."`, the value returned by the call `string1.length()` is 16.

Notice that two string expressions may be compared for equality using the standard relational operators. Each character in a string is stored in binary using either the ASCII or UNICODE code. Although these codes are different, they have some characteristics in common. In each of them, a blank precedes (is less than) all letters and numbers; the letters of the alphabet are stored in order from A to Z; and the digits are stored in order from 0 to 9. In both character codes the digits come before (that is, are less than) the uppercase characters, which are then followed by the lowercase characters. Thus, the uppercase characters are mathematically less than the lowercase characters.

When two strings are compared, their individual characters are compared a pair at a time (both first characters, then both second characters, and so on). If no differences are found, the strings are equal; if a difference is found, the string with the first lower character is considered the smaller string.

- `"Hello"` is greater than `"Good Bye"` because the first H in `Hello` is greater than the first G in `Good Bye`.
- `"Hello"` is less than `"hello"` because the first H in `Hello` is less than the first h in `hello`.
- `"Hello"` is less than `"Hello "` because the `'\0'` terminating the first string is less than the `' '` in the second string.
- `"SMITH"` is greater than `"JONES"` because the first S in `SMITH` is greater than the first J in `JONES`.
- `"123"` is greater than `"1227"` because the third character, the 3, in `123` is greater than the third character, the 2 in `1227`.
- `"1237"` is greater than `"123"` because the fourth character, the 7, in `1237` is greater than the fourth character, the \0 in `123`.
- `"Behop"` is greater than `"Beehive"` because the third character, the h, in `Behop` is greater than the third character, the e, in `Beehive`.

TABLE 7.4 The string **Class Processing Methods (Require the Header File** string**)**

Method/Operation	Description	Example
int length()	Returns the length of the implicit string.	string.length()
int size()	Same as above	string.size()
at(int index)	Returns the character at the specified index, and throws an exception if the index is non-existent	string.at(4)
int compare(string)	Compares two strings; returns a negative value if the implied string is less than str, zero if they are equal, and a positive value if the implied string is less than str	string1.compare(string2);
c_str()	Returns the string as a null terminated C-string	string1.c_str( );
bool empty	Returns true if the implied string is empty; otherwise, returns false	string1.empty();
erase(ind,n);	Removes n characters from the implied string, starting at index ind	string1.erase(2,3);
erase(ind)	Removes all characters from the implied string, starting from index ind until the end of the string; the length of the remaining string becomes ind	string1.erase(4);
int find(str)	Returns the index of the first occurrence of str within the implied object	string1.find("the")
int find(str, ind)	Returns the index of the first occurrence of str within the implied object, with the search beginning at index ind	string1.find("the", 5);
int find_first_of (str, ind)	Returns the index of the first occurrence of any character in str within the implied object, with the search starting at index ind	string1.find_first_of ("lt", 6)
int find_first_not_of(str, ind)	Returns the index of the first occurrence of any character not in str within the implied object, with the search starting at index ind	string1.find_first_not_of ("lt ,6)
void insert(ind, str)	Inserts the string str into the implied string, starting at index ind	string.insert (4, "there");
void replace(ind, n, str)	Removes n characters in the implied object, starting at index position ind, and insert the string str at index position ind	string1.replace (2,4,"okay");
string substr(ind,n)	Returns a string consisting of n characters extracted from the implied string starting at index ind; if n is greater than the remaining number of characters, the rest of the implied string is used	string2 = string1.substr(0,10);
void swap(str)	Swaps characters in str with the implied object	string1.swap(string2);
[ind]	Returns the character at index x, without checking if ind is a valid index	
=	Assignment (also converts a C-string to a string)	string1 = string
+	Concatenates two strings	string1 + string2
+=	Concatenation and assignment	string2 += string1
== != < <=	Relational operators; return true if the relation is satisfied; otherwise return false.	string1 == string2 string1 <= string2
> >=		string1 > string2

Program 7.6 uses `length()` and several relational expressions within the context of a complete program.

PROGRAM 7.6

```cpp
#include <iostream>
#include <string>
using namespace std;

int main()
{
  string string1 = "Hello";
  string string2 = "Hello there";

  cout << "string1 is the string: " <<  string1 << endl;
  cout << "The number of characters in string1 is " <<  string1.length()
       << endl << endl;

  cout << "string2 is the string: " <<  string2 << endl;
  cout << "The number of characters in string2 is " <<  string2.length()
       << endl << endl;

  if (string1 < string2)
    cout << string1 <<  " is less than " <<  string2 << endl << endl;
  else if (string1 == string2)
    cout << string1 <<  " is equal to " <<  string2 << endl << endl;
  else
    cout << string1 <<  " is greater than " <<  string2 << endl << endl;

  string1 = string1 + " there world!";
  cout << "After concatenation, string1 contains the characters: "
       << string1 << endl;
  cout << "The length of this string is " <<  string1.length() << endl;

  return 0;
}
```

Following is a sample output produced by Program 7.6:

```
string1 is the string: Hello
The number of characters in string1 is 5

string2 is the string: Hello there
The number of characters in string2 is 11

Hello is less than Hello there

After concatenation, string1 contains the characters: Hello there world!
The length of this string is 18
```

When reviewing this output, refer to Figure 7.5, which shows how the characters in `string1` and `string2` are stored in memory. Note that the length of each string refers to the total number of characters in the string and that the first character in each string is located at index position 0. Thus, the length of a string is always one more than the index number of the last character's position in the string.

| FIGURE 7.5 | The Initial Strings Used in Program 7.6 |

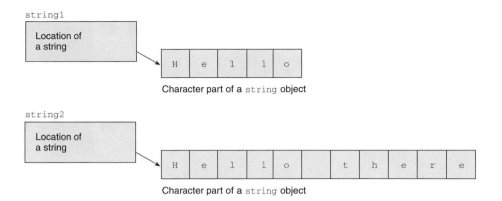

Character part of a string object

PROGRAM 7.7

```cpp
#include <iostream>
#include <string>
using namespace std;

int main()
{
  string str = "Counting the number of vowels";
  int i, numChars;
  int vowelCount = 0;

  cout << "The string: " <<  str << endl;

  numChars = str.length();
  for (i = 0; i < numChars; i++)
  {
    switch(str.at(i))    // here is where a character is retrieved
    {
      case 'a':
      case 'e':
      case 'i':
      case 'o':
      case 'u':
        vowelCount++;
    }
  }
  cout << "has " <<  vowelCount <<  " vowels." << endl;


  return 0;
}
```

Although you will mostly use the concatenation operator and `length()` method, there are times when you will find the other string methods, which are described in Table 7.4, useful. One of the more useful of these is the `at()` method, which permits you to retrieve individual characters in a string. Program 7.7 uses this method to select one character at a time from the string, starting at string position zero and ending at the index of the last character in the string. This last index value is always one less than the number of characters (that is, the string's length) in the string.

The expression `str.at(i)` in the `switch` statement above retrieves the character at position `i` in the string. This character is then compared to five different character values. The `switch` statement uses the fact that selected cases "drop through" in the absence of break statements. Thus, all selected cases result in an increment to `vowelCount`. The output displayed by Program 7.7 is:

```
The string: Counting the number of vowels
has 9 vowels.
```

As an example of inserting and replacing characters in a string using methods listed in Table 7.4, assume that you start with a string created by the statement:

```
string str = "This cannot be";
```

Figure 7.6 illustrates how this string is stored in the buffer created for it. As indicated, the initial length of the string is 14 characters.

FIGURE 7.6   Initial Storage of a String Object

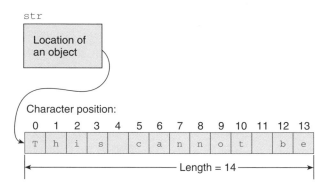

Now assume that the following statement is executed:

```
str.insert(4," I know");
```

This statement causes the designated seven characters, beginning with a blank, to be inserted, starting at index position 4, in the existing string. The resulting string, after the insertion, is as shown in Figure 7.7.

If the statement `str.replace(12, 6, "to");` is now executed, the existing characters in index positions 12 through 17 will be deleted and the two characters `to` inserted starting at index position 12. Thus, the net effect of the replacement is as shown in Figure 7.8. Note that the number of replacement characters, which in this particular case is two, can be less than, equal to, or greater than the characters that are being replaced, which in this case is six.

FIGURE 7.7 The String after the Insertion

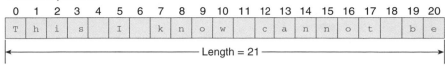

Character position:

0	1	2	3	4	5	6	7	8	9	10	11	12	13	14	15	16	17	18	19	20
T	h	i	s		I		k	n	o	w		c	a	n	n	o	t		b	e

Length = 21

FIGURE 7.8 The String after the Replacement

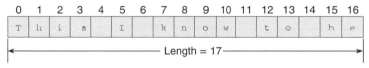

Character position:

0	1	2	3	4	5	6	7	8	9	10	11	12	13	14	15	16
T	h	i	s		I		k	n	o	w		t	o		h	e

Length = 17

FIGURE 7.9 The String after the Append

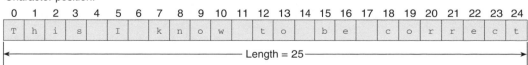

Character position:

0	1	2	3	4	5	6	7	8	9	10	11	12	13	14	15	16	17	18	19	20	21	22	23	24
T	h	i	s		I		k	n	o	w		t	o		b	e		c	o	r	r	e	c	t

Length = 25

Finally, if you append the string `"correct"` to the string shown in Figure 7.8 using the concatenation operator, +, the string illustrated in Figure 7.9 is obtained.

Program 7.8 illustrates using the statements within the context of a complete program.

PROGRAM 7.8

```cpp
#include <iostream>
#include <string>
using namespace std;

int main()
{
  string str = "This cannot be";
  int i, numChars;

  cout << "The original string is: " << str << endl
       << "   and has " << str.length() << " characters." << endl;

  // insert characters
  str.insert(4," I know");
  cout << "The string, after insertion is : " << str << endl
       << "   and has " << str.length() << " characters." << endl;

  // replace characters
  str.replace(12, 6, "to");
  cout << "The string, after replacement is: " << str << endl
       << "   and has " << str.length() << " characters." << endl;

  // append characters
  str = str + " correct";
  cout << "The string, after appending is: " << str << endl
       << "   and has " << str.length() << " characters." << endl;

  return 0;
}
```

The following output produced by Program 7.8 matches the strings shown in Figures 7.6 to 7.9.

```
The original string is: This cannot be
   This string has 14 characters.
The string, after insertion, is now: This I know cannot be
   This string has 21 characters.
The string, after replacement, is: This I know to be
   This string has 17 characters.
The string, after appending, is: This I know to be correct
   This string has 25 characters.
```

Of the remaining string methods listed in Table 7.4, the most commonly used are those that locate specific characters in a string and create substrings. Program 7.9 presents examples of how some of these other methods are used.

PROGRAM 7.9

```cpp
#include <iostream>
#include <string>
using namespace std;

int main()
{

  string string1 = "LINEAR PROGRAMMING THEORY";
  string s1, s2, s3;
  int j, k, l;

  cout << "The original string is " <<  string1 << endl;

  j = string1.find('I');
  cout << "  The first position of an 'I' is " <<  j << endl;

  k = string1.find('I', (j+1));
  cout << "  The next position of an 'I' is " <<  k << endl;

  j = string1.find("THEORY");
  cout << "  The first location of \"THEORY\" is " <<  j << endl;

  k = string1.find("ING");
  cout << "  The first index of \"ING\" is " <<  k << endl;

  s1 = string1.substr(2,5);
  s2 = string1.substr(19,3);
  s3 = string1.substr(6,8);

  cout << s1 + s2 + s3 << endl;

  return 0;
}
```

The output produced by Program 7.9 is:

```
The original string is LINEAR PROGRAMMING THEORY
  The first position of an 'I' is 1
  The next position of an 'I' is 15
  The first location of "THEORY" is 19
  The first index of "ING" is 15
NEAR THE PROGRAM
```

The main point illustrated in Program 7.9 is that both individual characters and sequences of characters can be located and extracted from a string.

Exercises 7.2

1. Enter and execute Program 7.4.

2. Determine the value of text.at(0), text.at(3), and text.at(10), assuming that text is, individually, each of the following strings:

   a. now is the time

   b. rocky raccoon welcomes you

     c. Happy Holidays

     d. The good ship

3. Enter and execute Program 7.7.

4. Modify Program 7.7 to count and display the individual numbers of each vowel contained in the string.

5. Modify Program 7.7 to display the number of vowels in a user-entered string.

6. Using the `at()` method, write a C++ program that reads in a string using `getline()` and then displays the string out in reverse order. (*Hint:* Once the string has been entered and saved, retrieve and display characters starting from the end of the string.)

7. Write a C++ program that accepts both a string and a single character from the user. The program should then determine how many times the character is contained in the string. (*Hint:* Search the string using the `find(str, ind)` method. This method should be used in a loop that starts the index value at zero and then changes the index to one value past the index of where the character was last found.)

8. Enter and execute Program 7.8.

9. Enter and execute Program 7.9.

10. Write a C++ program that accepts a string from the user and then replaces all occurrences of the letter e with the letter x.

11. Modify the program written for Exercise 10 to search for the first occurrence of a user-entered sequence of characters and replace this sequence, when it is found in the string, with a second set of a user-entered sequence. For example, if the entered string is `Figure 4.4 illustrates the output of Program 4.2` and the user enters that `4.` is to be replaced by `3.`, the resulting string will be `Figure 3.4 illustrates the output of Program 4.2`. (Note that only the first occurrence of the searched-for sequence has been changed.)

12. Modify the program written for Exercise 11 to replace all occurrences of the designated sequence of characters with the new sequence of characters. For example, if the entered string is `Figure 4.4 illustrates the output of Program 4.2` and the user enters that `4.` is to be replaced by `3.`, the resulting string will be `Figure 3.4 illustrates the output of Program 3.2`.

7.3 CHARACTER MANIPULATION METHODS

In addition to the `string` methods provided by the `string` class, the C++ language provides a number of very useful `character` class functions. These functions are listed in Table 7.5. The function declarations (prototypes) for each of these routines are contained in the header file `cctype`, which must be included in any program that uses these functions.

Because all of the `istype()` functions listed in Table 7.5 return a non-zero integer (which is interpreted as a Boolean `true` value) when the character meets the desired condition and a zero integer (or Boolean `false` value) when the condition is not met, these functions are typically used directly within an `if` statement. For example, consider the following code segment, which assumes that `ch` is a character variable:

```
if(isdigit(ch))
    cout << "The character just entered is a digit" << endl;
else if(ispunct(ch))
    cout << "The character just entered is a punctuation mark" << endl;
```

TABLE 7.5 Character Library Functions (Require the Header File `cctype`)

Function Prototype	Description	Example

`int isalnum(charExp)`	Returns a `true` (non-zero integer) if `charExp` evaluates to a letter or a digit; otherwise, it returns a `false` (zero integer)	`char key;`
		`cin >> key;`
		`isalnum(key);`

`int isalpha(charExp)`	Returns a `true` (non-zero integer) if `charExp` evaluates to a letter; otherwise, it returns a `false` (zero integer)	`isalpha('a')`
`int isascii(charExp)`	Returns a `true` (non-zero integer) if `charExp` evaluates to an ASCII character; otherwise returns a `false` (zero integer)	`isascii('a')`
`int isctrl(charExp)`	Returns a `true` (non-zero integer) if `charExp` evaluates to a control character; otherwise, it returns a false (zero integer)	`isctrl('a')`
`int isdigit(charExp)`	Returns a `true` (non-zero integer) if `charExp` evaluates to a a digit (0 through 9); otherwise it returns a `false` (zero integer)	`isdigit('a')`
`int isgraph(charExp)`	Returns a `true` (non-zero integer) if `charExp` evaluates to a printable character other than whitespace; otherwise `false` (zero integer)	`isgraph(' ')`
`int islower(charExp)`	Returns a `true` (non-zero integer) if `charExp` evaluates to a lowercase letter; otherwise it returns a `false` (zero integer)	`islower('a')`
`int isprint(charExp)`	Returns a `true` (non-zero integer) if `charExp` evaluates to a printable character; otherwise, returns a `false` (zero integer)	`isprint('a')`
`int ispucnt(charExp)`	Returns a `true` (non-zero integer) if `charExp` evaluates to a punctuation character; otherwise, returns a `false` (zero integer)	`ispucnt('!')`
`int isspace(charExp)`	Returns a `true` (non-zero integer) if `charExp` evaluates to a space; otherwise, returns a `false` (zero integer)	`isspace(' ')`
`int isupper(charExp)`	Returns a `true` (non-zero integer) if `charExp` evaluates to an uppercase letter; otherwise it returns a `false` (zero integer)	`isupper('a')`
`int tolower(charExp)`	Returns the lowercase equivalent if `charExp` evaluates to a uppercase character; otherwise it returns the character code without modification	`tolower('A')`
`int toupper(charExp)`	Returns the uppercase equivalent if `charExp` evaluates to a lowercase character; otherwise it returns the character code without `modification`	`toupper('a')`

In this example, if ch contains a digit character, the first cout statement is executed; if the character is a letter, the second cout statement is executed. In both cases, however, the character to be checked is included as an argument to the appropriate method. Program 7.10 illustrates this type of code within a program that counts the number of letters, digits, and other characters in a string. The individual characters to be checked are obtained using the string class at() method. In Program 7.10, this method is used in a for loop that cycles through the string from the first character to the last.

PROGRAM 7.10

```cpp
#include <iostream>
#include <string>
#include <cctype>
using namespace std;

int main()
{
    string str = "This  123/ is 567 A ?<6245> Test!";
    char nextChar;
    int i;
    int numLetters = 0, numDigits = 0, numOthers = 0;

    cout << "The original string is: " <<  str
         << "\nThis string contains " <<  str.length()
         <<  " characters," <<   " which consist of" << endl;

    // check each character in the string
    for (i = 0; i < str.length(); i++)
    {
      nextChar = str.at(i);   // get a character
      if (isalpha(nextChar))
        numLetters++;
      else if (isdigit(nextChar))
        numDigits++;
      else
        numOthers++;
    }

    cout << "      " <<  numLetters <<  " letters" << endl;
    cout << "      " <<  numDigits <<  " digits" << endl;
    cout << "      " <<  numOthers <<  " other characters." << endl;

  cin.ignore();
  return 0;
}
```

The output produced by Program 7.10 is:

```
The original string is: This 123/ is 567 A ?<6245> Test!
This string contains 33 characters, which consist of
    11 letters
    10 digits
    12 other characters.
```

As indicated by this output, each of the 33 characters in the string has correctly been categorized as a letter, digit, or other character.

Typically, as in Program 7.10, each of the functions in Table 7.5 is used in a character-by-character manner on each character in a string. This is again illustrated in Program 7.11, where each lowercase string character is converted to its uppercase equivalent using the `toupper()` function. This function only converts lowercase letters, leaving all other characters unaffected.

PROGRAM 7.11

```cpp
#include <iostream>
#include <string>
using namespace std;

int main()
{
  int i;
  string str;

  cout << "Type in any sequence of characters: ";
  getline(cin,str);

  // cycle through all elements of the string
  for (i = 0; i < str.length(); i++)
    str[i] = toupper(str[i]);

  cout << "The characters just entered, in uppercase, are: "
       << str << endl;

  cin.ignore();
  return 0;
}
```

A sample run of Program 7.11 produced the following output:

```
Type in any sequence of characters: this is a test OF 12345.
The characters just entered, in uppercase are: THIS IS A TEST OF 12345.
```

Pay particular attention in Program 7.11 to the statement `for (i = 0; i < str.length(); i++)` that is used to cycle through each of the characters in the string. This is typically how each element in a string is accessed, using the `length()` method to determine when the end of the string has been reached (review Program 7.10 to see that it is used in the same way). The only real difference is that in Program 7.11 each element is accessed using the subscript notation `str[i]`, whereas in Program 7.10 the `at()` method was used. Although these two notations are interchangeable, and which you use is a matter of choice, for consistency the two notations should not be mixed in the same program.

PROGRAMMING NOTE

Why the char Data Type Uses Integer Values

In C++, a character is stored as an integer value, which is sometimes confusing to beginning programmers. The reason for this is that, in addition to the standard English letters and characters, a program needs to store special characters that have no printable equivalents. One of these is the end-of-file sentinel that all computer systems use to designate the end of a file of data. These end-of-file sentinels can also be transmitted from the keyboard. For example, on Unix-based systems it is generated by pressing the Ctrl and D keys at the same time, whereas on Windows-based systems it is generated by simultaneously pressing the Ctrl and Z keys. Both of these sentinels are stored as the integer number −1, which has no equivalent character value. (You can check this by displaying the integer value of each entered character (see Program 7.12), and typing either Ctrl + D or Ctrl + Z, depending on the system you are using.)

By using a 16-bit integer value, over 64,000 different characters can be represented. This provides sufficient storage for multiple character sets that can include Arabic, Chinese, Hebrew, Japanese, Russian, and virtually almost all known language symbols. Thus, storing a character as an integer value has a very practical value.

A very important consequence of using integer codes for string characters is that characters can easily be compared for alphabetical ordering. For example, as long as each subsequent letter in an alphabet has a higher value than its preceding letter, the comparison of character values is reduced to the comparison of numeric values. If characters are stored in sequential numerical order, it ensures that adding one to a letter will produce the next letter in the alphabet.

Character I/O

Although you have used `cin` and `getline()` to accept data entered from the keyboard in a more or less "cookbook" manner, you also need to understand what data are actually being sent to the program and how the program must react to process the data correctly. At a very fundamental level, all input (as well as output) is done on a character-by-character basis as illustrated in Figure 7.10.

FIGURE 7.10 Accepting Keyboard-Entered Characters

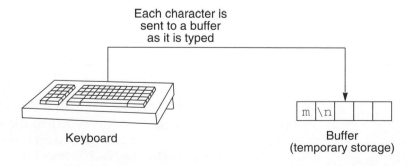

As illustrated in Figure 7.10, the entry of every piece of data, be it a string or a number, consists of typing individual characters. For example, the entry of the string `Hello` consists of pressing and releasing the six keys H, e, l, l, o, and the Enter key. Similarly, the output of the number `26.95` consists of the display of the five characters 2, 6, ., 9, and 5. Although the programmer typically doesn't think

A BIT OF BACKGROUND

A Notational Inconsistency

Notice that all of the character class methods listed in Table 7.6 use the standard object-oriented notation of preceding the method's name with an object name, as in `cin.get()`. This is not the case with the string class `getline()` method, which uses the notation `getline(cin, strVar)`. In this notation, the object, for example `cin`, appears as an argument. In terms of achieving consistency, you would expect `getline()` to be called as `cin.getline()`.

Unfortunately, the proper notation is already in use for a `getline()` method originally created for C-style strings (see next section); hence, a notational inconsistency has been provided.

of data in this manner, the program is always restricted to this character-by-character I/O, and all of C++'s higher-level I/O methods and streams are based on lower-level character I/O methods. These more elemental character methods, which can also be used directly by a programmer, are listed in Table 7.6.

TABLE 7.6 Basic Character I/O Methods (Require the Header File `cctype`)

Method	Description	Example
`cout.put(charExp)`	Places the character value of `charExp` on the output stream	`cout.put('A');`
`cin.get(charVar)`	Extracts the next character from the input stream, and assigns it to the variable `charVar`	`cin.get(key);`
`cin.peek(charVar)`	Assigns the next character from the input stream to the variable `charVar` *without* extracting the character from the stream	`cin.peek(nextKey);`
`cin.putback(charExp)`	Pushes a character value of `charExp` back onto the input stream	`cin.putback(cKey);`
`cin.ignore(n, char)`	Ignores a maximum of the next n input characters, up and including the detection of `char`; if no arguments are specified, ignores the next single character on the input stream	`cin.ignore(80,'\n');` `cin.ignore();`

The `get()` function reads the next character in the input stream and assigns it to the function's character variable. For example, a statement such as

```
cin.get(nextChar);
```

causes the next character entered at the key-board to be stored in the character variable `nextChar`. This function is extremely useful in inputting and checking individual characters before they are assigned to a complete string or the other C++ data type.

The character output function corresponding to `get()` is `put()`. This function expects a single character argument and displays the character passed to it on the terminal. For example, the statement `cout.put('A')` causes the letter A to be displayed on the screen.

Of the last three functions listed in Table 7.6, the `cin.ignore()` function is the most useful. This function permits skipping over input until a designated character, such as `'\n'` is encountered. For example, the statement `cin.ignore(80, '\n')` will skip up to a maximum of the next 80 characters, or stop the skipping if the newline character is encountered. Such a statement can be useful in skipping all further input on a line up to a maximum of 80 characters, or until the end of the current line is encountered. Input would then begin with the next line.

The `peek()` function returns the next character on the stream, but does not remove it from the stream's buffer (see Figure 7.6). For example, the expression `cin.peek(nextChar)` returns the next character input by the keyboard, but leaves it in the buffer. This is sometimes useful for "peeking" ahead and seeing what the next character is, while leaving it in place for the next input.

Finally, the `putback()` function places a character back on the stream so that it will be the next character read. The argument passed to `putback()` can be any character expression that evaluates to a legitimate character value, and need not be the last input character.

The Phantom newline Revisited

As you saw in the previous section, seemingly strange results are sometimes obtained when a `cin` stream input is followed by a `getline()` method call. This same result can occur when characters are input using the `get()` character method. To see how this can occur, consider Program 7.12, which uses the `get()` method to accept the next character entered at the keyboard and stores the character in the variable `fkey`.

PROGRAM 7.12

```
#include <iostream>
#include <cctype>
using namespace std;

int main()
{
  char fkey, skey;

  cout << "Type in a character: ";
  cin.get(fkey);
  cout << "The key just accepted is " << (int)fkey << endl;

  cin.ignore();
  return 0;
}
```

When Program 7.12 is run, the character entered in response to the prompt `Type in a character:` is stored in the character variable `fkey` and the decimal code for the character is displayed by explicitly casting the character into an integer, to force its display as an integer value. The following sample run illustrates this:

```
Type in a character: m
The key just accepted is 109
```

At this point, everything seems to be working just fine, although you might be wondering why the decimal value of m is displayed rather than the character itself. The reason for this will soon become apparent.

In typing m, two keys are usually pressed, the m key and the Enter key. As noted in the previous section, these two characters are stored in a buffer immediately after they are pressed (see Figure 7.4).

The first key pressed, m in this case, is taken from the buffer and stored in fkey. This, however, still leaves the code for the Enter key in the buffer. Thus, a subsequent call to get() for a character input will automatically pick up the code for the Enter key as the next character. For example, consider Program 7.13.

PROGRAM 7.13

```
#include <iostream>
#include <cctype>
using namespace std;

int main()
{
  char fkey, skey;

  cout << "Type in a character: ";
  cin.get(fkey);
  cout << "The key just accepted is " << (int)fkey << endl;

  cout << "Type in another character: ";
  cin.get(skey);
  cout << "The key just accepted is " << (int)skey << endl;

  cin.ignore();
  return 0;
}
```

The following is a sample run for Program 7.13:

```
Type in a character: m
The key just accepted is 109
Type in another character: The key just accepted is 10
```

After entering the letter m in response to the first prompt, the Enter key is also pressed. From a character standpoint this represents the entry of two distinct characters. The first character is m, which is coded and stored as the integer 109. The second character also gets stored in the buffer with the numerical code for the Enter key. The second call to get() picks up this code immediately, without waiting for any additional key to be pressed. The last cout stream displays the code for this key. The reason for displaying the numerical code rather than the character itself is because the Enter key has no printable character associated with it that can be displayed.

Remember that every key has a numerical code, including the Enter, Spacebar, Escape, and Control keys. These keys generally have no effect when entering numbers, because the input methods ignore them as leading or trailing input with numerical data. Nor do these keys affect the entry of a single character requested as the first user data to be input, as is the case in Program 7.12. Only when a character is requested after the user has already input some other data, as in Program 7.13, does the usually invisible Enter key become noticeable.

In Section 7.1 you learned some ways to prevent the Enter key from being accepted as a legitimate character input when the `getline()` method was used. The following ways can be used when the `get()` method is used within a program:

- Follow the `cin.get()` input with the call `cin.ignore()`.
- Accept the Enter key into a character variable, and then don't use further.

Program 7.14 applies the first solution to Program 7.13. Ignoring the Enter key immediately after the first character is read and displayed clears the buffer of the Enter key and gets it ready to store the next valid input character as its first character.

PROGRAM 7.14

```cpp
#include <iostream>
#include <cctype>
using namespace std;

int main()
{
  char fkey, skey;

  cout << "Type in a character: ";
  cin.get(fkey);
  cout << "The key just accepted is " << (int)fkey << endl;
  cin.ignore();

  cout << "Type in another character: ";
  cin.get(skey);
  cout << "The key just accepted is " << (int)skey << endl;

  cin.ignore();
  return 0;
}
```

In Program 7.14, observe that when the user types the letter m and presses the Enter key, the m is assigned to `fkey` and the code for the Enter key is ignored. The next call to `get()` stores the code for the next key pressed in the variable `skey`. From the user's standpoint, the Enter key has no effect except to signal the end of each character input. The following is a sample run for Program 7.14:

```
Type in a character: m
The key just accepted is 109
Type in another character: b
The key just accepted is 98
```

A Second Look at User-Input Validation

As mentioned in the first look at user-input validation (Section 3.4), programs that respond effectively to unexpected user input are formally referred to as robust programs and informally as "bulletproof" programs.

Code that validates user input and ensures that a program does not produce unintended results due to unexpected input is a sign of a well-constructed, robust program. One of your jobs as a programmer is to produce such programs. To see how such unintended results can occur, consider the following two code examples. First assume that your program contains the statements:

```
cout << "Enter an integer:";
cin  >> value;
```

Now assume that, by mistake, a user enters the characters e4. In earlier versions of C++, this would cause the program to unexpectedly terminate, or **crash**. While crashes can still occur with the current ANSI/ISO standard (see, for Example, Exercise 9), one will not occur in this case. Rather, a meaningless integer value will be assigned to the variable named `value`. This, of course, will invalidate any results obtained using this variable.

As a second example, consider the following code, which will cause an infinite loop to occur if the user enters a non-numeric value (the program can be halted by pressing the Control and C keys at the same time):

```
double value;

 do
 {
   cout << "Enter a number (enter 0 to exit): ";
   cin  >> value;

   cout << "The square root of this number is: " << sqrt(value) << endl;
 }while (value !=0);
```

The basic technique for handling invalid data input and preventing seemingly innocuous code, such as that in the two simple examples, from producing unintended results is referred to as **user-input validation**. Essentially this means validating the entered data either during or immediately after data entry and providing the user with a way of re-entering any invalid data. User-input validation is an essential part of any commercially viable program, and if done correctly, it will protect a program from attempting to process data types that can either cause a program to crash, create infinite loops, or produce more invalid results.

The central element in user-input validation is the checking of each entered character to verify that it qualifies as a legitimate character for the expected data-type. For example, if an integer is required, the only acceptable characters are a leading plus or minus sign and the digits 0 through 9. These characters can be checked as they are being typed, which means that the `get()` function is used to input a character at a time, or all of the characters can be accepted in a string, and then each string character checked for validity. Once all the entered characters have been validated, the entered string can then be converted into the correct data type.

There are two basic means of accomplishing the actual validation of the entered characters. Section 7.5 presents one of these ways: character-by-character checking. A second technique, which encompasses a broader scope of data processing tasks using exception handling, is presented in Section 7.6.

Exercises 7.3

1. Enter and execute Program 7.10.

2. Enter and execute Program 7.11.

3. Write a C++ program that counts the number of words in a string. A word is encountered whenever a transition from a blank space to a nonblank character is encountered. Assume that the string contains only words separated by blank spaces.

4. Generate 10 random numbers in the range 0 to 129. If the number represents a printable character print the character with an appropriate message that:

   The character is a lowercase letter
   The character is an uppercase letter
   The character is a digit
   The character is a space

   If the character is none of these, display its value in integer format.

5. a. Write a function named `length()` that determines and returns the length of a string, without using the string class `length()` method.

   b. Write a simple `main()` function to test the `length()` function written for Exercise 5a.

6. a. Write a function named `countlets()` that returns the number of letters in a string passed as an argument. Digits, spaces, punctuation, tabs, and newline characters should not be included in the returned count.

   b. Include the `countlets()` method written for Exercise 6a in an executable C++ program and use the program to test the method.

7. Write a program that accepts a string from the console and displays the hexadecimal equivalent of each character in the string.

8. Write a C++ program that accepts a string from the console and displays the string one word per line.

9. In response to the following code:

   ```
   cout << "Enter an integer: ";
   cin  >> value;
   ```

   suppose a user enters the data 12e4. What value will be stored in the integer variable `value`?

10. a. Write a C++ program that stops reading a line of text when a period is entered and then displays the sentence with correct spacing and capitalization. For this program correct spacing means that there should only be one space between words and that all letters should be in lowercase, except for the first letter of the first word. For example, if the user entered the text `i    am       going    to    Go    TO THe moVics.`, the displayed sentence should be `I am going to go to the movies.`

   b. Determine what characters, if any, are not correctly displayed by the program you created for Exercise 10a.

11. Write a C++ program that accepts a name as first name, last name and then displays the name as last name, first name. For example, if the user entered Gary Bronson, the output should be Bronson, Gary.

12. Modify the program written for Exercise 11 to include an array of five names.

7.4 STRINGS AND THE STANDARD TEMPLATE LIBRARY

Although not part of the STL section of C++'s library, the `string` class was designed to work directly with the STL (the STL is described in detail in Sections 12.6 and Chapter 16). In addition to providing a number of its own classes, the STL also provides a set of generic capabilities that can be applied to non-STL class objects. Table 7.7 lists a subset of these methods that are particularly useful in processing `string` class strings.[1]

TABLE 7.7 Template Library (STL) Methods Useful in Processing `string` Class Objects

Algorithm Name	Description
`binary_search (start, end, value)`	Returns a Boolean value of `true` if the specified value exists within the specified range; otherwise returns `false`; should only be used on a sorted set of values
`copy(srcStart, srcEnd, destStart)`	Copies elements from the source range specified by `srcStart` to `srcEnd`, to the range of elements starting at `destStart`
`copy_backward (srcStart, srcEnd, destStart)`	Copies elements in reverse order from the source range specified by `srcStart` to `srcEnd`, to the range of elements starting at `destStart`
`count(start, end, criterion)`	Returns the number of elements in the specified range that match the specified criterion
`equal(start1, end1, start2)`	Compares the elements in the range of elements specified by the range `start1` to `end1`, element by element, to the elements in the range starting with `start2`
`fill(start, end, value)`	Assigns every element in the range specified by `start` and `end` with the specified value
`find(start, end, value)`	Returns the position of the first occurrence of an element in a specified range having the specified value, if the value exists; performs a linear search, starting with the first element in a specified range and proceeds one element at a time until the complete range has been searched or the specified element has been found
`remove(start, end, value)`	Remove all elements in the range specified by `start` and `end` having the specified value, without changing the order of the remaining elements
`replace(start, end, oldVal, newVal)`	Replaces each element in the range specified by `start` and `end` that has the value `OldVal` with the value `newVal`
`reverse(start, end)`	Reverses elements in the range specified by `start` and `end`
`search(start, end, value)`	Finds the first occurrence of the specified value or sequence of values within a specified range
`sort(start end)`	Sorts elements in the range specified by `start` and `end` into an ascending order
`swap(srcStart, srcEnd, destStart)`	Swaps elements from the source range specified by `srcStart` to `srcEnd`, to the range of elements starting at `destStart`
`unique(start, end)`	Removes all elements in the range specified by `start` and `end` that are equal to the previous element; when the elements are in sorted order this will remove all duplicate entries

---

[1] These methods are formally referred to as STL algorithms. The reason for this terminology is presented in Chapter 16.

A BIT OF BACKGROUND

Anagrams and Palindromes

Some of the most challenging and fascinating word games are played with anagrams and palindromes.

An **anagram** is a rearrangement of the letters in a word or phrase that makes another word or phrase. Although the letters of the word *door* can be rearranged to spell *orod* and *doro*, it is more exciting to discover the words *odor* and *rood*. A word, phrase, or sentence that reads the same forward and backward, such as *top spot* is a **palindrome**.

The origins of most known anagrams and palindromes are lost to anonymity. Here are some collected by Richard Manchester in *The Mammoth Book of Fun and Games* (Hart Publishing Co. Inc., New York City, 1977; pages 229–231).

Apt Anagrams

The Mona Lisa → No hat, a smile
The United States of America → Attaineth its cause: freedom!

Interesting Palindromes

Live not on evil!
'Tis Ivan on a visit.
Yreka Bakery
Able was I ere I saw Elba.
Madam, I'm Adam.
A man, a plan, a canal: Panama!

Typically the ranges required as arguments to all of the methods listed in Table 7.7 must be specified as STL iterators. Two of the most useful iterators are returned by the STL iterator methods named `begin()` and `end()`. These are general purpose methods that return the positions of the first and last elements in a string, respectively.

To make this more tangible, you will apply the STL `reverse()` method to a `string` class object to illustrate how a rather challenging programming problem is solved very easily using the STL. The programming problem is to determine if a word or line of text is a palindrome.

A palindrome is a word or phrase in which the alphanumeric characters in the text are exactly the same in both the forward and reverse directions. By definition, alphanumeric characters consist of letters and digits only. Thus, all white space, punctuation marks, tabs, and nonprinting characters are not considered in determining if a palindrome exists. For example, the phrase "Madam I'm Adam" is a palindrome because, when the punctuation and white space is removed, the remaining sequence of characters is the same in both the forward and reverse directions.

For this example, you will write a program that accepts a line of text as input and then determines if it is a palindrome. The procedure to determine if the characters represent a palindrome is:

1. *Remove all non-alphanumeric characters from the string.*
2. *Convert all letters to lowercase (uppercase also works).*
3. *Make a copy of the resulting string.*
4. *Reverse the copy.*
5. *Compare the string, element-by-element, with its reversed copy.*

As shown in Program 7.15, Steps 1 and 2 are accomplished using character operations, Step 3 is accomplished using a one line `string` class assignment statement, Step 4 is accomplished using the STL `reverse()` algorithm, and Step 5 is accomplished using the `string` class equality operator.

PROGRAM 7.15

```cpp
#include <iostream>
#include <string>
#include <cctype>
#include <algorithm>
using namespace std;

int main()
{
  string text, savetext;
  int i;

  cout << "Enter the text: ";
  getline(cin, text);

  // Steps 1 and 2: remove all non alphanumeric characters
  // and then convert all alphanumerics to lowercase
  for (i = 0; i < text.length(); i++)
    if (isalnum(text.at(i)))
      text.at(i) = tolower(text.at(i));
    else
  {
      text.erase(i,1);
      i--;  // take into account that a character was removed
  }

  savetext = text; // Step 3: Make a copy of the cleaned up text

  reverse(text.begin(), text.end());  // Step 4: Reverse the
cleaned up text

  if (text == savetext)  // Step 5: Compare forward and reversed
texts
    cout << "The entered text is a palindrome.";
  else
    cout << "The entered text is not a palindrome.";

  cin.ignore();

  return 0;
}
```

Program 7.15 illustrates how easily STL algorithms can be used with string class objects to complete programming tasks that would otherwise take considerable time and effort, both to program and then verify. In Chapter 13 an additional set of STL provided classes is presented that also can use the same STL algorithms to solve more advanced programming tasks.

Exercises 7.4

1. Enter and execute Program 7.15. Verify that the program works correctly by entering the following text:

   a. Live not on evil!

   b. 'Tis Ivan on a visit.

   c. Yreka Bakery

   d. Able was I ere I saw Elba.

   e. Madam it's Tim Adam!!

   f. A man, a plan, a canal: Panama!

2. Modify Program 7.15 to remove all non-digits and then display the entered integer in reverse form. Thus, if the user enters the data 123abc45, the program should display 54321.

3. Modify Program 7.15 to display the entered text after it has been stripped of all non alphanumeric characters and all characters have been converted to lowercase.

4. Write a C++ program that swaps the text contained in two strings.

5. Write a C++ program that accepts a line of text into a string class object and then replaces every occurrence of the letter e with the letter x.

6. Modify the C++ program written for Exercise 5 so that the user can specify both the character that is to be replaced and the replacing character.

7. Write a C++ program that requests a line of text and then removes all the occurrences of a user-specified letter. Display the complete line of text after the removal to see how the order of the remaining elements has been affected. Additionally, display the size of the string both before and after the removal. Discuss why you might want to use the `string` class `erase()` method rather than the STL's `remove()` algorithm.

7.5 INPUT DATA VALIDATION

One of the major uses of strings in programs is for user-input validation. The necessity for validating user input is essential; even though a program prompts the user to enter a specific type of data, such as an integer, this does not ensure that the user will comply. What a user enters is, in fact, totally out of the programmer's control. What is in your control is how you deal with the entered data.

It certainly does no good to tell a frustrated user that "The program clearly tells you to enter an integer and you entered a date." Rather, successful programs always try to anticipate invalid data and isolate such data from being accepted and processed. This is typically accomplished by first validating that the data is of the correct type; if it is, the data is accepted; otherwise, the user is requested to re-enter the data, with a possible explanation of why the entered data was invalid.

One of the most common methods of validating input data is to accept all numbers as strings. Each character in the string can then be checked to ensure that it complies with the data type being requested. Only after this check is made and the data is verified for the correct type is the string converted to either an integer or floating-point value using the conversion functions listed in Table 13.4 (for data accepted using `string` class objects, the `c_str()` method must be applied to the string before the conversion function is invoked).

As an example, consider the input of an integer number. To be valid, the data entered must adhere to the following conditions:

- *The data must contain at least one character.*
- *If the first character is a + or - sign, the data must contain at least one digit.*
- *Only digits from 0 to 9 are acceptable following the first character.*

The following function, named `isvalidInt()`, can be used to check that an entered string complies with these conditions. This function returns the Boolean value of `true`, if the conditions are satisfied; otherwise, it returns a Boolean `false` value.

```
bool isvalidInt(string str)
{
  int start = 0;
  int i;
  bool valid = true;   // assume a valid
  bool sign = false;   // assume no sign

  // check for an empty string
  if (str.length() == 0)  valid = false;

  // check for a leading sign
  if (str.at(0) == '-'|| str.at(0) == '+')
  {
    sign = true;
    start = 1;  // start checking for digits after the sign
  }

  // check that there is at least one character after the sign
  if (sign && str.length() == 1) valid = false;

  // now check the string, which we know has at least one non-sign char
  i = start;
  while(valid && i < str.length())
  {
    if(!isdigit(str.at(i))) valid = false;  //found a non-digit character
    i++;  // move to next character
  }

  return valid;
}
```

In the code for the `isvalidInt()` method, pay attention to the conditions that are being checked. These are commented in the code and consist of checking that:

- *The string is not empty.*
- *A valid sign symbol (+ or -) is present.*
- *If a sign symbol is present, there is at least one digit following it.*
- *All of the remaining characters in the string are digits.*

Only if all of these conditions are met does the function return a Boolean `true` value. Once this value is returned, the string can be safely converted into an integer with the assurance that no unexpected value will result to hamper further data processing. Program 7.16 uses this method within the context of a complete program.

PROGRAM 7.16

```cpp
#include <iostream>
#include <string>
#include <cctype>
using namespace std;

int main()
{
  bool isvalidInt(string);  // function prototype (declaration)
  string value;
  int number;

  cout << "Enter an integer: ";
  getline(cin, value);

  if (!isvalidInt(value))
   cout << "The number you entered is not a valid integer.";
  else
  {
    number = atoi(value.c_str());
    cout << "The integer you entered is " << number;
  }

  return 0;
}

bool isvalidInt(string str)
{
  int start = 0;
  int i;
  bool valid = true;  // assume a valid
  bool sign = false;  // assume no sign


  // check for an empty string
  if (str.length() == 0)  valid = false;

  // check for a leading sign
  if (str.at(0) == '-'|| str.at(0) == '+')
  {
    sign = true;
    start = 1;  // start checking for digits after the sign
  }
```

(continued from previous page)

```
// check that there is at least one character after the sign
if (sign && str.length() == 1) valid = false;

 // now check the string, which we know has at least one non-sign char
i = start;
while(valid && i < str.length())
{
  if(!isdigit(str.at(i))) valid = false;  //found a non-digit character
  i++;  // move to next character
}

return valid;
}
```

Two sample runs using Program 7.16 produced the following:

```
Enter an integer: 12e45
The number you entered is not a valid integer.
```

and

```
Enter an integer: -12345
The number you entered is -12345
```

As illustrated by this output, the program successfully determines that an invalid character was entered in the first run.

Rather than accepting and then checking a complete string, an alternative is to check each character as it is typed. This is an especially useful method when a graphical user interface (GUI) is used for data input, because it permits the user to correct the data as it is being entered, rather than after all the complete number has been entered.

A second line of defense is to provide error processing code within the context of exception-handling code. This type of code is typically provided to permit the user to correct a problem such as invalid data entry by re-entering a new value. The means of providing this in C++ is referred to as exception handling and was presented in Section 7.1.

Exercises 7.5

1. Write a C++ program that prompts the user to type in an integer. Have your program accept the number, as an integer, using `cin` and, using `cout`, display the value your program actually accepted from the data entered. Run your program five times. The first time you run the program enter a valid integer number, the second time enter a floating-point number, and the third time enter a character. Next, enter the value 12e34 and then 31234.

2. Modify the program you wrote for Exercise 1 but have your program use a double-precision variable. Run the program four times. The first time enter an integer, the second time enter a decimal number, the third time enter a decimal number with an f as the last character entered, and the fourth time enter a character. Using the output display, keep track of what number your program actually accepted from the data you entered. What happened, if anything, and why?

3. a. Why do you think that successful application programs contain extensive data input validity checks? (*Hint:* Review Exercises 1 and 2.)

   b. What do you think is the difference between a data type check and a data reasonableness check?

   c. Assume that a program requests that a month, day, and year be entered by the user. What are some reasonable checks that could be made on the data entered?

4. a. Enter and execute Program 7.16.
   b. Run Program 7.16 five times, using the data referred to in Exercise 1 for each run.

5. Modify Program 7.16 to display any invalid characters that were entered.

6. Modify Program 7.16 to continually request an integer until a valid number is entered.

7. Modify Program 7.16 to remove all leading and trailing spaces from the entered string before it is checked for validity.

8. Write a function that checks each digit as it is entered, rather than checking the completed string, as done in Program 7.16.

9. Write a C++ function that checks for a valid floating-point number. Such a number can have an optional + or - sign, at most one decimal point, which can be the first character, and at least one digit between 0 and 9, inclusive.

7.6 FOCUS ON PROBLEM SOLVING

This section presents a complete means of ensuring that an integer number is entered by a user in response to a request for input that must be an integer value. The importance of this type of input data validation was presented in Section 3.4, which provided an introduction to data input validation, and Section 7.5, which provided a function named `isvalidInt()` that returned a Boolean `true` value if a user-entered string contained only those characters that could be converted into a valid integer. The technique presented in this section extends using the `isvalidInt()` function to ensure not only that an invalid integer value is detected, but also that the program provides the user with the option of re-entering values until a valid integer is obtained.

This technique can easily be applied to ensuring the entry of a valid floating-point number, which is the other numerical data type frequently requested as user-entered data.

For your convenience, the `isvalidInt()` function developed in Section 7.5 is repeated below.

```
bool isvalidInt(string str)
  {
    int start = 0;
    int i;
    bool valid = true;   // assume a valid
    bool sign = false;   // assume no sign

    // check for an empty string
    if (str.length() == 0)  valid = false;
```

```
    // check for a leading sign
    if (str.at(0) == '-'|| str.at(0) == '+')
    {
      sign = true;
      start = 1;  // start checking for digits after the sign
    }

    // check that there is at least one character after the sign
    if (sign && str.length() == 1) valid = false;

    // now check the string, which we know has at least one non-sign char
    i = start;
    while(valid && i < str.length())
    {
      if(!isdigit(str.at(i))) valid = false;  //found a non-digit character
      i++;  // move to next character
    }

  return valid;
}
```

As described in Section 7.5, when the isvalidInt() function is used, the code checks that:

- *The string is not empty.*
- *The string contains an optional valid sign symbol (1 or -).*
- *If a valid sign symbol is present, there is at least one digit following it.*
- *All of the remaining characters in the string are digits.*

If all of these conditions are met, the function returns a Boolean true value; otherwise, it returns a Boolean false value. Using this function, you can now develop a more comprehensive function, named getanInt(), that uses exception processing to continuously accept a user input until a string that corresponds to a valid integer is detected. Once such a string is entered, getanInt() converts the string to an integer and returns the integer value. This ensures that the program requesting an integer actually receives an integer and prevents any unwarranted effects, such as a program crash due to an invalid data type being entered.

The algorithm that you will use to accept the user's input is:

Set a Boolean variable named notanint to true
while (notanint is true)
    try
       Accept a string value
       If the string value does not correspond to an integer throw an exception
    catch the exception
       Display the error message "Invalid integer - Please re-enter:"
       Send control back to the while statement
    Set notanint to false (this causes the loop to terminate)
End while
Return the integer corresponding to the entered string

The code corresponding to this algorithm is highlighted in Program 7.17.

PROGRAM 7.17

```cpp
#include <iostream>
#include <string>
#include <cctype>
using namespace std;

int main()
{
  int getanInt();  // function declaration (prototype)
  int value;

  cout << "Enter an integer value: ";
  value = getanInt();
  cout << "The integer entered is: " << value << endl;

  return 0;
}

int getanInt()
{
  bool isvalidInt(string);  // function declaration (prototype)
  bool notanint = true;
  string svalue;

  while (notanint)
  {
    try
    {
      cin >> svalue;  // accept a string input
      if (!isvalidInt(svalue)) throw svalue;
    }
    catch (string e)
    {
      cout << "Invalid integer - Please re-enter: ";
      continue; // send control to the while statement
    }
    notanint = false;
  }
  return atoi(svalue.c_str());  // convert to an integer
}

bool isvalidInt(string str)
{
  int start = 0;
  int i;
  bool valid = true;  // assume a valid
  bool sign = false;  // assume no sign

  // check for an empty string
  if (str.length() == 0)  valid = false;
```

(continued from previous page)

```
      // check for a leading sign
      if (str.at(0) == '-'|| str.at(0) == '+')
      {
        sign = true;
        start = 1;  // start checking for digits after the sign
      }

      // check that there is at least one character after the sign
      if (sign && str.length() == 1) valid = false;

      // now check the string, which we know has at least one non-sign char
      i = start;
      while(valid && i < str.length())
      {
        if(!isdigit(str.at(i))) valid = false;  //
  found a non-digit character
        i++;  // move to next character
      }

    return valid;
}
```

Following is a sample output produced by Program 7.17:

```
Enter an integer value: abc
Invalid integer - Please re-enter: 12.
Invalid integer - Please re-enter: 12e
Invalid integer - Please re-enter: 120
The integer entered is: 120
```

As shown by this output, the getanInt() function works correctly. It continuously requests input until a valid integer is entered.

Exercises 7.6

1. Enter and execute Program 7.17.

2. Modify the isvalidInt() function used in Program 7.17 to remove all leading and trailing blank spaces from its string argument before determining if the string corresponds to a valid integer.

3. Modify the isvalidInt() function used in Program 7.17 to accept a string that ends in a decimal point. For example, input 12. should be accepted and converted to the integer number 12.

4. a. Write a C++ function named isvalidReal() that checks for a valid floating-point number. This kind of number can have an optional + or - sign, at most one decimal point, which can also be the first character, and at least one digit between 0 and 9 inclusive. The function should return a Boolean value of true if the entered number is a real number; otherwise, it should return a Boolean value of false.

b. Modify the `isvalidReal()` function written for Exercise 4a to remove all leading and trailing blank spaces from its string argument before determining if the string corresponds to a valid real number.

5. Write and execute a C++ function named `getaReal()` that uses exception handling to continuously accept an input string until a string that can be converted to a real number is entered. The function should return a double-precision value corresponding to the string value entered by the user.

7.7 NAMESPACES AND CREATING A PERSONAL LIBRARY

Until the introduction of personal computers in the early 1980s, with their extensive use of integrated circuits and microprocessors, both the speed of computers and their available memory were severely restricted. For example, the most advanced computers of the time had speeds measured in milliseconds (one-thousandth of a second), whereas current computers have speeds measured in nanoseconds (one-billionth of a second) and higher. Similarly, the memory capacity of early desktop computers consisted of 32,000 locations, with each location consisting of eight-bits. Today's computer memories consist of millions of memory locations, each consisting of from 32 to 64 bits.

These early hardware restrictions made it imperative that programmers use every possible trick to save memory space and make programs run more efficiently. Almost every program was handcrafted and included what was referred to as "clever code" to minimize run time and maximize the use of memory storage. Unfortunately, this individualized code, over time, became a liability. New programmers had to expend considerable time understanding existing code, and frequently even the original programmer had trouble figuring out code that was written only months before. This made modifications extremely time-consuming and costly and precluded cost-effective use of existing code for new installations.

The inability to reuse code efficiently combined with expanded hardware capabilities provided the incentive for discovering more efficient ways of programming. Initially this led to the structured programming concepts incorporated into procedural languages, such as Pascal, and currently to the object-oriented techniques that form the basis of C++. One of the early criticisms of C++, however, was that it did not provide a comprehensive library of classes. This has changed dramatically with the finalization of the ANSI/ISO standard and the inclusion of an extensive C++ library.

No matter how many useful classes or methods are provided, however, each major type of programming application, such as financial, marketing, engineering, and scientific areas, always have their own specialized requirements. For example, C++ provides rather good date and time functions in its `ctime` header file. For specialized needs, such as those encountered in the financial industry, however, these functions must be expanded. Thus, a more complete set of functions would include finding the number of business days between two dates that took into account both weekends and holidays. It would also require functions that implemented prior and next day algorithms that take into account leap years and the actual days in each month. These could either be provided as part of a more complete `Date` class or as non-class functions.

In situations like this, programmers create and share their own libraries of classes and functions with other programmers working on the same or similar projects. Once the classes and functions have been tested, they can be incorporated in any program without further expenditures of coding time.

At this stage in your programming career, you can begin to build your own library of specialized functions and classes. Sections 7.5 and 7.6 described how this can be accomplished by using the input validation functions, isvalidInt() and getanInt(), which are shown here:

```cpp
int getanInt()
{
  bool isvalidInt(string);  // function declaration (prototype)
  bool notanint = true;
  string svalue;

  while (notanint)
  {
    try
    {
      cin >> svalue;  // accept a string input
      if (!isvalidInt(svalue)) throw svalue;
    }
    catch (string e)
    {
      cout << "Invalid integer - Please re-enter: ";
     continue; // send control to the while statement
    }
    notanint = false;
  }
  return atoi(svalue.c_str());  // convert to an integer
}

bool isvalidInt(string str)
{
  int start = 0;
  int i;
  bool valid = true;  // assume a valid
  bool sign = false;  // assume no sign

  // check for an empty string
  if (str.length() == 0)  valid = false;

  // check for a leading sign
  if (str.at(0) == '-'|| str.at(0) == '+')
  {
    sign = true;
    start = 1;  // start checking for digits after the sign
  }

  // check that there is at least one character after the sign
  if (sign && str.length() == 1) valid = false;

  // now check the string, which we know has at least one non-sign char
  i = start;
  while(valid && i < str.length())
  {
    if(!isdigit(str.at(i))) valid = false;  //found a non-digit character
    i++;  // move to next character
  }

  return valid;
}
```

The first step in creating a library is to encapsulate all of the preferred functions and classes into one or more namespaces and then store the complete code (with or without using a namespace) into one or more files. For example you can create one namespace named `dataChecks` and save it in the file named `dataChecks.cpp`. Note that the file name under which the namespace is saved *need not* be the same as the namespace name used in the code.

The syntax for creating a namespace is:

```
namespace name
{
   funcions and/or classes in here
}   // end of namespace
```

Including the two functions `getanInt()` and `isvalidInt()` within a namespace named `dataChecks` and adding the appropriate `include` files and `using` declaration statement needed by the new namespace yield the following code (the syntax required to create the namespace is highlighted):

```cpp
namespace dataChecks
{
  #include <iostream>
  #include <string>
  #include <cctype>
  using namespace std;

  int getanInt()
  {
    bool isvalidInt(string);   // function declaration (prototype)
    bool notanint = true;
    string svalue;

    while (notanint)
    {
      try
      {
        cin >> svalue;   // accept a string input
        if (!isvalidInt(svalue)) throw svalue;
      }
      catch (string e)
      {
        cout << "Invalid integer - Please re-enter: ";
        continue; // send control to the while statement
      }
      notanint = false;
    }
    return atoi(svalue.c_str());   // convert to an integer
  }

  bool isvalidInt(string str)
  {
    int start = 0;
    int i;
    bool valid = true;   // assume a valid
    bool sign = false;   // assume no sign
```

```
        // check for an empty string
        if (str.length() == 0)  valid = false;

        // check for a leading sign
        if (str.at(0) == '-'|| str.at(0) == '+')
        {
          sign = true;
          start = 1;  // start checking for digits after the sign
        }

        // check that there is at least one character after the sign
        if (sign && str.length() == 1) valid = false;

        // now check the string, which we know has at least one non-sign char
        i = start;
        while(valid && i < str.length())
        {
          if(!isdigit(str.at(i))) valid = false;  //found a non-digit character
          i++;  // move to next character
        }
        return valid;
      }
    }  // end of dataChecks namespace
```

Once the namespace has been created and stored in a file, it can be included within another file by supplying a preprocessor directive informing the compiler where the desired namespace is to be found and including a using directive instructing the compiler to the particular namespace in the file to use. For the dataChecks namespace, which is stored in a file named dataChecks, you enter the following statements:

```
#include =c::\\mylibrary\\dataChecks>
using namespace dataChecks;
```

The first statement provides the full path name for the source code file. Notice that a full path name has been used and that two backslashes are used to separate path names. The double backslashes are required whenever providing either a relative or full path name. The only time that backslashes are not required is when the library code resides in the same directory as the program being executed. As indicated, the dataChecks source file is saved within a folder named mylibrary. The second statement tells the compiler to use the dataChecks namespace within the designated file. Program 7.18 includes these two statements within an executable program.

PROGRAM 7.18

```cpp
#include <c:\\mylibrary\\dataChecks.cpp>
using namespace dataChecks;

int main()
{
  int value;

  cout << "Enter an integer value: ";
  value = getanInt();
  cout << "The integer entered is: " << value << endl;

  return 0;
}
```

The only requirement for the include statement in Program 7.18 is that file name and location must correspond to an existing file having the same name in the designated path; otherwise a compiler error will occur. Should you want to name the source code file using a file extension, any extension can be used, as long as the following rules are maintained:

1. The file name under which the code is stored includes the extension.
2. The same file name, including extension, is used in the `include` statement.

Thus, if the file name used to store the functions were `dataLib.cpp`, the `include` statement in Program 7.18 would be `#include <c::\\mylibrary\\ dataChecks.cpp>` Also, a namespace is not required within the file. The designation of a namespace in the `using` statement tells the compiler to include only the code in the specified namespace, rather than all of the code in the file. In Program 7.18, if the data checking functions were not enclosed within a namespace, the `using` statement for the `dataChecks` namespace would have to be omitted.

Including the previously written and tested data checking functions within Program 7.18 as a separate file allows you to focus on the code within the program that uses these functions, rather than being concerned with the function code itself. This permits you to concentrate on using these functions as opposed to reexamining or even seeing the previously written and tested function code. In Program 7.18, the `main()` method simply exercises the data checking functions and produces the same output as Program 7.17. In creating the `dataChecks` namespace, you have included source code for the two functions. This is not required, and a compiled version of the source code can be saved instead. Finally, additions to a namespace defined in one file can be made in another file by using the same namespace name in the new file and including a `using` statement for the first file's namespace.

Exercises 7.7

1. Enter and compile Program 7.18. (*Hint:* Both the namespace header file dataChecks and the program file are available with the source code provided on the Course Technology Web site (www.course.com) for this text. See Exercise 4 for the downloading procedure.)

2. Why would a programmer supply a namespace file in its compiled form rather than as source code?

3. a. What is an advantage of namespaces?

   b. What is a possible disadvantage of namespaces?

4. What types of classes and functions would you include in a personal library? Why?

5. a. Write a C++ function named whole() that returns the integer part of any number passed to the function. (*Hint:* Assign the passed argument to an integer variable.)

   b. Include the function written in Exercise 5a in a working program. Make sure your function is called from main() and correctly returns a value to main(). Have main() use a cout statement to display the value returned. Test the function by passing various data to it.

   c. When you are confident that the whole() function written for Exercise 5a works correctly, save it in a namespace and a personal library of your choice.

6. a. Write a C++ function named fracpart() that returns the fractional part of any number passed to the function. For example, if the number 256.879 is passed to fracpart(), the number .879 should be returned. Have the function fracpart() call the whole() function that you wrote in Exercise 5. The number returned can then be determined as the number passed to fracpart() less the returned value when the same argument is passed to whole(). The completed program should consist of main() followed by fracpart() followed by whole().

   b. Include the function written in Exercise 6a in a working program. Make sure the function is called from main() and correctly returns a value to main(). Have main() use a cout statement to display the value returned. Test the function by passing various data to it.

   c. When you are confident that the fracpart() function written for Exercise 6a works correctly, save it in the same namespace and personal library selected for Exercise 5c.

7. Include the functions listed in Section 17.4 in the namespace and personal library selected for Exercise 5c. Add any other classes or functions that you think will be helpful to you in your programming work.

7.8 COMMON PROGRAMMING ERRORS

The common errors associated with defining and processing strings are:

1. Forgetting to include the string header file when using string class objects

2. Forgetting that the newline character, '\n', is a valid data input character

3. Forgetting to convert a string class object using the c_str() method when converting string class objects to numerical data types.

7.9 CHAPTER REVIEW

Key Terms

cctype
cin.get()
cin.getline()
getline()
isalpha()
isdigit()

length()
object
string class
tolower()
toupper()

Summary

1. A **string literal** is any sequence of characters enclosed in double quotation marks. A string literal is also referred to as a string value, a string constant, and more conventionally, simply as a string.

2. A string can be constructed as an object of the `string` class.

3. The `string` class is commonly used for constructing strings for input and output purposes, such as for prompts and displayed messages. Because of the provided capabilities, this class is also used when strings need to be compared or searched, or when individual characters in a string need to be examined or extracted as a substring. It is also used in more advanced situations when characters within a string need to be replaced, inserted, or deleted on a relatively regular basis.

4. Strings can be manipulated using either the methods of the class they are objects of or the general purpose string and character methods.

5. The `cin` object, by itself, tends to be of limited usefulness for string input because it terminates input when a blank is encountered.

6. For `string` class data input, use the `getline()` method.

7. The `cout` object can be used to display `string` class strings.

Exercises

1. Write a function that counts the number of lines entered using a `string` class object. Consider a line as any sequence of characters followed by the Enter key.

2. Read a sentence, one character at a time, from the keyboard into `string` class object. An entry will terminate with a period (.). Search the array to determine how many times a particular character, specified by the user at the keyboard, occurs in the sentence.

3. Write a function that counts the number of sentences entered into a `string` class object; assume a sentence ends in a period, question mark, or exclamation point.

4. Modify the function written for Exercise 3 to count the number of words as well as the number of sentences. The function should return the average words per sentence.

5. Write a function named `remove()` that returns nothing and deletes all occurrences of its character argument from a string. The function should take two arguments: the string name and the character to be removed. For

example, if `message` contains the string `Happy Holidays`, the function call `remove(message, 'H')` should place the string `appy olidays` into `message`.

6. Write a function named `addchars()` that adds n occurrences of a character to a string. For example, the function call `addchars(message, 4, '!")` should add four exclamation marks at the end of `message`.

7. Write a function named `extract()` that accepts two strings, `s1` and `s2`, and two integer numbers, `n1` and `n2`, as arguments. The function should extract `n2` characters from `s2`, starting at position `n1`, and place the extracted characters into `s1`. For example, if string `s1` contains the characters `05/18/95 D169254 Rotech Systems`, the function call `extract(s1, s2, 18, 6)` should create the string `Rotech` in `s2`. Note that the starting position for counting purposes is position one.

8. Using a `string` class object, write and execute a function that prints the elements in reverse order.

9. Write and execute a function that uses an array of characters and returns the position of the first occurrence of a user-specified letter in the array or a -1 if the letter does not occur.

PART II

Object-Oriented Programming in C++

For a programming language to be classified as object-oriented, it must provide three features: user-definable data types, inheritance, and polymorphism. The description of each of these features and their implementation in C++ is provided in this part of the text. Specifically, the fundamentals of constructing data types, which in C++ are referred to as classes, are presented in Chapters 8 and 9. Inheritance and polymorphism are then described in Chapter 10.*

In addition to providing the fundamentals of object-oriented programming, the fundamentals of using I/O streams as they apply to creating, reading, and writing data files are presented in Chapter 11. The material in Chapter 11 can be read independently of the material in Chapters 8 through 10.

---

* The material in both Parts II and III, with the notable exception of the advanced dynamically linked lists covered in Chapter 16 and other minor exceptions noted in the text, are essentially independent of each other. Both Parts II and III do, however, depend on the procedural aspects of C++ presented in Part I. Thus, Parts II and III need not be covered in sequence, and Part I can be followed equally well by either Part II or III.

Introduction to Classes

Besides being an improved version of C, the distinguishing characteristic of C++ is its support of object-oriented programming. Central to this object orientation is the concept of an abstract data type, which is a programmer-defined data type.

In this chapter, we explore the implications of permitting programmers to define their own data types and then present C++'s mechanism for constructing them. As we will see, the construction of a data type is based on both variables and functions; variables provide the means for creating new data configurations, and functions provide the means for performing operations on these configurations. What C++ provides is a unique way of combining variables and functions together in a self-contained, cohesive unit from which objects can be created.

8.1 ABSTRACT DATA TYPES IN C++ (CLASSES)

The programming environment has changed dramatically since the mid-1990s with the emergence of graphical screens and the subsequent interest in window applications. Providing a graphical user interface (GUI) where a user can easily move around in even a single window is a challenge when using procedural code. Programming multiple and possibly overlapping windows on the same graphical screen increases the complexity enormously when procedural code is used.

Unlike a procedural approach, however, an object-oriented approach works well on a graphical windowed environment, where each window can be specified as a self-contained rectangular object that can be moved and resized in relation to other objects on the screen. Additionally, within each window, other

Procedural, Hybrid, and Pure Object-Oriented Languages

Most high-level programming languages can be categorized into one of three main categories: procedural, hybrid, or object-oriented. FORTRAN, which was the first commercially available high-level programming language, is procedural. This makes sense because FORTRAN was designed to perform mathematical calculations that used standard algebraic formulas. These formulas were described as algorithms, and then the algorithms were coded using function and subroutine procedures. Other procedural languages that followed FORTRAN included BASIC, COBOL, and Pascal.

Currently, there are only two pure object-oriented languages: Smalltalk and Eiffel. The first requirement of a pure object-oriented language is that it contain three specific features: classes, inheritance, and polymorphism (each of these features is described in the next three chapters). In addition to providing these features, however, a "pure" object-oriented language must, at a minimum, always use classes. In a pure object-oriented language, all data types are constructed as classes, all data values are objects, all operators can be overloaded, and every data operation can only be executed using a class member function. *It is impossible in a pure object-oriented language not to use object-oriented features throughout a program.* This is not the case in a hybrid language.

In a hybrid language, such as C++, *it is impossible not to use elements of a procedural program.* This is because the use of any built-in data type or operation effectively violates the pure object-oriented paradigm. Although a hybrid language must have the ability to define classes, the distinguishing feature of a hybrid language is that it is possible to write a complete program using only procedural code. Additionally, hybrid languages need not even provide inheritance and polymorphic features—but they must provide classes. Languages that use classes but do not provide inheritance and polymorphic features are referred to as *object-based* languages rather than *object-oriented* languages.

graphical objects, such as check boxes, option buttons, labels, and text boxes, can easily be placed and moved.

To provide this object creation capability, extensions to the procedural language C were developed. These extensions became the new language named C++, which permits a programmer both to use and to create new objects.

Central to the creation of objects is the concept of an abstract data type, which is simply a user-defined data type, as opposed to the built-in data types provided by all languages (such as integer and floating-point types). Permitting a programmer to define new data types, such as a rectangular type, out of which specific rectangular objects can be created and displayed on a screen, forms the basis of C++'s object orientation.

Abstract Data Types

To gain a clear understanding of what an abstract data type is, consider the following four built-in data types supplied in C++: integers, doubles, Boolean, and characters. In using these data types, we typically declare one or more variables of the desired type, use them in their accepted ways, and avoid using them in ways that are not specified. Thus, for example, we do not use the modulus operator on two double-precision numbers. Because this operation makes no sense for double-precision numbers, it is never defined, in any programming language, for such numbers.

Thus, although we typically do not consider it, each data type consists of *both* a type of data, such as integer or floating-point, *and* specific operational capabilities provided for each type.

In computer terminology, the combination of data and their associated operations is defined as a **data type**. That is, a data type defines both the types of data and the types of operations that can be performed on the data. Seen in this light, the integer data type, the double-precision data type, and the character data type provided in C++ are all examples of built-in data types that are defined by a type of data and specific operational capabilities provided for initializing and manipulating the type. In a simplified form, this relationship can be described as:

data type = allowable data values + operational capabilities

Thus, the operations that we have been using in C++ are an inherent part of each data type. For each of these data types, the designers of C++ had to consider carefully, and then implement, specific operations.

To understand the importance of the operational capabilities provided by a programming language, let's take a moment to list some of those supplied with C++'s built-in data types (`ints`, `doubles`, `bools`, and `chars`). The minimum set of the capabilities provided by C++'s built-in data types is listed in Table 8.1.[1]

TABLE 8.1 C++ Built-in Data Type Capabilities

Capability	Example
Define one or more variables of the data type.	`int a, b;`
Initialize a variable at definition.	`int a = 5;`
Assign a value to a variable.	`a = 10;`
Assign one variable's value to another variable.	`a = b;`
Perform mathematical operations.	`a + b`
Perform relational operations.	`a > b`
Convert from one data type to another.	`a = int (7.2);`

After examining Table 8.1, let's look at how all of this relates to abstract data types (ADTs). By definition, an **abstract data type** is simply a user-defined type that defines both a type of data and the operations that can be performed on it. Such user-defined data types are required when we wish to create objects that are more complex than simple integers and characters. If we are to create our own data types, we must be aware of both the type of data we are creating and the capabilities that we provide to initialize and manipulate the data.

As a specific example, assume that we are programming an application that uses dates extensively. Clearly, from a data standpoint, a date must be capable of accessing and storing a month, day, and year designation. Although from an implementation standpoint there are a number of means of storing a date, from a

---

[1] You might notice the absence of reading and writing operations. In both C and C++, except for very primitive operations, input and output are provided by standard library routines and class functions.

user viewpoint the actual implementation is not relevant. For example, a date can be stored as three integers, one for the month, day, and year, respectively. Alternatively, a single long integer in the form yyyymmdd can also be used. Using the long integer implementation, assuming the date 5/16/07 corresponds to 5/16/2007 it would be stored as the long integer 20070516. For sorting dates, the long integer format is very attractive because the numerical sequence of the dates corresponds to their calendar sequence.

The method of internally structuring the date, unfortunately, supplies only a partial answer to our programming effort. We must still supply a set of operations that can be used with dates. Clearly, such operations could include assigning values to a date, subtracting two dates to determine the number of days between them, comparing two dates to determine which is earlier and which is later, and displaying a date in a conventional form such as 05/16/07 rather than as 05/16/2007.

Notice that the details of how each operation works are dependent on how we choose to store a date (formally referred to as its data structure) and are only of interest to us as we develop each operation. For example, the implementation of comparing two dates differs if we store a date using a single long integer as opposed to using separate integers for the month, day, and year, respectively.

The combination of the storage structure used for dates with a set of available operations appropriate to dates would then define an abstract date data type. Once this data type is developed, programmers who want to use it need never be concerned with *how* dates are stored or *how* the operations are performed. All they need to know is *what* each operation does and *how* to invoke it, much as they use C++'s built-in operations. For example, we do not really care how the addition of two integers is performed but only that it is done correctly.

In C++, an abstract data type is referred to as a **class**. Construction of a class is inherently easy, and we already have all the necessary tools in variables and functions. What C++ provides is a mechanism for packaging these two items into a self-contained unit. Let's see how this is done.

Class Construction

A class defines both data and functions. This is usually accomplished by constructing a class in two parts, consisting of a declaration section and an implementation section. As illustrated in Figure 8.1, the declaration section declares both the data types and functions for the class. The implementation section is then used to define the functions whose prototypes have been declared in the declaration

---

FIGURE 8.1   Format of a Class Definition

```
// class declaration section
class ClassName
{
    data members
        (variables)
    function members
        (prototypes)
};

// class implementation section
function definitions
```

section.[2] When a function is part of a class it is formally referred to as a **method** to clearly denote class membership. Frequently, however, you will still hear it referred to as a function.

Both the variables and functions listed in the class declaration section are collectively referred to as **class members**. Individually, the variables are referred to as both **data members** and **instance variables** (the terms are synonymous), whereas the functions are referred to as **member methods**. A member method name may not be the same as a data member name.

As a specific example of a class, consider the definition for a class named Date. This type of class is very important in financial programs where the calculation of settlement dates, interest payments, and dividend payments all depend on date determinations. Using such a class, the determination of whether a date falls on a weekend or holiday, for example, are easily answered.

```cpp
//--- class declaration section

class Date
{
  private:        // notice the colon after the word private
    int month;    // a data member
    int day;      // a data member
    int year;     // a data member
  public:         // again, notice the colon here
    Date(int = 7, int = 4, int = 2005);    // a member method - the constructor
    void setdate(int, int, int);  // a member method
    void showdate();              // a member method
};

//--- class implementation section

Date::Date(int mm, int dd, int yyyy)
{
  month = mm;
  day = dd;
  year = yyyy;
}

void Date::setdate(int mm, int dd, int yyyy)
{
  month = mm;
  day = dd;
  year = yyyy;

  return;
}

void Date::showdate()
{
  cout << "The date is ";
  cout << setfill ('0')
       << setw(2) << month << '/'
       << setw(2) << day << '/'
       << setw(2) << year % 100; // extract the last 2 year digits
  cout << endl;
  return;
}
```

---

[2] This separation into two parts is not mandatory because the implementation can be included within the declaration section, as described in the next section.

This definition may initially look overwhelming, but start simply by noticing that it does consist of two sections—a declaration section and an implementation section. Now consider each of these sections individually.

A class **declaration section** begins with the keyword `class` followed by a class name. Following the class name are the class's variable declarations and method prototypes, enclosed in a brace pair that is terminated with a semicolon. Thus, the general structure of the form that we have used is:[3]

```
class Name
{
  private:
    a list of variable declarations
  public:
    a list of function prototypes
};
```

Notice that this format is followed by our `Date` class, which for convenience we have listed below with no internal comments:

```
//--- class declaration section

class Date
{
  private:
    int month;
    int day;
    int year;
  public:
    Date(int = 7, int = 4, int = 2005);
    void setdate(int, int, int);
    void showdate();
};     // this is a declaration - don't forget the semicolon
```

The name of this class is `Date`. Although the initial capital letter is not required, it is conventionally used to designate a class. The body of the declaration section, which is enclosed within braces, consists of variable and function declarations. In this case, the data members `month`, `day`, and `year` are declared as integers and three functions named `Date()`, `setdate()`, and `showdate()` are declared via prototypes. The keywords `private` and `public` are access specifiers that define access rights. The `private` keyword specifies that the class members following, in this case the data members `month`, `day`, and `year`, may only be accessed by using the class functions (or friend functions, as will be discussed in Section 9.2).[4] The purpose of the `private` designation is specifically meant to enforce data security by requiring all access to private data members through the provided member functions. This type of access, which restricts a user from seeing how the data are actually stored, is referred to as **data hiding**. Once a class category such as `private` is designated, it remains in force until a new category is listed.

---

[3] Other forms are possible. Because this form is one of the most commonly used and easily understood, it serves as our standard model throughout the text.

[4] Note that the default membership category in a class is `private`, which means that this keyword can be omitted. In this text, we explicitly use the `private` designation to reinforce the idea of access restrictions inherent in class membership.

Specifically, we have chosen to store a date using three integers: one for the month, day, and year, respectively. In addition, we always store the year as a four-digit number. Thus, for example, we store the year 1998 as 1998 and not as 98. Making sure to store all years with their correct century designation eliminates a multitude of problems that can crop up if only the last two digits, such as 98, are stored. For example, the number of years between 1998 and 2006 can be quickly calculated as 2006-1998=8 years, while this same answer is not so easily obtained if only the year values 06 and 98 are used. We are sure of what the year 2006 refers to, whereas a two-digit value such as 06 could refer to either 1906 or 2006.

Following the `private` class data members, the method prototypes listed in the `Date` class have been declared as `public`. This means that these class methods *can* be called by any objects and functions not in the class. In general, all class functions should be public; as such they furnish the capabilities to manipulate the class variables from outside of the class. For our `Date` class, we have initially provided three functions named `Date()`, `setdate()`, and `showdate()`. Notice that one of these member functions has the same name, `Date`, as the class name. This particular function is referred to as a **constructor** function, and it has a specially defined purpose: It can be used to initialize class data members with values. The default values that are used for this function are the numbers 7, 4, and 2005, which, as we will shortly see, are used as the default `month`, `day`, and `year` values, respectively. One point to notice is that the default year is correctly represented as a four-digit integer that retains the century designation. Also notice that the constructor function has no return type, which is a requirement for this special function. The two remaining functions declared in our declaration example are `setdate()` and `showdate()`, both of which have been declared as returning no value (void). In the implementation section of the class, these three member functions are written to permit initialization, assignment, and display capabilities, respectively.

The **implementation section** of a class is where the member functions declared in the declaration section are written.[5] Figure 8.2 illustrates the general form of functions included in the implementation section. This format is correct for all functions except the constructor, which, as we have stated, has no return type.

FIGURE 8.2   Format of a Member Function

```
return-type ClassName::functionName(parameter list)
{
 function body
}
```

As shown in Figure 8.2, member methods defined in the implementation section have the same format as all user-written C++ functions with the addition of the class name and scope resolution operator, `::`, which identifies the method as a member of a particular class. Let us now reconsider the implementation section of our `Date` class, which is repeated below for convenience:

---

[5]It is also possible to define these functions within the declaration section by declaring and writing them as inline functions. Examples of inline member functions are presented in Section 8.2.

```
//--- class implementation section

Date::Date(int mm, int dd, int yyyy)
{
  month = mm;
  day = dd;
  year = yyyy;
}

void Date::setdate(int mm, int dd, int yyyy)
{
  month = mm;
  day = dd;
  year = yyyy;

  return;
}

void Date::showdate()
{
  cout << "The date is ";
  cout << setfill ('0')
       << setw(2) << month << '/'
       << setw(2) << day << '/'
       << setw(2) << year % 100; // extract the last 2 year digits
  cout << endl;
  return;
}
```

Notice that the first function in this implementation section has the same name as the class, which makes it a constructor function. Hence, it has no return type. The Date:: included at the beginning of the function header line identifies this function as a member of the Date class. The rest of the header line:

Date(int mm, int dd, int yyyy)

defines the function as having three integer parameters. The body of this function simply assigns the data member's month, day, and year with the values of the parameters mm, dd, and yyyy, respectively.

The next function header line:

void Date::setdate(int mm, int dd, int yyyy)

defines this as the setdate() function belonging to the Date class (Date::). This function returns no value (void) and expects three integer parameters, mm, dd, and yyyy. In a manner similar to the Date() function, the body of this function assigns the data member's month, day, and year with the values of these parameters.

Finally, the last function header line in the implementation section defines a function named showdate(). This function has no parameters, returns no value, and is a member of the Date class. The body of this function, however, needs a little more explanation.

Although we have chosen to internally store all years as four-digit values that retain century information, users are accustomed to seeing dates where the year is represented as a two-digit value, such as 12/15/99. To display the last two digits of the year value, the expression year % 100 can be used. For example, if the year is 1999, the expression 1999 % 100 yields the value 99, and if the year is 2006, the expression

2006 % 100 yields the value 6. Notice that if we had used an assignment such as year = year % 100; we would actually be altering the stored value of year to correspond to the last two digits of the year. Since we want to retain the year as a four-digit number, we must be careful only to manipulate the displayed value using the expression year % 100 within the cout stream. The setfill and setw manipulators are used to ensure that the displayed values correspond to conventionally accepted dates. For example, the date March 9, 2006 should appear as either 3/9/06 or 03/09/06. The setw manipulator forces each value to be displayed in a field width of two. Since this manipulator only remains in effect for the next insertion, we have included it before the display of each date value. As the setfill manipulator, however, remains in effect until the fill character is changed, we only have to include it once.[6] We have used the setfill manipulator here to change the fill character from its default of a blank space to the character 0. Doing this ensures that a date such as December 9, 2006 appears as 12/09/06 and not 12/ 9/ 6.

To see how our Date class can be used within the context of a complete program, consider Program 8.1. To make the program easier to read, it has been shaded in lighter and darker areas. The lighter area contains the class declaration and implementation sections that we have already considered. The darker area contains the header and main() function. For convenience, we will retain this shading convention for all programs using classes.[7]

The declaration and implementation sections contained in the lighter shaded region of Program 8.1 should look familiar to you because they contain the class declaration and implementation sections that we have already discussed. Notice, however, that this region only declares the class; it does not create any variables of this class type. This is true of all C++ types, including the built-in types such as integers and doubles. Just as a variable of an integer type must be defined, variables of a user-declared class must also be defined. Variables defined to be of a user-declared class are referred to as **objects**.

Using this new terminology, the first statement in Program 8.1's main() function, contained in the darker area, defines three objects, named a, b, and c, to be of class type Date. In C++, whenever a new object is defined, memory is allocated for the object, and its data members are automatically initialized. This is done by an automatic call to the class constructor function. For example, consider the definition Date a, b, c(4,1,2000); contained in main(). When the object named a is defined, the constructor function Date is automatically called. Because no arguments have been assigned to a, the default values of the constructor function are used, resulting in the initialization:

```
a.month = 7
a.day = 4
a.year = 2005
```

----

[6] This type of information is easily obtained using the on-line Help facility.

[7] This shading is not accidental. In practice, the lighter shaded region containing the class definition would be placed in a separate file. A single #include statement would then be used to include this class declaration in the program. Thus, the final program would consist of the two darker shaded regions illustrated in Program 8.1 with the addition of one more #include statement in the first region.

PROGRAM 8.1

```cpp
#include <iostream>
#include <iomanip>
using namespace std;

// class declaration

class Date
{
  private:
    int month;
    int day;
    int year;
  public:
    Date(int = 7, int = 4, int = 2005);        // constructor
    void setdate(int, int, int); // member function to copy a date
    void showdate();              // member function to display a date
};

// implementation section

Date::Date(int mm, int dd, int yyyy)
{
  month = mm;
  day = dd;
  year = yyyy;
}

void Date::setdate(int mm, int dd, int yyyy)
{
  month = mm;
  day = dd;
  year = yyyy;

  return;
}

void Date::showdate()
{
  cout << "The date is ";
  cout << setfill('0')
       << setw(2) << month << '/'
       << setw(2) << day << '/'
       << setw(2) << year % 100; // extract the last 2 year digits
  cout << endl;

  return;
}

int main()
{
  Date a, b, c(4,1,2000);  // declare 3 objects - initializes 1 of them

  b.setdate(12,25,2006);   // assign values to b's data members
  a.showdate();            // display object a's values
  b.showdate();            // display object b's values
  c.showdate();            // display object c's values

  return 0;
}
```

Notice the notation that we have used here. It consists of an object name and an attribute name separated by a period. This is the standard syntax for referring to an object's attribute, namely

```
objectName.attributeName
```

where `objectName` is the name of a specific object and `attributeName` is the name of a data member defined for the object's class. Thus, the notation `a.month = 7` refers to the fact that object a's `month` data member has been set to the value 7. Similarly, the notation `a.day = 4` and `a.year = 2005` refers to the fact that a's `day` and `year` data members have been set to the values 4 and 2005, respectively. In the same manner, when the object named b is defined, the same default arguments are used, resulting in the initialization of b's data members as:

```
b.month = 7
b.day = 4
b.year = 2005
```

The object named c, however, is defined with the arguments 4, 1, and 2000. These three arguments are passed into the constructor function when the object is defined, resulting in the initialization of c's data members as:

```
c.month = 4
c.day = 1
c.year = 2000
```

The next statement in `main()`, `b.setdate(12,25,2006)`, calls b's `setdate` function, which assigns the values 12, 25, and 2006 to b's data members, resulting in the assignment:

```
b.month = 12
b.day = 25
b.year = 2006
```

Notice the syntax for referring to an object's function. This syntax is

```
objectName.functionName(parameters)
```

where `objectName` is the name of a specific object and `functionName` is the name of one of the functions defined for the object's class. Since we have defined all class functions as `public`, a statement such as `b.setdate(12,25,2006)` is valid inside the `main()` function and is a call to the class's `setdate()` function. This statement tells the `setdate()` function to operate on the b object with the parameters 12, 25, and 2006. It is important to understand that because all class data members were specified as `private`, a statement such as `b.month = 12` is invalid from within `main()`. We are, therefore, forced to rely on member functions to access data member values.

The last three statements in `main()` call the `showdate()` function to operate on the a, b, and c objects. The first call results in the display of a's data values, the second call in the display of b's data values, and the third call in the display of c's data values. Thus, the output of Program 8.1 is:

```
The date is 07/04/05
The date is 12/25/06
The date is 04/01/00
```

Notice that a statement such as `cout << a;` is invalid within `main()` because `cout` does not know how to handle an object of class `Date`. Thus, we have sup-

▲ P O I N T   O F   I N F O R M A T I O N ▲

Interfaces, Implementations, and Information Hiding

The terms *interface* and *implementation* are used extensively in object-oriented programming literature. Each of these terms can be equated to specific parts of a class's declaration and implementation sections.

An *interface* consists of a class's public member function declarations and any supporting comments. Thus, the interface should be all that is required to tell a programmer how to use the class.

The *implementation* consists of both the class's implementation section, which consists of both private and public member definitions, *and* the class's private data members, which are contained in a class's declaration section.

The implementation is the essential means of providing information hiding. In its most general context, *information hiding* refers to the principle that *how* a class is internally constructed is not relevant to any programmer who wishes to use the class. That is, the implementation can and should be hidden from all class users precisely to ensure that the class is not altered or compromised in any way. All that a programmer need know to use the class correctly should be provided by the interface.

plied our class with a function that can be used to access and display an object's internal values.

Terminology

Because confusion sometimes arises about classes, objects, and other terminology associated with object-oriented programming, we will take a moment to clarify and review some terms. (Review Section 1.5 for additional information.)

A *class* is a programmer-defined data type out of which objects can be created. *Objects* are created from classes; they have the same relationship to classes as variables do to C++'s built-in data types. For example, in the declaration

```
int a;
```

a is said to be a variable, whereas in Program 8.1's declaration

```
Date a;
```

a is said to be an object. If it initially helps you to think of an object as a variable, do so.

Objects are also referred to as **instances of a class**, and the process of creating a new object is frequently referred to as an **instantiation** of the object. Each time a new object is instantiated (created), a new set of data members belonging to the object is created.[8] Individually, each data member represents an attribute of interest that is modeled by the class. The particular values contained in these data members for each object determine the object's **state**.

Seen in this way, a class can be thought of as a blueprint out of which particular instances (objects) can be created. Each instance (object) of a class will have its own set of particular values for the set of data members specified in the class declaration section.

---

[8] Note that only one set of class functions is created. These functions are shared between objects. The mechanism for using the same function on different objects' data members is presented in Section 10.3.

In addition to the data types allowed for an object, a class also defines **behavior**—that is, the operations that are permitted to be performed on an object's data members. Users of the object need to know *what* these functions can do and how to activate them through function calls, but unless run-time or space implications are relevant, they do not need to know *how* the operation is done. The actual implementation details of an object's operations are contained in the class implementation, which can be hidden from the user. Other names for the operations defined in a class implementation section are *procedures*, *functions*, *services*, and *methods*. We use these terms interchangeably throughout the remainder of the text.

Exercises 8.1

1. Define the following terms:

   a. class
   b. object
   c. declaration section
   d. implementation section
   e. instance variable
   f. member function
   g. data member
   h. constructor
   i. class instance
   j. services
   k. methods
   l. interface

2. Write a class declaration section for each of the following specifications. In each case, include a prototype for a constructor and a member function named `showdata()` that can be used to display member values.

   a. A class named `Time` that has integer data members named `secs`, `mins`, and `hours`.

   b. A class named `Complex` that has double-precision data members named `real` and `imaginary`.

   c. A class named `Circle` that has integer data members named `xcenter` and `ycenter` and a double-precision data member named `radius`.

   d. A class named `System` that has character data members named `computer`, `printer`, and `screen`, each capable of holding 30 characters (including the end-of-string `NULL`), and double-precision data members named `compPrice`, `printPrice`, and `scrnPrice`.

3. a. Construct a class implementation section for the constructor and `showdate()` function members corresponding to the class declaration created for Exercise 2a.

   b. Construct a class implementation section for the constructor and `showdate()` function members corresponding to the class declaration created for Exercise 2b.

   c. Construct a class implementation section for the constructor and `showdate()` function members corresponding to the class declaration created for Exercise 2c.

   d. Construct a class implementation section for the constructor and `showdate()` function members corresponding to the class declaration created for Exercise 2d.

4. a. Include the class declaration and implementation sections prepared for Exercises 2a and 3a in a complete working program.

   b. Include the class declaration and implementation sections prepared for Exercises 2b and 3b in a complete working program.

   c. Include the class declaration and implementation sections prepared for Exercises 2c and 3c in a complete working program.

   d. Include the class declaration and implementation sections prepared for Exercises 2d and 3d in a complete working program.

5. Determine the errors in the following class declaration section:

```
class employee
{
public:
   int empnum;
   char code;
private:
   class(int = 0);
   void showemp(int, char);
};
```

6. a. Add another member function named `convrt()` to the Date class in Program 8.1 that does the following: The function should access the `month`, `year`, and `day` data members and display and then return a long integer that is calculated as *year * 10000 + month * 100 + day*. For example, if the date is 4/1/2006, the returned value is 20060401. (Dates in this form are useful when performing sorts because placing the numbers in numerical order automatically places the corresponding dates in chronological order.)

   b. Include the modified Date class constructed for Exercise 6a in a complete C++ program.

7. a. Add an additional member function to Program 8.1's class definition named `leapyr()` that returns `true` when the year is a leap year and 0 if it is not. A leap year is any year that is evenly divisible by 4 but not evenly divisible by 100, with the exception that all years evenly divisible by 400 are leap years. For example, the year 2004 is a leap year because it is evenly divisible by 4 and not evenly divisible by 100. The year 2000 is a leap year because it is evenly divisible by 400.

   b. Include the class definition constructed for Exercise 7a in a complete C++ program. The `main()` function should display the message `The year is a leap year` or `The year is not a leap year` depending on the date object's year value.

8. Modify the Date class in Program 8.1 to contain a function that compares two Date objects and returns the later of the two. The function should be written according to the following algorithm:

   Comparison function
   　　Accept two Date values as arguments
   　　Determine the later date using the following procedure:
   　　　　Convert each date into an integer value having the form yyyymmdd
   　　　　This can be accomplished by using the algorithm described in Exercise 6a; compare the corresponding integers for each date; the larger integer corresponds to the later date.
   　　Return the later date

9. a. Add a member function to Program 8.1's class definition named `dayOfWeek()` that determines the day of the week for any date object. An algorithm for determining the day of the week is known as Zeller's algorithm. This algorithm assumes a date of the form mm/dd/ccyy, where mm is the month, dd is the day, cc is the century, and yy is the year in the century (for example, in the date 12/28/2000, mm = 12, dd= 28, cc = 20, and yy = 0).

   If the mm is less than 3,
   　　Set mm = mm + 12 and ccyy = ccyy–1
   EndIf
   Set cc = int(ccyy/100)
   Set year = ccyy % 100
   *Set the variable T = dd + int(26 * (mm+1)/10) + yy + int(yy/4) + int(cc/4) – 2 * cc*
   dayOfWeek = T % 7
   If dayOfWeek is less than 0
   　　dayOfWeek = dayOfWeek +7
   EndIf

   Using this algorithm the variable `dayOfWeek()` has a value of 0 if the date is a Saturday, 1 if a Sunday, etc.

b. Include the class definition constructed for Exercise 9a in a complete C++ program. The `main()` function should display the name of the day (Sun, Mon, Tue, etc.) for the `Date` object being tested.

8.2 CONSTRUCTORS

A *constructor* function is any function that has the same name as its class. Multiple constructors can be defined for each class as long as they are distinguishable by the number and types of their parameters.

The intended purpose of a constructor is to initialize a new object's data members. Thus, depending on the number and types of supplied arguments, one constructor function is automatically called each time an object is created. If no constructor function is written, the compiler supplies a default constructor. In addition to its initialization role, a constructor function may also perform other tasks when it is called and can be written in a variety of ways. In this section, we present the possible variations of constructor functions and introduce another function, the destructor, which is automatically called whenever an object goes out of existence.

Figure 8.3 illustrates the general format of a constructor. As shown in this figure, a constructor:

- must have the same name as the class to which it belongs
- must have no return type (not even void)

If you do not include a constructor in your class definition, the compiler supplies a do-nothing default one for you. For example, consider the following class declaration:

```cpp
class Date
{
  private:
    int month, day, year;
  public
    void setdate(int, int, int);
    void showdate();
};
```

Because no user-defined constructor has been declared here, the compiler creates a default constructor. For our `Date` class, this default constructor is equivalent to the implementation `Date(void){}`—that is, the compiler-supplied default constructor expects no parameters and has an empty body. Clearly, this default constructor is not very useful, but it does exist if no other constructor is declared.

FIGURE 8.3   Constructor Format

```cpp
ClassName::ClassName(parameter list)
{
 function body
}
```

The term **default constructor** is used quite frequently in C++. It refers to any constructor that does not require any parameters when it is called. This can be because no parameters are declared, which is the case for the compiler-supplied default, or because all parameters have been given default values. For example, the prototype Date(int = 7, int = 4, int = 2005) is valid for a default constructor. Here, each argument has been given a default value, and, when the corresponding constructor is written, an object can be declared as type Date without supplying any further arguments. Using such a constructor, the declaration Date a; initializes the a object with the default values 7, 4, and 2005.

To verify that a constructor function is automatically called whenever a new object is created, consider Program 8.2. Notice that in the implementation section the constructor function uses cout to display the message Created a new data object with data values. Thus, whenever the constructor is called, this message is displayed. Since the main() function creates three objects, the constructor is called three times, and the message is displayed three times.

PROGRAM 8.2

```cpp
#include <iostream>
using namespace std;

// class declaration section

class Date
{
  private:
    int month;
    int day;
    int year;
  public:
    Date (int = 7, int = 4, int = 2005);       // constructor
};

// implementation section

Date::Date(int mm, int dd, int yyyy)
{
  month = mm;
  day = dd;
  year = yyyy;
  cout << "Created a new data object with data values "
       << month << ", " << day << ", " << year << endl;
}

int main()
{
  Date a;                // declare an object
  Date b;                // declare an object
  Date c(4,1,2006);      // declare an object

  return 0;
}
```

The following output is produced when Program 8.2 is executed:

```
Created a new data object with data values 7, 4, 2005
Created a new data object with data values 7, 4, 2005
Created a new data object with data values 4, 1, 2006
```

Although any legitimate C++ statement can be used within a constructor function, such as the `cout` statement used in Program 8.2, it is best to keep constructors simple and use them only for initialization purposes. One further point needs to be made with respect to the constructor function in Program 8.2. According to the rules of C++, object members are initialized in the order in which they are declared in the class declaration section and *not* in the order in which they may appear in the function's definition within the implementation section. Usually, this is not an issue, unless one member is initialized using another data member's value.

Calling Constructors

As we have seen, constructors are called whenever an object is created. The actual declaration, however, can be made in a variety of ways. For example, the declaration

```
Date c(4,1,2006);
```

in Program 8.2 could also have been written as:

```
Date c = Date(4,1,2006);
```

This second form declares `c` as being of type `Date` and then makes a direct call to the constructor function with the arguments 4, 1, and 2006. This second form can be simplified when only one argument is passed to the constructor. For example, if only the `month` data member of the `c` object needed to be initialized with the value 8 and the `day` and `year` members can use the default values, the object can be created using the declaration:

```
Date c = 8;
```

Since this resembles declarations in C, it and its more complete form using the equal sign are referred to as the **C style of initialization**. The form of declaration in Program 8.2 is referred to as the **C++ style of initialization** and is the form we use predominantly throughout the remainder of the text.

Regardless of which initialization form you use, in no case should an object be declared with empty parentheses. For example, the declaration `Date a();` is not the same as the declaration `Date a;`. The latter declaration uses the default constructor values, while the former declaration results in no object being created.

Overloaded and Inline Constructors

The primary difference between a constructor and other user-written functions is how the constructor is called: Constructors are called automatically each time an object is created, whereas other functions must be explicitly called by name.[9] As a function, however, a constructor must still follow all of the rules applicable to user-written functions that were presented in Chapter 6. This means that constructors may have default argument values, as illustrated in Programs 8.1 and 8.2, may be overloaded, and may be written as inline functions.

---

[9] This is true for all functions except destructors, which are described later in this section. A destructor function is automatically called each time an object is destroyed.

Recall from Section 6.1 that function overloading permits the same function name to be used with different parameter lists. Based on the supplied argument types, the compiler determines which function to use when the call is encountered. Let's see how this can be applied to our `Date` class. For convenience, the appropriate class declaration is repeated below:

```
// class declaration section
class Date
{
  private:
    int month;
    int day;
    int year;
  public:
    Date(int = 7, int = 4, int = 2005);    // constructor
};
```

Here, the constructor prototype specifies three integer values, which are used to initialize the `month`, `day`, and `year` data members.

An alternate method of specifying a date is to use a long integer in the form *year * 10000 + month * 100 + day*. For example, the date 12/24/2005 using this form is 20051224 and the date 2/5/2006 is 20060205.[10] A suitable prototype for a constructor that uses dates of this form is:

```
Date(long); // an overloaded constructor
```

Here, the constructor is declared as receiving one long integer value. The code for this new `Date` function must, of course, correctly convert its single argument value into a month, day, and year, and is included within the class implementation section. The code for such a constructor is:

```
Date::Date(long yyyymmdd) // a second constructor
{
  year = int(yyyymmdd/10000.0);      // extract the year
  month = int( (yyyymmdd - year * 10000.0) / 100.00 ); // extract the month
  day = int(yyyymmdd - year * 10000.0 - month * 100.0); // extract the day
}
```

Do not be overly concerned with the conversion code within the function's body. The important point here is the concept of overloading the `Date()` function to provide two constructors. Program 8.3 contains a complete class definition that uses this new constructor function within the context of a working program.

The output provided by Program 8.3 is:

```
The date is 07/04/05
The date is 04/01/98
The date is 05/15/06
```

---

[10] The reasons for specifying dates in this manner are that only one number needs to be used per date and that sorting the numbers automatically puts the corresponding dates into chronological order.

PROGRAM 8.3

```cpp
#include <iostream>
#include <iomanip>
using namespace std;

// class declaration

class Date
{
  private:
    int month;
    int day;
    int year;
  public:
    Date(int = 7, int = 4, int = 2005);     // constructor
    Date(long);              // another constructor
    void showdate();       // member function to display a date
};

// implementation section

Date::Date(int mm, int dd, int yyyy)
{
  month = mm;
  day = dd;
  year = yyyy;
}

Date::Date(long yyyymmdd)
{
  year = int(yyyymmdd/10000.0);     // extract the year
  month = int( (yyyymmdd - year * 10000.0)/100.00 ); // extract the month
  day = int(yyyymmdd - year * 10000.0 - month * 100.0); // extract the day
}

void Date::showdate()
{
  cout << "The date is ";
  cout << setfill ('0')
       << setw(2) << month << '/'
       << setw(2) << day << '/'
       << setw(2) << year % 100; // extract the last 2 year digits
  cout << endl;

  return;
}

int main()
{
  Date a, b(4,1,1998), c(20060515L); // declare three objects

  a.showdate();     // display object a's values
  b.showdate();     // display object b's values
  c.showdate();     // display object c's values

  return 0;
}
```

Constructors

A *constructor* is any function that has the same name as its class. The primary purpose of a constructor is to initialize an object's member variables when an object is created. Hence, a constructor is automatically called when an object is declared.

A class can have multiple constructors provided that each constructor is distinguishable by having a different parameter list. A compiler error results when unique identification of a constructor is not possible. If no constructor is provided, the compiler supplies a do-nothing default constructor.

Every constructor function must be declared with *no return type* (not even void). Since they are functions, constructors may also be explicitly called in nondeclarative statements. When used in this manner, the function call requires parentheses following the constructor name, even if no parameters are used. However, when used in a declaration, parentheses *must not* be included for a zero parameter constructor. For example, the declaration Date a(); is incorrect. The correct declaration is Date a;. When parameters are used, however, they must be enclosed within parentheses in both declarative and nondeclarative statements. Default parameter values should be included within the constructor's prototype.

Three objects are created in Program 8.3's main() function. The first object, a, is initialized with the default constructor using its default argument values. Object b is also initialized with the default constructor, but it uses the argument values 4, 1, and 1998. Finally, object c, which is initialized with a long integer, uses the second constructor in the class implementation section. The compiler knows that it should use this second constructor because the argument specified, 20060515L, is clearly designated as a long integer. It is worthwhile pointing out that a compiler error occurs if both Date constructors had default values. In such a case, a declaration such as Date d; is considered ambiguous by the compiler because it is not able to determine which constructor to use. Thus, in each implementation section, only one constructor can be written as the default.

Just as constructors may be overloaded, they may also be written as **inline member functions.** Doing so simply means defining the function in the class declaration section. For example, making both of the constructors in Program 8.3 inline is accomplished by the declaration section:

```
// class declaration

class Date
{
  private:
    int month;
    int day;
    int year;
  public:
    Date(int mm = 7, int dd = 4, int yyyy = 2005)
    {
      month = mm;
      day = dd;
      year = yyyy;
    }
    Date(long yyyymmdd)   // here is the overloaded constructor
    {
      year = int(yyyymmdd/10000.0);    // extract the year
      month = int( (yyyymmdd - year * 10000.0)/100.00 );  // extract the month
      day = int(yyyymmdd - year * 10000.0 - month * 100.0); // extract the day
    }
};
```

▲ **P O I N T   O F   I N F O R M A T I O N** ▲

Accessor and Mutator Functions

An *accessor function* is any nonconstructor member function that accesses a class's private data members for purposes of retrieval or display. For example, the function `showdate()` in the `Date` class is an accessor function. Such functions are extremely important because they provide a means of displaying private data members' stored values.

When you construct a class, make sure to provide a complete set of accessor functions. Each accessor function does not have to return a data member's exact value, but it should return a useful representation of the value. For example, assume that a date such as 12/25/2006 is stored as a long integer member variable in the form 20062512. Although an accessor function could display this value, a more useful representation typically is either 12/25/06, or December 25, 2006.

A mutator function, or mutator for short, is any nonconstructor function that accesses a class's private data members for purposes of altering their stored values. As such, mutator functions can also provide a means of data input. For example, the `setdate()` function in the `Date` class is an example of mutator function. As we will see in Section 9.6, both the extraction and insertion operators can be overloaded to provide another means of object data input and output. Constructor functions, whose primary purpose is to initialize an object's member variables, are not considered as either accessor or mutator functions.

The keyword `inline` is not required in this declaration because member functions defined inside the class declaration are inline by default.

Generally, only functions that can be coded on a single line are good candidates for inline functions. This reinforces the convention that inline functions should be small. Thus, the first constructor is more conventionally written as:

```
Date(int mm = 7, int dd = 4, int yyyy = 2005)
{ month = mm; day = dd; year = yyyy; }
```

The second constructor, which extends over three lines, should not be written as an inline function.

Destructors

The counterpart to constructor functions is destructor functions. **Destructors** are functions that have the same class name as constructors, but are preceded by a tilde (~). Thus, for our `Date` class, the destructor name is `~Date()`. Like constructors, a default do-nothing destructor is provided by the C++ compiler in the absence of an explicit destructor. Unlike constructors, however, there can only be one destructor function per class. This is because destructors take no arguments and return no values.

Destructors are automatically called whenever an object goes out of existence and are meant to "clean up" any undesirable effects that might be left by the object. Generally, such effects only occur when an object contains a pointer member, which is the topic of Section 10.5.

Exercises 8.2

1. Determine whether the following statements are true or false:

   a. A constructor function must have the same name as its class.

   b. A class can only have one constructor function.

   c. A class can only have one default constructor function.

   d. A default constructor can only be supplied by the compiler.

e. A default constructor can have no parameters or all parameters must have default values.

f. A constructor must be declared for each class.

g. A constructor must be declared with a return type.

h. A constructor is automatically called each time an object is created.

i. A class can have only one destructor function.

j. A destructor must have the same name as its class, preceded by a tilde (~).

k. A destructor can have default argument values.

l. A destructor must be declared for each class.

m. A destructor must be declared with a return type.

n. A destructor is automatically called each time an object goes out of existence.

o. Destructors are not useful when the class contains a pointer data member.

2. For Program 8.3, what date is initialized for object `c` if the declaration `Date c(2006);` is used in place of the declaration `Date c(20060515L);`?

3. Modify Program 8.3 so that the only data member of the class is a long integer named `yyyymmdd`. Do this by substituting the declaration

```
long yyyymmdd;
```

for the existing declarations:

```
int month;
int day;
int year;
```

Then, using the same constructor function prototypes currently declared in the class declaration section, rewrite them so that the `Date(long)` function becomes the default constructor and the `Date(int, int, int)` function converts a month, day, and year into the proper form for the class data member.

4. a. Construct a `Time` class containing integer data members `seconds`, `minutes`, and `hours`. The class should contain two constructors: The first should be a default constructor having the prototype `Time(int, int, int)`, which uses default values of 0 for each data member. The second constructor should accept a long integer representing a total number of seconds and disassemble the long integer into hours, minutes, and seconds. The final function member should display the class data members.

   b. Include the class written for Exercise 4a within the context of a complete program.

5. a. Construct a class named `Student` consisting of an integer student identification number, an array of five floating-point grades, and an integer representing the total number of grades entered. The constructor for this class should initialize all `Student` data members to zero. Included in the class should be member functions to (1) enter a student ID number, (2) enter a single test grade and update the total number of grades entered, and (3) compute an average grade and display the student ID followed by the average grade.

   b. Include the class constructed in Exercise 5a within the context of a complete program. Your program should declare two objects of type `Student` and accept and display data for the two objects to verify operation of the member functions.

8.3 FOCUS ON PROBLEM SOLVING

Now that you have an understanding of how classes are constructed and the terminology used to describe them, let us apply this knowledge to two new applications. In the first application, we construct a single elevator object. We assume that the elevator can travel between the first and fifteenth floors of a building and that the location of the elevator must be known at all times. In the second application, we simulate the operation of a gas pump.

Problem 1: Constructing an Elevator Object

In this application, you are required to simulate the operation of an elevator. Output is required that describes the current floor on which the elevator is stationed or is passing. Additionally, an internal elevator button that is pushed as a request to move to another floor should be provided. The elevator can travel between the first and fifteenth floors of the building in which it is situated.

Analyze the Problem   For this application, we have one object, an elevator. The only attribute of interest is its location. A rider can request a change in the elevator's position (state). Additionally, we must be able to establish the initial floor position when a new elevator is put in service. Figure 8.4 illustrates an object diagram that includes both the required attributes and operations.

FIGURE 8.4   An Elevator Class Diagram

Elevator
Floor location
Initialize the floor position
Request a new floor

Develop a Solution   For this application, the location of the elevator, which corresponds to its current floor position, can be represented by an integer member variable whose value ranges between 1 and 15. The value of this variable, which we name `currentFloor`, effectively represents the current state of the elevator. The services that we provide for changing the state of the elevator are an initialization function to set the initial floor position when a new elevator is put in service and a request function to change the elevator's position (state) to a new floor. Putting an elevator in service is accomplished by declaring a single class instance (declaring an object of type `Elevator`), and requesting a new floor position is equivalent to pushing an elevator button.

The response to the elevator button should be as follows:

If a request is made for either a nonexistent floor or the current floor,
    Do nothing
Else if the request is for a floor above the current floor,
    Display the current floor number
    While not at the designated floor
        Increment the floor number
        Display the new floor number
    End While
    Display the ending floor number
Else   // the request must be for a floor below the current floor

(continued from previous page)

> *Display the current floor number*
> *While not at the designated floor*
>> *Decrement the floor number*
>> *Display the new floor number*
> *End While*
> *Display the ending floor number*

EndIf

Code the Solution   From the design, a suitable class declaration is:

```
// class declaration section
class Elevator
{
  private:
    int currentFloor;
  public:
    Elevator(int = 1);       // constructor
    void request(int);
};
```

Notice that we have declared one data member, `currentFloor`, and two class functions. The data member `currentFloor` is used to store the current floor position of the elevator. As a private member, it can only be accessed through member functions. The two declared public member functions, `Elevator()` and `request()`, are used to define the external services provided by each `Elevator` object. The `Elevator()` function, which has the same name as its class, becomes a constructor function that is automatically called when an object of type `Elevator` is created. We use this function to initialize the starting floor position of the elevator. The `request()` function is used to alter its position. To accomplish these services, a suitable class implementation section is:

```
// class implementation section

Elevator::Elevator(int cfloor)    // constructor
{
  currentFloor = cfloor;
}

void Elevator::request(int newfloor)  // access function
{
  if (newfloor < 1 ||  newfloor > MAXFLOOR || newfloor == currentFloor)
    ;  // do nothing
  else if ( newfloor > currentFloor)  // move elevator up
  {
    cout << "\nStarting at floor " << currentFloor << endl;
    while (newfloor > currentFloor)
    {
      currentFloor++;    // add one to current floor
      cout << "   Going Up - now at floor " << currentFloor << endl;
    }
    cout << "Stopping at floor " << currentFloor << endl;
  }
  else  // move elevator down
  {
```

(continued from previous page)

```
      cout << "\nStarting at floor " << currentFloor << endl;
      while (newfloor < currentFloor)
      {
        currentFloor--;   // subtract one from current floor
        cout << "   Going Down - now at floor " << currentFloor << endl;
      }
      cout << "Stopping at floor " << currentFloor << endl;
    }

  return;
  }
```

The constructor function is straightforward. When an `Elevator` object is declared, it is initialized to the floor specified; if no floor is explicitly given, the default value of 1 is used. For example, the declaration

`Elevator a(7);`

initializes the variable `a.currentFloor` to 7, whereas the declaration

`Elevator a;`

uses the default argument value and initializes the variable `a.currentFloor to 1`.

The `request()` function defined in the implementation section is more complicated and provides the class's primary service. Essentially, this function consists of an `if-else` statement having three parts: If an incorrect service is requested, no action is taken; if a floor above the current position is selected, the elevator is moved up; and if a floor below the current position is selected, the elevator is moved down. For movement up or down, the function uses a `while` loop to increment the position one floor at a time and reports the elevator's movement using a `cout` object stream. Program 8.4 includes this class in a working program.

Test and Correct the Program   Testing the `Elevator` class entails testing each class operation. To do this, we first include the `Elevator` class within the context of a working program, as given in Program 8.4.

PROGRAM 8.4

```
#include <iostream>
using namespace std;
const int MAXFLOOR = 15;

// class declaration

class Elevator
{
  private:
    int currentFloor;
  public:
    Elevator(int = 1);      // constructor
    void request(int);
};
```

(continued from previous page)

```cpp
// implementation section

Elevator::Elevator(int cfloor)
{
  currentFloor = cfloor;
}

void Elevator::request(int newfloor)
{
  if (newfloor < 1 || newfloor > MAXFLOOR || newfloor == currentFloor)
    ;   // do nothing
  else if ( newfloor > currentFloor)  // move elevator up
  {
    cout << "\nStarting at floor " << currentFloor << endl;
    while (newfloor > currentFloor)
    {
      currentFloor++;     // add one to current floor
      cout << "   Going Up - now at floor " << currentFloor << endl;
    }
    cout << "Stopping at floor " << currentFloor << endl;
  }
  else  // move elevator down
  {
    cout << "\nStarting at floor " << currentFloor << endl;
    while (newfloor < currentFloor)
    {
      currentFloor--;    // subtract one from current floor
      cout << "   Going Down - now at floor " << currentFloor << endl;
    }
    cout << "Stopping at floor " << currentFloor << endl;
  }

  return;
}
```

```cpp
int main()
{
  Elevator a;    // declare 1 object of type Elevator
  a.request(6);
  a.request(3);

  return 0;
}
```

The lightly shaded portion of Program 8.4 contains the class construction that we have already described. To see how this class is used, concentrate on the darker shaded section of the program. At the top of the program, we have included the `iostream` header file and declared a named constant `MAXFLOOR`, which corresponds to the highest floor that can be requested.

Within the `main()` function, three class function calls are included. The first statement creates an object named `a` of type `Elevator`. Since no explicit floor has been given, this elevator begins at floor 1, which is the default constructor argument.

A request is then made to move the elevator to floor 6, which is followed by a request to move to floor 3. The output produced by Program 8.4 is:

```
Starting at floor 1
    Going Up - now at floor 2
    Going Up - now at floor 3
    Going Up - now at floor 4
    Going Up - now at floor 5
    Going Up - now at floor 6
Stopping at floor 6

Starting at floor 6
    Going Down - now at floor 5
    Going Down - now at floor 4
    Going Down - now at floor 3
Stopping at floor 3
```

The basic requirements of object-oriented programming are evident in even as simple a program as Program 8.4. Before the `main()` function can be written, a useful class must be constructed. This is typical of programs that use objects. For such programs, the design process is front-loaded with the requirement that careful consideration of the class—its declaration and implementation—be given. Code contained in the implementation section effectively removes code that would otherwise be part of `main()`'s responsibility. Thus, any program that uses the object does not have to repeat the implementation details within its `main()` function. Rather, the `main()` function [and any function called by `main()`] is only concerned with sending messages to its objects to activate them appropriately. How the object responds to the messages and how the state of the object is retained are not `main()`'s concern; these details are hidden within the class construction.

One further point should be made concerning Program 8.4. Note that control is provided by the `main()` function. This control is sequential, with two calls made to the same object operation, using different argument values. This control is perfectly correct for testing purposes. However, by incorporating calls to `request()` within a `while` loop and using the random number function `rand()` to generate random floor requests, a continuous simulation of the elevator's operation is possible (see Exercise 3 at the end of this section).

Problem 2: A Single-Object Gas Pump Simulation

In this section, we present the first class required for a simulation that requires two separate classes. The first class, and the one developed in this section, models a gas pump. The second class, which completes the simulation and is developed in Section 9.6, models the arrival of multiple customers, each with various requests for differing amounts of gas to be pumped. The complete simulation is based on the following requirement:

We have been requested to write a program that simulates the operation of a gas pump. At any time during the simulation we should be able to determine, from the pump, the price per gallon of gas and the amount remaining in the supply tank from which the gas is pumped. If the amount of gas in the supply tank is greater than or equal to the amount of gas requested, the request should be filled; otherwise, only the available amount in the supply tank should be used. Once the gas is pumped, the total price of the gallons pumped should be displayed, and the amount of gas in gallons that was pumped should be subtracted from the amount in the supply tank.

For the simulation, assume that the pump is randomly idle between 1 to 15 minutes between customer arrivals and that a customer randomly requests between 3 and 20 gallons of gas. Although the default supply tank capacity is 500 gallons, assume that the initial amount of gas in the tank for this simulation is only 300 gallons. Initially, the program should simulate a one-half hour time frame.

Additionally, for each arrival and request for gas, we want to know the idle time before the customer arrived, how many gallons of gas were pumped, and the total price of the transaction. The pump itself must keep track of the price per gallon of gas and the amount of gas remaining in the supply tank. Typically, the price per gallon is $1.80, but the price for the simulation should be $2.00.

In developing this application, first notice that it involves two distinct object types. The first is a person who can arrive randomly between 1 and 15 minutes and can randomly request between 3 and 20 gallons of gas. The second object type is the gas pump. In this application, our goal will be to create a suitable gas pump class that can be used in the final simulation, which is completed in the next application.

The model for constructing a gas pump class that meets the requirements of the simulation is easily described in pseudocode as:

Put Pump *in Service*
  Initialize the amount of gas in the supply tank
  Initialize the price per gallon of gas

Display Values
  Display the amount of gas in the supply tank
  Display the price per gallon

Pump an Amount of Gas
  If the amount in the supply tank is greater than or equal to the requested amount
    Set the pumped amount of gas equal to the requested amount
  Else
    Set the pumped amount equal to the amount in the supply tank
  EndIf
  Subtract the pumped amount from the amount in the supply tank
  Calculate the total price as the price per gallon times the pumped amount
  Display the gallons of gas requested
  Display the gallons of gas pumped
  Display the amount remaining in the supply tank
  Display the total price for the amount of gas pumped

From the pseudocode description, the implementation of a `Pump` class is rather straightforward. The attributes of interest for the pump are the amount of gallons in the supply tank and the price per gallon. The required operations include supplying initial values for the pump's attributes, interrogating the pump for its attribute values, and satisfying a request for gas. The UML diagram for this class is shown as Figure 8.5.

FIGURE 8.5 `Pump` **Class UML Diagram**

```
                          Pump

  - amtInTank: double
  - price: double
  - AMOUNT_IN_TANK: static double = 500.0;
  - DEFAULT_PRICE: static double = 1.80;

  + Pump ( )
  + Pump (todaysPrice, amountInTank)
  + request (gallons)
  + getValues( )
```

Because the two attributes, the amount-in-the-tank and the price-per-gallon, can have fractional values, it is appropriate to make them double-precision values. Additionally, three services need to be provided. The first consists of initializing a pump's attributes, which consists of setting values for the amount in the supply tank and the price per gallon. The second consists of satisfying a request for gas, while the third service simply provides a reading of the pump's current attribute values. A suitable class definition that provides these services is:

PUMP.CPP

```cpp
#include <iostream>
#include <iomanip>
using namespace std;

const double AMOUNT_IN_TANK = 500;  // initial gallons in the tank
const double DEFAULT_PRICE = 1.80;  // price per gallon

class Pump
{
  // data declaration section
  private:
    double amtInTank;
    double price;

  // method declarations
  public:
    Pump(double = DEFAULT_PRICE, double = AMOUNT_IN_TANK);   // constructor
    void getValues();
    void request(double);
};

// methods implementation section

Pump::Pump(double todaysPrice, double amountInTank)
{
  amtInTank = amountInTank;
  price = todaysPrice;
}

void Pump::getValues()
{
  cout << "The gas tank has " << amtInTank << " gallons of gas." << endl;
  cout << "The price per gallon of gas is $" <<
setiosflags(ios::showpoint)
       << setprecision(2) << setiosflags(ios::fixed) << price << endl;
}

void Pump::request(double pumpAmt)
{
  double pumped;

  if (amtInTank >= pumpAmt)
    pumped = pumpAmt;
```

(continued from previous page)

```
  else
     pumped = amtInTank;

  amtInTank -= pumped;
  cout << pumpAmt << " gallons were requested " << endl;
  cout << pumped << " gallons were pumped" << endl;
  cout << amtInTank << " gallons remain in the tank" << endl;
  cout << "The total price is $" << setiosflags(ios::showpoint)
       << setprecision(2) << (pumped * price) << endl;

  return;
}
```

Let's analyze this class by individually inspecting both its data and method members. First, notice that we have declared two symbolic constants and two private instance variables. As private members, these data attributes can only be accessed through the class's member methods: `Pump()`, `getValues()`, and `request()`. It is these methods that provide the external services available to each `Pump` object.

The constructor function is straightforward. When a `Pump` object is declared it will be initialized to a given amount of gas in the supply tank and a given price per gallon. If no values are given, the defaults of $1.80 per gallon and 500 gallons are used; if only the price per gallon is provided, the constructor uses the default value of 500 for the missing second argument.

The `getvalues()` function defined in the implementation section simply provides a readout of the current attribute values. It is the `request()` function that is the most complicated because it provides the primary `Pump` service. The code follows the requirements of the pump and provides all of the gas required, unless the amount remaining in the supply tank is less the requested amount. Finally, it subtracts the amount pumped from the amount in the tank and calculates the total dollar value of the transaction.

To test the `Pump` class requires testing each class operation. To do this, consider Program 8.5.

PROGRAM 8.5

```
#include <c:\\cpcode\\Pump.cpp>
int main()
{
  Pump a(2.00, 300), b;    // declare 2 objects of type Pump

  a.getValues();
  cout << endl;
  a.request(20.0);
  cout << endl;
  a.request(290.0);
  b.getValues();

  return 0;
}
```

Notice that in Program 8.5 we have included the Pump class using the statement:

```
#include <c:\\cpcode\\Pump.cpp>
```

This assumes that the Pump class resides in the folder named cpcode on the C drive, and is saved as the file named Pump.cpp. An equivalent statement is:

```
#include "c:\\cpcode\\Pump.cpp"
```

In both include statements the double slashes are required, as a single slash would be interpreted as an escape character.

Within the main() method, eight statements are included. The first statement creates an object of type Pump. The supply tank for the first Pump object contains 300 gallons and the price per gallon is set to $2.00, while the second Pump object uses the default values AMOUNT_IN_TANK and DEFAULT_PRICE, which are 500 and 1.80, respectively.

A call is then made to getValues() to display the first pump's attribute values. The next statement is a request for gas of 20 gallons from the first Pump object. This is followed by a request for 290 gallons, which exceeds the remaining gas in the supply tank. Finally, the attribute values for the second pump are displayed. The output produced by Program 8.5 is:

```
The gas tank has 300 gallons of gas.
The price per gallon of gas is $2.00

20.00 gallons were requested
20.00 gallons were pumped
280.00 gallons remain in the tank
The total price is $40.00

290.00 gallons were requested
280.00 gallons were pumped
0.00 gallons remain in the tank
The total price is $560.00

The gas tank has 500 gallons of gas.
The price per gallon of gas is $1.80
```

As indicated by this output, all of the Pump class methods provide the correct functionality. Specifically, both Pump objects are initialized correctly by the constructor, and the request() method supplies the requested amount of gas, at the correct price, until the supply tank has been emptied.

Exercises 8.3

1. Enter Program 8.4 in your computer and execute it.

2. a. Modify the Elevator class in Program 8.4 to account for a second elevator. Put this elevator in service starting at the fifth floor. Have this second elevator move to the first floor and then move to the twelfth floor.

   b. Verify that the constructor function is called by adding a message within the constructor that is displayed each time a new object is created. Run your program to ensure its operation.

3. Modify Program 8.4 to use a `while` loop that calls the elevator's `request()` function with a random number between 1 and 15. If the random number is the same as the elevator's current floor, generate another request. The `while` loop should terminate after five valid requests have been made and satisfied by movement of the elevator. [*Hint:* Add a movement return code to the modified `request()` function.]

4. a. Modify the `main()` function in Program 8.5 to use a `while` loop that calls the pump's request function with a random number between 3 and 20. The `while` loop should terminate after five requests have been made.

   b. Modify the `main()` function written for Exercise 4a to provide a 30-minute simulation of the gas pump's operation. To do this, you have to modify the `while` loop to select a random number between 1 and 15 that represents the idle time between customer requests. Have the simulation stop once the idle time exceeds 30 minutes.

5. a. Construct a class definition of a Customer object type. The class is to have three member functions and no data members, as shown in Figure 8.6. The constructor function should simply call `srand()` with the argument `time(NULL)` to initialize the `rand()` function. The `arrive()` function should provide a random number between 1 and 15 as a return value, and the `gallons()` function should provide a random number between 3 and 20.

   b. Test the Customer class functions written for Exercise 5a in a complete working program.

   c. Use the Customer class function of Exercise 5a to simulate a random arrival of a person and a random request for gallons of gas within the program written for Exercise 4b.

6. Modify Program 8.5 so that the `Pump` class definition resides in a file named `Pump.cpp`. Then have Program 8.5 use an `#include` statement to include the class definition within the program. Make sure you use a full path name in the `include` statement. For example, if `Pump.cpp` resides in a directory named `foo` on the `C:` drive, the include statement should be `#include <<c:\\foo\\Pump.cpp>`.

7. Construct a class named `Light` that simulates a traffic light. The color attribute of the class should change from `Green` to `Yellow` to `Red` and then back to `Green` by the class's `change()` function. When a new `Light` object is created, its initial color should be `Red`.

FIGURE 8.6 Customer Class UML Diagram

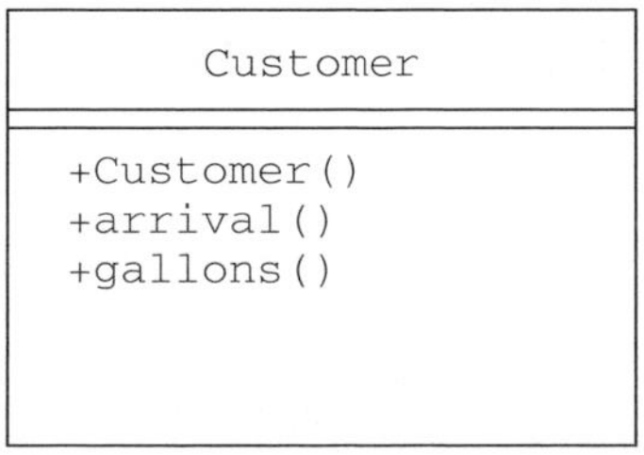

```
Customer

+Customer()
+arrival()
+gallons()
```

8. a. Construct a class definition that can be used to represent an employee of a company. Each employee is defined by an integer ID number, a floating-point pay rate, and the maximum number of hours the employee should work each week. The services provided by the class should be the ability to enter data for a new employee, the ability to change data for a new employee, and the ability to display the existing data for a new employee.

   b. Include the class definition created for Exercise 8a in a working C++ program that asks the user to enter data for three employees and displays the entered data.

   c. Modify the program written for Exercise 8b to include a menu that offers the user the following choices:

   ```
   1. Add an employee
   2. Modify employee data
   3. Delete an employee
   4. Exit this menu
   ```

   In response to a choice, the program should initiate appropriate action to implement the choice.

9. a. Construct a class definition that can be used to represent types of food. A type of food is classified as basic or prepared. Basic foods are further classified as either `Dairy`, `Meat`, `Fruit`, `Vegetable`, or `Grain`. The services provided by the class should be the ability to enter data for a new food, the ability to change data for a new food, and the ability to display the existing data for a new food.

   b. Include the class definition created for Exercise 9a in a working C++ that asks the user to enter data for four food items and displays the entered data.

   c. Modify the program written for Exercise 9b to include a menu that offers the user the following choices:

   ```
   1. Add a food item
   2. Modify a food item
   3. Delete a food item
   4. Exit this menu
   ```

   In response to a choice, the program should initiate appropriate action to implement the choice.

8.4 COMMON PROGRAMMING ERRORS

The more common programming errors initially associated with the construction of classes are as follows:

1. Failing to terminate the class declaration section with a semicolon.
2. Including a return type with the constructor's prototype or failing to include a return type with the other functions' prototypes.
3. Using the same name for a data member as for a member function.
4. Defining more than one default constructor for a class.
5. Forgetting to include the class name and scope operator, `::`, in the header line of all member functions defined in the class implementation section.

All of these errors result in a compiler error message.

8.5 CHAPTER REVIEW

Key Terms

abstract data type	destructor
class	implementation section
class members	inline member function
constructor	instance variables
data hiding	member functions
data members	method
data type	object
declaration section	private
default constructor	public

Summary

1. A *class* is a programmer-defined data type. *Objects* of a class may be defined and have the same relationship to their class as variables do to C++'s built-in data types.

2. A class definition consists of a declaration and implementation section. The most common form of a class definition is:

```
// class declaration section
class name
{
  private:
   a list of variable declarations;
  public:
    a list of function prototypes;
};


// class implementation section
class function definitions
```

The variables and functions declared in the class declaration section are collectively referred to as *class members.* The variables are individually referred to as class data members and the functions as class member functions. The terms `private` and `public` are *access specifiers.* Once an access specifier is listed, it remains in force until another access specifier is given. The `private` keyword specifies that the class members following it are private to the class and can only be accessed by the class's member functions. The `public` keyword specifies that the class members following may be accessed from functions outside the class. Generally, all data members should be specified as `private` and all member functions as `public`.

3. Class functions listed in the declaration section may be either written inline or their definitions included in the class implementation section. Except for constructor and destructor functions, all class functions defined in the class implementation section have the header line syntax:

```
return-type ClassName::functionName(parameter list);
```

Except for the addition of the class name and scope operator, `::`, which are required to associate the function name with the class, this header line is identical to the header line used for any user-written function.

4. A *constructor function* is a special function that is automatically called each time an object is declared. It must have the same name as its class and cannot have any return type. Its purpose is to initialize each declared object.

5. If no constructor is declared for a class, the compiler supplies a *default constructor*. This is a do-nothing function having the definition:

```
ClassName(void){ }
```

6. The term *default constructor* refers to any constructor that does not require any arguments when it is called. This can be because no parameters are declared (as is the case for the compiler-supplied default constructor) or because all arguments have been given default values.

7. Each class may only have one default constructor. If any constructor is user-defined, the compiler does not create its default constructor.

8. Objects are created using either a C++ or C style of declaration. The C++ style of declaration has the form:

```
ClassName list-of-objectNames(list of initializers);
```

where the list of initializers is optional. An example of this style of declaration, including initializers, for a class named `Date` is:

```
Date a, b, c(12,25,2006);
```

Here, the objects `a` and `b` are declared to be of type `Date` and are initialized using the default constructor values, whereas the object `c` is initialized with the values 12, 25, and 2006.

The equivalent C style of declaration, including the optional list of initializers, has the form:

```
ClassName objectName = ClassName(list of initializers);
```

An example of this style of declaration for a class named `Date` is:

```
Date c = Date(12,25,2006)
```

Here, the object `c` is created and initialized with the values 12, 25, and 2006.

9. Constructors may be overloaded in the same manner as any other user-written C++ function.

10. If a constructor is defined for a class, a user-defined default constructor also should be written because the compiler does not supply it.

11. A *destructor function* is called each time an object goes out of scope. Destructors must have the same name as their class, but are preceded by a tilde (~). There can only be one destructor per class.

12. A destructor function takes no arguments and returns no value. If a user-defined destructor is not included in a class, the compiler provides a do-nothing destructor.

Exercises

1. Define the following terms:
   a. attribute
   b. behavior
   c. state
   d. model
   e. class
   f. object
   g. interface

2. a. In place of specifying a rectangle's location by listing the position of two diagonal corner points, what other attributes could be used?
   b. What other attributes, besides length and width, might be used to describe a rectangle if the rectangle is to be drawn on a color monitor?
   c. Describe a set of attributes that could be used to define circles that are to be drawn on a black-and-white monitor.
   d. What additional attributes would you add to those selected in response to Exercise 2c if the circles were to be drawn on a color monitor?

3. a. For each of the following, determine what attributes might be of interest to someone considering buying the item:
   - a book
   - a can of soda
   - a pen
   - a cassette tape
   - a cassette tape player
   - an elevator
   - a car

   b. Do the attributes you used in Exercise 3a model an object or a class of objects?

4. For each of the following items, what behavior might be of interest to someone considering buying the item?
   a. a car
   b. a cassette tape player

5. All of the examples of classes considered in this chapter have consisted of inanimate objects. Do you think that animate objects such as pets and even human beings could be modeled in terms of attributes and behavior? Why or why not?

6. a. Given that *behavior* represents how an object of a class reacts to an external stimulus, what do you think is the mechanism by which one object "triggers" the designated behavior in another object? (*Hint:* Consider how one person typically gets another person to do something.)
   b. If behavior in C++ is constructed by defining an appropriate function, how do you think the behavior is activated in C++?

7. a. Construct a class named `Rectangle` that has floating-point data members named `length` and `width`. The class should have a constructor that sets each data member to 0, member functions named `perimeter()` and

`area()` to calculate the perimeter and area of a rectangle, respectively, a member function named `getdata()` to set a rectangle's length and width, and a member function named `showdata()` that displays a rectangle's length, width, perimeter, and area.

b. Include the `Rectangle` class constructed in Exercise 7a within a working C++ program.

8. a. Modify the `Date` class constructor defined in Program 8.1 to include a check that all day values reside between 1 and 31 and all month values reside between 1 and 12.

   b. Modify the day validation written for Exercise 8a to account for the month. Thus, for January (month 1) a day value between 1 and 31 is valid, whereas for February (month 2) a day value between 1 and 28 is valid, and so on.

   c. Modify the day validation written for Exercise 8b to account for leap years. (*Hint:* See Section 8.1, Exercise 7a.)

9. a. Modify the `Date` class defined in Program 8.1 to include a `nextDay()` function that increments a date by 1 day. Test your function to ensure that it correctly increments days into a new month and into a new year.

   b. Modify the `Date` class defined in Program 8.1 to include a `priorDay()` function that decrements a date by 1 day. Test your function to ensure that it correctly decrements days into a prior month and into a prior year.

10. a. In Exercise 4 of Section 8.2, you were asked to construct a `Time` class. For such a class, include a `tick()` function that increments the time by 1 second. Test your function to ensure that it correctly increments into a new minute and a new hour.

   b. Modify the `Time` class written for Exercise 10a to include a `detick()` function that decrements the time by 1 second. Test your function to ensure that it correctly decrements time into a prior hour and into a prior minute.

Class Functions and Conversions

The creation of a class requires that we provide the capability to declare, initialize, assign, manipulate, and display data members. In the previous chapter, the declaration, initialization, and display of objects were presented. In this chapter, we continue our construction of classes by providing the ability to create operator and conversion capabilities similar to those inherent in C++'s built-in types. With these additions, our user-defined types will have all of the functionality of built-in types.

9.1 ASSIGNMENT

In Chapter 3, we saw how C++'s assignment operator, =, performs assignment between variables. In this section, we see how assignment works when it is applied to objects and how to define our own assignment operator to override the default provided for user-defined classes.

For a specific assignment example, consider the `main()` function of Program 9.1. Notice that the implementation section of the `Date` class in Program 9.1 contains no assignment function. Nevertheless, we would expect the assignment statement `a = b;` in `main()` to assign b's data member values to their counterparts in a. This is, in fact, the case and is verified by the output produced when Program 9.1 is executed:

```
The date stored in a is originally 04/01/07
After assignment the date stored in a is 12/18/08
```

PROGRAM 9.1

```cpp
#include <iostream>
#include <iomanip>
using namespace std;

// class declaration

class Date
{
  private:
    int month;
    int day;
    int year;
  public:
    Date(int = 7, int = 4, int = 2005);     // constructor
    void showdate();        // member function to display a Date
};

// implementation section

Date::Date(int mm, int dd, int yyyy)
{
  month = mm;
  day = dd;
  year = yyyy;
}

void Date::showdate()
{
  cout << setfill('0')
       << setw (2) << month << '/'
       << setw (2) << day << '/'
       << setw (2) << year % 100;
  cout << endl;

  return;
}
```

```cpp
int main()
{
  Date a(4,1,2007), b(12,18,2008); // declare two objects

  cout << "The date stored in a is originally ";
  a.showdate();  // display the original date
  a = b;            // assign b's value to a
  cout << "After assignment the date stored in a is ";
  a.showdate();  // display a's values

  return 0;
}
```

The type of assignment illustrated in Program 9.1 is referred to as **memberwise assignment**. In the absence of any specific instructions to the contrary, the C++ compiler builds this type of default assignment operator for each class. If the class does *not* contain any pointer data members, this default assignment operator is adequate and can be used without further consideration. Before considering the problems that can occur with pointer data members, let's see how to construct our own explicit assignment operators. The information gained is then applicable to constructing all other user-defined operators.

Assignment operators, like all class members, are declared in the class declaration section and defined in the class implementation section. For the declaration of operators, however, the keyword `operator` must be included in the declaration. Using this keyword, a simple **assignment operator** declaration has the form:

```
void operator=(ClassName&);
```

The keyword `void` indicates that the assignment returns no value, `operator=` indicates that we are overloading the assignment operator with our own version, and the class name and ampersand within the parentheses indicate that the parameter to the operator is a class reference. For example, to declare a simple assignment operator for our `Date` class, the declaration

```
void operator=(Date&);
```

can be used.

The actual implementation of the assignment operator is defined in the implementation section. For our declaration, a suitable implementation is:

```
void Date::operator=(Date& newdate)
{
   day = newdate.day;      // assign the day
   month = newdate.month;  // assign the month
   year = newdate.year;    // assign the year
}
```

The use of the reference parameter in the definition of this operation is not accidental. In fact, one of the primary reasons for references in C++ is to facilitate the construction of overloaded operators and make the notation more natural.[1] In this definition, `newdate` is defined as a reference to a `Date` class. Within the body of the definition, the `day` member of the object referenced by `newdate` is assigned to the `day` member of the current object, which is then repeated for the `month` and `year` members. Assignments such as `a.operator=(b);` can then be used to call the overloaded assignment operator and assign b's member values to a. For convenience, the expression `a.operator=(b)` can be replaced with `a = b;`. Program 9.2 contains our new assignment operator within the context of a complete program.

Except for the addition of the overloaded assignment operator declaration and definition, Program 9.2 is identical to Program 9.1 and produces the same output. Its usefulness to us is that it illustrates how we can explicitly construct our own assignment definitions. In Section 10.5, when we introduce pointer data members, we will see how C++'s default assignment can cause troublesome errors that are circumvented by constructing our own assignment operators. Before moving on, however, two simple modifications to our assignment operator need to be made.

---

[1] Passing a reference is preferable to passing an object by value because it reduces the overhead required in making a copy of each object's data members.

PROGRAM 9.2

```cpp
#include <iostream>
#include <iomanip>
using namespace std;

// class declaration

class Date
{
  private:
    int month;
    int day;
    int year;
  public:
    Date(int = 7, int = 4, int = 2005);     // constructor
    void operator=(Date&);    // define assignment of a date
    void showdate();          // member function to display a date
};

// implementation section

Date::Date(int mm, int dd, int yyyy)
{
  month = mm;
  day = dd;
  year = yyyy;
}

void Date::operator=(Date& newdate)
{

  day = newdate.day;        // assign the day
  month = newdate.month;    // assign the month
  year = newdate.year;      // assign the year

  return;
}

void Date::showdate()
{
  cout << setfill('0')
       << setw(2) << month << '/'
       << setw(2) << day << '/'
       << setw(2) << year % 100;
  cout << endl;

  return;
}
```

```
int main()
{
  Date a(4,1,2007), b(12,18,2008); // declare two objects

  cout << "The date stored in a is originally ";
  a.showdate();   // display the original date
  a = b;          // assign b's value to a
  cout << "After assignment the date stored in a is ";
  a.showdate();   // display a's values

  return 0;
}
```

First, to preclude any inadvertent alteration to the object used on the right-hand side of the assignment, a constant reference parameter should be used. For our Date class, this takes the form:

```
void Date::operator=(const Date& newdate);
```

The final modification concerns the operation's return value. As constructed, our simple assignment operator returns no value, which precludes us from using it in multiple assignments such as a = b = c. The reason for this is that overloaded operators retain the same precedence and associativity as their equivalent built-in versions. Thus, an expression such as a = b = c is evaluated in the order a = (b = c). As we have defined assignment, unfortunately, the expression b = c returns no value, making subsequent assignment to a an error. To provide for multiple assignments, a more complete assignment operation would return a reference to its class type. Because the implementation of such an assignment requires a special class pointer, the presentation of this more complete assignment operator is deferred until the material presented in the next chapter is introduced. Until then, our simple assignment operator is more than adequate for our needs.

Copy Constructors

Although assignment looks similar to initialization, it is worthwhile noting that they are two entirely different operations. In C++, an initialization occurs every time a new object is created. In an assignment, no new object is created; the value of an existing object is simply changed. Figure 9.1 illustrates this difference.

One type of initialization that closely resembles assignment occurs in C++ when one object is initialized using another object of the same class. For example, in the declaration

```
Date b = a;
```

or its equivalent form

```
Date b(a);
```

the b object is initialized to a previously declared a object. The constructor that performs this type of initialization is called a **copy constructor**, and if you do not declare one, the compiler constructs one for you. The compiler's **default copy constructor** performs in a manner similar to the default assignment operator by doing a memberwise copy between objects. Thus, for the declaration Date b = a; the default copy constructor sets b's month, day, and year values to their respective counterparts in a. As with default assignment operators, default copy constructors work just fine unless the class contains pointer data members. Before considering the complications that can occur with pointer data members and how to handle them, it is helpful to look at how we can construct our own copy constructors.

FIGURE 9.1   Initialization and Assignment

$$c = a; \longleftarrow \text{Assignment}$$

$$\text{Type definition} \longrightarrow \text{Date } c = a; \longleftarrow \text{Initialization}$$

Copy constructors, like all class functions, are declared in the class declaration section and defined in the class implementation section. The declaration of a copy constructor has the general form:

```
ClassName(const ClassName&);
```

As with all constructors, the function name must be the class name. As further illustrated by the declaration, the parameter is a reference to the class, which is a characteristic of all copy constructors.[2] To ensure that the parameter is not inadvertently altered, it is always specified as a const. Applying this general form to our Date class, a copy constructor can be explicitly declared as:

```
Date(const Date&);
```

The actual implementation of this constructor, if it were to perform the same memberwise initialization as the default copy constructor, takes the form:

```
Date:: Date(const Date& olddate)
{
    month = olddate.month;
    day = olddate.day;
    year = olddate.year;
}
```

As with the assignment operator, the use of a reference parameter for the copy constructor is no accident: The reference parameter again facilitates a simple notation within the body of the function. Program 9.3 contains this copy constructor within the context of a complete program.

PROGRAM 9.3

```
#include <iostream>
#include <iomanip>
using namespace std;

// class declaration

class Date
{
  private:
    int month;
    int day;
    int year;
```

---

[2] A copy constructor is frequently defined as a constructor whose first parameter is a reference to its class type, with any additional parameters being defaults.

```cpp
  public:
    Date(int = 7, int = 4, int = 2005);     // constructor
    Date(const Date&);        // copy constructor
    void showdate();            // member function to display a date
};

// implementation section

Date::Date(int mm, int dd, int yyyy)
{
  month = mm;
  day = dd;
  year = yyyy;
}


Date::Date(const Date& olddate)
{
  month = olddate.month;
  day = olddate.day;
  year = olddate.year;
}

void Date::showdate()
{
  cout << setfill('0')
       << setw(2) << month << '/'
       << setw(2) << day << '/'
       << setw(2) << year % 100;
  cout << endl;

  return;
}
```

```cpp
int main()
{
  Date a(4,1,2007), b(12,18,2008); // use the constructor
  Date c(a);    // use the copy constructor
  Date d = b;  // use the copy constructor

  cout << "The date stored in a is ";
  a.showdate();
  cout << "The date stored in b is ";
  b.showdate();
  cout << "The date stored in c is ";
  c.showdate();
  cout << "The date stored in d is ";
  d.showdate();

  return 0;
}
```

The output produced by Program 9.3 is:

```
The date stored in a is 04/01/07
The date stored in b is 12/18/08
The date stored in c is 04/01/07
The date stored in d is 12/18/08
```

As illustrated by this output, c's and d's data members have been initialized by the copy constructor to a's and b's values, respectively. Although the copy constructor defined in Program 9.3 adds nothing to the functionality provided by the compiler's default copy constructor, it does provide us with the fundamentals of defining copy constructors. In Section 10.5, we will see how to modify this basic copy constructor to handle cases that are not adequately taken care of by the compiler's default.

Base/Member Initialization[3]

Except for the reference names `olddate` and `newdate`, a comparison of Program 9.3's copy constructor to Program 9.2's assignment operator shows them to be essentially the same function. The difference in these functions is that the copy constructor first creates an object's data members before the body of the constructor uses assignment to specify member values. Thus, the copy constructor does not perform a true initialization, but rather a creation followed by assignment.

A true initialization has no reliance on assignment whatsoever and is possible in C++ using a *base/member initialization list*. Such a list can only be applied to constructor functions and may be written in two ways.

The first way to construct a base/member initialization list is within a class's declaration section using the form:

```
className(parameter list) : list of data members(initializing values) {}
```

For example, using this form, a default constructor that performs a true initialization is:

```
// class declaration section

public:
  Date(int mo = 4, int da = 1, int yr = 2006) : month(mo), day(da), year(yr) {}
```

The second way is to declare a prototype in the class's declaration section followed by the initialization list in the implementation section. For our `Date` constructor, this takes the form:

```
// class declaration section

public:
  Date(int = 4, int = 1, int = 2006);  // prototype with defaults

// class implementation section

Date::Date(int mo, int da, int yr) : month(mo), day(da), year(yr) {}
```

---

[3] The material in this section is presented for completeness only and may be omitted without loss of subject continuity.

Notice that in both forms the body of the constructor function is empty. This is not a requirement, and the body can include any subsequent operations that you want the constructor to perform. The interesting feature of this type of constructor is that it clearly differentiates between the initialization tasks performed in the member initialization list contained between the colon and the braces and any subsequent assignments that might be contained within the function's body. Although we will not be using this type of initialization subsequently, it is required whenever there is a `const` class instance variable.

Exercises 9.1

1. Describe the difference between assignment and initialization.

2. a. Construct a class named `Time` that contains three integer data members named `hours`, `mins`, and `secs`, which will be used to store hours, minutes, and seconds. The function members should include a constructor that provides default values of 0 for each data member, a display function that prints an object's data values, and an assignment operator that performs a memberwise assignment between two `Time` objects.

   b. Include the `Time` class developed in Exercise 2a in a working C++ program that creates and displays two `Time` objects, the second of which is assigned the values of the first object.

3. a. Construct a class named `Complex` that contains two double-precision data members named `real` and `imag`, which will be used to store the real and imaginary parts of a complex number. The function members should include a constructor that provides default values of 0 for each member function, a display function that prints an object's data values, and an assignment operator that performs a memberwise assignment between two `Complex number` objects.

   b. Include the class written for Exercise 3a in a working C++ program that creates and displays the values of two `Complex` objects, the second of which is assigned the values of the first object.

4. a. Construct a class named `Car` that contains the following three data members: a double-precision variable named `engineSize`, a character variable named `bodyStyle`, and an integer variable named `colorCode`. The class methods should include a constructor that provides default values of 0 for each numeric data member and `'X'` for each character variable; a display function that prints the engine size, body style, and color code; and an assignment operator that performs a memberwise assignment between two `Car` objects for each instance variable.

   b. Include the class written for Exercise 4a in a working C++ program that creates and displays two `Car` objects, the second of which is assigned the values of the first object.

9.2 ADDITIONAL CLASS FEATURES

This section presents additional features pertaining to classes. These features include the scope of a class, creating static class members, and granting access privileges to nonmember functions. Each of these topics may be read independently of the others.

Class Scope

We have already encountered local and global scope in Chapter 6. As we saw there, the scope of a variable defines the portion of a program in which the variable can be accessed.

Values and Identities

Apart from any behavior that an object is supplied with, a characteristic feature that objects share with variables is that they always have a unique identity. It is an object's identity that permits one object to be distinguished from another. This is not true of a value, such as the number 5, because all occurrences of 5 are indistinguishable from one another. Hence, values are not considered objects in object-oriented programming languages such as C++.

Another distinguishing feature between an object and a value is that a value can never be a container whose value can change, whereas an object clearly can. A value is simply an entity that stands for itself.

Now consider a string such as `"Chicago"`. As a string, this is a value. However, since `Chicago` could also be a specific and identifiable object of type `City`, the context in which the name is used is important. Notice that if the string `"Chicago"` were assigned to an object's name attribute, it reverts to being a value.

For local variables, this scope is defined by any block contained within a brace pair, `{ }`. This includes both the complete function body and any internal sub-blocks. Additionally, all parameters of a function are considered to be local function variables.

Global variables are accessible from their point of declaration throughout the remaining portion of the file containing them, with three exceptions:

1. If a local variable has the same name as a global variable, the global variable can only be accessed within the scope of the local variable by using the scope resolution operator, `::`.

2. The scope of a nonstatic global variable can be extended into another file by using the keyword `extern`.

3. The same global name can be reused in another file to define a separate and distinct variable by using the keyword `static`. Static global variables are unknown outside of their immediate file.

In addition to local and global scopes, each class also defines an associated **class scope**. That is, the names of the data and function members are local to the scope of their class. Thus, if a global variable name is reused within a class, the global variable is hidden by the class data member in the same manner as a local function variable hides a global variable of the same name. Similarly, member function names are local to the class in which they are declared and can only be used by objects declared for the class. Additionally, local function variables also hide the names of class data members having the same name. Figure 9.2 illustrates the scope of the variables and functions for the following declarations:

```
double rate;    // global scope
// class declaration
class Test
{
  private:
    double amount, price, total;  // class scope
  public:
    double extend(double, double);  // class scope
};
```

FIGURE 9.2	Example of Scopes

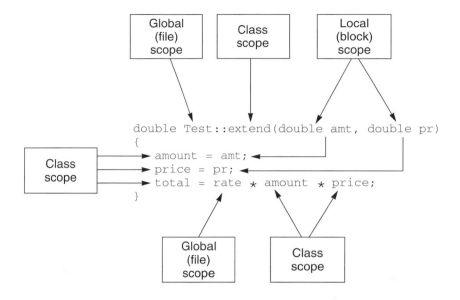

Static Class Members

As each class object is created, it gets its own block of memory for its data members. In some cases, however, it is convenient for every instantiation of a class to share the *same* memory location for a specific variable. For example, consider a class consisting of employee payment information, where each employee is subject to the same Social Security tax rate. Clearly, we could make the sales tax a global variable, but this is not very safe. Such data could be modified anywhere in the program, could conflict with an identical variable name within a function, and certainly violate C++'s principle of data hiding.

This type of situation is handled in C++ by declaring a class variable to be static. **Static class data members** share the same storage space for all objects of the class; as such, they act as global variables for the class and provide a means of communication between objects.

C++ requires that such static variables be declared within the class's declaration section. To actually create such variables, the declared static variable must be redeclared, with or without an initial value (this defines the variable, in contrast to a formal declaration statement that does not physically allocate storage for the variable), outside of the class's declaration sections.

For example, assuming the class declaration

```
//class declaration

class Employee
{
  private:
    static double taxRate;
    int idNum;
  public:
    Employee(int);   //constructor
    void display();
};
```

the definition and initialization of the `static` variable `taxRate` is accomplished using a statement such as:

```
double Employee::taxRate = 0.07;  // this defines taxRate
```

Here the scope resolution operator, `::`, is used to identify `taxRate` as a member of the class `Employee`, and the keyword `static` is not included. Program 9.4 uses this definition within the context of a complete program.

PROGRAM 9.4

```cpp
#include <iostream>
using namespace std;

// class declaration

class Employee
{
  private:
    static double taxRate;
    int idNum;
  public:
    Employee(int = 0); // constructor
    void display();     // access function
};

// static member definition
double Employee::taxRate = 0.07;  //this defines taxRate

// implementation section

Employee::Employee(int num)
{
  idNum = num;
}

void Employee::display()
{
  cout << "Employee number " << idNum
       << " has a tax rate of " << taxRate << endl;

  return;
}

int main()
{
  Employee emp1(11122), emp2(11133);

  emp1.display();
  emp2.display();

  return 0;
}
```

The output produced by Program 9.4 is

```
Employee number 11122 has a tax rate of 0.07
Employee number 11133 has a tax rate of 0.07
```

Once the definition (as opposed to the declaration) of a static class variable is made, any other definition will result in an error. Thus, the actual definition of a `static` member remains the responsibility of the class creator. A compiler error will occur if this definition is omitted. The storage sharing produced by the `static` data member and the objects created in Program 9.4 is illustrated in Figure 9.3.

FIGURE 9.3   Sharing the `static` **Data Member** taxRate

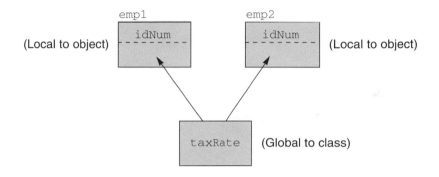

In addition to static data members, **static member functions** can also be created. Such functions apply to a class as a whole rather than to individual class objects and can only access static data members and other static member functions of the class.[4] An example of such a function is provided by Program 9.5.

The output produced by Program 9.5 is:

```
The static tax rate is 0.07
Employee number 11122 has a tax rate of 0.07
Employee number 11133 has a tax rate of 0.07
```

In reviewing Program 9.5, notice that the keyword `static` is used only when static data and function members are declared; it is not included in the definition of these members. Also notice that the static member function is called using the scope resolution operator with the function's class name. Finally, since static functions access only `static` variables that are not contained within a specific object, `static` functions may be called before any instantiations are declared.

Friend Functions

The only method we currently have for accessing and manipulating a class's private variables is through the class's member functions. Conceptually, this arrangement can be viewed as illustrated in Figure 9.4a. There are times, however, when it is

---

[4] The reason is that the `this` pointer, discussed in Section 10.3, is not passed to static member functions.

PROGRAM 9.5

```cpp
#include <iostream>
using namespace std;

// class declaration

class Employee
{
  private:
    static double taxRate;
    int idNum;
  public:
    Employee(int = 0);    // constructor
    void display();       // access function
    static void disp();   // static function
};

// static member definition
double Employee::taxRate = 0.07;    // this defines tax rate

// implementation section

Employee::Employee(int num)
{
  idNum = num;
}

void Employee::display()
{
  cout << "Employee number " << idNum
       << " has a tax rate of " << taxRate << endl;

  return;
}

void Employee::disp()
{
  cout << "The static tax rate is " << taxRate << endl;

  return;
}

int main()
{
  Employee::disp();    // call the static function
  Employee emp1(11122), emp2(11133);

  emp1.display();
  emp2.display();

  return 0;
}
```

useful to provide such access to selected nonmember functions. The procedure for providing this external access is rather simple: The class maintains its own approved list of nonmember functions that are granted the same privileges as a class's functions. The nonmember functions on the list are called **friend functions**, and the list is referred to as a friends list.

FIGURE 9.4a   Direct Access Is Provided to Member Functions

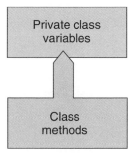

Figure 9.4b conceptually illustrates the use of such a list for nonmember access. Any nonmember function attempting access to an object's private variables is first checked against the friends list: If the function is on the list, access is approved; otherwise, access is denied.

From a coding standpoint, the friends list is simply a series of function prototype declarations that is preceded with the word `friend` and included in the class's declaration section. For example, if the functions named `addreal()` and `addimag()` are to be allowed access to the private members of a class named `Complex`, the following prototypes would be included within `Complex`'s declaration section:

```
friend double addreal(Complex&, Complex&);
friend double addimag(Complex&, Complex&);
```

Here, the friends list consists of two declarations. The prototypes indicate that each function returns a floating-point number and expects two references to objects of type `Complex` as arguments. Program 9.6 includes these two friend declarations in a complete program.

FIGURE 9.4b   Access Provided to Nonmember Functions

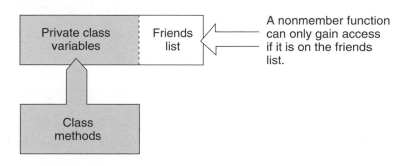

PROGRAM 9.6

```cpp
#include <iostream>
#include <cmath>
using namespace std;

// class declaration

class Complex
{
  // friends list
  friend double addreal(Complex&, Complex&);
  friend double addimag(Complex&, Complex&);
  private:
    double real;
    double imag;
  public:
    Complex(double = 0, double = 0);  // constructor
    void display();

};

// implementation section

Complex::Complex(double rl, double im)
{
  real = rl;
  imag = im;
}

void Complex::display()
{
  char sign = '+';

  if(imag < 0) sign = '-';
  cout << real << sign << abs(imag) << 'i';

  return;
}

// friend implementations

double addreal(Complex &a, Complex &b)
{
  return(a.real + b.real);
}

double addimag(Complex &a, Complex &b)
{
  return(a.imag + b.imag);
}
```

```
int main()
{
  Complex a(3.2, 5.6), b(1.1, -8.4);
  double re, im;

  cout << "\nThe first complex number is ";
  a.display();
  cout << "\nThe second complex number is ";
  b.display();


  re = addreal(a,b);
  im = addimag(a,b);
  Complex c(re,im);   // create a new Complex object
  cout << "\n\nThe sum of these two complex numbers is ";
  c.display();

  return 0;
}
```

The output produced by Program 9.6 is:

```
The first complex number is 3.2+5.6i
The second complex number is 1.1-8.4i


The sum of these two complex numbers is 4.3-2.8i
```

In reviewing Program 9.6, notice four items. The first is that since friends are not class members, they are unaffected by the access section in which they are declared—*they may be declared anywhere within the declaration section.* The convention we have followed is to include all `friend` declarations immediately following the class header. The second item to notice is that the keyword `friend` (like the keyword `static`) is used only within the class declaration and not in the actual function definition. Third, since a `friend` function is intended to have access to an object's private variables, at least one of the friend's parameters should be a reference to an object of the class that has made it a friend. Finally, as illustrated by Program 9.6, it is the class that grants `friend` status to a function and not the other way around. The function can never confer `friend` status on itself because to do so would violate the concepts of data hiding and access provided by a class.

Exercises 9.2

1. a. Rewrite Program 9.5 to include an integer static variable named numemps. This variable should act as a counter that is initialized to zero and is incremented by the class constructor each time a new object is declared. Rewrite the static function `disp()` to display the value of this counter.

   b. Test the program written for Exercise 1a. Have the `main()` function call `disp()` after each `Employee` object is created.

2. a. Construct a class named `Circle` that contains two integer variables named `xCenter` and `yCenter` and a double-precision data member named `radius`. Additionally, the class should contain a static variables named `scaleFactor`. Here, the `xCenter` and `yCenter` values represent the center point of a circle, `radius` represents the circle's actual radius, and `scaleFactor` represents a scale factor that will be used to scale the circle to fit on a variety of display devices.

   b. Include the class written for Exercise 2a in a working C++ program.

3. a. Answer whether the following three statements from Program 9.6:

   ```
   re = addreal(a,b);

   im = addimag(a,b);

   complex c(re,im);   // create a new complex object
   ```

   could be replaced by the single statement:

   ```
   complex(addread(a,b), addimag(a,b));
   ```

   b. Verify your answer to Exercise 3a by running Program 9.6 with the suggested replacement statement.

4. a. Rewrite the class written for Exercise 2a, but include a friend function that multiplies an object's `radius` by a static scale factor and then displays the actual radius value and the scaled value.

   b. Test the class written for Exercise 4a.

5. Rewrite Program 9.6 so that it has only one friend function named `addComplex()`. This function should accept two `Complex` objects and return a `Complex` object. The real and imaginary parts of the returned object should be the sum of the real and imaginary parts, respectively, of the two objects passed to `addComplex()`.

9.3 OPERATOR FUNCTIONS

A simple assignment operator was constructed in Section 9.1. In this section, we extend this capability and show how to broaden C++'s built-in operators to work with class objects. We will discover that class operators are themselves either member or friend functions.

The only symbols permitted for user-defined purposes are the subset of C++'s built-in symbols listed in Table 9.1. Each of these symbols can be adopted for class use with no limitation as to its meaning.[5] This is done by making each operation a function that can be overloaded like any other function.

The operation of the symbols listed in Table 9.1 can be redefined as we see fit for our classes, subject to the following restrictions:

- Symbols not in Table 9.1 cannot be redefined. For example, the ., ::, and ?: symbols cannot be redefined.

- New operator symbols cannot be created. For example, since %% is not an operator in C++, it cannot be defined as a class operator.

---

[5] The only limitation is that the syntax of the operator cannot be changed. Thus, a binary operator must remain binary and a unary operator must remain unary. Within this syntax restriction, an operator symbol can be used to produce any operation, whether or not the operation is consistent with the symbol's accepted usage. For example, we could redefine the addition symbol to provide multiplication. Clearly, this violates the intent and spirit of making these symbols available to us. We shall be very careful to redefine each symbol in a manner consistent with its accepted usage.

TABLE 9.1 Operators Available for Class Use

Operator	Description
()	Function call
[]	Array element
->	Structure member pointer reference
new	Dynamically allocate memory
delete	Dynamically deallocate memory
++	Increment
--	Decrement
-	Unary minus
!	Logical negation
~	One's complement
*	Indirection
*	Multiplication
/	Division
%	Modulus (remainder)
+	Addition
-	Subtraction
<<	Left shift
>>	Right shift
<	Less than
<=	Less than or equal to
>	Greater than
>=	Greater than or equal to
==	Equal to
!-	Not equal to
&&	Logical AND
||	Logical OR
&	Bitwise AND
^	Bitwise exclusive OR
|	Bitwise inclusive OR
=	Assignment
+= -= *=	Assignment
/= %= &=	Assignment
^= | =	Assignment
<<= >>=	Assignment
,	Comma

- Neither the precedence nor the associativity of C++'s operators can be modified. Thus, you cannot give the addition operator a higher precedence than the multiplication operator.
- Operators cannot be redefined for C++'s built-in types.
- A C++ operator that is unary cannot be changed to a binary operator and a binary operator cannot be changed to a unary operator.
- The operator must either be a member of a class or be defined to take at least one class member as an operand.

The first step in providing a class with operators from Table 9.1 is to decide which operations make sense for the class and how they should be defined. As a specific example, we continue to build on the `Date` class introduced previously. For this class, a small, meaningful set of class operations is defined.

Clearly, the addition of two dates is not meaningful. The addition of a date with an integer, however, does make sense if the integer is taken as the number of days to be added to the date. Likewise, the subtraction of an integer from a date makes sense. Also, the subtraction of two dates is meaningful if we define the difference to mean the number of days between the two dates. Similarly, it makes sense to compare two dates and determine if the dates are equal or if one date occurs before or after another date. Let's see how these operations can be implemented using C++'s operator symbols.

A user-defined operation is created as a function that redefines C++'s built-in operator symbols for class use. Functions that define operations on class objects and use C++'s built-in operator symbols are referred to as **operator functions**.

Operator functions are declared and implemented in the same manner as all member functions, with one exception: It is the function's name that connects the appropriate operator symbol to the operation defined by the function. An operator function's name is always of the form `operator<symbol>` where `<symbol>` is one of the operators listed in Table 9.1. The function name `operator+`, for example, is the name of the addition function, while the function name `operator==` is the name of the equal to comparison function.

Once the appropriate function name is selected, the process of writing the function amounts to having it accept the desired inputs and produce the correct returned value.[6] For example, in comparing two `Date` objects for equality, we would select C++'s equality operator. Thus, the name of our function becomes `operator==`. We would want our comparison operation to accept two `Date` objects, internally compare them, and return an integer value indicating the result of the comparison (for example, true for equality and false for inequality). As a member function, a suitable prototype that could be included in the class declaration section is:

```
bool operator==(Date&);
```

This prototype indicates that the function is named `operator==`, that it returns a Boolean value and that it accepts a reference to a `Date` object.[7] Only one `Date`

---

[6] As previously noted, this implies that the specified operator can be redefined to perform any operation. Good programming practice, however, dictates against such redefinitions.

[7] The prototype `bool operator==(Date)` also works. Passing a reference, however, is preferable to passing an object because it reduces the function call's overhead. This is because passing an object means that a copy of the object must be made for the called function, whereas passing a reference gives the function direct access to the object whose address is passed.

object is required here because the second `Date` object is the object that calls the function. Let's now write the function definition to be included in the class implementation section. Assuming our class is named `Date`, a suitable definition is:

```
int Date::operator==(Date& date2)
{
  if( day == date2.day && month == date2.month && year == date2.year)
    return 1;
  else
    return 0;
}
```

Once this function has been defined, it may be called using the same syntax that is used for C++'s built-in types. For example, if `a` and `b` are objects of type `Date`, the expression `if (a == b)` is valid. Program 9.7 includes this `if` statement as well as the declaration and definition of this operator function within the context of a complete program.

The output produced by Program 9.7 is:

```
Dates a and b are not the same.
Dates a and c are the same.
```

The first new feature illustrated in Program 9.7 is the declaration and implementation of the function named `operator==`. Except for its name, this operator function is constructed in the same manner as any other member function: It is declared in the declaration section and defined in the implementation section. The second new feature is how the function is called. Operator functions may be called using their associated symbols rather than in the way other functions are called. Since operator functions are true functions, however, the traditional method of calling them can also be used—by specifying their name and including appropriate arguments. Thus, in addition to being called by the expression `a == b` in Program 9.7, the call `a.operator==(b)` could also have been used.

Let's now create another operator for our `Date` class—an addition operator. As before, creating this operator requires that we specify three items:

1. The name of the operator function
2. The processing that the function is to perform
3. The data type, if any, that the function is to return

Clearly, for addition, we use the operator function named `operator+`. Having selected the function's name, we must now determine what we want this function to do, as it specifically relates to `Date` objects. As we noted previously, the sum of two dates is without meaning. Adding an integer to a date is meaningful, however, when the integer represents the number of days either before or after the given date. Here, the sum of an integer and a `Date` object is simply another `Date` object, which should be returned by the addition operation. Thus, a suitable prototype for our addition function is:

```
Date operator+(int);
```

This prototype is included in the class declaration section. It specifies that an integer is to be added to a class object and the operation returns a `Date` object. Thus, if `a` is a `Date` object, the function call `a.operator+(284)`, or its more commonly used alternative, `a + 284`, should cause the number 284 to be correctly added to `a`'s date value. We must now construct the function to accomplish this.

PROGRAM 9.7

```cpp
#include <iostream>
using namespace std;

// class declaration

class Date
{
  private:
    int month;
    int day;
    int year;
  public:
    Date(int = 7, int = 4, int = 2005);      // constructor
    int operator==(Date &);   // declare the operator== function
};

// implementation section

Date::Date(int mm, int dd, int yyyy)
{
  month = mm;
  day = dd;
  year = yyyy;
}

int Date::operator==(Date &date2)
{
  if(day == date2.day && month == date2.month && year == date2.year)
    return 1;
  else
    return 0;
}
```

```cpp
int main()
{
  Date a(4,1,2007), b(12,18,2008), c(4,1,2007); // declare 3 objects

  if (a == b)
    cout << "Dates a and b are the same." << endl;
  else
    cout << "Dates a and b are not the same." << endl;

  if (a == c)
    cout << "Dates a and c are the same." << endl;
  else
    cout << "Dates a and c are not the same." << endl;

  return 0;
}
```

Constructing the function requires that we first select a specific date convention. For simplicity, we adopt the financial date convention that considers each month to consist of 30 days and each year to consist of 360 days. Using this convention, our function will first add the integer number of days to the Date object's day value and then adjust the resulting day value to lie within the range 1 to 30 and the month value to lie within the range 1 to 12. A function that accomplishes this is:

```
Date Date::operator+(int days)
{
  Date temp;  // a temporary Date to store the result

  temp.day = day + days;  // add the days
  temp.month = month;
  temp.year = year;
  while (temp.day > 30)    // now adjust the months
  {
    temp.month++;
    temp.day -= 30;
  }
  while (temp.month > 12)  // adjust the years
  {
    temp.year++;
    temp.month -= 12;
  }
  return temp;      // the values in temp are returned
}
```

The important feature to notice here is the use of the temp object. The purpose of this object is to ensure that none of the function's arguments, which become the operator's operands, is altered. To understand this, consider a statement such as b = a + 284; that uses this operator function, where a and b are Date objects. This statement should never modify a's value. Rather, the expression a + 284 should yield a Date value that is then assigned to b. The result of the expression is, of course, the temp Date object returned by the operator+() function. Program 9.8 uses this function within the context of a complete program.

The output produced by Program 9.8 is:

```
The initial date is 04/01/07
The new date is 01/15/08
```

Operator Functions as Friends

The operator functions in both Programs 9.7 and 9.8 have been constructed as class members. An interesting feature of operator functions is that, except for the operator functions =, (), [], and ->, they may also be written as friend functions. For example, if the operator+() function used in Program 9.8 were written as a friend, a suitable declaration section prototype is:

```
friend Date operator+(Date&, int);
```

PROGRAM 9.8

```cpp
#include <iostream>
#include <iomanip>
using namespace std;

// class declaration

class Date
{
  private:
    int month;
    int day;
    int year;
  public:
    Date(int = 7, int = 4, int = 2005);      // constructor
    Date operator+(int);       // overload the + operator
    void showdate();              // member function to display a date
};
// implementation section

Date::Date(int mm, int dd, int yyyy)
{
  month = mm;
  day = dd;
  year = yyyy;
}

Date Date::operator+(int days)
{
  Date temp;  // a temporary date to store the result

  temp.day = day + days;  // add the days
  temp.month = month;
  temp.year = year;
  while (temp.day > 30)     // now adjust the months
  {
    temp.month++;
    temp.day -= 30;
  }
  while (temp.month > 12)  // adjust the years
  {
    temp.year++;
    temp.month -= 12;
  }
  return temp;      // the values in temp are returned
}
void Date::showdate()
{
```

(continued from previous page)

```
    cout << setfill('0')
         << setw(2) << month << '/'
         << setw(2) << day << '/'
         << setw(2) << year % 100;
    cout << endl;

    return;
}
```

```
int main()
{
    Date a(4,1,2007), b; // declare two objects

    cout << "The initial date is ";
    a.showdate();
    b = a + 284;    // add in 284 days = 9 months and 14 days
    cout << "The new date is ";
    b.showdate();

    return 0;
}
```

Notice that the friend version contains a reference to a `Date` object that is not contained in the member function version. In all cases, the equivalent friend version of a member operator function *must* contain an additional class reference that is not required by the member function.[8] This equivalence is listed in Table 9.2 for both unary and binary operators.

Table 9.2 Operator Function Parameter Requirements

	Member Function	Friend Function
Unary operator	1 implicit	1 explicit
Binary operator	1 implicit and 1 explicit	2 explicit

We now write Program 9.8's `operator+()` function as a friend function:

```
Date operator+(Date& op1, int days)
{
    Date temp;  // a temporary Date to store the result

    temp.day = op1.day + days;  // add the days
    temp.month = op1.month;
    temp.year = op1.year;
    while (temp.day > 30)    // now adjust the months
    {
        temp.month++;
        temp.day -= 30;
    }
```

---

[8] This extra parameter is necessary to identify the correct object. This parameter is not needed when using a member function because the member function "knows" on which object it is operating. The mechanism of this "knowing" is supplied by an implied member function parameter named `this`, which is explained in detail in Section 10.3.

```
    while (temp.month > 12)   // adjust the years
    {
      temp.year++;
      temp.month -= 12;
    }
    return temp;      // the values in temp are returned
}
```

The only difference between this version and the member version is the explicit use of a `Date` parameter named `op1` (the choice of this name is entirely arbitrary) in the friend version. This means that within the body of the friend function the first three assignment statements explicitly reference `op1`'s data members as `op1.day`, `op1.month`, and `op1.year`, whereas the member function simply refers to its parameters as `day`, `month`, and `year`.

In making the determination to overload a binary operator as either a friend or member operator function, the following convention can be applied: *Friend functions are more appropriate for binary functions that modify neither of their operands, such as `==`, `+`, `-`, etc., while member functions are more appropriate for binary functions, such as `=`, `+=`, `-=`, etc., which are used to modify one of their operands.*

Exercises 9.3

1. a. Define a greater than relational operator function named `operator>()` that can be used with the `Date` class declared in Program 9.7.

   b. Define a less than operator function named `operator<()` that can be used with the `Date` class declared in Program 9.7.

   c. Include the operator functions written for Exercises 1a and 1b in a working C++ program.

2. a. Define a subtraction operator function named `operator-()` that can be used with the `Date` class defined in Program 9.7. The subtraction should accept a long integer argument that represents the number of days to be subtracted from an object's date and return a `Date`. In doing the subtraction, use the convention that all months have 30 days and all years have 360 days. Additionally, an end-of-month adjustment should be made, if necessary, that converts any resulting day of 31 to a day of 30, except if the month is February. If the resulting month is February and the day is either 29, 30, or 31, it should be changed to 28.

   b. Define another subtraction operator function named `operator-()` that can be used with the `Date` class defined in Program 9.7. The subtraction should yield a long integer that represents the difference in days between two dates. In calculating the day difference, use the financial day count basis that assumes all months have 30 days and all years have 360 days.

   c. Include the overloaded operators written for Exercises 2a and 2b in a working C++ program.

3. a. Determine if the following addition operator function provides the same result as the function used in Program 9.8:

```
Date Date::operator+(int days)    // return a Date object
{
  Date temp;

  temp.day = day + days;    // add the days in
  temp.month = month + int(day/30);  // determine total months
  temp.day = temp.day % 30;           // determine actual day
  temp.year = year + int(temp.month/12);  // determine total years
  temp.month = temp.month % 12;       // determine actual month

  return temp;
}
```

      b. Verify your answer to Exercise 3a by including the function in a working C++ program.

  4. a. Rewrite the equality relational operator function in Program 9.7 as a friend function.

      b. Verify the operation of the friend operator function written for Exercise 4a by including it within a working C++ program.

  5. a. Rewrite the addition operator function in Program 9.8 to account for the actual days in a month, neglecting leap years.

      b. Verify the operation of the operator function written for Exercise 5a by including it within a working C++ program.

  6. a. Construct an addition operator for the `Complex` class declared in Program 9.6. This should be a member function that adds two complex numbers and returns a complex number.

      b. Add a member multiplication operator function to the class written for Exercise 6a that multiplies two complex numbers and returns a complex number.

      c. Verify the operation of the operator functions written for Exercises 6a and 6b by including them within a working C++ program.

9.4 TWO USEFUL ALTERNATIVES: `operator()` AND `operator[]`

There are times when it is convenient to define an operation having more than two arguments, which is the limit imposed on all binary operator functions. For example, each of our `Date` objects contains three integer data members: `month`, `day`, and `year`. For such an object, we might want to add an integer value to any of these three members, instead of just the day member as was done in Program 9.8. C++ provides for this possibility by supplying the **parentheses operator function**, `operator()`, which has no limits on the number of arguments that may be passed to it.

At the other end of the spectrum, the case illustrated by Program 9.8, in which only a single nonobject argument is required, occurs so frequently that C++ also provides an alternative means of achieving it. For this special case, C++ supplies the **subscript operator function,** `operator[]`, which permits a maximum of one argument. The only restriction imposed by C++ on the `operator()` and `operator[]` functions is that they must be defined as member (not friend) functions. For simplicity, we consider the `operator[]` function first.

The subscript operator function, `operator[]`, is declared and defined in the same manner as any other operator function, but it is called differently from the normal function and operator call. For example, if we wanted to use this operator function to accept an integer argument and return a `Date` object, the following prototype is valid:

```
Date operator[](int);  // declare the subscript operator
```

Except for the operator function's name, this is similar in construction to any other operator function prototype. Assuming we want this function to add its integer argument to a `Date` object, a suitable function implementation is:

```
Date Date::operator[](int days)
{
  Date temp;  // a temporary Date to store the result
```

```
            temp.day = day + days;   // add the days
            temp.month = month;
            temp.year = year;
            while (temp.day > 30)     // now adjust the months
            {
              temp.month++;
              temp.day -= 30;
            }
            while (temp.month > 12)  // adjust the years
            {
              temp.year++;
              temp.month -= 12;
            }
            return temp;        // the values in temp are returned
        }
```

Again, except for the initial header line, this is similar in construction to other operator function definitions. Once the function is created, however, it can only be called by passing the required argument through the subscript brackets. For example, if a is a Date object, the function call a[284] calls the subscript operator function and causes the function to operate on the a object using the integer value 284. This call is illustrated in Program 9.9.

PROGRAM 9.9

```
#include <iostream>
#include <iomanip>
using namespace std;

// class declaration

class Date
{
  private:
    int month;
    int day;
    int year;
  public:
    Date(int = 7, int = 4, int = 2005);   // constructor
    Date operator[](int);  // overload the subscript operator
     void showdate();        // member function to display a date
};

// implementation section

Date::Date(int mm, int dd, int yyyy)
{
  month = mm;
  day = dd;
  year = yyyy;
}
```

(continued from previous page)

```
Date Date::operator[](int days)
{
  Date temp;   // a temporary date to store the result

  temp.day = day + days;   // add the days
  temp.month = month;
  temp.year = year;
  while (temp.day > 30)     // now adjust the months
  {
    temp.month++;
    temp.day -= 30;
  }
  while (temp.month > 12)   // adjust the years
  {
    temp.year++;
    temp.month -= 12;
  }
  return temp;      // the values in temp are returned
}

void Date::showdate()
{
  cout << setfill('0')
       << setw(2) << month << '/'
       << setw(2) << day << '/'
       << setw(2) << year % 100;
  cout << endl;

  return;
}
```

```
int main()
{
  Date a(4,1,2007), b;  // declare two objects

  cout << "The initial date is ";
  a.showdate();
  b = a[284];   // add in 284 days = 9 months and 14 days
  cout << "The new date is ";
  b.showdate();

  return 0;
}
```

Program 9.9 is identical in every way to Program 9.8, except that we have used an overloaded subscript operator function in place of an overloaded addition operator function. Programs 9.9 and 9.8 produce identical output.[9]

The parentheses operator function, `operator()`, is almost identical in construction and calling to the subscript function, `operator[]`, with the substitution

---

[9] If you are familiar with arrays, notice that the expression `a[284]` used in Program 9.9 *appears* to indicate that `a` is an array, but it is not. It is simply the notation that is required to call an overloaded subscript function.

of parentheses for brackets. The difference between these two operator functions is in the number of allowable arguments. Whereas the subscript operator permits zero or one argument to be passed, the parentheses operator has no limit on the number of its arguments. For example, a suitable operator prototype to add an integer number of months, days, or years to a `Date` object is:

```
Date operator()(int, int, int);
```

Once such a function is implemented (which is left as an exercise), a call such as `a(2,4,3)` can be used to add 2 months, 4 days, and 3 years to the `Date` object named `a`.

These two extra functions provide a great deal of programming flexibility. In the case where only one argument is needed, they permit two different overloaded functions to be written, both of which have the same argument type. For example, we could use the `operator[]` function to add an integer number of days to a `Date` object and the `operator()` function to add an integer number of months. Because both functions have the same argument type, one function name could not be overloaded for both of these cases. These two functions also permit us the flexibility to restrict the other operator functions to class member arguments and use these two functions for any other argument types or operations, such as adding an integer to a `Date` object.

Exercises 9.4

1. Replace the subscript `operator[]` function in Program 9.9 with the parentheses `operator()` function.

2. a. Replace the subscript `operator[]` function in Program 9.9 with an `operator()` function that accepts integer month, day, and year values. Have the function add the input days, months, and years to the object's date and return the resulting date. For example, if the input is 3,2,1 and the object's date is 7/16/2006, the function should return the date 10/18/2007. Make sure that your function correctly handles an input such as 37 days and 15 months and adjusts the calculated day to be within the range 1 to 30 and the month within the range 1 to 12.

   b. Include the operator function written for Exercise 2a in a working C++ program and verify its operation.

3. a. Construct a class named `Student` consisting of the following private data members: an integer ID number, an integer count, and four double-precision grades. The constructor for this class should sct all data member values to zero. The class should also include a member function that displays all valid member grades, as determined by the grade count, and calculates and displays the average of the grades. Include the class in a working C++ program that declares three class objects named `a`, `b`, and `c`.

   b. Include a member `operator[]` function in the class constructed for Exercise 3a that has a double-precision grade count argument. The function should check the grade count data member, and if fewer than four grades have been entered, the function should store its argument into the next grade slot available. If four grades have already been entered, the function should return an error message indicating that the new grade cannot be accepted. Additionally, a new grade should force an increment to the count data member.

   c. Include a member `operator()` function in the class constructed for Exercise 3a that has a grade identification number and grade value as arguments. The function should force a change to the grade corresponding to the identification number and update the count if necessary. For example, an argument list of 4,98.5 should change the fourth test grade value to 98.5.

4. a. Add a member `operator[]` function to Program 9.6 that multiplies an object's complex number (both the real and imaginary parts) by a real number and returns a complex number. For example, if the real number is 2 and the complex number is 3+4i, the result is 6+8i.

   b. Verify the operation of the operator function written for Exercise 4a by including it within a working C++ program.

9.5 DATA TYPE CONVERSIONS

The conversion from one built-in data type to another was previously described in Chapter 3. With the introduction of user-defined data types, the possibilities for data type conversions expand to the following cases:

- Conversion from built-in type to built-in type
- Conversion from built-in type to user-defined type
- Conversion from user-defined type to built-in type
- Conversion from user-defined type to user-defined type

The first conversion is handled either by C++'s built-in implicit conversion rules or its explicit cast operator. The second conversion type is made using a *type conversion constructor*. The third and fourth conversion types are made using a *conversion operator function*. In this section, the specific means of performing each of these conversions is presented.

Built-In to Built-In Conversion

The conversion from one built-in data type to another has already been presented in Sections 3.1 and 3.3. To review this case briefly, this type of conversion is either implicit or explicit.

An implicit conversion occurs in the context of one of C++'s operations. For example, when a floating-point value is assigned to an integer variable, only the integer portion of the value is stored. The conversion is implied by the operation and is performed automatically by the compiler.

An explicit conversion occurs whenever a cast is used. In C++, two cast notations exist. Using the older C notation, a cast has the form *(dataType) expression*, and the newer C++ notation has the function-like form *dataType(expression)*. For example, both of the expressions `(int)24.32` and `int(24.32)` cause the floating-point value 24.32 to be truncated to the integer value 24.

Built-In to Class Conversion

User-defined casts for converting a built-in to a user-defined data type are created using constructor functions. A constructor whose first parameter is not a member of its class and whose remaining parameters, if any, have default values is a **type conversion constructor**. If the first argument of a type conversion constructor is a built-in data type, the constructor can be used to cast the built-in data type to a class object. Clearly, one restriction of such functions is that, as constructors, they must be member functions.

Although this type of cast occurs when the constructor is invoked to initialize an object, it is actually a more general cast than might be evident at first glance. This is because a constructor function can be explicitly invoked after all objects have been declared regardless of whether it was invoked previously as part of an object's declaration. Before exploring this further, let's first construct a type conversion constructor. We will then see how to use it as a cast independent of its initialization purpose.

The cast we construct converts a long integer into a `Date` object. Our `Date` object consists of dates in the form month/day/year and uses our by now familiar `Date` class. The long integer is used to represent dates in the form year * 10006 + month * 100 + day. For example, using this representation, the date 12/31/2006 becomes the long integer 20061231. Dates represented in this fashion are very useful for two reasons: First, a date can be stored as a single integer; second, such dates are in numerically increasing date order, making sorting extremely easy. For example, the date 01/03/2006, which occurs after 12/31/2005, becomes the integer 20060103, which is larger than 20051231. Since the integers representing dates can exceed the size of a normal integer, the integers are always declared as longs.

A suitable constructor function for converting from a long integer date to a date stored as a month, day, and year is:

```
// type conversion constructor from long to Date

Date::Date(long findate)
{
  year = int(findate/10000.0);
  month = int((findate - year * 10000.0)/100.0);
  day = int(findate - year * 10000.0 - month * 100.0);
}
```

Program 9.10 uses this type conversion constructor both as an initialization function at declaration time and as an explicit cast later in the program.

PROGRAM 9.10

```
#include <iostream>
#include <iomanip>
using namespace std;

// class declaration

class Date
{
  private:
    int month, day, year;
  public:
    Date(int = 7, int = 4, int = 2005);  // constructor
    Date(long);              // type conversion constructor
    void showdate();
};

// implementation section

// constructor
Date::Date(int mm, int dd, int yyyy)
{
  month = mm;
  day = dd;
  year = yyyy;
}
```

(continued from previous page)

```cpp
// type conversion constructor from long to date
Date::Date(long findate)
{
  year = int(findate/10000.0);
  month = int((findate - year * 10000.0)/100.0);
  day = int(findate - year * 10000.0 - month * 100.0);
}

// member function to display a date
void Date::showdate()
{
  cout << setfill('0')
       << setw(2) << month << '/'
       << setw(2) << day << '/'
       << setw(2) << year % 100;

  return;
}
```

```cpp
int main()
{
  Date a, b(20061225L), c(4,1,2007);  // declare 3 objects - initialize 2 of them

  cout << "Dates a, b, and c are ";
  a.showdate();
  cout << ", ";
  b.showdate();
  cout << ", and ";
  c.showdate();
  cout << ".\n";

  a = Date(20080103L);  // cast a long to a date

  cout << "Date a is now ";
  a.showdate();
  cout << ".\n";

  return 0;
}
```

The output produced by Program 9.10 is:

```
Dates a, b, and c are 07/04/05, 12/25/06, and 04/01/07.
Date a is now 01/03/08.
```

The change in a's date value illustrated by this output is produced by the assignment expression `a = Date(20060103L)`, which uses a type conversion constructor to perform the cast from `long` to `Date`.

Class to Built-In Conversion

Conversion from a user-defined data type to a built-in data type is accomplished using a conversion operator function. A **conversion operator function** is a member operator function having the name of a built-in data type or class. When the operator function has a built-in data type name, it is used to convert from a class to a built-in data type. For example, a conversion operator function for casting a class object to a long integer has the name `operator long()`. Here, the name of the operator function indicates that a conversion to a `long` will take place. If this function were part of a `Date` class, it would be used to cast a `Date` object into a long integer. This usage is illustrated by Program 9.11.

PROGRAM 9.11

```cpp
#include <iomanip>
#include <iostream>
using namespace std;

// class declaration

class Date
{
  private:
    int month, day, year;
  public:
    Date(int = 7, int = 4, int = 2005);     // constructor
    operator long();           // conversion operator function
    void showdate();
};

// implementation section

// constructor
Date::Date(int mm, int dd, int yyyy)
{
  month = mm;
  day = dd;
  year = yyyy;
}

// conversion operator function converting from Date to long
Date::operator long()    // must return a long
{
  long yyyymmdd;

  yyyymmdd = year * 10000.0 + month * 100.0 + day;

  return(yyyymmdd);
}

// member function to display a date
void Date::showdate()
{
  cout << setfill('0');
       << setw(2) << month << '/'
       << setw(2) << day << '/'
       << setw(2) << year % 100;

  return;
}
```

(continued from previous page)

```
int main()
{
  Date a(4,1,2007);  // declare and initialize one object of type date
  long b;            // declare an object of type long

  b = a;             // a conversion takes place here

  cout << "a's date is ";
  a.showdate();
  cout << "This date, as a long integer, is " << b << endl;

  return 0;
}
```

The output produced by Program 9.11 is:

```
a's date is 04/01/07
This date, as a long integer, is 20070401
```

The change in a's date value to a long integer illustrated by this output is produced by the assignment expression b = a. This assignment, which also could have been written explicitly as b = long(a), calls the conversion operator function long() to perform the cast from Date to long. In general, since explicit conversion more clearly documents what is happening, its use is preferred to implicit conversion.

Notice that the conversion operator function has no explicit parameters and has no explicit return type. This is true of any conversion operators: Its implicit parameter always is an object of the class being cast from, and the return type is implied by the name of the function. Additionally, as previously indicated, a conversion operator function *must* be a member function.

Class to Class Conversion

Converting from a user-defined data type to a user-defined data type is performed in the same manner as a cast from a user-defined to a built-in data type: It is done using a member *conversion operator function*. In this case, however, the operator function uses the class name being converted to rather than a built-in data name. For example, if two classes named Date and Intdate exist, the operator function named operator Intdate() could be placed in the Date class to convert from a Date object to an Intdate object. Similarly, the operator function named Date() could be placed in the Intdate class to convert from an Intdate to a Date.

Notice that, as before, in converting from a user-defined data type to a built-in data type, *the operator function's name determines the result of the conversion*; the class containing the operator function determines which type of data type is being converted.

Before providing a specific example of a class to class conversion, one additional point must be noted. Converting between classes clearly implies that we have two classes, one of which is always defined first and one of which is defined second. Having, within the second class, a conversion operator function with the name of the first class poses no problem because the compiler knows of the first class's existence. However, including a conversion operator function with the second class's name in the first class does pose a problem because the second class has not yet been defined. This is remedied by including a declaration for the second class prior to the first class's definition. This declaration, which is formally referred to as a **forward declaration**, is illustrated in Program 9.12, which also includes conversion operators between the two defined classes.

PROGRAM 9.12

```cpp
#include <iostream>
#include <iomanip>
using namespace std;

// forward declaration of class Intdate
class Intdate;

// class declaration for Date

class Date
{
  private:
    int month, day, year;
  public:
    Date(int = 7, int = 4, int = 2005);    // constructor
    operator Intdate();     // conversion operator Date to Intdate
    void showdate();
};

// class declaration for Intdate

class Intdate
{
  private:
    long yyyymmdd;
  public:
    Intdate(long = 0);     // constructor
    operator Date();   // conversion operator Intdate to Date
    void showint();
};

// implementation section for Date

Date::Date(int mm, int dd, int yyyy)   // constructor
{
  month = mm;
  day = dd;
  year = yyyy;
}

// conversion operator function converting from Date to Intdate class
Date::operator Intdate()    // must return an Intdate object
{
  long temp;

  temp = year * 10000.0 + month * 100.0 + day;
```

(continued from previous page)

```
    return(Intdate(temp));
}

// member function to display a Date
void Date::showdate()
{
  cout << setfill('0');
        << setw(2) << month << '/'
        << setw(2) << day << '/'
        << setw(2) << year % 100;

  return;
}

// implementation section for Intdate

Intdate::Intdate(long ymd)   // constructor
{
  yyyymmdd = ymd;
}

// conversion operator function converting from Intdate to Date class
Intdate::operator Date()     // must return a Date object
{
  int mo, da, yr;

  yr = int(yyyymmdd/10000.0);
  mo = int((yyyymmdd - yr * 10000.0)/100.0);
  da = int(yyyymmdd - yr * 10000.0 - mo * 100.0);

  return(Date(mo,da,yr));
}

// member function to display an Intdate
void Intdate::showint()
{
  cout << yyyymmdd;

  return;
}
```

```
int main()
{
  Date a(4,1,2007), b;       // declare two Date objects
  Intdate c(20081215L), d;   // declare two Intdate objects

  b = Date(c);       // cast c into a Date object
  d = Intdate(a);    // cast a into an Intdate object
```

(continued from previous page)

```
cout << " a's date is ";
a.showdate();
cout << "\n   as an Intdate object this date is ";
d.showint();

cout << "\n c's date is ";
c.showint();
cout << "\n   as a Date object this date is ";
b.showdate();
cout << endl;

return 0;
}
```

The output produced by Program 9.12 is:

```
a's date is 04/01/07
   as an Intdate object this date is 20070401
c's date is 20081215
   as a Date object this date is 12/15/08
```

As illustrated by Program 9.12, the cast from Date to Intdate is produced by the assignment b = Date(c) and the cast from Intdate to Date is produced by the assignment d = Intdate(a). Alternatively, the assignments b = c and d = a produce the same results. Notice also the forward declaration of the Intdate class prior to the Date class's declaration. This is required so that the Date class can reference Intdate in its operator conversion function.

Exercises 9.5

1. a. Define the four data type conversions available in C++ and the method of accomplishing each conversion.

   b. Define the terms *type conversion constructor* and *conversion operator function* and describe how they are used in user-defined conversions.

2. Write a C++ program that declares a class named Time having integer data members named hours, minutes, and seconds. Include in the program a type conversion constructor that converts a long integer, representing the elapsed seconds from midnight into an equivalent representation as hours:minutes:seconds. For example, the long integer 30336L should convert to the time 8:25:36. Use a military representation of time so that 2:30 P.M. is represented as 14:30:00. The relationship between time representations is

   elapsed seconds = hours * 3600 + minutes * 60 + seconds

3. A Julian date is a date represented as the number of days from a known base date. One algorithm for converting from a Gregorian date, in the form month/day/year, to a Julian date with a base date of 0/0/0 is given. All of the calculations in this algorithm use integer arithmetic, which means that the fractional part of all divisions must be discarded. In this algorithm, M = month, D = day, and Y = 4-digit year.

   If M is less than or equal to 2,
      set the variable MP = 0 and YP = Y−1
   Else
      *set MP = int(0.4 * M + 2.3) and YP = Y*

   T = int(YP/4) − int(YP/100) + int(YP/400)
   *Julian date = 365 * Y + 31 * (M − 1) + D + T − MP*

Using this algorithm, modify Program 9.11 to cast from a Gregorian `date` object to its corresponding Julian representation as a long integer. Test your program using the Gregorian dates 1/31/2005 and 3/16/2006, which correspond to the Julian dates 38381 and 38790, respectively.

4. Modify the program written for Exercise 2 to include a member conversion operator function that converts an object of type `Time` into a long integer representing the number of seconds from midnight.

5. Write a C++ program that has a `Date` class and a `Julian` class. Use the `Date` class from Program 9.12. The Julian class should represent a date as a long integer. For this program, include a member conversion operator function within the `Date` class that converts a `Date` object to a `Julian` object using the algorithm presented in Exercise 3. Test your program by converting the dates 1/31/2006 and 3/16/2007, which correspond to the Julian dates 38746 and 39155, respectively.

6. Write a C++ program that has a `Time` class and an `Ltime` class. The `Time` class should have integer data members named `hours`, `minutes`, and `seconds`, while the `Ltime` class should have a long data member named `elsecs`, which represents the number of elapsed seconds since midnight. For the `Time` class, include a member conversion operator function named `Ltime()` that converts a `Time` object to an `Ltime` object. For the `Ltime` class, include a member conversion operator function named `Time()` that converts an `Ltime` object to a `Time` object.

9.6 FOCUS ON PROBLEM SOLVING

The first problem presented in this section completes the gas pump simulation begun in Section 8.3. In place of a second design problem, an application is presented that shows how to overload both the extraction, `>>`, and the insertion, `<<`, operators for `Date` objects. Doing so permits us to input and output `Date` types as complete entities using `cout` and `cin` in the same manner as built-in data types use these two objects. Once you understand how the overloading is done, you will be able to provide standard input and output using the `cin` and `cout` stream objects for any class that you construct.

Problem 1: A Multiobject Gas Pump Simulation

In Problem 2 of Section 8.3, a requirement was made to construct a C++ program that simulated a gas pump's operation over the course of any 30-minute period. For convenience, this requirement is restated below:

We have been requested to write a program that simulates the operation of a gas pump. At any time during the simulation we should be able to determine, from the pump, the price per gallon of gas and the amount remaining in the supply tank from which the gas is pumped. If the amount of gas in the supply tank is greater than or equal to the amount of gas requested, the request should be filled; otherwise, only the available amount in the supply tank should be used. Once the gas is pumped, the total price of the gallons pumped should be displayed and the amount of gas in gallons that was pumped should be subtracted from the amount in the supply tank.

For the simulation, assume that the pump is randomly idle between 1 to 15 minutes between customer arrivals, and that a customer randomly requests between 3 and 20 gallons of gas. Although the default supply tank capacity is 500 gallons, assume that the initial amount of gas in the tank for this simulation is only 300 gallons. Initially, the program should simulate a one-half hour time frame.

Additionally, for each arrival and request for gas, we want to know the idle time before the customer arrived, how many gallons of gas were pumped, and the total price of the transaction. The pump itself must keep track of the price per gallon of gas and the amount of gas remaining in the supply tank. Typically, the price per gallon is $1.80, but the price for the simulation should be $2.00.

Having constructed a `Pump` class to model the operation of a gas pump, we can now use this class within the context of a complete simulation. We do so by first providing a `Customer` class and then controlling the interaction between these two classes using a `main()` function to create an actual multi-class simulation program.

Analyze the Problem   As specified, the problem entails two types of objects: a gas pump and a customer. Let's consider these object types separately.

The Pump   A `Pump` class was designed and implemented in Section 8.3 and is repeated here for convenience:

```
#include <iostream>
#include <iomanip>
using namespace std;

const double AMOUNT_IN_TANK = 500;   // initial gallons in the tank
const double DEFAULT_PRICE = 1.80;   // price per gallon

class Pump
{
 // data declaration section
 private:
  double amtInTank;
  double price;

 // method declarations
 public:
  Pump(double = DEFAULT_PRICE, double = AMOUNT_IN_TANK);  // constructor
  void getValues();
  void request(double);
};

// methods implementation section

Pump::Pump(double todaysPrice, double amountInTank)
{
 amtInTank = amountInTank;
 price = todaysPrice;
}
```

(continued from previous page)

```cpp
void Pump::getValues()
{
 cout << "The gas tank has " << amtInTank << " gallons of gas." << endl;
 cout << "The price per gallon of gas is $" << setiosflags(ios::showpoint)
       << setprecision(2) << setiosflags(ios::fixed) << price << endl;
}

void Pump::request(double pumpAmt)
{
 double pumped;

 if (amtInTank >= pumpAmt)
    pumped = pumpAmt;
  else
    pumped = amtInTank;

 amtInTank -= pumped;
 cout << pumpAmt << " gallons were requested " << endl;
 cout << pumped << " gallons were pumped" << endl;
 cout << amtInTank << " gallons remain in the tank" << endl;
 cout << "The total price is $" << setiosflags(ios::showpoint)
       << setprecision(2) << (pumped * price) << endl;

 return;
}
```

You should review Problem 2 in Section 8.3 if either the data or member methods of this `Pump` class are not clear. For later convenience in writing the required simulation program, assume that the code for the `Pump` class has been named `Pump.cpp` and is stored within a folder named `cpcode` on the C drive. Once this is done, you can include the Pump class definition with a program simply by using the single line preprocessor directive `#include <c:\\cpcode\Pump.cpp>`.[10]

The Customer For this simulation, there are multiple instances of customers arriving randomly between 1 and 15 minutes and requesting gas in amounts that vary randomly between 3 and 20 gallons. From an object viewpoint, however, we are not interested in storing the arrival and number of gallons requested by each customer. We simply need a customer object to present us with an arrival time and a request for gas in gallons. Thus, our `Customer` object type need have no attributes but must provide two operations. The first operation, which we will name `arrive()`, will provide a random arrival time between 1 and 15 minutes. The second operation, which we will call `gallons()`, will provide a random request of

---

[10] The reason we're using a full path name in the `#inlcude` statement is to ensure that the preprocessor accesses the `Pump.cpp` class that we have placed in the named folder. We do not want the preprocessor to search its default folder and possibly locate some other `Pump.cpp` class that we do not know about, or be unable to locate the `Pump.cpp` files at all.

between 3 and 20 gallons of gas. The UML class diagram for this class is presented in Figure 9.5.

FIGURE 9.5   Customer Class UML Diagram

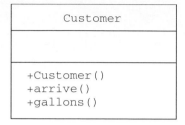

The actual class implementation can be coded as:

```
#include <ctime>
#include <cmath>
using namespace std;

//class declaration and implementation
class Customer
{
  public:
    Customer() {srand(time(NULL));};
    int arrive() {return(1 + rand() % 15);};
    int gallons() {return(3 + rand() % 18);};
};
```

In reviewing this code notice that the class constructor is used to randomize the `rand()` function (review Section 6.7 if you are unfamiliar with either the `srand()` or `rand()` functions). The `arrive()` function simply returns a random integer between 1 and 15, while the `gallons()` function returns a random integer between 3 and 20 (we leave it as an exercise for you to rewrite the `gallons()` function to return a non-integer value). Since all of the functions are single line, we have included their definitions within the declaration section as inline functions.

Again, for later convenience in writing the complete simulation program assume that the code for the `Customer` class is placed in a file named `Customer.cpp` within a folder named `cpcode` on the `C` drive. Once this is done, including the `Customer` class within a program requires the statement `#include <c:\\cpcode\\Customer.cpp`

Program Logic   Having analyzed and defined the two classes that we will be using, we still need to analyze and define the logic to correctly control the interaction between `Customer` and `Pump` objects for a valid simulation. In this particular case, the only interaction between a `Customer` object and a `Pump` object is that a customer's arrival, followed by a request, determines when the `Pump` is activated and how much gas is requested. Thus, each interaction between a `Customer` and a `Pump` can be expressed by the pseudocode:

Obtain a Customer arrival time
Obtain a Customer request for gas
Activate the Pump with the request

Program and Class Libraries

The concept of a program library began with FORTRAN, which was the first commercial high level language, introduced in 1954. The FORTRAN library consisted of a group of completely tested and debugged mathematical routines that were provided with the compiler. Since that time every programming language has provided its own library of functions. In both C and C++, this library is referred to as the *standard program library,* and includes more than 12,000 functions declared in fifteen different header files. Examples of standard library functions include `sqrt()`, `pow()`, `abs()`, `rand()`, `srand()`, and `time()`. The advantage of library functions is that they significantly enhance program development and design by providing code that is known to work correctly without the need for additional testing and debugging.

With the introduction of object-oriented languages the concept of a program library has been extended to include class libraries. A *class library* is a library of tested and debugged classes.

One of the key practical features of class libraries is that they help realize the goal of code reuse in a significant way. By providing tested and debugged code consisting of both data and function members, class libraries furnish large sections of pre-written and reusable code ready for incorporation within new applications. This shifts the focus of writing application programs from the creation of new code to understanding how to use predefined objects and stitch them together in a cohesive and useful way.

Although this repetition of events takes place continuously over the course of a day, we are only interested in a one-half hour period. Therefore, we must place these three events in a loop that is executed until the required simulation time has elapsed.

Develop a Solution   Having developed and coded the two required classes, `Pump` and `Customer`, what remains to be developed is the control logic within the `main()` function for correctly activating class events. This will require a loop controlled by the total arrival time for all customers. A suitable control structure for `main()` is described by the algorithm:

Create a Pump *object with the required initial supply of gas*
Display the values in the initialized Pump
Set the total time to 0
Obtain a Customer arrival time // first arrival
Add the arrival time to the total time
While the total time does not exceed the simulation time
   Display the total time
   Obtain a Customer request for gas
   Activate the Pump *with the request*
   Obtain a Customer arrival time // next arrival
   Add the arrival time to the total time
End While
Display a message that the simulation is over

Code the Solution   The C++ code corresponding to our design is listed as Program 9.13.

PROGRAM 9.13

```cpp
#include <c:\\cpcode\\Pump.cpp>      // note use of full path name here
#include <c:\\cpcode\\Customer.cpp>  // again - a full path name is used

const double SIMTIME = .5;   // simulation time in hours
const int MINUTES = 60;       // number of minutes in an hour

int main()
{
  Pump a(2.00, 300);  // declare 1 object of type Pump
  Customer b;          // declare 1 object of type Customer
  int totalTime = 0;
  int idleTime;
  int amtRequest;
  int SimMinutes;    // simulation time in minutes

  SimMinutes = SIMTIME * MINUTES;
  cout << "\nStarting a new simulation - simulation time is "
       << SimMinutes << " minutes" << endl;
  a.getValues();

  // get the first arrival
  idleTime = b.arrive();
  totalTime += idleTime;

  while (totalTime <= SimMinutes)
  {
    cout << "\nThe idle time is " << idleTime << " minutes" << endl
         << "  and we are " << totalTime
         << " minutes into the simulation." << endl;
    amtRequest = b.gallons();
    a.request(double(amtRequest));

    // get the next arrival
    idleTime = b.arrive();
    totalTime += idleTime;
  }
 cout << "\nThe idle time is " << idleTime << " minutes." << endl
      << "As the total time now exceeds the simulation time, " << endl
      << "  this simulation run is over." << endl;

  return 0;
}
```

Test and Correct the Program   Assuming that the Pump and Customer classes have been thoroughly tested and debugged, testing and debugging Program 9.13 is really restricted to testing and debugging the main() method. This specificity of testing is precisely one of the advantages of an object-oriented approach. Using previously written and tested class definitions allows us to focus our attention on the remaining code that controls the flow of events between objects, which in Program 9.13 centers on the main() method.

By itself, the `main()` method in Program 9.13 is a straightforward `while` loop where the `Pump` idle time corresponds to the time between customer arrivals. The output of a sample run, shown below, verifies that the loop is operating correctly:

```
Starting a new simulation - simulation time is 30 minutes
The gas tank has 300 gallons of gas.
The price per gallon of gas is $2.00

The idle time is 2 minutes
    and we are 2 minutes into the simulation.
7.00 gallons were requested
7.00 gallons were pumped
293.00 gallons remain in the tank
The total price is $14.00

The idle time is 1 minutes
    and we are 3 minutes into the simulation.
15.00 gallons were requested
15.00 gallons were pumped
278.00 gallons remain in the tank
The total price is $30.00


The idle time is 11 minutes
    and we are 14 minutes into the simulation.
13.00 gallons were requested
13.00 gallons were pumped
265.00 gallons remain in the tank
The total price is $26.00

The idle time is 8 minutes
    and we are 22 minutes into the simulation.
20.00 gallons were requested
20.00 gallons were pumped
245.00 gallons remain in the tank
The total price is $40.00

The idle time is 9 minutes.
As the total time now exceeds the simulation time,
    this simulation run is over.
```

In reviewing the operation of Program 9.13 it should be realized that we have used the same `Customer` object for each arrival and request. In Section 10.4 we will see how to dynamically create a new `Customer` object for each arrival and destroy the created object when it has completed its designated task.

Application 1: Overloading the Insertion, `<<`, and Extraction, `>>`, Operators

For all of the class examples seen so far, a display function has been used to output an object's attribute values. Since a user-defined type should provide all of the functionality of a built-in type, we should be able to input and output object values using `cin` and `cout`, respectively. This is, in fact, the case.

Every C++ compiler provides a class library that includes a number of predefined classes. Three of these classes are named `ostream`, `istream`, and `iostream`, respectively. The relationship between these classes is shown in Figure 9.6 and explained in detail in Section 11.7.[11] As you might have guessed, the `istream` name

---

[11] Notice that arrowheads point to the base classes.

is derived from *in*stream, the ostream name from *out*stream, and the iostream name from *input/output* stream. In this context, a **stream** is simply a one-way path between a source and a destination down which a sequence of bytes can be sent. A good analogy to a stream of bytes is a stream of water that provides a one-way path for the water from a source to a destination. Specifically, cin is the name of an input stream object of the class istream that connects data sent from the standard input device, which is the keyboard, to a program. Similarly, cout is an output stream object of class ostream that connects output from the program to the standard output device, which is the screen.[12]

FIGURE 9.6 The Relationship between Classes

For our current purposes, all we need know is that the insertion, or "put to," operator << is both defined and overloaded in the ostream class to handle the output of built-in types, while the extraction, or "get from," operator >> is both defined and overloaded in the istream class to handle input of built-in types. The capabilities of both the ostream and istream classes are available to the iostream class (through the process of inheritance, explained in the next chapter). Thus, we have access to the cin and cout streams and to the insertion and extraction operators through the iostream class that we have been including in all of our programs. This access permits us to create our own overloaded versions of the << and >> operator functions to handle user-defined object types.

Specifically, the process of making cin extractions and cout insertions available to a user-defined class consists of these steps:

1. Make each overloaded operator function a friend of the user-defined class (this ensures that these overloaded functions will have access to a class's private data members).
2. Construct an overloaded version for each operator function that is appropriate to the user-defined class.

What makes overloading the insertion and extraction operators so easy is that the function prototypes and header lines for each overloaded function are essentially "cookbook" steps. To understand how this is accomplished in practice, consider Program 9.14, which overloads the insertion and extraction operators to handle objects of type Date.

---

[12] A third object, cerr, is an output stream object of class ostream from the program to the standard output device, which is usually the screen. The major difference between cerr and cout is that the cout stream object is buffered while the cerr stream object is not.

PROGRAM 9.14

```cpp
#include <iostream>
using namespace std;

// class declaration

class Date
{
  friend ostream& operator<<(ostream&, const Date&);  // overload inserter operator
  friend istream& operator>>(istream&, Date&);          // overload extractor operator
  private:
    int month;
    int day;
    int year;
  public:
    Date(int = 7, int = 4, int = 2005);     // constructor
};

// implementation section

// overloaded insertion operator function
ostream& operator<<(ostream& out, const Date& adate)
{
  out << adate.month << '/' << adate.day << '/' << adate.year % 100;

  return out;
}

// overloaded extraction operator function
istream& operator>>(istream& in, Date& somedate)
{
  in >> somedate.month;    // accept the month part
  in.ignore(1);            // ignore 1 character, the / character
  in >> somedate.day;      // get the day part
  in.ignore(1);            // ignore 1 character, the / character
  in >> somedate.year;     // get the year part

  return in;
}

Date::Date(int mm, int dd, int yyyy)    // constructor
{
  month = mm;
  day = dd;
  year = yyyy;
}
```

(continued from previous page)

```
int main()
{
  Date a;
  cout << "Enter a date: ";
  cin  >> a;        // accept the date using cin
  cout << "The date just entered is " << a << endl;


  return 0;
}
```

A sample run of Program 9.14 follows:

```
Enter a date: 1/15/2006
The date just entered is 1/15/06
```

In reviewing Program 9.14, first notice that within the `main()` function a `Date` object is entered using `cin` and is output using `cout`. Now look at the class declaration for `Date` and notice that two friend functions have been included in the friends list using these function prototype declarations:

```
friend ostream& operator<<(ostream&, const Date&);
friend istream& operator>>(istream&, Date&);
```

The first declaration makes the overloaded insertion operator function `<<` a friend of the `Date` class, while the second statement does the same for the overloaded extraction operator function `>>`. In the first declaration, the `<<` operator has been declared to return a reference to an `ostream` object and to have two arguments, a reference to an `ostream` and a reference to a `Date` class, which is a constant. Similarly, in the second declaration, the `>>` operator has been declared to return a reference to an `istream` object and to have two arguments, a reference to an `istream` object and a reference to a `Date` object. By simply changing the class name `Date` to the name of any other class and including these declarations within the class's declaration section, these two prototypes can be used in any user-defined class. Thus, the general syntax of these declarations, applicable to any class, is:

```
friend ostream& operator<<(ostream&, const ClassName&);
friend istream& operator>>(istream&, ClassName&);
```

Now consider the implementations of these overloaded functions. Consider first the overloaded insertion operator function, which for convenience we repeat here:

```
ostream& operator<<(ostream& out, const Date& adate)
{
  out << adate.month << '/' << adate.day << '/' << adate.year % 100;

  return out;
}
```

Although the name of the reference to a `Date` object has been named `adate`, any user-selected name would do. Similarly, the parameter named `out`, which is a reference to an `ostream` object, can be any user-selected name. Within the body of the function, we insert the `month`, `day`, and `year` members of the `Date` object to the `out` object, which is then returned from the function. Also notice the notation used in inserting the `month`, `day`, and `year` to `out`, namely:

```
adate.month
adate.day
adate.year
```

This notation follows the dot notation introduced in Section 8.1 that includes both the object name and attribute name with the names separated by a period. This was the reason for making the overloaded operator function a friend of the `Date` class. By doing so, the overloaded insertion operator has direct access to a `Date` object's `month`, `day`, and `year` data members.

Now consider the implementations of the overloaded extraction operator function, which for convenience is repeated here:

```
// overloaded extraction operator function
istream& operator>>(istream& in, Date& somedate)
{
  in >> somedate.month;    // accept the month part
  in.ignore(1);            // ignore 1 character, the / character
  in >> somedate.day;      // get the day part
  in.ignore(1);            // ignore 1 character, the / character
  in >> somedate.year;     // get the year part
  return in;


}
```

The header line for this function declares that it returns a reference to an `istream` object and has two reference parameters: a reference to an `istream` object and a reference to a `Date` object. The parameter names, `in` and `somedate`, can be replaced by any other user-selected names.

The body of the function first extracts a value for the `month` member of the `Date`; then it uses the `ignore()` member function of `istream` to ignore the next input character, which is usually a slash, `/`. The value for the `day` member is then extracted, the next character is ignored, and finally the value of the `year` member is extracted. Thus, if the user typed in the date 1/15/2006 or the date 1-15-2006, the overloaded extractor function extracts 1, 15, and 2006 as the `month`, `day`, and `year` values, respectively. Although this same effect is produced by the single line

```
in >> somedate.month >> '/' >> somedate.day >> '/' >> somedate.year;
```

the coding used in Program 9.14 makes it clear that we are ignoring the delimiting character, whatever it might be.

Exercises 9.6

1. Enter Program 9.13 on your computer and execute it.

2. a. Remove the inline functions in the `Customer` class declaration and implementation section used in Program 9.13 by constructing individual declaration and implementation sections. Discuss which form of the `Customer` class you prefer and why.

   b. Rewrite the `gallons()` function in the Customer class so that it returns a floating-point number between 3.0 and 20.0 gallons.

3. Using the `Elevator` class defined in Section 8.3 and defining a new class name `Person`, construct a simulation whereby a person randomly arrives between 1 and 5 minutes on any floor and calls the elevator. If the elevator is not on the same floor as the person, it must move to the floor the person is on. Once inside the elevator, the person can select any floor except the current one. Run the simulation for three randomly arriving people and have the simulation display the movement of the elevator.

4. In place of the `main()` function used in Program 9.13, a student proposed the following:

```
int main()
{
  Pump a(AMT_IN_TANK, TODAYS_PRICE);   // declare 1 object of type Pump
  Customer b;                          // declare 1 object of type Customer
  int totalTime = 0;
  int idleTime;
  int amtRequest;
  int SimMinutes;   // simulation time in minutes

  SimMinutes = SIMTIME * MINUTES;
  cout << "\nStarting a new simulation - simulation time is "
       << SimMinutes << " minutes" << endl;
  a.values();

  do
  {
    idleTime = b.arrive();
    totalTime += idleTime;
    if (totalTime > (SimMinutes))
    {
      cout << "\nThe idle time is " << idleTime << " minutes." << endl
           << "As the total time now exceeds the simulation time, " << endl
           << "   this simulation run is over." << endl;
      break;
    }
    else
    {
      cout << "\nThe idle time is " << idleTime << " minutes" << endl
           << "    and we are " << totalTime
           << " minutes into the simulation." << endl;
      amtRequest = b.gallons();
      a.request(float(amtRequest));
    }
  } while (1);   // always true
  return 0;
}
```

Determine if this `main()` function produces a valid simulation. If it does not, discuss why not. If it does, discuss which version you prefer and why.

5. Enter Program 9.14 on your computer and execute it.

6. a. Modify the overloaded insertion operator function in Program 9.14 to use `setw(2)` and `setfill("0")` so that it displays a date, such as 12/5/2006, as 12/05/06.

   b. Modify the overloaded insertion operator function in Program 9.14 to accept a third character argument. If the actual argument is an E, the displayed date should be in European format of day-month-year; otherwise, it should be in the American standard form of month/day/year.

7. For the `Time` class constructed in Exercise 2 of Section 9.1, remove the display function and include overloaded extraction and insertion extraction operator functions for the input and output of `Time` objects using `cin` and `cout`, respectively. Times should be displayed in the form hrs:min:sec.

8. For the `Complex` class constructed in Exercise 3 of Section 9.1, remove the display function and include overloaded extraction and insertion extraction operator functions for the input and output of `Complex` objects using `cin` and `cout`, respectively.

9.7 COMMON PROGRAMMING ERRORS

1. Using a user-defined assignment operator in a multiple assignment expression when the operator has not been defined to return an object.

2. Using the keyword `static` when defining either a static data or function member. Here, the `static` keyword should be used only within the class declaration section.

3. Using the keyword `friend` when defining a friend function. The `friend` keyword should be used only within the class declaration section.

4. Failing to instantiate `static` data members before creating class objects that must access these data members.

5. Attempting to redefine an operator's meaning as it applies to C++'s built-in data types.

6. Redefining an overloaded operator to perform a function not indicated by its conventional meaning. Although this works, it is an example of extremely bad programming practice.

7. Attempting to make a conversion operator function a friend rather than a member function.

8. Attempting to specify a return type for a member conversion operator function.

9.8 CHAPTER REVIEW

Key Terms

assignment operator	memberwise assignment
class scope	operator functions
conversion operator function	operator()
copy constructor	operator[]
data type conversions	static class data member
default copy constructor	static member function
friend functions	type conversion constructor

Summary

1. An assignment operator may be declared for a class with the function prototype:

```
void operator=(ClassName&);
```

Here, the argument is a reference to the class name. The return type of `void` precludes the use of this operator in multiple assignment expressions such as `a = b = c`.

2. A type of initialization that closely resembles assignment occurs in C++ when one object is initialized using another object of the same class. The constructor that performs this type of initialization is called a *copy constructor* and has the function prototype:

```
ClassName(const ClassName&);
```

This is frequently represented using the notation X(X&).

3. Each class has an associated class scope, which is defined by the brace pair, { }, containing the class declaration. Data and function members are local to the scope of their class and can only be used by objects declared for the class. If a global variable name is reused within a class, the global variable is hidden by the class variable. Within the scope of the class variable, the global variable may be accessed using the scope resolution operator : :.

4. For each class object, a separate set of memory locations is reserved for all data members, except those declared as `static`. A `static` data member is shared by all class objects and provides a means of communication between objects. `Static` data members must be declared as such within the class declaration section and are defined outside of the declaration section.

5. `Static` function members apply to the class as a whole rather than to individual objects. Hence, a `static` function member can access only `static` data members and other `static` function members. `Static` function members must be declared as such within the class declaration section and are defined outside of the declaration section.

6. A nonmember function may access a class's private data members if it is granted `friend` status by the class. This is accomplished by declaring the function as a `friend` within the class's declaration section. Thus, it is always the class that determines which nonmember functions are friends; a function can never confer `friend` status on itself.

7. User-defined operators can be constructed for classes using member operator functions. An operator function has the form `operator<symbol>`, where `<symbol>` is one of the following:

```
()   []   ->   new   delete   ++  --  !~   ~   *   /   %   +   -
<<   >>   <   <=   >   >=   ++   !=   &&   ||   &   ^   |   =   +=
-=   *=   /=   %=   &=   ^=   |=   <<=   >>=   ,
```

For example, the function prototype `Date operator+(int);` declares that the addition operator is defined to accept an integer and return a `Date` object.

8. User-defined operators may be called in either of two ways: as a conventional function with arguments or as an operator expression. For example, for an operator having the header line

```
Date Date::operator+(int)
```

if `dte` is an object of type `Date`, the following two calls produce the same effect:

```
dte.operator+(284)
dte + 284
```

9. Operator functions may also be written as `friend` functions. The equivalent `friend` version of a member operator function always contains an additional class reference that is not required by the member function.

10. The subscript operator function, `operator[]`, permits a maximum of one nonclass argument. This function can only be defined as a member function.

11. The parentheses operator function, `operator()`, has no limits on the number of arguments. This function can only be defined as a member function.

12. There are four categories of data type conversions. They are conversions from:

   - Built-in types to built-in types
   - Built-in types to user-defined (class) types
   - User-defined (class) types to built-in types
   - User-defined (class) types to user-defined (class) types

   Built-in to built-in type conversions are performed using C++'s implicit conversion rules or explicitly using casts. Built-in to user-defined type conversions are performed using type conversion constructors. Conversions from user-defined types to either built-in or other user-defined types are performed using conversion operator functions.

13. A type conversion constructor is a constructor whose first parameter is not a member of its class and whose remaining parameters, if any, have default values.

14. A conversion operator function is a member operator function having the name of a built-in data type or class. It has no explicit parameters or return type; rather, the return type is the name of the function.

15. The `cout` insertion operator, `<<`, and the `cin` extraction operator, `>>`, can be overloaded to work with any class objects using this process:

   - Make each overloaded operator function a friend of the user-defined class (this ensures that these overloaded functions have access to a class's private data members).
   - Construct an overloaded version for each operator function that is appropriate to the user-defined class.

   The general function prototype syntax for providing these operator functions with friend status is:

   ```
   friend ostream& operator<<(ostream&, const ClassName&);
   friend istream& operator>>(istream&, ClassName&);
   ```

   These prototypes should be placed in the declaration section of the desired class and the `className` entry in each declaration changed to the actual class name.

Exercises

1. a. Construct a class named `Cartesian` that contains two floating-point data members named `x` and `y`, which are used to store the x and y values of a

point in rectangular coordinates. The function members should include a constructor that initializes the x and y values of an object to 0 and functions to input and display an object's x and y values. Additionally, there should be an assignment function that performs a memberwise assignment between two `Cartesian` objects.

b. Include the class written for Exercise 1a in a working C++ program that creates and displays the values of two Cartesian objects, the second of which is assigned the values of the first object.

2. a. Construct a class named `Savings` that contains three floating-point data members named `balance`, `rate`, and `interest` and a constructor that initializes each of these members to 0. Additionally, there should be a member function that inputs a balance and rate and then calculates an interest. The rate should be stored as a percentage, such as 6.5 for 6.5%, and the interest computed as *interest = balance × rate/100*. Additionally, there should be a member function to display all member values.

b. Include the class written for Exercise 2a in a working C++ program that tests each member function.

3. a. Redo Exercise 2 but make `rate` a static data member and include a static member function to input and alter `rate`'s value.

b. Include the class written for Exercise 3a in a working C++ program that tests each member function.

4. a. Construct a class named `Coord` that contains two floating-point data members named `xval` and `yval`, which are used to store the *x* and *y* values of a point in rectangular coordinates. The function members should include appropriate constructor and display functions and a friend function named `ConvPolar()`. The `ConvPolar()` function should accept two floating-point numbers that represent a point in polar coordinates and convert them into rectangular coordinates. For conversion from polar to rectangular coordinates, use the formulas:

$$x = r \cos \theta$$
$$y = r \sin \theta$$

b. Include the class written for Exercise 4a in a working C++ program.

5. a. Construct two classes named `RecCoord` and `PolarCoord`. The class named `RecCoord` should contain two floating-point data members named `xval` and `yval`, which are used to store the *x* and *y* values of a point in rectangular coordinates. The function members should include appropriate constructor and display functions and a friend function named `ConvPolar()`.

The class named `PolarCoord` should contain two floating-point data members named `dist` and `theta`, which are used to store the distance and angle values of a point represented in polar coordinates. The function members should include appropriate constructor and display functions and a friend function named `ConvPolar()`.

The friend function should accept an integer parameter named `dir`; two floating-point parameters named `val1` and `val2`; and two reference parameters named `recref` and `polref`, the first of which should be a reference to an object of type `RecCoord`, and the second to an object of type `PolarCoord`. If the value of `dir` is 1, `val1` and `val2` are to be considered as x and y rectangular coordinates that are to be converted to polar coordinates; if the value of `dir` is any other value, `val1` and `val2` are considered as distance and angle values that are to be converted to rectangular coordinates. For conversion from rectangular to polar coordinates, use these formulas:

$$r = \sqrt{x^2 + y^2}$$
$$\theta = \operatorname{atan}(y/x), x \neq 0$$

For conversion from polar to rectangular coordinates, use these formulas:

$$x = r \cos \theta$$
$$y = r \sin \theta$$

   b. Include the class written for Exercise 5a in a working C++ program.

6. List three C++ operators that cannot be overloaded.

7. a. Create a class named `Fractions` having two integer data members named for a fraction's numerator and denominator. The class's default constructor should provide both data members with default values of 1 if no explicit user initialization is provided. The constructor must also prohibit a 0 denominator value. Additionally, provide member functions for displaying an object's data values. Also provide the class with overloaded operators that are capable of adding, subtracting, multiplying, and dividing two `Fraction` objects according to the following formulas:

Sum of two fractions: $\quad \dfrac{a}{b} + \dfrac{c}{d} = \dfrac{ad + cb}{bd}$

Difference of two fractions: $\quad \dfrac{a}{b} + \dfrac{c}{d} = \dfrac{ad - cb}{bd}$

Product of two fractions: $\quad \dfrac{a}{b} \times \dfrac{c}{d} = \dfrac{ab}{bd}$

Division of two fractions: $\quad \dfrac{a}{b} \div \dfrac{c}{d} = \dfrac{ad}{cb}$

   b. Include the class written for Exercise 7a in a working C++ program that tests each of the class's member functions.

8. a. Include a member function named `gcd()` in the `Fraction` class constructed in Exercise 7 that reduces a fraction to its lowest common terms. Thus, a fraction such as 2/4 is reduced to 1/2. The means of doing this is to divide both the numerator and denominator values by their greatest common divisor. (See Exercise 6 in Section 6.10 for a description of how to obtain the greatest common divisor of two numbers.)

b. Modify the constructor written for Exercise 7a to include a call to gcd() so that every initialized fraction is in lowest common terms. Also make sure that each overloaded operator function also uses gcd() to return a fraction in lowest common terms.

c. Replace the display function with an overloaded insertion operator so that a Fraction object can be inserted directly into the cout stream. Also include an overloaded extraction operator that uses the cin stream with a Fraction object.

10

Inheritance and Dynamic Memory Allocation

This chapter shows how a class designed by one programmer can be altered by another in a way that retains the integrity and design of the original class. This is accomplished using inheritance, a new feature that is central to object-oriented programming. Inheritance permits the reuse and extension of existing code in a way that ensures the new code does not adversely affect what has already been written.

In addition to class construction and inheritance, the third required feature of all object-oriented languages is the ability to produce polymorphic behavior. This feature permits the same method name to invoke different responses in inherited class objects. Polymorphism is presented in Section 10.2.

Finally, the topic of dynamic creation and allocation of objects as a program is executing is presented.

10.1 CLASS INHERITANCE

The ability to create new classes from existing ones is the underlying motivation and power behind class and object-oriented programming techniques. This ability facilitates the reuse of existing code in new ways without the need for retesting and validation. It permits the designers of a class to make it available to others for additions and extensions without relinquishing control over the existing class features.

Constructing one class from another is accomplished using a capability called inheritance. Related to this capability is an equally important feature named polymorphism. Polymorphism provides the ability to redefine how member functions

Object-Based Versus Object-Oriented Languages

An *object-based language* is one in which data and operations can be incorporated in such a way that data values can be isolated and accessed through the specified class functions. The ability to bind the data members with operations in a single unit is referred to as *encapsulation.* In C++, encapsulation is provided by its class capability.

For a language to be classified as object-oriented, it must also provide inheritance and polymorphism. *Inheritance* is the capability to derive one class from another. A derived class is a completely new data type that incorporates all of the data members and member functions of the original class with any new data and function members unique to itself. The class used as the basis for the derived type is referred to as the *base* or *parent class*, and the derived data type is referred to as the *derived*, *child class, or subclass*.

Polymorphism permits the same method name to invoke one operation in objects of a parent class and a different operation in objects of a derived class.

C++, which provides encapsulation, inheritance, and polymorphism, is a true object-oriented language. Because C, which is C++'s predecessor, does not provide these features, it is neither an object-based nor an object-oriented language.

of related classes operate based on the class object being referenced. In fact, for a programming language to be classified as a true object-oriented language, it must provide the features of classes, inheritance, and polymorphism. In this section, we describe the inheritance features provided in C++. Polymorphism is presented in Section 10.2.

Inheritance is the ability to derive one class from another class. The initial class used as the basis for the derived class is referred to as either the **base class**, **parent class**, or **superclass**. The derived class is referred to as either the **derived class**, **child class**, or **subclass**.

A derived class is a completely new class that incorporates all of the data and member functions of its base class. It can, and usually does, however, add its own additional new data and function members, and it can override any base class function.

As an example of inheritance, consider three geometric shapes consisting of a circle, cylinder, and sphere. All of these shapes share a common characteristic, and we can make the circle a base type for the other two shapes, as illustrated in Figure 10.1.[1] Reformulating these shapes as class types, we make the circle the base class and derive the cylinder and sphere classes from it.

The relationships illustrated in Figure 10.1 are examples of simple inheritance. In **simple inheritance**, each derived type has only one immediate base type. The complement to simple inheritance is multiple inheritance. In **multiple inheritance**, a derived type has two or more base types. Figure 10.2 illustrates an example of multiple inheritance. In this text, we consider only simple inheritance.

The class derivations illustrated in both Figures 10.1 and 10.2 are formally referred to as **class hierarchies** because they illustrate the hierarchy, or order, in which one class is derived from another. Now we look at how to derive one class from another.

---

[1] By convention, arrows always point from the derived class to the base class.

FIGURE 10.1 Relating Object Types

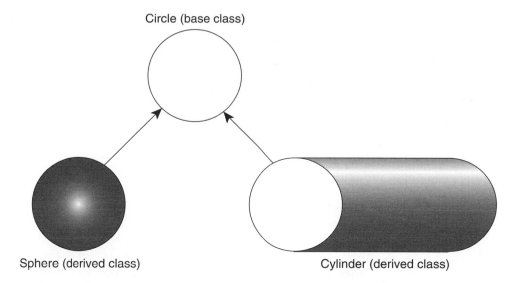

Circle (base class)

Sphere (derived class) Cylinder (derived class)

A derived class has the same form as any other class in that it consists of both a declaration and an implementation. The only difference is in the first line of the declaration section. For a derived class, this line is extended to include an access specification and a base class name using the syntax:

```
class DerivedClassName : class-access BaseClassName
```

For example, if `Circle` is the name of an existing class, a new class named `Cylinder` can be derived as follows:

```
class Cylinder : public Circle
{
    // add any additional data and
    // function members in here
};  // end of Cylinder class declaration
```

FIGURE 10.2 An Example of Multiple Inheritance

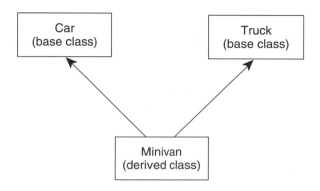

Car
(base class)

Truck
(base class)

Minivan
(derived class)

Except for the class-access specifier after the colon and the base class name, there is nothing inherently new or complicated about the construction of the `Cylinder` class. Before providing a description of the `Circle` class and adding data and function members to the derived `Cylinder` class, we need to reexamine access specifiers and how they relate to derived classes.

Access Specifications

Until now, we have used only private and public access specifiers within a class. Giving all data members private status ensured that they can only be accessed by either class member functions or friends. This restricted access prevents access by any nonclass functions (except friends), *which also precludes access by any derived class functions.* This is a sensible restriction because, if it did not exist, anyone could "jump around" the private restriction by simply constructing a derived class.

To retain a restricted type of access across derived classes, C++ provides a third access specification, protected. Protected access behaves identically to private access in that it only permits member or friend function access, but it permits this restriction to be inherited by any derived class. The derived class then defines the type of inheritance it is willing to take on, subject to the base class's access restrictions. This is done by the class-access specifier, which is listed after the colon at the start of its declaration section. Table 10.1 lists the resulting derived class member access based on a base class member's specification and the derived class-access specifier. In Table 10.1, we can see in the shaded region that if a base class member has a protected access and the derived class specifier is public, then the derived class member is protected to its class. Similarly, if a base class has a public access and the derived class specifier is public, the derived class member is public. This is the most commonly used type of specification for base class data and function members, respectively, and is the one we will use. This means that for all classes intended for use as a base class, we use a protected data member access in place of a private designation.

TABLE 10.1 Inherited Access Restrictions

Base Class Member	Derived Class Access	Derived Class Member
private ------------>	: private -------------->	inaccessible
protected ---------->	: private -------------->	private
public ------------->	: private -------------->	private
private ------------>	: public -------------->	inaccessible
protected ---------->	: public ---------------->	protected
public ------------->	: public ---------------->	public
private ------------>	: protected ------------->	inaccessible
protected ---------->	: protected ------------->	protected
public ------------->	: protected ------------->	protected

An Example

To illustrate the process of deriving one class from another, we will derive a `Cylinder` class from a base `Circle` class. The definition of the `Circle` class is:

```
// class declaration

class Circle
{
  protected:
    double radius;
  public:
    Circle(double = 1.0);  // constructor
    double calcval();
};

// class implementation

// constructor
Circle::Circle(double r)  // constructor
{
  radius = r;
}

// calculate the area of a circle
double Circle::calcval()
{
  return(PI * radius * radius);
}
```

Except for the substitution of the access specifier `protected` in place of the usual `private` specifier for the data member, this is a standard class definition. The only variable not defined is `PI`, which is used in the `calcval()` function. We define this as:

```
const double PI = 2.0 * asin(1.0);
```

This is simply a "trick" that forces the computer to return the value of `PI` accurate to as many decimal places as allowed by your computer. This value is obtained by taking the arcsin of 1.0, which is $\pi/2$, and multiplying the result by 2.

Having defined our base class, we can now extend it to a derived class. The definition of the derived class is:

```
// class declaration where
// Cylinder is derived from Circle

class Cylinder : public Circle
{
  protected:
    double length;  // add one additional data member and
  public:           // two additional function members
    Cylinder(double r = 1.0, double l = 1.0) : Circle(r), length(l) {}
    double calcval();
};

// class implementation

double Cylinder::calcval()   // this calculates a volume
{
  return (length * Circle::calcval()); // note the base function call
}
```

Relationship Between Circle and Cylinder Data Members

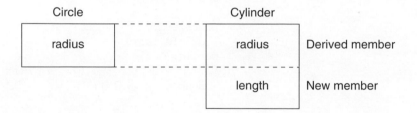

This definition encompasses several important concepts relating to derived classes. First, as a derived class, Cylinder contains all of the data and function members of its base class, Circle, plus any additional members that may be added. In this particular case, the Cylinder class consists of a radius data member, inherited from the Circle class, plus an additional length member. Thus, each Cylinder object contains *two* data members, as illustrated in Figure 10.3.

In addition to having two data members, the Cylinder class also inherits Circle's function members. This is illustrated in the Cylinder constructor, which uses a base member initialization list (see Section 8.1) that specifically calls the Circle constructor. It is also illustrated in Cylinder's calcval() function, which makes a call to Circle::calcval().

In both classes, the same function name, calcval(), has been specifically used to illustrate the overriding of a base function by a derived function. When a Cylinder object calls calcval(), it is a request to use the Cylinder version of the function, whereas a Circle object call to calcval() is a request to use the Circle version. In this case, the Cylinder class can only access the class version of calcval() using the scope resolution operator, as is done in the call Circle::calcval(). Program 10.1 uses these two classes within the context of a complete program.

PROGRAM 10.1

```cpp
#include <iostream>
#include <cmath>
using namespace std;

const double PI = 2.0 * asin(1.0);
// class declaration

class Circle
{
  protected:
    double radius;
  public:
    Circle(double = 1.0);   // constructor
    double calcval();
};
```

(continued from previous page)

```
// implementation section for Circle
Circle::Circle(double r)   // constructor
{
  radius = r;
}

// calculate the area of a circle
double Circle::calcval()
{
  return(PI * radius * radius);
}

// class declaration for the derived class
// Cylinder which is derived from Circle
class Cylinder : public Circle
{
  protected:
    double length;  // add one additional data member and
  public:           // two additional function members
    Cylinder(double r = 1.0, double l = 1.0) : Circle(r), length(l) {}
    double calcval();
};

// implementation for Cylinder

double Cylinder::calcval()    // this calculates a volume
{
  return (length * Circle::calcval()); // note the base function call
}
```

```
int main()
{
  Circle circle_1, circle_2(2);  // create two Circle objects
  Cylinder cylinder_1(3,4);       // create one Cylinder object

  cout << "The area of circle_1 is " << circle_1.calcval() << endl;
  cout << "The area of circle_2 is " << circle_2.calcval() << endl;
  cout << "The volume of cylinder_1 is " << cylinder_1.calcval() << endl;

  circle_1 = cylinder_1;  // assign a cylinder to a Circle

  cout << "\nThe area of circle_1 is now " << circle_1.calcval() << endl;

  return 0;
}
```

The output produced by Program 10.1 is:

```
The area of circle_1 is 3.141593
The area of circle_2 is 12.566371
The volume of cylinder_1 is 113.097336

The area of circle_1 is now 28.274334
```

The first three output lines are all straightforward and are produced by the first three `cout` statements in the program. As the output shows, a call to `calcval()` using a `Circle` object activates the `Circle` version of this function, whereas a call to `calcval()` using a `Cylinder` object activates the `Cylinder` version.

The assignment statement `circle_1 = cylinder_1;` introduces another important relationship between a base and derived class: *A derived class object can be assigned to a base class object.* This should not be surprising because both base and derived classes share a common set of data member types. In this type of assignment, it is only this set of data members, which consist of all the base class data members, that is assigned. Thus, as illustrated in Figure 10.4, our `Cylinder` to `Circle` assignment results in the following memberwise assignment:

```
circle_1.radius = cylinder_1.radius;
```

The length member of the `Cylinder` object is not used in the assignment because it has no equivalent variable in the `Circle` class. The reverse cast, from base to derived class, is not as simple and requires a constructor to correctly initialize the additional derived class members not in the base class.

Before leaving Program 10.1, one additional point should be made. Although the `Circle` constructor was explicitly called using a base/member initialization list for the `Cylinder` constructor, an implicit call could also have been made. In the absence of an explicitly derived class constructor, the compiler automatically calls the default base class constructor first, before the derived class constructor is called. This works because the derived class contains all of the base class data members. In a similar fashion, the destructor functions are called in the reverse order: first derived class and then base class.

FIGURE 10.4   Assignment from Derived to Base Class

Circle = Cylinder

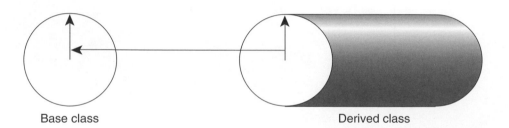

Base class   Derived class

Exercises 10.1

1. Define the following terms:

    a. inheritance

    b. base class

    c. derived class

    d. simple inheritance

    e. multiple inheritance

    f. class hierarchy

2. Describe the difference between a private and a protected class member.

3. What three features must a programming language provide for it to be classified as an object-oriented language?

4. a. Modify Program 10.1 to include a derived class named `Sphere` from the base `Circle` class. The only additional class members of `Sphere` should be a constructor and a `calcval()` function that returns the volume of the sphere. (*Note:* Volume = $4/3 \, \pi \, radius^3$.)

    b. Include the class constructed for Exercise 4a in a working C++ program. Have your program call all of the member functions in the `Sphere` class.

10.2 POLYMORPHISM

The overriding of a base member function using an overloaded derived member function, as illustrated by the `calcval()` function in Program 10.1, is an example of polymorphism. **Polymorphism** permits the same function name to invoke one response in objects of a base class and another response in objects of a derived class. In some cases, however, this method of overriding may not work as desired. To understand why this is so, consider Program 10.2.

PROGRAM 10.2

```
#include <iostream>
#include <cmath>
using namespace std;

// class declaration for the base class

class One
{
  protected:
    double a;
  public:
    One(double = 2.0);    // constructor
    double f1(double);    // a member function
    double f2(double);    // another member function
};
```

(continued from previous page)

```cpp
// class implementation for One

One::One(double val)    // constructor
{
  a = val;
}

double One::f1(double num)   // a member function
{
  return (num/2);
}
double One::f2(double num)   // another member function
{
  return( pow(f1(num),2) );   // square the result of f1()
}

// class declaration for the derived class

class Two : public One
{
  public:
    double f1(double);     // this overrides class One's f1()
};

// class implementation for Two

double Two::f1(double num)
{
  return (num/3);
}
```

```cpp
int main()
{
  One object_1;   // object_1 is an object of the base class
  Two object_2;   // object_2 is an object of the derived class

    // call f2() using a base class object call
  cout << "The computed value using a base class object call is "
       << object_1.f2(12) << endl;

    // call f2() using a derived class object call
  cout << "The computed value using a derived class object call is "
       << object_2.f2(12) << endl;

  return 0;
}
```

The output produced by this program is:

```
The computed value using a base class object call is 36
The computed value using a derived class object call is 36
```

As this output shows, the same result is obtained no matter which object type calls the f2() function. This result is produced because the derived class does not have an override to the base class f2() function. Thus, both calls to f2() result in the base class f2() function being called.

Once invoked, the base class f2() function always calls the base class version of f1() rather than the derived class override version. This behavior is due to a process referred to as *function binding.* In normal function calls, static binding is used. In **static binding**, the determination of which function is called is made at compile time. Thus, when the compiler first encounters the f1() function in the base class, it makes the determination that whenever f2() is called, either from a base or derived class object, it will subsequently call the base class f1() function.

In place of static binding, we want a binding method that is capable of determining which function should be invoked at run time based on the object type making the call. This type of binding is referred to as **dynamic binding**. To achieve dynamic binding, C++ provides virtual functions.

A **virtual function** specification tells the compiler to create a pointer to a function, but not fill in the value of the pointer until the function is actually called. Then, at run time, *and based on the object making the call,* the appropriate function address is used. Creating a virtual function is extremely easy; all that is required is that the keyword `virtual` be placed before the function's return type in the declaration section. For example, consider Program 10.3, which is identical to Program 10.2 except for the virtual declaration of the f1() function.

PROGRAM 10.3

```cpp
#include <iostream>
#include <cmath>
using namespace std;

// class declaration for the base class

class One
{
  protected:
    double a;
  public:
    One(double = 2.0);   // constructor
    virtual double f1(double);   // a member function
    float f2(double);   // another member function
};
```

(continued from previous page)

```cpp
// class implementation for One

One::One(double val)    // constructor
{
  a = val;
}

double One::f1(double num)   // a member function
{
  return (num/2);
}

double One::f2(double num)   // another member function
{
  return( pow(f1(num),2) );   // square the result of f1()
}



// class declaration for the derived class

class Two : public One
{
  public:
    virtual double f1(float);    // this overrides class One's f1()
};

// class implementation for Two

double Two::f1(double num)
{
  return (num/3);
}
```

```cpp
int main()
{
  One object_1;   // object_1 is an object of the base class
  Two object_2;   // object_2 is an object of the derived class

    // call f2() using a base class object call
  cout << "The computed value using a base class object call is "
       << object_1.f2(12) << endl;

    // call f2() using a derived class object call
  cout << "The computed value using a derived class object call is "
       << object_2.f2(12) << endl;

  return 0;
}
```

The output produced by Program 10.3 is:

```
The computed value using a base class object call is 36
The computed value using a derived class object call is 16
```

As illustrated by this output, the f2() function now calls different versions of the overloaded f1() function based on the object type making the call. This selection, based on the object making the call, is the classic definition of polymorphic function behavior and is caused by the dynamic binding imposed on f1() by virtue of its being a virtual function.

Once a function is declared as virtual, *it remains virtual for the next derived class with or without a virtual declaration in the derived class.* Thus, the second virtual declaration in the derived class is not strictly needed but should be included both for clarity and to ensure that any subsequently derived classes correctly inherit the function. Consider the inheritance diagram in Figure 10.5, where class C is derived from class B and class B is derived from class A.[2] In this situation, if function f1() is virtual in class A, but is not declared in class B, it will not be virtual in class C. The only other requirement is that, once a function has been declared as virtual, the return type and parameter list of all subsequent derived class override versions *must* be the same.

FIGURE 10.5 Inheritance Diagram

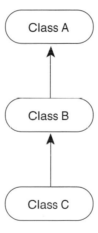

Exercises 10.2

1. Enter and execute Programs 10.2 and 10.3 on your computer so that you understand the relationship between function calls in each program.

2. Describe the two methods C++ provides for implementing polymorphism.

3. Describe the difference between static binding and dynamic binding.

4. Describe the difference between a virtual function and a nonvirtual function.

5. Describe what polymorphism is and provide an example of polymorphic behavior.

---

[2] By convention, as previously noted in Section 10.1, arrows point from the derived class to the base class.

10.3 THE this POINTER

Except for static data members, which are shared by all class objects, each object maintains its own set of member variables. This permits each object to have its own clearly defined state as determined by the values stored in its member variables.

For example, consider the `Date` class previously defined in Program 9.1 and repeated here for convenience:

```cpp
#include <iostream>
using namespace std;

// class declaration

class Date
{
  private:
    int month;
    int day;
    int year;
  public:
    Date(int = 7, int = 4, int = 2005);      // constructor
    void showdate();       // member function to display a Date
};

// implementation section

Date::Date(int mm, int dd, int yyyy)
{
  month = mm;
  day = dd;
  year = yyyy;
}

void Date::showdate()
{
  cout << "The date is";
  cout << setfill('0')
       << setw(2) << month << '/'
       << setw(2) << day << '/'
       << setw(2) << year % 100; // extract the last 2 year digits
  cout << endl;

  return;
}
```

Each time an object is created from this class, a distinct area of memory is set aside for its data members. For example, if two objects named a and b are created from this class, the memory storage for these objects is as illustrated in Figure 10.6. Notice that each set of data members has its own starting address in memory, which corresponds to the address of the first data member for the object.

This replication of data storage is not implemented for class functions. In fact, for each class, *only one copy of the member functions is retained in memory*, and each object uses these same functions.

Sharing member functions requires providing a means of identifying on which specific object class function should be operating. This is accomplished by providing address information to the function indicating where in memory the particular object is located. This address is provided by the name of the object, which is a reference name. For example, again using our Date class and assuming a is an object of this class, the statement a.showdate() passes the address of the a object into the showdate() member function. (Review Section 2.4 for information on memory addresses.)

FIGURE 10.6 The Storage of Two Date Objects in Memory

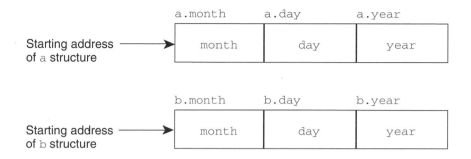

An obvious question at this point is how this address is passed to showdate() and where it is stored. The answer is that the address is stored in a special parameter named **this**, which is automatically supplied as a hidden parameter to each nonstatic member function when the function is called.

Unlike a reference parameter, which is effectively a named constant for an address, the this parameter is a pointer parameter. Although pointer parameters provide much more flexibility in using addresses than reference parameters and are explained in detail in Section 14.1, for our current purposes, all we need to know is that to gain access to the object whose address is provided by the this pointer we must apply C++'s dereference operator, *, to this.

Before proceeding to use the this pointer in a "cookbook" manner, let's take a moment to compare the differences between a pointer's address and a reference address. Recall from Section 6.5 that whenever a reference parameter is encountered, it is always *the contents of the reference address* that are accessed. This type of access is referred to as *automatic* or *implicit dereferencing* of the address and effectively hides the fact that a reference parameter is fundamentally a named constant for an address. When using a pointer parameter, dereferencing is not automatic. To access the contents of the address provided by the this pointer, the notation *this or its equivalent this-> must be used, which formally provides what is known as *explicit dereferencing*.

Returning now to our Date class, which has three member functions, the complete parameter list of the constructor Date() function is equivalent to:

                Date(Date *this, int mm, int dd, int yyyy)

where the declaration Date *this means that the this pointer contains the address of a specific Date object; similarly, the declaration Date& refarg means that the refarg reference parameter is the address of a Date object.[3] Similarly, the complete parameter list of showdate() is equivalent to:

                showdate(Date *this)

---

[3] Placing a space before the *, while a space is placed after the &, is by convention. Thus, Date& refarg can be written as Date &refarg and Date *this can be written as Date* this.

PROGRAM 10.4

```cpp
#include <iostream>
#include <iomanip>
using namespace std;

// class declaration

class Date
{
  private:
    int month;
    int day;
    int year;
  public:
    Date(int = 7, int = 4, int = 2005);      // constructor
    void showdate();      // member function to display a Date
};

// implementation section

Date::Date(int mm, int dd, int yyyy)
{
  (*this).month = mm;
  (*this).day = dd;
  (*this).year = yyyy;
}

void Date::showdate()
{
  cout << setfill('0')
       << setw(2) << (*this).month << '/'
       << setw(2) << (*this).day << '/'
       << setw(2) << (*this).year % 100;

  return;
}

int main()
{
  Date a(4,1,1999), b(12,18,2006); // declare two objects

  cout << "The date stored in a is originally ";
  a.showdate();  // display the original date
  a = b;          // assign b's value to a
  cout << "\nAfter assignment the date stored in a is ";
  a.showdate();  // display a's values
  cout << endl;

  return 0;
}
```

The important point here is to understand that when a member function is called, it actually receives an extra hidden argument that is the address of a Date object. Although it is usually not necessary to do so, this pointer data member can be explicitly used within all member functions. For example, consider Program 10.4, which uses the hidden argument this within the body of each member function to access the appropriate data member variables.

The output produced by Program 10.4 is:

```
The date stored in a is originally 04/01/99
After assignment the date stored in a is 12/18/06
```

This is the same output produced by Program 9.1, which does not use the this pointer to access the data members. Clearly, using the this pointer in Program 10.4 is unnecessary and simply clutters the member function code. There are times, however, when an object must pass its address to other functions. In these situations, one of which we now consider, the address stored in the this pointer must explicitly be used.[4]

The Assignment Operator Revisited

A simple assignment operator function was defined in Program 9.2 and is repeated here for convenience:

```
void Date::operator=(Date& newdate)
{
  day = newdate.day;      // assign the day
  month = newdate.month;  // assign the month
  year = newdate.year;    // assign the year
}
```

The drawback of this function is that it returns no value, making multiple assignments such as a = b = c impossible. Now that we have the this pointer at our disposal, we can fix our simple assignment operator function to provide an appropriate return type. In this case, the return value should be a Date rather than a void. Making this change in the function's prototype for our assignment operator yields:

```
Date operator=(const Date&);
```

Notice also that we have declared the function's argument to be a const, which ensures that this operand cannot be altered by the function. A suitable function definition for this prototype is:

```
Date Date::operator=(const Date& newdate)
{
  day = newdate.day;      // assign the day
  month = newdate.month;  // assign the month
  year = newdate.year;    // assign the year

  return *this;
}
```

In an assignment such as b = c or its equivalent form, b.operator=(c), the function first alters b's member values from within the function and then returns the value of this object, which may be used in a subsequent assignment. Thus, a multiple assignment expression such as a = b = c is possible and is illustrated in Program 10.5.

---

[4] The notation (*this). used in Program 10.4 can be replaced by the notation this ->.

PROGRAM 10.5

```cpp
#include <iostream>
#include <iomanip>
using namespace std;

// class declaration

class Date
{
  private:
    int month;
    int day;
    int year;
  public:
    Date(int = 7, int = 4, int = 2005);      // constructor
    Date operator=(const Date&);   // define assignment of a date
    void showdate();              // member function to display a date
};

// implementation section

Date::Date(int mm, int dd, int yyyy)
{
  month = mm;
  day = dd;
  year = yyyy;
}

Date Date::operator=(const Date& newdate)
{
  day = newdate.day;        // assign the day
  month = newdate.month;    // assign the month
  year = newdate.year;      // assign the year

  return *this;
}

void Date::showdate()
{
  cout << setfill('0')
       << setw(2) << this->month << '/'
       << setw(2) << this->day << '/'
       << setw(2) << this->year % 100;

  return;
}

int main()
{
  Date a(4,1,1999), b(12,18,2005), c(1,1,2006); // declare three objects
```

```
cout << "\nBefore assignment a's date value is ";
a.showdate();
cout << "\nBefore assignment b's date value is ";
b.showdate();
cout << "\nBefore assignment c's date value is ";
c.showdate();

a = b = c;   // multiple assignment

cout << "\nAfter assignment a's date value is ";
a.showdate();
cout << "\nAfter assignment b's date value is ";
b.showdate();
cout << "\nAfter assignment c's date value is ";
c.showdate();
cout << endl;

return 0;
}
```

The output produced by Program 10.5 is:

```
Before assignment a's date value is 04/01/99
Before assignment b's date value is 12/18/05
Before assignment c's date value is 01/01/06

After assignment a's date value is 01/01/06
After assignment b's date value is 01/01/06
After assignment c's date value is 01/01/06
```

As noted previously in Section 9.3, the only restriction on the assignment operator function is that it can only be overloaded as a member function. It cannot be overloaded as a friend function. Also notice that in the showdate() function we used the notation this > in place of the (*this). notation used in Program 10.4. You will see both types of notations used in your professional work.

Exercises 10.3

1. Discuss the difference between the automatic dereferencing that occurs when a reference parameter is used and the explicit dereferencing required by the this parameter.

2. Modify Program 10.4 so that the notation this-> is used in place of the notation (*this). within the body of both the constructor and showdate() functions. In doing so, notice that the -> symbol is constructed using a hyphen, -, followed by a right-facing arrowhead, >.

3. Rewrite the Date(), operator=(), and showdate() member functions in Program 9.2 to explicitly use the this pointer when referencing all data members. Run your program and verify that the same output as produced by Program 9.2 is achieved.

4. A problem with the assignment operator defined in this section is that it does not return a suitable l-value. (Recall from Section 3.1 that an l-value is a value that can be used on the left side of an assignment statement.) Although Program 10.5 defines a return type for the Date assignment operator, the return type is not used as an l-value because the expression a = b = c is evaluated as a = (b = c). Thus, in both the initial assignment b = c and the subsequent assignment a = b, the return value of the assignment operator is used as an r-value (that is, it is used on the right-hand side of an assignment). Modify the assignment operator so that the expression returns a correct l-value. This means that in the evaluation of the expression (a = b) = c, the initial l-value returned should be a.

10.4 PROGRAM DESIGN AND DEVELOPMENT

A multi-object simulation was presented in Section 9.6. In that simulation the same `Customer` object was reused to simulate multiple `Customer` arrivals. In the problem presented in this chapter different `Customer` objects are dynamically created as they are needed and deleted once their task has been completed.

To understand how the dynamic creation and deletion is accomplished we present an initial application that takes a first look at the dynamic allocation of memory storage. Dynamic allocation is presented a second time, as it applies to arrays (Chapter 12), and finally is considered once again as it applies to linked lists, stacks, and queues in Chapter 16. Each presentation can be read independently.

Application 1: Dynamic Object Creation and Deletion

As each variable or object is defined in a program, sufficient storage for it is designated by the compiler and assigned from a pool of computer memory locations before the program is executed. Once specific memory locations have been assigned they remain fixed for the lifetime of the variable and object or until the program has finished executing. For example, if a function requests storage for three non-static integers and five objects of a user-defined class, the storage for these integers and objects remains fixed from the point of their definition until the function finishes executing.

An alternative to this fixed allocation of memory is a dynamic allocation. Under dynamic allocation, the amount of allocated storage is determined and assigned as the function is executing, rather than being fixed prior to execution.

Although dynamic allocation of memory is most useful when dealing with lists where it allows the list to expand as new items are added and contracted as items are deleted, it can also be useful in simulation programs. For example, in simulating the arrival and departure of `Customer`, it is helpful to have a mechanism whereby a new `Customer` can be randomly created and then removed after being serviced. Two C++ operators, `new` and `delete`, provide this capability as described in Table 10.2.

Table 10.2   `new` **and** `delete` **Operators**

Operator Name	Description
`new`	Reserves the correct number of bytes for the variable or object type requested by the declaration. Returns the address of the first reserved location or a `NULL` value if sufficient memory is not available.
`delete`	Releases previously reserved memory.

From an operational viewpoint, dynamically allocated variables and objects created using the `new` operator are only accessible using the address returned by `new`. This means that, like the `this` pointer, the address of the newly created variable or object must be stored in a pointer variable. The mechanism for doing this is rather simple. For example, the statement `int *num = new int;` both reserves a memory area sufficient to hold one integer and places the address of this storage area into a pointer variable named `num`. This same dynamic allocation can also be made in two steps: Declare a pointer variable using a declaration statement, followed by a subsequent statement requesting dynamic allocation. Using this

PROGRAMMING NOTE

Using a `typedef` Statement

Among other uses, a `typedef` statement can be used to create a new and shorter name for pointer definitions. The syntax for a `typedef` statement is:

```
typedef dataType newTypeName;
```

For example, to make the name `PtrToInt` a synonym for the terms `int` `*` the following statement can be used:

```
typedef int *PtrToInt;
```

Such a statement would normally be placed at the top of a program file immediately after all `#include` statements. If this is done, the term `PtrToInt` can be used in place of the notation `int *`. Thus, for example, the declaration

```
PtrToInt pointerOne;
```

can replace the statement:

```
int *pointerOne;
```

Both statements declare that `pointerOne` is a pointer to an integer value.

By convention all `typedef` names are written in either initial or all uppercase letters, but this is not mandatory. The names used in a `typedef` statement can be any name that conforms to C++'s identifier naming rules.

---

two-step process, the single statement `int *num = new int;` can be replaced by the sequence of statements:

```
int *num;       // this declares a pointer variable that can
                // store the address of an integer
num = new int;  // this reserves memory for an integer and
                // puts the address of the memory area into num
```

In either case the allocated storage area comes from the computer's free storage area.[5] In a similar manner and of more usefulness is the dynamic allocation of a user-defined object. For example, the declaration

```
Customer *anotherCust;
```

declares `anotherCust` as a pointer variable that can be used to store the address of a `Customer` object. The actual creation of a new `Customer` object is completed by the statement:

```
anotherCust = new Customer;
```

This statement both creates a new `Customer` object and stores the address of the first reserved memory location into the pointer variable `anotherCust`. Program 10.6 illustrates this sequence of code within the context of a complete program.

---

[5] The free storage area of a computer is formally referred to as the heap. The heap consists of unallocated memory that can be allocated to a program, as requested, while the program is running.

▲ P O I N T   O F   I N F O R M A T I O N ▲

Pointers versus References

The distinguishing characteristic of a pointer, either as a formal parameter or variable, is that *every pointer contains a value that is an address*. Whereas a pointer is a variable or argument *whose contents are an address*, a reference *is an address*. As such, a reference can be thought of as a named constant, where the constant is a value that happens to be a valid memory address.

From an operational viewpoint pointers are much more flexible than references. This is because a pointer's contents can be manipulated in much the same manner as any other variable's value. For example, if foo is a pointer, the statement cout << foo; displays the value stored in the pointer variable. This is identical to the operation of displaying the value of an integer or floating-point variable. That the value stored in a pointer happens to be an address is irrelevant as far as cout is concerned.

The disadvantage of pointers is that their very flexibility makes them more complicated to understand and use than reference parameters or variables. Since references can only be used as a named address, they are easier to use. Thus, when the compiler encounters a reference it automatically dereferences the address to obtain the contents of the address. This is not the case with pointers. If you use a pointer's name, as we have noted, you access the pointer's contents. To correctly dereference the address stored in a pointer you must explicitly use C++'s dereference operator, *, in front of the pointer name. This informs the compiler that what you want is the item *whose address is in the pointer variable*.

Before looking at a sample output produced by Program 10.6 and analyzing how this output was produced by the main() function, consider the declaration of the Customer class. Notice that we have included an in-line constructor function to display the message

```
**** A new Customer has been created ****
```

whenever an object is created and an in-line destructor function to display the message

```
!!!! This Customer object has been deleted !!!!
```

whenever an object is deleted. These messages are only used to help you monitor the creation and deletion of an object when the program is executed. Also notice that we have not included the srand() function call within the constructor as we did in our original Customer class implementation presented in Section 9.6. Rather, we have made the calling of srand() a precondition to using any member method.

The primary reason for not including an srand() call in the Customer class constructor is that inclusion of this function would mean that it is called each time an object is created, when a single initial call to srand() is really all that is necessary for any single program execution. For large simulation runs where hundreds or even thousands of Customer objects can be created and deleted, execution times can be excessive and the savings in run times by careful placement of both function calls and calculations within repetitive loops can be dramatic.

PROGRAM 10.6

```cpp
#include <iostream>
#include <ctime>
#include <cmath>
using namespace std;

// Customer class
// precondition: srand() must be called once before any member methods
// postcondition: arrive() returns a random integer between 1 and 15
//              : gallons() returns a random integer between 3 and 20

class Customer
{
  public:
    Customer() {cout << "\n**** A new Customer has been created ****" << endl;};
    ~Customer() {cout << "!!!! This Customer object has been deleted !!!!" << endl;};
    int arrive() {return(1 + rand() % 15);};
    int gallons() {return(3 + rand() % 18);};
};

int main()
{
  Customer *anotherCust;  // declare 1 pointer to an object of type Customer
  int i, howMany;
  int interval, request;

  cout << "Enter the number of Customers to be created: ";
  cin >> howMany;
  srand(time(NULL));
  for(i = 1; i <= howMany; i++)
  {
    // create a new object of type Customer
    anotherCust = new Customer;

    // use the pointer to access the member methods
    interval = anotherCust->arrive();
    request = anotherCust->gallons();
    cout << "The arrival interval is " << interval << " minutes" << endl;
    cout << "The new Customer requests " << request << " gallons" << endl;
    cout << "The memory address of this object is: "<< anotherCust << endl;

    // delete the created object
    // delete anotherCust;
  }

  return 0;
}
```

Following is a sample output produced by Program 10.6:

```
Enter the number of Customers to be created: 4

**** A new Customer has been created ****
The arrival interval is 7 minutes
The new Customer requests 6 gallons
The memory address of this object is: 00323158

**** A new Customer has been created ****
The arrival interval is 10 minutes
The new Customer requests 9 gallons
The memory address of this object is: 00323200

**** A new Customer has been created ****
The arrival interval is 13 minutes
The new Customer requests 9 gallons
The memory address of this object is: 00323230

**** A new Customer has been created ****
The arrival interval is 4 minutes
The new Customer requests 13 gallons
The memory address of this object is: 00323260
```

As illustrated by this output, we can make the decision as to how many objects are to be created by Program 10.6 while the program is executing. Figure 10.7 illustrates the allocation of memory space corresponding to this sample output just before the program completes execution.

FIGURE 10.7 The Memory Allocation Produced by the Sample Execution of Program 10.6

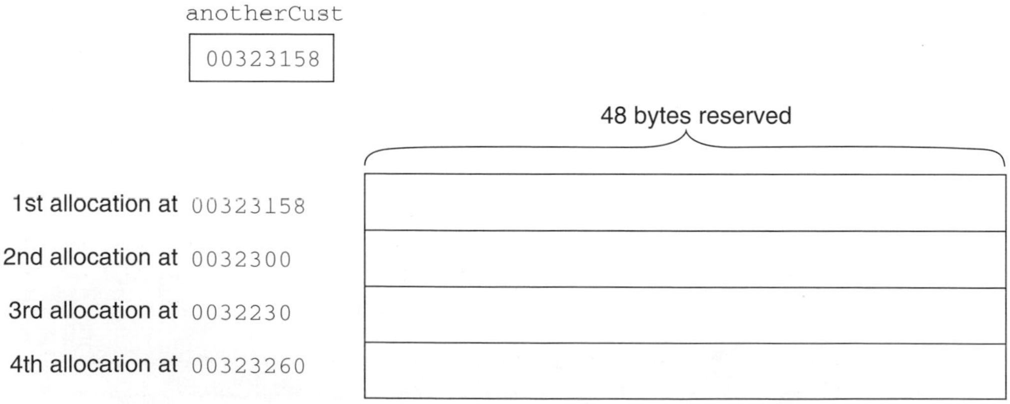

Now look at the `main()` function to see how this output was produced. First notice that new `Customer` objects are created using the statements:

```
Customer *anotherCust;
anotherCust = new Customer;
```

The first statement defines a single pointer variable named `anotherCust`. Each time the second statement is executed, a new object is created and its address is stored in the `anotherCust` variable (the old address is lost).[6] Notice also that this stored address can be displayed by inserting the pointer variable name in the `cout` stream as we have done in the last executable statement contained within `main()`'s body. Since the content of a pointer variable is a value, this value, even though it happens to be an address, can be displayed using the `cout` stream. Each time the value is displayed it simply represents the current address stored in the variable. Notice also that the last line in `main()`'s body comments out the statement `delete anotherCust;`. This was done intentionally to force each newly created object into a new memory area. If a `delete` had been used to release the previously allocated block of storage, the operating system would simply provide the same locations right back for the next allocation. In this case you would not see the assigned address change while the programming is executing.[7] In practice, however, it is very important to delete dynamically created objects when their usefulness ends. As you can see by the sample output, if you don't, the computer system starts to effectively "eat up" available memory space.

Finally, notice the notation used to access the member methods of each dynamically created object. For example, the notation `anotherCust->arrival()` calls the `arrival()` function of the object whose address resides in the pointer variable `anotherCust`. Since dynamically created objects do not have symbolic names they can only be accessed using the address information contained within the pointer variable. This can be done either using the notation `pointerName->methodName()` shown in Program 10.6 or by using the equivalent notation `(*pointerName).methodName()`.

Application 2: A Dynamic Gas Pump Simulation

In the multi-object simulation presented in Section 9.6 the same `Customer` object was used repeatedly to simulate multiple `Customer` arrivals. Using the information presented in the previous application, we now can write this simulation using dynamically created new and different `Customer` objects that are deleted once their request for gas has been fulfilled.

Analyze the Problem All dynamic allocations require that at least one pointer variable be available to store the address of the newly created object. The `new` operator is used to actually reserve this memory space and return the address, which should be assigned to the pointer variable. For example, the declaration

```
Customer *anotherCust;
```

declares a pointer variable named `anotherCust` that can be used to store an address of a `Customer` object.[8] Once this pointer has been defined, it can be used in an

---

[6] In practice the object whose address is currently in the pointer variable would have been deleted prior to reusing the pointer variable, so that the address being overwritten would be of no use anyway.

[7] The allocated storage would automatically be returned to the heap when the program has completed execution. It is, however, good practice to formally restore the allocated storage back to the heap using `delete` when the memory is no longer needed. This is especially true for larger programs that make numerous requests for additional storage areas.

[8] It should be noted that the width of all addresses is the same, be they addresses of `Customer` objects, `Pump` objects, or integer variables. Typically an address is either 32 or 64-bits wide. The reason for specifying the type of object is to inform the compiler of how many bytes must be accessed when the address is dereferenced. The actual allocation of memory for the object depends on how many data members it has, plus a fixed minimum size, which is typically 8 or 16 bytes.

assignment statement such as `anotherCust = new Customer;` that both allocates new storage and stores the address of the allocated area into the pointer variable.

For our simulation we will require both a `Pump` class and a `Customer` class. The `Customer` class, which is identical to that used in Program 10.6 except for the messages displayed by the constructor and destructor, is:

```cpp
#include <iostream>
#include <cmath>
using namespace std;

// Customer class declaration
// precondition: srand() must be called once before any function methods
// postcondition: arrive() returns a random integer between 1 and 15
//                : gallons() returns a random integer between 3 and 20

class Customer
{
  public:
     Customer() {cout << "\n**** A new Customer has arrived ****" << endl;};
     ~Customer() {cout << "!!!! The Customer has departed !!!!" << endl;};
     int arrive() {return(1 + rand() % 15);};
     int gallons() {return(3 + rand() % 18);};
};
```

For convenience we assume that this class is stored as `NewCustomer.cpp` in the `classes` directory of a C drive.

The `Pump` class is exactly the same as that used in Program 9.13 and is repeated below for convenience.

```cpp
// class declaration

#include <iostream>
#include <iomanip>
using namespace std;

const double AMOUNT_IN_TANK = 500;  // initial gallons in the tank
const double DEFAULT_PRICE = 1.80;   // price per gallon

class Pump
{
  // data declaration section
  private:
    double amtInTank;
    double price;

  // method declarations
  public:
    Pump(double = DEFAULT_PRICE, double = AMOUNT_IN_TANK);   // constructor
    void getValues();
    void request(double);
};
```

(continued from previous page)

```cpp
// methods implementation section

Pump::Pump(double todaysPrice, double amountInTank)
{
  amtInTank = amountInTank;
  price = todaysPrice;
}

void Pump::getValues()
{
  cout << "\nThe gas tank has " << amtInTank << " gallons of gas." << endl;
  cout << "The price per gallon of gas is $" << setiosflags(ios::showpoint)
       << setprecision(2) << setiosflags(ios::fixed) << price << endl;
}

void Pump::request(double pumpAmt)
{
  double pumped;

  if (amtInTank >= pumpAmt)
    pumped = pumpAmt;
  else
    pumped = amtInTank;

  amtInTank -= pumped;
  cout << pumpAmt << " gallons were requested " << endl;
  cout << pumped << " gallons were pumped" << endl;
  cout << amtInTank << " gallons remain in the tank" << endl;
  cout << "The total price is $" << setiosflags(ios::showpoint)
       << setprecision(2) << (pumped * price) << endl;

  return;
}
```

We assume that this class has been thoroughly tested and has been stored on a C drive in the `classes` directory as `Pump.cpp`.

Develop a Solution In using these preexisting `Pump` and `Customer` classes, all that remains to be developed is the control logic within the `main()` function for correctly creating `Pump` and `Customer` objects, and controlling the interaction between objects by appropriately activating class methods. A suitable control structure for `main()` is described by the psuedocode:

Create a Pump object with the required initial gallons of gas
Display the values in the initialized Pump
Set the total time to 0

Create the first Customer object
Obtain the Customer's interval arrival time
Add the arrival time to the total time

While the total time does not exceed the simulation time
  Display the total time
  Obtain a Customer request for gas
  Activate the Pump with the request
  Delete this Customer object

> Create a new Customer // next arrival
> Obtain the Customer's interval arrival time
> Add the arrival time to the total time
> EndWhile

> Display a message that the simulation is over

Code the Solution   The C++ code corresponding to our design is illustrated in Program 10.7.

PROGRAM 10.7

```cpp
#include <c:\\classes\\Pump.cpp>        // note use of full path name here
#include <c:\\classes\\NewCustomer.cpp>  // again a full path name is used

#include <ctime>

const double SIMTIME = .5;           // simulation time in hours
const int MINUTES = 60;              // number of minutes in an hour

int main()
{
  Pump a(2.00, 300);    // declare 1 object of type Pump
  Customer *anotherCust;  // declare 1 pointer to an object of type Customer
  int totalTime = 0;
  int idleTime;
  int amtRequest;
  int SimMinutes;  // simulation time in minutes

  SimMinutes = SIMTIME * MINUTES;
  cout << "\nStarting a new simulation - simulation time is "
       << SimMinutes << " minutes" << endl;
  a.getValues();

  srand(time(NULL));

  // create a new object of type Customer
  anotherCust = new Customer;

  // get the Customer's arrival time
  idleTime = anotherCust->arrive();
  totalTime += idleTime;

  while (totalTime <= SimMinutes)
  {

    cout << "The idle time is " << idleTime << " minutes" << endl
         << "    and we are " << totalTime
         << " minutes into the simulation." << endl;
    amtRequest = anotherCust->gallons();
    a.request(double(amtRequest));

    // delete this Customer
    delete anotherCust;
```

(continued from previous page)

```
    // create the next Customer
    anotherCust = new Customer;
    // get the next arrival
    idleTime = anotherCust->arrive();
    totalTime += idleTime;
  }
  cout << "The idle time is " << idleTime << " minutes." << endl
       << "\nAs the total time now exceeds the simulation time, " << endl
       << "   this simulation run is over." << endl;

  return 0;
}
```

Test and Correct the Program   Because the `Pump` and `Customer` classes are known to correctly meet their respective specifications, testing and debugging Program 10.7 can be restricted to testing and debugging the `main()` function. By itself, the `main()` function in Program 10.7 uses a straightforward `while` loop that creates and deletes `Customer` objects within a simulated time span of `SIMTIME` hours. Within the program the `Pump` idle time corresponds to the time between `Customer` arrivals. Notice that the notation used to dereference the address in the pointer variable `anotherCust` and activate the `arrival()` method is `anotherCust->arrival()`. In place of this notation, the alternative notation `(*anotherCust).arrival()` can be been used. The output of a sample run, shown below, verifies that the loop is operating correctly.

```
Starting a new simulation - simulation time is 30 minutes

The gas tank has 300 gallons of gas.
The price per gallon of gas is $2.00

**** A new Customer has arrived ****
The idle time is 2 minutes
   and we are 2 minutes into the simulation.
17.00 gallons were requested
17.00 gallons were pumped
283.00 gallons remain in the tank
The total price is $34.00
!!!! The Customer has departed !!!!

**** A new Customer has arrived ****
The idle time is 14 minutes
   and we are 16 minutes into the simulation.
9.00 gallons were requested
9.00 gallons were pumped
274.00 gallons remain in the tank
The total price is $18.00
!!!! The Customer has departed !!!!

**** A new Customer has arrived ****
The idle time is 12 minutes
   and we are 28 minutes into the simulation.
15.00 gallons were requested
15.00 gallons were pumped
259.00 gallons remain in the tank
The total price is $30.00
!!!! The Customer has departed !!!!
```

```
**** A new Customer has arrived ****
The idle time is 1 minutes
    and we are 29 minutes into the simulation.
14.00 gallons were requested
14.00 gallons were pumped
245.00 gallons remain in the tank
The total price is $28.00
!!!! The Customer has departed !!!!

**** A new Customer has arrived ****
The idle time is 3 minutes.

As the total time now exceeds the simulation time,
    this simulation run is over.
```

Exercises 10.4

1. a. Describe what a pointer is.

   b. For each of the following pointer declarations, identify the name of the pointer variable and the type of object that is accessed when the address in the pointer variable is dereferenced:

      ```
      float *b;
      int *addrOfInt;
      Customer *a;
      Pump *pointer1;
      Pump *addrOfAPump;
      ```

   c. If the asterisks, *, were removed from the declarations in Exercise 1b, what would the names immediately preceding the semicolon represent?

2. a. Describe dynamic allocation of memory.

   b. Describe the process of creating a dynamically allocated object. Specifically, discuss the roles of a pointer variable and the new operator in creating a dynamically allocated object.

   c. Discuss the importance of deleting dynamically allocated objects and what can happen if deletion is not used.

3. Programs 9.13 and 10.7 both produce a valid simulation. Since the type of simulation produced by each program is essentially the same, discuss the advantages and disadvantages of using multiple Customer objects in Program 10.7 as opposed to using a single Customer object in Program 9.13.

4. a. Modify Program 10.7 to use the Customer class defined in Program 9.13 [that is, put the srand() function call back into the constructor function]. Now run the program and notice that the same arrival times are obtained for each newly created customer object. What do you think is occurring to produce this effect?

   b. To correct for the problem noticed in Exercise 4a, place the following loop in the constructor function. (*Note:* Due to the loop, the constructor can no longer be written as an inline function.)

      ```
      for(int i = 0; i < 500000; i++);
      ```

      What does this loop accomplish? Run the program and notice that the randomness of customer arrivals has been restored. What do you notice about the time it takes to execute a complete simulation? Comment about the efficiency of your modified program as compared to Program 10.7.

10.5 POINTERS AS CLASS MEMBERS[9]

As we saw in Section 8.2, a class can contain any C++ data type. Thus, the inclusion of a pointer variable in a class should not seem surprising. For example, the class declaration:

```
class Test
{
  private:
    int idNum;
    double *ptPay;
  public:
    Test(int = 0, double * = NULL); //constructor
    void setvals(int a, double *b);
    void display();
};
```

declares a class consisting of two member variables and three member functions. The first member variable is an integer variable named idNum, and the second member variable is a pointer named ptPay, which is a pointer variable to a double-precision number. We use the setvals() member function to store values into the private member variables and the display() function for output purposes. The implementation of these two functions along with the constructor function Test() is contained in the class implementation section:

```
// class implementation

Test::Test(int id, double *pt)
{
  idNum = id;
  ptPay = pt;

   return;
}

void Test::setvals(int a, double *b)
{
  idNum = a;
  ptPay = b;

  return;
}

void Test::display()
{
  cout << "\nEmployee number " << idNum << " was paid $"
       << setiosflags(ios::showpoint)
       << setw(6) << setprecision(2)
       << *ptPay << endl;

  return;
}
```

---

[9] The material in this section requires a good grounding in pointer fundamentals. Thus, it should be read after the material in Section 14.1 is covered.

In this implementation, the `Test()` constructor initializes its `idNum` data member to its first parameter and its pointer member to its second parameter; if no parameters are given, these variables are initialized to 0 and `NULL`, respectively. The display function simply outputs the value pointed to by its pointer member. As defined in this implementation, the `setvals()` function is very similar to the constructor and is used to alter member values after the object has been declared: The function's first parameter (an integer) is assigned to `idNum` and its second parameter (an address) is assigned to `ptPay`.

The `main()` function in Program 10.8 illustrates the use of the `Test` class by first creating one object, named `emp`, which is initialized using the constructor's default arguments. The `setvals()` function is then used to assign the value 12345 and the address of the variable `pay` to the data members of this `emp` object. Finally, the `display()` function is used to display the value whose address is stored in `emp.ptPay`. As illustrated by the program, the pointer member of an object is used like any other pointer variable.

PROGRAM 10.8

```cpp
#include <iostream>
#include <iomanip>
using namespace std;

// class declaration

class Test
{
  private:
    int idNum;
    double *ptPay;
  public:
    Test(int = 0, double * = NULL);    // constructor
    void setvals(int, double *);   // access function
    void display();                // access function
};

// implementation section

Test::Test(int id, double *pt)
{
  idNum = id;
  ptPay = pt;
}

void Test::setvals(int a, double *b)
{
  idNum = a;
  ptPay = b;

  return;
}
```

(continued from previous page)

```cpp
void Test::display()
{
  cout << "\nEmployee number " << idNum << " was paid $"
       << setiosflags(ios::showpoint)
       << setw(6) << setprecision(2)
       << *ptPay << endl;

  return;
}
```

```cpp
int main()
{
  Test emp;
  double pay = 456.20;

  emp.setvals(12345, &pay);
  emp.display();

  return 0;
}
```

The output produced by Program 10.8 is:

```
Employee number 12345 was paid $456.20
```

Figure 10.8 illustrates the relationship between the data members of the `emp` object defined in Program 10.8 and the variable named `pay`. The value assigned to `emp.idNum` is the number 12345 and the value assigned to `pay` is 456.20. The address of the `pay` variable is assigned to the object member `emp.ptPay`. Since this member has been defined as a pointer to a double-precision number, placing the address of the double-precision variable `pay` in it is a correct use of this data member.

Although the pointer defined in Program 10.8 has been used in a rather trivial fashion, the program does illustrate the concept of including a pointer in a class.

FIGURE 10.8 Storing an Address in a Data Member

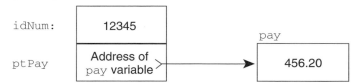

Clearly, it is more efficient to include the `pay` variable directly as a data member of the `Test` class rather than using a pointer to it. In some cases, however, pointers are advantageous. For example, assume we need to store a list of book titles. Rather than use a fixed length character array as a data member to hold each title, we could include a pointer member to a character array and then allocate the correct size array for each book title as it is needed. This arrangement is illustrated in Figure 10.9, which shows two objects, a and b, each of which consists of a single pointer data member. As depicted, object a's pointer contains the address of ("points to") a character array containing the characters `Windows Primer`, while object b's pointer contains the address of a character array containing the characters `A Brief History of Western Civilization`.

FIGURE 10.9 **Two Objects Containing Pointer Data Members**

Object a's data member:

Object b's data member:

A suitable class declaration section for a list of book titles that are to be accessed as illustrated in Figure 10.9 is:

```
// class declaration
class Book
{
  private:
    char *title;    // a pointer to a book title
  public:
    Book(char * = '\0');  // constructor
    void showtitle();    // display the title
};
```

The definitions of the constructor function, `Book()`, and the display function, `showtitle()`, are defined in the implementation section as:

```
// class implementation

Book::Book(char *name)
{
  title = new char[strlen(name)+1];  // allocate memory
  strcpy(title,name);                // store the string
}

void Book::showtitle()
{
  cout << title << endl;
}
```

The body of the `Book()` constructor contains two statements. The first statement, `title = new char[strlen(name)+1];` performs two tasks: First, the right-hand side of the statement allocates enough storage for the length of the name parameter plus one to accommodate the end-of-string null character, `'\0'`. Next, the address of the first allocated character position is assigned to the pointer variable `title`. These operations are illustrated in Figure 10.10. The second statement in the constructor copies the characters in the `name` argument to the newly created memory allocation. If no argument is passed to the constructor, then `title` is the empty string; that is, `title` is set to `NULL`. Program 10.9 uses this class definition within the context of a complete program.

FIGURE 10.10   Allocating Memory for `title = newchar[strlen(name)+1]`

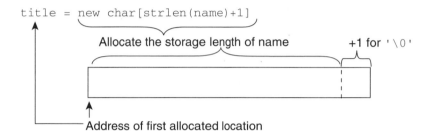

The output produced by Program 10.9 is:

```
Windows Primer
A Brief History of Western Civilization
```

Assignment Operators and Copy Constructors Reconsidered[10]

When a class contains no pointer data members, the compiler-provided defaults for the assignment operator and copy constructor adequately perform their intended tasks. Both of these defaults provide a member-by-member operation that produces no adverse side effects. This is not the case when a pointer member is included in the class declaration. Let's see why this is so.

Figure 10.11a illustrates the arrangement of pointers and allocated memory produced by Program 10.9 just before it completes execution. Let's assume that we insert the assignment statement `book2 = book1;` immediately before the `return` statement in the `main()` function. Since we have not defined an assignment operation, the compiler's default assignment is used. As we know, this assignment produces a memberwise copy (that is, `book2.title = book1.title`) and means that the address in `book1`'s pointer is copied into `book2`'s pointer. Thus, both pointers now "point to" the character array containing the characters `Windows Primer`, and the address of `A Brief History of Western Civilization` has been lost. This situation is illustrated in Figure 10.11b.

---

[10] The material in this section pertains to the problems that occur when using the default assignment, copy constructor, and destructor functions with classes containing pointer members and how to overcome these problems. On first reading, this section can be omitted without loss of subject continuity.

PROGRAM 10.9

```cpp
#include <iostream>
#include <string>
using namespace std;

// class declaration

class Book
{
  private:
    char *title;    // a pointer to a book title
  public:
    Book(char * = NULL);  // constructor
    void showtitle();     // display the title
};

// class implementation

Book::Book(char *strng)
{
  title = new char[strlen(strng)+1];  // allocate memory
  strcpy(title,strng);                // store the string
}

void Book::showtitle()
{
  cout << title << endl;

  return;
}
```

```cpp
int main()
{
  Book  book1("Windows Primer");    // create 1st title
  Book  book2("A Brief History of Western Civilization");   // 2nd
 title

  book1.showtitle();    // display book1's title
  book2.showtitle();    // display book2's title

  return 0;
}
```

Since the memberwise assignment illustrated in Figure 10.11b results in the loss of the address of A Brief History of Western Civilization, there is no way for the program to release this memory storage (it is cleaned up by the operating system when the program terminates). Worse, however, is the case where a destructor attempts to release the memory. Once the memory pointed to by book2 is released (again, referring to Figure 10.11b), book1 points to an undefined memory location. If this memory area is subsequently reallocated before `book1` is deleted, the deletion releases memory that another object is using. The results of this can create havoc.

What is typically desired is that the book titles themselves be copied and their pointers left alone, as shown in Figure 10.11c. This situation also removes all of the side effects of a subsequent deletion of any book object. To achieve the desired assignment, we must explicitly write our own assignment operator. A suitable definition for this operator is:

```
void Book::operator=(Book& oldbook)
{
  if(oldbook.title != NULL)  // check that it exists
    delete(title);           // release existing memory
  title = new char[strlen(oldbook.title) + 1];  // allocate new memory
  strcpy(title, oldbook.title);  // copy the title
}
```

This definition cleanly releases the memory previously allocated for the object and then allocates sufficient memory to store the copied title.

FIGURE 10.11a   **Before the Assignment** `book2 = book1;`

book1's pointer

| An address > | ────────► | Windows Primer |

book2's pointer

| An address > | ────────► | A Brief History of Western Civilization |

FIGURE 10.11b   **The Effect Produced by Default Assignment**

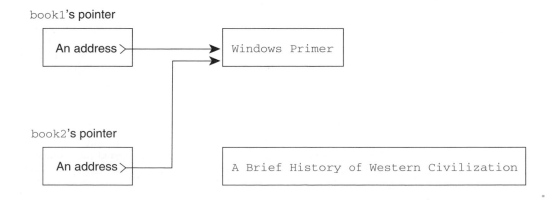

book1's pointer

| An address > | ────────► | Windows Primer |

book2's pointer

| An address > | | A Brief History of Western Civilization |

FIGURE 10.11c   The Desired Effect

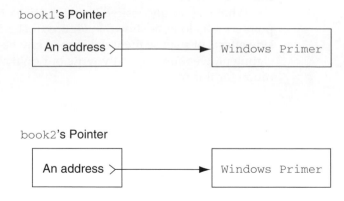

The problems associated with the default assignment operator also exist with the default copy constructor because it also performs a memberwise copy. As with assignment, these problems are avoided by writing our own copy constructor. For our Book class, such a constructor is:

```
Book::Book(Book& oldbook)
{
    title = new char[strlen(oldbook.title) + 1];   // allocate new memory
    strcpy(title, oldbook.title);   // copy the title
}
```

Comparing the body of this copy constructor to the assignment operator's function body reveals that they are identical except for the deallocation of memory performed by the assignment operator. This is because the copy constructor does not have to release the existing array prior to allocating a new one, since none exists when the constructor is called.

Exercises 10.5

1. Include the copy constructor and assignment operator presented in this section in Program 10.9 and run the program to verify their operation.

2. Write a suitable destructor function for Program 10.9.

3. a. Construct a class named Car that contains the following four data members: a floating-point variable named engineSize, a character variable named bodyStyle, an integer variable named colorCode, and a character pointer named vinPtr to a vehicle identification code. The function members should include a constructor that provides default values of 0 for each numeric data member, 'X' for each character variable, and NULL for each pointer; a display function that prints the engine size, body style, color code, and vehicle identification number; and an assignment operator that performs a memberwise assignment between two car objects that correctly handles the pointer member.

   b. Include the program written for Exercise 3a in a working C++ program that creates two Car objects, the second of which is assigned the values of the first object.

4. Modify Program 10.9 to include the assignment statement b = a and then run the modified program to assess the error messages, if any, that occur.

5. Using Program 10.9 as a start, write a program that creates five Book objects. The program should allow the user to enter five book titles interactively and then display the entered titles.

6. Modify the program written in Exercise 5 so that the program sorts the entered book titles in alphabetical order before it displays them. (*Hint:* You need to define a sort routine for the titles.)

10.6 COMMON PROGRAMMING ERRORS

The common programming errors associated with inheritance, polymorphism, pointers, and dynamic memory allocation are as follows:

1. Attempting to override a virtual function without using the same type and number of parameters as the original function.

2. Using the keyword virtual in the class implementation section. Functions are only declared as virtual in the class declaration section.

3. Using the default copy constructor and default assignment operators with classes containing pointer members. Since these default functions do a memberwise copy, the address in the source pointer is copied to the destination pointer. Typically, this is not what is wanted since both pointers end up pointing to the same memory area.

4. Forgetting that this is a pointer that must be dereferenced using either (*this). or this->.

10.7 CHAPTER REVIEW

Key Terms

base class	polymorphism
class hierarchy	simple inheritance
derived class	static binding
dynamic binding	this pointer
inheritance	virtual function
multiple inheritance	

Summary

1. *Inheritance* is the capability of deriving one class from another class. The initial class used as the basis for the derived class is referred to as the *base*, *parent*, or *superclass*. The derived class is referred to as the *derived*, *child*, or *subclass*.

2. Base class functions can be overridden by derived class functions with the same name. The override function is simply an overloaded version of the base class function defined in the derived class.

3. *Polymorphism* is the ability for the same function name to invoke different responses based on the object making the function call. It can be accomplished using overloaded and virtual functions.

4. In *static binding*, the determination of which function is invoked is made at compile time. In *dynamic binding*, the determination is made at run time.

5. A *virtual function* specification designates that dynamic binding should take place. The specification is made in the function's prototype by placing the keyword `virtual` before the function's return type. Once a function has been declared as virtual, it remains so for all derived classes as long as there is a continuous trail of function declarations through the derived chain of classes.

6. For each class, only one copy of each class function is retained in memory. The address of an object's data members is provided to a class function by passing a hidden parameter, corresponding to the memory address of the selected object, to the class function. The address is passed in a special pointer parameter named `this`. The `this` pointer may be used explicitly by a class function to access a data member.

7. Pointers may be included as class data members. A pointer member adheres to the same rules as a pointer variable.

8. The default copy constructor and default assignment operators are typically not useful with classes containing pointer members. This is because these default functions do a memberwise copy in which the address in the source pointer is copied to the destination pointer, resulting in both pointers "pointing to" the same memory area. For these situations, you must define your own copy constructor and assignment operator.

Exercises

1. Describe the difference between static and dynamic binding.

2. a. Create a base class named `Point` that consists of an *x* and *y* coordinate. From this class, derive a class named `Circle` that has an additional data member named `radius`. For this derived class, the x and y data members represent the center coordinates of a circle. The function members of the first class should consist of a constructor and a `distance()` function that returns the distance between two points, where:

$$distance = \sqrt{(x2 - x1)^2 + (y2 - y1)^2}$$

Additionally, the derived class should have a constructor, an override `distance()` function that calculates the distance between circle centers, and a function named `area` that returns the area of a circle.

b. Include the classes constructed for Exercise 2a in a working C++ program. Have your program call all of the member functions in each class. In addition, call the base class distance function with two `Circle` objects and explain the result returned by the function.

3. a. Using the classes constructed for Exercise 2a, derive a class named `Cylinder` from the derived `Circle` class. The `Cylinder` class should have a constructor and a member function named `area` that determines

the surface area of the cylinder. For this function, use the algorithm *surface area* = $2\pi r\,(l + r)$, where r is the radius of the cylinder and l is the length.

b. Include the classes constructed for Exercise 3a in a working C++ program. Have your program call all of the member functions in the `Cylinder` class.

c. What do you think the result might be if the base class distance function were called with two `Cylinder` objects?

4. a. Create a base class named `Rectangle` that contains `length` and `width` data members. From this class, derive a class named `Box` having an additional data member named `depth`. The function members of the base `Rectangle` class should consist of a constructor and an area function. The derived `Box` class should have a constructor and an override function named `area` that returns the surface area of the box and a `volume()` function.

b. Include the classes constructed for Exercise 4a in a working C++ program. Have your program call all of the member functions in each class and explain the result when the `distance()` function is called using a `Box` object.

5. a. Construct a class named `TelBook` that contains data members capable of holding a last name, first name, and telephone number. The constructor should set each of these members to "x". Additionally, create member functions to input data values, to display data values, and to assign one object's data values to another object.

b. Include the class written for Exercise 5a in a working C++ program that tests each member function.

11 | I/O File Streams and Data Files

The data for the programs we have used so far has either been assigned internally within the programs or entered by the user during program execution. As such, the data used in these programs is stored only in the computer's main memory, and ceases to exist once the program using it finishes executing. This type of data entry is fine for small amounts of data. Imagine, however, a company having to pay someone to type in the names and addresses of hundreds or thousands of customers every month each time bills are prepared and sent.

As you'll learn in this chapter, it makes more sense to store such data outside of a program, on a convenient storage medium. Data that is stored together under a common name on a storage medium other than the computer's main memory is called a data file. Typically data files are stored on disks, tapes, or CD-ROMs. Besides providing a permanent storage for the data, another great advantage of data files is that they can be shared between programs, so that the data output by one program can be input directly to another program. You'll begin this chapter by learning how data files are created and maintained in C++. Because one major concern about using data files has to do with ensuring that your programs open and connect correctly to them before any data processing begins, you'll also learn how to use exception handling for this task. This type of error detection and correction is a major concern of all professionally written programs.

A BIT OF BACKGROUND

Privacy, Security, and Files

Data files have been around a long time before computers were used, but were primarily stored as paper records in filing cabinets. Terms such as *open*, *close*, *records*, and *lookup* that are used in handling computer files are reminders of these older techniques for accessing paper files stored in drawers.

Today most files are stored electronically, and the amount of information that is collected and stored proliferates wildly. Because it is much easier to transit large amounts of data electronically than to ship paper folders, increasingly serious problems of privacy and security have arisen.

Whenever an individual fills out a government form or a credit application, submits a mail order, applies for a job, writes a check, or uses a credit card, an electronic data trail is created. Each time those files are shared among government agencies or private enterprises the individual loses more of his or her privacy.

In order to help protect U.S. citizens' constitutional rights, the Fair Credit Reporting Act was passed in 1970, followed by the Federal Privacy Act in 1974. These acts specify that it is illegal for a business to keep secret files, that you are entitled to examine and correct any data collected about you, and that government agencies and contractors must show justification for accessing your records. Efforts continue to create mechanisms that will serve to preserve an individual's security and privacy.

11.1 I/O FILE STREAM OBJECTS AND METHODS

To store and retrieve data outside a C++ program you need two things:

- A file
- A file stream object

You'll learn about these important topics in the following two sections.

Files

A **file** is a collection of data that is stored together under a common name, usually on a disk, magnetic tape, or CD-ROM. For example, the C++ programs that you store on disk are examples of files. The stored data in a program file is the program code that becomes input data to the C++ compiler. In the context of data processing, however, the C++ program is not usually considered data, and the term file, or data file, is typically used to refer only to external files that contain the data used in a C++ program.

A file is physically stored on an external medium such as a disk. Each file has a unique file name referred to as the file's **external name**. The external name is the name of the file as it is known by the operating system. When you review the contents of a directory or folder (for example, in Windows Explorer) you see files listed by their external names. Each computer operating system has its own specification as to the maximum number of characters permitted for an external file name. Table 11.1 lists these specifications for the more commonly used operating systems.

To ensure that the examples presented in this text are compatible with all of the operating systems listed in Table 11.1 we will generally, but not exclusively, adhere to the more restrictive DOS and VMX specifications. If you are using one of the other operating systems, however, you should take advantage of the increased length specification to create descriptive file names. Very long file names should be avoided, however, because they take more time to type and can result in typing errors. A manageable length for a file name is 12 to 14 characters, with an outside maximum of 25 characters.

TABLE 11.1   Maximum Allowable File Name Characters

Operating System	Maximum Length
DOS	8 characters plus an optional period and 3-character extension
Windows 98, 2000, XP	255 characters
UNIX	
Early versions	14 characters
Current versions	255 characters

Using the DOS convention then, the following are all valid computer data file names:

```
prices.dat    records      info.txt
exper1.dat    scores.dat   math.mem
```

Choose file names that indicate both the type of data in the file and the application for which it is used. Frequently, the first eight characters describe the data themselves, and an extension (the characters after the decimal point) describes the application. For example, the Excel spreadsheet program automatically applies an extension of xls to all spreadsheet files, Microsoft's Word and the WordPerfect word processing programs use the extensions doc and wpx (where x refers to the version number), respectively, and C++ compilers require a program file to have the extension cpp. When creating your own file names, you should adhere to this practice. For example, using the DOS convention, the name exper1.dat is appropriate in describing a file of data corresponding to experiment number 1.

There are two basic types of files: **text files**, which are also known as **character-based files**, and **binary-based** files. Both file types store data using a binary code; the difference is in what the codes represent. Briefly, text-based files store each individual character, such as a letter, digit, dollar sign, decimal point, and so on, using an individual character code (typically ASCII or UNICODE). The use of a character code allows such files to be displayed by a word processing program or text editor so that a person can read them. Binary-based files use the same code as your C++ compiler uses for its primitive data types. This means that numbers appear in their true binary form, while strings retain their ASCII or UNICODE form. The advantage of binary-based files is compactness, because it takes less space to store most numbers using their binary code than as individual character values. In general, the vast majority of files used by programmers are text files, simply because the file's data can be displayed by word processing programs and simple text editors. The default file type in C++ is alwayways a text file, and is the type presented in this chapter.

FIGURE 11.1   Input and Output File Streams

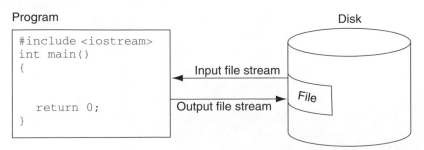

PROGRAMMING NOTE

Input and Output Streams

A *stream* is a one-way transmission path between a source and a destination. What gets sent down this transmission path is a stream of bytes. A good analogy to this "stream of bytes" is a stream of water that provides a one-way transmission path of water from a source to a destination.

Stream objects are created from stream classes. Two stream objects that we have used extensively are the input stream object named `cin` and the output stream object named `cout`. The `cin` object provides a transmission path from keyboard to program while the `cout` object provides a transmission path from program to terminal screen. These two objects are created from the stream classes `istream` and `ostream`, respectively, which are parent classes to the `iostream` class. When the `iostream` header file is included in a program using the `#include <iostream>` directive, the `cin` and `cout` stream objects are automatically declared and opened by the C++ compiler for the compiled program.

File stream objects provide the same capabilities as the `cin` and `cout` objects, except they connect a program to a file rather than the keyboard or terminal screen. Also file stream objects must be explicitly declared. File stream objects that will be used for input must be declared as objects of the class `ifstream`, while file stream objects that will be used for output must be declared as objets of the class `ofstream`. The classes `ifstream` and `ofstream` are made available to a program by inclusion of the `fstream` header file using the directive `#include <fstream>`. The `fstream` class is derived from both the `ifstream` and `ofstream` classes (see Section 11.7).

File Stream Objects

A **file stream** is a one-way transmission path that is used to connect a file stored on a physical device, such as a disk or CD-ROM, to a program. Each file stream has its own mode, which determines the direction of data on the transmission path—that is, whether the path will move data from a file into a program or whether the path will move data from a program to a file. A file stream that receives or reads data from a file into a program is referred to as an **input file stream**. A file stream that sends or writes data to a file is referred to as an **output file stream**. Notice that the direction, or mode, is always defined in relation to the program and not the file; data that go into a program are considered input data, and data sent out from the program are considered output data. Figure 11.1 illustrates the data flow from and to a file using input and output streams.

For each file that your program uses, a distinct file stream object must be created. If you are going to read and write to a file, both an input and output file stream object are required.

For each file that your program uses, regardless of the file's type (text or binary), a distinct file stream object must be created. If you want your program to both read and write to a file, both an input and output file stream object are required. Input file stream objects are declared to be of type `ifstream` while output file streams are declared to be of type `ofstream`. For example, the declaration

```
ifstream inFile;
```

declares an input file stream object named `inFile` to be an object of the class `ifstream`. Similarly, the declaration

```
ofstream outFile;
```

declares an output file stream object named `outFile` to be an object of the class `ofstream`. Within a C++ program a file stream is always accessed by its appropriate stream object name, one name for reading the file and one name for writing to the file. Object names, such as `inFile` and `outFile`, can be any programmer selected names that conform to C++'s identifier rules.

File Stream Methods

Each file stream object has access to the methods defined for its respective `ifstream` or `ofstream` class. These methods include connecting a stream object name to an external file name (called **opening a file**), determining if a successful connection has been made, closing a connection (called **closing a file**), getting the next data item into the program from an input stream, putting a new data item from the program onto an output stream, and detecting when the end of a file has been reached.

Opening a file connects each file stream object to a specific external file name. This is accomplished using a file stream's `open` method, which is a straight forward procedure that accomplishes two purposes. First, opening a file establishes the physical connecting link between a program and a file. Since details of this link are handled by the computer's operating system and are transparent to the program, the programmer normally need not consider them.

From a coding perspective, the second purpose of opening a file is more relevant. Besides establishing the actual physical connection between a program and a data file, opening a file connects the file's external computer name to the stream object name used internally by the program. The method that performs this task is named `open()` and is provided by both the `ifstream` and `ofstream` classes.

In using the `open()` method to connect the file's external name to its internal object stream name, only one argument is required, which is the external file name. For example, the statement

```
inFile.open("prices.dat");
```

connects the external text file named `prices.dat` to the internal program file stream object named `inFile`. This assumes, of course, that `inFile` has been declared as either an `ifstream` or `ofstream` object. If a file has been opened with the preceding statement, the program accesses the file using the internal object name `inFile`, while the computer saves the file under the external name `prices.dat`. Notice that the external file name argument passed to `open()` is a string contained between double quotes. Also notice that calling the `open()` method requires the standard object notation where the name of the desired method, in this case `open()`, is preceded by a period and an object name.

When an existing file is connecting to an input file stream, the file's data is made available for input, starting at the first data item in the file. Similarly, a file connected to an output file stream creates a new file and makes the file available for output. If a file exists with the same name as a file opened in output mode, the old file is erased and all its data is lost.

When opening a file, for input or output, good programming practice requires that you check that the connection has been established before attempting to use the file in any way. You can do this via the `fail()` method, which will return a `true` value if the open was unsuccessful, or a `false` value if the open was successful. Typically the `fail()` method is used in code similar to the following, which attempts to open a file named `prices.dat` for input, checks that a valid connection was made, and reports an error message if the file was not successfully opened for input:

```
ifstream inFile;  // any object name can be used here

inFile.open("prices.dat");  // open the file
// check that the connection was successfully opened
if (inFile.fail())
{
  cout << "\nThe file was not successfully opened"
       << "\n Please check that the file currently exists."
       << endl;
  exit(1);
}
```

If the `fail()` method returns a `true`, which indicates that the open failed, a message is displayed by this code and the `exit()` function, which is a request to the operating system to end program execution immediately, is called. The `exit()` function requires inclusion of the `cstdlib` header function in any program that uses this function, and `exit()`'s single integer argument is passed directly to the operating system for possible further operating system program action or user inspection. Throughout the remainder of the text we will include this type of error checking whenever a file is opened. (In Section 11.3 we show how to use exception handling for the same type of error checking.)

In addition to the `fail()` method, C++ provides three other methods (all listed in Table 11.2) that can be used to detect a file's status. The use of these additional methods is presented at the end of the next section.

Program 11.1 illustrates the statements required to open a file for input, including an error checking routine to ensure that a successful open was obtained. A file opened for input is said to be in **read mode**.

TABLE 11.2 File Status Methods

Prototype	Description
fail()	Returns a Boolean true if the file has not been successfully opened; otherwise returns a Boolean false value.
eof()	Returns a Boolean true if a read has been attempted past the end-of-file; otherwise returns a Boolean false value. The value becomes true only when the first character after the last valid file character is read.
good()	Returns a Boolean true value while the file is available for program use. Returns a Boolean false value if a read has been attempted past the end-of-file. The value becomes false only when the first character after the last valid file character is read.
bad()	Returns a Boolean true value if a read has been attempted past the end-of-file; otherwise returns a false. The value becomes true only when the first character after the last valid file character is read.

PROGRAM 11.1

```cpp
#include <iostream>
#include <fstream>
#include <cstdlib>   // needed for exit()
using namespace std;

int main()
{
  ifstream inFile;

  inFile.open("prices.dat");  // open the file with the
                              // external name prices.dat
  if (inFile.fail())  // check for a successful open
  {
    cout << "\nThe file was not successfully opened"
         << "\n Please check that the file currently exists."
         << endl;
    exit(1);
  }

  cout << "\nThe file has been successfully opened for reading."
       << endl;

  // statements to read data from the file would be placed here

  return 0;
}
```

A sample run using Program 11.1 produced the output:

```
The file has been successfully opened for reading.
```

A slightly different check is required for output files, because if a file exists having the same name as the file to be opened in output mode, the existing file is erased and all its data is lost. To avoid the situation the file is first opened in input mode, simply to see if it exists. If it does, the user is given the choice of explicitly permitting it to be overwritten when it is later opened in output mode. The code used to accomplish this is highlighted in Program 11.2.

PROGRAM 11.2

```cpp
#include <iostream>
#include <fstream>
#include <cstdlib>   // needed for exit()
using namespace std;

int main()
{
  ifstream inFile;
  ofstream outFile;
```

(continued from previous page)

```
inFile.open("prices.dat");  // attempt to open the file for input

char response;

if (!inFile.fail())  // if it doesn't fail, the file exists
{
 cout << "A file by the name prices.dat exists.\n"
      << "Do you want to continue and overwrite it\n"
      << " with the new data (y or n): ";
 cin >> response;
 if (tolower(response) == 'n')
 {
   cout << "The existing file will not be overwritten." << endl;
    exit(1);  //terminate program execution
 }
}
outFile.open("prices.dat"); // now open the file for writing

if (inFile.fail())  // check for a successful open
{
   cout << "\nThe file was not successfully opened"
        << endl;
   exit(1);
}

cout << "The file has been successfully opened for output."
     << endl;

// statements to write to the file would be placed here

return 0;
}
```

Following are two runs made with Program 11.2:

```
A file by the name prices.dat exists.
Do you want to continue and overwrite it
 with the new data (y or n): n
The existing file will not be overwritten.
```

and

```
A file by the name prices.dat exists.
Do you want to continue and overwrite it
 with the new data (y or n): y
The file has been successfully opened for output.
```

Although Programs 11.1 and 11.2 can be used to open an existing file for reading and writing, respectively, both programs lack statements to actually perform a read or write and close the file. These topics are discussed shortly. Before leaving these programs, however, it is worthwhile noting that it is possible to combine the declaration

> ## PROGRAMMING NOTE

Using C-strings as File Names

If you choose to use a C-string to store an external file name, you must be aware of the following restrictions. The maximum length of the C-string must be specified within brackets immediately after it is declared. For example, in the declaration

```
char filename[21] = "prices.dat";
```

the number 21 limits the number of characters that can be stored in the C-string. The number in brackets, in this example, 21, always represents one more than the maximum number of characters that can be assigned to the variable. This is because the compiler always adds a final end-of-string character to terminate the string. Thus the string value `"prices.dat"`, which consists of 10 characters, is actually stored as 11 characters. The extra character is an end-of-string marker supplied by the compiler. In our example, the maximum string value assignable to the string variable `filename` is a string value consisting of 20 characters.

of either an `ifstream` or `ofstream` object and its associated open statement into one statement. For example, the following two statements in Program 11.1

```
ifstream inFile;
inFile.open("prices.dat");
```

can be combined into the single statement:

```
ifstream inFile("prices.dat");
```

Embedded and Interactive File Names

Two practical problems with Programs 11.1 and 11.2 are:

1. The external file name is embedded within the program code.
2. There is no provision for a user to enter the desired file name while the program is executing.

As both programs are written, if the file name is to change a programmer must modify the external file name in the call to `open()` and recompile the program. Both of these problems can be alleviated by assigning the file name to a string variable.

A string variable as we have used it throughout the text (see especially Chapter 9) is a variable that can hold a string value, which is any sequence of zero or more characters enclosed within double quotes. For example, `"Hello  World"`, `"prices.dat"`, and `""` are all strings. Notice that strings are always written with double quotes that delimit the beginning and end of a string but are not stored as part of the string.

In declaring and initializing a string variable for use in an `open()` method, the string is always considered as a C-string. The Programming Note on C-strings (this page) presents the precautions that must be understood when using a C-string. A much safer alternative, and one that we will use throughout this text, is to use a `string` class object and then convert this object to a C-string using the `c_str()` method.

Once a string variable is declared to store a file name it can be used in one of two ways. First, as shown in Program 11.3a, it can placed at the top of a program to clearly identify a file's external name, rather than embed it within an `open()` method call.

PROGRAM 11.3a

```cpp
#include <iostream>
#include <fstream>
#include <cstdlib>    // needed for exit()
#include <string>
using namespace std;

int main()
{
  string filename = "prices.dat"; // place the file name up front
  ifstream inFile;

  inFile.open(filename.c_str());  // open the file

  if (inFile.fail())  // check for successful open
  {
    cout << "\nThe file named " << filename << " was not successfully opened"
         << "\n Please check that the file currently exists."
         << endl;
    exit(1);
  }

  cout << "\nThe file has been successfully opened for reading.\n";

  return 0;
}
```

In reviewing Program 11.3a notice that we have declared and initialized the string object named `filename` at the top of `main()` for easy file identification. Next, notice that when a string object is used, as opposed to a string literal, the variable name *is not* enclosed within double quotes in the `open()` method call. Also notice that within the `open()` call, the string object is converted to a C-string using the expression `filename.c_str()`. Finally, notice that in the `fail()` method code the file's external name is displayed by inserting the string object's name in the `cout` output stream. For all of these reasons we will continue to identify the external names of files in this manner.

Another extremely useful role played by string objects is to permit the user to enter the file name as the program is executing. For example, the code

```cpp
string filename;

cout << "Please enter the name of the file you wish to open: ";
cin  >> filename;
```

allows a user to enter a file's external name at run time. The only restriction in this code is that the user must not enclose the entered string value in double quotes, which is a plus, and that the entered string value cannot contain any blanks. The reason for this is that when using `cin` the compiler will terminate the string when it encounters a blank. Program 11.3b uses this code in the context of a complete program.

PROGRAM 11.3b

```cpp
#include <iostream>
#include <fstream>
#include <cstdlib>    // needed for exit()
#include <string>
using namespace std;

int main()
{
  string filename;
  ifstream inFile;

  cout << "Please enter the name of the file you wish to open: ";
  cin  >> filename;

  inFile.open(filename.c_str());  // open the file

  if (inFile.fail())  // check for successful open
  {
    cout << "\nThe file named " << filename << " was not successfully opened"
         << "\n Please check that the file currently exists."
         << endl;
    exit(1);
  }
  cout << "\nThe file has been successfully opened for reading.\n";

  return 0;
}
```

Following is a sample output provided by Program 11.3b:

```
Please enter the name of the file you wish to open: foobar

The file named foobar was not successfully opened
 Please check that the file currently exists.
```

Closing a File

A file is closed using the close() method. This method breaks the connection between the file's external name and the file stream object, which can then be used for another file. For example, the statement

```
inFile.close();
```

closes the inFile stream's connection to its current file. As indicated, the close() method takes no argument.

Because all computers have a limit on the maximum number of files that can be open at one time, closing files that are no longer needed makes good sense. Any open files existing at the end of normal program execution will be automatically closed by the operating system.

PROGRAMMING NOTE

Checking for a Successful Connection

It is important to check that the `open()` method successfully established a connection between a file stream and an external file. This is because the `open()` call is really a request to the operating system that can fail for a variety of reasons. (Chief among these reasons is a request to open an existing file for reading that the operating system cannot locate or attempting to open a file for output in a non-existent folder.) If the operating system cannot satisfy the open request you need to know about it and gracefully terminate your program. Failure to do so almost always results in abnormal program behavior or a subsequent program crash. There are two styles of coding for checking the return value.

The most common method for checking that a fail did not occur when attempting to use a file for input is the one coded in Program 11.1. It is used to clearly distinguish the `open()` request from the check made via the `fail()` call, and is repeated below for convenience:

```
inFile.open("prices.dat");  // request to open the file

if (inFile.fail())   // check for a failed connection
{
   cout << "\nThe file was not successfully opened"
        << "\n Please check that the file currently exists."
        << endl;
   exit(1);
}
```

Similarly, the check made in Program 11.2 is typically included when a file is being opened in output mode.

Alternatively, you may encounter programs that use `fstream` objects in place of both `ifstream` and `ofstream` objects (see Programming Note on page 586). When using `fstream`'s `open()` method two arguments are required: a file's external name and an explicit mode indication. Using an `fstream` object, the open request and check for an input file typically appear as follows:

```
fstream inFile;

inFile.open("external file name", ios::in);
if (inFile.fail())
{
 cout << "\nThe file was not successfully opened"
      << "\n Please check that the file currently exists."
      << endl;
 exit(1);
}
```

Many times the conditional expression `inFile.fail()` is replaced by the equivalent expression `!inFile`. Although we will always use `ifstream` and `ofstream` objects, be prepared to encounter the styles that use `fstream` objects.

PROGRAMMING NOTE

Using `fstream` Objects

In using both `ifstream` and `ofstream` objects the mode, input or output, is implied by the object. Thus `ifstream` objects can only be used for input, while `ofstream` objects can only be used for output.

Another means of creating file streams is to use `fstream` objects that can be used for input or output, but require an explicit mode designation. An `fstream` object is declared using the syntax:

```
fstream objectName;
```

When using the `fstream` class's `open()` method, two arguments are required: a file's external name and a mode indicator. Permissible mode indicators are:

Indicator	Description
`ios::in`	Open a text file in input mode
`ios::out`	Open a text file in output mode
`ios::app`	Open a text file in append mode
`ios::ate`	Go to the end of the opened file
`ios::binary`	Open a binary file in input mode (default is text file)
`ios::trunc`	Delete file contents if file exists
`ios::nocreate`	If file does not exist, open fails
`ios::noreplace`	If file exists, open for output fails

As with `ofstream` objects, an `fstream` object in output mode creates a new file and makes the file available for writing. If a file exists with the same name as a file opened for output, the old file is erased. For example, assuming that `file1` has been declared as an object of type `fstream` using the statement

```
fstream file1;
```

then the statement

```
file1.open("prices.dat",ios::out);
```

attempts to open the text file named `prices.dat` for output. Once this file has been opened, the program accesses the file using the internal object name `file1`, while the computer saves the file under the external name `prices.dat`.

An `fstream` file object opened in append mode means that an existing file is available for data to be added to the end of the file. If the file opened for appending does not exist, a new file with the designated name is created and made available to receive output from the program. For example, again assuming that `file1` has been declared to be of type `fstream`, the statement

```
file1.open("prices.dat",ios::app);
```

attempts to open a text file named `prices.dat` and makes it available for data to be appended to the end of the file.

Finally, an `fstream` object opened in input mode means that an existing external file has been connected and its data is available as input. For example, assuming that `file1` has been declared to be of type `fstream`, the statement

```
file1.open("prices.dat",ios::in);
```

attempts to open a file named `prices.dat` for input. The mode indicators can be combined by the bit Or operation (see Section 17.2). For example, the statement

```
file1.open("prices.dat", ios::in | ios::binary)
```

opens the `file1` stream, which can be either an `fstream` or `ifstream`, as an input binary stream. If the mode indicator is omitted as the second argument for an `ifstream` object, the stream is automatically opened as a text input file, while if it is omitted for an `ofstream` object, the stream is, by default, opened as a text output file.

Exercises 11.1

1. Write individual declaration and open statements that link the following external data file names to their corresponding internal object names. Assume that all the files are text-based.

External Name	Object Name	Mode
coba.mem	memo	output
book.let	letter	output
coupons.bnd	coups	append
yield.bnd	yield	append
prices.dat	priFile	input
rates.dat	rates	input

2. a. Write a set of two statements that first declares the following objects as `ifstream` objects and then opens them as text input files: `inData.txt`, `prices.txt`, `coupons.dat`, and `exper.dat`.

   b. Rewrite the two statements for Exercise 2a using a single statement.

3. a. Write a set of two statements that first declares the following objects as `ofstream` objects and then opens them as text output files: `outDate.txt`, `rates.txt`, `distance.txt`, and `file2.txt`.

   b. Rewrite the two statements for Exercise 3a using a single statement.

4. Enter and execute Program 11.1 on your computer.

5. Enter and exectue Program 11.2 on your computer

6. a. Enter and execute Program 11.3a on your computer.

   b. Add a `close()` method to Program 11.3a and then execute the program.

7. Enter and execute Program 11.3b on your computer.

   b. Add a `close()` method to Program 11.3b and then execute the program.

8. Using the reference manuals provided with your computer's operating system, determine:

   a. The maximum number of characters that can be used to name a file for storage by the computer system

   b. The maximum number of data files that can be open at the same time

9. Would it be appropriate to call a saved C++ program a file? Why or why not?

10. a. Write individual declaration and open statements to link the following external data file names to their corresponding internal object names. Use only `ifstream` and `ofstream` objects.

External Name	Object Name	Mode
coba.mem	memo	binary and output
coupons.bnd	coups	binary and append
prices.dat	priFile	binary and input

   b. Redo Exercise 10a using only `fstream` objects.

   c. Write `close` statements for each of the files opened in Exercise 10a.

11.2 READING AND WRITING CHARACTER-BASED FILES

Reading or writing character-based files involves almost the identical operations for reading input from a terminal and writing data to a display screen. For writing to a file, the `cout` object is replaced by the `ofstream` object name declared in the program. For example, if outFile is declared as an object of type ofstream the following output statements are valid:

```
outFile << 'a';
outFile << "Hello World!";
outFile << descrip << ' ' << price;
```

The file name in each of these statements, in place of cout, simply directs the output stream to a specific file instead of to the standard display device Program 11.4 illustrates the use of the insertion operator, <<, to write a list of descriptions and prices to a file.

PROGRAM 11.4

```cpp
#include <iostream>
#include <fstream>
#include <cstdlib>    // needed for exit()
#include <string>
#include <iomanip>   // needed for formatting
using namespace std;

int main()
{
  string filename = "prices.dat";   // put the file name up front
  ofstream outFile;

  outFile.open(filename.c_str());

  if (outFile.fail())
  {
    cout << "The file was not successfully opened" << endl;
    exit(1);
  }

    // set the output file stream formats
  outFile << setiosflags(ios::fixed)
          << setiosflags(ios::showpoint)
          << setprecision(2);

    // send data to the file
  outFile << "Mats " << 39.95 << endl
          << "Bulbs " << 3.22 << endl
          << "Fuses " << 1.08 << endl;

  outFile.close();
  cout << "The file " << filename
       << " has been successfully written." << endl;

  return 0;
}
```

PROGRAMMING NOTE

Formatting Text File Output Stream Data

Output file streams can be formatted in the same manner as the `cout` standard output stream. For example, if an output stream named `fileOut` has been declared, the statement

```
fileOut << setiosflags(ios::fixed)
        << setiosflags(ios::showpoint)
        << setprecision(2);
```

formats all data inserted in the `fileOut` stream in the same way that these parameterized manipulators work for the `cout` stream. The first manipulator parameter, `ios::fixed`, causes the stream to output all numbers as if they were floating-point values. The next parameter, `ios::showpoint`, tells the stream always to provide a decimal point. Thus, a value such as 1.0 will appear as 1.0, and not 1. Finally, the `setprecision` manipulator tells the stream always to display 2 decimal values after the decimal point. Thus, the number 1.0 for example, will appear as 1.00.

Instead of using manipulators, you can also us the stream methods `setf()` and `precision()`. For example, the previous formatting can also be accomplished using the code:

```
fileOut.setf(ios::fixed);
fileOut.setf(ios::showpoint);
fileOut.precision(2);
```

Which style you select is a matter of preference. In both cases the formats need only be specified once and remain in effect for every number subsequently inserted into the file stream.

When Program 11.4 is executed, a file named `prices.dat` is created and saved by the computer as a text file (which is the default file type). The file is a sequential file consisting of the following data:

```
Mats 39.95
Bulbs 3.22
Fuses 1.00
```

The actual storage of characters in the file depends on the character codes used by the computer. Although only 30 characters appear to be stored in the file, corresponding to the descriptions, blanks, and prices written to the file, the file actually contains 36 characters. The extra characters consist of the newline escape sequence at the end of each line that is created by the `endl` manipulator, which is created as a carriage return character (`cr`) and linefeed (`lf`). Assuming characters are stored using the ASCII code, the `prices.dat` file is physically stored as illustrated in Figure 11.2. For convenience, the character corresponding to each hexadecimal code is listed below the code. A code of 20 represents the blank character. Additionally, both C and C++ append the low-value hexadecimal byte 0x00 as the end-of-file (EOF) sentinel when the file is closed. This end-of-file sentinel is never counted as part of the file.

FIGURE 11.2   The `prices.dat` File as Stored by the Computer

```
42 61 74 74 65 72 69 65 73 20 33 39 2e 32 35 0D 0A 42 75 6c 62 73
 M  a  t  t  e  r  i  e  s        3  9  .  2  5 cr lf  B  u  l  b  s
4D 61 74 73 32 0D 0A 46 75 73 65 73 20 31 2e 30 32 0D 0A
 3  .  2  2 cr lf  F  u  s  e  s        1  .  0  0 cr lf
```

PROGRAMMING NOTE

The put() Method

All output streams have access to the fstream class's put() method, which permits character by character output to a stream. This method works in the same manner as the character insertion operator, <<. The syntax of this method call is:

```
ofstreamName.put(characterExpression);
```

where *characterExpression* can be either a character variable or literal value. For example, the following code can be used output an 'a' to the standard output stream:

```
cin.put('a');
```

In a similar manner, if outFile is an ofstream object file that has been opened, the following code outputs the character value in the character variable named keycode to this output:

```
char keycode;
     .
     .
outFile.put(keycode);
```

Reading from a Text File

Reading data from a character-based file is almost identical to reading data from a standard keyboard, except that the cin object is replaced by the ifstream object declared in the program. For example, if inFile is declared as an object of type ifstream that is opened for input, the input statement

```
inFile >> descrip >> price;
```

will read the next two items in the file and store them in the variables descrip and price.

The file stream name in this statement, in place of cin, simply directs the input to come from the file stream rather than the standard input device stream. Other methods that can be used for stream input are listed in Table 11.3. Each of these methods must, of course, be preceded by a stream object name.

TABLE 11.3 fstream **Methods**

Method Name	Description
get()	Returns the next character extracted from the input stream as an int.
get(charVar)	Overloaded version of get() that extracts the next character from the input stream and assigns it to the specified character variable, charVar.
getline(streamObj, strObj, termChar)	Extracts characters from the specified input stream, strObj, until the terminating character, termChar, is encountered. Assigns the characters to the specified string class object, strObj.
peek()	Returns the next character in the input stream without extracting it from the stream.
ignore(int n)	Skips over the next n characters. If n is omitted, the default is to skip over the next single character.

Program 11.5 illustrates how the `prices.dat` file that was created in Program 11.4 can be read. The program also illustrates one method of detecting the end-of-file (EOF) marker using the `good()` function (see Table 11.2). Because this function returns a Boolean `true` value before the EOF marker has been either read or passed over, it can be used to verify that the data just read is valid file data. Only after the EOF marker has been read or passed over, does this function return a Boolean `false`. Thus, the notation `while(infile.good())` used in Program 11.5 ensures that the data is from the file before the EOF has been read.

PROGRAM 11.5

```cpp
#include <iostream>
#include <fstream>
#include <cstdlib>    // needed for exit()
#include <string>
using namespace std;

int main()
{
  string filename = "prices.dat";  // put the file name up front
  string descrip;
  double price;

  ifstream inFile;

  inFile.open(filename.c_str());

  if (inFile.fail())  // check for successful open
  {
    cout << "\nThe file was not successfully opened"
         << "\n Please check that the file currently exists."
         << endl;
    exit(1);
  }

    // read and display the file's contents
  inFile >> descrip >> price;
  while (inFile.good()) // check next character
  {
    cout << descrip << ' ' << price << endl;
    inFile >> descrip >> price;
  }

  inFile.close();

  return 0;
}
```

The display produced by Program 11.5 is:

```
Mats 39.95
Bulbs 3.22
Fuses 1.08
```

PROGRAMMING NOTE

A Way to Clearly Identify a File's Name and Location

During program development test files are usually placed in the same directory as the program. Therefore, a method call such as `inFile.open("exper.dat")` causes no problems to the operating system. In production systems, however, it is not uncommon for data files to reside in one directory while program files reside in another. For this reason it is always a good idea to include the full path name of any file opened.

For example, if the `exper.dat` file resides in the directory `C:\test\files`, the `open()` call should include the full path name, viz: `inFile.open("c:\\test\\files\\exper.dat")`. Then, no matter where the program is run from, the operating system will know where to locate the file. Notice that the double backslashes are required in the path name.

Another important convention is to list all file names at the top of a program instead of embedding the names deep within the code. This can easily be accomplished by string variables to store each file name. note the use of the double backslashes, which are required.

For example, if the statements

```
string filename = "c:\\test\\files\\exper.dat";
```

are placed at the top of a program file, the declaration statement clearly lists both the name of the desired file and its location. Then, if some other file is to be tested, all that is required is a simple one line change at the top of the program.

Using a string variable for the file's name is also useful for the `fail()` method check. For example, consider the following code:

```
string filename;
ifstream infile;

inFile.open(filename.c_str());

if (inFile.fail())
{
   cout << "\n The file named " << filename
        << was not successfully opened"
        <<\n Please check that this file currently exists."
   exit(1);
}
```

In this code the name of the file that failed to open is directly displayed within the error message without the name being embedded as a string value.

Re-examine the expression `inFile.good()` used in the `while` statement. This expression is `true` as long as the EOF marker has not been read. Thus, as long as the item read was good, the loop continues to read the file. Within the loop, the items just read are first displayed and then a new string and a double-precision number are input to the program. When the EOF has been detected, the expression returns a Boolean value of `false` and the loop terminates. This ensures that data is read and displayed up to, but not including, the end-of-file marker.

A direct replacement for the statement while(inFile.good()) is the statement while(!inFile.eof()), which is read as "while the end of file has not been reached." This works because the eof() function returns a true only after the EOF marker has been read or passed over. In effect then, the relational expression checks that the EOF has not been read; hence, the use of the NOT, !, operator.

Alternatively, another means of detecting the EOF is to use the fact that the extraction operation, >>, returns a Boolean value of `true` if data was extracted from a stream; otherwise, it returns a Boolean `false` value. Using this return value, the following code can be used within Program 11.5 to read the file:

```
// read and display the file's contents
  while (inFile >> descrip >> price) // check next character
    cout << descrip << ' ' << price << endl;
```

Although initially a bit cryptic, this code makes perfect sense when you understand that the expression being tested not only extracts data from the file, but returns a Boolean value to indicate if the extraction was successful or not.

Finally, in either the above `while` statement or in Program 11.5, the expression `inFile >> descrip >> price` can be replaced by a `getline()` method (see Section 9.1). For file input this method has the syntax:

```
getline(fileObject, strObj, terminatingChar)
```

where *fileObject* is the name of the `ifstream` file, *strObj* is a string class object, and *terminatingChar* is an optional character constant or variable specifying the terminating character. If this optional third argument is omitted, the default terminating character is the newline (`'\n'`) character. Program 11.6 illustrates using `getline()` within the context of a complete program.

PROGRAM 11.6

```cpp
#include <iostream>
#include <fstream>
#include <cstdlib>    // needed for exit()
#include <string>
using namespace std;

int main()
{
  string filename = "prices.dat";  // put the file name up front
  string line;
  ifstream inFile;

  inFile.open(filename.c_str());

  if (inFile.fail())  // check for successful open
  {
    cout << "\nThe file was not successfully opened"
         << "\n Please check that the file currently exists."
         << endl;
    exit(1);
  }

    // read and display the file's contents
  while (getline(inFile,line))
    cout << line << endl;

  inFile.close();

  return 0;
}
```

> ## P R O G R A M M I N G   N O T E

The `get()` **and** `putback()` **Methods**

All input streams have access to the `fstream` class's `get()` method, which permits character-by-character input from an input stream. This method works in a similar manner to character extraction using the `>>` operator with two important differences: if a newline character, `'\n'`, or a blank character, `' '`, are encountered, these characters are read in the same manner as any other alphanumeric character. The syntax of this method call is:

```
istreamName.get(characterVariable);
```

For example, the following code can be used to read the next character from the standard input stream and store the character into the variable `ch`:

```
char ch;
cin.get(ch);
```

In a similar manner, if `inFile` is an `ifstream` object that has been opened to a file, the following code reads the next character in the stream and assigns it to the character `keycode`:

```
char keycode;
inFile.get(keycode);
```

In addition to the `get()` method, all input streams have a `putback()` method that can be used to put the last character read from an input stream back on the stream. This method has the syntax

```
ifstreamName.putback(characterExpression);
```

where `characterExpression` can be any character variable or character value.

The `putback()` method provides an output capability to an input stream. It should be noted that the putback character need not be the last character read; rather, it can be any character. All putback characters, however, have no effect on the data file but only on the open input stream. Thus, the data file characters remain unchanged, although the characters subsequently read from the input stream can change.

Program 11.6 is really a line-by-line text-copying program, which reads a line of text from the file and then displays it on the terminal. The output of Program 11.6 is:

```
Mats 39.95
Bulbs 3.22
Fuses 1.00
```

If it were necessary to obtain the description and price as individual variables, either Program 11.5 should be used or the string returned by `getline()` in Program 11.6 must be processed further to extract the individual data items (see Section 10.7 for parsing procedures).

Standard Device Files

The file stream objects we have used have all been logical file objects. A logical file object is a stream that connects a file of logically related data such as a data file to a program. In addition to logical file objects, C++ also supports physical file objects. A physical file object is a stream that connects to a hardware device, such as a keyboard, screen, or printer.

The actual physical device assigned to your program for data entry is formally called the **standard input** file. Usually this is the keyboard. When a `cin` object method call is encountered in a C++ program, it a request to the operating system to go to this standard input file for the expected input. Similarly, when a `cout` object method call is encountered, the output is automatically displayed or "written to" a device that has been assigned as the **standard output** file. For most systems this is a terminal screen, although it can be a printer.

When a program is executed, the standard input stream `cin` is automatically connected to the standard input device. Similarly, the standard output stream `cout` is automatically connected to the standard output device. These two object streams are always available for programmer use, as are the standard error stream, `cerr`, and the standard log stream, `clog`. Both of these streams also connect to the terminal screen.

Other Devices

The keyboard, display, error-reporting, and logging streams are automatically connected to the internal stream objects named `cin`, `cout`, `cerr`, and `clog` respectively, by a C++ program by including the `iostream` header file. Additionally, other devices can be used for input or output if the name assigned by the system is known. For example, most IBM or IBM-compatible personal computers assign the name `prn` to the printer connected to the computer. For these computers a statement such as `outFile.open("prn")` connects the printer to the `ofstream` object named `outFile`. A subsequent statement, such as `outFile << "Hello World!";` would then cause the string `Hello World!` to be printed directly on the printer. Notice that as the name of an actual file, `prn` must be enclosed in double quotes in the `open()` function call.

Exercises 11.2

1. a. Enter and execute Program 11.5.

   b. Modify Program 11.5 to use the expression `!inFile.eot()` in place of the expression `inFile.good()`, and execute the program to see that it operates correctly.

2. a. Enter and execute Program 11.6.

   b. Modify Program 11.6 by replacing the identifier `cout` with `cerr`, and verify that the output for the standard error file stream is the screen.

   c. Modify Program 11.6 by replacing the identifier `cout` with `clog`, and verify that the output for the standard log stream is the screen.

3. a. Write a C++ program that accepts lines of text from the keyboard and writes each line to a file named `text.dat` until an empty line is entered. An empty line is a line with no text that is created by pressing the Enter (or Return) key.

   b. Modify Program 11.6 to read and display the data stored in the `text.dat` file created in Exercise 3a.

4. Determine the operating system command or procuedure provided by your computer to display the contents of a saved file.

5. a. Create a text file named `employee.dat` containing the following data:

Anthony	A	10031	7.82	12/18/05
Burrows	W	10067	9.14	6/09/05
Fain	B	10083	8.79	5/18/04
Janney	P	10095	10.57	9/28/05
Smith	G	10105	8.50	12/20/03

   b. Write a C++ program to read the `employee.dat` file created in Exercise 5a and produce a duplicate copy of the file named `employee.bak`.

   c. Modify the program written in Exercise 5b to accept the names of the original and duplicate files as user input.

d. Since the program written for Exercise 5c always copies data from an original file to a duplicate file, can you think of a better method of accepting the original and duplicate file names than prompting the user for them each time the program is executed?

6. a. Write a C++ program that opens a file and displays the contents of the file with associated line numbers. That is, the program should print the number 1 before displaying the first line, then print the number 2 before displaying the second line, and so on for each line in the file.

b. Modify the program written in Exercise 6a to list the contents of the file on the printer assigned to your computer.

7. a. Create a text file containing the following data (without the headings):

Names	Social Security Number	Hourly Rate	Hours Worked
B Caldwell	555-88-2222	7.32	37
D Memcheck	555-88-4444	8.32	40
R Potter	555-88-6666	6.54	40
W Rosen	555-88-8888	9.80	35

b. Write a C++ program that reads the data file created in Exercise 7a and computes and displays a payroll schedule. The output should list the Social Security number, name, and gross pay for each individual, where gross pay is calculated as *Hourly Rate × Hours Worked*.

8. a. Create a text file containing the following car numbers, number of miles driven, and number of gallons of gas used by each car (do not include the headings in the file):

Car Number	Miles Driven	Gallons Used
54	250	19
62	525	38
71	123	6
85	1,322	86
97	235	14

b. Write a C++ program that reads the data in the file created in Exercise 8a and displays the car number, miles driven, gallons used, and the miles per gallon for each car. The output should additionally contain the total miles driven, total gallons used, and average miles per gallon for all the cars. These totals should be displayed at the end of the output report.

9. a. Create a text file with the following data (without the headings):

Part Number	Initial Amount	Quantity Sold	Minimum Amount
QA310	95	47	50
CM145	320	162	200
MS514	34	20	25
EN212	163	150	160

b. Write a C++ program to create an inventory report based on the data in the file created in Exercise 9a. The display should consist of the part number, current balance, and the amount that is necessary to bring the inventory to the minimum level.

10. a. Create a text file containing the following data (without the headings):

Name	Rate	Hours
Callaway, G.	6.00	40
Hanson, P.	5.00	48
Lasard, D.	6.50	35
Stillman, W.	8.00	50

b. Write a C++ program that uses the information contained in the file created in Exercise 10a to produce the following pay report for each employee:

```
Name    Pay Rate   Hours    Regular Pay    Overtime Pay    Gross Pay
```

Regular pay is to be computed as any hours worked up to and including 40 hours times the pay rate. Overtime pay is to be computed as any hours worked above 40 hours times a pay rate of 1.5 times the regular rate, and the gross pay is the sum of regular and overtime pay. At the end of the report, the program should display the totals of the regular, overtime, and gross pay columns.

11. a. Store the following data in a file:

```
5 96 87 78 93 21 4 92 82 85 87 6 72 69 85 75 81 73
```

b. Write a C++ program to calculate and display the average of each group of numbers in the file created in Exercise 11a. The data is arranged in the file so that each group of numbers is preceded by the number of data items in the group. Thus, the first number in the file, 5, indicates that the next five numbers should be grouped together. The number 4 indicates that the following four numbers are a group, and the 6 indicates that the last six numbers are a group. (*Hint:* Use a nested loop. The outer loop should terminate when the end-of-file has been encountered.)

11.3 EXCEPTIONS AND FILE CHECKING[1]

Error detection and processing using with exception handling is used extensively within C++ programs that use one or more files. For example, if a user deletes or renames a file using the operating system, this action will cause a C++ program to fail when an open() function call attempts to open the file under its original name. (A typical file processing application is one that allows, for example, a user to delete a file or change its data from outside a program using operating system commands.) Such file processing actions can easily cause a C++ program to fail, as for example, if a user deletes a file that will be opened for reading.

Recall from Section 7.1 that the code for general exception handling looks like this:

```
try
{
   // one or more statements,
   // at least one of which should
   // throw an exception
}
catch(exceptionDataType parameterName)
{
   // one or more statements
}
```

In this code the try block statements are executed. If no error occurs, the catch block statements are omitted and processing continues with the statement following the catch block. However, if any statement within the try block throws an exception, the catch block whose exceptionDataType matches the exception is executed. If no catch block is defined for a try block, a compiler error occurs. If no catch block exists that catches a thrown data type, a program crash occurs only if the exception is thrown. Most times, but not always, the catch block displays an error message and terminates processing with a call to the exit() function.

---

[1] This topic can be omitted on the first reading without loss of subject continuity.

Program 11.7 illustrates the statements required to open a file in read mode that includes exception handling.

PROGRAM 11.7

```cpp
#include <iostream>
#include <fstream>
#include <cstdlib>    // needed for exit()
#include <string>
using namespace std;

int main()
{
  string filename = "prices.dat";  // put the file name up front
  string descrip;
  double price;

  ifstream inFile;

  try  // this block tries to open the file, read, and display the file's data
  {
    inFile.open(filename.c_str());

    if (inFile.fail()) throw filename; // this is the exception being checked

      // read and display the file's contents
    inFile >> descrip >> price;
      while (inFile.good()) // check next character
    {
       cout << descrip << ' ' << price << endl;
       inFile >> descrip >> price;
    }
    inFile.close();

    return 0;
  }
  catch (string e)
  {
    cout << "\nThe file "<< e << " was not successfully opened"
         << "\n Please check that the file currently exists."
         << endl;
    exit(1);
  }
}
```

The exception message produced by Program 11.7 when it was executed and the prices.dat file was not found is:

```
The file prices.dat was not successfully opened
   Please check that the file currently exists.
```

PROGRAMMING NOTE

Checking That the File Was Successfully Opened

Using Exception handling is the most common method for checking that the operating system successfully located the designated file is the one coded in Program 11.7, the key coding points of which are repeated here for convenience:

```
try  // this block tries to open the file, read, and display the file's data
  {
    // open the file, throwing an exception if the open fails
    // perform all required file processing
    // close the file
  }
  catch (string e)
  {
    cout << "\nThe file "<< e << " was not successfully opened"
         << "\n Please check that the file currently exists."
         << endl;
    exit(1);
  }
```

Although the exception handling code in Program 11.7 can be used to check for a successful file open for both input and output, a more rigorous check is usually required for output files. This is because, on output, the file is almost guaranteed to be found. If it exists it will be found, and if it does not exist, the operating system will create it (unless append mode is specified and the file already exists or the operating system cannot find the indicated folder). Knowing that the file has been successfully found and opened, however, is insufficient for output purposes when an existing output file *must not* be overwritten. For these cases, the file can first be opened for input, and then, if the file is found, a further check can be made to ensure that the user explicitly provides approval for overwriting it. How this is accomplished is illustrated in highlighted code within Program 11.8.

PROGRAM 11.8

```cpp
#include <iostream>
#include <fstream>
#include <cstdlib>   // needed for exit()
#include <string>
#include <iomanip>  // needed for formatting
using namespace std;

int main()
{
  char response;
  string filename = "prices.dat";  // put the file name up front
  ifstream inFile;
  ofstream outFile;
```

(continued from previous page)

```cpp
try // open a basic input stream simply to check if the file exists
{
    inFile.open(filename.c_str());
    if (inFile.fail()) throw 1; // this means the file doesn't exist
        // only get here if the file was found;
        // otherwise the catch block takes control
    cout << "A file by the name " << filename << " currently exists.\n"
         << "Do you want to overwrite it with the new data (y or n): ";
    cin >> response;
    if (tolower(response) == 'n')
    {
        inFile.close();
        cout << "The existing file has not been overwritten." << endl;
        exit(1);
    }
}
catch(int e) {};   // a do-nothing block that permits
                   // processing to continue
try
{
        // open the file in write mode and continue with file writes
    outFile.open(filename.c_str());
    if (outFile.fail()) throw filename;
        // set the output file stream formats
    outFile << setiosflags(ios::fixed)
            << setiosflags(ios::showpoint)
            << setprecision(2);
        // write the data to the file
    outFile << "Mats " << 39.95 << endl
            << "Bulbs "  << 3.22 << endl
            << "Fuses " << 1.08 << endl;
    outFile.close();
    cout << "The file " << filename
         << " has been successfully written." << endl;

    return 0;
}
catch(string e)
{
    cout << "The file " << filename
         << " was not opened for output and has not been written."
         << endl;
}
}
```

Notice in Program 11.8 that the `try` blocks are separate. Because a `catch` block is affiliated with the closest previous `try` block, there is no ambiguity about unmatched `try` and `catch` blocks.

Opening Multiple Files

As an example of applying exception handling to the opening of two files at the same time, assume that we wish to read the data from a character-based file named `info.txt`, one character at a time, and write this data to a file named `backup.txt`. Essentially, this application is a file copy program that reads the data from one file in a character-by-character manner and writes them to a second file. For purposes of illustration, assume that the characters stored in the input file are as shown in Figure 11.3.

FIGURE 11.3 | The Data Stored in `info.txt`

```
Now is the time for all good people
   to come to the aid of their party.
Please call (555) 888-6666 for
   further information.
```

Figure 11.4 illustrates the structure of the streams that are necessary for producing our file copy. In this figure, the input stream object referenced by the variable `inFile` will read data from the `info.txt` file, and the output stream object referenced by the variable `outFile` will write data to the `backup.txt` file.

FIGURE 11.4 | The File Copy Stream Structure

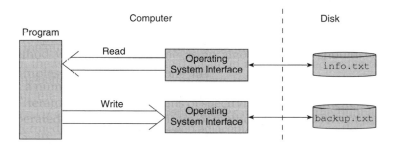

Now consider Program 11.9, which creates the `backup.txt` file as an exact duplicate of the `info.txt` file using the procedure illustrated in Figure 11.4.

PROGRAM 11.9

```cpp
#include <iostream>
#include <fstream>
#include <cstdlib>   // needed for exit()
#include <string>
using namespace std;
```

(continued from previous page)

```cpp
int main()
{
  string fileOne = "info.txt";  // put the file name up front
  string fileTwo = "info.bak";
  char ch;
  ifstream inFile;
  ofstream outFile;

  try  //this block tries to open the input file
  {
    // open a basic input stream
    inFile.open(fileOne.c_str());
      if (inFile.fail()) throw fileOne;
  } // end of outer try block
  catch (string in)  // catch for outer try block
  {
    cout << "The input file " << in
         << " was not successfully opened." << endl
         << " No backup was made." << endl;
    exit(1);
  }

  try  // this block tries to open the output file and
  {    // perform all file processing

    outFile.open(fileTwo.c_str());
    if (outFile.fail())throw fileTwo;
    while ((ch = inFile.get())!= EOF)
      outFile.put(ch);;

    inFile.close();
    outFile.close();
  }
  catch (string out)  // catch for inner try block
  {
    cout << "The backup file " << out
         << " was not successfully opened." << endl;
    exit(1);
  }

  cout << "A successful backup of " << fileOne
       << " named " << fileTwo << " was successfully made." << endl;

  return 0;
}
```

For simplicity, Program 11.9 attempts to open both the input and output files within individually separate and non-nested `try` blocks. More generally, the second file would be opened in a nested inner `try` block so that the attempt to open this second file would not be made if the opening of the first file threw an exception. How this is accomplished is explained in this section's Programming Note on nesting `try` blocks.

PROGRAMMING NOTE

Nesting `try` **Blocks**

When more than one file stream is involved, opening each file stream in its own `try` block permits exact isolation and identification of which file caused an exception, should one occur. In doing so, the `try` blocks can be nested. For example, consider Program 11.9, which is rewritten here using nested `try` blocks. Notice that in this case the `catch` block for the inner `try` block must also be nested in the same block scope as its `try` block.

```cpp
#include <iostream>
#include <fstream>
#include <cstdlib>   // needed for exit()
#include <string>
using namespace std;

int main()
{
  string fileOne = "info.text";  // put the file name up front
  string fileTwo = "info.bak";
  char ch;
  ifstream inFile;
  ofstream outFile;

  try  //this block tries to open the input file
  {
    // open a basic input stream
    inFile.open(fileOne.c_str());
      if (inFile.fail()) throw fileOne;
    try  // this block tries to open the output file and
    {    // perform all file processing
         // open a basic output stream
      outFile.open(fileTwo.c_str());
      if (outFile.fail())throw fileTwo;
      while ((ch = inFile.get()) != EOF)
      outFile.put(ch);;

    inFile.close();
    outFile.close();
  }  // end of inner try block
  catch (string out)  // catch for inner try block
  {
    cout << "The backup file " << out
         << " was not successfully opened." << endl;
    exit(1);
  }
}  // end of outer try block
catch (string in)  // catch for outer try block
{
  cout << "The input file " << in
       << " was not successfully opened." << endl
       << " No backup was made." << endl;
  exit(1);
}
```

(continued from previous page)

```
      cout << "A successful backup of " << fileOne
          << " named " << fileTwo << "was successfully made." << endl;

      return 0;
    }
```

The important point to notice in this program is the nesting of the `try` blocks. If the two `try` blocks are not nested and the input stream declaration `ifstream inFile;` was placed in the first block, it could not be used in the second `try` block without producing a compiler error. The reason for this is that all variables declared in a block of code, which is defined by an opening and closing brace pair, are local to the block in which they are declared.

In reviewing Program 11.9, pay particular attention to the statement:

```
        while((ch = inFile.get())!= EOF)
```

This statement continually reads a value from the input stream until the EOF value is detected. As long as the returned value does not equal the EOF value, the value is written to the output object stream. The parentheses surrounding the expression `(ch = inFile.get())` are necessary to ensure that a value is first read and assigned to the variable `ch` before the retrieved value is compared to the EOF value. In their absence, the complete expression would be `ch = inFile.get()!= EOF`. Due to the precedence of operations, the relational expression `inFile.get()!= EOF` would be executed first. Because this is a relational expression, its result is either a Boolean `true` or `false` value based on the data retrieved by the `get()` method. Attempting to assign this Boolean result to the character variable `ch` is an invalid conversion across an assignment operator.

Exercises 11.3

1. List two conditions that will cause a fail condition when a file is opened for input.

2. List two conditions that will cause a fail condition when a file is opened for output.

3. If a file that exists is opened for output in write mode, what happens to the data currently in the file?

4. Modify Program 11.7 to use an identifier name of your choice, in place of the letter e, for the `catch` block's exception parameter name.

5. Enter and execute Program 11.8.

6. Determine why the two `try` blocks in Program 11.8, which are not nested, cause no problems in either compilation or execution. (*Hint:* Place the declaration for the file name within the first `try` block and compile the program.)

7. a. If the nested `try` blocks in the program listed in this section's Programming Note on nested `try` blocks are separated into non-nested blocks the program will not compile. Determine why this is so.

   b. What additional changes would have to be made to the program listed in this section's Programming Note on nested `try` blocks to allow the program to be written with un-nested blocks (*Hint:* See Exercise 6)?

8. Either enter the data for the `info.txt` file in Figure 11.3 or obtain it from this text's Web site (see Preface for the URL). Then enter and execute Program 11.9 and verify that the backup file was written.

9. Modify Program 11.9 to use a `getline()` method in place of the `get()` method currently in the program.

11.4 RANDOM FILE ACCESS

The term **file access** refers to the process of retrieving data from a file. There are two types of file access: sequential access and random access. To understand these two types of file access, you first need to understand some concepts related to how data is organized within a file.

The term **file organization** refers to the way data is stored in a file. The files we have used, and will continue to use, all have a **sequential organization**. This means that the characters within the file are stored in a sequential manner, one after another.

In addition to being sequentially organized, we have also read each file, after it has been opened, in a sequential manner. That is, we have accessed each character sequentially, one after another. This type of access is referred to as **sequential access**. The fact that the characters in the file are stored sequentially, however, does not force us to access them sequentially. In fact, we can skip over characters and read a sequentially organized file in a non-sequential manner.

In **random access**, any character in the opened file can be read directly, without first having to sequentially read all the characters stored ahead of it. To provide random access to files, each `ifstream` object automatically creates a file position marker. This marker is a long integer that represents an offset from the beginning of each file and keeps track of where the next character is to be read from or written to. The functions that are used to access and change the file position marker are listed in Table 11.4. The suffixes `g` and `p` in these function names denote `get` and `put`, respectively, where `get` refers to an input (get from) file and `put` refers to an output (put to) file.

The `seek()` functions allow the programmer to move to any position in the file. In order to understand this method, you must first clearly understand how data is referenced in the file using the file position marker.

Each character in a data file is located by its position in the file. The first character in the file is located at position 0, the next character at position 1, and so on. A character's position is also referred to as its offset from the start of the file. Thus, the first character has a 0 offset, the second character has an offset of 1, and so on for each character in the file.

The `seek()` functions require two arguments: the offset, as a long integer, into the file; and where the offset is to be calculated from, as determined by the mode. The three possible alternatives for the mode are `ios::beg`, `ios::cur`, and

TABLE 11.4 File Position Marker Functions

Name	Description
`seekg(offset, mode)`	For input files, move to the offset position as indicated by the mode.
`seekp(offset, mode)`	For output files, move to the offset position as indicated by the mode.
`tellg(void)`	For input files, return the current value of the file position marker.
`tellp(void)`	For output files, return the current value of the file position marker.

`ios::end`, which denote the beginning, current position, and the end of the file, respectively. Thus, a mode of `ios::beg` means the offset is the true offset from the start of the file. A mode of `ios::cur` means that the offset is relative to the current position in the file, and an `ios::end` mode means the offset is relative to the end of the file. A positive offset means move forward in the file and a negative offset means move backward. Examples of `seek()` function calls are shown below. In these examples, assume that `inFile` has been opened as an input file and `outFile` as an output file. Notice, in these examples, that the offset passed to `seekg()` and `seekp()` must be a long integer.

```
inFile.seekg(4L,ios::beg);     // go to the fifth character in the input file
outFile.seekp(4L,ios::beg);    // go to the fifth character in the output file
inFile.seekg(4L,ios::cur);     // move ahead five characters in the input file
outFile.seekp(4L,ios::cur);    // move ahead five characters in the output file
inFile.seekg(-4L,ios::cur);    // move back five characters in the input file
outFile.seekp(-4L,ios::cur);   // move back five characters in the output file
inFile.seekg(0L,ios::beg);     // go to start of the input file
outFile.seekp(0L,ios::beg);    // go to start of the output file
inFile.seekg(0L,ios::end);     // go to end of the input file
outFile.seekp(0L,ios::end);    // go to end of the output file
inFile.seekg(-10L,ios::end);   // go to 10 characters before the input file's end
outFile.seekp(-10L,ios::end);  // go to 10 characters before the output file's end
```

As opposed to the `seek()` functions that move the file position marker, the `tell()` functions simply return the offset value of the file position marker. For example, if ten characters have already been read from an input file named `inFile`, the function call

```
inFile.tellg();
```

returns the long integer 10. This means that the next character to be read is offset 10 byte positions from the start of the file, and is the eleventh character in the file.

Program 11.10 illustrates the use of `seekg()` and `tellg()` to read a file in reverse order, from last character to first. As each character is read it is also displayed.

PROGRAM 11.10

```cpp
#include <iostream>
#include <fstream>
#include <string>
#include <cstdlib>
using namespace std;

int main()
{
   string filename = "test.dat";
   char ch;
   long offset, last;
   ifstream inFile(filename.c_str());
```

(continued from previous page)

```
if (inFile.fail())    // check for successful open
{
  cout << "\nThe file was not successfully opened"
          << "\n Please check that the file currently exists"
          << endl;
  exit(1);
}

inFile.seekg(0L,ios::end);    // move to the end of the file
last = inFile.tellg();        // save the offset of the last character

for(offset = 1L; offset <= last; offset++)
{
  inFile.seekg(-offset, ios::end);
  ch = inFile.get();
  cout << ch << " : ";
}

inFile.close();
cout << endl;

return 0;
}
```

Assuming the file `test.dat` contains the following data:

The grade was 92.5

the output of Program 11.10 is:

```
5 : . : 2 : 9 : : s : a : w : : e : d : a : r : g : : e : h : T :
```

Program 11.10 initially goes to the last character in the file. The offset of this character, which is the end-of-file character, is saved in the variable `last`. Since `tellg()` returns a long integer, `last` has been declared as long integer.

Starting from the end of the file, `seekg()` is used to position the next character to be read, referenced from the end of the file. As each character is read, the character is displayed and the offset adjusted in order to access the next character. It should be noted that the first offset used is -1, which represents the character immediately preceding the EOF marker.

Exercises 11.4

1. a. Create a file named `test.dat` on the directory that contains your program files. You can do this by using a text editor by copying the file `test.dat` on the data disk provided with this book.

   b. Enter and execute Program 11.10 on your computer.

2. Rewrite Program 11.10 so that the origin for the `seekg()` function used in the `for` loop is the start of the file rather than the end.

3. Modify Program 11.10 to display an error message if `seekg()` attempts to reference a position beyond the end of the file.

4. Write a program that will read and display every second character in a file named `test.dat`.

5. Using the seek() and tell() functions, write a function named fileChars() that returns the total number of characters in a file.

6. a. Write a function named readBytes() that reads and displays n characters starting from any position in a file. The function should accept three arguments: a file object name, the offset of the first character to be read, and the number of characters to be read. (*Note:* the prototype for readBytes should be void readBytes(fstream&, long, int).)

   b. Modify the readBytes() function written in Exercise 6a to store the characters read into a string or an array. The function should accept the address of the storage area as a fourth argument.

11.5 FILE STREAMS AS FUNCTION ARGUMENTS

A file stream object can be used as a function argument. The only requirement is that the function's formal parameter be a reference (see Section 6.5) to an the appropriate stream, either as ifstream& or ofstream&. For example, in Program 11.11 an ofstream object named outFile is opened in main() and this stream object is passed to the function inOut(). Notice that the function prototype and header line for inOut() both declare the formal parameter as a reference to an ostream object type. The inOut() function is then used to write five lines of user-entered text to the file.

PROGRAM 11.11

```cpp
#include <iostream>
#include <fstream>
#include <cstdlib>
#include <string>
using namespace std;

int main()
{
  string fname = "list.dat";  // here is the file we are working with

  void inOut(ofstream&);    // function prototype

  ofstream outFile;

  outFile.open(fname.c_str());
  if (outFile.fail())    // check for a successful open
  {
    cout << "\nThe output file " << fname << " was not successfully opened"
         << endl;
    exit(1);
  }

  inOut(outFile);  // call the function

  return 0;
}
```

(continued from previous page)

```
void inOut(ofstream& fileOut)
{

  const int NUMLINES = 5;  // number of lines of text
  string line;
  int count;

  cout << "Please enter five lines of text:" << endl;
  for (count = 0; count < NUMLINES; count++)
  {
    getline(cin,line);
    fileOut << line << endl;
  }

  cout << "\nThe file has been successfully written." << endl;
  return;
}
```

Within `main()` the file is an `ostream` object named `outFile`. This object is passed to the `inOut()` function and is accepted as the formal parameter named `fileOut`, which is declared to be a reference to an `ostream` object type. The function `inOut()` then uses its reference parameter `outFile` as an output file stream name in an identical manner as `main()` would use the `fileOut` stream object. Notice also that Program 11.11 uses the `getline()` method introduced in Section 11.2 (see Table 11.3).

In Program 11.12 we have expanded on Program 11.11 by adding a `getOpen()` function to perform the open. Notice that `getOpen()`, like `inOut()`, accepts a reference argument to an `ofstream` object. After the `getOpen()` function completes execution, this reference is passed to `inOut()`, as it was in Program 11.11. Although you might be tempted to write `getOpen()` to return a reference to an `ofstream`, this will not work because it ultimately results in an attempt to assign a returned reference to an existing one.

PROGRAM 11.12

```
#include <iostream>
#include <fstream>
#include <cstdlib>
#include <string>
using namespace std;

int main()
{
  int getOpen(ofstream&);   // pass a reference to an fstream
  void inOut(ofstream&);    // pass a reference to an fstream

  ofstream outFile;     // file name is an fstream object
```

(continued from previous page)

```cpp
  getOpen(outFile);     // open the file
  inOut(outFile);       // write to it

  return 0;
}

int getOpen(ofstream& fileOut)
{
  string name;

  cout << "\nEnter a file name: ";
  getline(cin,name);

  fileOut.open(name.c_str());       // open the file

  if (fileOut.fail())       // check for successful open
  {
    cout << "Cannot open the file" << endl;
    exit(1);
  }
  else
    return 1;
}

void inOut(ofstream& fileOut)
{
  const int NUMLINES = 5;   // number of lines
  int count;
  string line;

  cout << "Please enter five lines of text:" << endl;
  for (count = 0; count < NUMLINES; ++count)
  {
    getline(cin,line);
    fileOut << line << endl;
  }
  cout << "\nThe file has been successfully written.";
  return;
}
```

Program 11.12 is simply a modified version of Program 11.11 that now allows the user to enter a file name from the standard input device and then opens the `ofstream` connection to the external file. If the name of an existing data file is entered, the file will be destroyed when it is opened for output. A useful trick that you may employ to prevent this type of mishap is to open the entered file using an input file stream. Then, if the file exists, the `fail()` method will indicate a successful open (i.e., the open does not fail), which indicates that the file is available for input. This can be used to alert the user that a file with the entered name currently exists in the system and to request confirmation that the data in the file can be destroyed and the file opened for output. Before the file is reopened for output the input file stream should be closed. The implementation of this algorithm is left as an exercise.

1. A function named pFile() is to receive a file name as a reference to an ifstream object. What declarations are required to pass a file name to pFile()?

2. Write a function named fcheck() that checks whether a file exists. The function should accept an ifstream object as a formal reference parameter. If the file exists, the function should return a value of 1, otherwise the function should return a value of zero.

3. Assume that a data file consisting of a group of individual lines has been created. Write a function named printLine() that will read and display any desired line of the file. For example, the function call printLine(fstream& fName,5); should display the fifth line of the passed object stream.

4. Rewrite the function getOpen() used in Program 11.12 to incorporate the file-checking procedures described in this section. Specifically, if the entered file name exists, an appropriate message should be displayed. The user should then be presented with the option of entering a new file name or allowing the program to overwrite the existing file. Use the function written for Exercise 2 in your program.

11.6 FOCUS ON PROBLEM SOLVING

Once a data file has been created, application programs are typically written to read and update the file with current data. In this section, two such program requirements are presented. The first problem uses a file as a database for storing the ten most recent pollen counts, which are used in the summer as allergy "irritability" measures. As a new reading is obtained, it is added to the file and the oldest stored reading is deleted.

The second program requirement concerns an expanded file update procedure. In this application, a file containing inventory data, consisting of book identification numbers and quantities in stock, is updated by information contained in a second file. This application requires that identification numbers in the two files be matched before a record is updated.

Problem 1: Single-File Update of Pollen Counts

Pollen count readings, which are taken from August through September in the northeastern region of the United States, measure the number of ragweed pollen grains in the air. Pollen counts in the range of 10 to 200 grains per cubic meter of air are usual during this time of year. Typically, pollen counts above 10 begin to affect a small percentage of hay fever sufferers, counts in the range of 30 to 40 noticeably bother approximately 30% of hay fever sufferers, and counts between 40 and 50 adversely affect over 60% of all hay fever sufferers.

Program Requirement   A program is to be written that updates a file containing the ten most recent pollen counts. As a new count is obtained, it is added to the end of the file and the oldest count deleted from the file.[2] Additionally, the average of the new file's data is calculated and displayed. The existing file is named `pollen.in` and contains the data shown in Figure 11.5.

Analyze the Problem   The input data for this problem consist of a file of ten integer numbers and a user-input value of the most recent integer value pollen count. There are two required outputs:

1. A file of the ten most recent integer values
2. The average of the data in the updated file

FIGURE 11.5   Data Currently in the Pollen File

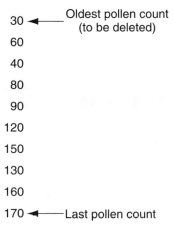

Develop a Solution   The algorithm for solving this problem is straightforward and is described by the following pseudocode:

main( ) function
    Display a message indicating what the program does
    Call the Input stream function
    Call the Output stream function
    Call the Update function
    Display the new 10-week average

Input stream function
    Request the name of the input data file
    Open an input file stream and validate a successful connection

---

[2] This type of data storage is formally referred to as a first-in/first-out (FIFO) list, which is also called a *queue*. If the list is maintained in last-in/first-out order (LIFO), it is called a *stack*.

Output stream function
    Request the name of the output data file
    Open an output file stream and validate a successful connection

Update function
    Request a new pollen count reading
    Read the oldest pollen count from the input data file
    For the remaining input file pollen counts
        Read an input value
        Add the value to a total
        Write the input value to the output file stream
    Endfor
    Write the new pollen count to the output file stream
    Add the new pollen count to the total
    Calculate the average as total / number of pollen counts
    Return the new 10-week average
    Close all files

In reviewing this algorithm, notice that the oldest pollen count is read but never used in any computation. The remaining pollen counts are read, "captured" in a total, and individually written to the output data file. The last pollen count is then added to the total and also written to the output data file. Finally, the average of the most recent pollen counts is computed and displayed, and all file streams are closed.

Code the Solution   Program 11.13 presents a C++ representation of the selected design where the selected algorithm has been coded as the function pollenUpdate.

PROGRAM 11.13

```cpp
#include <iostream>
#include <fstream>
#include <cstdlib>
#include <string>
using namespace std;

void openInput(ifstream&);    // pass a reference to an ifstream
void openOutput(ofstream&);   // pass a reference to an ofstream
float pollenUpdate(ifstream&, ofstream&);   // pass two references

int main()
{
   ifstream inFile;    // inFile is an istream object
   ofstream outFile;   // outFile is an ofstream object
   double average;
```

(continued from previous page)

```cpp
      // display a user message
   cout << "\n\nThis program reads the old pollen count file, "
        << "creates a current pollen"
        << "\n    count file, and calculates and displays "
        << "the latest ten week average.";

   openInput(inFile);
   openOutput(outFile);

   average = pollenUpdate(inFile, outFile);

   cout << "\nThe new ten week average is: " << average << endl;

   return 0;
}

// this function gets an external file name and opens the file for input
void openInput(ifstream& fname)
{
   string filename;

   cout << "\n\nEnter the input pollen count file name: ";
   cin >> filename;

   fname.open(filename.c_str());

   if (fname.fail())    // check for a successful open
   {
     cout << "\nFailed to open the file named " << filename << "for input"
          << "\n Please check that this file exits"
          << endl;
     exit(1);
   }

   return;
}


// this function gets an external file name and opens the file for output
void openOutput(ofstream& fname)
{
   string filename;

   cout << "Enter the output pollen count file name: ";
   cin >> filename;

   fname.open(filename.c_str());

   if (fname.fail())    // check for a successful open
   {
     cout << "\nFailed to open the file named " << filename << "for output"
          << endl;
     exit(1);
   }
```

(continued from previous page)

```cpp
    return;
}

// the following function reads the pollen file
// writes a new file
// and returns the new weekly average
float pollenUpdate(ifstream& infile, ofstream& outfile)
{
    const int POLNUMS = 10; // maximum number of pollen counts

    int i, polreading;
    int oldreading, newcount;
    double sum = 0;
    double average;

       // get the latest pollen count
    cout << "Enter the latest pollen count reading: ";
    cin >> newcount;


       // read the oldest pollen count
    infile >> oldreading;

    // read, sum and write out the rest of the pollen counts
    for(i = 0; i < POLNUMS - 1; i++)
    {
        infile >> polreading;
        sum += polreading;
        outfile << polreading << endl;
    }
       // write out the latest reading
    outfile << newcount << endl;

       // compute and display the new average
    average = (sum + newcount) / double(POLNUMS);

    infile.close();
    outfile.close();

    cout << "\nThe output file has been written.\n";

    return average;
}
```

Test and Correct the Program   Testing Program 11.13 requires that we provide both valid and invalid input data for the program. Invalid data consist of both a nonexistent input data file name and a data file that contains fewer than ten items. Valid data consist of a file containing ten integers. A sample run of Program 11.13 follows with a valid input file:

```
This program reads the old pollen count file, creates a current pollen
    count file, and calculates and displays the latest ten-week average.

Enter the input pollen count file name: pollen.in
Enter the output pollen count file name: pollen.out
Enter the latest pollen count reading: 200

The output file has been written.

The new ten week average is: 120
```

The updated file created by Program 11.13 is illustrated in Figure 11.6. In reviewing the contents of this file, notice that the most current reading has been added to the end of the file and that the other pollen readings obtained from the original file shown in Figure 11.6 have been moved up one position in the new file. Also notice that the output of our sample run correctly calculates the new 10-week average.

FIGURE 11.6   The Updated Pollen File

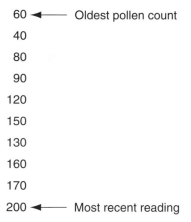

60 ◄——— Oldest pollen count
40
80
90
120
150
130
160
170
200 ◄——— Most recent reading

Problem 2: Master/Transactions File Update

A common form of file update occurs when the current data are themselves contained in a file. Here, the file to be updated is referred to as a **master file**, and the file containing the current data is referred to as a **transactions file**. As a specific example of this type of update, consider the following.

Program Requirement   Assume that a current master file, named `oldbook.mas`, consists of book identification numbers and quantities in stock, as illustrated in Table 11.5. A transactions file, named `book.trn`, contains the quantities of each book bought, sold, or returned to stock each day. This file is sorted by ID number at the end of each month and contains the data illustrated in Table 11.6.

Write a program that uses the data in the transaction file to update the data in the master file so that at the end of the update, the master file contains a correct count of books for each identification number.

TABLE 11.5   Master File Data

Book ID No.	Quantity in Stock
125	98
289	222
341	675
467	152
589	34
622	125

TABLE 11.6   Transaction File Data

ID No.	Date	Sold	Returned	Bought
289	1/10/05	125	34	50
341	1/10/05	300	52	0
467	1/15/05	50	20	200
467	1/20/05	225	0	160
589	1/31/05	75	10	55

Analyze the Problem   Since this application requires more than a simple modification of existing techniques, we present additional background information and perform an exploratory analysis to ensure that we understand the problem.

A standard solution when updating a master file with the data in a transactions file must first have all the transactions in the same identification (ID) number order as the records in the master file. In this case, since the records in the master file, as illustrated in Table 11.5, are in increasing (ascending) identification number order, the transactions must also be kept in ascending order. As illustrated in Table 11.6, this is the case for the `book.trn` file.

Once the two files are in the same ID number order, the standard procedure for creating an updated master file consists of reading a master record from the existing master file and one record from the transaction file. If the ID numbers of the two records match, the transaction record's information is applied to the data in the master record and another transaction record is read. As long as the transaction record's ID number matches the master record's ID number, the update of the master record continues. When the transaction record's ID number does not match the master record's ID number, which indicates that there is no further update data to be applied to the master record, an updated record is written to the new master file. Let's see how this procedure works by doing a hand calculation with the data shown in Tables 11.5 and 11.6.

The first record read from the master file has ID number 125, while the first transaction record has ID number 289. Since the ID numbers do not match, the update of this first master record is complete (in this case, there is no update information), and the existing master record is written, without modification, to the new master file. Then the next master record is read, which has an ID number of 289. Since this ID number matches the transaction ID number, the inventory balance for book number 289 is updated, yielding a new balance of 181 books. Because the transaction file can contain multiple update records for the same ID number (notice the two records for ID number 467), the next transaction record is read and checked before writing an updated record to the new master file. Since the ID number of the next transaction record is not 289, the update of this book number is complete and an updated master record is written to the new master file.

This procedure continues, record by record, until the last master record has been updated. Should the end of the transaction file be encountered before the last master record is read from the existing master file, the remaining records in the existing master file are written directly to the new master file with no need to check for update information. The new master file can be a completely new file, or each updated record can be written back to the old master file. In our update procedure, we will create a new master file so that the original data in the old master file are left intact. Now let's formalize this algorithm using a pseudocode description.

Develop a Solution   Since we are using two master files, the old and new masters, a notation must be established to clearly distinguish between them. By convention, the existing master file is always referred to as the old master file, and the updated master file is called the new master file. Using these terms, the pseudocode description of the update procedure found in the analysis step is:

Open the old master file
Open the transaction file
Open the new master file (initially blank)
Read the first old master record
While not at the end of the transaction file,
   Read a transaction record
   While the transaction ID does not match the old master ID,
      Write an updated master record to the new master file
      Read the next transaction record
   Endwhile
   If the ID numbers do match,
    Calculate a new balance
   Endwhile
*** *To get here the last transaction record has just been read*
   Write the last updated master to the new master file
   While there are any remaining records in the old master file,
      Read an old master record
      Write a new master record
   Endwhile
   Close all files

Code the Solution   In C++, the selected design is implemented by Program 11.14.

PROGRAM 11.14

```cpp
#include <iostream>
#include <fstream>
#include <iomanip>
#include <cstdlib>
#include <string>
using namespace std;

string oldMaster = "oldbook.mst";  // here are the files we will be
string newMaster = "newbook.mst";  // working with
string transactions = "book.trn";

void doUpdate();

int main()
{
  doUpdate();

  return 0;
}

// update function
// precondition: both a master file named oldbook.mas and
//               : a transaction file named bok.trn exist on
//               : the current directory
//               : and both files are in date order
// postcondition: a new master file named newbook.mas is created

void doUpdate(void)
{
  int idmast, idtrans, balance, sold, returned, bought;
  int ch;
  string date;
  ifstream oldmast, trans;
  ofstream newmast,

    // open and check the oldMaster file
  oldmast.open(oldMaster.c_str());
  if (oldmast.fail())
  {
    cout << "\nThe input file " << oldMaster << "was not successfully opened"
         << "\n Please check that the file currently exists." << endl;
    exit(1);
  }
    // open and check the newMaster file
  newmast.open(newMaster.c_str());
  if (newmast.fail())
  {
    cout << "\nFailed to open the new master file " << newMaster
         << " for output." << endl;
    exit(1);
  }
```

(continued from previous page)

```
      // open and check the transactions file
  trans.open(transactions.c_str());
  if (trans.fail())
  {
    cout << "\nThe input file " << trans <<" was not successfully opened"
         << "\n Please check that the file currently exits." << endl;
    exit(1);
  }
      // read the first old master file record
  oldmast >> idmast >> balance;
  while( (ch = trans.peek()) != EOF)
  {
      // read one transactions record
    trans >> idtrans >> date >> sold >> returned >> bought;
      // if no match keep writing and reading the master file
    while (idtrans > idmast)
    {
      newmast << '\n' << idmast << setw(6) << balance;
      oldmast >> idmast >> balance;
    }
    balance = balance + bought - sold + returned;
  }
    // write the last updated new master file
  newmast << '\n' << idmast << setw(6) << balance;
    // write any remaining old master records to the new master
  while ( (ch = oldmast.peek()) != EOF)
  {

    oldmast >> idmast >> balance;
    newmast << '\n' << idmast << setw(6) << balance;
  }

  oldmast.close();
  newmast.close();
  trans.close();
  cout << "\n....File update complete...\n";

  return;
}
```

Test and Correct the Program   A sample run using Program 11.14 with an old master file containing the data illustrated in Table 11.5 and a transactions data file containing the data illustrated in Table 11.6 yielded the following data in the file `newbook.mas`:

125	98
289	181
341	427
467	257
589	24
622	125

A hand calculation using the data in Tables 11.5 and 11.6 verifies that the data in the second column reflect the correct new balance for the book identification numbers in the first column. Additional runs should now be made with the transactions file containing data for only the first book in the master file and then with data for only the last book in the master file. These two runs would successfully test the extreme values of the `while` loops.

Exercises 11.6

1. Write a C++ program to create the pollen file illustrated in Figure 11.5.

2. Either using the file created in Exercise 1, or using the `pollen.in` file provided on the source code disk supplied with this text, enter and run Program 11.13 on your computer.

3. a. A file named `polar.dat` contains the polar coordinates needed in a graphics program. Currently, this file contains the following data:

Distance (inches)	Angle (degrees)
2.0	45.0
6.0	30.0
10.0	45.0
4.0	60.0
12.0	55.0
8.0	15.0

Write a C++ program to create this file on your computer system.

   b. Using the `polar.dat` file created in Exercise 3a, write a C++ program that accepts distance and angle data from the user and adds the data to the end of the file.

   c. Using the `polar.dat` file created in Exercise 3a, write a C++ program that reads this file and creates a second file named `xycord.dat`. The entries in the new file should contain the rectangular coordinates corresponding to the polar coordinates in the `polar.dat` file. Polar coordinates are converted to rectangular coordinates using the equations

$$x = r \cos \theta$$

$$y = r \sin \theta$$

where r is the distance coordinate and θ is the radian equivalent of the angle coordinate in the `polar.dat` file.

4. a. Write a C++ program to create both the `oldbook.mas` file, illustrated in Table 11.5, and the `book.trn` file, illustrated in Table 11.6. (*Note:* Do not include the column headings in the file.)

   b. Using the files created in Exercise 4a, enter and run Program 11.14 to verify its operation.

   c. Modify Program 11.14 to prompt the user for the names of the old master file, the new master file, and the transactions file. The modified program should accept these file names as input while the program is executing.

   d. Using the `book.trn` file created in Exercise 4a, write a C++ program that reads this file and displays the transaction data in it, including the heading lines shown in Table 11.6.

5. a. Write a C++ program to create a data file containing the following information:

Student ID Number	Student Name	Course Code	Course Credits	Course Grade
2333021	BOKOW, R.	NS201	3	A
2333021	BOKOW, R.	MG342	3	A
2333021	BOKOW, R.	FA302	1	A
2574063	FALLIN, D.	MK106	3	C
2574063	FALLIN, D.	MA208	3	B
2574063	FALLIN, D.	CM201	3	C
2574063	FALLIN, D.	CP101	2	B
2663628	KINGSLEY, M.	QA140	3	A
2663628	KINGSLEY, M.	CM245	3	B
2663628	KINGSLEY, M.	EQ521	3	A
2663628	KINGSLEY, M.	MK341	3	A
2663628	KINGSLEY, M.	CP101	2	B

b. Using the file created in Exercise 5a, write a C++ program that creates student grade reports. The grade report for each student should contain the student's name and identification number, a list of courses taken, the credits and grade for each course, and a semester grade-point average. For example, the grade report for the first student is:

```
Student Name: BOKOW, R.
Student ID Number: 2333021


Course Code    Course Credits    Course Grade

  NS201              3                 A
  MG342              3                 A
  FA302              1                 A


Total Semester Course Credits Completed: 7
Semester Grade-Point Average: 4.0
```

The semester grade-point average is computed in two steps. First, each course grade is assigned a numerical value (A = 4, B = 3, C = 2, D = 1, F = 0) and the sum of each course's grade value times the credits for each course is computed. This sum is then divided by the total number of credits taken during the semester.

6. a. Write a C++ program to create a data file containing the following information:

Student ID Number	Student Name	Course Credits	Grade-Point Average (GPA)
2333021	BOKOW, R.	48	4.0
2574063	FALLIN, D.	12	1.8
2663628	KINGSLEY, M.	36	3.5

b. Using the file created in Exercise 6a as a master file and the file created in Exercise 5a as a transactions file, write a file update program to create an updated master file.

11.7 A CLOSER LOOK AT THE `iostream` CLASS LIBRARY

The `iostream` class library provided as part of each C++ compiler is not part of the C++ language. By convention, each C++ compiler provides an input/output library, named `iostream`, that contains a number of classes that adhere to a common ANSI specification.

As we have already seen, the classes contained within the `iostream` class library access files using entities called streams. For most systems, the data bytes transferred on a stream represent either ASCII characters or binary numbers.

When the data transfer between a computer and an external data file modifies the data so that the data stored in the file are *not* an exact representation of the data as they are stored internally within the computer, the file is referred to as a **formatted file**. Examples of this are files that store their data using ASCII codes. Such files are also referred to as **text files**, and the terms **text** and **formatted** are sometimes used interchangeably.

When the data transfer between a computer and an external data file is done without modification so that the data stored in the file *are* an exact representation of the data as they are stored internally within the computer, the file is referred to as a **binary file** or **unformatted file**.

The mechanism for reading a byte stream from a file or writing a byte stream to a file, with or without formatting, is always hidden when using a high-level language such as C++. Nevertheless, it is useful to understand this mechanism so that we can place the services provided by the `iostream` class library in their appropriate context.

File Stream Transfer Mechanism

The mechanism for transferring data between a program and a data file is illustrated in Figure 11.7. As shown, transferring data between a program and a file involves an intermediate file buffer contained in the computer's memory. Each opened file is assigned its own file buffer, which is simply a storage area that is used to hold the data transferred between the program and the file.

From its side, the program either writes a set of data bytes to the file buffer or reads a set of data bytes from the file buffer using a stream object.

On the other side of the buffer, the transfer of data between the device storing the actual data file (usually a tape, disk, or CD-ROM) and the file buffer is handled by special operating system programs that are referred to as **device drivers**.[3] Typically, a disk device driver only transfers data between the disk and file buffer in fixed sizes, such as 1024 bytes at a time. Thus, the file buffer provides a convenient means of permitting a device driver to transfer data in blocks of one size while the program can access them using a different size (typically as individual characters or as a fixed number of characters per line).

---

[3] Device drivers are not stand-alone programs but are an integral part of the operating system. Essentially, the device driver is a section of operating system code that accesses a hardware device, such as a disk unit, and handles the data transfer between the device and the computer's memory. Hence, it must correctly synchronize the speed of the data transferred between the computer and the device sending or receiving the data. This is because the computer's internal data transfer rate is generally much faster than any device connected to it.

FIGURE 11.7   The Data Transfer Mechanism

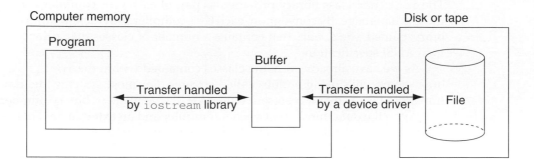

Components of the iostream **Class Library**

The iostream class library consists of two primary base classes, the streambuf class and the ios class. The streambuf class provides the file buffer illustrated in Figure 11.7 and a number of general routines for transferring data when little or no formatting is required. The ios class contains a pointer to the file buffers provided by the streambuf class and a number of general routines for transferring data with formatting. From these two base classes, numerous other classes are derived and included in the iostream class library.

Figure 11.8 illustrates an inheritance diagram for the ios family of classes as it relates to the ifstream, ofstream, and fstream classes. The inheritance diagram for the streambuf family of classes is shown in Figure 11.9. As described in the previous chapter, the convention adopted for inheritance diagrams is that the arrows point from a derived class to a base class. The correspondence between the classes illustrated in Figures 11.8 and 11.9, including the header files that define them, is listed in Table 11.7.

Thus, the ifstream, ofstream, and fstream classes that we have used for file access all use a buffer provided by the filebuf class defined in the fstream header file. Similarly, the cin, cout, and cerr iostream objects that we have been using throughout the text use a buffer provided by the streambuf class and defined in both the iostream and fstream header files.

In-Memory Formatting

In addition to the classes illustrated in Figure 11.8, a class named strstream is also derived from the ios class. This class uses the strstreambuf class illustrated in Figure 11.8, requires the strstream header file, and provides capabilities for writing and reading strings to and from in-memory defined streams.

As an output stream, such streams are typically used to "assemble" a string from smaller pieces until a complete line of characters is ready to be inserted, either to cout or to a file stream. Attaching a strstream object to a buffer for this purpose is done in a manner similar to that of attaching an fstream object to an output file. For example, the statement

```
strstream inmem(buf, 72, ios::out);
```

attaches a strstream object to an existing buffer of 72 bytes in output mode. Program 11.15 illustrates using this statement within the context of a complete program.

FIGURE 11.8 The Base Class `ios` and Its Derived Classes (not all derived classes are shown—arrowheads point to base classes)

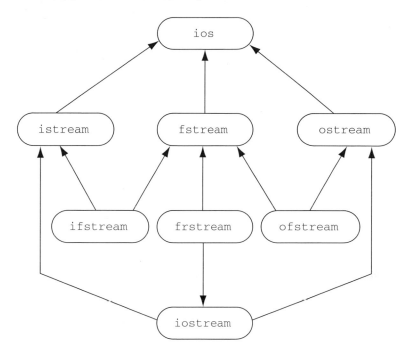

TABLE 11.7 Correspondence between Classes

ios Class	streambuf Class	Header File

`istream`
`ostream`
`iostream`
	`streambuf`	`iostream`
		or
		`fstream`

`ifstream`
`ofstream`
`fstream`
	`filebuf`	`fstream`

FIGURE 11.9 The Base Class `streambuf` and Its Derived Classes (not all derived classes are shown)

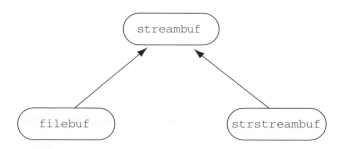

PROGRAM 11.15

```
#include <strstream>
#include <iomanip>
using namespace std;

int main()
{
  const int MAXCHARS = 81;   // one more than the maximum characters in a line
  int units = 10;
  float price = 36.85;
  char buf[MAXCHARS];

  strstream inmem(buf, MAXCHARS, ios::out);   // open an in-memory stream

    // write to the buffer through the stream
  inmem << "No. of units = "
        << setw(3) << units
        << "   Price per unit = $"
        << setw(8) << setprecision(2) << price << '\0';

  cout << '|' << buf << '|';

  return 0;
}
```

The output produced by Program 11.15 is:

```
|No. of units = 10 Price per unit = $ 36.85|
```

As illustrated by this output, the character buffer has been correctly filled in by insertions to the inmem stream. (Note that the end-of-string NULL '\0' which is the last insertion to the stream, is required to correctly close off the string.) Once the desired character array has been filled, it is typically written out to a file as a single string.

In a similar manner, a strstream object can be opened in input mode. Typically, such a stream is used as a working storage area, or buffer, for storing a complete line of text from either a file or standard input. Once the buffer has been filled, the extraction operator is used to "disassemble" the string into component parts and convert each data item into its designated data type. Doing this permits the input of data from a file on a line-by-line basis prior to assigning individual data items to their respective variables.

11.8 COMMON PROGRAMMING ERRORS

The common programming errors with respect to files are:

1. Using a file's external name in place of the internal file stream object name when accessing the file. The only stream method that uses the data file's external name is the open() function. As always, all stream methods presented in this chapter must be preceded by a stream object name and the dot operator.

2. Opening a file for output without first checking that a file with the given name already exists. Not checking for a pre-existing file name ensures that the file will be overwritten.

3. Not understanding the end of a file is only detected until after the EOF sentinel has either been read or passed over.

4. Attempting to detect the end of a file using character variable for the EOF marker. Any variable used to accept the EOF must be declared as an integer variable. For example, if `ch` is declared as a character variable the expression

```
while ( (ch = in.file.peek()) != EOF )
```

produces an infinite loop.[4] This occurs because a character variable can never take on an EOF code. EOF is an integer value (usually -1) that has no character representation. This ensures that the EOF code can never be confused with any legitimate character encountered as normal data in the file. To terminate the loop created by the above expression, the variable `ch` must be declared as an integer variable.

5. Using an integer argument with the `seekg()` and `seekp()` functions. This offset must be a long integer constant or variable. Any other value passed to these functions can result in an unpredictable effect.

11.9 CHAPTER REVIEW

Key Terms

binary file	output file stream
close( ) method	random access
data file	seekg( ) method
external file name	seekp( ) method
file access	sequential organization
file organization	string variable
file stream	tellg( ) method
input file stream	tellp( ) method
open( ) method	text file

Summary

1. A *data file* is any collection of data stored in an external storage medium under a common name.

2. A data file is connected to a file stream using an `open()` method. This method connects a file's external name with an internal object name. After the file is opened, all subsequent accesses to the file require the internal object name.

3. A file can be opened and connected to either an input or output file stream. An opened output file stream either creates a new data file or erases the data in an existing opened file. An opened input file stream makes an existing file's data available for input. An error condition results if the file does not exist and can be detected using the file stream's `fail()` method.

---

[4] This will not occur on UNIX systems where characters are stored as signed integers.

4. All file streams must be declared as objects of either the `ifstream` or `ofstream` classes. This means that a declaration similar to either of these statements

```
ifstream inFile;
ofstream outFile;
```

must be included with the declarations in which the file is opened. The stream object names `inFile` and `outFile` can be replaced with any user-selected object name.

5. In addition to any files opened within a function, the standard stream objects `cin`, `cout`, and `cerr` are automatically declared and opened when a program is run. `cin` is the object name of an input file stream used for data entry (usually from the keyboard), `cout` is the object name of an output file stream used for default data display (usually the terminal screen), and `cerr` is the object name of an output file stream used for displaying system error messages (usually the terminal screen).

6. Data files can be accessed randomly using the `seekg()`, `seekp()`, `tellg()`, and `tellp()` methods. The `g` versions of these functions are used to alter and query the file position marker for input file streams, and the `p` versions do the same for output file streams.

7. Table 11.8 lists the methods supplied by the `fstream` class for file manipulation.

TABLE 11.8   `fstream` **Methods**

Method Name	Description
`get()`	Extract the next character from the input stream and return it as an `int`.
`get(chrVar)`	Extract the next character from the input the input stream and assign it to `chrVar`.
`getline(fileObj, string, termChar)`	Extract the next string of characters from the input file stream object and assign then to string until the specified terminating character is detected. If omitted, the default terminating character is a newline.
`getline(C-stringVar,int n,'\n')`	Extract and return characters from the input stream until either n 1 characters are read or a newline is encountered (terminates the input with a '\0').
`peek()`	Return the next character in the input stream without extracting it from the stream.
`put(chrExp)`	Put the character specified by `chrExp` on the output stream.
`putback(chrExp)`	Push the character specified by `chrExp` back onto the input stream. Does not alter the data in the file.
`ignore(int n)`	Skip over the next characters. If n is omitted, the default is to skip over the next single character.
`eof()`	Returns a Boolean `true` value if a read has been attempted past the end-of-file; otherwise returns a Boolean `false` value. The value becomes `true` only when the first character after the last valid file character is read.
`good()`	Returns a Boolean `true` value while the file is available for program use. Returns a Boolean `false` value if a read has been attempted past the end-of-file. The value becomes `false` only when the first character after the last valid file character is read.
`bad()`	Returns a Boolean `true` value if a read has been attempted past the end-of-file; otherwise returns a `false`. The value becomes `true` only when the first character after the last valid file character is read.
`fail()`	Returns a Boolean `true` if the file has not been successfully opened; otherwise returns a Boolean `false` value.

Exercises

1. You are to write a C++ program that allows the user to enter the following information from the keyboard for each of up to 20 students in a class:

   ```
   Name   Exam_1_Grade   Exam_2_Grade   Homework_Grade   Final_Exam_Grade
   ```

   For each student, your program should first calculate a final grade, using the formula:

   $$Final\_Grade = 0.20 * Exam\_1 + 0.20 * Exam\_2 + 0.35 * Homework + 0.25 * Final\_Exam\_Grade$$

   and then assign a letter grade on the basis of $90 - 100 = A$, $80 - 89 = B$, $70 - 79 = C$, $60 - 69 = D$, less than 60 = F. All of the information, including the final grade and the letter grade, should then be displayed and written to a file.

2. Write a C++ program that permits a user to enter the following information about your small company's ten employees and writes the sorted information to a file:

   ```
   ID No.    Sex (M/F)    Hourly Wage    Years with the Company
   ```

3. Write a C++ program that allows you to read the file created in Exercise 2, change the hourly wage or years for each employee, and create a new updated file.

4. Write a C++ program that reads the file created in Exercise 2 one record at a time, asks for the number of hours worked by that employee each month, and calculates and displays each employee's total pay for the month.

5. a. You have collected information about cities in your state. You decide to store each city's name, population, and the name of its mayor in a file. Write a C++ program to accept the data for a number of cities from the keyboard and store the data in a file in the order in which they are entered.

   b. Read the file created in Exercise 5a, sort the data alphabetically by city name, and display the data.

6. A bank's customer records are to be stored in a file and read into a set of arrays so that an individual's record can be accessed randomly by account number. Create the file by entering five customer records, with each record consisting of an integer account number (starting with account number 1000), a first name having a maximum of 10 characters, a last name having a maximum of 15 characters, and a floating-point balance.

   Once the file is created, write a C++ program that requests a user-input account number and displays the corresponding name and account balance from the file.

7. Create a text file with the following data or use the file named `shipped.txt` on the diskette provided with this text. The headings are not part of the file but indicate what the data represent.

Shipped Date	Tracking Number	Part Number	First Name	Last Name	Company
04/12/05	D50625	74444	James	Lehoff	Rotech
04/12/05	D60752	75255	Janet	Lezar	Rotech
04/12/05	D40295	74477	Bill	McHenry	Rotech
04/12/05	D23745	74470	Diane	Kaiser	Rotech
04/12/05	D50892	75155	Helen	Richardson	NipNap

The format of each line in the file is identical with fixed length fields defined as follows:

Field Position	Field Name	Starting Col. No.	Ending Col. No.	Field Length
1	Shipped Date	1	8	8
2	Tracking Number	12	17	6
3	Part Number	22	26	5
4	First Name	31	35	5
5	Last Name	39	48	10
6	Company	51	64	14

Using this data file, you are to write a C++ program that reads the file and produces a report listing the date, part number, first name, last name, and company name.

P A R T

III

Data Structures and Additional Features

The variables that we have used so far have all had a common characteristic: Each variable can only be used to store a single value at a time. For example, although the variables key, count, and grade declared in the statements

```
char key;
int count;
double grade;
```

are of different data types, each variable can only store one value of the declared data type. These types of variables are called atomic variables. An **atomic variable**, which is also referred to as a **scalar variable**, is a variable whose value cannot be further subdivided or separated into a legitimate data type.

Another method of storing and retrieving data is to use a data structure. A **data structure** is a data type whose values can be decomposed into individual data elements, each of which is either atomic or another data structure, *and* it provides an access scheme for locating individual data elements within the structure. One such data structure is a class, which was presented in Part II.

In Chapter 12, we look at a data structure referred to as an **array**, which uses built-in procedural operations for both access and individual element manipulation. An array whose individual elements are characters is the method C++ uses to store strings. These array types are presented in Chapter 13. Additionally, in Chapter 14, a complete description of pointers is presented. In addition to other very useful tasks, pointers provide a very powerful access method for array processing in general and strings in particular.

In Chapter 15, we present record structures. Although record structures can be defined as classes having no member functions and all of whose data members are public, C++ provides a nonclass, procedural method of defining record structures. It is this method that is described.

Finally, in Chapter 16, we present advanced data structures named *stacks* and *queues*. Although these two structures can also be defined as special cases of record structures, we show how to construct and process these structures using STL classes.

Arrays

Frequently, we may have a set of values, all of the same data type, that forms a logical group. For example, Figure 12.1 illustrates three groups of items. The first group is a list of five floating-point temperatures, the second group is a list of four character codes, and the last group is a list of six integer grades.

A simple list containing individual items of the same data type is called a **one-dimensional array**. In this chapter, we describe how one-dimensional arrays are declared, initialized, stored inside a computer, and used. Additionally, we explore the use of one-dimensional arrays with example programs and present the procedures for declaring and using multidimensional arrays.

FIGURE 12.1 Three Lists of Items

Temperatures	Codes	Grades
95.75	Z	98
83.0	C	87
97.625	K	92
72.5	L	79
86.25		85
		72

12.1 ONE-DIMENSIONAL ARRAYS

A **one-dimensional array**, which is also referred to as either a **single-dimensional array** or a **vector**, is a list of related values with the same data type that is stored using a single group name.[1] In C++, as in other computer languages, the group name is referred to as the array name. For example, consider the list of temperatures in Figure 12.2. All temperatures in the list are floating-point numbers and must be declared as such. However, the individual items in the list do not have to be declared separately. The items in the list can be declared as a single unit and stored under a common variable name called the **array name**. For convenience, we choose `temp` as the name for the list shown in Figure 12.2.

FIGURE 12.2   A List of Temperatures

Temperatures
95.75
83.0
97.625
72.5
86.25

To specify that `temp` is to store five individual floating-point values, we must use the declaration statement `float temp[5]`. Notice that this declaration statement gives the array (or list) name, the data type of the items in the array, and the number of items in the array. Good programming practice requires that the number of array items be defined as a named constant before declaring the array. Thus, in practice, the previous array declaration is declared using two statements, such as:

```
const int NUMELS = 5;
float temp[NUMELS];
```

Further examples of array declarations are:

```
const int NUMELS = 6;
int grade[NUMELS];

const int ARRAYSIZE = 4;
char code[ARRAYSIZE];

const int SIZE = 100;
double amount[SIZE];
```

In these declaration statements, each array is allocated sufficient memory to hold the number of data items given in the declaration statement. Thus, the array named

---

[1] Note that lists can be implemented in a variety of ways, some of which are further described in Chapter 16. An array is simply one implementation of a list in which all of the list elements are of the same type and each element is stored consecutively in a set of contiguous memory locations.

grade has storage reserved for six integers, the array named code has storage reserved for four characters, and the array named amount has storage reserved for 100 double-precision numbers. The named constant NUMELS, ARRAYSIZE, and SIZE are programmer-selected names.

Figure 12.3 illustrates the storage reserved for the code and grade arrays. Each item in an array is called an *element* or *component* of the array. The individual elements stored in the arrays illustrated in Figure 12.3 are stored sequentially, with the first array element stored in the first reserved location, the second element stored in the second reserved location, and so on until the last element is stored in the last reserved location. This contiguous storage allocation is a key feature of arrays because it provides a simple mechanism for easily locating any single element in the array.

FIGURE 12.3 The code and grade Arrays in Memory

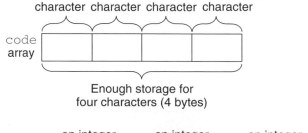

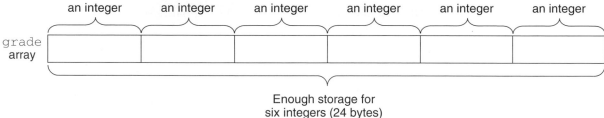

Because elements in the array are stored sequentially, any individual element can be accessed by giving the name of the array and the element's position. This position is called the element's **index** or **subscript** value (the terms are synonymous). For a single-dimensional array, the first element has an index of 0, the second element has an index of 1, and so on. In C++, the array name and index of the desired element are combined by listing the index in braces after the array name. For example, given the declaration double temp[5]:

temp[0] refers to the first temperature stored in the temp array.

temp[1] refers to the second temperature stored in the temp array.

temp[2] refers to the third temperature stored in the temp array.

temp[3] refers to the fourth temperature stored in the temp array.

temp[4] refers to the fifth temperature stored in the temp array.

Figure 12.4 illustrates the temp array in memory with the correct designation for each array element. Each individual element is referred to as an **indexed variable** or a **subscripted variable** because both a variable name and an index or subscript value must be used to reference the element. Remember that the index or subscript value gives the *position* of the element in the array.

FIGURE 12.4 Identifying Individual Array Elements

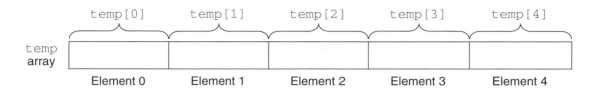

The subscripted variable `temp[0]` is read as both "temp sub zero" and "temp zero." This is a shortened way of saying "the temp array subscripted by zero." Similarly, `temp[1]` is read as either "temp sub one" or "temp one," `temp[2]` as either "temp sub two" or "temp two," and so on.

Although it may seem unusual to refer to the first element with an index of zero, doing so increases the computer's speed when it accesses array elements. Internally, unseen by the programmer, the computer uses the index as an offset from the array's starting position. As illustrated in Figure 12.5, the index tells the computer how many elements to skip, starting from the beginning of the array, to get to the desired element.

FIGURE 12.5 Accessing Individual Array—Element 3

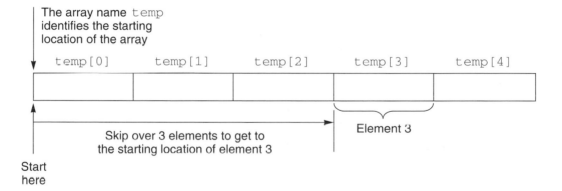

Subscripted variables can be used anywhere scalar variables are valid. Examples using the elements of the `temp` array are:

```
temp[0] = 95.75;
temp[1] = temp[0] - 11.0;
temp[2] = 5.0 * temp[0];
temp[3] = 79.0;
temp[4] = (temp[1] + temp[2] - 3.1) / 2.2;
sum = temp[0] + temp[1] + temp[2] + temp[3] + temp[4];
```

The subscript contained within brackets need not be an integer constant; any expression that evaluates to an integer may be used as a subscript.[2] In each case, of course, the value of the expression must be within the valid subscript range

---

[2] Some compilers permit floating-point variables as subscripts; in these cases, the floating-point value is truncated to an integer value.

defined when the array is declared. For example, assuming that `i` and `j` are `int` variables, the following subscripted variables are valid:

```
temp[i]
temp[2*i]
temp[j-i]
```

One extremely important advantage of using integer expressions as subscripts is that it allows sequencing through an array by using a loop. This makes statements such as

```
sum = temp[0] + temp[1] + temp[2] + temp[3] + temp[4];
```

unnecessary. The subscript values in this statement can be replaced by a `for` loop counter to access each element in the array sequentially. For example, the code

```
const int NUMELS = 5

sum = 0;                          // initialize the sum to zero
for (i = 0; i < NUMELS; i++)
   sum = sum + temp[i];          // add value
```

sequentially retrieves each array element and adds the element to `sum`. Here, the variable `i` is used both as the counter in the `for` loop and as a subscript. As `i` increases by 1 each time through the loop, the next element in the array is accessed. The procedure for adding the array elements within the `for` loop is similar to the accumulation procedure we have used many times before.

The advantage of using a `for` loop to sequence through an array becomes apparent when working with larger arrays. For example, if the `temp` array contained 100 values rather than just 5, simply changing the number 5 to 100 in the `const` statement is sufficient to sequence through the 100 elements and add each temperature to the sum.

As another example of using a `for` loop to sequence through an array, assume that we want to locate the maximum value in an array of 1000 elements named `grade`. To locate the maximum value, we assume initially that the first element in the array is the largest number. Then, as we sequence through the array, the maximum is compared to each element. When an element with a higher value is located, it becomes the new maximum. The following code does the job:

```
const int NUMELS = 1000;

maximum = grade[0];               // set the maximum to element zero
for (i = 1; i < NUMELS; i++)      // cycle through the rest of the array
   if (grade[i] > maximum)        // compare each element to the maximum
      maximum = grade[i];         // capture the new high value
```

In this code, the `for` statement consists of one `if` statement. The search for a new maximum value starts with element 1 of the array and continues through the last element. Each element is compared to the current maximum, and when a higher value is encountered, it becomes the new maximum.

Input and Output of Array Values

Individual array elements can be assigned values interactively using the `cin` object. Examples of individual data entry statements are:

```
cin >> temp[0];
cin >> temp[1] >> temp[2] >> temp[3];
cin >> temp[4] >> grade[6];
```

Structured Data Types

In contrast to atomic data types, such as integers and floating-point built-in types that cannot be decomposed into simpler types, *structured types* can be decomposed into simpler types that are related within a defined structure. (Another term used for a structured type is a data structure.) Because a structured type consists of one or more simpler types, operations must be available for retrieving and updating the individual types that make up a data structure.

Single-dimensional arrays are examples of a structured type. In a single-dimensional array, such as an array of integers, the array is composed of individual integer values. In an array, where the values are related by their position in the array, index numbers provide the means of accessing and modifying individual elements.

In the first statement, a single value is read and stored in the variable named `temp[0]`. The second statement causes three values to be read and stored in the variables `temp[1]`, `temp[2]`, and `temp[3]`, respectively. Finally, the last `cin` statement can be used to read values into the variables `temp[4]` and `grade[6]`.

Alternatively, a `for` loop can be used to cycle through the array for interactive data input. For example, the code

```
const int NUMELS = 5;

for (i = 0; i < NUMELS; i++)
{
  cout << "Enter a temperature: ";
  cin >> temp[i];
}
```

prompts the user for five temperatures. The first temperature entered is stored in `temp[0]`, the second in `temp[1]`, and so on until five temperatures have been input.

One caution should be mentioned about storing data in an array. C++ does not check the value of the index being used (called a **bounds check**). If an array has been declared as consisting of 10 elements, for example, and you use an index of 12, which is outside the bounds of the array, C++ does not notify you of the error when the program is compiled. The program attempts to access element 12 by skipping over the appropriate number of bytes from the start of the array. Usually, this results in a program crash—but not always. If the accessed memory location itself contains a value of the correct data type, the program simply uses the value in the accessed location. This leads to more errors, which are particularly troublesome to locate when the value legitimately assigned to the storage location is retrieved and processed. Using named constants, as we have done, helps eliminate this problem because the `for` loop's range is restricted to the array's declared size.

During output, individual array elements can be displayed using a `cout` statement, or complete sections of the array can be displayed by including a `cout` statement within a `for` loop. Examples of this are

```
cout << grade[6];
```

and

```
cout << "The value of element " << i << " is " << temp[i];
```

and

```
const int NUMELS = 20;
for (k = 5; k < NUMELS; k++)
  cout <<  k << "   " << amount[k] << endl;
```

The first statement displays the value of the subscripted variable grade[6]. The second statement displays the value of the subscript i and the value of temp[i]. Before this statement can be executed, i needs an assigned value. Finally, the last example includes a cout statement within a for loop. Both the value of the index and the value of the elements from 5 to 19 are displayed.

Program 12.1 illustrates these input and output techniques using an array named grade that is defined to store five integer numbers. Included in the program are two for loops. The first for loop is used to cycle through each array element and allows the user to input individual array values. After five values have been entered, the second for loop is used to display the stored values.

PROGRAM 12.1

```
#include <iostream>
using namespace std;

int main()
{
  const int MAXGRADES = 5;

  int i, grade[MAXGRADES];

  for (i = 0; i < MAXGRADES; i++)     // Enter the grades
  {
    cout << "Enter a grade: ";
    cin  >> grade[i];
  }

  cout << endl;

  for (i = 0; i < MAXGRADES; i++)     // Print the grades
    cout << "grade " << i << " is " << grade[i] << endl;

  return 0;
}
```

A sample run of Program 12.1 is:

```
Enter a grade: 85
Enter a grade: 90
Enter a grade: 78
Enter a grade: 75
Enter a grade: 92

grade 0 is 85
grade 1 is 90
grade 2 is 78
grade 3 is 75
grade 4 is 92
```

In reviewing the output produced by Program 12.1, pay particular attention to the difference between the displayed index value and the numerical value stored at that index position. The index value refers to the location of the element in the array, whereas the subscripted variable refers to the value stored in the designated location.

In addition to simply displaying the values stored in each array element, the elements can also be processed by appropriately referencing the desired element. For example, in Program 12.2, the value of each element is accumulated in a total, which is displayed upon completion of the individual display of each array element.

PROGRAM 12.2

```
#include <iostream>
using namespace std;

int main()
{
  const int MAXGRADES = 5;

  int i, grade[MAXGRADES], total = 0;

  for (i = 0; i < MAXGRADES; i++)     // Enter the grades
  {
    cout << "Enter a grade: ";
    cin  >> grade[i];
  }

  cout << "\nThe total of the grades";

  for (i = 0; i < MAXGRADES; i++)     // Display and total the grades
  {
    cout << "   " << grade[i];
    total =  total + grade[i];
  }

  cout << " is " << total << endl;

  return 0;
}
```

A sample run of Program 12.2 is:

```
Enter a grade: 85
Enter a grade: 90
Enter a grade: 78
Enter a grade: 75
Enter a grade: 92

The total of the grades  85  90  78  75  92 is 420
```

A BIT OF BACKGROUND

Handling Lists with LISP

Methods of handling lists have been especially important in the development of computer science and applications. In fact, in 1958, John McCarthy developed a language at the Massachusetts Institute of Technology specifically for manipulating lists. This language was named *LISP*, the acronym for *LISt Processing*. It has proved valuable for handling problems based on mathematical logic and is used extensively in artificial intelligence and pattern recognition projects.

One simple language related to LISP is named *LOGO* and has been made particularly user friendly. It incorporates a technique called "turtle graphics," by which a pointer is moved around the screen to plot geometric figures. LOGO has been used widely to teach programming fundamentals to children.

Notice that in Program 12.2, unlike Program 12.1, only the values stored in each array element are displayed. Although the second `for` loop was used to accumulate the total of each element, the accumulation could also have been accomplished in the first loop by placing the statement `total = total + grade[i];` after the `cin` statement used to enter a value. Also notice that the `cout` statement used to display the total is made outside of the second `for` loop so that the total is displayed only once, after all values have been added to the total. If this `cout` statement is placed inside of the `for` loop, five totals are displayed, with only the last displayed total containing the sum of all of the array values.

Exercises 12.1

1. Write array declarations for the following:

   a. a list of 100 double-precision grades

   b. a list of 50 double-precision temperatures

   c. a list of 30 integers, each representing a code

   d. a list of 100 integer years

   e. a list of 32 double-precision velocities

   f. a list of 1000 double-precision distances

   g. a list of six integer code numbers

2. Write appropriate notation for the first, third, and seventh elements of the following arrays:

   a. `int grade[20]`

   b. `double prices[10]`

   c. `double amps[16]`

   d. `int dist[15]`

   e. `double velocity[25]`

   f. `double time[100]`

3. a. Write individual `cin` statements that can be used to enter values into the first, third, and seventh elements of each of the arrays declared in Exercises 2a through 2f.

   b. Write a `for` loop that can be used to enter values for the complete array declared in Exercise 2a.

4. a. Write individual `cout` statements that can be used to print the values from the first, third, and seventh elements of each of the arrays declared in Exercises 2a through 2f.

   b. Write a `for` loop that can be used to display values for the complete array declared in Exercise 2a.

5. List the elements that are displayed by the following sections of code:

   a. ```
for (m = 1; m <= 5; m++)
    cout << a[m] << " ";
```

   b. ```
for (k = 1; k <= 5; k = k + 2)
    cout <<   a[k] << " ";
```

   c. ```
for (j = 3; j <= 10; j++)
    cout << b[j] << " ";
```

   d. ```
for (k = 3; k <= 12; k = k + 3)
    cout << b[k] << " ";
```

   e. ```
for (i - 2; i < 11; i = i | 2)
    cout << c[i] << " ";
```

6. a. Write a program to input the following values into an array named `prices`: 10.95, 16.32, 12.15, 8.22, 15.98, 26.22, 13.54, 6.45, 17.59. After the data are entered, have your program output the values.

   b. Repeat Exercise 6a, but after the data are entered, have your program display them in the following form:

   ```
   10.95         16.32         12.15
    8.22         15.98         26.22
   13.54          6.45         17.59
   ```

7. Write a program to input eight integer numbers into an array named `grade`. As each number is input, add the number into a total. After all numbers are input, display the numbers and their average.

8. a. Write a program to input ten integer numbers into an array named `fmax` and determine the maximum value entered. Your program should contain only one loop, and the maximum should be determined as array element values are being input. (*Hint:* Set the maximum equal to the first array element, which should be input before the loop used to input the remaining array values.)

   b. Repeat Exercise 8a, keeping track of both the maximum element in the array and the index number for the maximum. After displaying the numbers, print these two messages:

   ```
   The maximum value is: ____
   This is element number ____ in the list of numbers
   ```

   Have your program display the correct values in place of the underlines in the messages.

   c. Repeat Exercise 8b, but have your program locate the minimum of the data entered.

9. a. Write a program to input the following integer numbers into an array named `grades`: 89, 95, 72, 83, 99, 54, 86, 75, 92, 73, 79, 75, 82, 73. As each number is input, add the number to a total. After all numbers are input and the total is obtained, calculate the average of the numbers and use the average to determine the deviation of each value from the average. Store each deviation in an array named `deviation`. Each deviation is obtained as the element value less the average of all the data. Have your program display each deviation alongside its corresponding element from the `grades` array.

   b. Calculate the variance of the data used in Exercise 9a. The variance is obtained by squaring each individual deviation and dividing the sum of the squared deviations by the number of deviations.

10. Write a program that specifies three one-dimensional arrays named `prices`, `quantity`, and `amount`. Each array should be capable of holding ten elements.
   ```

Using a `for` loop, input values for the `prices` and `quantity` arrays. The entries in the `amount` array should be the product of the corresponding values in the `prices` and `quantity` arrays (thus, `amount[i] = price[i] * quantity[i]`). After all of the data have been entered, display the following output:

```
Price          Quantity          Amount
-----          --------          ------
```

Under each column heading, display the appropriate value.

11. a. Write a program that inputs ten floating-point numbers into an array named `raw`. After ten user-input numbers are entered into the array, your program should cycle through `raw` ten times. During each pass through the array, your program should select the lowest value in `raw` and place the selected value in the next available slot in an array named `sorted`. Thus, when your program is complete, the sorted array should contain the numbers in `raw` in sorted order from lowest to highest. (*Hint:* Make sure to reset the lowest value selected during each pass to a very high number so that it is not selected again. You need a second `for` loop within the first `for` loop to locate the minimum value for each pass.)

    b. The method used in Exercise 11a to sort the values in the array is very inefficient. Can you determine why? What might be a better method of sorting the numbers in an array?

12.2 ARRAY INITIALIZATION

Array elements can be initialized within their declaration statements in the same manner as for scalar variables, except that the initializing elements must be included in braces. Examples of such initializations are:

```
const int NUMGRADES = 5;
int grade[NUMGRADES] = {98, 87, 92, 79, 85};

const int NUMCODES = 6;
char codes[NUMCODES] = {'s', 'a', 'm', 'p', 'l', 'e'};

const int SIZE = 7;
double width[SIZE] = {10.96, 6.43, 2.58, .86, 5.89, 7.56, 8.22};
```

Initializers are applied in the order in which they are written, with the first value used to initialize element 0, the second value used to initialize element 1, and so on, until all values have been used. Thus, in the declaration

```
int grade[NUMGRADES] = {98, 87, 92, 79, 85};
```

`grade[0]` is initialized to 98, `grade[1]` is initialized to 87, `grade[2]` is initialized to 92, `grade[3]` is initialized to 79, and `grade[4]` is initialized to 85.

Because white space is ignored in C++, initializations may be continued across multiple lines. For example, in the declarations

```
const int NUMGALS = 20;
int gallons[NUMGALS] = {19, 16, 14, 19, 20, 18,   // initializing values
                        12, 10, 22, 15, 18, 17,   // may extend across
                        16, 14, 23, 19, 15, 18,   // multiple lines
                        21, 5};
```

four lines are used to initialize all of the array elements.

If the number of initializers is less than the declared number of elements listed in square brackets, the initializers are applied starting with array element 0. Thus, in the declaration

```
const int ARRAYSIZE = 7;
double length[ARRAYSIZE] = {7.8, 6.4, 4.9, 11.2};
```

only length[0], length[1], length[2], and length[3] are initialized with the listed values. The other array elements are initialized to zero.

Unfortunately, there is no method of either indicating repetition of an initialization value or initializing later array elements without first specifying values for earlier elements.

A unique feature of initializers is that the size of an array may be omitted when initializing values are included in the declaration statement. For example, the declaration

```
int gallons[] = {16, 12, 10, 14, 11};
```

reserves enough storage room for five elements. Similarly, the following two declarations are equivalent

```
const int NUMCODES = 6;
char codes[NUMCODES] = {'s', 'a', 'm', 'p', 'l', 'e'};
```

and

```
char codes[] = {'s', 'a', 'm', 'p', 'l', 'e'};
```

Both of these declarations set aside six character locations for an array named codes. An interesting and useful simplification can also be used when initializing character arrays. For example, the declaration

```
char codes[] = "sample";   // no braces or commas
```

uses the string "sample" to initialize the codes array. Recall that a string is any sequence of characters enclosed in double quotes. This last declaration creates an array named codes having seven elements and fills the array with the seven characters illustrated in Figure 12.6. The first six characters, as expected, consist of the letters s, a, m, p, l, and e. The last character, which is the escape sequence \0, is called the **Null character**. The Null character is automatically appended to all strings that are used to initialize a character array, and is what distinguishes a C-string from a string class value. This character has an internal storage code that is numerically equal to zero (the storage code for the zero character has a numerical value of decimal 48, so the two cannot be confused by the computer), and it is used as a marker, or sentinel, to mark the end of a string. As we shall see in Chapter 13, this marker is invaluable when manipulating arrays of characters, which is how C-strings are stored in C++.

Once values have been assigned to array elements, either through initialization within the declaration statement or by using interactive input, the array elements can be processed as described in the previous section. For example, Program 12.3 illustrates the initialization of array elements within the declaration of the array and then uses a for loop to locate the maximum value stored in the array.

FIGURE 12.6 Initializing a Character Array with a String Adds a Terminating \0 Character

codes[0]	codes[1]	codes[2]	codes[3]	codes[4]	codes[5]	codes[6]
s	a	m	p	l	e	\0

PROGRAM 12.3

```cpp
#include <iostream>
using namespace std;

int main()
{
  const int MAXELS = 5;

  int i, max, nums[MAXELS] = {2, 18, 1, 27, 16};

  max = nums[0];

  for (i = 1; i < MAXELS; i++)
    if (max < nums[i])
      max = nums[i];

  cout << "The maximum value is " << max << endl;

  return 0;
}
```

The output produced by Program 12.3 is:

```
The maximum value is 27
```

Exercises 12.2

1. Write array declarations, including initializers, for the following:

   a. a list of ten integer grades: 89, 75, 82, 93, 78, 95, 81, 88, 77, 82

   b. a list of five double-precision amounts: 10.62, 13.98, 18.45, 12.68, 14.76

   c. a list of 100 double-precision interest rates; the first six rates are 6.29, 6.95, 7.25, 7.35, 7.40, 7.42

   d. a list of 64 double-precision temperatures; the first ten temperatures are 78.2, 69.6, 68.5, 83.9, 55.4, 67.0, 49.8, 58.3, 62.5, 71.6

   e. a list of 15 character codes; the first seven codes are f, j, m, q, t, w, z

2. Write an array declaration statement that stores the following values in an array named `prices`: 16.24, 18.98, 23.75, 16.29, 19.54, 14.22, 11.13, 15.39. Include these statements in a program that displays the values in the array.

3. Write a program that uses an array declaration statement to initialize the following numbers in an array named `slopes`: 17.24, 25.63, 5.94, 33.92, 3.71, 32.84, 35.93, 18.24, 6.92. Your program should locate and display both the maximum and minimum values in the array.

4. Write a program that stores the following prices in an array named `prices`: 9.92, 6.32, 12.63, 5.95, 10.29. Your program should also create two arrays named `units` and `amounts`, each capable of storing five double-precision numbers. Using a `for` loop and a `cin` statement, have your program accept five user-input numbers into the `units` array when the program is run. Your program should store the product of the corresponding values in the `prices` and `units` arrays in the `amounts` array (for example, `amounts[1] = prices[1] * units[1]`) and display the following output (fill in the table appropriately):

```
Price         Units         Amount
-----         -----         ------
 9.92           .             .
 6.32           .             .
12.63           .             .
 5.95           .             .
10.29           .             .
                            ------
Total:                        .
```

5. The string of characters "Good Morning" is to be stored in a character array named goodstr1. Write the declaration for this array in three different ways.

6. a. Write declaration statements to store the string "Input the Following Data" in a character array named message1, the string "------------" in an array named message2, the string "Enter the Date: " in an array named message3, and the string "Enter the Account Number: " in an array named message4.

   b. Include the array declarations written in Exercise 6a in a program that uses cout statements to display the messages. For example, the statement

   $$\text{cout} << \text{message1};$$

   causes the string stored in the message1 array to be displayed. Your program requires four such statements to display the four individual messages. (*Hint:* Using a cout statement to display a string requires that the last character in the string be the end-of-string marker \0.)

7. a. Write a declaration to store the string "This is a test" into an array named strtest. Include the declaration in a program to display the message using the following loop:

   ```
   for (i = 0; i < NUMDISPLAY; i++)
     cout << strtest[i];
   ```

   where NUMDISPLAY is a symbolic constant for the number 14.

   b. Modify the for statement in Exercise 7a to display only the array characters t, e, s, and t.

   c. Include the array declaration written in Exercise 7a in a program that uses the cout object to display characters in the array. For example, the statement cout << strtest; causes the string stored in the strtest array to be displayed. Using this statement requires that the last character in the array be the end-of-string marker \0.

   d. Repeat Exercise 7a using a while loop. (*Hint:* Stop the loop when the \0 escape sequence is detected. The expression while(strtest[i] != '\0') can be used.)

12.3 ARRAYS AS FUNCTION ARGUMENTS

Individual array elements are passed to a called function in the same manner as individual scalar variables; they are simply included as subscripted variables when the function call is made. For example, the function call

$$\text{findMin}(\text{grade}[2], \text{grade}[6]);$$

passes the values of the elements grade[2] and grade[6] to the function findMin().

Passing a complete array of values to a function is in many respects an easier operation than passing individual elements. The called function receives access to the actual array rather than a copy of the values in the array. For example, if grade is an array, the function call `findMax(grade);` makes the complete `grade` array available to the `findMax()` function. This is different from passing a single variable to a function.

Recall that when a single scalar argument is passed to a function, the called function receives only *a copy* of the passed value, which is stored in one of the function's parameters. If arrays were passed in this manner, a copy of the complete array would have to be created. For large arrays, making duplicate copies of the array for each function call wastes computer storage and frustrates the effort to return multiple element changes made by the called program (recall that a function directly returns at most one value). To avoid these problems, the called function is given direct access to the original array.[3] Thus, any changes made by the called function are made directly to the array itself. For the following specific examples of function calls, assume that the arrays `nums`, `keys`, `units`, and `prices` are declared as:

```
int nums[5];                        // an array of five integers
char keys[256];                     // an array of 256 characters
double units[500], prices[500];     // two arrays of 500 doubles
```

For these arrays, the following function calls can be made:

```
findMax(nums);
findChar(keys);
calcTotal(nums, units, prices);
```

In each case, the called function receives direct access to the named array.

On the receiving side, the called function must be alerted that an array is being made available. For example, suitable function header lines for the previous functions are:

```
int findMax(int vals[5])
char findChar(char inKeys[256])
void calcTotal(int arr1[5], double arr2[500], double arr3[500])
```

In each of these function header lines, the names in the parameter list are chosen by the programmer. However, the parameter names used by the functions still refer to the original array created outside the function. This is made clear in Program 12.4.

Notice that the function prototype for `findMax()` declares that `findMax()` returns an integer and expects an array of five integers as an argument. It is also important to know that only one array is created in Program 12.4. In `main()`, this array is known as `nums`, and in `findMax()`, the array is known as `vals`. As illustrated in Figure 12.7, both names refer to the same array. Thus, in Figure 12.7, `vals[3]` is the same element as `nums[3]`.

The argument and parameter declarations in the `findMax()` prototype and the function header line, respectively, in Program 12.4 actually contain extra information that is not required by the function. All that `findMax()` must know is that the parameter `vals` refers to an array of integers. Because the array has been created in `main()` and no additional storage space is needed in `findMax()`, the declaration for `vals` can omit the size of the array. Thus, an alternative function header line is:

```
int findMax(int vals[])
```

---

[3] This is accomplished because the starting address of the array is actually passed as an argument. The formal parameter receiving this address argument is a pointer. The intimate relationship between array names and pointers is presented in Chapter 14.

PROGRAM 12.4

```cpp
#include <iostream>
using namespace std;

const int MAXELS = 5; //global-used in main() and findMax()

int findMax(int [MAXELS]);        // function prototype

int main()
{
  int nums[MAXELS] = {2, 18, 1, 27, 16};

  cout << "The maximum value is " << findMax(nums) << endl;

  return 0;
}

// find the maximum value
int findMax(int vals[MAXELS])
{
  int i, max = vals[0];

  for (i = 1; i < MAXELS; i++)
    if (max < vals[i])
      max = vals[i];

  return max;
}
```

This form of the function header makes more sense when you realize that only one item is actually passed to findMax() when the function is called, which is the starting address of the nums array. This is illustrated in Figure 12.8.

Because only the starting address of the nums array is passed to findMax(), the number of elements in the array need not be included in the declaration for vals.[4] In fact, it is generally advisable to omit the size of the array in the function header line. For example, consider the more general form of findMax(), which can be used to find the maximum value of an integer array of arbitrary size:

```cpp
int findMax(int vals[], int numEls)    // find the maximum value
{
  int i, max = vals[0];

  for (i = 1; i < numEls; i++)
   if (max < vals[i])
     max = vals[i];

  return max;
}
```

---

[4] An important consequence is that findMax() has direct access to the passed array. This means that any change to an element of the vals array actually is a change to the nums array. This is significantly different than the situation with scalar variables, where the called function does not receive direct access to the passed variable.

FIGURE 12.7   Only One Array Is Created

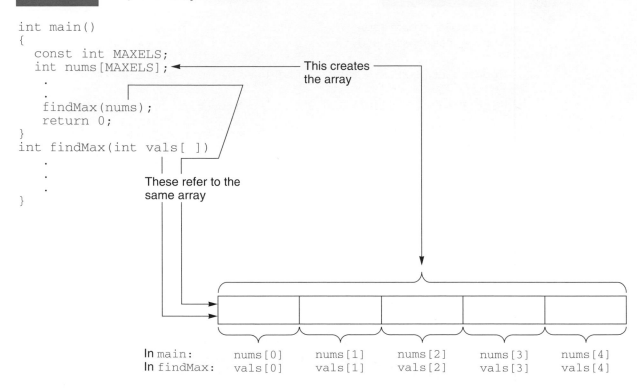

The more general form of `findMax()` declares that the function returns an integer value. The function expects the starting address of an integer array and the number of elements in the array as arguments. Then, using the number of elements as the boundary for its search, the function's `for` loop causes each array element to be examined in sequential order to locate the maximum value. Program 12.5 illustrates the use of `findMax()` in a complete program.

FIGURE 12.8   The Starting Address of the Array Is Passed

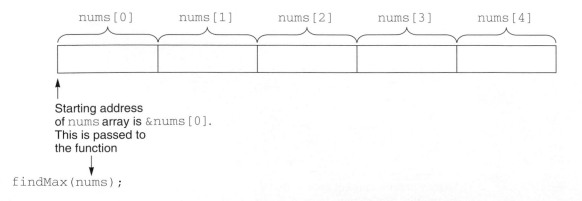

PROGRAM 12.5

```cpp
#include <iostream>
using namespace std;

int findMax(int [], int);    // function prototype

int main()
{
  const int MAXELS = 5;

  int nums[MAXELS] = {2, 18, 1, 27, 16};

  cout << "The maximum value is "
       << findMax(nums, MAXELS) << endl;

  return 0;
}

// find the maximum value
int findMax(int vals[], int numEls)
{
  int i, max = vals[0];

  for (i = 1; i < numEls; i++)
    if (max < vals[i])
      max = vals[i];

 return max;
}
```

The output displayed by both Programs 12.4 and 12.5 is:

```
The maximum value is 27
```

Exercises 12.3

1. The following declarations were used to create the `prices` array:

   ```cpp
   const int NUMGRADES = 500;
   double prices[NUMGRADES];
   ```

   Write two different function header lines for a function named `sortArray()` that accepts the `prices` array as a parameter named `inArray` and returns no value.

2. The following declarations were used to create the `keys` array:

   ```cpp
   const int NUMKEYS = 256;
   char keys[NUMKEYS];
   ```

   Write two different function header lines for a function named `findKey()` that accepts the `keys` array as a parameter named `select` and returns no value.

3. The following declarations were used to create the `rates` array:

   ```cpp
   const int NUMRATES = 256;
   double rates[NUMRATES];
   ```

   Write two different function header lines for a function named `prime()` that accepts the `rates` array as a parameter named `rates` and returns a double-precision value.

4. a. Modify the `findMax()` function in Program 12.4 to locate the minimum value of the passed array. Rename the function `findMin()`.

    b. Include the function written in Exercise 4a in a complete program and run the program on a computer.

5. Write a program that has a declaration in `main()` to store the following numbers into an array named `rates`: 6.5, 7.2, 7.5, 8.3, 8.6, 9.4, 9.6, 9.8, 10.0. There should be a function call to `show()` that accepts the `rates` array as a parameter named `rates` and then displays the numbers in the array.

6. a. Write a program that has a declaration in `main()` to store the string `"Vacation is near"` into an array named `message`. There should be a function call to `display()` that accepts `message` in a parameter named `strng` and then displays the message.

    b. Modify the `display()` function written in Exercise 6a to display the first eight elements of the `message` array.

7. Write a program that declares three single-dimensional arrays named `price`, `quantity`, and `amount`. Each array should be declared in `main()` and should be capable of holding ten double-precision numbers. The numbers that should be stored in `price` are 10.62, 14.89, 13.21, 16.55, 18.62, 9.47, 6.58, 18.32, 12.15, 3.98. The numbers that should be stored in `quantity` are 4, 8.5, 6, 7.35, 9, 15.3, 3, 5.4, 2.9, 4.8. Your program should pass these three arrays to a function called `extend()`, which should calculate the elements in the `amount` array as the product of the corresponding elements in the `price` and `quantity` arrays (`amount[1] = price[1] * quantity[1]`, for example). After `extend()` has put values into the `amount` array, the values in the array should be displayed from within `main()`.

8. Write a program that includes two functions named `calcAvg()` and `variance()`. The `calcAvg()` function should calculate and return the average of the values stored in an array named `testvals`. The array should be declared in `main()` and include the values 89, 95, 72, 83, 99, 54, 86, 75, 92, 73, 79, 75, 82, 73. The `variance()` function should calculate and return the variance of the data. The variance is obtained by subtracting the average from each value in `testvals`, squaring the differences obtained, adding their squares, and dividing by the number of elements in `testvals`. The values returned from `calcAvg()` and `variance()` should be displayed from within `main()`.

12.4 USING STL ALGORITHMS FOR SEARCHING AND SORTING[5]

At some time in their career, programmers find that they need to both sort and search arrays of data items. For example, experimental results might have to be arranged in either increasing (ascending) or decreasing (descending) order for statistical analysis; an array of names, as string data, may have to be sorted in alphabetical order; or an array of dates may have to be rearranged in ascending date order. Similarly, an array of names may have to be searched to find a particular name in the list, or a list of dates may have to be searched to locate a particular date.

Sorting and searching arrays can be accomplished either by using a prewritten function or by writing the code from scratch (referred to in programming as "rolling your own"). C++'s Standard Template Library (STL) provides a set of generic capabilities that can be applied to both STL data structures, such as the `vector` type presented in Section 12.6, as well as non-STL data structures, such as an array. Table 12.1 lists three of these capabilities (a more complete list is provided in Section 12.6) that are directly applicable to searching and sorting arrays. These capabilities are provided as methods and are formally referred to as STL algorithms.

---

[5] This topic may be omitted on first reading without loss of subject continuity.

TABLE 12.1 Standard Template Library (STL) search and sort Algorithms

Algorithm Name	Description
binary_search (start, end, value)	Returns a Boolean value of `true` if the specified value exists within the specified range; otherwise returns `false`. Can only be used on a sorted set of values.
find (start, end, value)	Returns the position of the first occurrence of an element in a specified range having a specified value, if the value exists. Performs a linear search, starting with the first element in a specified range and proceeds one element at a time until the complete range has been searched or the specified element has been found.
sort(start, end)	Sorts elements in the specified range into an ascending order.

The basics underlying the search and sort functions listed in Table 12.1 are presented in Section 12.8. You will need to understand these concepts in order to create a specialized sort or search function. This section presents sorting and searching array elements using the STL functions, which is the preferred technique because it relies on tested and reliable code. In general it is not necessary to sort a list before searching it, although, in many cases, much faster searches can be performed if an array's elements are in sorted (either ascending or descending) order.

Notice that all of the STL algorithms listed in Table 12.1 operate on elements within a designated range. This range is always specified by providing the first element in the range and one element beyond the last desired element. When used with arrays, these first and last elements are easily specified as offsets using the array's name as the starting point. Examples of various ranges, assuming an array named `names`, are:

First Element	Last Element	Specified Range
names + 0	names + 3	names[0] through names[2], inclusive
names	names + 3	same as above, because a 0 offset for the first element can be omitted
names + 1	names + 11	names[1] through names[10], inclusive

This notation permits the first and last elements to be passed to the selected algorithm using the same procedure as arrays were passed into a called function (that is, by the array's name) presented in the last section. For example, the statement `sort(names, names + 11);` calls the `sort` algorithm and specifies that the elements from `names[0]` to `names[10]` should be replaced in a sorted order. Notice that in all cases the specified range starts at the first element and ends at one element *less than* the last specified element.

The function prototypes for each of the algorithms listed in Table 12.1 are provided in a header file named `algorithm`; thus, this file must be included in any program that uses these algorithms. This is accomplished by including the statement `#include <algorithm>`.

The `sort()` method uses a modified quick sort algorithm (described in Section 12.8) to arrange an array's elements into an ascending (increasing) order, while the `binary_search()` method (also described in Section 12.8) requires a sorted list for its search. Thus, in practice, the sort() method is almost always called immediately before the binary_search() method is invoked, unless the array is known to be in a sorted order to begin with. The find() method not only searches for a designated value, but returns the position of the first match. Because this method performs a linear search, starting at the first element in the specified range and moving sequentially, element-by-element through the list, it does not require the list to be in a sorted order. However, for large lists it will frequently save time if the list is first sorted and a binary_search() performed to establish that a desired element is present, before invoking the slower find() method to sequentially search each item in the list.

As a specific example of this, and to see how each of the algorithms listed in Table 12.1 is used, consider Program 12.6. This program first permits keyboard entry of a user-specified number of names that are entered into an array. The sort() method is then called to rearrange the elements into ascending order. Once the sort has been completed, the program requests the entry of a name that is subsequently used as an argument to the binary_search() method. This method returns a Boolean true value if the specified name is contained in the array; otherwise, it returns a false value. Then, and only if the binary_search() method determines that the value is in the array, the find() method is called to determine where the name is actually located. The statements in Program 12.6 that use the sort(), binary_search(), and find() methods have been highlighted for easy identification.

PROGRAM 12.6

```cpp
#include <iostream>
#include <string>
#include <algorithm>   // needed to access STL algorithms
using namespace std;

int main()
{
  const int NUMELS = 5;
  string names[NUMELS];   //an array of string values
  string value;
  int i, offset;
  bool found;

  // read the array values
  for (i = 0; i < NUMELS; i++)
  {
    cout << "Enter name " << (i+1) << ": ";
    cin  >> names[i];
  }

  // sort the array
  sort(names, names + NUMELS);
```

(continued from previous page)

```
   cout << "\nEnter the name you are looking for: ";
   cin  >> value;

   found = binary_search(names, names + NUMELS, value);
   if (found)
   {
     offset = find(names, names + NUMELS, value) - names;
      cout << "\nThe name " << value << " is located at position "
           << offset + 1 << " in the sorted array." << endl;
   }
   else
      cout << "\nThe name " << value << " is not in the array."
           << endl;

   // display the sorted array
   cout << "\nThe values in sorted order are:";
   for (i = 0; i < NUMELS; i++)
     cout << "  " << names[i];
   cout << endl;

   return 0;
}
```

Following is a sample run using Program 12.6, where the user enters five names into the array and then requests that the sorted array names be searched for the name Menning.

```
Enter name 1: Williams
Enter name 2: Menning
Enter name 3: Able
Enter name 4: Jones
Enter name 5: Smith

Enter the item you are looking for: Menning

The name Menning is located at position 3 in the sorted array.

The values in sorted order are:  Able  Jones  Menning  Smith  Williams
```

In reviewing Program 12.6, notice that the `sort()` method arranges array elements into alphabetical order for string elements and in increasing numerical order for primitive data types. In addition, when the `binary_search()` method is used to locate a specified value, the method returns either a Boolean `true (1)` or `false (0)` value—it does not return the location of the value. Also notice that all three functions use the array's name as their first argument, and the name plus an offset as their second argument, while the `binary_search()` and `find()` functions require an additional third argument, which is the searched for value. If only a section of the array is desired to be sorted or searched, the first two arguments in all three function calls can be specified with offsets. For example, if only the 3rd through 5th array elements were to be sorted, the appropriate method call would be `sort(nums + 2, nums + 4)`.

Finally, the `find()` method returns the location of the designated element, which is equivalent to the array's name plus an offset to the element. The offset to the element is then determined by subtracting the array's name from the returned value, which is done in the statement:

```
offset = find(names, names + NUMELS, value) - names;
```

Adding one to this value converts this offset to the exact position of the located element.

Exercises 12.4

1. Enter and run Program 12.6 on your computer.

2. Execute Program 12.6 but enter names with both lowercase and uppercase letters and determine if the correct alphabetical order is produced. What does this tell you about the `sort()` function?

3. Execute Program 12.6, entering all names in the array with an initial capital letter. Then enter the searched for name in all lowercase letters. What does the output display tell you about the `binary_search()` function?

4. Modify Program 12.6 to enter and sort an array of integers.

5. Modify Program 12.6 to enter and sort an array of characters.

6. Using either the Internet or the on-line documentation provided with your compiler, obtain documentation on the STL and the list of algorithms provided by this library.

12.5 DECLARING AND PROCESSING TWO-DIMENSIONAL ARRAYS

A **two-dimensional array**, which is sometimes referred to as a **table**, consists of both rows and columns of elements. For example, the following array of numbers

8	16	9	52
3	15	27	6
14	25	2	10

is a two-dimensional array of integers. This array consists of three rows and four columns. To reserve storage for this array, both the number of rows and the number of columns must be included in the array's declaration. Calling the array `val`, the correct specification for this two-dimensional array is:

```
const int NUMROWS = 3;
const int NUMCOLS = 4;
int val[NUMROWS][NUMCOLS];
```

Similarly, the declarations

```
const int NUMROWS = 10;
const int NUMCOLS = 5;
double prices[NUMROWS][NUMCOLS];
```

and

```
const int ROWS = 6;
const int COLS = 26;
char code[ROWS][COLS];
```

declare that the array `prices` consists of 10 rows and 5 columns of floating-point numbers and that the array `code` consists of 6 rows and 26 columns, with each element capable of holding one character. Again, notice that we have used named constants in declaring each array's size.

Each element in a two-dimensional array is located by identifying its position in the array. As illustrated in Figure 12.9, the term `val[1][3]` uniquely identifies the element in row 1, column 3. As with single-dimensional array variables, double-dimensional array variables can be used anywhere scalar variables are valid. Examples that use elements of the `val` array are:

```
amount = val[2][3];
val[0][0] = 62;
newnum = 4 * (val[1][0] - 5);
sumRow0 = val[0][0] + val[0][1] + val[0][2] + val[0][3];
```

The last statement causes the values of the four elements in row 0 to be added and the sum to be stored in the scalar variable `sumRow0`.

As with single-dimensional arrays, two-dimensional arrays can be initialized from within their declaration statements. This is done by listing the initial values within braces and separating them by commas. Additionally, braces can be used to separate individual rows. For example, the declaration

```
const int NUMROWS = 3;
const int NUMCOLS = 4;
int val[NUMROWS][NUMCOLS] = { {8,16,9,52},
                              {3,15,27,6},
                              {14,25,2,10} };
```

declares `val` to be an array of integers with three rows and four columns, with the initial values given in the declaration. The first set of internal braces contains the values for row 0 of the array, the second set of braces contains the values for row 1, and the third set contains the values for row 2.

Although the commas in the initialization braces are always required, the inner braces can be omitted. Thus, the initialization for `val` may be written as:

```
int val[NUMROWS][NUMCOLS] = {8,16,9,52,
                             3,15,27,6,
                             14,25,2,10};
```

FIGURE 12.9 Each Array Element Is Identified by Its Row and Column Position

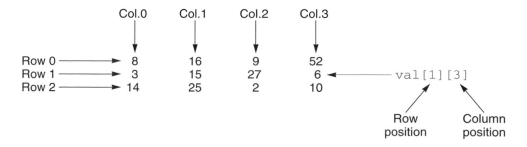

FIGURE 12.10	Storage and Initialization of the val Array

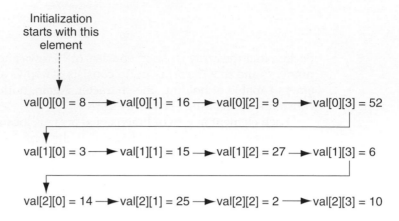

Initialization
starts with this
element

val[0][0] = 8 ⟶ val[0][1] = 16 ⟶ val[0][2] = 9 ⟶ val[0][3] = 52

val[1][0] = 3 ⟶ val[1][1] = 15 ⟶ val[1][2] = 27 ⟶ val[1][3] = 6

val[2][0] = 14 ⟶ val[2][1] = 25 ⟶ val[2][2] = 2 ⟶ val[2][3] = 10

The separation of initial values into rows in the declaration statement is not necessary because the compiler assigns values beginning with the [0][0] element and proceeds row by row to fill in the remaining values. Thus, the initialization

```
int val[NUMROWS][NUMCOLS] = {8,16,9,52,3,15,27,6,14,25,2,10};
```

is equally valid but does not clearly illustrate to another programmer where one row ends and another begins.

As illustrated in Figure 12.10, the initialization of a two-dimensional array is done in row order. First, the elements of the first row are initialized, then the elements of the second row are initialized, and so on until the initializations are completed. This row ordering is also the same ordering used to store two-dimensional arrays. That is, array element [0][0] is stored first, followed by element [0][1], followed by element [0][2], and so on. Following the first row's elements are the second row's elements and so on for all the rows in the array.

As with single-dimensional arrays, two-dimensional arrays may be displayed by individual element notation or by using loops (either while or for loops). This is illustrated by Program 12.7, which displays all of the elements of a 3 × 4 two-dimensional array using two different techniques. Notice in Program 12.7 that we have used symbolic constants to define the array's rows and columns.

PROGRAM 12.7

```
#include <iostream>
#include <iomanip>
using namespace std;

int main()
{
  const int NUMROWS = 3;
  const int NUMCOLS = 4;

  int i, j;
  int val[NUMROWS][NUMCOLS] = {8,16,9,52,3,15,27,6,14,25,2,10};
```

(continued from previous page)

```cpp
  cout << "\nDisplay of val array by explicit element"
       << endl << setw(4) << val[0][0] << setw(4) << val[0][1]
       << setw(4) << val[0][2] << setw(4) << val[0][3]
       << endl << setw(4) << val[1][0] << setw(4) << val[1][1]
       << setw(4) << val[1][2] << setw(4) << val[1][3]
       << endl << setw(4) << val[2][0] << setw(4) << val[2][1]
       << setw(4) << val[2][2] << setw(4) << val[2][3];

  cout << "\n\nDisplay of val array using a nested for loop";

  for (i = 0; i < NUMROWS; i++)
  {
    cout << endl;        // print a new line for each row
    for (j = 0; j < NUMCOLS; j++)
      cout << setw(4) <<  val[i][j];
  }

  cout << endl;

  return 0;
}
```

The display produced by Program 12.7 is:

```
Display of val array by explicit element
    8 16   9 52
    3 15  27   6
   14 25   2 10
Display of val array using a nested for loop
    8 16   9 52
    3 15  27   6
   14 25   2 10
```

The first display of the `val` array produced by Program 12.7 is constructed by explicitly designating each array element. The second display of array element values, which is identical to the first, is produced using a nested `for` loop. Nested loops are especially useful when dealing with two-dimensional arrays because they allow the programmer to designate and cycle through each element easily. In Program 12.7, the variable `i` controls the outer loop and the variable `j` controls the inner loop. Each pass through the outer loop corresponds to a single row, with the inner loop supplying the appropriate column elements. After a complete row is printed, a newline is started for the next row. The effect is a display of the array in a row-by-row fashion.

Once two-dimensional array elements have been assigned, array processing can begin. Typically, `for` loops are used to process two-dimensional arrays because, as previously noted, they allow the programmer to designate and cycle through each array element easily. For example, the nested `for` loop in Program 12.8 is used to multiply each element in the `val` array by the scalar number 10 and display the resulting value.

PROGRAM 12.8

```cpp
#include <iostream>
#include <iomanip>
using namespace std;

int main()
{
  const int NUMROWS = 3;
  const int NUMCOLS = 4;

  int i, j;
  int val[NUMROWS][NUMCOLS] = {8,16,9,52,
                               3,15,27,6,
                               14,25,2,10};

// multiply each element by 10 and display it
  cout << "\nDisplay of multiplied elements";
  for (i = 0;  i < NUMROWS;  i++)
  {
    cout << endl;    // start each row on a new line
    for (j = 0; j < NUMCOLS; j++)
    {
      val[i][j] = val[i][j] * 10;
      cout << setw(5) << val[i][j];
    }  // end of inner loop
  }    // end of outer loop
  cout << endl;

  return 0;
}
```

The output produced by Program 12.8 is:

```
Display of multiplied elements
  80 160  90 520
  30 150 270  60
 140 250  20 100
```

Passing two-dimensional arrays into a function is a process identical to passing single-dimensional arrays. The called function receives access to the entire array. For example, the function call display(val); makes the complete val array available to the function named display(). Thus, any changes made by display() are made directly to the val array. Assuming that the following two-dimensional arrays named test, code, and stocks are declared as

```cpp
int test[7][9];
char code[26][10];
double stocks[256][52];
```

the following function calls are valid:

```cpp
findMax(test);
obtain(code);
price(stocks);
```

On the receiving side, the called function must be alerted that a two-dimensional array is being made available. For example, assuming that each of the previous functions returns an integer, suitable function header lines for the functions are:

```
int findMax(int nums[7][9])
int obtain(char key[26][10])
int price(double names[256][52])
```

In each of these function header lines, the parameter names chosen are local to the function. However, the internal parameter names used by the function still refer to the original array created outside the function. Program 12.9 illustrates passing a two-dimensional array into a function that displays the array's values.

Only one array is created in Program 12.9. This array is known as `val` in `main()` and as `nums` in `display()`. Thus, `val[0][2]` refers to the same element as `nums[0][2]`. The named constants `ROWS` and `COLS` are declared globally because they are used by both `main()` and `display()`.

Notice the use of the nested `for` loop in Program 12.9 for cycling through each array element. In Program 12.9, the variable `rowNum` controls the outer loop and the variable `colNum` controls the inner loop. For each pass through the outer loop, which corresponds to a row, the inner loop makes one pass through the column elements. After a complete row is printed, the `endl` manipulator causes a newline to be started for the next row. The effect is a display of the array in a row-by-row fashion:

```
 8 16  9 52
 3 15 27  6
14 25  2 10
```

The parameter declaration for `nums` in `display()` contains extra information not required by the function. The declaration for `nums` can omit the row size of the array. Thus, an alternative function prototype is

```
display(int nums[][COLS]);
```

and an alternative function header line is:

```
void display(int nums[][COLS])
```

PROGRAM 12.9

```cpp
#include <iostream>
#include <iomanip>
using namespace std;

const int ROWS = 3;
const int COLS = 4;

void display(int [ROWS][COLS]);    // function prototype

int main()
{
  int val[ROWS][COLS] = {8,16,9,52,
                         3,15,27,6,
                         14,25,2,10};

  display(val);

  return 0;
}
```

(continued from previous page)

```cpp
void display(int nums[ROWS][COLS])
{
  int rowNum, colNum;

  for (rowNum = 0; rowNum < ROWS; rowNum++)
  {
    for(colNum = 0; colNum < COLS; colNum++)
      cout << setw(4) <<nums[rowNum][colNum];
    cout << endl;
  }

  return;
}
```

The reason the column size must be included whereas the row size is optional becomes obvious when you consider how the array elements are stored in memory. Starting with element `val[0][0]`, each succeeding element is stored consecutively, row by row, as `val[0][0]`, `val[0][1]`, `val[0][2]`, `val[0][3]`, `val[1][0]`, `val[1][1]`, etc., as illustrated in Figure 12.11.

As with all array accesses, an individual element of the `val` array is obtained by adding an offset to the starting location of the array. For example, element `val[1][3]` of the `val` array illustrated in Figure 12.11 is located at an offset of 28 bytes from the start of the array (assuming four bytes for an `int`). Internally, the compiler determines this offset using the following calculation:

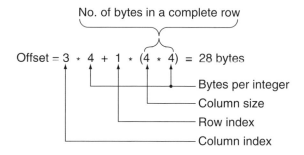

The column size is necessary in the offset calculation so that the compiler can determine the number of positions to skip over to get to the desired row.

FIGURE 12.11   **Storage of the val Array**

	Column 0	Column 1	Column 2	Column 3	
Row 0					`val[1][3]`
Row 1					
Row 2					

Internal Array Element Location Algorithm[6]

Internally, each individual element in an array is obtained by adding an offset to the starting address of the array. Thus, the memory address of each array element is internally calculated as:

Address of element i = starting array address + the offset

For single-dimensional arrays, the offset to the element with index `i` is calculated as:

*Offset = i * the size of an individual element*

For two-dimensional arrays, the same address calculation is made, except that the offset is determined as follows:

*Offset = column index value * the size of an individual element*
*+ row index value * number of bytes in a complete row*

where the number of bytes in a complete row is calculated as:

number of bytes in a complete row =
*maximum column specification * the size of an individual element*

For example, as illustrated in Figure 12.12, for an array of integers where each integer is stored using four bytes, the offset to the element whose index value is 5 is 5 * 4 = 20.

Using the address operator, `&`, we can check this address algorithm. For example, consider Program 12.10.

FIGURE 12.12   The Offset to the Element with an Index Value of 5

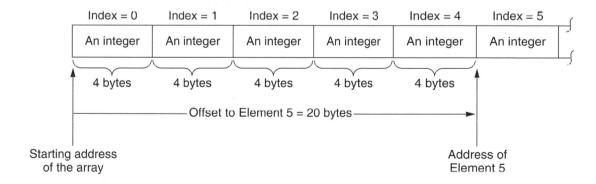

PROGRAM 12.10

```
#include <iostream>
using namespace std;

int main()
{
   const int NUMELS = 20;

   int arr[NUMELS];
```

---

[6] This topic is optional and may be omitted with no loss of subject continuity.

(continued from previous page)

```cpp
    cout << "The starting address of the arr array is: "
         << int (&arr[0]) << endl;
    cout << "The storage size of each array element is: "
         << sizeof(int) << endl;
    cout << "The address of element number 5 is: "
         << int (&arr[5]) << endl;
    cout << "The starting address of the array, "
         << "\ndisplayed using the notation arr, is: "
         << int (arr) << endl;

    return 0;
}
```

A sample output produced by Program 12.10 is:

```
The starting address of the arr array is: 1244796
The storage size of each array element is: 4
The address of element number 5 is: 1244916
The starting address of the array,
displayed using the notation arr, is: 1244796
```

Notice that the addresses have been displayed in decimal form and that element 5 is 20 bytes beyond the starting address of the array. Also notice that the starting address of the array is the same as the address of the zeroth element, which is coded as `&arr[0]`. Alternatively, as illustrated by the displayed line, the starting array address can also be obtained as `arr`, which is the name of the array. This is because an array name is a pointer constant, which is an address. (The close association of array names and pointers is explained in depth in Chapter 14.)

Larger Dimensional Arrays

Although arrays with more than two dimensions are not commonly used, C++ does allow any number of dimensions to be declared. This is done by listing the maximum size of all dimensions for the array. For example, the declaration `int response[4][10][6];` declares a three-dimensional array. The first element in the array is designated as `response[0][0][0]` and the last element as `response[3][9][5]`.

Conceptually, as illustrated in Figure 12.13, a three-dimensional array can be viewed as a book of data tables. Using this visualization, the first index value can be thought of as the location of the desired row in a table, the second index value as the desired column, and the third index value, which is often called the *rank,* as the page number of the selected table. Similarly, arrays of any dimension can be declared. Conceptually, a four-dimensional array can be represented as a shelf of books, where the fourth dimension is used to declare a desired book on the shelf, and a five-dimensional array can be viewed as a bookcase filled with books, where the fifth dimension refers to a selected shelf in the bookcase. Using the same analogy, a six-dimensional array can be considered as a single row of bookcases, where the sixth dimension refers to the desired bookcase in the row, a seven-dimensional array can be considered as multiple rows of bookcases, where the seventh dimension refers to the desired row, and so on. Alternatively, arrays of three, four, five, six, or more dimensions can be viewed as mathematical *n*-tuples of order three, four, five, six, and so on, respectively.

FIGURE 12.13   Representation of a Three-Dimensional Array

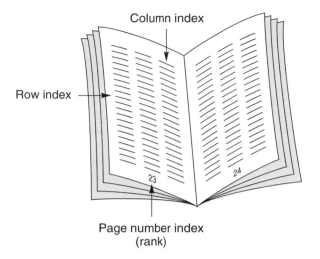

Column index

Row index

23   24

Page number index
(rank)

Exercises 12.5

1. Write appropriate specification statements for:

   a. an array of integers with 6 rows and 10 columns

   b. an array of integers with 2 rows and 5 columns

   c. an array of characters with 7 rows and 12 columns

   d. an array of characters with 15 rows and 7 columns

   e. an array of double-precision numbers with 10 rows and 25 columns

   f. an array of double-precision numbers with 16 rows and 8 columns

2. Determine the output produced by the following program:

```
#include <iostream>
int main()
{
  const int ROWS = 3;
  const int COLS = 4;
  int i, j, val[ROWS][COLS] = {8,16,9,52,3,15,27,6,14,25,2,10};

  for (i = 0; i < ROWS; i++)
  {
    for (j = 0; j < COLS; j++)
      cout << val[i][j] << " ";
    cout << endl;
  }

  return 0;
}
```

3. a. Write a C++ program that adds the values of all elements in the `val` array used in Exercise 2 and displays the total.

   b. Modify the program written for Exercise 3a to display the total of each row separately.

4. Write a C++ program that adds equivalent elements of the two-dimensional arrays named `first` and `second`. Both arrays should have two rows and three columns. For example, element `[1][2]` of the resulting array should be the sum of `first[1][2]` and `second[1][2]`. The first and second arrays should be initialized as follows:

	First			Second	
16	18	23	24	52	77
54	91	11	16	19	59

5. a. Write a C++ program that finds and displays the maximum value in a two-dimensional array of integers. The array should be declared as a 4 × 5 array of integers and initialized with these data: 16, 22, 99, 4, 18, −258, 4, 101, 5, 98, 105, 6, 15, 2, 45, 33, 88, 72, 16, 3.

   b. Modify the program written in Exercise 5a so that it also displays the maximum value's row and column subscript numbers.

6. Write a C++ program to select the values in a 4 × 5 array of integers in increasing order and store the selected values in the single-dimensional array named sort. Use the data given in Exercise 5a to initialize the two-dimensional array.

7. a. A professor has constructed a two-dimensional array of floating-point numbers having three rows and five columns. This array currently contains the test grades of the students in the professor's advanced compiler design class. Write a C++ program that reads 15 array values and then determines the total number of grades in these ranges: less than 60, greater than or equal to 60 and less than 70, greater than or equal to 70 and less than 80, greater than or equal to 80 and less than 90, and greater than or equal to 90.

   b. Entering 15 grades each time the program written for Exercise 7a is run is cumbersome. What method, therefore, is appropriate for initializing the array during the testing phase?

   c. How might the program you wrote for Exercise 7a be modified to include the case of no grade being present? That is, what grade could be used to indicate an invalid grade and how does your program have to be modified to exclude counting such a grade?

8. a. Write a function that finds and displays the maximum value in a two-dimensional array of integers. The array should be declared as a 10-row × 20-column array of integers in main(), and the starting address of the array should be passed to the function.

   b. Modify the function written in Exercise 8a so that it also displays the row and column number of the element with the maximum value.

   c. Can the function you wrote for Exercise 8a be generalized to handle any size two dimensional array?

12.6 THE STL VECTOR CLASS[7]

Many programming applications require lists that must constantly be expanded and contracted as items are added to and removed from the list. Although expanding and contracting an array can be accomplished by creating, copying, and deleting arrays, this solution tends to be costly in terms of both initial programming, maintenance, and testing time. To meet the need of providing a completely tested and generic set of data structure that can be easily modified, expanded, and contracted, C++ provides a useful set of classes in its Standard Template Library (STL).

Each STL class is coded as a template (see Section 6.1) that permits the construction of a generic type of data structure, which is referred to as a **container**. The terms **list** and **collection** are frequently used as synonyms for a container, with each term referring to a set of data items that form a natural unit or group. Using this definition an array is also a container; however, it is a container that is provided as a built-in type as contrasted to the containers created using STL. Figure 12.14 illustrates the container types provided by the STL.

---

[7] This topic may be omitted on first reading without loss of subject continuity.

FIGURE 12.14   The Collection STL Container Types

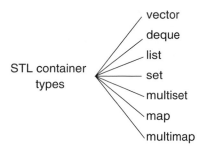

In this section the vector container class is presented, along with the most commonly used algorithms for this class and the arguments, known as iterators, required for these algorithms. You have already encountered three of these algorithms (`sort`, `find`, and `binary_search`) and their required iterator arguments in Section 12.4.

A vector is similar to an array in that it stores elements that can be accessed using an integer index that starts at zero, but dissimilar in that a vector will automatically expand as needed, and is provided with a number of extremely useful class methods (functions) for operating on the vector. Table 12.2 lists these vector class methods, with highlighting used to identify the methods that we will use in our demonstration program.

In addition to the specific vector class methods listed in Table 12.2, vectors also have access to the complete set of generic STL algorithms, three of which were presented in Section 12.4. Table 12.3 summarizes the most commonly used of these algorithms.

Notice that there is both a swap algorithm (Table 12.3) and a swap vector class method (Table 12.2). Because a class's method is targeted to work specifically with its container type and generally will execute faster, whenever a container class provides a method with the same name as an algorithm, you should use the class method.

Finally, a number of additional items, referred to as iterators, are also provided by the STL. Iterators provide the means of specifying which elements in a container are to be operated on when an algorithm or method is called. Two of the most useful iterators are returned by the STL iterator functions named `begin()` and `end()`. These are general purpose functions that return the positions of the first and last elements in a container, respectively.

To make this more tangible and provide a meaningful introduction to using an STL container class, we will use the vector container class to create a vector for holding a list of names. As we shall see, a vector is very similar to a C++ array, except that it can automatically expand as needed.

Program 12.11 initially constructs a vector and initializes it with names stored in a string array. Once it is initialized, various vector methods and STL algorithms are used to operate on the vector. Specifically, one method is used to change an existing name, another to insert a name within the vector, and a third method to append a name to the end of the list of names. After each method and algorithm is applied, a `cout` object is employed to display the results.

TABLE 12.2 Summary of Vector Class Methods (Functions) and Operations

Functions (Class Methods) and Operations	Description
`Vector<DataType> name`	Creates an empty vector with compiler dependent initial size
`vector<DataType> name(source)`	Creates a copy of the source vector
`vector<DataType> name(n)`	Creates a vector of size `n`
`vector<DataType> name(n, elem)`	Creates a vector of size `n` with each element initialized as `elem`.
`vector<DataType> name(src.beg, src.end)`	Creates a vector initialized with elements from a source container beginning at `src.beg` and ending at `src.end`
`~vector(DataType>()`	Destroys the vector and all elements it contains
`at[index]`	Returns the element at the designated index, and throws an exception if the index is out of bounds
`name[index]`	Returns the element at the designated index, with no bounds checking
`at(index)`	Returns the element at the specified index argument, with bounds checking on the index value
`front()`	Returns the first element in the vector
`back()`	Returns the last element in the vector
`dest = src`	Assigns all elements of `src` vector to `dest` vector
`assign(n, elem)`	Assigns `n` copies of `elem`
`assign(src.begin, src.end)`	Assigns the elements of the src container (need not be a vector) between the range `src.begin` and `src.end`, to the name vector
`insert(pos, elem)`	Inserts `elem` at position `pos`
`insert(pos, n, elem)`	Inserts `n` copies of `elem` starting at position `pos`
`insert(pos, src.begin, src.end)`	Insert, starting at position `pos`, a copy of the elements that start at `src.begin`, and stop at `src.end`
`push_back(elem)`	Appends `elem` at the end of the vector
`erase(pos)`	Removes the element at the specified position
`erase(begin, end)`	Removes the elements within the specified range
`resize(value)`	Resizes the vector to a larger size, with new elements instantiated using the default constructor
`resize(value, elem)`	Resizes the vector to a larger size, with new elements instantiated as `elem`
`clear()`	Removes all elements from the vector
`swap(nameB)`	Swaps the elements of the implied and `nameB` vectors; can be performed using the `swap()` algorithm
`nameA == nameB`	Returns a Boolean `true` if `nameA` elements all equal `nameB` elements; otherwise, returns `false`
`nameA != nameB`	Returns a Boolean `false` if `nameA` elements all equal `nameB` elements; otherwise, returns `true`; same as `!(nameA == nameB)`
`nameA < nameB`	Returns a Boolean `true` if `nameA` is less than `nameB`; otherwise, returns `false`
`nameA > nameB`	Returns a Boolean `true` if `nameA` is greater than `nameB`; otherwise, returns `false`; same as `nameB < nameA`
`nameA <= nameB`	Returns a Boolean `true` if `nameA` is less than or equal to `nameB`
`nameA >= nameB`	Returns a Boolean `true` if `nameA` is greater than or equal to `nameB`
`name.size()`	Returns the size of the vector as an `int`
`name.empty()`	Returns a Boolean `true` if vector is empty; otherwise, returns `false`
`name.max_size()`	Returns the maximum possible elements as an integer
`name.capacity()`	Returns the maximum possible elements, as an integer, without relocation of the vector

PROGRAMMING NOTE

When to Use an Array or a Vector

An array is the data structure of first choice whenever you have a list of primitive data types or objects that does not have to be expanded or contracted.

A vector is the data structure of first choice whenever you have a list of primitive data types or objects that can be grouped as an array, but must be expanded or contracted.

Whenever possible, always use STL's algorithms to operate on both arrays (see Section 12.4) and vectors (described in this section). Both STL's classes and algorithms provide verified and reliable code that can significantly shorten program development time.

TABLE 12.3 Commonly Used Standard Template Library (STL) Algorithms

Algorithm Name	Description
accumulate	Returns the sum of the numbers in a specified range
binary_search	Returns a Boolean value of true if the specified value exists within the specified range, otherwise returns false; can only be used on a sorted set of values
copy	Copies elements from a source range to a destination range
copy_backward	Copies elements from a source range to a destination range in a reverse direction
count	Returns the number of elements in a specified range that match a specified value
equal	Compares the elements in one range of elements, element by element, to the elements in a second range
fill	Assigns every element in a specified range to a specified value
find	Returns the position of the first occurrence of an element in a specified range having a specified value, if the value exists; performs a linear search, starting with the first element in a specified range and proceeds one element at a time until the complete range has been searched or the specified element has been found
max_element	Returns the maximum value of the elements in the specified range
min_element	Returns the minimum value of the elements in the specified range
random_shuffle	Randomly shuffles element values in a specified range
remove	Removes a specified value within a specified range without changing the order of the remaining elements
replace	Replaces each element in a specified range having a specified value with a newly specified value
reverse	Reverses elements in a specified range
search	Finds the first occurrence of a specified value or sequence of values within a specified range
sort	Sorts elements in a specified range into an ascending order
swap	Exchanges element values between two objects
unique	Removes duplicate adjacent elements within a specified range

PROGRAM 12.11

```cpp
#include <iostream>
#include <string>
#include <vector>
#include <algorithm>
using namespace std;

int main()
{
 const int NUMELS = 4;
 string n[] ={"Donavan", "Michaels", "Smith", "Jones"};
 int i;

  // instantiate a vector of strings using the n[] array
  vector<string> names(n, n + NUMELS);
 cout << "\nThe vector initially has a size of "
      << names.size() << ",\n and contains the elements:\n";
  for (i = 0; i < names.size(); i++)
   cout << names[i] << "   ";

  // modify the element at position 3 (i.e. index = 2) in the vector
  names[2] = "Farmer";
  cout << "\n\nAfter replacing the third element, the vector has a size of "
       << names.size() << ",\n and contains the elements:\n";
  for (i = 0; i < names.size(); i++)
   cout << names[i] << " ";

  // insert an element into the vector at position 2 (i.e. index = 1)
  names.insert(names.begin()+1, "Williams");
  cout << "\n\nAfter inserting an element into the second position,"
       << "\n the vector has a size of " << names.size() << ","
       << " and contains the elements:\n";
  for (i = 0; i < names.size(); i++)
   cout << names[i] << " ";

  // add an element to the end of the vector
  names.push_back("Adams");
  cout << "\n\nAfter adding an element to the end of the list,"
       << "\n the vector has a size of " << names.size() << ","
       << " and contains the elements:\n";
  for (i = 0; i < names.size(); i++)
   cout << names[i] << " ";

  // sort the vector
  sort(names.begin(), names.end());
  cout << "\n\nAfter sorting, the vector's elements are:\n";
  for (i = 0; i < names.size(); i++)
   cout << names[i] << " ";

  cout << endl;

  return 0;
}
```

In reviewing Program 12.11, first notice the inclusion of the four header files `<iostream>`, `<string>`, `<vector>`, and `<algorithm>` and the `using namespace std;` statement. The `<iostream>` header is needed to create and use the `cout` stream; the `<string>` header is required for constructing strings; the `<vector>` header is required to create one or move `vector` objects; and the `<algorithm>` header is required for the `sort` algorithm that is applied after we have completed adding and replacing `vector` elements.

The statement in Program 12.11 that is used to create and initialize the vector named `names` is:

```
vector<int> names(n, n + NUMELS);
```

Here, the vector `names` is declared as a vector of type `int` and is initialized with elements from the `n` array, starting with the first element of the array (element `n[0]`), and ending with the last array element, which is located at position `n + NUMELS`. Thus, the vector `names` now has a size sufficient for four string values and has been initialized with the strings `"Donavan"`, `"Michaels"`, `"Smith"`, and `"Jones"`. The next set of statements in Program 12.11 displays the initial values in the vector, using standard subscripted vector notation that is identical to the notation used for accessing array elements. Displaying the vector values in this manner, however, requires knowing how many elements each vector contains. As we insert and remove elements we would like the vector itself to keep track of where the first and last elements are; this capability is, in fact, automatically provided by two iterator methods furnished for each STL container, named `begin()` and `end()`.

The next major set of statements, consisting of

```
// modify the element at position 3 (i.e. index = 2) in the vector
names[2] = "Farmer";
```

and

```
// insert an element into the vector at position 2 (i.e. index = 1)
names.insert(names.begin()+1, "Williams");
```

are used to both modify an existing vector value and insert a new value into the vector. Specifically, the `names[2]` notation uses standard indexing, while the `insert()` method requires an iterator and the value to be inserted, as arguments. Thus, `names[2]` specifies that the third element in the vector will be changed (remember that vectors, like arrays, begin at index position 0). The `insert()` method is then used to insert the string literal `Williams` in the second position of the vector. Notice that iterator arithmetic is allowed. Thus, because the `begin()` method returns the iterator value corresponding to the start of the vector, adding 1 to it designates the second position in the vector. It is at this position that the new value is inserted with all subsequent values moved up by one position in the vector, with the vector automatically expanding to accept the inserted value. At this point in the program, the vector `names` now contains the elements:

```
Donavan Williams Michaels Farmer Jones
```

This arrangement of values was obtained by replacing the original value `Smith` with `Farmer` and then inserting the string `Williams` into the second position, which automatically moves all subsequent elements up by one position and increases the total vector size to accommodate 5 strings.

Next, the statement `names.push_back("Adams");` is used to append the string literal Adams to the end of the vector, which results in the elements:

```
Donavan Williams Michaels Farmer Jones Adams
```

Finally, the last section of code used in Program 12.11 uses the `sort` algorithm to sort the elements in each vector and then randomly shuffle them. Notice that this algorithm uses iterator values to determine the sequence of elements to be operated upon. After the algorithm is applied, the values in the vector are once again displayed. Following is the complete output produced by Program 12.11:

```
The vector initially has a size of 4,
 and contains the elements:
Donavan  Michaels  Smith  Jones

After replacing the third element, the vector has a size of 4,
 and contains the elements:
Donavan Michaels Farmer Jones

After inserting an element into the second position,
 the vector has a size of 5, and contains the elements:
Donavan Williams Michaels Farmer Jones

After adding an element to the end of the list,
 the vector has a size of 6, and contains the elements:
Donavan Williams Michaels Farmer Jones Adams

After sorting, the vector's elements are:
Adams Donavan Farmer Jones Michaels Williams
```

Using Vectors with Objects[8]

Program 12.11 is useful in illustrating the construction and maintenance of a vector. From a practical standpoint, however, one important element is missing from the program, which is the inclusion of a programmer designed record type. For example, assume a list of employee records must be maintained where each record consists of an employee's name and pay rate (Figure 12.15).

For this UML description, a class must be first be created from which individual programmer-defined objects can be constructed and added into the list. Once the desired class has been constructed and compiled, a vector for objects constructed from this class can be created.

---

[8] This topic requires understanding of classes presented in Chapter 9, and can be omitted on first reading without loss of subject continuity.

FIGURE 12.15	A NameRate Class UML Diagram

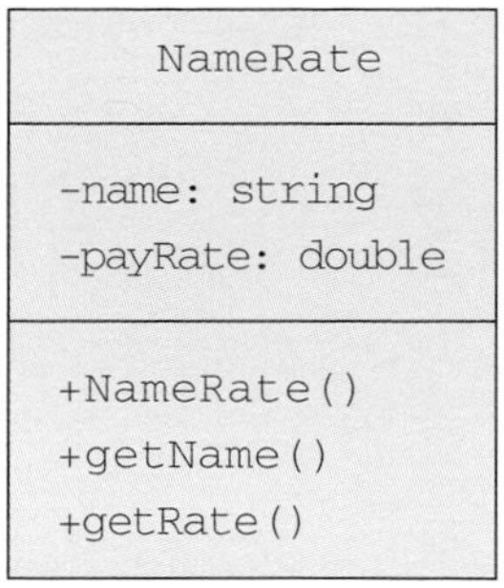

```
           NameRate
─────────────────────────────
-name: string
-payRate: double
─────────────────────────────
+NameRate()
+getName()
+getRate()
```

Class 12.1 provides the code for Figure 12.15's class diagram.

CLASS 12.1

```cpp
#include <string>
using namespace std;

class NameRate
{
  // data declarations
  private:
    string name;
    double payRate;

  // method definitions
  public:
    NameRate(string nn, double rate) // constructor
        {name = nn; payRate - rate;};
    string getName(){return name;};      // accessor
    double getRate(){return payRate;}; // accessor

};
```

In reviewing Class 12.1, make special note that all of the class's data members have been declared as public. This is necessary because we will be placing them into a vector in which we specifically want anyone with access to the list to be able to change, remove, and add instantiated objects. Having developed a class for our employee records, we can now construct a vector container for storing objects created from this class. This, of course, requires two distinct operations: instantiating actual objects and then storing each object within the vector.

Program 12.12 shows how this can be accomplished. Initially, four records of the NameRate type are created. These records have been created individually and added into the list using the vector class's push_back() method.

PROGRAM 12.12

```cpp
#include <iostream>
#include <string>
#include <vector>
#include <algorithm>
using namespace std;

class NameRate
{
  // data declarations
  private:
    string name;
    double payRate;

  // method definitions
  public:
     NameRate(string nn, double rate) // constructor
        {name = nn; payRate = rate;};
    string getName(){return name;};   // accessor
    double getRate(){return payRate;}; // accessor

};

int main()
{
  NameRate a("Bender, Jim", 18.55);
  NameRate b("Acme, Sam", 26.58);
  NameRate c("Mening, Stephen", 15.85);
  NameRate d("Zeman, Harold", 17.92);

  vector<NameRate> empRecords; // add an individual object into the list

  cout << "The size of the instantiated vector is "
       << empRecords.size() << endl << " and its capacity is "
       << empRecords.capacity() << endl << endl;
  empRecords.push_back(a);
  empRecords.push_back(b);
  empRecords.push_back(c);
  empRecords.push_back(d);

  cout << "After adding four objects, the size of the list is "
       << empRecords.size() << endl << " and its capacity is "
       << empRecords.capacity() << endl << endl;

  cout << "The data stored in the vector is:" << endl << endl;
  cout << "    Name              Pay Rate\n";
  cout << "---------------    -------------\n";
```

(continued from previous page)

```
  // use accessor methods to extract the name and pay rate
  for(int i = 0; i < empRecords.size(); i++)
  {
    cout << empRecords[i].getName()
         << "\t\t" << empRecords[i].getRate() << endl;
  }

  return 0;
}
```

In reviewing Program 12.12 note that the statement

```
                    vector<NameRate> empRecords;
```

creates an empty vector named `empRecords`. After the list has been created, the program inserts four `NameRate` objects into the list. This is one of the distinguishing advantages of vectors over arrays: elements can be inserted, appended, and removed from the list without the programmer having to explicitly write the code underlying all of these operations, as is required by arrays.

Now review the `for` loop coded at the end of Program 12.12. Specifically, notice that the loop is terminated by the expression `empRecords.size()`, which uses the vector class's `size()` method to determine the actual number of elements in the vector. The individual data items in each retrieved `NameRate` object are then accessed using `NameRate`'s accessor methods. In Program 12.12 this is restricted to accessing the `name` and `payRate` data using the `getName()` and `getRate()` accessors. That this is successfully accomplished is verified by the following output produced by the program:

```
     The size of the instantiated vector is 0
       and its capacity is 0

     After adding four objects, the size of the list is 4
       and its capacity is 4

     The data stored in the vector is:

           Name                 Pay Rate
     ---------------          ------------
     Bender, Jim                 18.55
     Acme, Sam                   26.58
     Mening, Stephen             15.85
     Zeman, Harold               17.92
```

Parallel Arrays

Consider the data provided in Table 12.4. Clearly, it is possible to store this information using three individual arrays, where one array is used for storing the integer employee numbers, one for the string names, and one for the double-precision pay rates (Figure 12.16). Such arrays, where corresponding data in a record resides in the same position in more than one array, are referred to as **parallel arrays**. The separation of an individual record into parallel arrays was required in earlier programming languages that only supported array data structures. Unfortunately, it sometimes also becomes the first choice of beginning programmers who are familiar with arrays and how to program them.

TABLE 12.4 A Table of Employee Data

Employee Number	Employee Name	Employee Pay Rate
12479	Adams, C	15.72
13623	Brenner, D.	17.54
14145	Dunson, P.	16.55
15987	Franklin, S.	18.43
16203	Jamason, T.	15.72
16417	Kline, H.	19.64
17634	Opper, G.	17.29
18321	Smith, S.	18.67
19435	Voelmer, L.	15.50
19567	Wilson, R.	17.35

If you find yourself thinking in terms of parallel arrays, use it only as a design aid to help you structure the data as an object. For example, using an object approach, each record that is divided across the three arrays in Figure 12.16 can be combined into an object, which accurately encapsulates each employee's data as a single record (see Figure 12.17). Once you have correctly captured a record's structure, the usefulness of the parallel array as a design aid is completed. Except for very simple or specialized applications, you should rarely ever code a set of parallel arrays.

FIGURE 12.16   Employee Records Represented Using Three Parallel Arrays

Employee Number	Employee Name	Employee Pay Rate
12479	ADAMS, C.	15.72
13623	BRENNER, D.	17.54
14145	DUNSON, P.	16.56
15987	FRANKLIN, S.	18.43
16203	JAMASON, T.	15.72
16417	KLINE, H.	19.64
17634	OPPER, G.	17.29
18321	SMITH, S.	18.67
19435	VOELMER, L.	15.50
19567	WILSON, R.	17.35

FIGURE 12.17   Employee Records Represented as Objects

		Employee Number	Employee Name	Employee Pay Rate
1st	Object →	12479	ADAMS, C.	15.72
2nd	Object →	13623	BRENNER, D.	17.54
3rd	Object →	14145	DUNSON, P.	16.56
4th	Object →	15987	FRANKLIN, S.	18.43
5th	Object →	16203	JAMASON, T.	15.72
6th	Object →	16417	KLINE, H.	19.64
7th	Object →	17634	OPPER, G.	17.29
8th	Object →	18321	SMITH, S.	18.67
9th	Object →	19435	VOELMER, L.	15.50
10th	Object →	19567	WILSON, R.	17.35

Exercises 12.6

1. Define the terms "container" and "Standard Template Library."

2. What `include` statements should be included with programs that use the Standard Template Library?

3. Enter and execute Program 12.11.

4. Modify Program 12.11 so that the initial set of names is input by the user when the program executes. Either have the program first request the number of initial names that will be entered or terminate name entry with a sentinel value.

5. Modify Program 12.11 to use and display the results reported by the vector class's `capacity()` and `max_size()` methods.

6. Modify Program 12.11 to use `random_shuffle()` algorithm.

7. Modify Program 12.11 to use the `binary_search()` and `find()` algorithms. Have your program request the name that is to be searched.

8. Using Program 12.11 as a starting point, create an equivalent program that uses a vector of integers. Initialize the vector using the array `int values[] = {10, 14, 98, 64, 88, 2, 20,17}`.

9. Use the `max_element()` and `min_element()` algorithms to determine the maximum and minimum values in the vector created for Exericise 8. (*Hint:* Use the expression `max_element(vectorName.begin(), vectorName.end())` to determine the maximum value stored in the vector. Then use the same arguments for the `min_element()` algorithm.)

10. Enter and execute Program 12.12.

11. a. Modify Program 12.12 to display the size of the vector and its capacity immediately after the vector is instantiated and after each `NameRate` object has been added to the vector. What does the displayed capacity tell you about how your compiler resizes the vector when its capacity needs to be increased due to the addition of a new element?

    b. What vector class methods can you use to explicitly set a vector's capacity, both when the vector is instantiated and after it has been created?

12. For the following class

```
public class Inventory
{
  public:
    string description;
    int prodnum;
    int quantity;
    double price;
};
```

write the following:

a. An accessor method for each instance variable

b. A declaration for a vector of `Inventory` objects, named `invRecords`

c. A statement that reads and displays the price of the 15th `Inventory` object stored in the vector

13. Define a vector for factory employee objects, in which each object contains the name, age, Social Security number, hourly wage, and number of years an employee has been with the company. Write the following:

a. An accessor method for each instance variable

b. Statements that display the name and number of years with the company for the 25th employee in the vector

c. A loop that, for every employee, adds 1 to the number of years with the company and that adds 50 cents to the hourly wage

12.7 FOCUS ON PROBLEM SOLVING

The next two applications are presented to illustrate single-dimensional array processing and further our understanding of using arrays as function arguments. In the first application, two statistical functions are created to determine the average and standard deviation of an array of numbers. In the second application, a function is used to insert an identification number into an existing array that is maintained in a sorted order.

Application 1: Statistical Analysis

Two functions are to be developed to determine the average and standard deviation of a list of integer numbers. Each function must be capable of accepting the numbers as an array and returning their calculated values to the calling function. We now apply the top-down development procedure to develop the required functions.

Analyze the Problem   The statement of the problem indicates that two output values are required: an average and a standard deviation.

The input item defined in the problem statement is a list of integer numbers. Because the size of the list is not specified in the problem statement and to make our functions as general as possible, both functions will be designed to handle any size list passed to them. This requires that the exact number of elements in the array must also be passed to each function at the time of the function call. From each function's viewpoint, this means that it must be capable of receiving at least two input items as parameters: an array of arbitrary size and an integer number corresponding to the number of elements in the passed array.

Develop a Solution The I/O specifications determined when we analyzed the problem imply that the parameter list of each function must be capable of receiving at least two items: one parameter to accommodate the integer array and the second parameter to accept an integer. The first function returns the average of the numbers in the passed array and the second function returns the standard deviation. These items are determined as follows:

Calculate the average by adding the grades and dividing by the number of grades that was added
Determine the standard deviation by:
   Subtracting the average from each individual grade (this results in a set
      of new numbers, each of which is called a deviation)
   Squaring each deviation found in the previous step
   Adding the squared deviations and dividing the sum by the number of
      deviations
   The square root of the number found in the previous step is the
      standard deviation

The standard deviation can be calculated only after the average has been computed. Thus, in addition to requiring the array of integers and the number of values in the array, the standard deviation function also requires that the average be passed to it. This is the advantage of specifying the algorithm, in detail, before any coding is done; it ensures that all necessary inputs and requirements are discovered early in the programming process.

To ensure that we understand the required processing, we do a hand calculation. For this calculation, we arbitrarily assume that the average and standard deviation of the following ten grades are to be determined: 98, 82, 67, 54, 78, 83, 95, 76, 68, and 63. The average of these data is:

$$\text{Average} = (98 + 82 + 67 + 54 + 78 + 83 + 95 + 76 + 68 + 63)/10$$
$$= 76.4$$

The standard deviation is calculated by first determining the sum of the squared deviations. It is then obtained by dividing the resulting sum by 10 and taking its square root.

$$
\begin{aligned}
\text{Sum of squared deviations} = {} & (98 - 76.4)^2 + (82 - 76.4)^2 \\
& + (67 - 76.4)^2 + (54 - 76.4)^2 \\
& + (78 - 76.4)^2 + (83 - 76.4)^2 \\
& + (95 - 76.4)^2 + (76 - 76.4)^2 \\
& + (68 - 76.4)^2 + (63 - 76.4)^2 \\
& = 1730.400700
\end{aligned}
$$

$$\text{Standard deviation} = \sqrt{1730.4007/10} = \sqrt{173.04007} = 13.154470$$

Having specified the algorithm required of each function, we are now in a position to code them.

Code the Solution In writing functions, it is convenient to concentrate initially on the header line. The body of the function can then be written to process the input parameters correctly to produce the desired results.

Naming our averaging function `findAvg()` and arbitrarily selecting the parameter names `nums` and `numel` for the passed array and the number of elements, respectively, the function header becomes:

```
double findAvg(int nums[], int numel)
```

This begins the definition of the averaging function, and it allows the function to accept an array of integer values and an integer number. As illustrated by the hand calculation, the average of a set of integer numbers can be a double-precision number; therefore, the function is defined as returning a double-precision value. The body of the function calculates the average as described by the algorithm developed earlier. Thus, the completed `findAvg()` function becomes:

```
double findAvg(int nums[], int numel)
{
  int i;
  double sumnums = 0.0;

  for (i = 0; i < numel; i++)  // calculate the sum of the grades
    sumnums = sumnums + nums[i];

  return (sumnums / numel);    // calculate and return the average
}
```

In the body of the function is a `for` loop to sum the individual numbers. Notice also that the termination value of the loop counter in the `for` loop is `numel`, the number of integers in the array passed to the function through the parameter list. The use of this parameter gives the function its generality and allows it to be used for input arrays of any size. For example, calling the function with the statement

```
findAvg(values,10)
```

tells the function that `numel` is 10 and that the `values` array consists of 10 values, whereas the statement

```
findAvg(values,1000)
```

tells `findAvg()` that `numel` is 1000 and that the `values` array consists of 1000 numbers. In both calls, the actual argument named `values` corresponds to the parameter named `nums` within the `findAvg()` function.

Using similar reasoning as that for the averaging function, the function header for the standard deviation routine, which we name `stdDev()`, becomes:

```
double stdDev(int nums[], int numel, float av)
```

This header begins the definition of the stdDev() function. It defines the function as returning a double-precision value and accepting an array of integers, an integer value, and a double-precision value as inputs to the function. The body of the stdDev() function must calculate the standard deviation as described in the development step. The complete standard deviation function becomes:

```
double stdDev(int nums[], int numel, float av)
{
  int i;
  double sumdevs = 0.0;

  for (i = 0; i < numel; i++)
    sumdevs = sumdevs + pow((nums[i] - av),2.0);

  return(sqrt(sumdevs/numel));
}
```

Test and Correct the Program   Testing a program's function requires writing a main() program unit to call the function and display the returned results. Program 12.13 uses such a main() unit to set up a grade array with the data previously used in our hand calculation and to call the findAvg function.

PROGRAM 12.13

```
#include <iostream>
#include <iomanip>
#include <cmath>
using namespace std;

double findAvg(int [], int);          // function prototype
double stdDev(int [], int, double);   // function prototype

int main()
{
  const int NUMELS = 10;
  int values[NUMELS] = {98, 82, 67, 54, 78, 83, 95, 76, 68, 63};
  double average, stdDev;

  average = findAvg(values, NUMELS); // call the function
  stdDev = stdDev(values, NUMELS, average); // call the function

  cout << "The average of the numbers is "
       << setw(5) << setiosflags(ios::showpoint)
       << setprecision(2) << average << endl;

  cout << "The standard deviation of the numbers is "
       << setw(5) << setiosflags(ios::showpoint)
       << setprecision(2) << stdDev << endl;

  return 0;
}
```

(continued from previous page)

```
double findAvg(int nums[], int numel)
{
  int i;
  double sumnums = 0.0;

  for (i = 0; i < numel; i++)  // calculate the sum of the grades
    sumnums = sumnums + nums[i];

  return (sumnums / numel);    // calculate and return the average
}

double stdDev(int nums[], int numel, double av)
{
  int i;
  double sumdevs = 0.0;

  for (i = 0; i < numel; i++)
    sumdevs = sumdevs + pow((nums[i] - av),2);

  return(sqrt(sumdevs/numel));
}
```

A test run using Program 12.13 produced the following display:

```
The average of the numbers is 76.40
The standard deviation of the numbers is 13.15
```

Although this result agrees with our previous hand calculation, testing is really not complete without verifying the calculation at the boundary points. In this case, such a test consists of checking the calculation with all of the same values, such as all 0s and all 100s. Another simple test is to use five 0s and five 100s. We leave these tests as an exercise.

Application 2: List Maintenance

A common programming problem is to maintain a list in either numerical or alphabetical order. For example, telephone lists are traditionally kept in alphabetical order, whereas lists of part numbers are kept in numerical order.

As part of an overall maintenance program, a function is to be written that correctly inserts a three-digit identification code within a list of numbers. The list is maintained in increasing number order and duplicate identification codes are not allowed. In this application, such a function will be written. A maximum list size of 100 values is allowed and a sentinel value of 9999 is used to indicate the end of the list. Thus, for example, if the current list contains nine identification codes, the tenth position in the list contains the sentinel value.

We again use the top-down function development approach.

Analyze the Problem   The required output is an updated list of three-digit codes in which the new code has been inserted correctly into the existing list.

The input items for this function are the existing array of identification codes and the new code to be inserted into the list.

Develop a Solution   Insertion of an identification code into the existing list requires the following processing:

> *Determine where in the list the new code should be placed*
> > *This is done by comparing the new code to each value in the current list*
> > *until either a match is found, an identification code larger than the new*
> > *code is located, or the end of the list is encountered*
> *If the new code matches an existing code,*
> > *display a message that the code already exists*
> *Else*
> > *To make room for the new element in the array, move*
> > *each element one position over (this is done by*
> > *starting from the sentinel value and moving each*
> > *item one position over towards the end of the list*
> > *until the desired position in the list is reached)*
> > *Insert the new code in the desired position*
> *Endif*

For our hand calculation, assume that the list of identification codes consists of the numbers in Figure 12.18a. If the number code 142 is to be inserted into this list, it must be placed in the fourth position, after 136. To make room for the new code, all of the codes from the fourth position to the end of the list must be moved one position toward the end of the list, as illustrated in Figure 12.18b. The move is always started from the end of the list and proceeds from the sentinel value back until the desired position in the list is reached. (You can convince yourself that if the copy proceeded forward from the fourth element, 144 is reproduced in all subsequent locations until the sentinel value is reached.) After the movement of the necessary elements, the new code is inserted in the correct position. This creates the updated list shown in Figure 12.18c.

Code the Solution   For this problem, we use the parameter named idcode for the passed array of identification numbers and the parameter named newcode

---

FIGURE 12.18   Updating an Ordered List of Identification Numbers

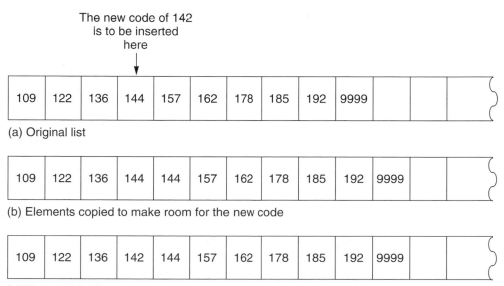

The new code of 142
is to be inserted
here

| 109 | 122 | 136 | 144 | 157 | 162 | 178 | 185 | 192 | 9999 | | | |

(a) Original list

| 109 | 122 | 136 | 144 | 144 | 157 | 162 | 178 | 185 | 192 | 9999 | | |

(b) Elements copied to make room for the new code

| 109 | 122 | 136 | 142 | 144 | 157 | 162 | 178 | 185 | 192 | 9999 | | |

(c) The updated list

for the new code number to be inserted into the array. Here, the passed array is used for both receiving the original array of numbers and as the final updated array. Internal to the function, we use a variable named `newpos` to hold the position in the list where the new code is to be inserted and the variable named `trlpos` to hold the position value of the sentinel. The variable `i` is used as a running index value.

Using these argument and variable names, the function named `insert()` performs the required processing. After accepting the array and the new code value as parameters, `insert()` performs the four major tasks described by the pseudocode selected in the design step.

```
void insert(int idcode[], int newcode)
{
  int i, newpos, trlpos;

  // find correct position to insert the new code
  i = 0;
  while (idcode[i] < newcode)
    i++;
  if (idcode[i] == newcode)
    cout << "\nThis identification code is already in the list";
  else
  {
    newpos = i;     // found the position for the new code

    // find the end of the list
    while (idcode[i] != 9999)
      i++;
    trlpos = i;

    // move idcodes over one position
    for (i = trlpos; i >= newpos; --i)
      idcode[i+1] = idcode[i];

    // insert the new code
    idcode[newpos] = newcode;
  }
}
```

The first task accomplished by the function is to determine the correct position for the new code. This is done by cycling through the list as long as each value encountered is less than the new code. Because the sentinel value of 9999 is larger than any new code, the looping must stop when the sentinel value is reached.

After the correct position is determined, the position of the sentinel value, which is the last element in the list, is found. Starting from this last position, each element in the list is moved over by one position until the value in the required new position is reached. Finally, the new identification code is inserted in the correct position.

Test and Correct the Program   Program 12.14 incorporates the `insert()` function within a complete program. This allows us to test the function with the same data used in our hand calculation.

PROGRAM 12.14

```cpp
#include <iostream>
using namespace std;

void insert(int [], int);      // function prototype

int main()
{
  const int MAXNUM = 100;

  int id[MAXNUM] = {109, 122, 136, 144, 157, 162, 178, 185, 192, 9999};
  int newcode, i;

  cout << "\nEnter the new identification code: ";
  cin  >> newcode;

  insert(id, newcode);

  cout << "\nThe updated list is: ";
  i = 0;
  while(id[i] != 9999)
  {
    cout << " " << id[i];
    i++;
  }
  cout << endl;

  return 0;
}

void insert(int idcode[], int newcode)
{
  int i, newpos, trlpos;

  // find correct position to insert the new code
  i = 0;
  while (idcode[i] < newcode)
    i++;
  if (idcode[i] == newcode)
    cout << "\nThis identification code is already in the list";
  else
  {
    newpos = i;    // found the position for the new code

    // find the end of the list
    while (idcode[i] != 9999)
      i++;
    trlpos = i;
```

(continued from previous page)

```
    // move idcodes over one position
    for (i = trlpos; i >= newpos; --i)
      idcode[i+1] = idcode[i];

    // insert the new code
    idcode[newpos] = newcode;
  }

  return;
}
```

A sample run of Program 12.14 is:

```
Enter the new identification code: 142
The updated list is: 109 122 136 142 144 157 162 178 185 192
```

Although this result agrees with our previous hand calculation, it does not constitute full testing of the program. To be sure that the program works for all cases, test runs should be made that:

1. Duplicate an existing code.
2. Place a new identification code at the beginning of the list.
3. Place a new identification code at the end of the list.

Exercises 12.7

1. Modify Program 12.13 so that the grades are entered into the `values` array using a function named `entvals`.

2. Rewrite Program 12.13 to determine the average and standard deviation of the following list of 15 grades: 68, 72, 78, 69, 85, 98, 95, 75, 77, 82, 84, 91, 89, 65, 74.

3. Modify Program 12.13 so that a `high()` function is called that determines the highest value in the passed array and returns this value to the main program unit for display.

4. Modify Program 12.13 so that a function named `sort()` is called after the call to the `stdDev()` function. The `sort` function should sort the grades into increasing order for display by `main()`.

5. a. Test Program 12.14 using an identification code of 86, which should place this new code at the beginning of the existing list.

   b. Test Program 12.14 using an identification code of 200, which should place this new code at the end of the existing list.

6. a. Determine an algorithm for deleting an entry from an ordered list of numbers.

   b. Write a function named `delete()`, which uses the algorithm selected in Exercise 6a, to delete an identification code from the list of numbers illustrated in Figure 12.14a.

7. Assume the following letters are stored in an array named `alphabet`: B, J, K, M, S, Z. Write and test a function named `adlet()`, which accepts both the `alphabet` array and a new letter as parameters and inserts the new letter in the correct alphabetical order in the `alphabet` array.

12.8 SEARCHING AND SORTING

In this section, we introduce the underlying algorithms for both sorting and searching lists. Note that it is not necessary to sort a list before searching it, although, as we shall see, much faster searches are possible if the list is in sorted order.

Search Algorithms

A common requirement of many programs is to search a list for a given element. For example, in a list of names and telephone numbers, we might search for a specific name so that the corresponding telephone number can be printed, or we might wish to search the list simply to determine if a name is there. The two most common methods of performing such searches are the linear and binary search algorithms.

Linear Search

In a **linear search,** which is also known as a **sequential search,** each item in the list is examined in the order in which it occurs until the desired item is found or the end of the list is reached. This is analogous to looking at every name in the phone directory, beginning with Aardvark, Aaron, until you find the one you want or until you reach Zzxgy, Zora. Obviously, this is not an efficient way to search a long alphabetized list. However, a linear search has two advantages:

1. The algorithm is simple.
2. The list need not be in any particular order.

In a linear search, the search begins at the first item and continues sequentially, item by item, through the list. The pseudocode for a function performing a linear search is:

For all the items in the list
* Compare the item with the desired item*
* If the item was found,*
*   Return the index value of the current item*
* EndIf*
EndFor
Return −1 because the item was not found

Notice that the function's return value indicates whether the item was found or not. If the return value is −1, the item was not in the list; otherwise, the return value within the `for` loop provides the index of where the item is located within the list.

The function `linearSearch()` illustrates this procedure as a C++ function:

```
// this function returns the location of key in the list
// a -1 is returned if the value is not found
int linearSearch(int list[], int size, int key)
{
  int i;

  for (i = 0; i < size; i++)
  {
    if (list[i] == key)
      return i;
  }

  return -1;
}
```

In reviewing `linearSearch()`, notice that the `for` loop is simply used to access each element in the list, from first element to last, until a match is found with the desired item. If the desired item is located, the index value of the current item is returned, which causes the loop to terminate; otherwise, the search continues until the end of the list is encountered.

To test this function, we have written a `main()` driver function to call it and display the results returned by `linearSearch()`. The complete test program is illustrated in Program 12.15.

PROGRAM 12.15

```
#include <iostream>
using namespace std;

int linearSearch(int [], int, int);  // function prototype

int main()
{
  const int NUMEL = 10;

  int nums[NUMEL] = {5,10,22,32,45,67,73,98,99,101};
  int item, location;


  cout << "Enter the item you are searching for: ";
  cin  >> item;

  location = linearSearch(nums, NUMEL, item);

  if (location > -1)
    cout << "The item was found at index location "
         << location << endl;
  else
    cout << "The item was not found in the list\n";

  return 0;
}
```

(continued from previous page)

```
// this function returns the location of key in the list
// a -1 is returned if the value is not found
int linearSearch(int list[], int size, int key)
{
  int i;

  for (i = 0; i < size; i++)
  {
    if (list[i] == key)
      return i;
  }

  return -1;
}
```

Sample runs of Program 12.15 are

```
Enter the item you are searching for: 101
The item was found at index location 9
```

and

```
Enter the item you are searching for: 65
The item was not found in the list
```

As has already been pointed out, an advantage of linear searches is that the list does not have to be in sorted order to perform the search. Another advantage is that if the desired item is located toward the front of the list, only a small number of comparisons are done. The worst case, of course, occurs when the desired item is at the end of the list. On average, however, and assuming that the desired item is equally likely to be anywhere within the list, the number of required comparisons are $N/2$, where N is the list's size. Thus, for a ten-element list, the average number of comparisons needed for a linear search is five, and for a 10,000-element list, the average number of comparisons is 5000. As we show next, this average can be significantly reduced using a binary search algorithm.

Binary Search

In a **binary search**, the list must be in sorted order. Starting with an ordered list, the desired item is first compared to the element in the middle of the list (for lists with an even number of elements, either of the two middle elements can be used). Three possibilities present themselves once the comparison is made: (1) the desired item may be equal to the middle element, (2) it may be greater than the middle element, or (3) it may be less than the middle element.

In the first case, the search has been successful, and no further searches are required. In the second case, because the desired item is greater than the middle element, if it is found at all, it must be in the upper part of the list. This means that the lower part of the list consisting of all elements from the first to the midpoint element can be discarded from any further search. In the third case, because the desired item is less than the middle element, if it is found at all, it must be found in the lower part of the list. For this case, the upper part of the list containing all elements from the midpoint element to the last element can be discarded from any further search.

FIGURE 12.19   The Binary Search Algorithm

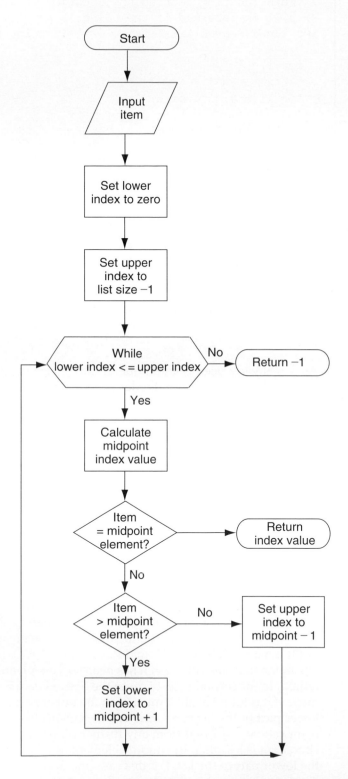

The complete algorithm for implementing this search strategy is illustrated in Figure 12.19 and defined by the following pseudocode:

Set the lower index to 0
Set the upper index to 1 less than the size of the list
Begin with the first item in the list
While the lower index is less than or equal to the upper index,
   Set the midpoint index to the integer average of the lower and upper
      index values
   Compare the desired item to the midpoint element
      If the desired element equals the midpoint element,
         Return the index value of the current item
      Else if the desired element is greater than the midpoint element,
         Set the lower index value to the midpoint value plus 1
      Else if the desired element is less than the midpoint element,
         Set the upper index value to the midpoint value less 1
      Endif
EndWhile
Return −1 because the item was not found

As illustrated by both the pseudocode and the flowchart in Figure 12.19, a `while` loop is used to control the search. The initial list is defined by setting the lower index value to 0 and the upper index value to 1 less than the number of elements in the list. The midpoint element is then taken as the integerized average of the lower and upper values. Once the comparison to the midpoint element is made, the search is subsequently restricted by moving either the lower index to one integer value above the midpoint or by moving the upper index to one integer value below the midpoint. This process is continued until the desired element is found or the lower and upper index values become equal. The function `binarySearch()` presents the C++ version of this algorithm. In this function the variables named `left` and `right` correspond to the lower and upper indices, respectively.

```cpp
// this function returns the location of key in the list
// a -1 is returned if the value is not found
int binarySearch(int list[], int size, int key)
{
  int left, right, midpt;

  left = 0;
  right = size - 1;

  while (left <= right)
  {
    midpt = (int) ((left + right) / 2);
    if (key == list[midpt])
    {
      return midpt;
    }
    else if (key > list[midpt])
      left = midpt + 1;
    else
      right = midpt - 1;
  }

  return -1;
}
```

For purposes of testing this function, Program 12.16 is used.

PROGRAM 12.16

```cpp
#include <iostream>
using namespace std;

int binarySearch(int [], int, int);  // function prototype

int main()
{
  const int NUMEL = 10;

  int nums[NUMEL] = {5,10,22,32,45,67,73,98,99,101};
  int item, location;

  cout << "Enter the item you are searching for: ";
  cin  >> item;
  location = binarySearch(nums, NUMEL, item);
  if (location > -1)
    cout << "The item was found at index location "
         << location << endl;
  else
    cout << "The item was not found in the array\n";

  return 0;
}

// this function returns the location of key in the list
// a -1 is returned if the value is not found
int binarySearch(int list[], int size, int key)
{
  int left, right, midpt;

  left = 0;
  right = size - 1;

  while (left <= right)
  {
    midpt = (int) ((left + right) / 2);
    if (key == list[midpt])
    {
      return midpt;
    }
    else if (key > list[midpt])
      left = midpt + 1;
    else
      right = midpt - 1;
  }

  return -1;
}
```

A sample run using Program 12.16 yields:

```
Enter the item you are searching for: 101
The item was found at index location 9
```

The value of using a binary search algorithm is that the number of elements that must be considered is cut in half each time through the `while` loop. Thus, the first time through the loop, N elements must be considered; the second time through the loop, $N/2$ of the elements have been eliminated and only $N/2$ remain. The third time through the loop, another half of the remaining elements have been eliminated and so on.

In general, after p passes through the loop, the number of values remaining to be searched is $N/(2^p)$. In the worst case, the search can continue until there is less than or equal to 1 element remaining to be searched. Mathematically, this can be expressed as $N/(2^p) \leq 1$. Alternatively, it may be rephrased as p is the smallest integer such that $2^p \geq N$. For example, for a 1000-element array, N is 1000 and the maximum number of passes, p, required for a binary search is ten. Table 12.5 compares the number of loop passes needed for a linear and binary search for various list sizes. As illustrated, the maximum number of loop passes for a 50-item list is almost ten times more for a linear search than for a binary search, and the difference is even more spectacular for larger lists. As a rule of thumb, 50 elements are usually taken as the switchover point: For lists smaller than 50 elements, linear searches are acceptable; for larger lists, a binary search algorithm should be used.

Big O Notation

On average, over a large number of linear searches with N items in a list, we expect to examine half $(N/2)$ of the items before locating the desired item. In a binary search, the maximum number of passes, p, occurs when $N/2^p = 1$. This relationship can be algebraically manipulated to $2^p = N$, which yields $p = \log_2 N$, which approximately equals $3.33 \log_{10} N$.

For example, finding a particular name in an alphabetical directory with $N = 1000$ names requires an average of $500 = (N/2)$ comparisons using a linear search. With a binary search, only about 10 ($\approx 3.3 \times \log_{10} 1000$) comparisons are required.

A common way to express the number of comparisons required in any search algorithm using a list of N items is to give the order of magnitude of the number of comparisons required, on average, to locate a desired item. Thus, the linear search is said to be of order N and the binary search of order $\log_2 N$. Notationally, this is expressed as $O(N)$ and $O(\log_2 N)$, where the O is read as "the order of," and the notation is called **Big O notation**.

Sort Algorithms

For sorting data, two major categories of sorting techniques exist, called internal and external sorts. **Internal sorts** are used when the data list is not too large and the complete list can be stored within the computer's memory, usually in an array. **External sorts** are used for much larger data sets that are stored in large external disk or tape files and cannot be accommodated within the computer's memory as a complete unit. Here, we present three internal sort algorithms that range from the simple and slow to the complex and fast. The first two algorithms presented are all quite commonly used when sorting lists with less than approximately 50 elements. For larger lists, more sophisticated sorting algorithms, such as the third algorithm, are typically employed.

TABLE 12.5 A Comparison of `while` Loop Passes for Linear and Binary Searches

Array Size	10	50	500	5,000	50,000	500,000	5,000,000	50,000,000
Average linear search passes	5	25	250	2,500	25,000	250,000	2,500,000	25,000,000
Maximum linear search passes	10	50	500	5,000	50,000	500,000	5,000,000	50,000,000
Maximum binary search passes	4	6	9	13	16	19	23	26

Selection Sort

One of the simplest sorting techniques is the selection sort. In a **selection sort**, the smallest value is initially selected from the complete list of data and exchanged with the first element in the list. After this first selection and exchange, the next smallest element in the revised list is selected and exchanged with the second element in the list. The smallest element is thus already in the first position in the list, so this second pass need consider only the second through the last elements. For a list consisting of N elements, this process is repeated $N - 1$ times, with each pass through the list requiring one less comparison than the previous pass.

For example, consider the list of numbers in Figure 12.20. The first pass through the initial list results in 32 being selected and exchanged with the first element in the list. The second pass, made on the reordered list, results in 155 being selected from the second through fifth elements. This value is then exchanged with the second element in the list. The third pass selects 307 from the third through fifth elements in the list and exchanges this value with the third element. Finally, the fourth and last pass through the list selects the remaining minimum value and exchanges it with the fourth list element. Although each pass in this example resulted in an exchange, no exchange is made in a pass if the smallest value is already in the correct location.

In pseudocode, the selection sort is described as:

Set interchange count to zero (not required, but done just to keep track of the
interchanges)
For each element in the list from first to next-to-last,
  Find the smallest element from the current element being
    referenced to the last element by:
      Setting the minimum value equal to the current element
      Saving (storing) the index of the current element
      For each element in the list from the current element + 1
        to the last element in the list,
        If element [inner loop index] < minimum value,
          Set the minimum value = element [inner loop index]
          Save the index of the new found minimum value
        EndIf
      EndFor
      Swap the current value with the new minimum value
      Increment the interchange count
EndFor
Return the interchange count

The function `selectionSort()` incorporates this procedure into a C++ function:

```
int selectionSort(int num[], int numel)
{
  int i, j, min, minidx, temp, moves = 0;

  for ( i = 0; i < (numel - 1); i++)
  {
    min = num[i];    // assume minimum is the first array element
    minidx = i;       // index of minimum element
    for(j = i + 1; j < numel; j++)
    {
      if (num[j] < min)    // if we've located a lower value
      {                      // capture it
        min = num[j];
        minidx = j;
      }
    }
    if (min < num[i])   // check if we have a new minimum
    {                     // and if we do, swap values
      temp = num[i];
      num[i] = min;
      num[minidx] = temp;
      moves++;
    }
  }

  return moves;
}
```

The selectionSort() function expects two parameters: the list to be sorted and the number of elements in the list. As specified by the pseudocode, a nested set of for loops performs the sort. The outer for loop causes one less pass through the list than the total number of data items in the list. For each pass, the variable min is initially assigned the value num[i], where i is the outer for loop's counter variable. Because i begins at 0 and ends at one less than numel, each element in the list, except the last, is successively designated as the current element.

The inner loop cycles through the elements below the current element and is used to select the next smallest value. Thus, this loop begins at the index value i + 1 and continues through the end of the list. When a new minimum is found, its value and position in the list are stored in the variables named min and minidx, respectively. Upon completion of the inner loop, an exchange is made only if a value less than that in the current position was found.

For purposes of testing selectionSort(), Program 12.17 was constructed. This program implements a selection sort for the same list of ten numbers that was previously used to test our search algorithms. For later comparison to the other sorting algorithms that are presented, the number of actual moves made by the program to get the data into sorted order is counted and displayed.

| **FIGURE 12.20** | A Sample Selection Sort |

Initial List	Pass 1	Pass 2	Pass 3	Pass 4
690	32	32	32	32
307	307	155	144	144
32	690	690	307	307
155	155	307	690	426
426	426	426	426	690

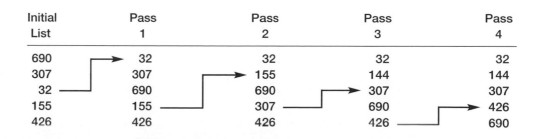

PROGRAM 12.17

```cpp
#include <iostream>
using namespace std;

int selectionSort(int [], int);

int main()
{
  const int NUMEL = 10;

  int nums[NUMEL] = {22,5,67,98,45,32,101,99,73,10};
  int i, moves;

  moves = selectionSort(nums, NUMEL);

  cout << "The sorted list, in ascending order, is:\n";
  for (i = 0; i < NUMEL; i++)
    cout << "   " <<nums[i];

  cout << endl << moves << " moves were made to sort this list\n";

  return 0;
}

int selectionSort(int num[], int numel)
{
  int i, j, min, minidx, temp, moves = 0;

  for ( i = 0; i < (numel - 1); i++)
  {
    min = num[i];   // assume minimum is the first array element
    minidx = i;     // index of minimum element
    for(j = i + 1; j < numel; j++)
    {
      if (num[j] < min)   // if we've located a lower value
      {                   // capture it
        min = num[j];
        minidx = j;
      }
    }
    if (min < num[i])  // check if we have a new minimum
    {                  // and if we do, swap values
      temp = num[i];
      num[i] = min;
      num[minidx] = temp;
      moves++;
    }
  }

  return moves;
}
```

The output produced by Program 12.17 is:

```
The sorted list, in ascending order, is:
  5 10 22 32 45 67 73 98 99 101
8 moves were made to sort this list
```

Clearly, the number of moves displayed depends on the initial order of the values in the list. An advantage of the selection sort is that the maximum number of moves that must be made is $N - 1$, where N is the number of items in the list. Further, each move is a final move that results in an element residing in its final location in the sorted list.

A disadvantage of the selection sort is that $N(N - 1)/2$ comparisons are always required, regardless of the initial arrangement of the data. This number of comparisons is obtained as follows: The last pass always requires one comparison, the next-to-last pass requires two comparisons, and so on to the first pass, which requires $N - 1$ comparisons. Thus, the total number of comparisons is:

$$1 + 2 + 3 + \ldots + (N - 1) = N(N - 1)/2 = N^2/2 - N/2$$

For large values of N, the N^2 dominates, and the order of the selection sort is $O(N^2)$.

Exchange (Bubble) Sort

In an **exchange sort**, adjacent elements of the list are exchanged with one another in such a manner that the list becomes sorted. One example of such a sequence of exchanges is provided by the **bubble sort**, where successive values in the list are compared, beginning with the first two elements. If the list is to be sorted in ascending (from smallest to largest) order, the smaller value of the two being compared is always placed before the larger value. For lists sorted in descending (from largest to smallest) order, the smaller of the two values being compared is always placed after the larger value.

For example, assume that a list of values is to be sorted in ascending order. If the first element in the list is larger than the second, the two elements are interchanged. Then the second and third elements are compared. Again, if the second element is larger than the third, these two elements are interchanged. This process continues until the last two elements have been compared and exchanged, if necessary. If no exchanges were made during this initial pass through the data, the data are in the correct order and the process is finished; otherwise, a second pass is made through the data, starting from the first element and stopping at the next-to-last element. The reason for stopping at the next-to-last element on the second pass is that the first pass always results in the most positive value "sinking" to the bottom of the list.

As a specific example of this process, consider the list of numbers in Figure 12.21. The first comparison results in the interchange of the first two element values, 690 and 307. The next comparison, between elements 2 and 3 in the revised list, results in the interchange of values between the second and third elements, 690 and 32. This comparison and possible switching of adjacent values are continued until the last two elements have been compared and possibly switched. This process completes the first pass through the data and results in the largest number moving to the bottom of the list. As the largest value sinks to its resting place at the bottom of the list, the smaller elements slowly rise, or "bubble," to the top of the list. This bubbling effect of the smaller elements is what gave rise to the name "bubble" sort for this sorting algorithm.

FIGURE 12.21   The First Pass of a Bubble Sort

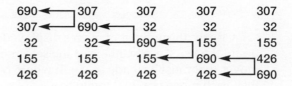

Because the first pass through the list ensures that the largest value always moves to the bottom of the list, the second pass stops at the next-to-last element. This process continues with each pass stopping at one higher element than the previous pass, until $N - 1$ passes through the list have been completed. In both cases, the resulting list is in sorted order. The pseudocode describing this sort is:

Set interchange count to zero (not required, but done just to
 keep track of the interchanges)
For the first element in the list to one less than the last element (i index)
  For the second element in the list to the last element (j index)
  If num[j] < num[j − 1]
  {
    swap num[j] with num[j − 1]
    increment interchange count
  }
  EndFor
EndFor
Return interchange count

This sort algorithm is coded in C++ as the function `bubbleSort()`, which is included within Program 12.18 for testing purposes. This program tests `bubbleSort()` with the same list of ten numbers used in Program 12.17 to test `selectionSort()`. For comparison to the earlier selection sort, the number of adjacent moves (exchanges) made by `bubbleSort()` is also counted and displayed.

PROGRAM 12.18

```
#include <iostream>
using namespace std;

int bubbleSort(int [], int);

int main()
{
  const int NUMEL = 10;

  int nums[NUMEL] = {22,5,67,98,45,32,101,99,73,10};
  int i, moves;

  moves = bubbleSort(nums, NUMEL);

  cout << "The sorted list, in ascending order, is:\n";
  for (i = 0; i < NUMEL; i++)
    cout << "   " <<nums[i];

  cout << endl << moves << " moves were made to sort this list\n";
```

(continued from previous page)

```
    return 0;
}

int bubbleSort(int num[], int numel)
{
    int i, j, temp, moves = 0;

    for ( i = 0; i < (numel - 1); i++)
    {
        for(j = 1; j < numel; j++)
        {
            if (num[j] < num[j-1])
            {
                temp = num[j];
                num[j] = num[j-1];
                num[j-1] = temp;
                moves++;
            }
        }
    }

    return moves;
}
```

Here is the output produced by Program 12.18:

```
The sorted list, in ascending order, is:
  5 10 22 32 45 67 73 98 99 101
18 moves were made to sort this list
```

As with the selection sort, the number of comparisons using a bubble sort is $O(N^2)$, and the number of required moves depends on the initial order of the values in the list. In the worst case, when the data are in reverse sorted order, the selection sort performs better than the bubble sort. Here, both sorts require $N(N - 1)/2$ comparisons, but the selection sort needs only $N - 1$ moves, whereas the bubble sort needs $N(N - 1)/2$ moves. The additional moves required by the bubble sort result from the intermediate exchanges between adjacent elements to "settle" each element into its final position. In this regard, the selection sort is superior because no intermediate moves are necessary. For random data, such as those used in Programs 12.17 and 12.18, the selection sort generally performs equal to or better than the bubble sort.

A modification to the bubble sort (see Exercise 4) that causes the sort to terminate whenever no exchanges have been made in a pass, indicating the list is in order, can make the bubble sort operate as an $O(N)$ sort in specialized cases.

Quicksort

The selection and exchange sorts both require $O(N^2)$ comparisons, which make them very slow for long lists. The **quicksort** algorithm, which is also called a *partition sort*, divides a list into two smaller sublists and sorts each sublist by partitioning into smaller sublists and so on.[9] The order of a quicksort is $N \log_2 N$. Thus,

---

[9] This algorithm was developed by C. A. R. Hoare and first described by him in an article entitled "QuickSort" in *Computer Journal* (Vol. 5, pp. 10–15) in 1962.

for a 1000-item list, the total number of comparisons for a quicksort is of the order of $1000(3.3 \log_{10} 1000) \approx 1000(10) = 10,000$ compared to $1000(1000) = 1,000,000$ for a selection or exchange sort.

The quicksort puts a list into sorted order by a partitioning process. At each stage, the list is partitioned into sublists so that a selected element, called the *pivot*, is placed in its correct position in the final sorted list. To understand the process, consider the list in Figure 12.22. The original list consists of seven numbers. Designating the first element in the list, 98, as the pivot element, the list is rearranged as shown in the first partition. Notice that this partition results in all values less than 98 residing to its left and all values greater than 98 to its right. For now, disregard the exact order of the elements to the left and right of 98 (in a moment, we will see how the arrangement of the numbers came about).

FIGURE 12.22   A First Quicksort Partition

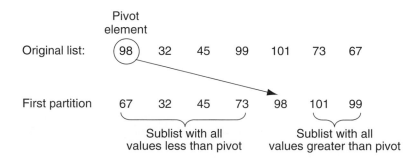

The numbers to the left of the pivot constitute one sublist and the numbers to the right are another sublist, which individually must be reordered by a partitioning process. The pivot for the first sublist is 67 and the pivot for the second sublist is 101. Figure 12.23 shows how each of these sublists is partitioned using their respective pivot elements. The partitioning process stops when a sublist has only one element. In the case illustrated in Figure 12.23, a fourth partition is required for the sublist containing the values 45 and 32 because all other sublists have only one element. Once this last sublist is partitioned, the quicksort is completed and the original list is in sorted order.

As we have illustrated, the key to the quicksort is its partitioning process. An essential part of this process is that each sublist is rearranged in place; that is, elements are rearranged within the existing list. This rearrangement is facilitated by first saving the value of the pivot, which frees its slot to be used by another element.

FIGURE 12.23   Completing the Quicksort

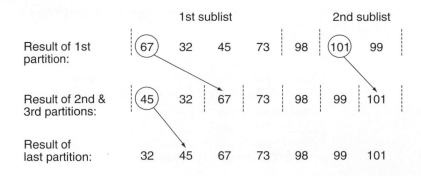

The list is then examined from the right, starting with the last element in the list, for a value less than the pivot; when one is found, it is copied to the pivot slot. This copy frees a slot at the right of the list for use by another element. The list is now examined from the left for any value greater than the pivot; when one is found, it is copied to the last freed slot. This right-to-left and left-to-right scan is continued until the right and left index values meet. The saved pivot element is then copied into this slot. At that point, all values to the left of the index are smaller than the pivot value and all values to the right are greater. Before providing the pseudocode for this process, we will show all of the steps required to complete one partition using our previous list of numbers.

Consider Figure 12.24, which shows our original list from Figure 12.22 and the positions of the initial left and right indices. As shown in the figure, the pivot value has been saved into a variable named `pivot`; the right index points to the last list element and is the active index. Using this index, the scan for elements less than the pivot value of 98 begins.

FIGURE 12.24 Start of the Scanning Process

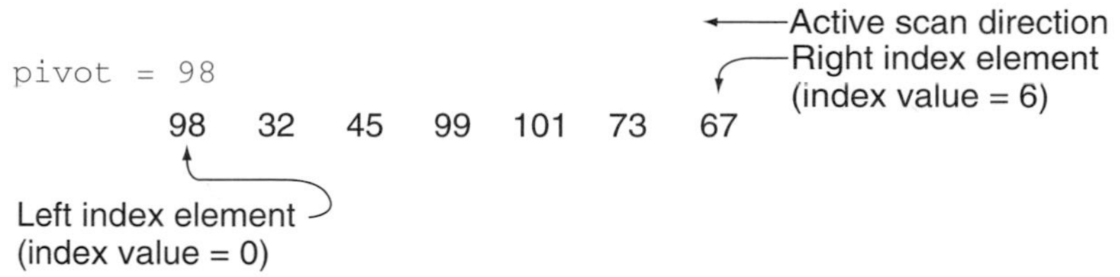

```
pivot = 98
                                              Active scan direction
                                              Right index element
                                              (index value = 6)
          98   32   45   99   101   73   67

Left index element
(index value = 0)
```

Since 67 is less than the pivot value of 98, the 67 is moved into the pivot slot (the pivot value is not lost because it has been assigned to the variable `pivot`) and the left index is incremented. This results in the arrangement shown in Figure 12.24. Notice that the element pointed to by the right index is now available for the next copy because its value, 67, has been reproduced as the first element. (This is always the case; when a scan stops, its index indicates the position available for the next move.)

Scanning the list shown in Figure 12.25 continues from the left for a search of all values greater than 98. This occurs when 99 is reached. Since 99 is greater than the pivot value of 98, the scan stops and 99 is copied into the position indicated by the right index. The right index is then decremented, which produces the situation illustrated in Figure 12.26.

Scanning the list shown in Figure 12.26 now continues from the right in a search for values less than the pivot. Since 73 qualifies, the right scan stops, 73 is moved into the position indicated by the left index, and the left index is incremented. This results in the list shown in Figure 12.27.

FIGURE 12.25 List after the First Copy

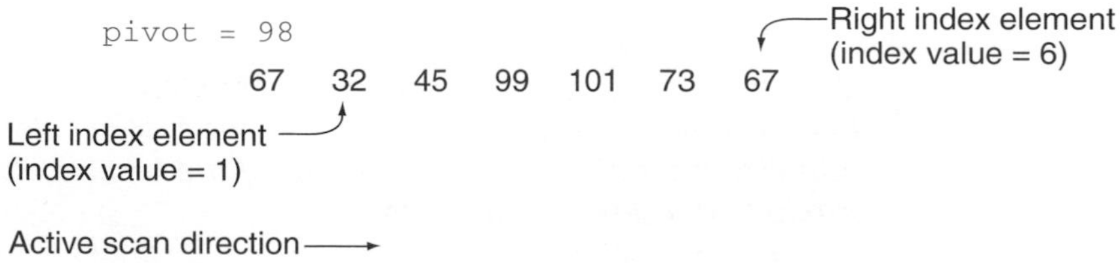

```
          pivot = 98
                                              Right index element
                                              (index value = 6)
          67   32   45   99   101   73   67

Left index element
(index value = 1)

Active scan direction
```

FIGURE 12.26   Start of Second Right-Side Scan

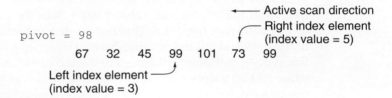

FIGURE 12.27   Start of Second Left-Side Scan

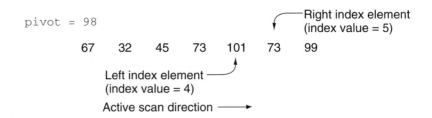

FIGURE 12.28   Position of List Elements after 101 Is Moved

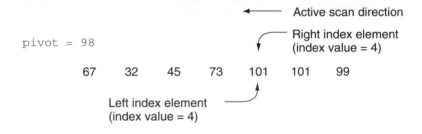

Scanning of the list shown in Figure 12.28 now resumes from the left in a search for values greater than 98. Because 101 qualifies, this scan stops, 101 is moved into the slot indicated by the right index, and the right index is incremented. This results in the list illustrated in Figure 12.27. Notice in this figure that left and right indices are equal. This is the condition that stops all scanning and indicates the position where the pivot should be placed. Doing so results in completion of this partition with the list in the following order:

67 32 45 73 98 101 99

Compare this list with the one previously shown for the first partition in Figure 12.22. As is seen, they are the same. Here, the pivot has been placed so that all elements less than it are to its left and all values greater than it are to its right. The same partitioning process would now be applied to the sublists on either side of the partition.

The pseudocode describing this partitioning process is:

Set the pivot to the value of the first list element
Initialize the left index to the index of the first list element
Initialize the right index to the index of the last list element
While (left index ≠ right index)

>   *// scan from the right, skipping over larger values*
>   *While (right index element ≤ pivot) // skip over larger values*
>   *Decrement right index*
>   *EndWhile*
>   *If (right index ≠ left index)*
>   *Move the lower value into the slot indicated by the left index*
>   *Increment the left index*
>   *EndIf*
>   *// scan from the left, skipping over smaller values*
>   *While (left index element ≤ pivot) // skip over smaller values*
>   *Increment left index*
>   *EndWhile*
>   *If (left index ≠ right index)*
>   *Move the higher value into the slot indicated by the right index*
>   *Decrement the right index*
>   *EndIf*
> *EndWhile*
> *Move the pivot into the slot indicated by the left or right index (they are*
>   *equal here)*
> *Return the left (or right) index*

The function partition, contained within Program 12.19, codes this algorithm in C++.

PROGRAM 12.19

```cpp
#include <iostream>
using namespace std;

int partition(int [], int, int);  // function prototype

int main()
{
  const int NUMEL = 7;

  int nums[NUMEL] = {98,32,45,99,101,73,67};
  int i, pivot;

  pivot = partition(nums, 0, NUMEL-1);

  cout << "\nThe returned pivot index is " << pivot;
  cout << "\nThe list is now in the order:\n";
  for (i = 0; i < NUMEL; i++)
    cout << "   " <<nums[i];
  cout << endl;

  return 0;
}
```

(continued from previous page)

```
int partition(int num[], int left, int right)
{
  int pivot, temp;

  pivot = num[left];  // "capture" the pivot value, which frees up one slot
  while (left < right)
  {
      // scan from right to left
    while(num[right] >= pivot && left < right)  // skip over larger or equal values
      right--;
    if (right != left)
    {
      num[left] = num[right];   // move the higher value into the available slot
      left++;
    }
      // scan from left to right
    while (num[left] <= pivot && left < right) // skip over smaller or equal values
      left++;
    if (right != left)
    {
      num[right] = num[left];  // move lower value into the available slot
  }   right--;
  }
  num[left] = pivot;  // move pivot into correct position

  return left;       // return the pivot index
}
```

Program 12.19 is simply used to test the function. Notice that it contains the same list that we used in our hand calculation. A sample run using Program 12.19 produced this output:

```
The returned pivot index is 4
The list is now in the order:
  67 32 45 73 98 101 99
```

Notice that this output produces the result previously obtained by our hand calculation. The importance of the returned pivot index is that it defines the sub-lists that are subsequently partitioned. The first sublist consists of all elements from the first list element to the element whose index is 3 (1 less than the returned pivot index), and the second sublist consists of all elements starting at index value 5 (1 more than the returned pivot index) and ending at the last list element.

The quicksort uses the returned pivot value in determining whether additional calls to partition are required for each sublist defined by the list segments to the left and right of the pivot index. This is done using the following recursive logic:

Quicksort(list, lower index, upper index)
  Calculate a pivot index calling partition(list, lower index, upper index)
  If (lower index < pivot index),
      quicksort(list, pivot index − 1, lower)
  If (upper index > pivot index),
      quicksort(list, pivot index + 1, upper)

The C++ code for this logic is described by the quicksort function contained within Program 12.20. As indicated, quicksort requires a partition to both rearrange lists and return its pivot value.

PROGRAM 12.20

```cpp
#include <iostream>
using namespace std;

void quicksort(int [], int, int);   // function prototypes
int partition(int [], int, int);

int main()
{
  const int NUMEL = 7;

  int nums[NUMEL] = {67,32,45,73,98,101,99};
  int i;

  quicksort(nums, 0, NUMEL-1);

  cout << "\nThe sorted list, in ascending order, is:\n";
  for (i = 0; i < NUMEL; i++)
    cout << "   " <<nums[i];
  cout << endl;

  return 0;
}

void quicksort(int num[], int lower, int upper)
{
  int i, j, pivot;

  pivot = partition(num,lower, upper);

  if (lower < pivot)
     quicksort(num, lower, pivot - 1);
  if (upper > pivot)
     quicksort(num, pivot + 1, upper);

  return;
}
```

(continued from previous page)

```
int partition(int num[], int left, int right)
{
  int pivot, temp;

  pivot = num[left];  // "capture" the pivot value, which frees up one slot
  while (left < right)
  {
      // scan from right to left
    while(num[right] >= pivot && left < right)  // skip over larger or equal values
      right--;
    if (right != left)
    {
      num[left] = num[right];   // move the higher value into the available slot
      left++;
    }
      // scan from left to right
    while (num[left] <= pivot && left < right) // skip over smaller or equal values
      left++;
    if (right != left)
    {
      num[right] = num[left];  // move lower value into the available slot
      right--;
    }
  }
  num[left] = pivot;  // move pivot into correct position

  return left;       // return the pivot index
}
```

Here is the output produced by Program 12.20:

```
The sorted list, in ascending order, is:
32 45 67 73 98 99 101
```

As indicated by this output, quicksort correctly sorts the test list of numbers. Figure 12.29 shows the sequence of calls made to quicksort by Program 12.20. In this figure, left-pointing arrows indicate calls made because the first if condition (lower < pivot) was true, and right-pointing arrows indicate calls made because the second if condition (upper > pivot) was true.

FIGURE 12.29 The Sequence of Calls Made by Program 12.20

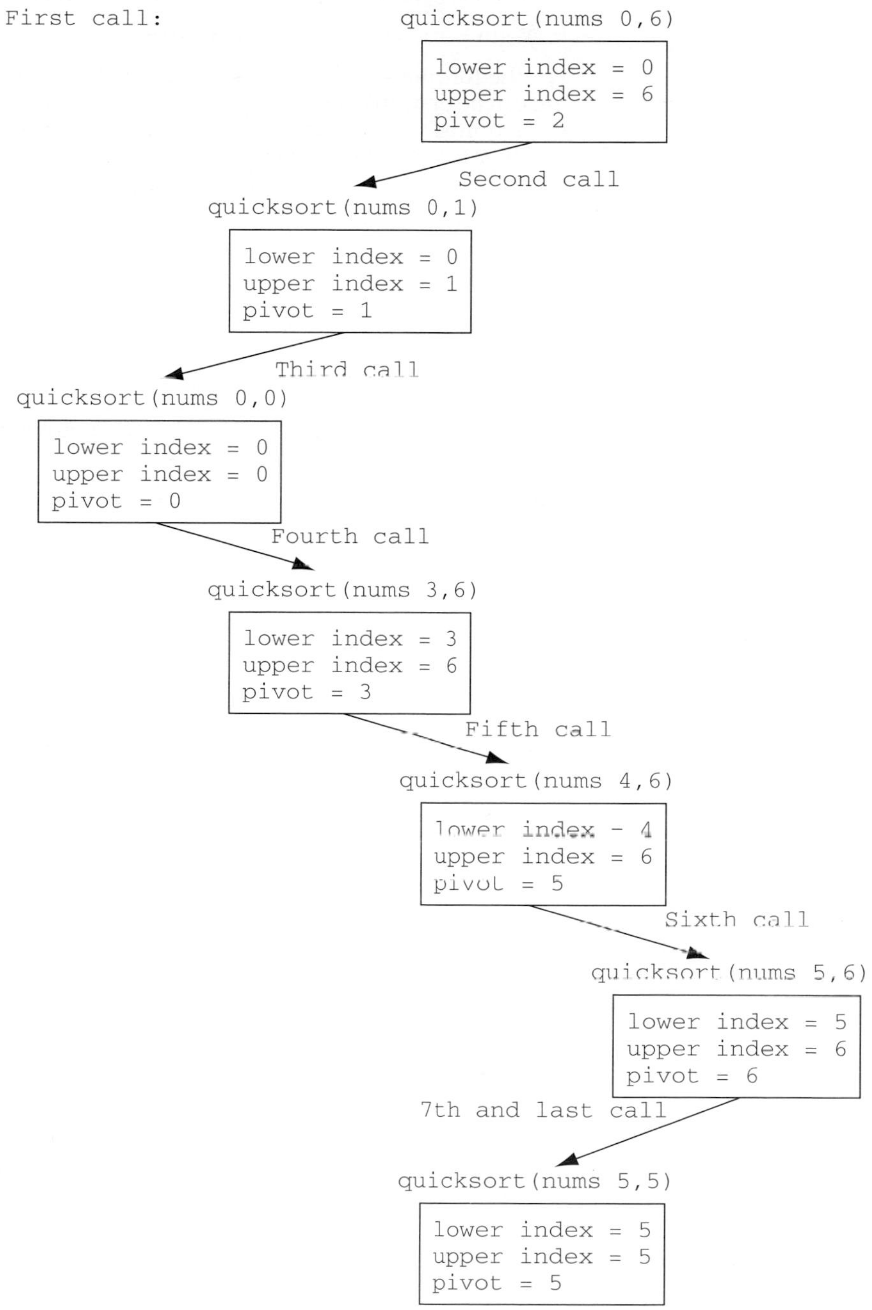

Exercise 12.8

1. a. Modify Program 12.17 to use a list of ten randomly generated numbers and determine the number of moves required to put the list in order using a selection sort. Display both the initial list and the reordered list.

   b. Redo Exercise 1a using a bubble sort.

2. For the functions `selectionSort()`, `bubbleSort()`, and `quicksort()`, the sorting can be done in decreasing order by a simple modification. In each case, identify the required changes and then rewrite each function to accept a flag indicating whether the sort should be in increasing or decreasing order. Modify each routine to receive and use this flag parameter correctly.

3. a. The selection and bubble sort both use the same technique for swapping list elements. Replace the code in these two functions that performs the swap by a call to a function named `swap`. The prototype for swap should be:

   ```
   void swap(int&, int&)
   swap()
   ```

   `swap()` itself should be constructed using the algorithm presented in Section 6.5.

   b. Describe why the quicksort function does not require the swapping algorithm used by the selection and bubble sorts.

4. An alternate form of the bubble sort is presented in the following program:

```cpp
#include <iostream>
using namespace std;
int main()
{
  const int TRUE = 1;
  const int FALSE = 0;

  int nums[10] = {22,5,67,98,45,32,101,99,73,10};
  int i, temp, moves, npts, outord;

  moves = 0;
  npts = 10;
  outord = TRUE;
  while (outord && npts > 0)
  {
    outord = FALSE;
    for ( i = 0; i < npts - 1; i++)
      if (nums[i] > nums[i+1])
      {
        temp = nums[i+1];
        nums[i+1] = nums[i];
        nums[i] = temp;
        outord = TRUE;
        moves++;
      }
    npts--;
  }
  cout << "The sorted list, in ascending order, is:\n";
  for (i = 0; i < 10; i++)
    cout << "   " << nums[i];
  cout << endl << moves
       << " moves were made to sort this list\n";
  return 0;
}
```

An advantage of this version of the bubble sort is that processing is terminated whenever a sorted list is encountered. In the best case, when the data are in sorted order to begin with, an exchange sort requires no moves (the same for the selection sort) and only $N - 1$ comparisons. (The selection sort always requires $N(N - 1)/2$ comparisons.)

After you have run this program to convince yourself that it correctly sorts a list of integers, rewrite the sort algorithm it contains as a function named `newBubble()` and test your function using the driver function contained in Program 12.15.

5. a. Modify Program 12.20 to use a larger test list consisting of 20 numbers.

   b. Modify Program 12.20 to use a list of 100 randomly selected numbers.

6. A company currently maintains two lists of part numbers, where each part number is an integer. Write a C++ program that compares these lists of numbers and displays the numbers, if any, that are common to both. (*Hint:* Sort each list prior to making the comparison.)

7. Redo Exercise 6, but display a list of part numbers that appear only on one list, but not both.

8. Rewrite the binary search algorithm to use recursion rather than iteration.

12.9 COMMON PROGRAMMING ERRORS

Four common errors are associated with using arrays:

1. Forgetting to declare the array. This error results in a compiler error message equivalent to "Invalid indirection" each time a subscripted variable is encountered within a program. The exact meaning of this error message will become clear in Chapter 13 when the correspondence between arrays and pointers is established.

2. Using a subscript that references a nonexistent array element. For example, declaring the array to be of size 20 and using a subscript value of 25. This error is not detected by most C++ compilers. However, it causes a run-time error that results either in a program crash or a value that has no relation to the intended element being accessed from memory. In either case, it is usually an extremely troublesome error to locate. The only solution to this problem is to make sure, either by specific programming statements or by careful coding, that each subscript references a valid array element. Using named constants for an array's size and for the maximum subscript value helps eliminate this problem.

3. Not using a large enough conditional value in a `for` loop counter to cycle through all the array elements. This error usually occurs when an array is initially specified to be of size n and there is a `for` loop within the program of the form `for (i = 0; i < n; i++)`. The array size is then expanded but the programmer forgets to change the interior `for` loop parameters. Declaring an array's size using a named constant and consistently using the named constant throughout the function in place of the variable n eliminates this problem.

4. Forgetting to initialize the array. Although many compilers automatically set all elements of integer and real valued arrays to zero and all elements of character arrays to blanks, it is up to the programmer to ensure that each array is correctly initialized before the processing of array elements begins.

12.10 CHAPTER REVIEW

Key Terms

Big O notation	one-dimensional array
binary search	quicksort
exchange (bubble) sort	selection sort
index	single-dimensional array
indexed variable	subscript
linear (sequential) search	subscripted variable
Null character (`'\0'`)	two-dimensional array

Summary

1. A single-dimensional array is a data structure that can be used to store a list of values of the same data type. Such arrays must be declared by giving the data type of the values that are stored in the array and the array size. For example, the declaration:

```
int num[100];
```

creates an array of 100 integers. A preferable approach is first to use a named constant for the array size and then use this constant in the definition of the array. For example

```
const int MAXSIZE = 100;
```

and

```
int num[MAXSIZE];
```

2. Array elements are stored in contiguous locations in memory and referenced using the array name and a subscript, for example, `num[22]`. Any nonnegative integer value expression can be used as a subscript and the subscript 0 always refers to the first element in an array.

3. A two-dimensional array is declared by listing both a row and a column size with the data type and name of the array. For example, the declarations

```
const int ROWS = 5;
const int COLS = 7;
int mat[ROWS][COLS];
```

create a two-dimensional array consisting of five rows and seven columns of integer values.

4. Two-dimensional arrays may be initialized when they are declared. This is accomplished by listing the initial values, in a row-by-row manner, within braces and separating them with commas. For example, the declaration

```
int vals[3][2] = { {1, 2},
                   {3, 4},
                   {5, 6} };
```

produces the following three-row by two-column array:

```
1 2
3 4
5 6
```

As C++ uses the convention that initialization proceeds in row-wise order, the inner braces can be omitted. Thus, an equivalent initialization is provided by the statement:

```
int vals[3][2] = {1, 2, 3, 4, 5, 6};
```

5. Arrays are passed to a function by passing the name of the array as an argument. The value actually passed is the address of the first array storage location. Thus,

the called function receives direct access to the original array and not a copy of the array elements. Within the called function, a parameter must be declared to receive the passed array name. The declaration of the parameter can omit the row size of the array.

6. The linear search is an O(N) search. It examines each item in a list until the searched item is found or until it is determined that the item is not in the list.

7. The binary search is an $O(\log_2 N)$ search. It requires that a list be in sorted order before it can be applied.

8. The selection and exchange sort algorithms require an order of magnitude of N^2 comparisons for sorting a list of N items.

9. The quicksort algorithm requires an order of magnitude of $N \log_2 N$ comparisons to sort a list of N items.

Exercises

1. a. Write a C++ program that reads a list of floating-point grades from the keyboard into an array named `grade`. The grades are to be counted as they are read, and entry is to be terminated when a negative value has been entered. Once all of the grades have been input, your program should find and display the sum and average of the grades. The grades should then be listed with an asterisk (*) placed in front of each grade that is below the average.

   b. Extend the program written for Exercise 1a to display each grade and its letter equivalent. Assume the following scale:

   A grade between 90 and 100 is an A.
   A grade greater than or equal to 80 and less than 90 is a B.
   A grade greater than or equal to 70 and less than 80 is a C.
   A grade greater than or equal to 60 and less than 70 is a D.
   A grade less than 60 is an F.

2. Define an array named `peopleTypes` that can store a maximum of 50 integer values that are entered at the keyboard. Enter a series of 1s, 2s, 3s, and 4s into the array, where 1 represents an infant, 2 represents a child, 3 represents a teenager, and 4 represents an adult that was present at a local school function. Any other integer value should not be accepted as valid input, and data entry should stop when a negative value has been entered.

   Your program should count the number of each 1, 2, 3, and 4 in the array and output a list of how many infants, children, teenagers, and adults were at the school function.

3. Given a one-dimensional array of integer numbers, write and test a function that prints the elements in reverse order.

4. Write and test a function that returns *the position* of the largest and smallest values in an array of floating-point numbers.

5. Read a set of numerical grades from the keyboard into an array. The maximum number of grades is 50, and data entry should be terminated when a negative number has been entered. Have your program sort and print the grades in *descending* order.

6. a. Define an array with a maximum of 20 integer values and either fill the array with numbers input from the keyboard or assigned by the program. Then write a function named `split()` that reads the array and places all zero or positive numbers into an array named `positive` and all negative numbers

into an array named `negative`. Finally, have your program call a function that displays the values in both the `positive` and `negative` arrays.

b. Extend the program written for Exercise 6a to sort the `positive` and `negative` arrays into ascending order before they are displayed.

7. Using the `srand()` and `rand()` C++ library functions, fill an array of 1000 floating-point numbers with random numbers that have been scaled to the range 1 to 100. Then determine and display the number of random numbers having values between 1 and 50 and the number having values greater than 50. What do you expect the output counts to be?

8. In many statistical analysis programs, data values that are considerably outside the range of the majority of values are simply dropped from consideration. Using this information, write a C++ program that accepts up to ten floating-point values from a user and determines and displays the average and standard deviation of the input values. All values that are more than four standard deviations away from the computed average are to be displayed and dropped from any further calculation, and a new average and standard deviation should be computed and displayed.

9. Given a one-dimensional array of floating-point numbers named `num`, write a function that determines the sum of the numbers:

    a. using repetition

    b. using recursion (*Hint:* If $n = 1$, then the sum is `num[0]`; otherwise, the sum is `num[n]` plus the sum of the first $n - 1$ elements.)

10. Your professor has asked you to write a C++ program that can be used to determine grades at the end of the semester. For each student, who is identified by an integer number between 1 and 60, four examination grades must be kept. Additionally, two final grade averages must be computed. The first grade average is simply the average of all four grades. The second grade average is computed by weighting the four grades as follows: the first grade gets a weight of 0.2, the second grade gets a weight of 0.3, the third grade a weight of 0.3, and the fourth grade a weight of 0.2; that is, the final grade is computed as:

```
0.2 * grade1 + 0.3 * grade2 + 0.3 * grade3 + 0.2 * grade4
```

Using this information, you are to construct a 60 × 6 two-dimensional array, in which the first column is used for the student number, the next four columns for the grades, and the last two columns for the computed final grades. The output of the program should be a display of the data in the completed array.

For test purposes, the professor has provided the following data:

Student	Grade 1	Grade 2	Grade 3	Grade 4
1	100	100	100	100
2	100	0	100	0
3	82	94	73	86
4	64	74	84	94
5	94	84	74	64

11. Modify the program written for Exercise 10 by adding an eighth column to the array. The grade in the eighth column should be calculated by computing the average of the top three grades only.

12. a. You are to create a two-dimensional list of integer part numbers and quantities of each part in stock and write a function that displays the data in the array in *decreasing* quantity order. Assume that no more than 100 different parts are being kept track of and test your program with the following data:

Part No.	Quantity
1001	62
949	85
1050	33
867	125
346	59
1025	105

b. Modify the function written in Exercise 12a to display the data in part number order.

13. Assume that the answers to a true–false test are as follows: T T F F T. Given a two-dimensional answer array where each row corresponds to the answers provided on one test, write a function that accepts the two-dimensional array and the number of tests as parameters, and returns a one-dimensional array containing the grades for each test. (Assume each question is worth 5 points so that the maximum possible grade is 25.) Test your function using the following data:

Test 1:	T	F	T	T	T
Test 2:	T	T	T	T	T
Test 3:	T	T	F	F	T
Test 4:	F	T	F	F	F
Test 5:	F	F	F	F	F
Test 6:	T	T	F	T	F

14. Modify the function that you wrote for Exercise 13 so that each test is stored in column order rather than row order.

15. Write a function that can be used to sort the elements of a 3 × 4 two-dimensional array of integers so that the lowest value is in element position [0][0], the next highest value in element position [0][1], and the highest value in element position [2][3].

16. A magic square is a square of numbers with N rows and N columns in which each of the integer values from 1 to ($N * N$) appears exactly once and the sum of each column, each row, and each diagonal is the same value. For example, Figure 12.30 shows a magic square in which $N = 3$ and the sum of the rows, columns, and diagonal is 15. Write a program that constructs and displays a magic square for any given odd number N. The algorithm is:

Insert the value 1 in the middle of the first row (element [0][N%2])
   After a value, x, has been placed, move up one row and to the right one column. Place the next number, x + 1, there, unless:
      (1) You move off the top (row = –1) in any column, then move to the bottom row and place the next number, x + 1, in the bottom row of that column
      (2) You move off the right end (column = N) of a row, then place the next number, x + 1, in the first column of that row
      (3) You move to a position that is already filled or out of the upper right corner, then place the next number, x + 1, immediately below x
   Stop when you have placed as many elements as there are in the array

17. Among other applications, Pascal's triangle (see Figure 12.31) provides a means of determining the number of possible combinations of n things taken r at a time. For example, the number of possible combinations of five people ($n = 5$) taken two at a time ($r = 2$) is 10.

Each row of the triangle begins and ends with 1. Every other element in a row is the sum of the element directly above it with the element to the left of the one above it. That is,

```
element[n][r] = element[n-1][r] + element[n-1][r-1]
```

Using this information, write and test a C++ program to create the first 11 rows of a two-dimensional array representing Pascal's triangle. For any given value of *n* less than 11 and *r* less than or equal to *n*, the program should display the appropriate element. Use your program to determine in how many ways a committee of eight can be selected from a group of ten people.

FIGURE 12.30 A Magic Square

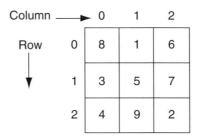

FIGURE 12.31 Pascal's Triangle

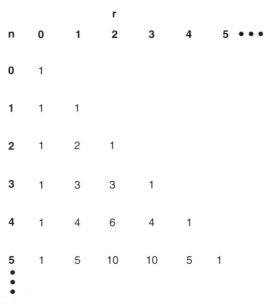

---

18. A three-dimensional weather array for the first two weeks of January 2005 uses the first index, which can have a value of 0 or 1, to represent the first and second week, respectively. The second index, numbered 0 through 6, represents the day. And the last index, which can be either 0 or 1, represents the day's high and low temperature, respectively.

Use this information to write a C++ program that either prompts for or assigns the high and low temperatures for each element of the arrays. Then allow the user to request:

- any day's high and low temperatures
- average high and low temperatures for a given month
- month and day with the highest temperature
- month and day with the lowest temperature

CHAPTER
13 | C-Strings

Each computer language has its own method of handling strings of characters. Some languages, such as C++, have an extremely rich set of string manipulation functions and capabilities. Other languages, such as FORTRAN, which is predominantly used for numerical calculations, added string handling capabilities with later versions of the compiler. Languages such as LISP, which are targeted for list handling applications, provide an exceptional string manipulation capability.

C++ has two different ways of storing and manipulating strings. The second, and newer way, using the `string` class was presented in Chapter 7. The original procedure for storing a string in C++, and the one described in this chapter, is as an array of characters that is terminated by a sentinel value, which is the escape sequence `'\0'`. This representation permits strings to be manipulated using standard element-by-element array-processing techniques. Strings stored in this manner are now referred to as character strings, or C-strings, for short. Additionally, a `cstring` class was introduced with the latest ANSI/ISO standard that provides a number of useful methods, such as inserting, deleting, and extracting characters from a C-string. This class is also presented in this chapter. Finally, the character-based methods previously presented in Chapter 7, which can also be used to process individual elements of C-strings, are summarized in this chapter.

13.1 C-STRING FUNDAMENTALS

A **string literal**, as described in section 2.1, is any sequence of characters enclosed in double quotes. A string literal is also referred to as a string value and more conventionally as a **string**. Examples of strings are `"This is a string"`, `"Hello World!"`, and `"xyz 123 *!#@&"`.

713

FIGURE 13.1 Storing a C-String in Memory

| G | o | o | d | | M | o | r | n | i | n | g | ! | \0 |

A C-string is stored as an array of characters terminated by a special end-of-string symbolic constant named NULL. The value assigned to the NULL constant is the escape sequence '\0' and is the sentinel that marks the end of every string. For example, Figure 13.1 illustrates how the string "Good Morning!" is stored in memory. The string uses 14 storage locations, with the last character in the string being the end-of-string marker \0. The double quotes surrounding the string literal are not stored as part of the string.

Because a C-string is stored as an array of characters, the individual characters in the array can be input, manipulated, or output using standard array-handling techniques. The end-of-string NULL character is useful for detecting the end of the string when handling strings in this fashion.

C-String Input and Output

Inputting a string from a keyboard and displaying a string requires using either a standard library function or class method. In addition to the standard input and output streams, cin and cout, Table 13.1 lists the commonly used library methods for both character-by-character and complete C-string input/output. These are contained in the iostream header file.

As listed in Table 13.1, in addition to the cout and cin streams, C++ provides the methods cin.getline(), cin.get(), and cin.peek() input (these are not the same as the methods defined for the string class having the same name). The character output functions, put() and putback(), however, are the same as those provided for the string class.

TABLE 13.1   String and Character I/O Functions (Requires the iostream Header File)

C++ Routine	Description	Example
cin.getline(str, n, ch)	C-string input from the keyboard	cin.getline(str, 81, '\n');
cin.get()	Character input from the keyboard	nextChar = cin.get();
cin.peek()	Returns the next character from the input stream without extracting it from the stream	nextKey = cin.peek();
cout.put(charExp)	Places the character on the output stream	cout.put('A');
cin.putback(charExp)	Pushes a character back onto the input stream	cin.putback(cKey);
cin.ignore(n, char)	Ignores a maximum of the next n input characters, up and including the detection of char; if no arguments are specified, ignores the next character on the input stream	cin.ignore(80,'\n'); cin.ignore();

> ## PROGRAMMING NOTE

Should You Use a `string` Class Object or a C-String?

The reasons for using a `string` class object are:

- The `string` class does an automatic bounds check on every index used to access string elements. This is not true for C-strings, and using an invalid C-string index can result in a system crash.
- The `string` class automatically expands and contracts storage as needed. C-strings are fixed in length and are subject to overrunning the allocated storage space.
- The `string` class provides a rich set of methods for operating on a string. C-strings almost always require a subsidiary set of functions.
- When necessary, It is easy to convert to a C-string using the `string` class's `c_str()` method. Conversely, a C-string can easily be converted to a `string` class object by assigning it to a `string` object.

The reasons for using a C-string are:

- The programmer has ultimate control over how the string is stored and manipulated.
- A large number of extremely useful functions exist to input, examine, and process C-strings.
- C-strings are an excellent way to explore advanced programming techniques using pointers (see Chapter 14).
- You will encounter them throughout your programming career, as they are embedded in almost all existing C++ code.
- They are fun to program.

Program 13.1 illustrates using `cin.getline()` and `cout` to input and output a string entered at the user's terminal.

PROGRAM 13.1

```cpp
#include <iostream>
using namespace std;

int main()
{
  const int MAXCHARS = 81;
  char message[MAXCHARS];  // an array of characters large
                           // enough storage for a complete line

  cout << "Enter a string:\n";

  cin.getline(message,MAXCHARS,'\n');

  cout << "The string just entered is:\n"
       << message << endl;

  cin.ignore();
  return 0;
}
```

PROGRAMMING NOTE

Initializing and Processing C-Strings

Each of the following declarations produce the same result:

```
char test[5] = "abcd";
char test[] = "abcd";
char test[5] = {'a', 'b', 'c', 'd', '\0'};
char test[] = {'a', 'b', 'c', 'd', '\0'};
```

Each declaration creates storage for exactly five characters and initialize this storage with the characters 'a', 'b', 'c', 'd', and '\0'. Since a string literal is used for initialization in the first two declarations, the compiler automatically supplies the end-of-string NULL character.

String variables declared in either of these ways shown preclude the use of any subsequent assignments, such as test = "efgh";, to the character array. In place of an assignment you can use the strcpy() function, such as strcpy(test, "efgh"). The only restriction on using strcpy() is the size of the declared array cannot be exceeded, which in this case is 5 elements. Attempting to copy a larger string value into test causes the copy to overflow the destination array beginning with the memory area immediately following the last array element. This overwrites whatever was in these memory locations and typically causes a runtime crash when the overwritten areas are accessed via their legitimate identifier name(s).

The same problem can arise when using the strcat() function. It is your responsibility to ensure that the concatenated string will fit into the original string.

An interesting situation arises when string variables are defined using pointers (see Programming Note in Section 12.2). In these situations assignments can be made after the declaration statement.

The following is a sample run of Program 13.1:

```
Enter a string:
This is a test input of a string of characters.
The string just entered is:
This is a test input of a string of characters.
```

The cin.getline() method used in Program 13.1 continuously accepts and stores characters typed at the terminal into the character array named message until either 80 characters are entered (the 81st character is then used to store the end-of-string NULL character, \0), or the ENTER key is detected. Pressing the ENTER key at the terminal generates a newline character, \n, which is interpreted by cin.getline() as the end-of-line entry. All the characters encountered by cin.getline(), except the newline character, are stored in the message array. Before returning, the cin.getline() function appends a NULL character, '\0', to the stored set of characters, as illustrated in Figure 13.2. The cout object is then used to display the C-string.

FIGURE 13.2   Inputting a C-string with cin.getline()

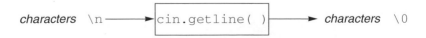

characters \n ⟶ cin.getline( ) ⟶ *characters* \0

cin.getline( ) substitutes \0 for the entered \n

Although the `cout` object is used in Program 13.1 for C-string output, `cin` could not be used in place of `cin.getline()` for C-string input. This is because the `cin` object reads a set of characters up to either a blank space or a newline character. The `cin.getline()` function has the syntax

```
cin.getline(str, terminatingLength, terminatingChar)
```

where *str* is a C-string or character pointer variable (presented in Chapter 14), *terminatingLength* is an integer constant or variable indicating the maximum number of input characters that can be input, and *terminatingChar* is an optional character constant or variable specifying the terminating character. If this optional third argument is omitted, the default terminating character is the newline (`'\n'`) character. Thus, the statement

```
cin.getline(message,MAXCHARS);
```

can be used in place of the longer statement:

```
cin.getline(message,MAXCHARS,'\n');
```

Both of these function calls stop reading characters when the ENTER key is pressed or until MAXCHARS characters have been read, whichever comes first. Since `cin.getline()` permits specification of any terminating character for the input stream, a statement such as `cin.getline(message,MAXCHARS,'x');` is also valid. This particular statement will stop accepting characters whenever the x key is pressed. In all future programs we will assume that input is terminated by the ENTER key, which generates a newline character. As such the optional third argument passed to `getline()`, which is the terminating character, will be omitted.

C-String Processing

C-strings can be manipulated using either standard library functions or standard array-processing techniques. The library functions typically available for use are presented in the next section. For now, we concentrate on processing a C-string in a character-by-character fashion. This allows us to understand how the standard library functions are constructed and to create our own library functions. For a specific example, consider the function `strcopy()`, which copies the contents of `string2` to `string1`.

```
// copy string2 to string 1
void strcopy(char string1[], char string2[])
{
  int i = 0;                       // i will be used as a subscript

  while (string2[i] != '\0')   // check for the end-of-string
  {
    string1[i] = string2[i];   // copy the element to string1
    i++;
  }
  string1[i] = '\0';               // terminate the first string

  return;
}
```

Although this C-string copy function can be shortened considerably and written more compactly, which is done later in this section, it does illustrate the main features of C-string manipulation. The two C-strings are passed to `strcopy()` as arrays. Each element of `string2` is then assigned to the equivalent element of string1 until the end-of-string marker is encountered. The detection of the Null character forces the termination of the while loop controlling the copying of elements. Because the Null character is not copied from string2 to string1, the last statement in strcopy() appends an end-of-string character to string1. Prior to calling strcopy(), the programmer must ensure that sufficient space has been allocated for the string1 array to store the elements of the string2 array. Program 13.2 includes the strcopy() function in a complete program. Notice that the function prototype for strcopy() declares that the function expects to receive two character arrays.

PROGRAM 13.2

```cpp
#include <iostream>
using namespace std;

void strcopy(char [], char []); // function prototype

int main()
{
  const int MAXCHARS = 81;
  char message[MAXCHARS];       // enough storage for a complete line
  char newMessage[MAXCHARS];   // enough storage for a copy of message
  int i;

  cout << "Enter a sentence: ";
  cin.getline(message,MAXCHARS);          // get the string
  strcopy(newMessage,message);    // pass two array addresses
  cout << "The copied string is:\n"
       << newMessage << endl;

  return 0;
}

void strcopy(char string1[], char string2[])    // copy string2 to string1
{
  int i = 0;                      // i will be used as a subscript

  while (string2[i] != '\0')     // check for the end-of-string
  {
    string1[i] = string2[i];     // copy the element to string1
    i++;
  }
  string1[i] = '\0';             // terminate the first string

  return;
}
```

The following is a sample run of Program 13.2:

```
Enter a sentence: How much wood could a woodchuck chuck.
The copied string is:
How much wood could a woodchuck chuck.
```

Detecting the End-of-String NULL Character   The NULL character that marks the end of each string is extremely important in user-created string processing functions. Frequently, however, it is effectively disguised by C++ programmers. This is because the numerical value of the NULL character is zero, which is considered false in relational expressions.

To understand how the NULL character is typically used by C++ programmers, reconsider the strcopy() function in Program 13.2. This function, which is repeated below for convenience, is used to copy the characters from one array to another array, one character at a time, until the end-of-string NULL character is detected.

```
void strcopy(char string1[], char string2[])    // copy string2 to string1
{
  int i = 0;

  while (string2[i] != '\0')    // check for the end-of-string
  {
    string1[i] = string2[i];    // copy the element to string1
    i++;
  }
  string1[i] = '\0';            // terminate the first string

  return;
}
```

As currently written, the subscript i in the strcopy() function is used successively to access each character in the array named string2 by "marching along" the string one character at a time. The while statement in strcopy() tests each character to ensure that the end of the string has not been reached. As with all relational expressions, the tested expression, string2[i] != '\0', is either true or false. Using the string this is a string illustrated in Figure 13.3 as an example, as long as string2[i] does not access the end-of-string character, the value of the expression is nonzero and is considered true. The expression is only false when the value of the expression is zero. This occurs when the last element in the string is accessed.

Recall that C++ defines false as zero and true as anything else. Thus, the expression string2[i] != '\0' becomes zero, or false, when the end of the string is reached. It is nonzero, or true, everywhere else. Because the NULL character has an internal value of zero by itself, the comparison to '\0' is not necessary. When string2[i] accesses the end-of-string character, the value of string2[i] is zero. When string2[i] accesses any other character, the value of string2[i] is the value of the code used to store the character and is nonzero. Figure 13.4 lists the ASCII codes for the C-string this is a string. As seen in the figure, each element has a nonzero value except for the NULL character.

Because expression string2[i] is only zero at the end of a string and nonzero for every other character, the expression while (string2[i] != '\0') can be replaced by the simpler expression while (string2[i]). Although this may appear confusing at first, the revised test expression is certainly more compact than the longer version. End-of-string tests are frequently written by professional C++ programmers in this shorter form, so it is worthwhile to become familiar with this expression. Including this expression in strcopy() results in the following version:

```
void strcopy(char string1[], char string2[])   // copy string2 to string1
{
  int i = 0;

  while (string2[i])
  {
    string1[i] = string2[i];    // copy the element to string1
    i++;
  }
  string1[i] = '\0';            // terminate the first string

  return;
}
```

FIGURE 13.3 The `while` Test Becomes False at the End of the String

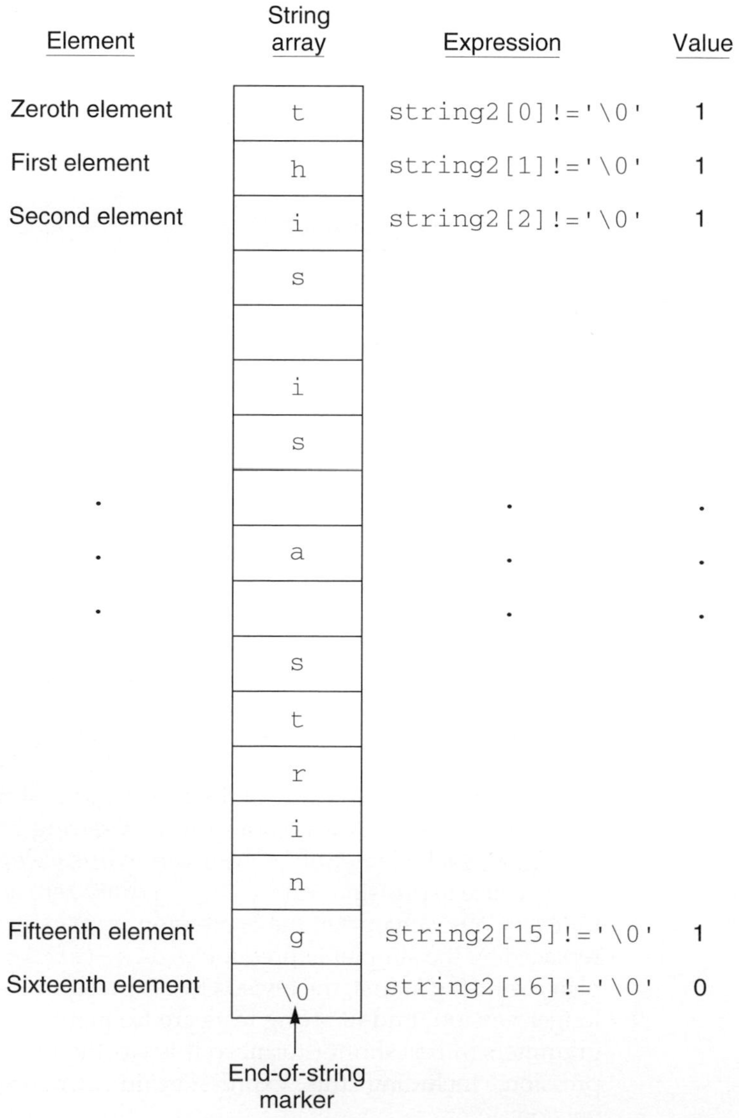

Element	String array	Expression	Value
Zeroth element	t	`string2[0]!='\0'`	1
First element	h	`string2[1]!='\0'`	1
Second element	i	`string2[2]!='\0'`	1
	s		
	i		
	s		
.		.	.
.	a	.	.
.		.	.
	s		
	t		
	r		
	i		
	n		
Fifteenth element	g	`string2[15]!='\0'`	1
Sixteenth element	\0	`string2[16]!='\0'`	0

End-of-string marker

FIGURE 13.4   **The ASCII Codes Used to Store** this is a string

String array	Stored codes	Expression	Value
t	116	string2[0]	116
h	104	string2[1]	104
i	105	string2[2]	105
s	115		
	32		
i	105		
s	115		
	32	.	.
a	97	.	.
	32	.	.
s	115		
t	116		
r	114		
i	105		
n	110		
g	103	string2[15]	103
\0	0	string2[16]	0

The second modification that would be made to this C-string copy function by an experienced C++ programmer is to include the assignment inside the test portion of the while statement. Our new version of the string copy function is:

```
void strcopy(char string1[], char string2[])    // copy string2 to string1
{
  int i = 0;

  while (string1[i] = string2[i])
    i++;

  return;
}
```

Notice that including the assignment statement within the test part of the while statement eliminates the necessity of separately terminating the copied string with the NULL character. The assignment within the parentheses ensures that the NULL character is copied from string2 to string1. The value of the assignment expression becomes zero only after the NULL character is assigned to string1, at which point the while loop is terminated.

Character-by-Character Input

Just as C-strings can be processed using character-by-character techniques, they can also be entered and displayed in this manner. For example, consider Program 13.3, which uses the character-input function cin.get() to accept a string one character at a time. The shaded portion of Program 13.3 essentially replaces the cin.getline() function previously used in Program 13.2.

PROGRAM 13.3

```cpp
#include <iostream>
using namespace std;

int main()
{
  const int MAXCHARS = 81;
  char message[MAXCHARS], c;

  cout << "Enter a sentence:\n";

  int i = 0;
  while(i < MAXCHARS && (c = cin.get()) != '\n')
  {
    message[i] = c;    // store the character
    i++;
  }
  message[i] = '\0';   // terminate the string

  cout << "\nThe sentence just entered is: "
       << message << endl;

  return 0;
}
```

The following is a sample run of Program 13.3:

```
Enter a sentence:
This is a test input of a string of characters.
The sentence just entered is:
This is a test input of a string of characters.
```

The while statement in Program 13.3 causes characters to be read provided the number of characters entered is less than MAXCHARS and the character returned by cin.get() is not the newline character. The parentheses surrounding the expression c = cin.get() are necessary to assign the character returned by cin.get() to the variable c prior to comparing it to the newline escape sequence. Without the surrounding parentheses, the comparison operator, !=, which takes precedence over the assignment operator, causes the entire expression to be equivalent to

$$c = (cin.get() != '\backslash n')$$

which is an invalid application of `cin.get()`.[1]

Program 13.3 also illustrates a very useful technique for developing functions. The shaded statements constitute a self-contained unit for entering a complete line of characters from a terminal. As such, these statements can be removed from `main()` and placed together as a new function. Program 13.4 illustrates placement of these statements in a separate function named `getaline()`.

PROGRAM 13.4

```
#include <iostream>
using namespace std;

const int MAXCHARS = 81;   // global constant used in both
                           // main() and getaline()

void getaline(char []);   // function prototype

int main()
{
  char message[MAXCHARS];   // enough storage for a complete line
  int i;

  cout << "Enter a sentence: ";
  getaline(message);
  cout << "\nThe sentence just entered is: "
  cout << message << endl;

  return 0;
}

void getaline(char strng[])
{
  int i = 0;
  char c;

  while(i < MAXCHARS && (c = cin.get()) != '\n')
  {
    strng[i] = c;          // store the character entered
    i++;
  }
  strng[i] = '\0';         // terminate the string

  return;
}
```

----

[1] The equivalent statement in C is `c = (getchar() != '\n')`, which is a valid expression that produces an unexpected result for most beginning programmers. Here, the character returned by `getchar()` is compared to `'\n'`, and the value of the comparison is either 0 or 1, depending on whether or not `getchar()` received the newline character. This value, either 0 or 1, is then assigned to `c`.

Exercises 13.1

1. a. The following function can be used to select and display all vowels contained within a user-input string:

```
void vowels(char strng[])
{
  int i = 0;
  char c;
  while ((c = strng[i++]) != '\0')
    switch(c)
    {
      case 'a':
      case 'e':
      case 'i':
      case 'o':
      case 'u':
          cout << c;
    } // end of switch
  cout << endl;
  return;
}
```

Notice that the `switch` statement in `vowels()` uses the fact that selected cases "drop through" in the absence of `break` statements. Thus, all selected cases are displayed by the single `cout` statement within the `switch` statement. Include `vowels()` in a working program that accepts a user-input string and then displays all vowels in the string. Your program should display `ouieiooo` in response to the input `How much is the little worth worth?`

   b. Modify the `vowels()` function to count and display the total number of vowels contained in the C-string passed to it.

2. Modify the `vowels()` function of Exercise 1 to count and display the individual numbers of each vowel contained in the C-string.

3. a. Write a C++ function to count the total number of characters, including blanks, contained in a C-string. Do not include the end-of-string marker in the count.

   b. Include the function written for Exercise 3a in a complete working program.

4. Write a program that accepts a string of characters from a terminal and displays the hexadecimal equivalent of each character.

5. Write a C++ program that accepts a string of characters from a terminal and displays the string one word per line.

6. Write a function that reverses the characters in a C-string. (*Hint:* This can be considered as a string copy starting from the back end of the first string.)

7. Write a function called `delChar()` that can be used to delete characters from a C-string. The function should accept three arguments: the C-string name, the number of characters to delete, and the starting position in the C-string where characters should be deleted. For example, the function call `delChar(strng,13,5)`, when applied to the string `all enthusiastic people`, should result in the string `all people`.

8. Write a function called `addChar()` to insert one C-string of characters into another C-string. The function should accept three arguments: the string to be inserted, the original string, and the position in the original string where the insertion should begin. For example, the call `addChar(" for all",message,6)` should insert the characters `for all` in `message` starting at `message[5]`.

9. a. Write a C++ function named `toUpper()` that converts lowercase letters into uppercase letters. The expression `c - 'a' + 'A'` can be used to make the conversion for any lowercase character stored in c.

   b. Add a data input check to the function written in Exercise 9a to verify that a valid lowercase letter is passed to the function. A character, in ASCII, is lowercase if it is greater than or equal to a and less than or equal to z. If the character is not a valid lowercase letter, have the function `toUpper()` return the passed character unaltered.

    c. Write a C++ program that accepts a string from a terminal and converts all low-ercase letters in the string to uppercase letters.

10. Write a C++ program that accepts a string from a terminal and converts all upper-case letters in the string to lowercase letters.

11. Write a C++ program that counts the number of words in a C-string. A word is encountered whenever a transition from a blank space to a nonblank character is encountered. Assume the string contains only words separated by blank spaces.

13.2 LIBRARY FUNCTIONS

C++ does not provide built-in operations for complete arrays, such as array assign-ments or array comparisons. Because a C-string is just an array of characters termi-nated with a `'\0'` character and not a data type in its own right, this means that as-signment and relational operations *are not* provided for strings. Extensive collections of C-string handling functions and routines, however, that effectively supply string assignment, comparison, and other very useful string operations are included as part of C++'s student library. The more commonly used routines are listed in Table 13.2.

TABLE 13.2   String Library Routines (Required Header File Is `cstring`)

Name	Description	Example
`strcpy(stringVar, stringExp)`	Copies `stringExp` to `stringVar`, including the `'\0'`.	`strcpy(test, "efgh")`
`strcat(stringVar, stringExp)`	Appends `strExp` to the end of the string value contained in `stringVar`.	`strcat(test, "there")`
`strlen(stringExp)`	Returns the length of the string. Does not include the `'\0'` in the length count.	`strlen("Hello World!")`
`strcmp(stringExp1, stringExp2)`	Compares `stringExp1` to `stringExp2`. Returns a negative integer if `stringExp1 <` `stringExp2`, 0 if `stringExp1 ==` `stringExp2`, and a positive integer if `stringExp1 >` `stringExp2`.	`strcmp("Bebop", "Beehive")`
`strncpy(stringVar, stringExp, n)`	Copies at most n characters of `stringExp` to `stringVar`. If `stringExp` has fewer than n char-acters it pads `stringVar` with `'\0'`s.	`strncpy(str1, str2, 5)`
`strncmp(stringExp1, stringExp2, n)`	Compares at most n characters of `stringExp1` to `stringExp2`. Returns the same values as `strcmp()` based on the number of characters compared.	`strncmp("Bebop", "Beehive", 2)`
`strchr(stringExp, character)`	Locates the position of the first occurrence of the character within the `stringExp`. Returns the address of the character.	`strchr("Hello", 'l')`
`strtok(stringExp, character)`	Parses `stringExp` into tokens. Returns the next sequence of characters contained in `stringExp` up to but not including the delimiter character ch.	`strtok("Hello there World!, ' ')`

String library functions are called in the same manner as all C++ functions. This means that the appropriate declarations for these functions, which are contained in the standard header files `<cstring>`, must be included in your program before the function is called.

The most commonly used functions listed in Table 13.2 are the first four. The `strcpy()` function copies a source C-string expression, which consists of either a string literal or the contents of a C-string variable, into a destination C-string variable. For example, in the function call `strcpy(string1, "Hello World!")`, the source string literal `"Hello World!"` is copied into the destination C-string variable `string1`. Similarly, if the source C-string is a C-string variable named `srcString`, the function call `strcpy(string1, srcString)` copies the contents of `srcString` into `string1`. In both cases, it is the programmer's responsibility to ensure that `string1` is large enough to contain the source C-string (see accompanying Programming Note).

The `strcat()` function appends a string expression onto the end of a C-string variable. For example, if the contents of a C-string variable named `destString` are `"Hello"`, then the function call `strcat(destString, " there World!")` results in the string value `"Hello there World!"` being assigned to `destString`. As with the `strcpy()` function, it is the programmer's responsibility to ensure that the destination C-string has been defined large enough to hold the additional concatenated characters.

The `strlen()` function returns the number of characters in its C-string argument but does not include the terminating NULL character in the count. For example, the value returned by the function call `strlen("Hello World!")` is 12.

Finally, two C-string expressions may be compared for equality using the `strcmp()` function. Each character in a C-string is stored in binary using either the ASCII or ANSI code. The first 128 characters of the extended 8-bit ANSI code are identical to the complete 128 character ASCII code. In both of them, a blank precedes (is less than) all letters and numbers, the letters of the alphabet are stored in order from A to Z, and the digits are stored in order from 0 to 9.

When two strings are compared, their individual characters are compared a pair at a time (both first characters, then both second characters, and so on). If no differences are found, the strings are equal; if a difference is found, the string with the first lower character is considered the smaller string. Thus,

`"Good Bye"` is less than `"Hello"` because the first `'G'` in `Good Bye` is less than the first `'H'` in `Hello`.

`"Hello"` is less than `"hello"` because the first `'H'` in `Hello` is less than the first `'h'` in `hello`.

`"Hello"` is less than `"Hello "` because the `'\0'` terminating the first string is less than the `' '` in the second string.

`"SMITH"` is greater than `"JONES"` because the first `'S'` in `SMITH` is greater than the first `'J'` in `JONES`.

`"123"` is greater than `"1227"` because the third character, `'3'`, in `123` is greater than the third character, `'2'`, in `1227`.

`"1237"` is greater than `"123"` because the fourth character, `'7'`, in `1237` is greater than the fourth character, `'\0'`, in `123`.

`"Behop"` is greater than `"Beehive"` because the third character, `'h'`, in `Behop` is greater than the third character, `'e'`, in `Beehive`.

Program 13.5 uses the C-string functions we have discussed within the context of a complete program.

PROGRAM 13.5

```cpp
#include <iostream>
#include <cstring>   // required for the cstring function library
using namespace std;

int main()
{
  const int MAXELS = 50;
  char string1[MAXELS] = "Hello";
  char string2[MAXELS] = "Hello there";
  int n;

  n = strcmp(string1, string2);

  if (n < 0)
    cout << string1 << " is less than " << string2 << endl;
  else if (n == 0)
    cout << string1 << " is equal to " << string2 << endl;
  else
    cout << string1 << " is greater than " << string2 << endl;

  cout << "\nThe length of string1 is " << strlen(string1)
       << " characters" << endl;
  cout << "The length of string2 is " << strlen(string2)
       << " characters" << endl;

  strcat(string1," there World!");

  cout << "\nAfter concatenation, string1 contains "
       << "the string value\n" << string1
       << "\nThe length of this string is "
       << strlen(string1) << " characters" << endl;

  cout << "\nType in a sequence of characters for string2: ";
  cin.getline(string2, MAXELS);

  strcpy(string1, string2);

  cout << "After copying string2 to string1, "
       << "the string value in string1 is:\n" << string2
       << "\nThe length of this string is "
       << strlen(string1) << " characters" << endl;

  cout << "\nThe starting address of the string1 string is: "
       << (void *) string1 << endl;

  return 0;
}
```

Sample output produced by Program 13.5 is:

```
Hello is less than Hello there

The length of string1 is 5 characters
The length of string2 is 11 characters

After concatenation, string1 contains the string value
Hello there World!
The length of this string is 18 characters

Type in a sequence of characters for string2: It's a wonderful day
After copying string2 to string1, the string value in string1 is:
It's a wonderful day
The length of this string is 20 characters

The starting address of the string1 string is: 0012FEA4
```

Except for the last displayed line, the output of Program 13.5 follows the discussion presented for the C-string library functions. As demonstrated by this output, the extraction operator << automatically dereferences a C-string variable and displays the contents in the variable. Sometimes, however, we really want to see the address of the C-string. As shown in Program 13.5, this can be done by casting the string variable name using the expression (void *). Another method is to send the expression &string1[0] to the cout object. This expression is read as "the *address* of the string[0] element," which is also the starting address of the complete character array.

Character Routines

In addition to string manipulation functions, the standard C++ library includes the character handling routines previously presented in Section 7.3 and summarized in Table 13.3. The prototypes for each of these routines are contained in the header file cctype, which should be included in any program that uses these routines.

All of the routines listed in Table 13.3 return a nonzero integer (that is, a true value) if the character meets the desired condition and a zero integer (that is, a false value) if the condition is not met; therefore, these functions can be used directly within an if statement. For example, consider the following code segment:

```
char ch;

ch = cin.get();  // get a character from the keyboard

if(isdigit(ch))
  cout < "The character just entered is a digit" << endl;
else if(ispunct(ch))
  cout << "The character just entered is a punctuation mark" << endl;
```

Notice that the character routine is included as a condition within the if statement because the function effectively returns either a true (nonzero) or false (zero) value.

Program 13.6 illustrates the use of the toupper() routine within the function ConvertToUpper(), which is used to convert all lowercase C-string characters into their uppercase form.

TABLE 13.3 Character Library Routines (Required Header File Is `cctype`)

Required Prototype	Description	Example
`int isalpha(char)`	Returns a nonzero number if the character is a letter; otherwise, it returns zero	`isalpha('a')`
`int isupper(char)`	Returns a nonzero number if the character is uppercase; otherwise, it returns zero	`isupper('a')`
`int islower(char)`	Returns a nonzero number if the character is lowercase; otherwise, it returns zero	`islower('a')`
`int isdigit(character)`	Returns a nonzero number if the character is a digit (0 through 9); otherwise, it returns zero	`isdigit('a')`
`int isascii(character)`	Returns a nonzero number if the character is an ASCII character; otherwise, it returns zero	`isascii('a')`
`int isspace(character)`	Returns a nonzero number if the character is a space; otherwise, it returns zero	`isspace(' ')`
`int isprint(character)`	Returns a nonzero number if the character is a printable character; otherwise, it returns zero	`isprint('a')`
`int iscntrl(character)`	Returns a nonzero number if the character is a control character; otherwise, it returns zero	`iscntrl('a')`
`int ispunct(character)`	Returns a nonzero number if the character is a punctuation character; otherwise, it returns zero	`ispunct('!')`
`int toupper(char)`	Returns the uppercase equivalent if the character is lowercase; otherwise, it returns the character unchanged	`toupper('a')`
`int tolower(char)`	Returns the lowercase equivalent if the character is uppercase; otherwise, it returns the character unchanged	`tolower('A')`

PROGRAM 13.6

```
#include <iostream>
#include <cctype>      // required for the character function library
using namespace std;

void ConvertToUpper(char []);

int main()
{
  const int MAXCHARS = 100;
  char message[MAXCHARS];

  cout << "\nType in any sequence of characters: ";
  cin.getline(message,MAXCHARS);

  ConvertToUpper(message);

  cout << "The characters just entered, in uppercase are: "
       << message << endl;

  return 0;
}
```

(continued on next page)

(continued from previous page)

```
// this function converts all lowercase characters to uppercase
void ConvertToUpper(char message[])
{
  for(int i = 0; message[i] != '\0'; i++)
    message[i] = toupper(message[i]);

  return;
}
```

The output produced by Program 13.6:

```
Type in any sequence of characters: this is a test OF 12345.
The characters just entered, in uppercase are: THIS IS A TEST OF 12345.
```

Notice that the `toupper()` library function only converts lowercase letters and that all other characters are unaffected.

Conversion Routines

The last group of standard C-string library routines, listed in Table 13.4, is used to convert C-strings to and from integer and double-precision data types. The prototypes for each of these routines are contained in the header file `cstdlib`, which should be included in any program that uses these routines.

TABLE 13.4   String Conversion Routines (Required Header File Is `cstdlib`)

Prototype	Description	Example
`int atoi(string-exp)`	Converts an ASCII string to an integer. Conversion stops at the first noninteger character.	`atoi("1234")`
`double atof(string-exp)`	Converts an ASCII string to a double-precision number. Conversion stops at the first character that cannot be interpreted as a double.	`atof("12.34")`
`char[] itoa(string-esp)`	Converts an integer to an ASCII string. The space allocated for the returned string must be large enough for the converted value.	`itoa(1234)`

Program 13.7 illustrates the use of the `atoi()` and `atof()` functions. The output produced by Program 13.7 is:

```
The string "1234" as an integer number is: 1234
This number divided by 3 is: 411
The string "1234.96" as a double number is: 1234.96
This number divided by 3 is: 411.653
```

As this output illustrates, once a string has been converted to either an integer or double-precision value, mathematical operations on the numerical value are valid.

PROGRAM 13.7

```cpp
#include <iostream>
#include <cstring>
#include <cstdlib>    // required for string conversion function library
using namespace std;

int main()
{
  const int MAXELS = 20;
  char string[MAXELS] = "1234";
  int num;
  double dnum;

  num = atoi(string);

  cout << "The string \"" << string << "\" as an integer number is: "
       << num;
  cout << "\nThis number divided by 3 is: " << num / 3 << endl;

  strcat(string, ".96");

  dnum = atof(string);

  cout << "The string \"" << string << "\" as a double number is: "
       << dnum;
  cout << "\nThis number divided by 3 is: " << dnum / 3 << endl;

  return 0;
}
```

Exercises 13.2

1. Enter and execute Program 13.5 on your computer.

2. Enter and execute Program 13.6 on your computer.

3. Enter and execute Program 13.7 on your computer.

4. Write the following declaration statement in three additional ways:

   ```cpp
   char string[] = "Hello World";
   ```

5. a. Write a function named length() that returns the length of a C-string without using any standard library functions.

   b. Write a simple main() function to test the length() function written for Exercise 5a.

6. a. Write a function named compare() that compares two C-strings and returns an integer value of:

      −1 if the first string is less than the second string.
       0 if the two strings are equal.
       1 if the first string is greater than the second string.

      Do not use any standard library functions in the compare() function.

   b. Write a simple main() function to test the compare() function written for Exercise 6a.

7. a. Write a C++ function named ctype() that determines the ASCII type of any integer in the range 0 to 127. If the number represents a printable ASCII character, print the character with one of the following appropriate messages:

```
The ASCII character is a lowercase letter.
The ASCII character is an uppercase letter.
The ASCII character is a digit.
The ASCII character is a punctuation mark.
The ASCII character is a space.
```

If the ASCII character is a nonprintable character, display its ASCII code in decimal format and the message, The ASCII character is a nonprintable character.

b. Write a simple main() function to test the function written for Exercise 7a. The main() function should generate 20 random numbers in the range 0 to 127 and call ctype() for each generated number.

8. a. Include the C-string library functions strlen(), strcat(), and strncat() within a function having the prototype int concat(char string1[], char string2[], int maxlength). The concat() function should perform a complete concatenation of string2 to string1 only if the length of the concatenated C-string does not exceed maxlength, which is the maximum length defined for string1. If the concatenated string exceeds maxlength, concatenate only the characters in string2 so that the maximum combined string length is equal to maxlength - 1, which provides enough room for the end-of-string NULL character.

b. Write a simple main() function to test the concat() function written for Exercise 8a.

9. a. Write a function named countlets() that returns the number of letters in an entered string. Digits, spaces, punctuation, tabs, and newline characters should not be included in the returned count.

b. Write a simple main() function to test the countlets() function written for Exercise 9a.

13.3 FOCUS ON PROBLEM SOLVING

In this section, we focus on constructing two string processing functions. The first function will be used to count the number of characters in a string. The purpose of this problem is to reinforce our concept of a C++ string and how characters can be accessed one at a time. The second function will be used to count words. Although this seems a simple problem at first glance, it is more typical in that it brings up a set of issues that must be addressed before a final algorithm can be selected. Chief among these issues is coming up with suitable criteria for what constitutes a word. This is necessary so that the function can correctly identify and count a word when it encounters one.

Problem 1: Character Counting

In this problem, we want to pass a string to a function and have the function return the number of characters in the string. For our current purposes, any character in the string, whether it is a blank, printable, or nonprintable character, is counted. The end-of-string null is not included in the final count. Although this problem can be solved using the strlen() function, we want a user-written version both to illustrate how such functions are constructed and for further modification in Problem 2.

Analyze the Problem   This problem is rather straightforward in its I/O requirements: The input to the function is a string and the output returned by the function is the number of characters in the string. Since a string in C++ is simply an array of characters, we can pass the string to our function by passing the character array. Because the function is to return an integer value, the number of characters in the string, we define it as returning an `int`.

Develop a Solution   Once the function receives the string, it must start at the beginning of the string and count each character it encounters as it "marches along" to the end of the string. Because each C++ string is terminated by a `'\0'` character, we can use this as a sentinel to tell us when the count should stop. As illustrated in Figure 13.5, we examine each character by indexing through the array until the sentinel is reached.

FIGURE 13.5	Counting Characters in a String

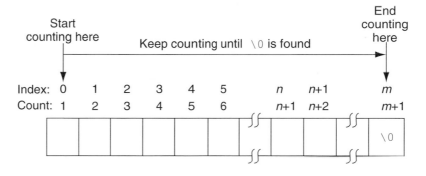

The pseudocode describing our character counting algorithm is:

Accept the string as an array parameter
Initialize a count to 0
For all the characters in the array,
   Increment the count
EndFor
Return the count

Code the Solution   The C++ code corresponding to our pseudocode solution is:

```cpp
int countchar(char list[])
{
    int i, count = 0;

    for(i = 0; list[i] != '\0'; i++)
        count++;

    return(count);
}
```

Notice that we have used a `for` loop within `countchar()`. We could just as easily replace this with a `while` loop.

Test and Correct the Program   To test the function, we create a main driver function whose sole purpose is to exercise `countchar()`. Program 13.8 includes both the `main()` driver and `countchar()`.

PROGRAM 13.8

```cpp
#include <iostream>
using namespace std;

int countchar(char []);   // function prototype

int main()
{
  const int MAXNUM = 1000;
  char message[MAXNUM];
  int numchar;

  cout << "\nType in any number of characters: ";

  cin.getline(message,MAXNUM);
  numchar = countchar(message);
  cout << "The number of characters just entered is "
       << numchar << endl;

  return 0;
}

int countchar(char list[])
{
  int i, count = 0;

  for(i = 0; list[i] != '\0'; i++)
    count++;

  return count;
}
```

A sample run using Program 13.8 is:

```
Type in any number of characters: This is a test of character counts
The number of characters just entered is 34
```

Problem 2: Word Counting

This problem is more complicated than the previous problem because we must first determine the criteria for identifying a word. At first glance, since each word is followed by a blank space, we might be tempted simply to count spaces. For example, consider the situation pictured in Figure 13.6. The problem with this approach is that the last word does not have a trailing blank. Even more troublesome are the cases where more than one blank is used between words and leading blanks are used before the first word. We have to keep these situations in mind when we develop a solution for counting words.

FIGURE 13.6   A Sample Line of Words

| t | h | i | s | | i | s | | t | h | e | | t | y | p | i | c | a | l | | c | a | s | e |

Analyze the Problem   From an I/O standpoint, this problem is straightforward: The input to the function is a string and the output returned by the function is the number of words in the string. Since a string in C++ is simply an array of characters, we can pass the string to our function by passing the character array. Because the function is to return an integer value, the number of words in the string, we define it as returning an `int`.

Develop a Solution   As we have seen in Figure 13.6, we must come up with an algorithm for determining when to increment our word counter; that is, we must algorithmically define what constitutes a word. Counting spaces does not work without a modification that accounts for extra blanks. An alternative is to increment a counter only when the first character of a word is detected. This approach has the advantages of a positive test for a word and is the approach we take.

Once this first character is found, we can set a flag indicating that we are in a word. This flag can stay on until we come out of a word, which is signified by detecting a blank space. At this point, we set the flag to not-in-a-word. The not-in-a-word condition remains true until a nonblank character is again detected. A pseudocode description of this algorithm is:

Set an inword flag to false
Set the word count to 0
For all the characters in the array,
   If the current character is a blank,
    Set inword to false
   Else if (inword equals false),
    Set inword to true
    Increment the word count
   EndIf
EndFor
Return the count

The key to this algorithm is the `if-else` condition. If the current character is a blank, the inword flag is set to NO, *regardless* of what it was on the previous character. The else condition is only executed if the current character is not a blank and checks if we are not in a word. In this case (current character not a blank and we are not in a word), we must be making the transition from a blank to a nonblank character. Because this is the criterion for determining that we are in a word, the inword flag is set to YES and the word count is incremented.

Code the Solution   The C++ code corresponding to our solution is:

```
int countword(char list[])
{
  bool inaword;
  int i, count = 0;

  inaword = false;
  for(i = 0; list[i] != '\0'; i++)
  {
    if (list[i] == ' ')
      inaword = false;
```

(continued from previous page)

```
          else if (inaword == false)
          {
            inaword = true;
            count++;
          }
        }
      return(count);
    }
```

Test and Correct the Problem   To test the function, we create a `main()` driver function whose sole purpose is to exercise `countword()`. Program 13.9 includes both the `main()` driver and `countword()`.

PROGRAM 13.9

```
include <iostream>
using namespace std;

int countword(char []);   // function prototype

int main()
{
  const int MAXNUM = 1000;
  char message[MAXNUM];
  int numword;

  cout << "\nType in any number of words: ";

  cin.getline(message,MAXNUM);

  numword = countword(message);

  cout << "The number of words just entered is "
       << numword << endl;

  return 0;
}

int countword(char list[])
{
  bool inaword;
  int i, count = 0;

  inaword = false;
  for(i = 0; list[i] != '\0'; i++)
  {
    if (list[i] == ' ')
      inaword = false;
```

(continued from previous page)

```
      else if (inaword == false)
      {
         inaword = true;
         count++;
      }
   }

   return count;
}
```

A sample run using Program 13.9 is:

```
Type in any number of words: This is a test line with a bunch of words
The number of words just entered is 10
```

Further tests that should be performed using Program 13.9 are:

- Enter words with multiple spaces between them.
- Enter words with leading spaces before the first word.
- Enter words with trailing spaces after the last word.
- Enter a sentence that ends in a period or question mark.

Exercises 13.3

1. Modify the countchar() function in Program 13.8 to omit blank spaces from the count.

2. Create a function named cvowels() that counts and returns the number of vowels in a passed string.

3. Modify the countword() function in Program 13.9 so that it counts both characters and words. (*Hint:* Refer to Section 6.5 for how to return multiple values.)

4. Modify the countword() function in Program 13.9 to indirectly return the number of words and characters entered, excluding blank spaces, and to directly return the average number of characters per word.

5. Write a function to count the number of lines entered.

6. Write a function to count the number of sentences entered; assume a sentence ends in either a period, question mark, or exclamation point.

7. Modify the function written for Exercise 6 to count the number of words as well as the number of sentences. The function should return the average words per sentence.

8. The Fog index is an index used by editors to grade the reading level difficulty of an article and is described in detail in the boxed article on the next page.[2]

   For this exercise, obtain samples of at least ten sentences from any four textbooks you are currently using. For each of these samples, manually determine the number of words and big words (these are defined in the accompanying boxed article) contained in the sample. Then write a C++ function to accept the sentences, calculate a Fog index, and return it. Check the value returned by your function against your hand calculations.

---

[2] The *NLA News*, Vol. 7, No. 9, May 1991. Permission to reproduce this article was kindly granted by Dr. John Truxal, codirector of the New Liberal Arts Program of the Alfred P. Sloan Foundation.

Editors worry about the reading level of their publications. For example, the *Wall Street Journal* aims for a Fog index of 11, the *New York Times* about 15, and the *New York Daily News* 9. The Fog index is a formula generally used to find an approximate reading grade level by measuring the sentence length and the fraction of words with three or more syllables. While reading difficulty is critically dependent on concepts and the presentation, neither factor enters the Fog index.

We looked at one recent issue of *NLA News* and worked out the Fog index for several articles:

Quantitative methods:	10
Museum staff member:	12
Political scientist:	18
Sociologist:	19

In other words, the last sample is read easily by someone reading at grade 19 level (roughly the doctorate).

To find the Fog index, pick a sample of at least 100 words. Omit all proper names, and then:

1. Count the number of sentences. Clauses separated by colons or semicolons are treated as separate sentences.
2. Count the number of "Big Words"—words of three or more syllables. Do not include words that reach three syllables because of "es" or "ed" endings, or because they are compounds of simple words, such as everything or seventeen.
3. Substitute into this formula:

$$\text{Fog index} = 0.4 \left[\frac{\text{number of words}}{\text{number of sentences}} + 100 \, \frac{\text{number of big words}}{\text{number of words}} \right]$$

As an example, we look at the first three paragraphs of this article. After we leave out numbers and proper names, we have the sample shown in the following shaded region. There are 102 words, 6 sentences, and 19 big words (italicized in the following box).

Editors worry about the reading level of their *publications*. For example, the *Wall Street Journal* aims for a Fog index of 11, the *New York Times* about 15, and the *New York Daily News 9*. The Fog index is a *formula generally* used to find an *approximate* reading grade level by measuring the sentence length and the fraction of words with three or more *syllables*. While reading *difficulty* is *critically dependent* on concepts and the *presentation,* neither factor enters the Fog index.

We looked at one recent issue of *NLA News* and worked out the Fog index for *several articles*:

Quantitative methods:	10
Museum staff member:	12
Political scientist:	18
Sociologist:	19

In other words, the last sample is read *easily* by someone reading at grade 19 level (roughly the *doctorate*).

For this case the formula gives

$$0.4 * (102/6 + 100 * 19/102) = 14$$

The reading level is grade 14 (college sophomore).

In applying the Fog index to an "I Can Read It All By Myself" book, we find an index of 2—second grade reading level.

13.4 COMMON PROGRAMMING ERRORS

The common errors associated with defining and processing strings are:

1. Not providing sufficient space for the C-string to be stored. A simple variation of this is not providing space for the end-of-C-string NULL character when a string is defined as an array of characters.

2. Not including the ' \0 ' terminating character when an array is initialized character by character. For example, the definition

```
char string[] = {'H', 'e', 'l', 'l', 'o'};
```

does not create a valid C-string because a terminating NULL character, '\0', is not included in the initialization.

3. Not realizing that the strcmp() function returns a value of 0, which is equivalent to false, when the strings being compared are equal. Thus, the condition !stcmp(string1, string2) should be used to determine if the strings are equal.

13.5 CHAPTER REVIEW

Key Terms

cin.get()	strcpy()
cin.getline()	string
isalpha()	strlen()
isdigit()	tolower()
NULL	toupper()
strcat()	

Summary

1. A C-string is an array of characters that is terminated by the NULL character.

2. C-strings can always be processed using standard array-processing techniques. The input and display of a C-string, however, always require reliance on a standard library function.

3. The cin object and the cin.get() and cin.getline() methods can be used to input a C-string. The cin object tends to be of limited usefulness for C-string input because it terminates input when a blank is encountered.

4. The cout object can be used to display C-strings.

5. Many standard library functions exist for processing C-strings as a complete unit. Internally, these functions manipulate C-strings in a character-by-character manner.

6. Character arrays can be initialized using string assignment of the form:

```
char arrayName[ ] = "text";
```

This initialization is equivalent to:

```
char arrayName[ ] = {'t','e','x','t','\0'};
```

Exercises

1. Determine the value of `text[0]`, `text[3]`, and `text[10]`, assuming that `text` is an array of characters and the following have been stored in the array:

    a. now is the time

    b. rocky raccoon welcomes you

    c. Happy Holidays

    d. The good ship

2. Write a function named `remove()` that returns nothing and deletes all occurrences of a specific character from a C-string. The function should use two parameters: the C-string name and the character to be removed. For example, if `message` contains the string `"Happy Holidays"`, the function call `remove(message, 'H')` should place the string `"appy  olidays"` into `message`.

3. Write a function that adds a single character at the end of an existing C-string. The function should replace the existing `'\0'` character with the new character and append a new `'\0'` at the end of the C-string. The function returns nothing.

4. Write a function that deletes a single character from the end of a C-string. This is effectively achieved by moving the `'\0'` character one position closer to the start of the string. The function returns nothing.

5. Write a function named `trimfrnt()` that deletes all leading blanks from a C-string.

6. Write a function named `trimrear()` that deletes all trailing blanks from a C-string.

7. Write a function named `addchars()` that adds n occurrences of a character to a C-string. For example, the call `addchars(message, 4, '!")` should add four exclamation points at the end of `message`.

8. Write a function named `extract()` that accepts two C-strings, s1 and s2, and two integer numbers, n1 and n2, as arguments. The function should extract n2 characters from s2, starting at position n1, and place the extracted characters into s1. For example, if C-string s1 contains the characters `05/18/06 D169254 Rotech Systems`, the function call `extract(s1, s2, 18, 6)` should create the string `Rotech` in s2. Note that the starting position for counting purposes is in position one. Be sure to close off the returned C-string with `'\0'` and make sure that string s1 is defined in the calling function to be large enough to accept the extracted values.

9. Given a one-dimensional array of characters, write and test a function that prints the elements in reverse order.

10. Write and test a function that uses an array of characters and returns the position of the first occurrence of a user-specified letter in the array or −1 if the letter does not occur.

11. A word or phrase in which the letters spell the same message (with changes in the white space permitted and punctuation not considered) when written both forward and backward is a palindrome. For example, Madam I'm Adam and A man, a plan, a canal: Panama! are both palindromes. Write a C++ program that accepts a line of text as a C-string and examines the entered text to determine if it is a palindrome. If it is, display the message `This is a palindrome`. If a palindrome was not entered, the message `This is not a palindrome` should be displayed.

12. Write a C++ program that first initializes a two-dimensional array defined as `list[5][30]` with the following five strings:

```
"04/12/07 74444 Bill Barnes"
"12/28/06 75255 Harriet Smith"
"10/17/05 74477 Joan Casey"
"02/18/06 74470 Deane Fraser"
"06/15/07 75155 Jan Smiley"
```

Your program should include a function named `printit()` that displays each string in the array. (*Hint:* `&list[i][0]` is the address of the *i*th string in the array.)

14 Addresses, Pointers, and Arrays

High-level languages all provide a feature called *pointers,* which permit the construction of dynamically linked lists (see Section 15.4). One of C++'s advantages is that it also allows the programmer to access the addresses of variables directly and manipulate them using pointer arithmetic; that is, addresses can be added, subtracted, and compared. This feature is not provided by other high-level languages.

   This chapter presents the basics of declaring pointer variables to store addresses. Additionally, methods of using pointer variables to access and use their stored addresses in meaningful ways are presented.

14.1 ADDRESSES AND POINTERS

As we saw in Section 2.4, to display the address of a variable, we can use C++'s **address operator,** &, which means "the address of." When used in a nondeclarative statement, the address operator placed in front of a variable's name refers to the address of the variable.[1] For example, in a nondeclarative statement, &num means *the address of* num, &miles means *the address of* miles, and &foo means *the address of* foo. Program 14.1, which is a copy of Program 2.9, uses the address operator to display the address of the variable num.

---

[1]As we saw in Chapter 6, when used in declaring a reference parameter, the ampersand, &, refers to the data type *preceding* it. Thus, both the declarations double& num and double # are read as "num is the address of a double" or, more commonly, as "num is a reference to a double."

742

PROGRAM 14.1

```cpp
#include <iostream>
using namespace std;

int main()
{
  int num;

  num = 22;
  cout << "num = " << num << endl;
  cout << "The address of num = " << &num << endl;

  return 0;
}
```

The output of Program 14.1 is:

```
num = 22
The address of num = 0012FED4
```

Figure 14.1 illustrates both the contents and address of the num variable provided by the output of Program 14.1.

As was mentioned in Section 2.4, address information changes depending on what computer is executing the program and how many other programs are currently loaded into memory.

FIGURE 14.1 A More Complete Picture of the Variable num

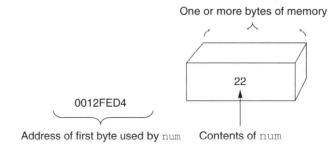

Storing Addresses

Besides displaying the address of a variable, as was done in Program 14.1, we can also store addresses in suitably declared variables. For example, the statement

```
numAddr = &num;
```

stores the address corresponding to the variable num in the variable numAddr, as illustrated in Figure 14.2. Similarly, the statements

```
d = &m;
tabPoint = &list;
chrPoint = &ch;
```

store the addresses of the variables m, list, and ch in the variables d, tabPoint, and chrPoint, respectively, as illustrated in Figure 14.3. The variables numAddr, d, tabPoint, and chrPoint are formally called **pointer variables,** or *pointers* for short. **Pointers** are simply variables that are used to store the addresses of other variables.

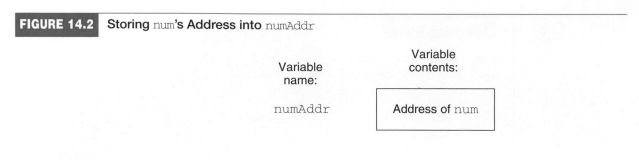

FIGURE 14.2 Storing num's Address into numAddr

Variable
name:

Variable
contents:

numAddr

Address of num

FIGURE 14.3 Storing More Addresses

Variable:

Contents:

d

Address of m

tabPoint

Address of list

chrPoint

Address of ch

Using Addresses

To use a stored address, C++ provides us with an **indirection operator**, *. The
* symbol, when followed by a pointer (with a space permitted both before and after the *), means *the variable whose address is stored in.* Thus, if numAddr is a pointer
(remember that a pointer is a variable that stores an address), *numAddr means *the
variable whose address is stored in* numAddr. Similarly, *tabPoint means *the variable
whose address is stored in* tabPoint, and *chrPoint means *the variable whose address is stored in* chrPoint. Figure 14.4 shows the relationship between the address
contained in a pointer variable and the variable ultimately addressed.

Although *d literally means *the variable whose address is stored in* d, this is commonly shortened to the statement *the variable pointed to by* d. Similarly, referring to
Figure 14.4, *y can be read as *the variable pointed to by* y. The value ultimately
obtained, as shown in Figure 14.4, is qqqq.

When using a pointer variable, the value that is finally obtained is always
found by first going to the pointer variable (or pointer, for short) for an address.
The address contained in the pointer is then used to get the desired contents. Certainly, this is a rather indirect way of getting to the final value, and not unexpectedly, the term **indirect addressing** is used to describe this procedure.

Because the use of a pointer requires the computer to do a double lookup (first
the address is retrieved and then the address is used to retrieve the actual data), a
worthwhile question is: Why bother to store an address in the first place and not just
use variables directly, as we have done throughout the text? The answer to this
question rests on the intimate relationship between pointers and arrays and the ability of pointers to create and delete new variable storage locations dynamically while
a program is running. Both of these topics are presented later in this chapter. For
now, however, given that each variable has a memory address associated with it, the
idea of storing an address should not seem overly strange.

FIGURE 14.4 Using a Pointer Variable

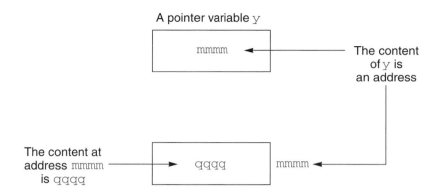

Declaring Pointers

Like all variables, pointers must be declared before they can be used to store an address. When we declare a pointer variable, C++ requires that we also specify the type of variable that is pointed to. For example, if the address in the pointer `numAddr` is the address of an integer, the correct declaration for the pointer is:

```
int *numAddr;
```

This declaration is read as *the variable pointed to by* `numAddr` (from the `*numAddr` in the declaration) *is an integer.*[2]

Notice that the declaration `int *numAddr;` specifies two things: first, that the variable pointed to by `numAddr` is an integer and second, that `numAddr` must be a pointer (because it is used with the indirection operator `*`). Similarly, if the pointer `tabPoint` points to (contains the address of) a floating-point number and `chrPoint` points to a character variable, the required declarations for these pointers are, respectively:

```
double *tabPoint;
char *chrPoint;
```

These two declarations can be read, respectively, as *the variable pointed to by* `tabPoint` *is a double* and *the variable pointed to by* `chrPoint` *is a char.* Consider Program 14.2.

---

[2] Pointer declarations may also be written in the form `dataType* pointerName;` where a space is placed between the indirection operator symbol and the pointer variable name. This form, however, becomes error prone when multiple pointer variables are declared in the same declaration statement and the asterisk is inadvertently omitted after the first pointer name is declared. For example, the declaration `int* num1, num2;` declares `num1` as a pointer variable and `num2` as an integer variable. To more easily accommodate multiple pointers in the same declaration and clearly mark a variable as a pointer, we adhere to the convention that places an asterisk directly in front of each pointer variable name. This type of error rarely occurs with reference declarations because references are almost exclusively used as parameters and single declarations of parameters are mandatory.

PROGRAM 14.2

```cpp
#include <iostream>
using namespace std;

int main()
{
  int *numAddr;        // declare a pointer to an int
  int miles, dist;     // declare two integer variables

  dist = 158;          // store the number 158 into dist
  miles = 22;          // store the number 22 into miles
  numAddr = &miles;    // store the 'address of miles' in numAddr

  cout << "The address stored in numAddr is " << numAddr << endl;
  cout << "The value pointed to by numAddr is " << *numAddr << "\n\n";

  numAddr = &dist;   // now store the address of dist in numAddr
  cout << "The address now stored in numAddr is " << numAddr << endl;
  cout << "The value now pointed to by numAddr is " << *numAddr << endl;

  return 0;
}
```

The output of Program 14.2 is:

```
The address stored in numAddr is 0012FECB
The value pointed to by numAddr is 22

The address now stored in numAddr is 0012FEBC
The value now pointed to by numAddr is 158
```

The only use for Program 14.2 is to help us understand "what gets stored where." Let's review the program to see how the output was produced.

The declaration statement `int *numAddr;` declares `numAddr` to be a pointer variable used to store the address of an integer variable. The statement `numAddr = &miles;` stores the address of the variable `miles` into the pointer `numAddr`. The first `cout` statement causes this address to be displayed. The second `cout` statement in Program 14.2 uses the indirection operator to retrieve and print out *the value pointed to by* `numAddr`, which is, of course, the value stored in `miles`.

Because `numAddr` has been declared as a pointer to an integer variable, we can use this pointer to store the address of any integer variable. The statement `numAddr = &dist` illustrates this by storing the address of the variable `dist` in `numAddr`. The last two `cout` statements verify the change in `numAddr`'s value and that the new stored address does point to the variable `dist`. As illustrated in Program 14.2, only addresses should be stored in pointers.

It certainly would have been much simpler if the pointer used in Program 14.2 could have been declared as `pointer numAddr;`. Such a declaration, however, conveys no information as to the storage used by the variable whose address is stored in `numAddr`. This information is essential when the pointer is used with the indirection operator, as it is in the second `cout` in Program 14.2. For example, if the address of an integer is stored in `numAddr`, then only four bytes of storage are typically retrieved when the address is used. If the address of a character is stored in `numAddr`, only one byte of storage is retrieved, and a double typically requires the retrieval of eight bytes of storage. The declaration of a pointer must, therefore, include the type of variable being pointed to. Figure 14.5 illustrates this concept.

FIGURE 14.5   Addressing Different Data Types Using Pointers

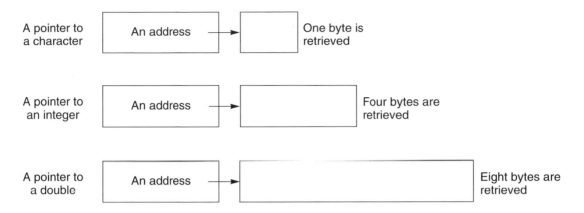

References and Pointers

At this point, you might be asking what the difference is between a pointer and a reference. Essentially, a reference is a named constant for an address; hence, the address named as a reference cannot be altered. But because a pointer is a variable, the address in the pointer can be changed. For simple applications, the use of references over pointers is easier and clearly preferred. Another difference is that references don't require the indirection operator to locate the final value being accessed, whereas pointers do. Technically this is designated by saying that references are *automatically dereferenced* or *implicitly dereferenced* (the terms are synonymous), whereas pointers must be *explicitly dereferenced.*

In passing a scalar variable's address as a function argument, references provide a simpler notational interface and are usually preferred. The same is true when we consider references to structures, which is the topic of the next chapter. For other situations, such as dynamically allocating new sections of memory for additional variables as a program is running or using alternatives to array notation (both topics are presented in this chapter), pointers are required.

Reference Variables[3]   References are used almost exclusively as function parameters and return types. Nevertheless, reference variables are also available in C++. For completeness, we now show how such variables can be declared and used.

Once a variable has been declared, it may be given additional names. This is accomplished using a reference declaration, which has the form:

```
dataType& newName = existingName;
```

For example, the reference declaration

```
double& sum = total;
```

equates the name sum to the name total—both now refer to the same variable, as illustrated in Figure 14.6.

---

[3] This topic may be omitted with no loss of subject continuity.

FIGURE 14.6   sum **Is an Alternative Name for** total

Two names for the
same memory area

total **or** sum

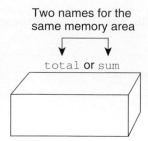

Once another name has been established for a variable using a reference declaration, the new name, which is referred to as an *alias,* can be used in place of the original name. For example, consider Program 14.3.

PROGRAM 14.3

```
#include <iostream>
using namespace std;

int main()
{
  double total = 20.5;    // declare and initialize total
  double& sum = total;    // declare another name for total

  cout << "sum = " << sum << endl;
  sum = 18.6;                // this changes the value in total
  cout << "total = " << total << endl;

  return 0;
}
```

The following output is produced by Program 14.3:

```
sum = 20.5
total = 18.6
```

Because the variable sum is simply another reference to the variable total, it is the value stored in total that is obtained by the first cout statement in Program 14.3. Changing the value in sum then changes the value in total, which is displayed by the second cout object in Program 14.3.

In constructing reference variables, two considerations must be kept in mind. First, the reference variable should be of the same data type as the variable it refers to. For example, the sequence of declarations

```
int num = 5;
double& numref = num; // = INVALID - CAUSES A COMPILER ERROR
```

does not equate numref to num; rather it causes a compiler error because the two variables are of different data types. Secondly, a compiler error is also produced when an attempt is made to equate a reference to a constant. For example, the declaration

```
int& val = 5;  // INVALID - CAUSES A COMPILER ERROR
```

is also invalid.

A BIT OF BACKGROUND

Admiral Grace Hopper, USN

Grace Hopper received a PhD from Yale University and joined the Naval Reserve in 1943. In her assignment to the Bureau of Ordnance Computation Project at Harvard University, she programmed the Mark I, the first large-scale, electromechanical, digital computer. Later she applied her outstanding talents in mathematics as senior programmer of the UNIVAC I.

Commodore Hopper became a pioneer in the development of computer languages and served on the Conference of Data Systems Languages (CODASYL) committee. She helped develop COBOL and is credited with producing the first practical program in that language. In 1959, she developed a COBOL compiler, which allowed programs written in a standardized language to be transported between different computers for the first time.

An interesting sidelight to her career was that her log book entry, dated September 19, 1945, at 15:45 hours, recorded "First actual case of bug being found." It was an actual insect that had shorted a relay in the Mark I.

Admiral Hopper remained a colorful figure in the computing community after her retirement from active duty in the U.S. Navy in August 1986 at the age of 79.

Once a reference name has been correctly equated to one variable name, the reference cannot be changed to refer to another variable.

As with all declaration statements, multiple references may be declared in a single statement as long as each reference name is preceded by an ampersand. Thus, the declaration

```
double& sum = total, & average;
```

creates two reference variables named sum and average.[4]

Another way of looking at references is to consider them as pointers with restricted capabilities that implicitly hide a lot of explicit dereferencing that is required with pointers. For example, consider the statements:

```
int b;      // b is an integer variable
int& a = b; // a is a reference variable that stores b's address
a = 10;     // this changes b's value to 10
```

Here, a is declared as a reference variable that is effectively a named constant for the address of the b variable. The compiler knows from the declaration that a is a reference variable, so it automatically assigns the address of b (rather than the contents of b) to a in the declaration statement. Finally, in the statement a = 10; the compiler uses the address stored in a to change the value stored in b to 10. The advantage of using the reference is that it automatically performs an indirect access of b's value without the need for explicitly using the indirection symbol, *. As noted previously, this type of access is referred to as an *automatic dereference*.

Implementing this same correspondence between a and b using pointers is done by the following sequence of instructions:

```
int b;      // b is an integer variable
int *a = &b; // a is a pointer - store b's address in a
*a = 10;     // this changes b's value to 10 by explicit
             // dereference of the address in a
```

---

[4] Reference declarations may also be written with a space before the ampersand and the reference variable in the form dataType &newName = existingName. This form is not used much, however, probably to distinguish reference variable address notation from that used in assigning addresses to pointer variables.

Here, a is defined as a pointer that is initialized to store the address of b. Thus, *a, which can be read as either *the variable whose address is in* a or *the variable pointed to by* a, is b, and the expression *a = 10 changes b's value to 10. Notice in the pointer case that the stored address can be altered to point to another variable; whereas in the reference case the reference variable cannot be altered to refer to any variable except the one to which it is initialized. Also notice that to dereference a, we must explicitly use the indirection operator, *. As you might expect, * is also referred to as the *dereferencing operator.*

Exercises 14.1

1. If average is a variable, what does &average mean?

2. For the variables and addresses illustrated in Figure 14.7, determine &temp, &dist, &date, and &miles.

3. a. Write a C++ program that includes the following declaration statements. Have the program use the address operator and the cout object to display the addresses corresponding to each variable.

   ```
   int num, count;
   long date;
   float yield;
   double price;
   ```

   b. After running the program written for Exercise 3a, draw a diagram of how your computer has set aside storage for the variables in the program. On your diagram, fill in the addresses displayed by the program.

   c. Modify the program written in Exercise 3a to display the amount of storage your computer reserves for each data type [use the sizeof() operator]. With this information and the address information provided in Exercise 3b, determine if your computer set aside storage for the variables in the order in which they were declared.

4. If a variable is declared as a pointer, what must be stored in the variable?

FIGURE 14.7 Memory Bytes for Exercise 2

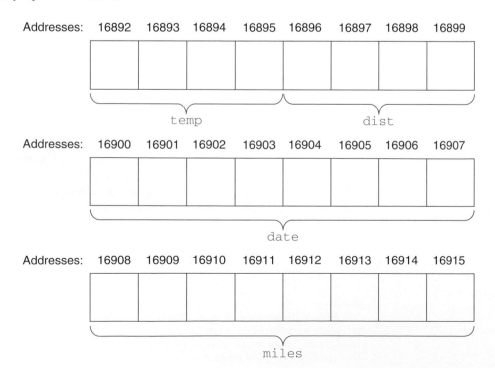

5. Using the indirection operator, write expressions for the following:

   a. the variable pointed to by xAddr

   b. the variable whose address is in yAddr

   c. the variable pointed to by ptYld

   d. the variable pointed to by ptMiles

   e. the variable pointed to by mptr

   f. the variable whose address is in pdate

   g. the variable pointed to by distPtr

   h. the variable pointed to by tabPt

   i. the variable whose address is in hoursPt

6. Write declaration statements for the following:

   a. The variable pointed to by yAddr is an integer.

   b. The variable pointed to by chAddr is a character.

   c. The variable pointed to by ptYr is a long integer.

   d. The variable pointed to by amt is a double-precision variable.

   e. The variable pointed to by z is an integer.

   f. The variable pointed to by qp is a floating-point variable.

   g. datePt is a pointer to an integer.

   h. yldAddr is a pointer to a double-precision variable.

   i. amtPt is a pointer to a floating-point variable.

   j. ptChr is a pointer to a character.

7. a. What are the variables yAddr, chAddr, ptYr, amt, z, qp, datePtr, yldAddr, amtPt, and ptChr in Exercise 6 called?

   b. Why are the variable names amt, z, and qp in Exercise 6 not good choices for pointer variable names?

8. Write English sentences that describe what is contained in the following declared variables:

   a. char *keyAddr;

   b. int *m;

   c. double *yldAddr;

   d. long *yPtr;

   e. float *pCou;

   f. int *ptDate;

9. Which of the following are declarations for pointers?

   a. long a;

   b. char b;

   c. char *c;

   d. int x;

   e. int *p;

   f. double w;

   g. float *k;

    h. `float 1;`

    i. `double *z;`

10. For the following declarations:

```
int *xPt, *yAddr;
long *dtAddr, *ptAddr;
double *ptZ;
int a;
long b;
double c;
```

determine which of the following statements are valid:

    a. `yAddr = &a;`

    b. `yAddr = &b;`

    c. `yAddr = &c;`

    d. `yAddr = a;`

    e. `yAddr = b;`

    f. `yAddr = c;`

    g. `dtAddr = &a;`

    h. `dtAddr = &b;`

    i. `dtAddr = &c;`

    j. `dtAddr = a;`

    k. `dtAddr = b;`

    l. `dtAddr = c;`

    m. `ptZ = &a;`

    n. `ptAddr = &b;`

    o. `ptAddr = &c;`

    p. `ptAddr = a;`

    q. `ptAddr = b;`

    r. `ptAddr = c;`

    s. `yAddr = xPt;`

    t. `yAddr = dtAddr;`

    u. `yAddr = ptAddr;`

11. For the variables and addresses illustrated in Figure 14.8, fill in the appropriate data as determined by the following statements:

    a. `ptNum = &m;`

    b. `amtAddr = &amt;`

    c. `*zAddr = 25;`

    d. `k = *numAddr;`

    e. `ptDay = zAddr;`

    f. `*ptYr = 1987;`

    g. `*amtAddr = *numAddr;`

12. Using the `sizeof()` operator, determine the number of bytes used by your computer to store the address of an integer, character, and double-precision number. (*Hint:* `sizeof(*int)` can be used to determine the number of memory bytes used for a pointer to an integer.) Do you expect the size of each address to be the same? Why or why not?

FIGURE 14.8 Memory Locations for Exercise 11

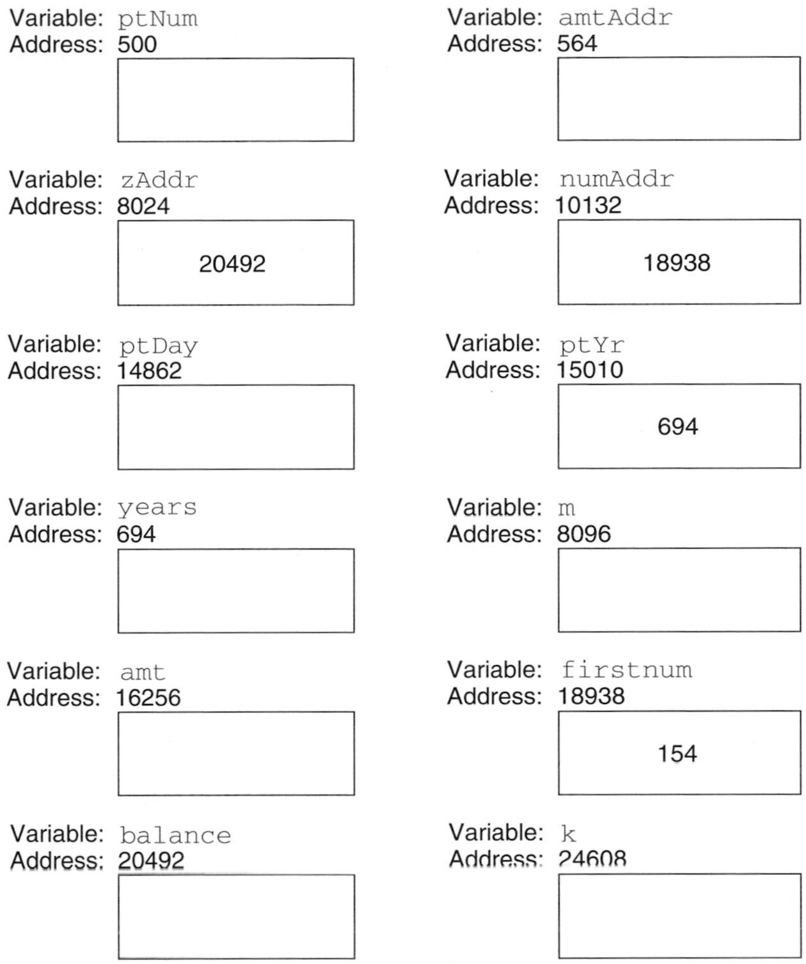

Variable: ptNum
Address: 500

Variable: amtAddr
Address: 564

Variable: zAddr
Address: 8024

20492

Variable: numAddr
Address: 10132

18938

Variable: ptDay
Address: 14862

Variable: ptYr
Address: 15010

694

Variable: years
Address: 694

Variable: m
Address: 8096

Variable: amt
Address: 16256

Variable: firstnum
Address: 18938

154

Variable: balance
Address: 20492

Variable: k
Address: 24608

14.2 ARRAY NAMES AS POINTERS

Although pointers are simply, by definition, variables used to store addresses, there is also a direct and intimate relationship between array names and pointers. In this section, we describe this relationship in detail.

Figure 14.9 illustrates the storage of a single-dimensional array named grade, which contains five integers. Assume that each integer requires 4 bytes of storage.

FIGURE 14.9 The grade Array in Storage

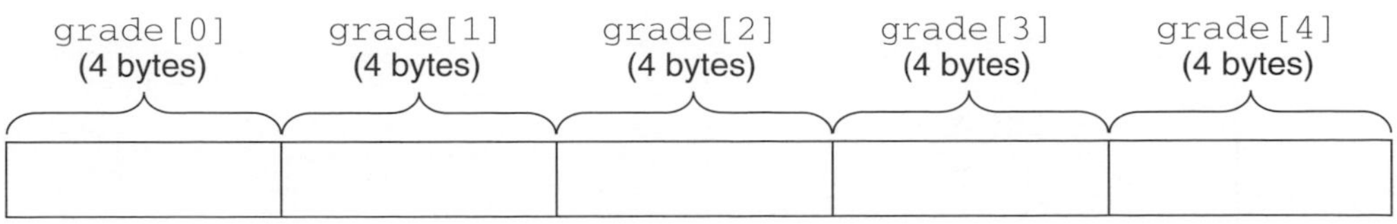

grade[0] (4 bytes)	grade[1] (4 bytes)	grade[2] (4 bytes)	grade[3] (4 bytes)	grade[4] (4 bytes)

FIGURE 14.10   Using a Subscript to Obtain an Address

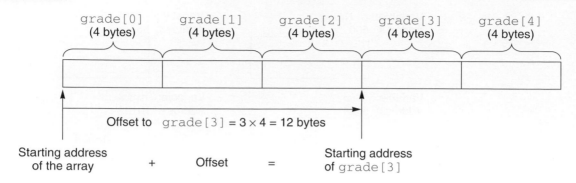

Using subscripts, the fourth element in the `grade` array is referred to as `grade[3]`. The use of a subscript, however, conceals the extensive use of addresses by the computer. Internally, the computer immediately uses the subscript to calculate the address of the desired element based on both the starting address of the array and the amount of storage used by each element. Accesssing the element `grade[3]` forces the compiler, internally, to make the address computation:

$$\&grade[3] = \&grade[0] + (3 * 4)$$

Remembering that the address operator, &, means *the address of*, this last statement is read "*the address of* `grade[3]` *equals the address of* `grade[0]` *plus 12*. Figure 14.10 illustrates the address computation used to locate `grade[3]`.

Recall that a pointer is a variable used to store an address. If we create a pointer to store the address of the first element in the `grade` array, we can mimic the operation used by the computer to access the array elements. Before we do this, let us first consider Program 14.4.

When Program 14.4 is run, the following display is obtained:

```
Element 0 is 98
Element 1 is 87
Element 2 is 92
Element 3 is 79
Element 4 is 85
```

PROGRAM 14.4

```cpp
#include <iostream>
using namespace std;

int main()
{
  const int ARRAYSIZE = 5;

  int i, grade[ARRAYSIZE] = {98, 87, 92, 79, 85};

  for (i = 0; i < ARRAYSIZE; i++)
    cout << "\nElement " << i << " is " << grade[i];
  cout << endl;

  return 0;
}
```

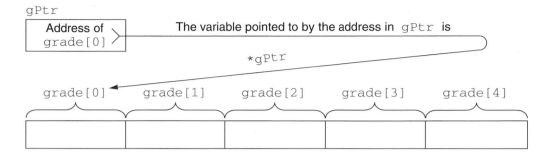

FIGURE 14.11 The Variable Pointed to by *gPtr **Is** grade[0]

Program 14.4 displays the values of the array grade using standard subscript notation. Now, let us store the address of array element 0 in a pointer. Then, using the indirection operator, *, we can use the address in the pointer to access each array element. For example, if we store the address of grade[0] into a pointer named gPtr (using the assignment statement gPtr = &grade[0];), then, as illustrated in Figure 14.11, the expression *gPtr, which means *the variable pointed to by* gPtr, refers to grade[0].

One unique feature of pointers is that offsets may be included in expressions using pointers. For example, 1 in the expression *(gPtr + 1) is an *offset*. The complete expression refers to the integer that is one beyond the variable pointed to by gPtr. Similarly, as illustrated in Figure 14.12, the expression *(gPtr + 3) refers to the variable that is three integers beyond the variable pointed to by gPtr. This is the variable grade[3].

Table 14.1 lists the complete correspondence between elements accessed by subscripts and by pointers and offsets. The relationships listed in Table 14.1 are illustrated in Figure 14.13.

Using the correspondence between pointers and subscripts illustrated in Figure 14.13, the array elements previously accessed in Program 14.4 using subscripts can now be accessed using pointers. This is done in Program 14.5.

PROGRAM 14.5

```cpp
#include <iostream>
using namespace std;

int main()
{
  const int ARRAYSIZE = 5;

  int *gPtr;               // declare a pointer to an int

  int i, grade[ARRAYSIZE] = {98, 87, 92, 79, 85};

  gPtr = &grade[0];      // store the starting array address
  for (i = 0; i < ARRAYSIZE; i++)
    cout << "\nElement " << i << " is " << *(gPtr + i);
  cout << endl;

  return 0;
}
```

FIGURE 14.12 An Offset of Three from the Address in `gPtr`

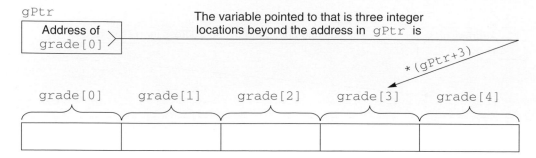

When Program 14.5 is run, the following display is obtained:

```
Element 0 is 98
Element 1 is 87
Element 2 is 92
Element 3 is 79
Element 4 is 85
```

Notice that this is the same display produced by Program 14.4.

TABLE 14.1 Array Elements May Be Accessed in Two Ways

Array Element	Subscript Notation	Pointer Notation
Element 0	grade[0]	*gPtr and *(gPtr + 0)
Element 1	grade[1]	*(gPtr + 1)
Element 2	grade[2]	*(gPtr + 2)
Element 3	grade[3]	*(gPtr + 3)
Element 4	grade[4]	*(gPtr + 4)

FIGURE 14.13 The Relationship Between Array Elements and Pointers

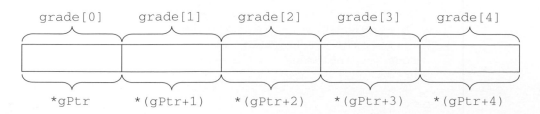

The method used in Program 14.5 to access individual array elements simulates how the compiler internally accesses all array elements. Any subscript used by a programmer is automatically converted to an equivalent pointer expression by the compiler. In our case, because the declaration of gPtr included the information that integers are pointed to, any offset added to the address in gPtr is automatically scaled by the size of an integer. Thus, *(gPtr + 3), for example, refers to the address of grade[0] plus an offset of 12 bytes (3 * 4), where we have assumed that sizeof(int) = 4. This is the address of grade[3], as illustrated in Figure 14.10.

The parentheses in the expression *(gPtr + 3) are necessary to access the desired array element correctly. Omitting the parentheses results in the expression *gPtr + 3. Due to the precedence of the operators, this expression adds 3 to "the variable pointed to by gPtr." Since gPtr points to grade[0], this expression adds the value of grade[0] and 3 together. Note also that the expression *(gPtr + 3) does not change the address stored in gPtr. Once the computer uses the offset to locate the correct variable from the starting address in gPtr, the offset is discarded and the address in gPtr remains unchanged.

Although the pointer gPtr used in Program 14.5 was specifically created to store the starting address of the grade array, this was, in fact, unnecessary. When an array is created, the compiler automatically creates an internal pointer constant for it and stores the starting address of the array in this pointer. In almost all respects, a pointer constant is identical to a pointer variable created by a programmer, but as we shall see, there are some differences.

For each array created, the name of the array becomes the name of the pointer constant created by the compiler for the array, and the starting address of the first location reserved for the array is stored in this pointer. Thus, declaring the grade array in both Programs 14.4 and 14.5 actually reserved enough storage for five integers, created an internal pointer named grade, and stored the address of grade[0] in the pointer. This is illustrated in Figure 14.14.

FIGURE 14.14   Creating an Array Also Creates a Pointer

grade

&grade[0]

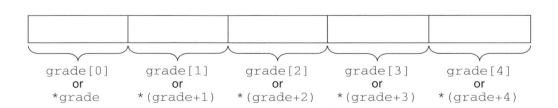

grade[0]   grade[1]   grade[2]   grade[3]   grade[4]
   or   or   or   or   or
*grade   *(grade+1)   *(grade+2)   *(grade+3)   *(grade+4)

The implication is that every access to grade using a subscript can be replaced by an equivalent access using grade as a pointer. Thus, wherever the expression grade[i] is used, the expression *(grade + i) can also be used. This is illustrated in Program 14.6, where `grade` is used as a pointer to access all of its elements.

Program 14.6 produces the same output as Programs 14.4 and 14.5. However, using `grade` as a pointer made it unnecessary to declare and initialize the pointer `gPtr` used in Program 14.5.

PROGRAM 14.6

```cpp
#include <iostream>
using namespace std;

int main()
{
  const int ARRAYSIZE = 5;

  int i, grade[ARRAYSIZE] = {98, 87, 92, 79, 85};

  for (i = 0; i < ARRAYSIZE; i++)
    cout << "\nElement " << i << " is " << *(grade + i);
  cout << endl;

  return 0;
}
```

In most respects, an array name and pointer can be used interchangeably. *A true pointer, however, is a variable and the address stored in it can be changed. An array name is a pointer constant and the address stored in the pointer cannot be changed by an assignment statement.* Thus, a statement such as `grade = &grade[2];` is invalid. This should come as no surprise. Since the whole purpose of an array name is to correctly locate the beginning of the array, allowing a programmer to change the address stored in the array name defeats this purpose and leads to havoc whenever array elements are accessed. Also, expressions taking the address of an array name are invalid because the pointer created by the compiler is internal to the computer and not stored in memory as are pointer variables. Thus, trying to store the address of `grade` using the expression `&grade` results in a compiler error.

An interesting sidelight to the observation that elements of an array can be accessed using pointers is that a pointer access can always be replaced using subscript notation. For example, if `numPtr` is declared as a pointer variable, the expression `*(numPtr + i)` can also be written as `numPtr[i]`. This is true even though `numPtr` is not created as an array. As before, when the compiler encounters the subscript notation, it replaces it internally with the pointer notation.

Dynamic Array Allocation[5]

As each variable is defined in a program, sufficient storage for it is assigned from a pool of computer memory locations made available to the compiler. Once specific memory locations have been reserved for a variable, these locations are fixed for

---

[5] This topic may be omitted on first reading with no loss of subject continuity.

the life of that variable, whether they are used or not. For example, if a function requests storage for an array of 500 integers, the storage for the array is allocated and fixed from the point of the array's definition. If the application requires fewer than 500 integers, the unused allocated storage is not released back to the system until the array goes out of existence. If, on the other hand, the application requires more than 500 integers, the size of the integer array must be increased and the function defining the array recompiled.

An alternative to this fixed or static allocation of memory storage locations is the dynamic allocation of memory. Under a dynamic allocation scheme, the amount of storage to be allocated is determined and adjusted as the program is run rather than fixed at compile time.

The dynamic allocation of memory is extremely useful when dealing with lists because it allows the list to expand as new items are added and contract as items are deleted. For example, in constructing a list of grades, the exact number of grades ultimately needed may not be known. Rather than creating a fixed array to store the grades, it is extremely useful to have a mechanism whereby the array can be enlarged and shrunk as necessary. Two C++ operators, `new` and `delete`, that provide this capability are described in Table 14.2. (These operators require the `new` header file.)

Explicit dynamic storage requests for scalar variables or arrays are made either as part of a declaration or assignment statement.[6] For example, the declaration statement `int *num = new int;` reserves an area sufficient to hold one integer and places the address of this storage area into the pointer `num`. This same dynamic allocation can be made by first declaring the pointer using the declaration statement `int *num;` and subsequently assigning the pointer an address with the assignment statement `num = new int;`. In either case, the allocated storage area comes from the computer's free storage area.[7]

In a similar manner and of more usefulness is the dynamic allocation of arrays. For example, the declaration

```
int *grades = new int[200];
```

reserves an area sufficient to store 200 integers and places the address of the first integer into the pointer `grades`. Although we have used the constant 200 in this example declaration, both a named constant and a variable dimension can be used. For example, consider the following sequence of instructions:

```
cout << "Enter the number of grades to be processed: ";
cin  >> numgrades;
int *grades = new int[numgrades];
```

In this sequence, the size of the array that is created depends on the number input by the user. Because pointer and array names are related, each value in the newly created storage area can be accessed using standard array notation, such as `grades[i]`, rather than the equivalent pointer notation `*(grades + i)`. Program 14.7 illustrates this sequence of code in the context of a complete program.

---

[6] Note that the compiler automatically provides this dynamic allocation and deallocation from the stack for all auto variables.

[7] The free storage area of a computer is formally referred to as the *heap*. The heap consists of unallocated memory that can be allocated to a program, as requested, while the program is running.

TABLE 14.2   Dynamic Allocation Operators (requires `new` header file)

Operator Name	Description
new	Reserves the number of bytes requested by the declaration. Returns the address of the first reserved location or `NULL` if sufficient memory is not available.
delete	Releases a block of bytes previously reserved. The address of the first reserved location must be passed as an argument to the operator.

PROGRAM 14.7

```cpp
#include <iostream>
#include <new>
using namespace std;

int main()
{
  int numgrades, i;

  cout << "Enter the number of grades to be processed: ";
  cin  >> numgrades;

  int *grades = new int[numgrades];  // create the array

  for(i = 0; i < numgrades; i++)
  {
    cout << "  Enter a grade: ";
    cin  >> grades[i];
  }
  cout << "\nAn array was created for " << numgrades << "integers\n";
  cout << " The values stored in the array are:";
  for (i = 0; i < numgrades; i++)
    cout << "\n    " << grades[i];
  cout << endl;

  delete[] grades;   // return the storage to the heap

  return 0;
}
```

Notice in Program 14.7 that the `delete` operator is used with braces whenever the `new` operator was previously used to delete an array. The `delete[]` statement restores the allocated block of storage to the operating system while the programming is executing.[8] The only address required by `delete` is the starting address of the block of storage that was dynamically allocated. Thus, any address returned by `new` can subsequently be used by `delete` to restore the reserved memory to the

---

[8] The allocated storage should automatically be returned to the heap, by the operating system, when the program has completed execution. Since this is not always the case, however, it is extremely important to formally restore dynamically allocated memory to the heap when the storage is no longer needed. The term *memory leak* is used to describe the condition that occurs when dynamically allocated memory is not formally returned using the `delete` operator and the operating system does not reclaim the allocated memory area.

computer. The `delete` operator does not alter the address passed to it, but simply removes the storage that the address references. Following is a sample run using Program 14.7:

```
Enter the number of grades to be processed: 4
    Enter a grade: 85
    Enter a grade: 96
    Enter a grade: 77
    Enter a grade: 92

An array was created for 4 integers
 The values stored in the array are:
    85
    96
    77
    92
```

Exercises 14.2

1. Replace each of the following references to a subscripted variable with a pointer reference:

   a. `prices[5]`

   b. `grades[2]`

   c. `yield[10]`

   d. `dist[9]`

   e. `mile[0]`

   f. `temp[20]`

   g. `celsius[16]`

   h. `num[50]`

   i. `time[12]`

2. Replace each of the following pointer notations with a subscript notation:

   a. `*(message + 6)`

   b. `*amount`

   c. `*(yrs + 10)`

   d. `*(stocks + 2)`

e. `*(rates + 15)`

f. `*(codes + 19)`

3. a. List the three things that the declaration statement `double prices[5];` causes the compiler to do.

   b. If each double-precision number uses 8 bytes of storage, how much storage is set aside for the prices array?

   c. Draw a diagram similar to Figure 14.14 for the prices `array`.

   d. Determine the byte offset relative to the start of the `prices` array corresponding to the offset in the expression `*(prices + 3)`.

4. a. Write a declaration to store the string `"This is a sample"` into an array named `samtest`. Include the declaration in a program that displays the values in `samtest` in a `for` loop that uses a pointer to access each element in the array.

   b. Modify the program written in Exercise 4a to display only array elements 10 through 15 (these are the letters s, a, m, p, l, and e).

5. Write a declaration to store the following values into an array named `rates`: 12.9, 18.6, 11.4, 13.7, 9.5, 15.2, 17.6. Include the declaration in a program that displays the values in the array using pointer notation.

14.3 POINTER ARITHMETIC

Pointer variables, like all variables, contain values. The value stored in a pointer is, of course, an address. Thus, by adding and subtracting numbers to pointers, we can obtain different addresses. Additionally, the addresses in pointers can be compared using any of the relational operators (`==`, `!=`, `<`, `>`, etc.) that are valid for comparing other variables. In performing arithmetic on pointers, we must be careful to produce addresses that point to something meaningful. In comparing pointers, we must also make comparisons that make sense. Consider these declarations:

```
const int ARRAYSIZE-100;
int nums[ARRAYSIZE];
int *nPt;
```

To set the address of `nums[0]` into `nPt`, either of the following two assignment statements can be used:

```
nPt = &nums[0];
nPt = nums;
```

The two assignment statements produce the same result because `nums` is a pointer constant that itself contains the address of the first location in the array. This is, of course, the address of `nums[0]`. Figure 14.15 illustrates the allocation of memory resulting from the previous declaration and assignment statements, assuming that each integer requires 4 bytes of memory and that the location of the beginning of the `nums` array is at address 18934.

Once `nPt` contains a valid address, values can be added to and subtracted from the address to produce new addresses. When adding or subtracting numbers to pointers, the computer automatically adjusts the number to ensure that the result still "points to" a value of the correct type. For example, the statement `nPt = nPt + 3;` forces the computer to scale the 3 by the correct number to ensure that the resulting address is the address of an integer. Assuming that each integer requires 4 bytes of storage, as illustrated in Figure 14.15, the computer multiplies 3 by 4 and adds the result, 12, to the address in nPt. The resulting address is 18946, which is the correct address of nums[3].

This automatic scaling by the computer ensures that the expression nPt + i, where i is any positive integer, correctly points to the *i*th element beyond the one currently being pointed to by nPt. Thus, if nPt initially contains the address of nums[0], nPt + 4 is the address of nums[4], nPt + 50 is the address of nums[50], and nPt + i is the address of nums[i]. Although we have used actual addresses in Figure 14.15 to illustrate the scaling process, the programmer need never know or care about the actual addresses used by the computer. The manipulation of addresses using pointers generally does not require knowledge of the actual address.

FIGURE 14.15   The nums **Array in Memory**

nPt

18934 ◀── The address of nums[0]

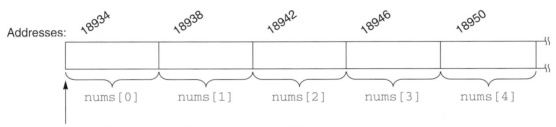

Addresses: 18934   18938   18942   18946   18950

      nums[0]   nums[1]   nums[2]   nums[3]   nums[4]

The starting address of the nums array is 18934

Addresses can also be incremented or decremented using both prefix and postfix increment and decrement operators. Adding 1 to a pointer causes the pointer to point to the next element of the type being pointed to. Decrementing a pointer causes the pointer to point to the previous element. For example, if the pointer variable p is a pointer to an integer, the expression p++ causes the address in the pointer to be incremented to point to the next integer. This is illustrated in Figure 14.16. In reviewing this figure, notice that the increment added to the pointer is correctly scaled to account for the fact that the pointer is used to point to integers. It is, of course, up to the programmer to ensure that the correct type of data is stored in the new address contained in the pointer.

The increment and decrement operators can be applied as both prefix and postfix pointer operators. All of the following combinations using pointers are valid:

```
*ptNum++      // use the pointer and then increment it
*++ptNum      // increment the pointer before using it
*ptNum--      // use the pointer and then decrement it
*--ptNum      // decrement the pointer before using it
```

Of the four possible forms, the most commonly used is *ptNum++. This is because such an expression allows each element in an array to be accessed as the address is "marched along" from the starting address of the array to the address of the last array element. The use of the increment operator is shown in Program 14.8. In this program, each element in the nums array is retrieved by successively incrementing the address in nPt.

FIGURE 14.16   Increments Are Scaled when Used with Pointers

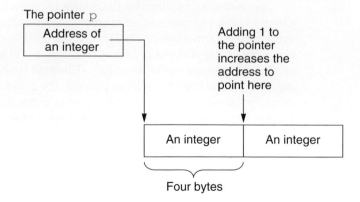

PROGRAM 14.8

```
#include <iostream>
using namespace std;

int main()
{

  const int NUMS = 5;
  int nums[NUMS] = {16, 54, 7, 43, -5};
  int i, total = 0, *nPt;

  nPt = nums;     // store address of nums[0] in nPt
  for (i = 0; i < NUMS; i++)
    total = total + *nPt++;
  cout << "The total of the array elements is " << total << endl;

  return 0;
}
```

The output produced by Program 14.8 is:

```
The total of the array elements is 115
```

The expression `total = total + *nPt++` used in Program 14.8 accumulates the values "pointed to" by the `nPt` pointer variable. Within this expression, the term `*nPt++` first causes the program to retrieve the integer pointed to by `nPt`. This is done by the `*nPt` part of the term. The postfix increment, `++`, then adds 1 to the address in `nPt` so that `nPt` now contains the address of the next array element. The increment is, of course, scaled by the compiler so that the actual address in `nPt` is the correct address of the next array element.

Pointers may also be compared. This is particularly useful when dealing with pointers used to access elements in the same array. For example, rather than using a counter in a `for` loop to access each element in an array correctly, the address in a pointer can be compared to the starting and ending address of the array itself. The expression

$$nPt <= \&nums[4]$$

is true (nonzero) as long as the address in `nPt` is less than or equal to the address of `nums[4]`. Because `nums` is a pointer constant that contains the address of `nums[0]`, the term `&nums[4]` can be replaced by the equivalent term `nums + 4`. Using either of these forms, Program 14.8 can be rewritten as Program 14.9 to continue adding array elements while the address in `nPt` is less than or equal to the address of the last array element.

Notice that in Program 14.9 `total += *nPt++`, the compact form of the accumulating expression, was used in place of the longer form, `total = total + *nPt++`. Also, the expression `nums + (NUMS - 1)` does not change the address in `nums`. Because `nums` is an array name and not a pointer variable, its value cannot be changed. The expression `nums + (NUMS - 1)` first retrieves the address in `nums`, adds 4 to this address (appropriately scaled), and uses the result for comparison purposes. Expressions such as `*nums++` that attempt to change the address are invalid. Expressions such as `*nums` or `*(nums + i)`, which use the address without attempting to alter it, are valid. It should be noted that the expression `nPt <= nums + (NUMS - 1)` used in the `while` statement can be replaced by the expression `nPt < nums + NUMS`.

PROGRAM 14.9

```
#include <iostream>
using namespace std;

int main()
{
  const int NUMS = 5;
  int nums[NUMS] = {16, 54, 7, 43, -5};
  int total = 0, *nPt;

  nPt = nums;    // store address of nums[0] in nPt
  while (nPt <= nums + (NUMS - 1))
    total += *nPt++;
  cout << "The total of the array elements is " << total << endl;

  return 0;
}
```

Pointer Initialization

Like all variables, pointers can be initialized when they are declared. When initializing pointers, however, you must be careful to set an address in the pointer. For example, an initialization such as

$$int\ *ptNum = \&miles;$$

is only valid if `miles` is declared as an integer variable prior to `ptNum` being declared. Here, we are creating a pointer to an integer and setting the address in the pointer to the address of an integer variable. Notice that if the variable `miles` is declared subsequently to `ptNum`, as follows:

```
int *ptNum = &miles;
int miles;
```

an error occurs. This is because the address of `miles` is used before `miles` has even been defined. Since the storage area reserved for `miles` has not been allocated when `ptNum` is declared, the address of `miles` does not yet exist.

Pointers to arrays can also be initialized within their declaration statements. For example, if `prices` has been declared as an array of double-precision numbers, either of the following two declarations can be used to initialize the pointer named `zing` to the address of the first element in `prices`:

```
double *zing = &prices[0];
double *zing = prices;
```

The last initialization is correct because `prices` is itself a pointer constant containing an address of the proper type. (The variable name `zing` was selected in this example to reinforce the idea that any variable name can be selected for a pointer.)

Exercises 14.3

1. Replace the `while` statement in Program 14.9 with a `for` statement.

2. a. Write a program that stores the following numbers in an array named `rates`: 6.25, 6.50, 6.8, 7.2, 7.35, 7.5, 7.65, 7.8, 8.2, 8.4, 8.6, 8.8, 9.0. Display the values in the array by changing the address in a pointer called `dispPt`. Use a `for` statement in your program.

   b. Modify the program written in Exercise 2a to use a `while` statement.

3. a. Write a program that stores the string `Hooray for All of Us` into an array named `strng`. Use the declaration `strng[] = "Hooray for All of Us";`, which ensures that the end-of-string escape sequence `\0` is included in the array. Display the characters in the array by changing the address in a pointer called `messPt`. Use a `for` statement in your program.

   b. Modify the program written in Exercise 3a to use the `while` statement: `while (*messPt++ != '\0')`.

   c. Modify the program written in Exercise 3a to start the display with the word `All`.

4. Write a program that stores the following numbers in an array named `miles`: 15, 22, 16, 18, 27, 23, 20. Have your program copy the data stored in `miles` to another array named `dist` and then display the values in the `dist` array.

5. Write a program that stores the following letters in an array named `message`:

   This is a test.

   Have your program copy the data stored in `message` to another array named `mess2` and then display the letters in the `mess2` array. Use pointers for copying and editing all array elements.

14.4 PASSING ADDRESSES

We have already seen one method of passing addresses to a function. This was accomplished using references, as described in Section 6.5. Although passing references to a function provides the function with the address of the passed variables, it is an implied use of addresses because the function call does not reveal the fact that reference parameters are being used. For example, the function call `swap(num1, num2);` does not reveal whether `num1` or `num2` is a passed value or a reference. Only by looking at the function prototype or examining the function header line for `swap()` is the type of pass revealed.

In contrast to passing addresses implicitly using references, addresses can be passed explicitly using pointers. Let us see how this is accomplished.

To explicitly pass an address to a function, we place the address-of operator, `&`, in front of the variable being passed. For example, the function call

```
swap(&firstnum, &secnum);
```

passes the addresses of the variables `firstnum` and `secnum` to `swap()`, as illustrated in Figure 14.17. Explicitly passing addresses using the address operator is referred to as *pass by reference* because the called function can reference, or access, variables in the calling function using the passed addresses.[9] As we saw in Section 6.5, calls by reference are also accomplished using reference parameters. Here, we will use the passed addresses and pointers to directly access the variables `firstnum` and `secnum` from within `swap()` and exchange their values—a procedure that was previously accomplished in Program 6.12 using reference parameters.

FIGURE 14.17 **Explicitly Passing Addresses to** `swap()`

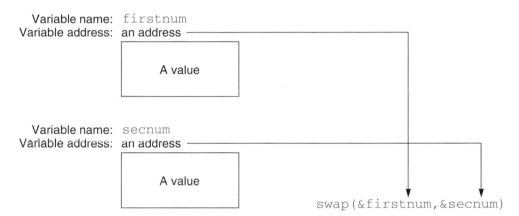

One of the first requirements in writing `swap()` is to construct a function header line that correctly receives and stores the passed values, which in this case are two addresses. As we saw in Section 14.1, addresses are stored in pointers, which means that the parameters of `swap()` must be declared as pointers.

Assuming that `firstnum` and `secnum` are double-precision variables, and that `swap()` returns no value, a suitable function header line for `swap()` is:

```
void swap(double *nm1Addr, double *nm2Addr)
```

The choice of the parameter names `nm1Addr` and `nm2Addr` is, as with all parameter names, up to the programmer. The declaration `double *nm1Addr`, however, declares that the parameter named `nm1Addr` is used to store the address of a double-precision value. Similarly, the declaration `double *nm2Addr` declares that `nm2Addr` also stores the address of a double-precision value.

---

[9] The term *pass by reference* here does not imply that a reference parameter is being used. It implies that an address is being passed, either as a reference or pointer, and the address permits the called function to directly reference (access) the calling function's argument.

Before writing the body of swap() to exchange the values in firstnum and secnum, let's first check that the values accessed using the addresses in nm1Addr and nm2Addr are correct. This is done in Program 14.10.

PROGRAM 14.10

```cpp
#include <iostream>
using namespace std;

void swap(double *, double *);        // function prototype

int main()
{
  double firstnum = 20.5, secnum = 6.25;

  swap(&firstnum, &secnum);                 // call swap

  return 0;
}

// this function illustrates passing pointer arguments
void swap(double *nm1Addr, double *nm2Addr)
{

  cout << "The number whose address is in nm1Addr is "
       << *nm1Addr << endl;
  cout << "The number whose address is in nm2Addr is "
       << *nm2Addr << endl;

  return;
}
```

The output displayed by Program 14.10 is:

```
The number whose address is in nm1Addr is 20.5
The number whose address is in nm2Addr is 6.25
```

In reviewing Program 14.10, note two things. First, the function prototype for swap():

```
void swap(double *, double *);
```

declares that swap() returns no value directly and that its parameters are two pointers that "point to" double-precision values. Thus, when the function is called, it requires that two addresses be passed and that each address be the address of a double-precision value.

The second item to notice is that within swap() the indirection operator is used to access the values stored in firstnum and secnum. swap() itself has no knowledge of these variable names, but it does have the address of firstnum stored in nm1Addr and the address of secnum stored in nm2Addr. The expression *nm1Addr used in the first cout statement means *the variable whose address is in* nm1Addr. This is, of course, the variable firstnum. Similarly, the second cout statement obtains the value stored in `secnum` as *the variable whose address is in* `nm2Addr`. Thus, we have successfully used pointers to allow `swap()` to access variables in `main()`. Figure 14.18 illustrates the concept of storing addresses in parameters.

Storing Addresses in Parameters

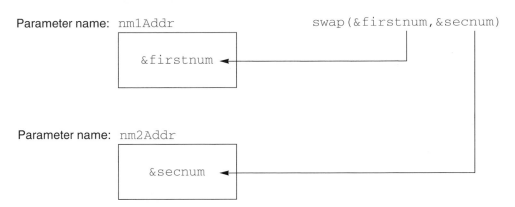

Having verified that `swap()` can access `main()`'s local variables `firstnum` and `secnum`, we can now expand `swap()` to exchange the values in these variables. The values in `main()`'s variables `firstnum` and `secnum` can be interchanged from within `swap()` using the three-step interchange algorithm previously described in Section 6.5, which for convenience is relisted here:

1. Store `firstnum`'s value in a temporary location.
2. Store `secnum`'s value in `firstnum`.
3. Store the temporary value in `secnum`.

Using pointers from within `swap()`, this takes the form:

1. Store the value of the variable pointed to by `nm1Addr` in a temporary location. The statement `temp = *nm1Addr;` does this (see Figure 14.19).

2. Store the value of the variable whose address is in `nm2Addr` in the variable whose address is in `nm1Addr`. The statement `*nm1Addr = *nm2Addr;` does this (see Figure 14.20).

3. Move the value in the temporary location into the variable whose address is in `nm2Addr`. The statement `*nm2Addr = temp;` does this (see Figure 14.21).

Indirectly Storing `firstnum`'s Value

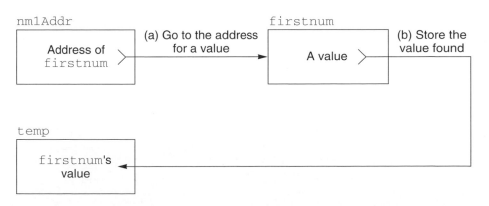

FIGURE 14.20   Indirectly Changing `firstnum`'s Value

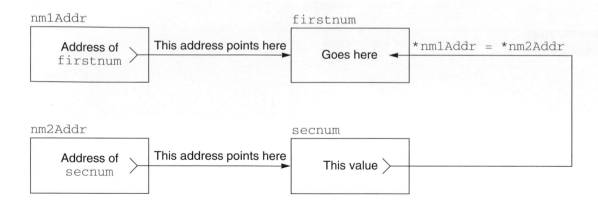

FIGURE 14.21   Indirectly Changing `secnum`'s Value

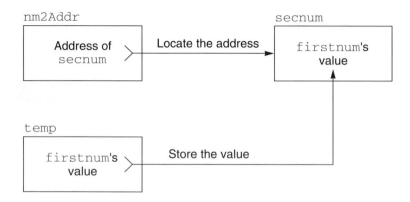

Program 14.11 contains the final form of `swap()`, written according to our description.

PROGRAM 14.11

```
#include <iostream>
using namespace std;

void swap(double *, double *);      // function prototype

int main()
{
  double firstnum = 20.5, secnum = 6.25;

  cout << "The value stored in firstnum is: " << firstnum << endl;
  cout << "The value stored in secnum is: " << secnum << "\n\n";
  swap(&firstnum, &secnum);              // call swap

  cout << "The value stored in firstnum is now: "
```

(continued from previous page)

```
          << firstnum <<  endl;
   cout << "The value stored in secnum is now: "
          << secnum << endl;

   return 0;
}

// this function swaps the values in its two arguments
void swap(double *nm1Addr, double *nm2Addr)
{
   double temp;

   temp = *nm1Addr;            // save firstnum's value
   *nm1Addr = *nm2Addr;        // move secnum's value into firstnum
   *nm2Addr = temp;            // change secnum's value

   return;
}
```

The following sample run was obtained using Program 14.11:

```
The value stored in firstnum is: 20.5
The value stored in secnum is: 6.25

The value stored in firstnum is now: 6.25
The value stored in secnum is now: 20.5
```

As illustrated in this output, the values stored in `main()`'s variables have been modified from within `swap()`, which was made possible by the use of pointers. The interested reader should compare this version of `swap()` with the version using references that was presented in Program 6.12. The advantage of using pointers in preference to references is that the function call itself explicitly designates that addresses are being used, which is a direct alert that the function will most likely alter variables of the calling function. The advantage of using references is that the notation is much simpler.

Generally, for functions such as `swap()`, the notational convenience wins out, and references are used. In passing arrays to functions, however, which is our next topic, the compiler automatically passes an address. This dictates that a pointer parameter is used to store the address.

Passing Arrays

When an array is passed to a function, its address is the only item actually passed. By this we mean the address of the first location used to store the array, as illustrated in Figure 14.22. Because the first location reserved for an array corresponds to element 0 of the array, the "address of the array" is also the address of element 0.

For a specific example in which an array is passed to a function, consider Program 14.12. In this program, the `nums` array is passed to the `findMax()` function using conventional array notation.

FIGURE 14.22 The Address of an Array, which Is the Address of the First Location Reserved for the Array, Becomes a Function's Parameter

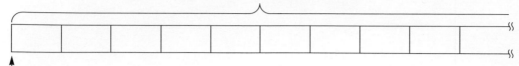

An array is a series of memory locations

The address of the first location
is passed as an argument and
stored in a pointer parameter

PROGRAM 14.12

```cpp
#include <iostream>
using namespace std;

int findMax(int [], int);     // function prototype

int main()
{
  const int NUMPTS = 5;
  int nums[NUMPTS] = {2, 18, 1, 27, 16};

  cout << "\nThe maximum value is "
       << findMax(nums,NUMPTS) << endl;
}

// this function returns the maximum value in an array of ints
int findMax(int vals[], int numEls)
{
  int i, max = vals[0];

  for (i = 1; i < numEls; i++)
   if (max < vals[i])
     max - vals[i];

  return max;
}
```

The output displayed by Program 14.12 is:

```
The maximum value is 27
```

The parameter named `vals` in the header line declaration for `findMax()` actually receives the address of the array `nums`. Hence, `vals` is really a pointer because pointers are variables (or parameters) used to store addresses. Since the address passed into `findMax()` is the address of an integer, another suitable header line for `findMax()` is:

```cpp
int findMax(int *vals, int numEls) // here vals is declared as
                                   // a pointer to an integer
```

The declaration `int *vals` in the header line declares that `vals` is used to store an address of an integer. The address stored is, of course, the location of the beginning of an array. The following is a rewritten version of the `findMax()` function that uses the new pointer declaration for `vals` but retains the use of subscripts to refer to individual array elements:

```
int findMax(int *vals, int numEls)    // find the maximum value
{
  int i, max = vals[0];

  for (i = 1; i < numEls; i++)
   if (max < vals[i])
     max = vals[i];

  return max;
}
```

Regardless of how `vals` is declared in the function header or how it is used within the function body, it is truly a pointer parameter. Thus, the address in `vals` may be modified. This is not true for the name `nums`. Because `nums` is the name of the originally created array, it is a pointer constant. As described in Section 14.2, this means that the address in `nums` cannot be changed and that the address of `nums` itself cannot be taken. No such restrictions, however, apply to the pointer parameter named `vals`. All the address arithmetic that we learned in the previous section can be legitimately applied to `vals`.

We shall write two additional versions of `findMax()`, both using pointers instead of subscripts. In the first version, we simply substitute pointer notation for subscript notation. In the second version, we use address arithmetic to change the address in the pointer.

As previously stated, the subscript notation `arrayName[i]` can always be replaced by the pointer notation `*(arrayName + i)` for access to an array element. In our first modification to `findMax()`, we make use of this correspondence by simply replacing all notations of the form `vals[i]` with the equivalent notation `*(vals + i)`.

```
int findMax(int *vals, int numEls)    // find the maximum value
{
  int i, max = *vals;

  for (i = 1; i < numEls; i++)
   if (max < *(vals + i) )
     max = *(vals + i);

  return max;
}
```

Our next version of `findMax()` makes use of the fact that the address stored in `vals` can be changed. After each array element is retrieved using the address in `vals`, the address itself is incremented by 1 in the altering list of the `for` statement. The expression `max = *vals` previously used to set `max` to the value of `vals[0]` is replaced by the expression `max = *vals++`, which adjusts the address in `vals` to point to the second element in the array. The element assigned to `max` by this expression is the array element pointed to by `vals` before `vals` is incremented. The postfix increment, `++`, does not change the address in `vals` until after the address has been used to retrieve the first array element.

```
int findMax(int *vals, int numEls)    // find the maximum value
{
  int i, max = *vals++;    // get the first element and increment
  for (i = 1; i < numEls; i++, vals++)
  {
    if (max < *vals)
      max = *vals;
  }
  return max;
}
```

Let us review this version of findMax(). Initially, the maximum value is set to "the thing pointed to by vals." Since vals initially contains the address of the first element in the array passed to findMax(), the value of this first element is stored in max. The address in vals is then incremented by 1. The 1 that is added to vals is automatically scaled by the number of bytes used to store integers. Thus, after the increment, the address stored in vals is the address of the next array element. This is illustrated in Figure 14.23. The value of this next element is compared to the maximum, and the address is again incremented, this time from within the altering list of the for statement. This process continues until all the array elements have been examined.

FIGURE 14.23 | **Pointing to Different Elements**

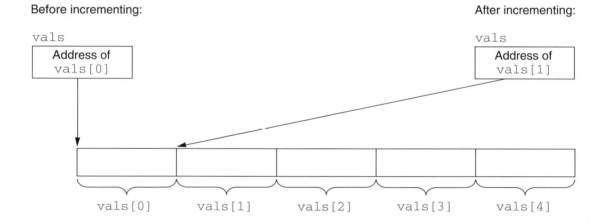

Before incrementing: After incrementing:

vals   vals

| Address of vals[0] | | Address of vals[1] |

| | vals[0] | | vals[1] | | vals[2] | | vals[3] | | vals[4] |

The version of findMax() that you should choose is a matter of personal style and taste. Generally, beginning programmers feel more at ease using subscripts rather than pointers. Also, if the program uses an array as the natural storage structure for the application and data at hand, an array access using subscripts is more appropriate to clearly indicate the intent of the program. In other situations, one of which is described in the next section, the use of pointers becomes an increasingly useful and powerful tool in its own right.

One further "neat trick" can be gleaned from our discussion. Because passing an array to a function really involves passing an address, we can just as well pass any valid address. For example, the function call findMax(&nums[2],3) passes the address of nums[2] to findMax(). Within findMax(), the pointer vals stores the address, and the function starts the search for a maximum at the element corresponding to this address. Thus, from findMax()'s perspective, it has received an address and proceeds appropriately.

Advanced Pointer Notation[10]

Access to multidimensional arrays can also be made using pointer notation, although the notation becomes more and more cryptic as the array dimensions increase. An extremely useful application of this notation occurs with two-dimensional character arrays, one of the topics in Section 14.6. Here, we consider pointer notation for two-dimensional numeric arrays. For example, consider the declarations:

```
const int ROWS = 2;
const int COLS = 3;
int nums[ROWS][COLS] = { {16,18,20},
                         {25,26,27} };
```

These declarations create an array of elements and a set of pointer constants named nums, nums[0], and nums[1]. The relationship between these pointer constants and the elements of the nums array is illustrated in Figure 14.24.

FIGURE 14.24   Storage of the nums Array and Associated Pointer Constants

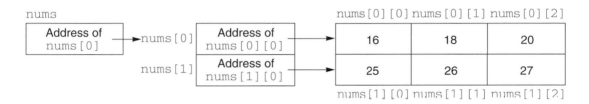

The availability of the pointer constants associated with a two-dimensional array allows us to access array elements in a variety of ways. One way is to consider the two-dimensional array as an array of rows, where each row is itself an array of three elements. Considered in this light, the address of the first element in the first row is provided by nums[0] and the address of the first element in the second row is provided by nums[1]. Thus, the variable pointed to by nums[0] is nums[0][0] and the variable pointed to by nums[1] is nums[1][0]. Once the nature of these constants is understood, each element in the array can be accessed by applying an appropriate **offset** to the appropriate pointer. Thus, the following notations are equivalent:

Pointer Notation	Subscript Notation	Value
*nums[0]	nums[0][0]	16
*(nums[0] + 1)	nums[0][1]	18
*(nums[0] + 2)	nums[0][2]	20
*nums[1]	nums[1][0]	25
*(nums[1] + 1)	nums[1][1]	26
*(nums[1] + 2)	nums[1][2]	27

We can now go even further and replace nums[0] and nums[1] with their respective pointer notations, using the address of nums. As illustrated in Figure 14.24,

---

[10] This topic may be omitted without loss of subject continuity.

the variable pointed to by `nums` is `nums[0]`. That is, `*nums is nums[0]`. Similarly, `*(nums + 1)` is `nums[1]`. Using these relationships leads to the following equivalences:

Pointer Notation	Subscript Notation	Value
`*(*nums)`	`nums[0][0]`	16
`*(*nums + 1)`	`nums[0][1]`	18
`*(*nums + 2)`	`nums[0][2]`	20
`*(*(nums + 1))`	`nums[1][0]`	25
`*(*(nums + 1) + 1)`	`nums[1][1]`	26
`*(*(nums + 1) + 2)`	`nums[1][2]`	27

The same notation applies when a two-dimensional array is passed to a function. For example, assume that the two-dimensional array `nums` is passed to the function `calc()` using the call `calc(nums);`. Here, as with all array passes, an address is passed. A suitable function header line for the function `calc()` is:

```
calc(int pt[2][3])
```

As we have already seen, the parameter declaration for `pt` can also be:

```
calc(int pt[][3])
```

Using pointer notation, another suitable declaration is:

```
calc(int (*pt)[3])
```

In this last declaration, the inner parentheses are required to create a single pointer to arrays of three integers. Each array is, of course, equivalent to a single row of the `nums` array. By suitably offsetting the pointer, each element in the array can be accessed. Notice that without the parentheses the declaration becomes:

```
int *pt[3]
```

which creates an array of three pointers, each one pointing to a single integer.

Once the correct declaration for `pt` is made (any of the three valid declarations can be used), the following notations within the function `calc()` are all equivalent:

Pointer Notation	Subscript Notation	Value
`*(*pt)`	`pt[0][0]`	16
`*(*pt+1)`	`pt[0][1]`	18
`*(*pt+2)`	`pt[0][2]`	20
`*(*(pt+1))`	`pt[1][0]`	25
`*(*(pt+1)+1)`	`pt[1][1]`	26
`*(*(pt+1)+2)`	`pt[1][2]`	27

The last two notations using pointers are encountered in more advanced C++ programs. The first of these occurs because functions can return any valid C++ scalar data type, including pointers to any of these data types. If a function returns a pointer, the data type being pointed to must be declared in the function's declaration. For example, the declaration

```
int *calc()
```

declares that `calc()` returns a pointer to an integer value. This means that an address of an integer variable is returned. Similarly, the declaration

```
double *taxes()
```

declares that taxes() returns a pointer to a double-precision value. This means that an address of a floating-point variable is returned.

In addition to declaring pointers to integers, floating-point numbers, and C++'s other data types, pointers can also be declared that point to (contain the address of) a function. Pointers to functions are possible because function names, like array names, are themselves pointer constants. For example, the declaration

```
int (*calc)()
```

declares calc() to be a pointer to a function that returns an integer. This means that calc contains the address of a function, and the function whose address is in the variable calc returns an integer value. If, for example, the function sum() returns an integer, the assignment calc = sum; is valid.

Exercises 14.4

1. The following declarations were used to create the prices array:

   ```
   const int SIZE = 500;
   double prices[SIZE];
   ```

   Write three different header lines for a function named sortArray that accepts the prices array as a parameter named inArray and returns no value.

2. The following declarations were used to create the keys array:

   ```
   const int SIZE = 256;
   char keys[SIZE];
   ```

   Write three different header lines for a function named findKey() that accepts the keys array as a parameter named select and returns no value.

3. The following declarations were used to create the rates array:

   ```
   const int SIZE = 256;
   float rates[SIZE];
   ```

   Write three different header lines for a function named prime that accepts the rates array as a parameter named rates and returns no value.

4. Modify the findMax() function to locate the minimum value of the passed array. Write the function using only pointers and rename the function findMin().

5. In the last version of findMax() presented, vals was incremented inside the altering list of the for statement. Instead, suppose that we do the incrementing within the condition expression of the if statement as follows:

   ```
   int findMax(int *vals, int numEls)     // incorrect version
   {
     int i, max = *vals++;    // get the first element and increment

     for (i = 1; i < numEls; i++)
       if (max < *vals++)
         max = *vals;
     return (max);
   }
   ```

   This version produces an incorrect result. Determine why.

6. a. Write a program that has declarations in main() to store the following numbers into an array named rates: 6.5, 7.2, 7.5, 8.3, 8.6, 9.4, 9.6, 9.8, 10.0. There should be a function call to show() that accepts rates as a parameter named rates and then displays the numbers using the pointer notation *(rates + i).

   b. Modify the show() function written in Exercise 6a to alter the address in rates. Use the expression *rates rather than *(rates + i) to retrieve the correct element.

14.5 POINTERS AND C-STRING LIBRARY FUNCTIONS

Pointers are exceptionally useful in constructing functions that manipulate C-strings (recall that the term C-string is short for character string, and consists of text stored in a character array whose last character is `'\0'`). When pointer notation is used in place of subscripts to access individual characters in a string, the resulting statements are both more compact and more efficient. In this section, we describe the equivalence between subscripts and pointers when accessing individual characters in a C-string.

Consider the `strcopy()` function introduced in Section 13.1. This function was used to copy the characters of one string to a second string. For convenience, this function is repeated below:

```
void strcopy(char string1[], char string2[])    // copy string2 to string1
{
  int i = 0;

  while (string1[i] = string2[i])
    i++;
  return;
}
```

The conversion of `strcopy()` from subscript notation to pointer notation is now straightforward. Although each subscript version of `strcopy()` can be rewritten using pointer notation, the following is the equivalent of our last subscript version:

```
void strcopy(char *string1, char *string2)    // copy string2 to string1
{
  while (*string1 = *string2)
  {
    string1++;
    string2++;
  }
  return;
}
```

In both subscript and pointer versions of `strcopy()`, the function receives the name of the array being passed. Recall that passing an array name to a function actually passes the address of the first location of the array. In our pointer version of `strcopy()`, the two passed addresses are stored in the pointer parameters `string1` and `string2`, respectively.

The declarations `char *string1;` and `char *string2;` used in the pointer version of `strcopy()` indicate that `string1` and `string2` are both pointers containing the address of a character and stress the treatment of the passed addresses as pointer values rather than array names. These declarations are equivalent to the declarations `char string1[]` and `char string2[]`, respectively.

Internal to `strcopy()`, the pointer expression `*string1`, which refers to *the element whose address is in* `string1`, replaces the equivalent subscript expression `string1[i]`. Similarly, the pointer expression `*string2` replaces the equivalent subscript expression `string2[i]`. The expression `*string1 = *string2` causes the element pointed to by `string2` to be assigned to the element pointed to by `string1`. Because the starting addresses of both strings are passed to `strcopy()` and stored in `string1` and `string2`, respectively, the expression `*string1` initially refers to `string1[0]` and the expression `*string2` initially refers to `string2[0]`.

Consecutively incrementing both pointers in `strcopy()` with the expressions `string1++` and `string2++` simply causes each pointer to "point to" the next consecutive character in the respective C-string. As with the subscript version, the pointer version of `strcopy()` steps along, copying element by element, until the end of the C-string is copied. One final change to the C-string copy function can be made by including the pointer increments as postfix operators within the test part of the `while` statement. The final form of the C-string copy function is:

```
void strcopy(char *string1, char *string2)   // copy string2 to string1
{
  while (*string1++ = *string2++)
    ;
  return;
}
```

There is no ambiguity in the expression `*string1++ = *string2++` even though the indirection operator, `*`, and the increment operator, `++`, have the same precedence. Here, the character pointed to is accessed before the pointer is incremented. Only after completion of the assignment `*string1 = *string2` are the pointers incremented to correctly point to the next characters in the respective strings.

The C-string copy function included in the standard library supplied with C++ compilers is typically written exactly like our pointer version of `strcopy()`.

Exercises 14.5

1. Determine the value of `*text`, `*(text + 3)`, and `*(text + 10)`, assuming that `text` is an array of characters and the following have been stored in the array:

   a. now is the time

   b. rocky raccoon welcomes you

   c. Happy Holidays

   d. The good ship

2. a. The following function, `convert()`, "marches along" the C-string passed to it and sends each character in the string one at a time to the `toUpper()` function until the `Null` character is encountered:

   ```
   void convert(char strng[])    // convert a string to uppercase letters
   {
     int i = 0;
     while (strng[i] != '\0')
     {
       strng[i] = toUpper(strng[i]);
       i++;
     }
     return;
   }

   char toUpper(char letter)  // convert a character to uppercase
   char letter;
   {
     if( (letter >= 'a') && (letter <= 'z') )
       return (letter - 'a' + 'A');
     else
       return (letter);
   }
   ```

   The `toUpper()` function takes each character passed to it and examines it to determine if the character is a lowercase letter (a lowercase letter is any character between *a* and *z*, inclusive). Assuming that characters are stored using the standard ASCII character codes, the expression `letter - 'a' + 'A'` converts a lowercase letter to its uppercase equivalent. Rewrite the `convert()` function using pointers.

b. Include the `convert()` and `toUpper()` functions in a working program. The program should prompt the user for a string and echo the string back to the user in uppercase letters.

3. Using pointers, repeat Exercise 1b from Section 13.1.

4. Using pointers, repeat Exercise 2 from Section 13.1.

5. Using pointers, repeat Exercise 3 from Section 13.1.

6. Write a function named `remove()` that returns nothing and deletes all occurrences of a character from a C-string. The function should use two parameters: the C-string name and the character to be removed. For example, if `message` contains the C-string `Happy Holidays`, the function call `remove(message, 'H')` should place the C-string `appy olidays` into message. Use pointer notation in your function.

7. Using pointers, repeat Exercise 6 from Section 13.1.

8. Write a function that uses pointers to add a single character at the end of an existing C-string. The function should replace the existing `'\0'` character with the new character and append a new `'\0'` at the end of the C-string. The function returns nothing.

9. Write a function that uses pointers to delete a single character from the end of a C-string. This is effectively achieved by moving the `'\0'` character one position closer to the start of the string. The function returns nothing.

10. Determine the C-string handling functions that are available with your C++ compiler. For each available function, list the data types of the parameters expected by the function and the data type of any returned value.

14.6 C-STRING DEFINITIONS AND POINTER ARRAYS

The definition of a C-string automatically involves a pointer. For example, the definition `char message1[80];` both reserves storage for 80 characters and automatically creates a pointer constant, `message1`, which contains the address of `message1[0]`. As a pointer constant, the address associated with the pointer cannot be changed—it must always "point to" the beginning of the created array.

It is also possible to create a C-string using a pointer instead of creating a C-string as an array. For example, the definition `char *message2;` creates a pointer to a character. In this case, `message2` is a true pointer variable. Assignment statements, such as `message2 = "this is a string";`, can be made once a pointer to a character is defined. In this assignment, `message2`, which is a pointer, receives the address of the first character in the string.

The main difference in the definitions of `message1` as an array and `message2` as a pointer is in the way the pointer is created. Defining `message1` using the declaration `char message1[80]` explicitly calls for a fixed amount of storage for the array. This causes the compiler to create a pointer constant. Defining `message2` using the declaration `char *message2` explicitly creates a pointer variable first. This pointer is then used to hold the address of a string when the string is actually specified. This difference in definitions has both storage and programming consequences.

From a programming perspective, defining `message2` as a pointer to a character allows C-string assignments, such as `message2 = "this is a string";`, to be made within a program. Similar assignments are not allowed for C-strings defined as arrays. Thus, the statement `message1 = "this is a string";` is not valid. Both definitions, however, allow initializations to be made using a C-string assignment. For example, both of the following initializations are valid:

```
char message1[80] = "this is a string";
char *message2 = "this is a string";
```

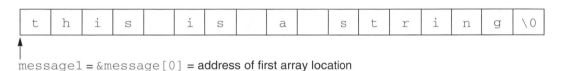
FIGURE 14.25 String Storage Allocation

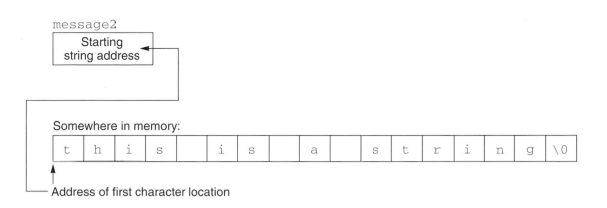

message1 = &message[0] = address of first array location

a. Storage allocation for a C-string defined as an array

message2

Starting
string address

Somewhere in memory:

Address of first character location

b. Storage of a C-string using a pointer

From a storage perspective, the allocation of space for message1 and for message2 is quite different. As illustrated in Figure 14.25, both initializations cause the computer to store the same C-string internally. In the case of message1, a specific set of 80 storage locations is reserved and the first 17 locations are initialized. For message1, different strings can be stored, but each C-string overwrites the previously stored characters. The same is not true for message2.

The definition of message2 reserves enough storage for one pointer. The initialization then causes the C-string to be stored in memory and the address of the string's first character (in this case, the address of the t) to be loaded into the pointer. If a later assignment is made to message2, the initial C-string remains in memory and new storage locations are allocated to the new string. For example, consider the following sequence of instructions:

```
char *message2 = "this is a string";
message2 = "A new message";
```

The first statement defines message2 as a pointer variable, stores the initialization C-string in memory, and loads the starting address of the string (the address of the t, in this case) into message2. The next assignment statement causes the computer to store the second C-string and change the address in message2 to point to the starting location of this new C-string.

It is important to realize that the second C-string assigned to message2 does not overwrite the first C-string but simply changes the address in message2 to point to the new string. As illustrated in Figure 14.26, both C-strings are stored inside the computer. Any additional C-string assignment to message2 results in the additional storage of the new C-string and a corresponding change in the address stored in `message2`. Doing so also means that we no longer have access to the original C-string memory storage location.

FIGURE 14.26   Storage Allocation Using a Pointer Variable

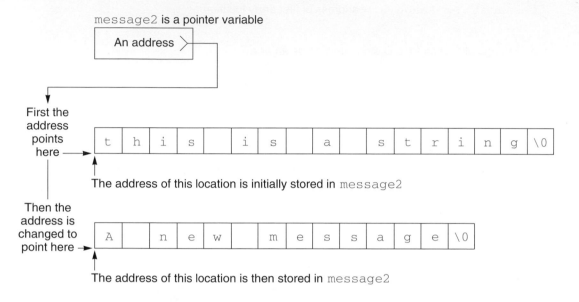

`message2` is a pointer variable

An address

First the address points here →

| t | h | i | s | | i | s | | a | | s | t | r | i | n | g | \0 |

The address of this location is initially stored in `message2`

Then the address is changed to point here →

| A | | n | e | w | | m | e | s | s | a | g | e | \0 |

The address of this location is then stored in `message2`

Pointer Arrays

The declaration of an array of character pointers is an extremely useful extension to single string pointer declarations. For example, the declarations

```
const int NUMSEASONS = 4;
char *seasons[NUMSEASONS];
```

create an array of four elements, where each element is a pointer to a character. As individual pointers, each pointer can be assigned to point to a string using string assignment statements. Thus, the statements

```
seasons[0] = "Winter";
seasons[1] = "Spring";
seasons[2] = "Summer";
seasons[3] = "Fall";   // note: string lengths may differ
```

set appropriate addresses into the respective pointers. Figure 14.27 illustrates the addresses loaded into the pointers for these assignments. The `seasons` array, as illustrated, does not contain the actual strings assigned to the pointers. These strings are stored elsewhere in the computer, in the normal data area allocated to the program. The array of pointers contains only the addresses of the starting location for each string.

The initializations of the `seasons` array can also be incorporated directly within the definition of the array as follows:

```
const int NUMSEASONS = 4;
char *seasons[NUMSEASONS] = {"Winter",
                             "Spring",
                             "Summer",
                             "Fall"};
```

FIGURE 14.27 The Addresses Contained in the seasons[] Pointers

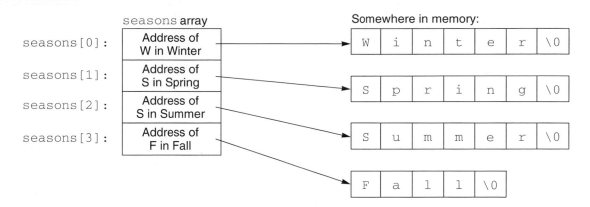

These declarations both create an array of pointers and initialize the pointers with appropriate addresses. Once addresses have been assigned to the pointers, each pointer can be used to access its corresponding string. Program 14.13 uses the seasons array to display each season using a for loop.

PROGRAM 14.13

```cpp
#include <iostream>
using namespace std;

int main()
{

   const int NUMSEASONS = 4;
   int n;
   char *seasons[] = {"Winter",
                      "Spring",
                      "Summer",
                      "Fall"};

   for(n = 0; n < NUMSEASONS; n++)
     cout << "\nThe season is " << seasons[n];
   cout << endl;

   return 0;
}
```

The output obtained from Program 14.13 is:

```
The season is Winter
The season is Spring
The season is Summer
The season is Fall
```

The advantage of using a list of pointers is that logical groups of data headings can be collected and accessed with one array name. For example, the months in a year can be collectively grouped in one array called months, and the days in a

PROGRAMMING NOTE

Allocating Space for a String

Although the declarations

```
const int SIZE = 5;
char test[SIZE] = "abcd";
```

and

```
char *test = "abcd";
```

both create storage for the characters `'a'`, `'b'`, `'c'`, `'d'`, and `'\0'`, there is a subtle difference between the two declarations and how values can be assigned to `test`. An array declaration such as `char test[SIZE];` precludes the use of any subsequent assignment expression, such as `test = "efgh"`, to assign values to the array. The use of a `strcpy()`, such as `strcpy(test,"efgh")`, however, is subsequently valid. The only restriction on `strcpy()` is the size of the array, which in this case is five elements. This situation is reversed when a pointer is created.

A pointer declaration, such as `char *test;`, precludes the use of `strcpy()` to initialize the memory locations pointed to by the pointer, but it does allow assignments. For example, the following sequence of statements is valid:

```
char *test;
test = "abcd";
test = "here is a longer string";
```

Once a string of characters has been assigned to `test`, `strcpy()` can be used provided the copy uses no more elements than are currently contained in the string.

The difference in usage is explained by the fact that the compiler automatically allocates sufficient new memory space for any string pointed to by a pointer variable but does not do so for an array of characters. For arrays the array size is fixed by the definition statement.

Formally, any expression that yields a value that can be used on the left side of an assignment expression is said to be an *lvalue*. (Similarly, any expression that yields a value that can be used on the right side of an assignment statement is said to be an *rvalue*.) Thus, a pointer variable can be an *lvalue*, but an array name cannot.

---

week collectively grouped in an array called `days`. The grouping of like headings allows the programmer to access and print an appropriate heading by simply specifying the correct position of the heading in the array. Program 14.14 uses the seasons array to correctly identify and display the season corresponding to a user-input month.

Except for the expression $n = (n \% 12) / 3$, Program 14.14 is straightforward. The program requests the user to input a month and accepts the number corresponding to the month using a `cin` statement. The expression $n = (n \% 12) / 3$ uses a common programming "trick" to scale one set of numbers into a second more useful set. In this case, the first set is the numbers 1 through 12 and the second set is the numbers 0 through 3. Thus, the months of the year, which correspond to the numbers 1 through 12, are adjusted to the correct season subscript. The expression $n \% 12$ adjusts the month entered so that it lies within the range 0 through 11, with 0 corresponding to December, 1 to January, and so on. Dividing by 3 causes the resulting number to range between 0 and 3, corresponding to the possible seasons elements. The result of the division by 3 is assigned to the integer variable n. The months 0, 1, and 2, when divided by 3, are set to 0; the months 3, 4, and

5 are set to 1; the months 6, 7, and 8 are set to 2; and the months 9, 10, and 11 are set to 3. This is equivalent to the following assignments:

Months	Season
December, January, February	Winter
March, April, May	Spring
June, July, August	Summer
September, October, November	Fall

PROGRAM 14.14

```
#include <iostream>
using namespace std;

int main()
{
  int n;
  char *seasons[] = {"Winter",
                     "Spring",
                     "Summer",
                     "Fall"};

  cout << "\nEnter a month (use 1 for Jan., 2 for Feb., etc.): ";
  cin  >> n;
  n = (n % 12) / 3;    // create the correct subscript
  cout << "The month entered is a "<< seasons[n]
       << " month." << endl;

  return 0;
}
```

The following is a sample output obtained from Program 14.14:

```
Enter a month (use 1 for Jan., 2 for Feb., etc.): 12
The month entered is a Winter month.
```

Exercises 14.6

1. Write two declaration statements that can be used in place of the declaration `char text[] = "Hooray!";`.

2. Determine the value of `*text`, `*(text + 3)`, and `*(text + 7)` for each of the following sections of code:

   a. `char *text;`
      `char message[] = "the check is in the mail";`
      `text = message;`
   b. `char *text;`
      `char formal[] = {'t','h','i','s',' ','i','s',' ','a','n',' ',`
      `                 'i','n','v','i','t','a','t','i','o','n','\0'};`
      `text = &formal[0];`
   c. `char *test;`
      `char more[] = "Happy Holidays";`
      `text = &more[4];`
   d. `char *text, *second;`
      `char blip[] = "The good ship";`
      `second = blip;`
      `text = ++second;`

3. Determine the error in the following program:

```
#include <iostream>

int main()
{
  int i = 0;
  char message[] = {'H','e','l','l','o','\0'};

  for( ; i < 5; i++)
  {
    cout << *message;
    message++;
  }

  return 0;
}
```

4. a. Write a C++ function that displays the day of the week corresponding to a user-entered input number between 1 and 7. That is, in response to an input of 2, the program displays the name Monday. Use an array of pointers in the function.

   b. Include the function written for Exercise 4a in a complete working program.

   c. Modify the function written in Exercise 4a so that the function returns the address of the character string containing the proper day to be displayed.

5. Write a function that accepts ten lines of user-input text and stores the entered lines as ten individual strings. Use a pointer array in your function.

14.7 COMMON PROGRAMMING ERRORS

When using the material presented in this chapter, be aware of the following possible errors:

1. Attempting to store an address in a variable that has not been declared as a pointer.

2. Using a pointer to access nonexistent array elements. For example, if `nums` is an array of ten integers, the expression `*(nums + 15)` points six integer locations beyond the last element of the array. Because C++ does not do any bounds checking on array accesses, this type of error is not caught by the compiler. This is the same error, disguised in pointer notation form, that occurs when using a subscript to access an out-of-bounds array element.

3. Incorrectly applying the address and indirection operators. For example, if `pt` is a pointer variable, the expressions

```
pt = &45             // INVALID
pt = &(miles + 10)   // INVALID
```

are both invalid because they attempt to take the address of a value.

Notice that the expression `pt = &miles + 10`, however, is valid. Here, 10 is added to the address of `miles`. Again, it is the programmer's responsibility to ensure that the final address "points to" a valid data element.

4. Taking addresses of pointer constants. For example, given the declarations

```
const int SIZE = 25;
int nums[SIZE];
int *pt;
```

the assignment

```
pt = &nums;   // INVALID
```

is invalid. `nums` is a pointer constant that is itself equivalent to an address. The correct assignment is `pt = nums`.

5. Taking addresses of a reference parameter, reference variable, or register variable. The reason is that reference parameters and variables are essentially the same as pointer constants in that they are named address values. Similarly, the address of a register variable cannot be taken. Thus, for the declarations

```
register total;
int *ptTot;
```

the assignment

```
ptTot = &total;   // INVALID
```

is invalid. The reason is that register variables are stored in a computer's internal registers, and these storage areas do not have standard memory addresses.

6. Initializing pointer variables incorrectly. For example, the initialization

```
int *pt = 5;   // INVALID
```

is invalid. Because `pt` is a pointer to an integer, it must be initialized with a valid address.

7. Becoming confused about whether a variable *contains* an address or *is* an address. Pointer variables and pointer parameters contain addresses. Although a pointer constant is synonymous with an address, it is useful to treat pointer constants as pointer variables with two restrictions:

- The address of a pointer constant cannot be taken.
- The address "contained in" the pointer constant cannot be altered.

Except for these two restrictions, pointer constants and variables can be used almost interchangeably. Therefore, when an address is required, any of the following can be used:

- A pointer variable name
- A pointer parameter name
- A pointer constant name
- A nonpointer variable name preceded by the address operator (e.g., `&variable`)
- A nonpointer argument name preceded by the address operator (e.g., `&argument`)

Some of the confusion surrounding pointers is caused by the cavalier use of the word *pointer*. For example, the phrase "a function requires a pointer parameter" is more clearly understood when it is realized that the phrase really means "a function requires an address as an argument." Similarly, the phrase "a function returns a pointer" really means "a function returns an address."

If you are ever in doubt as to what is really contained in a variable or how it should be treated, use the `cout` object to display the contents of the variable, the "thing pointed to," or "the address of the variable." Seeing what is displayed frequently helps sort out what is really in the variable.

8. Misunderstanding the terminology. For example, if `text` is defined as

    ```
    char *text;
    ```

    the variable `text` is sometimes referred to as a string. Thus, the terminology "store the characters `Hooray for the Hoosiers` into the `text` string" may be encountered. Strictly speaking, calling `text` a string or a string variable is incorrect. The variable `text` is a pointer that contains the address of the first character in the string. Nevertheless, referring to a character pointer as a string occurs frequently enough that you should be aware of it.

9. Using the default copy constructor and default assignment operators with classes containing pointer members. Since these default functions do a memberwise copy, the address in the source pointer is copied to the destination pointer. Typically, this is not desirable because both pointers end up pointing to the same memory area.

10. Forgetting to use the bracket set, `[]`, following the `delete` operator when dynamically deallocating memory that was previously allocated using the `new []` operator.

14.8 CHAPTER REVIEW

Key Terms

address operator	offset
indirect addressing	pointer
indirection operator	pointer variable

Summary

1. Every variable has a data type, an address, and a value. In C++, the address of a variable can be obtained by using the address operator `&`.

2. A *pointer* is a variable that is used to store the address of another variable. Pointers, like all C++ variables, must be declared. The indirection operator, `*`, is used both to declare a pointer variable and to access the variable whose address is stored in a pointer.

3. An array name is a pointer constant. The value of the pointer constant is the address of the first element in the array. Thus, if `val` is the name of an array, `val` and `&val[0]` can be used interchangeably.

4. Any access to an array element using subscript notation can always be replaced using pointer notation. That is, the notation `a[i]` can always be replaced by the notation `*(a + i)`. This is true whether `a` was initially declared explicitly as an array or as a pointer.

5. Arrays can be dynamically created as a program is executing. For example, the sequence of statements:

    ```
    cout << "Enter the array size: ";
    cin  >> num;
    int *grades = new int[num];
    ```

    creates an array named `grades` of size `num`. The area allocated for the array can be dynamically destroyed using the `delete[]` operator. For example, the statement `delete[] grades;` releases the allocated area for the `grades` array.

6. Arrays are passed to functions as addresses. The called function always receives direct access to the originally declared array elements.

7. When a single-dimensional array is passed to a function, the parameter declaration for the array can be either an array declaration or a pointer declaration. Thus, the following parameter declarations are equivalent:

```
float a[];
float *a;
```

8. Pointers can be incremented, decremented, compared, and assigned. Numbers added to or subtracted from a pointer are automatically scaled. The scale factor used is the number of bytes required to store the data type originally pointed to.

Exercises

1. Write a function named `trimfrnt()` that deletes all leading blanks from a string. Write the function using pointers with a return type of `void`.

2. Write a function named `trimrear()` that deletes all trailing blanks from a string. Write the function using pointers with a return type of `void`.

3. Write a C++ program that asks for two lowercase characters. Pass the two entered characters using pointers to a function named `capit()`. The `capit()` function should capitalize the two letters and return the capitalized values to the calling function through its pointer arguments. The calling function should then display all four letters.

4. Write a program that declares three single-dimensional arrays: `miles`, `gallons`, and `mpg`. Each array should be capable of holding ten elements. In the `miles` array, store the numbers 240.5, 300.0, 189.6, 310.6, 280.7, 216.9, 199.4, 160.3, 177.4, 192.3. In the `gallons` array, store the numbers 10.3, 15.6, 8.7, 14, 16.3, 15.7, 14.9, 10.7, 8.3, 8.4. Each element of the `mpg` array should be calculated as the corresponding element of the `miles` array divided by the equivalent element of the `gallons` array. For example, `mpg[0]` = `miles[0]` / `gallons[0]`. Use pointers when calculating and displaying the elements of the `mpg` array.

5. a. Write a program that has a declaration in `main()` to store the string `Vacation is near` into an array named `message`. There should be a function call to display that accepts `message` in a parameter named `strng` and then displays the message using the pointer notation `*(strng + i)`.

   b. Modify the display function written in Exercise 5a to alter the address in `message`. Also use the expression `*strng` rather than `*(strng + i)` to retrieve the correct element.

6. Write a program that declares three single-dimensional arrays named `price`, `quantity`, and `amount`. Each array should be declared in `main()` and be capable of holding ten double-precision numbers. The numbers to be stored in `price` are 10.62, 14.89, 13.21, 16.55, 18.62, 9.47, 6.58, 18.32, 12.15, 3.98. The numbers to be stored in `quantity` are 4, 8.5, 6, 7.35, 9, 15.3, 3, 5.4, 2.9, 4.8. Have your program pass these three arrays to a function called `extend()`, which calculates the elements in the `amount` array as the product of the equivalent elements in the `price` and `quantity` arrays. For example, `amount[1]` = `price[1]` * `quantity[1]`.

After `extend()` has put values into the `amount` array, display the values in the array from within `main()`. Write the `extend` function using pointers.

7. a. Determine the output of the following program:

```cpp
#include <iostream>

void arr(int [] []); // equivalent to void arr(int (*) []);

int main()
{
    const int ROWS = 2;
    const int COLS = 3;
    int nums[ROWS][COLS] = { {33,16,29},
                             {54,67,99}};
    arr(nums);

    return 0;
}
void arr(int (*val) [3])
{
    cout << endl << *(*val);
    cout << endl << *(*val + 1);
    cout << endl << *(*(val + 1) + 2);
    cout << endl << *(*val) + 1;

    return;
}
```

b. Given the declaration for `val` in the `arr` function, is the notation `val[1][2]` valid within the function?

8. Define an array of ten pointers to floating-point numbers. Then read ten numbers into the individual locations accessed by the pointers. Now add all of the numbers and store the result in a pointer-accessed location. Display the contents of all of the locations.

15 | Data Structures

A structure is a historical holdover from C. It provided, and still does, for storing information of varying types—such as a string name, an integer part number, and a real price—together under one name. Commercially, this type of data storage is called a **record**.

To make the discussion more tangible, consider data items that might be stored for a video game character, as illustrated in Figure 15.1.

Each of the individual data items listed in Figure 15.1 is an entity by itself that is referred to as a **data field**. Taken together, all the data fields form a single unit that is referred to as a **structure**. In both C and C++ languages, a structure is referred to as a **record**, and the two terms are used interchangeably. The major difference between C and C++ structures is that C++ permits methods to be included in a structure. When methods are added, the only real difference between a C++ structure and a class is the default access used by each. In a structure, the default for variables is public, while in a class this default is private. The implication of this is that a structure can be used to create a class and a class can be made to create a structure. This, however, is rarely if ever done.

FIGURE 15.1 | Typical Components of a Video Game Character

```
Name:
Type:
Location in Dungeon:
Strength Factor:
Intelligence Factor:
Type of Armor:
```

Structures are now primarily used for their historical purpose, which is to create a publicly available record. In this chapter the C++ statements required to create, use, and manipulate structures, in their role as records, is presented.

15.1 STRUCTURES

In its original form, and the one considered in this chapter, a structure can be considered as a class that has no methods and all of whose variables are public. In dealing with structures, as such, it is important to distinguish between form and content.

If a structure is considered as a record, as the term is used commercially, a structure's form consists of the symbolic names, data types, and arrangement of individual data items in the structure. The structure's contents refers to the actual data values in the symbolic names. For example, Figure 15.2 shows acceptable contents for the structure whose form was illustrated in Figure 15.1.

FIGURE 15.2   The Form and Contents of a Record

```
Name: Golgar
Type: Monster
Location in Dungeon: G7
Strength Factor: 78
Intelligence Factor: 15
Type of Armor: Chain Mail
```

Creating and using a structure requires the same two steps needed for creating and using any variable. First the structure's type must be declared. Then specific values can be assigned to the individual structure elements. Declaring a structure requires listing the data types, data names, and arrangement of data items. For example, the statement

```
struct birth
{
   int month;
   int day;
   int year;
} birth;
```

declares the form of a structure named `birth` and reserves storage for the individual data items listed in the structure. The `birth` structure consists of three data items or fields, which are called members of the structure.

Assigning actual data values to the data items of a structure is called **populating the structure** and is a relatively straightforward procedure. Each member of a structure is accessed by giving both the structure name and individual data item name, separated by a period. Thus, `birth.month` refers to the first member of the `birth` structure, `birth.day` refers to the second member of the structure, and `birth.year` refers to the third member. Program 15.1 illustrates assigning values to the individual members of the `birth` structure.

The output produced by Program 15.1 is:

```
My birth Date is 12/28/86
```

As in most C++ statements, the spacing of a structure definition is not rigid. For example, the `birth` structure could just as well have been defined:

```
struct {int month; int day; int year;} birth;
```

PROGRAM 15.1

```
// a program that defines and populates a record
#include <iostream>
using namespace std;

int main()
{
  struct
  {
    int month;
    int day;
    int year;
  } birth;

  birth.month = 12;
  birth.day = 28;
  birth.year = 86;

  cout << "My birth date is "
       << birth.month << '/'
       << birth.day   << '/'
       << birth.year  << endl;

  return 0;
}
```

Also, as with all C++ definition statements, multiple variables can be defined in the same statement. For example, the definition statement

```
struct
{
  int month;
  int day;
  int year;
} birth, current;
```

creates two structure variables having the same form. The members of the first structure are referenced by the individual names `birth.month`, `birth.day`, and `birth.year`, while the members of the second structure are referenced by the names `current.month`, `current.day`, and `current.year`. Notice that the form of this particular structure definition statement is identical to the form used in defining any program variable: The data type is followed by a list of variable names.

A useful and commonly used modification for defining structure types is to list the form of the structure with no following variable names. In this case, however, the list of structure members must be preceded by a user selected data type name. For example, in the declaration

```
struct Date
{
  int month;
  int day;
  int year;
};
```

the term `Date` is a structure type name: It defines a new data type that is a data structure of the declared form.[1] By convention the first letter of a user selected data type name is uppercase, as in the name `Date`, which helps to identify them when they are used in subsequent definition statements. Here, the declaration for the `Date` structure creates a new data type without actually reserving any storage locations. As such it is not a definition statement. It simply declares a `Date` structure type and describes how individual data items are arranged within the structure. Actual storage for the members of the structure is reserved only when specific variable names are assigned. For example, the definition statement

`Date birth, current;`

reserves storage for two `Date` structure variables named `birth` and `current`, respectively. Each of these individual structures has the form previously declared for the `Date` structure.

The declaration of a structure data type, like all declarations, may be global or local. Program 15.2 illustrates the global declaration of a `Date` data type. Internal to `main()`, the variable `birth` is defined as a local variable of `Date` type.

PROGRAM 15.2

```cpp
#include <iostream>
using namespace std;

struct Date     // this is a global declaration
{
  int month;
  int day;
  int year;
};

int main()
{
  Date birth;

  birth.month = 12;
  birth.day = 28;
  birth.year = 86;

  cout << "My birth Date is " << birth.month << '/'
               << birth.day   << '/'
               << birth.year  << endl;

  return 0;
}
```

---

[1] For completeness it should be mentioned that a C++ structure can also be declared as a class with no member methods and all public data members. Similarly, a C++ class can be declared as a `struct` having all private data members and all public member methods. Thus, C++ provides two syntaxes for both structs and classes. The convention, however, is not to mix notations and always use structures for creating record types and classes for providing true information and implementation hiding.

The output produced by Program 15.2 is identical to the output produced by Program 15.1.

The initialization of structures follows the same rules as for the initialization of arrays; structures may be initialized by following the definition with a list of initializers. For example, the definition statement

```
Date birth = {12, 28, 86};
```

can be used to replace the first four statements internal to `main()` in Program 15.2. Notice that the initializers are separated by commas, not semicolons.

The individual members of a structure are not restricted to integer data types, as illustrated by the `Date` structure. Any valid C++ data type can be used. For example, consider an employee record consisting of the following data items:

```
Name:
Identification Number:
Regular Pay Rate:
Overtime Pay Rate:
```

A suitable declaration for these data items is:

```
struct PayRec
{
    string name;
    int idNum;
    double regRate;
    double otRate;
};
```

Once the `PayRec` data type is declared, a specific structure variable using this type can be defined and initialized. For example, the definition

```
PayRec employee = {"H. Price",12387,15.89,25.50};
```

creates a structure named `employee` of the `PayRec` data type. The individual members of `employee` are initialized with the respective data listed between braces in the definition statement.

Notice that a single structure is simply a convenient method for combining and storing related items under a common name. Although a single structure is useful in explicitly identifying the relationship among its members, the individual members could be defined as separate variables. One of the real advantages to using structures is only realized when the same data type is used in a list many times over. Creating lists with the same data type is the topic of the next section.

Before leaving single structures, it is worth noting that the individual members of a structure can be any valid C++ data type, including both arrays and structures. An array of characters was used as a member of the `employee` structure defined previously. Accessing an element of a member array requires giving the structure's name, followed by a period, followed by the array designation.

Including a structure within a structure follows the same rules for including any data type in a structure. For example, assume that a structure is to consist of a name and a date of birth, where a `Date` structure has been declared as:

```
struct Date
{
    int month;
    int day;
    int year;
};
```

A suitable definition of a structure that includes a `name` and a `Date` structure is:

```
struct
{
    string name;
    Date birth;
} person;
```

Notice that in declaring the `Date` structure, the term `Date` is a data type name; thus it appears before the braces in the declaration statement. In defining the `person` structure variable, `person` is a variable name; thus it is the name of a specific structure. The same is true of the variable named `birth`. This is the name of a specific `Date` structure. Individual members in the `person` structure are accessed by preceding the desired member with the structure name followed by a period. For example, `person.birth.month` refers to the `month` variable in the `birth` structure contained in the `person` structure.

Exercises 15.1

1. Declare a structure data type named `Stemp` for each of the following records:

   a. A student record consisting of a student identification number, number of credits completed, and cumulative grade-point average

   b. A student record consisting of a student's name, date of birth, number of credits completed, and cumulative grade-point average

   c. A mailing list consisting of a person's name and address (street, city, state, and zip code)

   d. A stock record consisting of the stock's name, the price of the stock, and the date of purchase

   e. An inventory record consisting of an integer part number, part description, number of parts in inventory, and an integer reorder number

2. For the individual data types declared in Exercise 1, define a suitable structure variable name and initialize each structure with the appropriate following data:

   a. `Identification Number: 4672`
      `Number of Credits Completed: 68`
      `Grade-Point Average: 3.01`

   b. `Name: Rhona Karp`
      `Date of Birth: 8/4/1980`
      `Number of Credits Completed: 96`
      `Grade-Point Average: 3.89`

   c. `Name: Kay Kingsley`
      `Street Address: 614 Freeman Street`
      `City: Indianapolis`
      `State: IN`
      `Zip Code: 07030`

```
     d. Stock: IBM
        Price Purchased: 115.375
        Date Purchased: 12/7/1999

     e. Part Number: 16879
        Description: Battery
        Number in Stock: 10
        Reorder Number: 3
```

3. a. Write a C++ program that prompts a user to input the current month, day, and year. Store the data entered in a suitably defined record and display the date in an appropriate manner.

   b. Modify the program written in Exercise 3a to use a record that accepts the current time in hours, minutes, and seconds.

4. Write a C++ program that uses a structure for storing the name of a stock, its estimated earnings per share, and its estimated price-to-earnings ratio. Have the program prompt the user to enter these items for five different stocks, each time using the same structure to store the entered data. When the data have been entered for a particular stock, have the program compute and display the anticipated stock price based on the entered earnings and price-per-earnings values. For example, if a user entered the data XYZ 1.56 12, the anticipated price for a share of XYZ stock is (1.56)*(12) = $18.72.

5. Write a C++ program that accepts a user-entered time in hours and minutes. Have the program calculate and display the time 1 minute later.

6. a. Write a C++ program that accepts a user-entered date. Have the program calculate and display the date of the next day. For purposes of this exercise, assume that all months consist of 30 days.

   b. Modify the program written in Exercise 6a to account for the actual number of days in each month.

15.2 ARRAYS OF STRUCTURES

The real power of structures is realized when the same structure is used for lists of data. For example, assume that the data shown in Figure 15.3 must be processed. Clearly, the employee numbers can be stored together in an array of integers, the names in an array of strings, and the pay rates in an array of double-precision numbers. In organizing the data in this fashion, each column in Figure 15.3 is considered to be a separate list, which is stored in its own array. The correspondence between items for each individual employee is maintained by storing an employee's data in the same array position in each array.

The separation of the complete list into three individual arrays is unfortunate because all of the items relating to a single employee constitute a natural organization of data into structures, as illustrated in Figure 15.4. Using a structure, the integrity of the data organization as a record can be maintained and reflected by the program. Under this approach, the list in Figure 15.4 can be processed as a single array of ten structures.

Declaring an array of structures is the same as declaring an array of any other variable type. For example, if the data type PayRecord is declared as

```
struct PayRecord
{
    int idNum;
    string name;
    double rate;
};
```

FIGURE 15.3 A List of Employee Data

Employee Number	Employee Name	Employee Pay Rate
32479	Abrams, B.	6.72
33623	Bohm, P.	7.54
34145	Donaldson, S.	5.56
35987	Ernst, T.	5.43
36203	Gwodz, K.	8.72
36417	Hanson, H.	7.64
37634	Monroe, G.	5.29
38321	Price, S.	9.67
39435	Robbins, L.	8.50
39567	Williams, B.	7.20

then an array of ten such structures can be defined as:

```
PayRecord employee[10];
```

This definition statement constructs an array of ten elements, each of which is a structure of the data type `PayRecord`. Notice that the creation of an array of ten structures has the same form as the creation of any other array. For example, creating an array of ten integers named `employee` requires the declaration:

```
int employee[10];
```

FIGURE 15.4 A List of Structures

	Employee Number	Employee Name	Employee Pay Rate
1st structure ⟶	32479	Abrams, B.	6.72
2nd structure ⟶	33623	Bohm, P.	7.54
3rd structure ⟶	34145	Donaldson, S.	5.56
4th structure ⟶	35987	Ernst, T.	5.43
5th structure ⟶	36203	Gwodz, K.	8.72
6th structure ⟶	36417	Hanson, H.	7.64
7th structure ⟶	37634	Monroe, G.	5.29
8th structure ⟶	38321	Price, S.	9.67
9th structure ⟶	39435	Robbins, L.	8.50
10th structure ⟶	39567	Williams, B.	7.20

In this declaration, the data type is int, whereas in the earlier declaration for employee, the data type is PayRecord.

Once an array of structures is declared, a particular data item is accessed by giving the position of the desired structure in the array followed by a period and the appropriate structure member. The variable employee[0].rate, for example, accesses the rate member of the first employee structure in the employee array. Including structures as elements of an array permits a list of structures to be processed using standard array programming techniques. Program 15.3 displays the first five employee records listed in Figure 15.4.

PROGRAM 15.3

```cpp
#include <iostream>
#include <iomanip>
using namespace std;

struct PayRecord    // this is a global declaration
{
  int id;
  string name;
  double rate;
};

int main()
{
  const int NUMRECS = 5;    // maximum number of records
  int i;
  PayRecord employee[NUMRECS] = {
                        { 32479, "Abrams, B.", 6.72 },
                        { 33623, "Bohm, P.", 7.54},
                        { 34145, "Donaldson, S.",  5.56},
                        { 35987, "Ernst, T.", 5.43 },
                        { 36203, "Gwodz, K.", 8.72 }
                        };

  cout << endl;    // start on a new line
  cout << setiosflags(ios::left);  // left justify the output
  for ( i = 0; i < NUMRECS; i++)
    cout << setw(7)  << employee[i].id
         << setw(15) << employee[i].name
         << setw(6)  << employee[i].rate << endl;

  return 0;
}
```

The output displayed by Program 15.3 is:

```
32479      Abrams, B.      6.72
33623      Bohm, P.        7.54
34145      Donaldson, S.   5.56
35987      Ernst, T.       5.43
36203      Gwodz, K.       8.72
```

In reviewing Program 15.3, notice the initialization of the array of structures. Although the initializers for each structure have been enclosed in inner braces, these are not strictly necessary because all members have been initialized. As with all external and static variables, in the absence of explicit initializers, the numeric elements of both static and external arrays or structures are initialized to zero and their character elements are initialized to NULLs. The etiosflags(ios::left) manipulator included in the cout object stream forces each name to be displayed left-justified in its designated field width.

Exercises 15.2

1. Define arrays of 100 structures for each of the data types described in Exercise 1 of the previous section.

2. a. Using the data type

```
struct MonthDays
{
  char name[10];
  int days;
};
```

define an array of 12 structures of type MonthDays. Name the array convert() and initialize the array with the names of the 12 months in a year and the number of days in each month.

b. Include the array created in Exercise 2a in a program that displays the names and number of days in each month.

3. Using the data type declared in Exercise 2a, write a C++ program that accepts a month from a user in numeric form and displays the name of the month and the number of days in the month. Thus, in response to an input of 3, the program displays March has 31 days.

4. a. Declare a single structure data type suitable for an Employee structure of the following type:

Number	Name	Rate	Hours
3462	Jones	4.62	40
6793	Robbins	5.83	38
6985	Smith	5.22	45
7834	Swain	6.89	40
8867	Timmins	6.43	35
9002	Williams	4.75	42

b. Using the data type declared in Exercise 4a, write a C++ program that interactively accepts the Exercise 4a data into an array of six structures. Once the data have been entered, the program should create a payroll report listing each employee's name, number, and gross pay. Include the total gross pay of all employees at the end of the report.

5. a. Declare a single structure data type suitable for a `Car` structure of the following type:

Car Number	Miles Driven	Gallons Used
25	1450	62
36	3240	136
44	1792	76
52	2360	105
68	2114	67

b. Using the data type declared for Exercise 5a, write a C++ program that interactively accepts these data into an array of five structures. Once the data have been entered, the program should create a report listing each car number and the miles per gallon achieved by the car. At the end of the report, include the average miles per gallon achieved by the complete fleet of cars.

15.3 STRUCTURES AS FUNCTION ARGUMENTS

Individual structure members may be passed to a function in the same manner as any scalar variable. For example, given the structure definition

```
struct
{
    int idNum;
    double payRate;
    double hours;
} emp;
```

the statement

```
display(emp.idNum);
```

passes a copy of the structure member `emp.idNum` to a function named `display()`. Similarly, the statement

```
calcPay(emp.payRate,emp.hours);
```

passes copies of the values stored in structure members `emp.payRate` and `emp.hours` to the function `calcPay()`. Both functions, `display()` and `calcPay()`, must declare the correct data types for their respective parameters.

Complete copies of all members of a structure can also be passed to a function by including the name of the structure as an argument to the called function. For example, the function call

```
calcNet(emp);
```

passes a copy of the complete `emp` structure to `calcNet()`. Internal to `calcNet()`, an appropriate declaration must be made to receive the structure. Program 14.4 declares a global data type for an `employee` structure. This type is then used by both the `main()` and `calcNet()` functions to define specific structures with the names `emp` and `temp`, respectively.

The output produced by Program 15.4 is:

```
The net pay for employee 6782 is $361.66
```

In reviewing Program 15.4, observe that both `main()` and `calcNet()` use the same data type to define their individual structure variables. The structure variable defined in `main()` and the structure variable defined in `calcNet()` are two completely different structures. Any changes made to the local `temp` variable in calcNet() are not reflected in the emp variable of main(). In fact, because both structure variables are local to their respective functions, the same structure variable name could have been used in both functions with no ambiguity.

When calcNet() is called by main(), copies of emp's structure values are passed to the temp structure. calcNet() then uses two of the passed member values to calculate a number, which is returned to main().

PROGRAM 15.4

```cpp
#include <iostream>
#include <iomanip>
using namespace std;

struct Employee        // declare a global structure type
{
  int idNum;
  double payRate;
  double hours;
};

double calcNet(Employee);   // function prototype

int main()
{
  Employee emp = {6782, 8.93, 40.5};
  double netPay;

  netPay = calcNet(emp);       // pass copies of the values in emp

    // set output formats
  cout << setw(10)
       << setiosflags(ios::fixed)
       << setiosflags(ios::showpoint)
       << setprecision(2);

  cout << "The net pay for employee " << emp.idNum
       << " is $" << netPay << endl;

  return 0;
}

double calcNet(Employee temp)  // temp is of data type Employee
{
  return (temp.payRate * temp.hours);
}
```

An alternative to the pass-by-value function call illustrated in Program 15.4, in which the called function receives a copy of a structure, is a pass-by-reference that passes a reference to a structure. Doing so permits the called function to directly access and alter values in the calling function's structure variable. For example, referring to Program 15.4, the prototype of calcNet() can be modified to:

```cpp
double calcNet(Employee&);
```

If this function prototype is used and the calcNet() header line is rewritten to conform to it, the main() function in Program 15.4 may be used as is. Program 15.4a illustrates these changes within the context of a complete program.

PROGRAM 15.4a

```cpp
#include <iostream>
#include <iomanip>
using namespace std;

struct Employee        // declare a global structure type
{
  int idNum;
  double payRate;
  double hours;
};

double calcNet(Employee&);    // function prototype

int main()
{
  Employee emp = {6782, 8.93, 40.5};
  double netPay;

  netPay = calcNet(emp);         // pass a reference

    // set output formats
  cout << setw(10)
       << setiosflags(ios::fixed)
       << setiosflags(ios::showpoint)
       << setprecision(2);

  cout << "The net pay for employee " << emp.idNum
       << " is $" <<  netPay << endl;

  return 0;
}

double calcNet(Employee& temp)    // temp is a reference variable
{
  return (temp.payRate * temp.hours);
}
```

Program 15.4a produces the same output as Program 15.4, except that the `calcNet()` function in Program 15.4a receives direct access to the `emp` structure rather than a copy of it. This means that the variable name `temp` within `calcNet` is an alternate name for the variable `emp` in `main()`, and any changes to `temp` are direct changes to `emp`. Although the same function call, `calcNet(emp)`, is made in both programs, the call in Program 15.4a passes a reference, whereas the call in Program 15.4 passes values.

Passing a Pointer

In place of passing a reference, a pointer can be passed. To use a pointer, we must, in addition to modifying the function's prototype and header line, modify the call to `calcNet()` in Program 15.4 to:

```cpp
calcNet(&emp);
```

Here, the function call clearly indicates that an address is being passed (which is not the case in Program 15.4a). The disadvantage, however, is in the dereferencing notation required internal to the function. However, because pointers are widely used in practice, it is worthwhile to become familiar with the notation used.

To store the passed address correctly, `calcNet()` must declare its parameter as a pointer. A suitable function definition for `calcNet()` is:

```
double calcNet(Employee *pt)
```

Here, the declaration for `pt` declares this parameter as a pointer to a structure of type `Employee`. The pointer `pt` receives the starting address of a structure whenever `calcNet()` is called. Within `calcNet()`, this pointer is used to directly access any member in the structure. For example, `(*pt).idNum` refers to the `idNum` member of the structure, `(*pt).payRate` refers to the `payRate` member of the structure, and `(*pt).hours` refers to the `hours` member of the structure. These relationships are illustrated in Figure 15.5. The parentheses around the expression `*pt` in this figure are necessary to initially access *the structure whose address is in* `pt`. This is followed by an identifier to access the desired member within the structure. In the absence of the parentheses, the structure member operator . . . takes precedence over the indirection operator. Thus, the expression `*pt.hours` is another way of writing `*(pt.hours)`, which refers to *the variable whose address is in the* `pt.hours` *variable*. This last expression clearly makes no sense because there is no structure named `pt`, and `hours` does not contain an address.

FIGURE 15.5 **A Pointer Can Be Used to Access Structure Members**

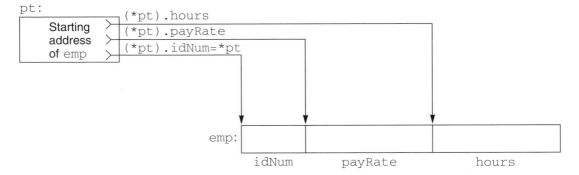

As illustrated in Figure 15.5, the starting address of the `emp` structure is also the address of the first member of the structure.

The use of pointers in this manner is so common that a special notation exists for it. The general expression *(*pointer).member* can always be replaced with the notation `pointer->member`, where the `->` operator is constructed using a minus sign followed by a right-facing arrow (greater than symbol). Either expression can be used to locate the desired member. For example, the following expressions are equivalent:

```
(*pt).idNum      can be replaced by     pt->idNum
(*pt).payRate    can be replaced by     pt->payRate
(*pt).hours      can be replaced by     pt->hours
```

Program 15.5 illustrates how to pass a structure's address and use a pointer with the new notation to access the structure directly.

The name of the pointer parameter declared in Program 15.5 is, of course, selected by the programmer. When `calcNet()` is called, `emp`'s starting address is passed to the function. Using this address as a starting point, individual members of the structure are accessed by including their names with the pointer.

As with all C++ expressions that access a variable, the increment and decrement operators can also be applied to them. For example, the expression

$$++pt->hours$$

adds one to the hours member of the emp structure. Because the -> operator has a higher priority than the increment operator, the hours member is accessed first and then the increment is applied.

PROGRAM 15.5

```cpp
#include <iostream>
#include <iomanip>
using namespace std;

struct Employee    // declare a global structure type
{
  int idNum;
  double payRate;
  double hours;
};
double calcNet(Employee *);    //function prototype

int main()
{
  Employee emp = {6782, 8.93, 40.5};
  double netPay;

  netPay = calcNet(&emp);        // pass an address

    // set output formats
  cout << setw(10)
       << setiosflags(ios::fixed)
       << setiosflags(ios::showpoint)
       << setprecision(2);

  cout << "The net pay for employee " << emp.idNum
       << " is $" << netPay << endl;

  return 0;
}

double calcNet(Employee *pt) // pt is a pointer to a
{                            // structure of Employee type
  return (pt->payRate * pt->hours);
}
```

Alternatively, the expression (++pt)->hours uses the prefix increment operator to increment the address in pt before the hours member is accessed. Similarly, the expression (pt++)->hours uses the postfix increment operator to increment the address in pt after the hours member is accessed. In both of these cases, however, a sufficient number of defined structures must exist to ensure that the incremented pointers actually point to legitimate structures.

FIGURE 15.6   Changing Pointer Addresses

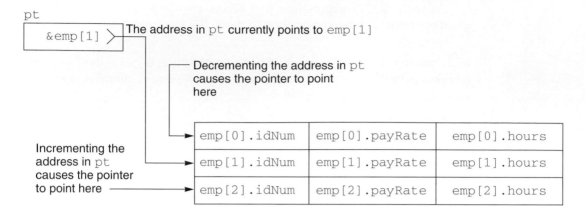

As an example, Figure 15.6 illustrates an array of three structures of type employee. Assuming that the address of emp[1] is stored in the pointer pt, the expression ++pt changes the address in pt to the starting address of emp[2], while the expression --pt changes the address to point to emp[0].

Returning Structures

In practice, most structure handling functions receive direct access to a structure by receiving a structure's address. Then any changes to the structure can be made directly from within the function. If you want to have a function return a separate structure, however, you must follow the same procedures for returning complete data structures as for returning scalar values. These procedures include declaring the function appropriately and alerting any calling function to the type of data structure being returned. For example, the function getValues() in Program 15.6 returns a complete structure to main().

The following output is displayed by Program 15.6:

```
The employee ID number is 6789
The employee pay rate is $16.25
The employee hours are 38
```

Because the getValues() function returns a structure, the function header for getValues() must specify the type of structure being returned. Because getValues() does not receive any arguments, the function header has no parameter declarations and consists of the line:

```
Employee getValues();
```

Within getValues(), the variable next is defined as a structure of the type to be returned. After values have been assigned to the next structure, the structure values are returned by including the structure name within the return statement.

On the receiving side, main() must be alerted that the getValues() function is returning a structure. This is handled by the function prototype for getValues(). Notice that these steps for returning a structure from a function are identical to the normal procedures for returning scalar data types described in Chapter 6.

PROGRAM 15.6

```cpp
#include <iostream>
#include <iomanip>
using namespace std;

struct Employee    // declare a global structure type
{
  int idNum;
  double payRate;
  double hours;
};

Employee getValues();    // function prototype

int main()
{
  Employee emp;

  emp = getValues();
  cout << "\nThe employee ID number is " << emp.idNum
       << "\nThe employee pay rate is $" << emp.payRate
       << "\nThe employee hours are " << emp.hours << endl;

  return 0;
}

Employee getValues() // return an employee structure
{
  Employee next;

  next.idNum = 6789;
  next.payRate = 16.25;
  next.hours = 38.0;

  return next;
}
```

Exercises 15.3

1. Write a C++ function named `days()` that determines the number of days from the date 1/1/1900 for any date passed as a structure. Use the `Date` structure:

```cpp
struct Date
{
  int month;
  int day;
  int year;
};
```

In writing the `days()` function, use the convention that all years have 360 days and each month consists of 30 days. The function should return the number of days for any `Date` structure passed to it.

2. Write a C++ function named `difDays()` that calculates and returns the difference between two dates. Each date is passed to the function as a structure using the following global type:

```
struct Date
{
  int month;
  int day;
  int year;
};
```

The `difDays()` function should make two calls to the `days()` function written for Exercise 1.

3. a. Rewrite the `days()` function written for Exercise 1 to receive a reference to a `Date` structure rather than a copy of the complete structure.

   b. Redo Exercise 3a using a pointer rather than a reference.

4. a. Write a C++ function named `larger()` that returns the later date of any two dates passed to it. For example, if the dates 10/9/2005 and 11/3/2005 are passed to `larger()`, the second date is returned.

   b. Include the `larger()` function written for Exercise 4a in a complete program. Store the `Date` structure returned by `larger()` in a separate `Date` structure and display the member values of the returned `Date`.

5. a. Modify the function `days()` written for Exercise 1 to account for the actual number of days in each month. Assume, however, that each year contains 365 days (that is, do not account for leap years).

   b. Modify the function written for Exercise 5a to account for leap years.

15.4 DYNAMIC DATA STRUCTURE ALLOCATION

We have already encountered the concept of explicitly allocating and deallocating memory space using the `new` and `delete` operators (see Section 13.2). For convenience, the description of these operators is repeated in Table 15.1. This ability to allocate memory dynamically is especially useful when dealing with a list of structures because it permits the list to expand as new records are added and contract as records are deleted.

TABLE 15.1

Operator Name	Description
new	Reserves the number of bytes required by the requested data type. Returns the address of the first reserved location or NULL if sufficient memory is not available.
delete	Releases a block of bytes previously reserved. The address of the first reserved location is required as an argument to the operator.

In requesting additional storage space, the user must provide the `new` function with an indication of the amount of storage needed. This is done by requesting enough space for a particular type of data. For example, either of the two expressions `new(int)` or `new int` (the two forms may be used interchangeably) requests enough storage to store an integer number. A request for enough storage for a data structure is made in the same fashion. For example, using the declaration

```
struct TeleType
{
  char name[30];
  char phoneNo[16];
};
```

the expressions `new TeleType` and `new(TeleType)` both reserve enough storage for one `TeleType` data structure.

In allocating storage dynamically, we have no advance indication as to where the computer system will physically reserve the requested number of bytes, and we have no explicit name to access the newly created storage locations. To provide access to these locations, `new` returns the address of the first location that has been reserved. This address must be assigned to a pointer. The return of an address by `new` is especially useful for creating a linked list of data structures. As each new structure is created, the address returned by `new` to the structure can be assigned to a pointer member of the previous structure in the list. Program 15.7 illustrates the use of `new` to create a structure dynamically in response to a user-input request.

A sample session produced by Program 15.7 is:

```
Do you wish to create a new record (respond with y or n): y
Enter a name: Monroe, James
Enter the phone number: (555) 555-1817
The contents of the record just created is:
Name: Monroe, James
Phone Number: (555) 555-1817
```

In Program 15.7, notice that only two variable declarations are made in `main()`. The variable `key` is declared as a character variable and the variable `recPoint` is declared as a pointer to a structure of the `TeleType` type. Because the declaration for the type `TeleType` is global, `TeleType` can be used within `main()` to define `recPoint` as a pointer to a structure of the `TeleType` type.

If a user enters `y` in response to the first prompt in `main()`, a call to `new` is made for the required memory to store the designated structure. Once `recPoint` has been loaded with the proper address, this address can be used to access the newly created structure. The function `populate()` is used to prompt the user for data needed in filling the structure and to store the user-entered data in the correct members of the structure. The argument passed to `populate()` in `main()` is the pointer `recPoint`. Like all passed arguments, the value contained in `recPoint` is passed to the function. Since the value in `recPoint` is an address, `populate()` receives the address of the newly created structure and can directly access the structure members.

Within `populate()`, the value received by it is stored in the parameter named `record`. Because the value to be stored in `record` is the address of a structure, `record` must be declared as a pointer to a structure. This declaration is provided by the statement `TeleType *record;`. The statements within `populate()` use the address in `record` to locate the respective members of the structure.

The `dispOne()` function in Program 15.7 is used to display the contents of the newly created and populated structure. The address passed to `dispOne()` is the same address that was passed to `populate()`. Because this passed value is the address of a structure, the parameter name used to store the address is declared as a pointer to the correct structure type.

PROGRAM 15.7

```cpp
// a program illustrating dynamic structure allocation
#include <iostream>
#include <string>
using namespace std;

struct TeleType
{
  string name;
  string phoneNo;
};

void populate(TeleType *); // function prototype needed by main()
void dispOne(TeleType *); // function prototype needed by main()

int main()
{
  char key;
  TeleType *recPoint;      // recPoint is a pointer to a
                           // structure of type TeleType

  cout << "Do you wish to create a new record (respond with y or n): ";
  key = cin.get();
  if (key == 'y')
  {
    key = cin.get();       // get the Enter key in buffered input
    recPoint = new TeleType;
    populate(recPoint);
    dispOne(recPoint);
  }
  else
    cout << "\nNo record has been created.";

  return 0;
}

  // input a name and phone number
  void populate(TeleType *record) // record is a pointer to a
  {                               // structure of type TeleType
  cout << "Enter a name: ";
  getline(cin, record->name);
  cout << "Enter the phone number: ";
  getline(cin, record->phoneNo);

  return;
}
  // display the contents of one record

void dispOne(TeleType *contents)  // contents is a pointer to a
{                                 // structure of type TeleType
  cout << "\nThe contents of the record just created is:"
       << "\nName: " << contents->name
       << "\nPhone Number: " << contents->phoneNo << endl;

  return;
}
```

Exercises 15.4

1. Enter and execute Program 15.7.

2. As described in Table 15.1, the new operator returns either the address of the first new storage area allocated or NULL if insufficient storage is available. Modify Program 15.7 to check that a valid address has been returned before a call to `populate()` is made. Display an appropriate message if sufficient storage is not available.

3. Write a C++ function named `modify()` that can be used to modify the name and phone number members of a structure of the type created in Program 15.7. The argument passed to `modify()` should be the address of the structure to be modified. The `modify()` function should first display the existing name and phone number in the selected structure and then request new data for these members.

15.5 FOCUS ON PROBLEM SOLVING

In this section, we focus on two problems that use and manipulate data structures. The first problem is concerned with obtaining data for a single record that is to be used in preparing a set of shipping instructions. The second problem addresses the processing of an array of records.

Problem 1: Populating and Processing a Structure

In this problem, a customer calls in an order for bicycles, giving his or her name, address, number of bicycles desired, and the kind of bicycle. For now, all bicycles on one order must be the same kind (a restriction removed in Exercise 3 at the end of this section). Mountain bikes cost $269.95 each and street bikes $149.50. The total bill is to be calculated for the order. Additionally, based on the user's knowledge of the customer, the customer is classified as either a good or bad credit risk. Based on the input data, the program is to prepare shipping instructions listing the customer's name, address, number and type of bikes, and the total amount due. Based on the creditworthiness of the customer, the program must indicate on the shipping instructions if this is a C.O.D. (cash on delivery) shipment or whether the customer will be billed separately.

Analyze the Problem   The input and output requirements of this problem are relatively simple. On the input side, the items that must be obtained are:

1. Customer's name
2. Customer's address
3. Number of bicycles ordered
4. Type of bicycle (mountain or street)
5. Creditworthiness of the customer (good or bad)

For output, a set of shipping instructions is to be generated. The instructions must contain the first four input items, the total cost of the order, and the type of billing. The total cost is obtained as the number of bicycles ordered (input item 3) times the appropriate cost per bicycle, and the type of billing is determined by the creditworthiness of the customer (input item 5). If the customer is creditworthy, a bill will be sent; otherwise, the order requires cash payment on delivery.

FIGURE 15.7	Customer Record Layout

Field No.	Field Contents	Field Type
1	Customer name	Character[50]
2	Customer address	Character[50]
3	Bicycles ordered	Integer
4	Bicycle type	Character—M or S
5	Creditworthiness	Character—Y or N
6	Dollar value of order	Float

Develop a Solution   The input data can be considered to be a record, with the five input items as fields within the record. Additionally, we will add a sixth field to contain the total dollar value of the order. Figure 15.7 illustrates the data types that we will use for this customer record.

A suitable data structure for the record layout of Figure 15.7 is:

```
struct Customer
{
    string name;
    string address;
    int numbikes;
    char biketype;
    char goodrisk;
    double amount;
};
```

Having developed a suitable layout for the data, the design of the program is rather straightforward. The program has to request the input data, determine the total dollar value of the order, and then print the shipping instructions. For this problem, we use one function to populate the structure and a second function to print the shipping instructions. Figure 15.8 presents a structure chart for this solution. In pseudocode, the solution is:

Define the record

Function main
  Populate the data using the function recvorder
  Print the shipping instructions using the function shipslip

Function recvorder
  Input data for name, address, number of bicycles, type of bicycle, and credit type
  Calculate dollar value of order

Function shipslip
  Print name, address, number of bicycles, and type of bicycle
  Determine if this is a C.O.D. or separate billable order
  Print the order type and the dollar value of the order

FIGURE 15.8   Structure Chart

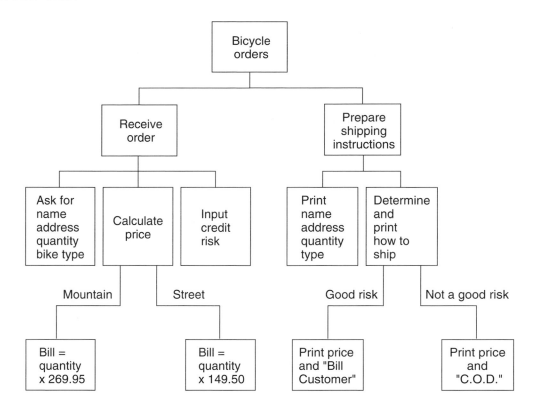

Code the Solution   The C++ code corresponding to our solution is contained in Program 15.8. Notice that the code uses named constants for the maximum string length and the prices of the bicycles. This is in keeping with good programming practice that "magic" numbers are not buried deep within the code where they are hard to locate. Also notice that the function `recvorder()` validates the data entered for bike and credit risk type before storing values in the appropriate data fields.

Notice in Program 15.8 that the function `recvorder()` returns a single data structure to `main()`, whereas `shipslip()` receives a single data structure as its argument. Also notice that within each function, assignments and displayed values are performed for *individual* values in the fields, not for the entire record.

Test and Correct the Program   The errors most likely to be encountered in a program that uses records are those related to undefined or incompatible variables. Such errors occur when the user attempts to use a field name alone (such as `numbikes`) without specifying the record to which it belongs (`record.numbikes`). Another common mistake is to attempt to use a record name without specifying the field (such as writing `record` instead of `record.name`).

PROGRAM 15.8

```cpp
#include <iostream>
#include <iomanip>
#include <iomanip>
using namespace std;

const float MPRICE = 269.95;  // price of a mountain bike
const float SPRICE = 149.50;  // price of a street bike

struct Customer
{
  string name;
  string address;
  int numbikes;
  char biketype;
  char goodrisk;
  double amount;
};

Customer recvorder();  // function prototype needed for main()
void shipslip(Customer);   // function prototype needed for main()

int main()
{
  Customer client;
  client = recvorder();  // enter the order
  shipslip(client);      // prepare shipping instructions

  return 0;
}

 // enter an order
 // precondition: requires MPRICE, which is the price of a mountain bike
 //              : and SPRICE, which is the price of a street bike

Customer recvorder() // return a structure of type Customer
{
  Customer record;  // record is local to this function
  char btype = 'N';
  char risk = 'U';
  double price;

  cout << "\nEnter customer information: ";
  cout << "\nName: ";
  getline(cin, record.name);
  cout << " Address: ";
  getline(cin, record.address);
  cout << "\nHow many Bicycles are ordered: ";
  cin  >> record.numbikes;
  cout << "Type of Bicycle ordered:";
  while( !(btype == 'M' || btype == 'S') )
```

(continued from previous page)

```cpp
   {
     cout << "\n M Mountain";
     cout << "\n S Street";
     cout << "\nChoose one (M or S): ";
     cin  >> btype;
     btype = toupper(btype);    // make sure it's in uppercase
   }
      // determine the price of the bike
   if (btype == 'M')
     price = MPRICE;
   else if (btype == 'S')
     price = SPRICE;

   record.amount = record.numbikes * price;
   record.biketype = btype;

   while( !(risk == 'Y' || risk == 'N') )
   {
     cout << "\nIs this customer a good risk (Y or N): ";
     cin >> risk;
     risk = toupper(risk);
   }
   record.goodrisk = risk;

   return record;
}
 // prepare a shipping list
void shipslip(Customer record)
{
  cout << "\n        Shipping Instructions:";
  cout << "\nTo: " << record.name;
  cout << "\n     " << record.address;
  cout << "\nShip: " << record.numbikes;
  if (record.biketype == 'M')
    cout << " Mountain Bikes";
  else if (record.biketype == 'S')
    cout << " Street Bikes";

    // set output formats
  cout << setw(6)
       << setiosflags(ios::fixed)
       << setiosflags(ios::showpoint)
       << setprecision(2);

  if (record.goodrisk == 'Y')
    cout << "\nby freight, and bill the customer $"
         << record.amount << endl;
  else
    cout << "\nC.O.D.   Amount due on delivery = $"
         << record.amount << endl;

  return;
}
```

Testing should include valid data as well as illegal values for `record.biketype` and `record.goodrisk` and perhaps addresses that exceed 50 characters. Check some results to make sure that the final dollar amount of the bill is calculated correctly. Here is a sample run:

```
Enter customer information:
Name: Jim Watson
Address: 2 Hopper Lane, Rye NH 86662

How many Bicycles are ordered: 6
Type of Bicycle ordered:
   M Mountain
   S Street
Choose one (M or S): S

Is this customer a good risk (Y or N): Y


        Shipping Instructions:
To: Jim Watson
    2 Hopper Lane, Rye NH 86662
Ship: 6 Street Bikes
by freight, and bill the customer $897.00
```

Problem 2 : Sorting and Searching an Array of Structures

Arrays of records can be sorted and searched just like an array of any other type of data. An entire record can be assigned, as a single unit, to another record variable of the same type, and when that is done, all of the fields within it are copied. This is a distinct advantage of records over parallel arrays, where each field must be copied individually.

Usually, when sorting or searching a database consisting of an array of records, you are interested in a particular field in each record. For example, you may want to sort in order of increasing age or alphabetically by last name. The field sorted on is referred to as the **key field**, and sorting and searching are said to be performed "by record key."

Different fields can be designated as keys at different times for different purposes. Searching is facilitated when the key is unique in each record, that is, when no two records have the same key value. Therefore, it is common for unique values, such as Social Security number, employee number, or account number, to be designated as the primary key of a record. If a primary key (such as a last name) is not unique, then another field is often designated as a secondary key, and the sorting and searching occur first in order by the primary key and then by the secondary key.

In this problem, we are going to sort an array of employee records by name and then search for all employees making less than a user-entered hourly rate. For this problem, assume that our database consists of the records shown in Figure 15.9.

Analyze the Problem   The inputs to this problem consist of the records contained within the database, which are listed in Figure 15.9, and a user-input hourly rate.

The required outputs are the list of employee records, sorted by name, and a list of all employees having an hourly rate less than the input value.

Develop a Solution   The data shown in Figure 15.9 will be stored in an array of data structures. We use a selection sort (see Section 12.8) to sort the array into alphabetical order by name; thus, the name field is our primary key field. The sorted array is then displayed to the screen.

FIGURE 15.9	An Unsorted Array of Employee Records

Employee Number	Employee Name	Hourly Rate
34145	Donaldson, S.	5.56
33623	Bohm, P.	7.54
36203	Gwodz, K.	8.72
32479	Abrams, B.	6.72
35987	Ernst, T.	5.43

A linear search through the sorted array of records is then performed, using the rate field as the key field, to find and display all employees having a lower hourly rate than a user-input value. Thus, our program will do the following:

- Define the array of employee records.
- Sort the array by the name field and display the sorted array.
- Prompt the user for an hourly rate and accept the input data.
- Search the sorted array and display all employees making less than the input hourly rate.

Refining this initial algorithm, the following pseudocode expands on how the program will input and process the data.

Function main
   Define an array of data structures and populate it
   Sort the array of data structures using the function selsort
   Display the sorted array using the function display
   Prompt the user for an hourly rate and accept the data
   Perform a linear search for records having a lower hourly rate
      and display the employee number and name for all records
      found

Function selsort
   Perform a selection sort on the array based on the name field

Function display
   For each record in the array,
      Display the record's contents
   EndFor

Function linsearch
   Search each record and examine its rate field
   If the rate value is less than the input value,
      Display the record's number and name fields
   EndIf

Code the Solution   Program 15.9 illustrates C++ code that performs the steps indicated by our program solution. In examining the code, notice that we have used a named constant for the array size, and that we have made all functions general purpose in that they are not restricted for sorting and searching only five records; they can be used for any array size. If you are unfamiliar with the code used in the `selsort()` function, you should review Section 12.8.

```cpp
#include <iostream>
#include <iomanip>
#include <string>
using namespace std;

const int ARRAYSIZE = 5;   // maximum no. of records in the array

struct PayRecord // construct a global structure type

{
  int id;
  string name;
  double rate;
};

  // function prototypes needed by main()
void selsort(PayRecord [], int); // 1st parameter is an array of records
void display(PayRecord [], int);
void linsearch(PayRecord [], int, double);

int main()
{
  PayRecord employee[ARRAYSIZE] = { { 34145, "Donaldson, S.", 5.56},
                                    { 33623, "Bohm, P.", 7.54},
                                    { 36203, "Gwodz, K.", 8.72 },
                                    { 32479, "Abrams, B.", 6.72 },
                                    { 35987, "Ernst, T.", 5.43 } };
  double cutrate;
  selsort(employee, ARRAYSIZE);
  display(employee, ARRAYSIZE);
  cout << "\nEnter the cutoff pay rate: ";
  cin  >> cutrate;
  linsearch(employee, ARRAYSIZE, cutrate);

  return 0;
}

void selsort(PayRecord array[], int numel)
{
  int i, j, minidx;
  char minstrng[MAXNAME];
  PayRecord temp;

  for(i = 0; i < (numel - 1); i++)
  {
    strcpy(minstrng, array[i].name); //assume minimum is first name in list
    minidx = i;
    for(j = i + 1; j < numel; j++)
```

(continued from previous page)

```
    {
      if ( strcmp(array[j].name, minstrng) < 0 ) // if we've located a
      {                                           // lower name, capture it
       strcpy(minstrng, array[j].name);
       minidx = j;
      }
    }
    if ( strcmp(minstrng, array[i].name) < 0 ) // check for a new minimum
    {
      temp = array[i];
      array[i] = array[minidx];
      array[minidx] = temp;
    }
  }
}
void linsearch(PayRecord array[], int numel, double minrate)
{
  int i;
  cout << "\nThe employees making less than this rate are:";
  for (i = 0; i < numel; i++)
    if (array[i].rate < minrate)
      cout << "\n  " << array[i].id << " "
           << setw(20) << setiosflags(ios::left) << array[i].name;
  cout << endl;

  return;
}


void display(PayRecord array[], int numel)
{
  int i;

  cout << "\nThe sorted array of structures is:";
  for (i = 0; i < numel; i++)
    cout << "\n  " << array[i].id << " "
         << setw(20) << setiosflags(ios::left) << array[i].name
         << setw(8) << setprecision(2) << array[i].rate;
    cout << endl;

  return;
}
```

Test and Correct the Program   The sort and search procedures are modifications of those in Section 12.8. Compare these to see what changes have been made to accommodate record arrays.

This is clearly a lengthy program, but debugging can be straightforward if you begin with the `main()` function and then follow through each called function. Substituting stub functions (or just inserting `cout` statements to indicate when you enter and exit each function) helps you trace the program's flow and locate errors. Here is a sample run:

```
The sorted array of structures is:
    32479     Abrams, B.              6.72
    33623     Bohm, P.               7.54
    34145     Donaldson, S.          5.56
    35987     Ernst, T.              5.43
    36203     Gwodz, K.              8.72

Enter the cutoff pay rate: 7.00

The employees making less than this rate are:
    32479     Abrams, B.
    34145     Donaldson, S.
    35987     Ernst, T.
```

Exercises 15.5

1. Write a C++ program that defines a record for a single-item inventory in a store. The record should contain fields for the description, inventory number, storage bin location, quantity on hand, and wholesale cost of the item. A function should allow you to request a new wholesale cost and quantity on hand. If the quantity drops below ten, display a warning message that the stock is low.

2. Develop a program that handles a single record describing the produce in your store. The record should have fields for the produce name (such as apples, oranges, and bananas), quantity on hand, and retail price. As you order or sell each type, the quantity on hand changes. If the amount on hand of any type falls below 30, print a message suggesting that more be ordered. If the amount on hand increases to more than 200, print a message that advertises them for sale at 25% off the regular retail price.

3. Modify Program 15.8 so that a customer may order a variety of kinds of bicycles. (*Hint:* Change the record so that there is a number field for each bicycle type containing how many of that type were ordered. Name these fields `nummtnbikes` and `numstbikes`, and eliminate the `biketype` field.)

4. Construct a data structure that contains all of the short biographical information about yourself that you might think is important, such as name, age, height, hair color, eye color, monthly salary, address, and so on. Write a C++ program that allows you to enter data into the record and to change the contents of the fields when necessary.

5. Expand the inventory problem of Exercise 1 to handle an array of up to five records and populate the five records. Have the program give you a report of all of the inventory items and make up order forms for those whose quantity is fewer than ten items on hand.

6. Modify Program 15.8 to handle an array of records so that you can take five orders for bicycles during the day and prepare shipping orders for all of them at once at the end of the day.

7. a. Representative information about a group of medical patients is shown in Figure 15.10. Define a data structure that records this information for five patients.

   b. Using the data defined in Exercise 7a, write a C++ program that displays the patient's name, address, total days of care (`Inpatient + Outpatient`), and total charges (`Hospital + Doctor + Pharmacy`). Print bills for all patients 65 or older, with their name, address, and a listing of their hospital, doctor, and pharmacy charges. Then calculate and print on the bill a display of the total charges less a 20% senior-citizen discount.

| FIGURE 15.10 | Patient Information for Exercise 7 |

Name	Address	Age	Amount owed	Days of care
First Last	Street City State Zip code		Hospital Doctor Pharmacy	Inpatient Outpatient
Robert Sorenson	1182 25th Street Remington OR 98762	61	$217.90 84.25 63.44	2 6

Test your program using the following data:

```
Robert Sorensen
1182 25th Street
Remington OR 98762
61        217.90        84.25        63.44        2        6
Rita Martinez
815 Buchanan Ave
Williams AZ 82173
27        582.96        479.63        84.90        29       0
Francine Appleton
513 Perington Blvd
St. Francis MN 21394-3005
68        2123.23       654.00        228.21       32       5
George Thomas
10865 Doughboy St
Los Angeles CA 90413-8273
53        105.49        486.88        241.56       2        45
Gary Allred
226 Mountain Road
Hoover NE 70014-1275
78        409.54        441.32        142.09       31       0
```

15.6 UNIONS[2]

A **union** is a data type that reserves the same area in memory for two or more variables, each of which can be a different data type. A variable that is declared as a union data type can be used to hold a character variable, an integer variable, a double-precision variable, or any other valid C++ data type. Each of these types—but only one at a time—can actually be assigned to the union variable.

The definition of a union has the same form as a structure definition, with the keyword union used in place of the keyword structure. For example, the declaration

```
union
{
  char key;
  int num;
  double price;
} val;
```

---

[2] This topic may be omitted on first reading with no loss of subject continuity.

creates a union variable named val. If val were a structure, it would consist of three individual members. As a union, however, val contains a single member that can be either a character variable named key, an integer variable named num, or a double-precision variable named price. In effect, a union reserves sufficient memory locations to accommodate its largest member's data type. This same set of locations is then accessed by different variable names depending on the data type of the value currently residing in the reserved locations. Each value stored overwrites the previous value, using as many bytes of the reserved memory area as necessary.

Individual union members are accessed using the same notation as structure members. For example, if the val union is currently used to store a character, the correct variable name to access the stored character is val.key. Similarly, if the union is used to store an integer, the value is accessed by the name val.num, and a double-precision value is accessed by the name val.price. With union members, it is the programmer's responsibility to ensure that the correct member name is used for the data type currently residing in the union.

Typically, a second variable keeps track of the current data type stored in the union. For example, the following code could be used to select the appropriate member of val for display. Here, the value in the variable uType determines the currently stored data type in the val union:

```
switch(uType)
{
  case 'c': cout << val.key;
            break;
  case 'i': cout << val.num;
            break;
  case 'd': cout << val.price;
            break;
  default : cout << "Invalid type in uType : " << uType;
}
```

As they are in structures, a data type can be associated with a union. For example, the declaration

```
union DateAndTime
{
  int days;
  double time;
};
```

provides a union data type without actually reserving any storage locations. This data type can then be used to define any number of variables. For example, the definition

```
DateAndTime first, second, *pt;
```

creates a union variable named first, a union variable named second, and a pointer that can be used to store the address of any union having the form of DateAndTime. Once a pointer to a union has been declared, the same notation used to access structure members can access union members. For example, if the assignment pt = &first; is made, then pt->days refers to the days member of the union named first.

Unions may themselves be members of structures or arrays, or structures, arrays, and pointers may be members of unions. In each case, the notation used to access a member must be consistent with the nesting employed. For example, in the structure defined by

```
struct
{
  char uType;
  union
  {
    char *text;
    double rate;
  } uTax;
} flag;
```

the variable rate is referenced as:

```
flag.uTax.rate
```

Similarly, the first character of the string whose address is stored in the pointer text is accessed as:

```
(*flag.uTax).text
```

Exercises 15.6

1. Assume the following definition has been made:

```
union
{
  double rate;
  double taxes;
  int num;
} flag;
```

For this union, write appropriate cout streams to display the various members of the union.

2. Define a union variable named car that contains an integer named year, an array of ten characters named name, and an array of ten characters named model.

3. Define a union variable named lang that allows a floating-point number to be accessed by both the variable names interest and rate.

4. Declare a union data type named Amt that contains an integer variable named intAmt, a double-precision variable named dblAmt, and a pointer to a character named ptKey.

5. a. What do you think will be displayed by the following section of code?

```
union
{
  char ch;
  double btype;
} alt;
alt.ch = 'y';
cout << alt.btype;
```

b. Include the code presented in Exercise 5a in a program and run the program to verify your answer to Exercise 5a.

15.7 COMMON PROGRAMMING ERRORS

Three common errors are often made when using structures or unions.

1. Structures and unions, as complete entities, cannot be used in relational expressions. For example, even if `TeleType` and `PhoneType` are two structures of the same type, the expression `TeleType == PhoneType` is invalid. Individual members of a structure or union can, of course, be compared, if they are of the same data type, using any of C++'s relational operators.

2. This error is really an extension of a pointer error as it relates to structures and unions. Whenever a pointer is used to "point to" either of these data types, or whenever a pointer is itself a member of a structure or a union, take care to use the address in the pointer to access the appropriate data type. Should you be confused about just what is being pointed to, remember: If in doubt, print it out.

3. Because a union can store only one of its members at a time, you must be careful to keep track of the currently stored variable. Storing one data type in a union and accessing it by the wrong variable name can result in an error that is particularly troublesome to locate.

15.8 CHAPTER REVIEW

Key Terms

data field	structure
key field	structure member
record	union

Summary

1. A *structure* allows individual variables to be grouped under a common variable name. Each variable in a structure is accessed by its structure variable name, followed by a period, followed by its individual variable name. Another term for a data structure is a *record*. One form for declaring a structure is:

```
struct
{
  individual member declarations;
} structureName;
```

2. A data type can be created from a structure using the declaration form:

```
struct DataTypeName
{
  individual member declarations;
};
```

Individual structure variables may then be defined as this `DataTypeName` name. By convention, the first letter of the `DataTypeName` name is always capitalized.

3. Structures are particularly useful as elements of arrays. Used in this manner, each structure becomes one record in a list of records.

4. Complete structures can be used as function arguments, in which case the called function receives a copy of each element in the structure. The address of a structure may also be passed, either as a reference or a pointer, which provides the called function with direct access to the structure.

5. Structure members can be any valid C++ data type, including other structures, unions, arrays, and pointers. When a pointer is included as a structure member, a linked list can be created. Such a list uses the pointer in one structure to "point to" (contain the address of) the next logical structure in the list.

6. Unions are declared in the same manner as structures. The definition of a union creates a memory overlay area, with each union member using the same memory storage locations. Thus, only one member of a union can be active at a time.

Exercises

1. Define a structure data type and member variables for a business, including fields for the business name, description of the product or services, address, number of employees, and annual revenue.

2. Define a structure data type and member variables for a single kind of screw in your parts inventory, with fields for inventory number, screw length, diameter, kind of head (Phillips or standard slot), material (steel, brass, other), and cost.

3. A structure type is defined as:

```
struct Inventory
{
  char description[50];
  int prodnum;
  int quantity;
  float price;
};
```

   Write the following:

   a. A declaration for an array of 100 structures of type Inventory

   b. An assignment of inventory number 4355 to the 83rd Inventory item

   c. A statement that displays the price of the 15th Inventory item

4. Define an array of structures for up to 50 factory employees, in which each record contains fields for name, age, Social Security number, hourly wage, and years with the company. Write the following:

   a. Statements that display the name and number of years with the company for the 25th employee in the array

   b. A loop that, for every employee, adds 1 to the number of years with the company and that adds 50 cents to the hourly wage

FIGURE 15.11   Two Mathematical Vectors

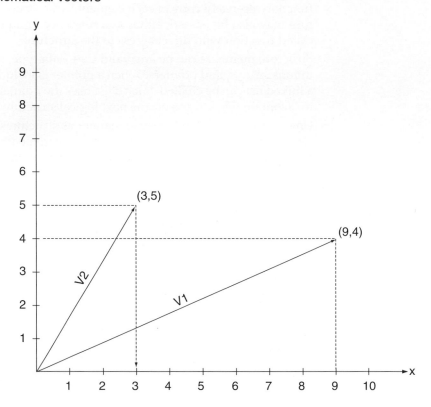

5. a. In two dimensions, a mathematical vector is a pair of numbers that represents directed arrows in a plane, as shown by the mathematical vectors V1 and V2 in Figure 15.11.

Two-dimensional mathematical vectors can be written in the form (*a,b*), where *a* and *b* are called the *x* and *y* components of the vector. For example, for the vectors illustrated in Figure 15.11, V1 = (9,4) and V2 = (3,5). For mathematical vectors, the following operations apply:

If `V1=(a,b)` and `V2=(c,d)`

`V1+V2=(a,b)+(c,d)=(a + c, b + d)`

`V1-V2=(a,b)2(c,d)=(a - c, b - d)`

Using this information, write a C++ program that defines an array of two mathematical vector structures, where each record consists of two double-precision components *a* and *b*. Your program should permit a user to enter two vectors, call two functions that return the sum and difference of the entered vectors, and display the results calculated by these functions.

b. In addition to the operations defined in Exercise 5a, two other vector operations are negation and absolute value. For a vector V1 with components (*a,b*), these operations are defined as follows:

```
negation: -V1 = -(a,b) = (-a,-b)
absolute value: |V1| = sqrt(a * a + b * b)
```

Using this information, modify the program that you wrote for Exercise 5a to display the negation and absolute values of both vectors input by a user as well as the negation and absolute value of the sum of the two input vectors.

16 | The Standard Template Library

As described in Section 12.6, C++ provides a vector class for storing, ordering, and retrieving objects that permits the list to expand or contract as objects are added to or removed from it. This chapter presents two additional types of list maintenance classes, both of which are supported by the same Standard Template Library (STL) from which vectors are derived. You'll learn about these two new classes by studying three specific list handling applications: linked lists, stacks, and queues. You'll also study the underlying algorithm for a linked list. The advantage of using STL classes is that the advanced programming capabilities underlying linked lists, stacks, and queues are all provided as part of the STL class implementations.

This chapter is intended as an introduction to the STL. A complete textbook would be required to cover the complete set of classes and capabilities provided by the STL. The applications presented in this chapter represent an extremely small subset of those that can be addressed using the STL. Typically, the second course in a computer science curriculum is specifically devoted to presenting the advanced applications that are programmed using either the STL or similarly constructed classes.

16.1 THE STANDARD TEMPLATE LIBRARY

You've already worked with one kind of list, an array, which is the list of choice for a fixed-length set of related data. Many programming applications, however, require variable-length lists that must constantly be expanded and contracted as items are added to and removed from the list. Although expanding and contracting an array can be accomplished by creating, copying, and deleting arrays, this solution tends to be costly in terms of initial programming, maintenance, and testing time.

In all but the simplest of situations, it is almost always more efficient to use the STL to create and manipulate lists. Among other uses, one of the purposes of the STL is to provide a completely tested and generic set of easily used lists that can be maintained in various configurations. This is accomplished by calling either prewritten class methods or generalized algorithms applicable to all STL-created list types. The STL is one component of the larger Standard Library of header files and classes. It provides a broad range of generic capabilities for rapidly constructing and manipulating lists of objects—objects consisting of either built-in variables or objects. These STL capabilities allow you to maintain lists and perform operations on them, such as sorting and searching, without having to fully understand or program the advanced and frequently complicated underlying algorithms.

Currently the STL provides seven different types of lists, each supported by its own class. These seven list types are summarized in Table 16.1.

As listed in the Classification column of Table 16.1, the seven different list types are categorized as either sequence or associative. A **sequence list** is one in which a list object is solely determined by its position in the list—that is, by where the object was placed in the list and how it may have been subsequently moved. For example, both arrays and vectors are sequence lists, where an object's position in the list is determined by the exact order in which it was added into the array or vector or subsequently moved. An **associative list** is automatically maintained in a sorted order. An object's position in an associative list depends on its value and a selected sorting criterion. For example, an alphabetical list of names depends on the name and a sorting criteria, rather than on the exact order that individual names were entered into the list. In this chapter you will only be concerned with STL's sequence types. You already learned about one kind of sequence list, the vector type, in Section 12.6.

Before you begin working with lists and the STL, it's helpful to understand the difference between the lists provided by the STL and arrays. An array is a built-in list type. By contrast, the lists provided by the STL are class types. Although arrays are most often used to directly store built-in numerical data types, they still retain general characteristics common to the more advanced lists provided by the STL. For example, like an array, an STL list can be empty, which means that it currently holds no items. As it applies to both arrays and lists provided by the STL, a list is considered to be a container that can hold a collection of zero or more items, each of which is of the same type. For this reason, STL lists and arrays are referred to as both **containers** and **collections**, and in this text, these terms are used interchangeably. A list must also provide a means for accessing individual objects.

TABLE 16.1 STL Lists

List Type	Classification	Usage
vector	Sequence	Dynamic arrays
list	Sequence	Linked lists
deque	Sequence	Stacks and queues
set	Associative	Binary trees without duplicate objects
multiset	Associative	Binary trees that may have duplicate objects
map	Associative	Binary trees with a unique key that does not permit duplicate objects
multimap	Associative	Binary trees with a unique key that permits duplicate objects

When a list provides this individual data location capability, the list becomes a data structure. In an array, this location ability is provided by the position of each object in the array, which is designated using an integer index value.

Although STL lists can also store built-in data types, they are more commonly used to store and maintain objects. In commercial applications these objects are usually referred to as records. Once an object's structure has been defined, some means for collecting all of the objects into a single list is required. For example, the objects that are stored could be students' academic records. In addition to the individual records, a means is needed to store all of the records in some order so that individual records can be located, displayed, printed, and updated.

Before describing specific types of applications in detail, however, it is worthwhile emphasizing that only objects—and not a class's methods—are stored in a list. The methods, which apply to the class as a whole, simply provide a means of initializing each object before it is placed into the list and reporting and modifying an object either before it is inserted into or after it has been extracted from the list. Figure 16.1 illustrates the complete process of creating and using both objects and lists.

Each STL class provides its own set of methods, as illustrated by the `vector` class presented in Section 8.6. The STL also provides a general set of methods, referred to as algorithms, that can be applied to any range of objects stored in any STL created list. These algorithms, previously introduced in Section 7.6, are repeated in Table 16.2, for your convenience.

Finally, the last major set of components provided as part of the STL is iterators. Iterators provide the means of specifying the objects in a container and operate in a similar manner as indices do for arrays.

To create and use STL lists, you must do the following:

1. Use the STL class to construct the desired container type.

2. Store objects within the list.

3. Apply either the STL class's methods or the more general STL algorithms to the stored objects.

You will put these steps into practice in the following sections as you construct the three kinds of lists: linked lists, stacks, and queues.

FIGURE 16.1 **The List Creation Process**

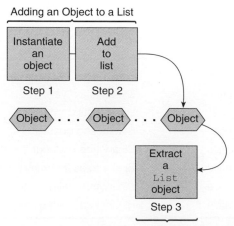

Adding an Object to a List

Instantiate an object — Step 1

Add to list — Step 2

Object . . . Object . . . Object

Extract a List object — Step 3

Extracting an Object from a List

> ### PROGRAMMING NOTE

Homogeneous and Heterogeneous Data Types

Lists and objects are both data structures. A data structure is a container of data organized in a way that facilitates the insertion, retrieval, and deletion of the data. The difference between a list and an object is in the types of objects they contain. A list is a **homogeneous** data structure, which means that its components must be of the same data type. An object is a **heterogeneous** data structure, which means that each of its internal objects can be of different data types. For example, an object could contain a name stored as a string data type, a pay rate stored as a double-precision data type, and an identification number stored as an integer data type. Because an object can be composed of different data types, it is a heterogeneous data structure. However, the list holding all of the objects is a homogeneous data structure, where each object has the same heterogeneous structure.

TABLE 16.2 Commonly Used STL Algorithms

Algorithm Name	Description
accumulate	Returns the sum of the numbers in a specified range
binary_search	Returns a Boolean value of `true` if the specified value exists within the specified range, otherwise, returns `false`; can only be used on a sorted set of values
copy	Copies objects from a source range to a destination range
copy_backward	Copies objects from a source range to a destination range in a reverse direction
count	Returns the number of objects in a specified range that match a specified value
equal	Compares the objects in one range of objects, object by object, to the objects in a second range
fill	Assigns every object in a specified range to a specified value
find	Returns the position of the first occurrence of an object in a specified range having a specified value, if the value exists; performs a linear search, starting with the first object in a specified range and proceeds one object at a time until the complete range has been searched or the specified object has been found
max_object	Returns the maximum value of the objects in the specified range
min_object	Returns the minimum value of the objects in the specified range
random_shuffle	Randomly shuffles object values in a specified range
remove	Removes a specified value within a specified range without changing the order of the remaining objects
replace	Replaces each object in a specified range having a specified value with a newly specified value
reverse	Reverses objects in a specified range
search	Finds the first occurrence of a specified value or sequence of values within a specified range
sort	Sorts objects in a specified range into ascending order
swap	Exchanges object values between two objects
unique	Removes duplicate adjacent objects within a specified range

1. Define the following terms:

   a. container

   b. collection

   c. data structure

   d. iterator

   e. list

   f. STL

2. What sequential container types are supported in STL?

3. What associative container types are supported in STL?

4. For each of the following, define a class that contains only a data declaration section and can be used to create the following objects:

   a. An object, known as a student record, containing a student identification number, the number of credits completed, and a cumulative grade point average

   b. An object, known as a student record, capable of holding a student's name, date of birth, number of credits completed, and cumulative grade point average

   c. A mailing list containing a title field, last name field, first name field, two street address fields, a city field, a state field, and a zip code field

   d. A stock object containing the stock's name, the price of the stock, and the date of purchase

   e. An inventory object containing an integer part number, a string part description, an integer number of parts in inventory, and an integer re-order value

5. For each of the individual classes declared in Exercise 4, add a suitable constructor and accessor method. Test each method to initialize and display the following data:

   a. `Identification Number: 4672`
      `Number of Credits Completed: 68`
      `Grade Point Average: 3.01`

   b. `Name: Rhona Karp`
      `Date of Birth: 8/4/60`
      `Number of Credits Completed: 96`
      `Grade Point Average: 3.89`

   c. `Title: Dr.`
      `Last Name: Kingsley`
      `First Name: Kay`
      `Street Address: 614 Freeman Street`
      `City: Indianapolis`
      `State: IN`
      `Zip Code: 07030`

   d. `Stock: IBM`
      `Price Purchased: 134.5`
      `Date Purchased: 10/1/86`

   e. `Part Number: 16879`
      `Description: Battery`
      `Number in Stock: 10`
      `Reorder Number: 3`

6. a. Write a C++ program that prompts a user to input the current month, day, and year. Store the data entered in a suitably defined object and display the date in an appropriate manner.

   b. Modify the program written in Exercise 6a to use an object that accepts the current time in hours, minutes, and seconds.

7. Define a class capable of creating objects that can store a business's name, description of the business's product or services, address, number of employees, and annual revenue.

8. Define a class capable of creating objects for various screw types held in inventory. Each object should contain a field for an integer inventory number, double-precision screw length, double-precision diameter, kind of head (Phillips or standard slot), material (steel, brass, other), and cost.

9. Write a C++ program that defines a class capable of creating objects for storing the name of a stock, its estimated earnings per share, and its estimated price-to-earnings ratio. Have the program prompt the user to enter these items for five different stocks. When the data has been entered for a particular stock, have the program compute and display the anticipated stock price based on the entered earnings and price-per-earnings values. For example, if a user entered the data XYZ 1.56 12, the anticipated price for a share of XYZ stock is (1.56)*(12) = $18.72.

16.2 LINKED LISTS

A classic data-handling problem is making additions or deletions to existing objects that are maintained in a specific order. This is best illustrated by considering the alphabetical telephone list shown in Figure 16.2. Starting with this initial set of names and telephone numbers, assume that you now need to add new objects to the list such that the alphabetic ordering of the objects is always maintained.

Although the insertion or deletion of ordered objects can be accomplished using an array or vector, these containers are not efficient representations for adding or deleting objects internal to the list, because deleting an object creates an empty slot that requires shifting up all objects below the deleted object to close the empty slot. Similarly, adding an object internally to the list requires that all objects after the addition be shifted down to make room for the new entry. Thus, either adding or deleting objects in an array or a vector requires restructuring objects within the container—an inherently inefficient practice even though it is automatically handled by the `vector` class.

FIGURE 16.2 A Telephone List in Alphabetical Order

Acme, Sam
(555) 898-2392
Dolan, Edith
(555) 682-3104
Lanfrank, John
(555) 718-4581
Mening, Stephen
(555) 382-7070
Zemann, Harold
(555) 219-9912

A linked list provides a convenient method for maintaining a constantly changing list without the need for continually reordering and restructuring. In a **linked list** each object contains one variable that specifies the location of the next object in the list. Thus, with a linked list it is not necessary to physically store each object in the proper order; instead, each new object is physically stored in whatever memory space is currently free. If an object is added to the list, it's only necessary to update the variables for the objects immediately preceding and following the newly

FIGURE 16.3   Using Pointer Variables to Link Structures

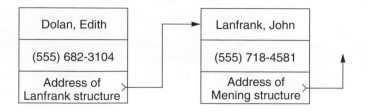

inserted object with the new location information. Therefore, from a programming standpoint, information is always contained within one object that permits location of the next object, no matter where this next object is actually stored.

A linked list is illustrated in Figure 16.3, where each object consists of a name and telephone number, plus an additional variable that stores the address of the next object in the list. Although the actual data for the Lanfrank object shown in the figure may be physically stored anywhere in the computer, the variable included at the end of the Dolan object maintains the proper alphabetical order and provides the location of the Lanfrank object. A variable used in this way is called a **pointer variable** and is described in the next chapter. All that you need to know at this point, however, is that each object in a linked list must contain information to locate the next object.

To see the usefulness of the pointer variable in the Dolan object, assume a telephone number for June Hagar has been added to the alphabetical list, as shown in Figure 16.4. The data for June Hagar is stored in a data object using the same type as that used for the existing objects. To ensure that the telephone number for Hagar is correctly displayed after the Dolan telephone number, the value in the pointer variable in the Dolan object must be altered to locate the Hagar object, and the pointer variable in the Hagar object must be set to the location of the Lanfrank object. As illustrated in Figure 16.4, the pointer variable in each object simply locates the object in the list, even if that object is not physically located in the correct order. Removal of an object from a linked list is the reverse process of adding an object. The actual object is logically removed from the list by simply changing the pointer variable's value in the object preceding it to the location of the object immediately following the deleted object.

FIGURE 16.4   Adjusting Addresses to Point to Appropriate Objects

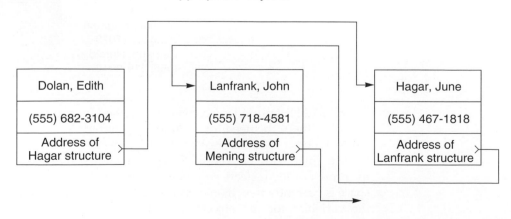

There are two fundamentally different approaches to actually constructing a linked list. The first approach is to use the STL `list` class; the second approach is to "make your own," in which the programmer provides a class that includes an object's declaration and the code for creating and maintaining the list.

The usefulness of the STL `list` class is that the linked list, as shown in Figure 16.4, can be constructed without the programmer having either to understand or to program the internal details of the pointer variables. The programmer doesn't even have to understand the details of how the STL list is created and maintained. This is, of course, the major benefit of object-oriented programming using existing classes. Thus, except for exceedingly specialized cases, you should almost always use the STL `list` class, which is described next. However, because it is useful to understand what is actually being provided by this class and the concepts underlying it, the basics of creating your own linked lists after the `list` class is also described.

STL `list` Class Implementation

Figure 16.5 presents the internal structure used by the STL `list` class to maintain a list of linked objects. The important point to notice is that the access through the list only occurs via variables in each object that contain location information for an object. These variables are referred to as **link variables**. This structure makes it possible to insert a new object into the list simply by storing the new object in any available memory location and adjusting the location information in at most two link variables. Unlike an array implementation, it is not necessary to store list objects in contiguous memory locations. Similarly, an object can be removed by adjusting the link information in two link variables. As explained earlier, this means that expansion and contraction of the list are more efficient than the same operations using a vector approach.

FIGURE 16.5 Class Showing Four Link Variables

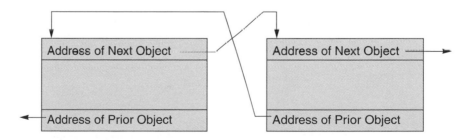

Table 16.3 lists the methods provided by the `list` class. These methods deal with adding, removing, and locating objects from the front and rear of the list. Note that linked lists provide no random access methods. To get to any internal object, the list must be sequentially traversed, object-by-object, starting at either the front or back of the list.

Also note that the `list` class provides no method for returning any object except the first and last objects. Instead, to access an internal object, not only must the list be traversed from one end, but all objects before the desired object must be removed from the list. Technically, when an item is removed in this fashion, it is

TABLE 16.3 Summary of STL `list` Class Methods and Operations

Methods and Operations	Type	Description
`list<DataType> name`	constructor	Creates an empty list named name with compiler-dependent initial size
`list<DataType> name(source)`	constructor	Creates a copy of the source list
`list<DataType> name(n)`	constructor	Creates a list of size n
`list<DataType> name(n, object)`	constructor	Creates a list of size n with each object initialized as `object`
`list<DataType> name(src.beg, src.end)`	constructor	Creates a list initialized with objects from a source container beginning at `src.beg` and ending at `src.end`
`~list(DataType>()`	destructor	Destroys the list and all objects it contains
`name.front()`	accessor	Returns the object at the front of the list (the first object) with no check for the existence of a first object
`name.pop_front()`	mutator	Removes, but does not return, the object at the front of the list
`name.push_front(object)`	mutator	Inserts `object` at the front of the list
`name.back()`	accessor	Returns the object at the back of the list with no check for the existence of a last object
`name.pop_back()`	mutator	Removes, but does not return, the object at the back of the list (the last object)
`name.push_back(object)`	mutator	Inserts `object` at the back of the list
`name.insert(itr, object)`	mutator	Inserts `object` at the iterator position `itr`
`name.insert(itr, src.beg, src.end)`	mutator	Inserts copies of objects from a source container, beginning at `src.beg` and ending at `src.end`, at iterator position `itr`
`name.insert(itr, n, object)`	mutator	Inserts n copies of `object` at iterator position `itr`
`name.assign(n, object)`	mutator	Assigns n copies of `object`
`name.(src.begin, src.end)`	mutator	Assigns the objects of the `src` container (need not be a list), between the range `src.begin` and `src.end`, to the named list
`name.erase(pos)`	mutator	Removes the object at the specified position
`name.erase(begin, end)`	mutator	Removes the objects within the specified range
`name.resize(value)`	mutator	Resizes the list to a larger size with new objects instantiated using the default constructor
`name.resize(value, object)`	mutator	Resizes the list to a larger size with new objects instantiated as `object`
`name.clear()`	mutator	Removes all objects from the list
`nameA.swap(nameB)`	mutator	Swaps the objects of `nameA` and `nameB` lists; can be performed using the `swap()` algorithm
`name.begin()`	accessor	Returns an iterator to the first object in the list
`name.end()`	accessor	Returns an iterator to the position after the last object in the list

TABLE 16.3 *(continued)*

Methods and Operations	Type	Description
`name.rbegin()`	accessor	Returns a reverse iterator for the first object in the list
`name.rend()`	accessor	Returns a reverse iterator for the position after the last object in the list
`name.unique()`	mutator	Removes consecutive duplicate objects
`name.merge(name2)`	mutator	Merges the sorted objects of `name2` into the sorted objects of `name`, creating a final sorted list
`name.reverse()`	mutator	Reverses the objects in the list
`name.splice(itr, name1)`	mutator	Inserts `name1` objects into `name` at position `itr`
`name.splice(itr, name2, beg, end)`	mutator	Inserts `name2` objects in the position range from `beg` to `end` into `name` at position `itr`
`name.sort()`	mutator	Sorts the objects in the list
`nameA == nameB`	relational	Returns a Boolean `true` if `nameA` objects all equal `nameB` objects; otherwise, returns `false`
`nameA != nameB`	relational	Returns a Boolean `false` if `nameA` objects all equal `nameB` objects; otherwise, returns `true`; same as `!(nameA == nameB)`
`nameA < nameB`	relational	Returns a Boolean `true` if `nameA` is less than `nameB`; otherwise, returns `false`
`nameA > nameB`	relational	Returns a Boolean `true` if `nameA` is greater than `nameB`; otherwise, returns `false`; same as `nameB < nameA`
`nameA <= nameB`	relational	Returns a Boolean `true` if `nameA` is less than or equal to `nameB`
`nameA >= nameB`	relational	Returns a Boolean `true` if `nameA` is greater than or equal to `nameB`
`name.size()`	capacity	Returns the number of objects in the list as an integer
`name.empty()`	capacity	Returns a Boolean `true` if list is empty; otherwise, returns `false`
`name.max_size()`	capacity	Returns the maximum possible objects as an Integer
`name.capacity()`	capacity	Returns the maximum possible objects as an integer without relocation of the list

referred to as "popping" the object from the list. Generally, not to lose the removed objects, a copy of the list is made, either as a complete list or object by object as each object is removed, or popped.

Now consider the following two example programs. Program 16.1 creates and displays a single linked list of names, stored as strings, whereas Program 16.2 shows how to store and retrieve user-created objects. Because of the STL's structure, the two applications are virtually the same. Later, in Program 16.3, we show how to construct your own linked list of objects without using the STL classes.

PROGRAMMING NOTE

List Application Considerations

Vectors are the preferred list type whenever you need random access to objects without the need for many insertions or deletions. The reason is that an index value can be used to go directly to the desired object. Insertions and deletions require modifying the underlying array supporting the vector and can be costly in terms of overhead time required to perform these operations when many insertions and deletions are required

Because the only way to get to an object in the middle of a list is by traversing all of the objects either before it or by traversing objects from the back of the list toward the desired object, attempts at random access tends to be costly in terms of access time. Thus, a list is the preferred list type whenever many object insertions and deletions need to be made *and* object access tends to be sequential.

Finally, if you only need to store primitive data types, such as integers or double-precision values, a simple array should be your first choice.

PROGRAM 16.1

```cpp
#include <iostream>
#include <list>
#include <algorithm>
#include <string>
using namespace std;

int main()
{
  list<string> names, addnames;
  string n;

  // add names to the original list
  names.push_front("Dolan, Edith");
  names.push_back("Lanfrank, John");

  // create a new list
  addnames.push_front("Acme, Sam");
  addnames.push_front("Zebee, Frank");

  names.sort();
  addnames.sort();

  // merge the second list into the first
  names.merge(addnames);
  cout << "The first list size is: " <<  names.size() << endl;
  cout << "This list contains the names:\n";

  while (!names.empty())
  {
    cout << names.front() << endl;
    names.pop_front();  // remove the object
  }
}
```

The output produced by Program 16.1 is:

```
The first list size is: 4:
This list contains the names:
Acme, Sam
Dolan, Edith
Lanfrank, John
Zebee, Frank
```

Using User-Defined Objects

In practice, the majority of real-life applications using linked lists require a user-defined object consisting of a combination of data types. For example, consider the problem of creating a linked list for the simplified telephone objects class illustrated in Figure 16.6.

FIGURE 16.6   UML Class Diagram for a Telephone Directory Object

```
                          NameTele
------------------------------------------------
-name: string
-phoneNum: string
------------------------------------------------
+NameTele(name, phoneNum)
+string getName(): return name
+string getPhone(): return phoneNum
```

A suitable class definition corresponding to Figure 16.6's UML diagram is:

CLASS 16.1

```
class NameTele
{
  // data declaration section
  private:
    string name;
    string phoneNum;

  // methods declaration and implementation section
  public:
    NameTele(string nn, string phone)  // constructor
    {
      name = nn;
      phoneNum = phone;
    }
    string getName(){return name;}
    string getPhone(){return phoneNum;}
};
```

This class permits constructing objects consisting of name and phoneNumber instance variables using a constructor, as well as accessor methods for setting and retrieving these variables. Program 16.2 instantiates four objects of this class and stores them within a linked list. After it is created, the complete list is displayed.

PROGRAM 16.2

```cpp
#include <iostream>
#include <list>
#include <string>
using namespace std;

class NameTele
{
  // data declaration section
  private:
    string name;
    string phoneNum;

  // methods declaration and implementation section
  public:
    NameTele(string nn, string phone)  // constructor
    {
      name = nn;
      phoneNum = phone;
    }
    string getName(){return name;}
    string getPhone(){return phoneNum;}
};

  int main()
  {
      // instantiate a list and initialize the list
    // using the objects in the array
    list<NameTele> employee;

    employee.push_front( NameTele("Acme, Sam", "(555) 891-2392"));
    employee.push_back( NameTele("Dolan, Edith", "(555) 682-3104"));
    employee.push_back( NameTele("Mening, Stephen", "(555) 382-7070"));
    employee.push_back( NameTele("Zeman, Harold", "(555) 219-9912"));

    // retrieve all list objects
    // use accessor methods to extract the name and pay rate
      cout <<"The size of the list is " << employee.size() << endl;
    cout <<"\n     Name                Telephone";
    cout <<"\n-------------        -------------\n";

    while (!employee.empty())
    {
      cout << employee.front().getName()
          << "\t     " << employee.front().getPhone() << endl;
      employee.pop_front();  // remove the object
    }
  }
```

The output produced by Program 16.2 is:

```
                    The size of the list is 4

             Name                      Telephone
        ---------------             ---------------
        Acme, Sam                   (555) 891-2392
        Dolan, Edith                (555) 682-3104
        Mening, Stephen             (555) 382-7070
        Zeman, Harold               (555) 219-9912
```

Notice in Program 16.2 that after each object is retrieved from the list, the underlying class's `accessor` methods extract individual name and telephone values. Because the dot operator has a left-to-right associativity, an expression such as `employee.front().getName()` is interpreted as `(employee.front()).getName()`. Thus, the STL's `list` class's `front()` method is used to return the front object from the list, which is then further processed by the `NameTele` class's `getName()` method.

Constructing a Programmer-Defined Linked List[1]

The key to constructing a linked list is to provide each object with at least one pointer variable. For example, to use the `NameTele` class (Class 16.1) in a user-created linked list, you first have to provide a link from one object to the next. This is accomplished by adding an extra variable to each object. As this variable must be capable of storing the address value of a `NameTele` object, a suitable declaration for the required instance variable is:

```
NameTele *link; // create a pointer variable to a NameTele object
```

The inclusion of a pointer variable in a data declaration section should not be surprising, because an object is permitted to contain any C++ data type. In this case, the variable named `link` will be used to locate an object of type `NameTele`. In addition to this new variable, you need to supply the class with a set of constructor, mutator, and accessor methods that include setting and retrieving the value stored in `link`. Class 16.2 provides a complete class definition to meet these additional requirements.

CLASS 16.2

```cpp
#include <iostream>
#include <string>
using namespace std;

class NameTele
{
  // data declaration section
  private:
    string name;
    string phoneNum;
    NameTele *link;
```

---

[1] This topic can be omitted without loss of subject continuity.

(continued from previous page)

```
      // methods declaration and implementation section
      public:
        NameTele(string nn, string phone)   // constructor
        {
          name = nn;
          phoneNum = phone;
          link = NULL;
        }
        string getName(){return name;}
        string getPhone(){return phoneNum;}
        NameTele *getLink(){return link;}
        void setLink(NameTele *ll){link = ll;}
    };
```

Because each object in a linked list has the same format, it is clear that the last object cannot have a pointer value that points to another object because there is none. To satisfy this requirement, the last object in the list will always have a NULL value in its pointer variable. The NULL value is interpreted as a sentinel indicating the end of the list has been reached. Similarly, an initial pointer variable must be available for storing the address of the first object in the list.

Program 16.3 illustrates using the NameTele class by specifically defining four objects having this form, which have been named head, r1, r2, and r3, respectively. The name and telephone members of three of these objects are initialized with actual name and telephone numbers when the objects are defined.

PROGRAM 16.3

```
#include <iostream>
#include <string>
using namespace std;

class NameTele
{
  // data declaration section
  private:
    string name;
    string phoneNum;
    NameTele *link;

  // methods declaration and implementation section
  public:
    NameTele(string nn, string phone)   // constructor
    {
      name = nn;
      phoneNum = phone;
      link = NULL;
    }
    string getName(){return name;}
    string getPhone(){return phoneNum;}
    NameTele *getLink(){return link;}
    void setLink(NameTele *ll){link = ll;}
};
```

(continued from previous page)

```cpp
int main()
{
  NameTele head = NameTele("xx", "xx");  // create an empty object

  // create three objects
  NameTele r1 = NameTele("Acme, Sam", "(555) 898 2392");
  NameTele r2 = NameTele("Dolan, Edith", "(555) 682 3104");
  NameTele r3 = NameTele("Lanfrank, John", "(555) 718 4581");

  // link all of the objects
  head.setLink(&r1);  // have the head link point to the first object;
  r1.setLink(&r2);
  r2.setLink(&r3);

  // retrieve each object using the link from the prior object
  cout << head.getLink()->getName() << endl
       << r1.getLink()->getName() << endl
       << r2.getLink()->getName() << endl;
}
```

The output produced by executing Program 16.3 is:

```
Acme, Sam
Dolan, Edith
Lanfrank, John
```

The important concept illustrated by Program 16.3 is the use of a pointer variable in one object to access the next object in the list, as illustrated in Figure 16.7.

FIGURE 16.7 The Relationship Between Objects in Program 16.3

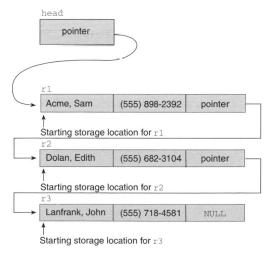

The initialization of the names and telephone numbers for each of the objects defined in Program 16.3 is straightforward. Although each object consists of three variables, only the first two variables in each are explicitly initialized when an object is instantiated. The remaining variable, which is a pointer, is only assigned an explicit address after the next object is placed in the list.

The three assignment statements in Program 16.3 perform the correct pointer assignments. The expression `head.setLink(&r1);` stores the address of the first telephone object in the pointer variable of the object named `head`. The expression `r1.setLink(&r2);` stores the address of the `r2` object in the pointer member of the `r1` object. Similarly, the expression `r2.setLink(&r3);` stores the address of the `r3` object in the pointer member of the `r2` object.

Once name and telephone values have been assigned to each object, and correct location information has been stored in the appropriate pointers, the pointers are then used to access each object's name member. For example, the expression `head.getLink()->getName()` is used to locate the `r1` object and then to extract its `name` value. Often the links in a linked list of objects can be used to loop through the complete list. As each object is accessed, it can be either examined to select a specific value or used to print out a complete list. Equally important is that a linked list can easily expand as new objects are added and contract as existing objects are deleted.

For objects that need to be inserted internally within a list, the new object's link would also have to be set to locate the next object in the list, and the prior object's link would also have to be adjusted to correctly locate the inserted object. Deleting an object is accomplished by removing the link to the object and adjusting the prior object's link to locate the next valid object in the list.

Programming all of the required insertion and deletion methods takes time and care. Using the STL's `list` class removes all of this programming effort from you, while providing a complete set of tested methods for performing all the maintenance tasks associated with a linked list.

Exercises 16.2

1. Modify Program 16.2 to prompt the user for a name. Have the program search the existing list for the entered name. If the name is in the list, display the corresponding phone number; otherwise, display this message: The name is not in the current phone list.

2. Write a C++ program that contains a linked list of 10 integer numbers. Have the program display the numbers in the list.

3. Using the linked list of objects shown in Figure 16.4, write the sequence of steps necessary to delete the object for John Lanfrank from the list.

4. Generalize the description provided in Exercise 3 to describe the sequence of steps necessary to remove the nth object from a list of linked objects. The nth object is preceded by the (n−1)st object and followed by the (n+1)st object.

5. Determine the output of the following program:

```
#include <iostream>
#include <list>
using namespace std;

int main()
{
    int intValue;
    double sum = 0.0;
    double average;

    // create an array of integer values
    int nums[] = {1, 2, 3, 4, 5 };

    // instantiate a list of ints using a
    // constructor that initializes the list with values from the array
    list<int> x(nums, nums + 4);

    cout <<"\nThe list x initially has a size of " << x.size()
         << "," << "\n and contains the objects: " ;
```

(continued from previous page)

```
      while (!x.empty())
      {
        cout << x.front() << "  ";
        x.pop_front();
      }
      cout << endl;
  }
```

16.3 STACKS

A **stack** is a special type of list in which objects can only be added to and removed from the top of the list. As such, it is a **last-in, first-out (LIFO)** list—that is, a list in which the last item added to the list is the first item that can be removed. An example of this type of operation is a stack of dishes in a cafeteria, where the last dish placed on top of the stack is the first dish removed. Another example is the "in basket" on a desk, where the last paper placed in the basket is typically the first one removed. In computer programming, stacks, among other uses, are used in all function calls to store and retrieve data to and from the function.

As a specific stack example, consider Figure 16.8, which illustrates an existing list of three last names. As shown, the top name on this list is Barney.

FIGURE 16.8   A List of Names

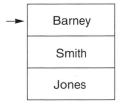

If you now restrict access to the list so that names can only be added and removed from the top of the list, then the list becomes a stack. This requires that you designate which end of the list is the top and which the bottom. Because the name Barney is physically placed above the other names, this is considered the top of the list. To explicitly signify this, an arrow has been used, so the list's top is clearly indicated.

FIGURE 16.9   An Expanding and Contracting List of Names

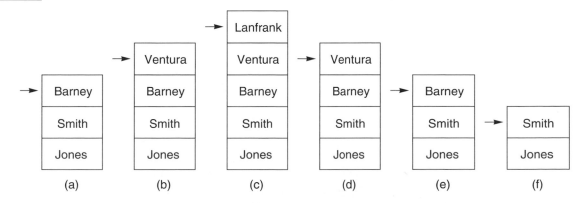

(a)   (b)   (c)   (d)   (e)   (f)

Figure 16.9 (which consists of six parts, labeled a through f) illustrates how the stack expands and contracts as names are added and deleted. For example, in part

A BIT OF BACKGROUND

Dr. Lukasiewicz and RPN

Dr. Jan Lukasiewicz, born in 1878, studied and taught mathematics at the University of Lvov, in Poland, before becoming a respected professor at the University of Warsaw. He received an appointment in 1919 to the post of Minister of Education in Poland and, with Stanislaw Lesniewski, founded the Warsaw School of Logic.

After World War II, Dr. Lukasiewicz and his wife, Regina, found themselves exiled in Belgium. When he was offered a professorship at the Royal Academy in Dublin, they moved to Ireland, where they remained until his death in 1956.

In 1951 Dr. Lukasiewicz developed a new set of postfix algebraic notation, which was critical in the design of early microprocessors in the 1960s and 1970s.

The actual implementation of postfix algebra was done using stack arithmetic, in which data were pushed on a stack and popped off when an operation needed to be performed. Such stack handling instructions require no address operands and made it possible for very small computers to handle large tasks effectively.

Stack arithmetic, which is based on Dr. Lukasiewicz's work, reverses the more commonly known prefix algebra and became known as Reverse Polish Notation (RPN). Early pocket calculators developed by the Hewlett-Packard Corporation were especially notable for their use of RPN and made stack arithmetic the favorite of many scientists and engineers.

b, the name Ventura has been added to the list. By part c, a total of two new names have been added and the top of the list has changed accordingly. By next removing the top name, Lanfrank, from the list in part c, the stack shrinks to that shown in part d, where Ventura now resides at the top of the stack. As names continue to be removed from the list (parts e and f), the stack continues to contract.

Although Figure 16.9 is an accurate representation of a list of names, it contains additional information that is not provided by a true stack object. When names are added to or removed from a stack, no count is kept of how many names have been added or deleted or of how many items the stack actually contains at any one time.

For example, by examining each part of Figure 16.9, you can determine how many names are on the list. In a true stack, the only item that can be seen and accessed is the top item on the list. To find out how many items the list contains would require continual removal of the top item until no more items exist.

Stack Class Implementation

Creating a stack requires the following four components:

- A container for holding items in the list
- A method of designating the current top stack item
- An operation for placing a new item on the stack
- An operation for removing an item from the stack

By convention, the operation of placing a new item on the top of a stack is called a **push**, and the operation of removing an item from a stack is called a **pop**. How each of these operations is actually implemented depends on the container type used to represent a stack. In C++, a stack can be easily created using the STL's deque class. This class creates a double-ended list, where objects can be pushed and popped from either end of the list. To create a stack, only the front end of the deque is used. A summary of the deque class's methods and operations are listed in Table 16.4.

Stacking the Deque

Stacks and queues are two special forms of a more general data object called a *deque* (pronounced "deck"). Deque stands for *double-ended queue*.

In a deque object, data can be handled in one of four ways:

1. Insert at the beginning and remove from the beginning. This is the last-in, first-out (LIFO) stack.
2. Insert at the beginning and remove form the end. This is the first-in, first-out (FIFO) queue.
3. Insert at the end and remove from the end, which represents an inverted LIFO technique.

4. Insert at the end and remove from the beginning, which represents an inverted FIFO queue.

Implementation 1 (stack object) is presented in this section and implementation 2 (queue object) is presented in the next section. Implementations 3 and 4 are sometimes used for keeping track of memory addresses, such as when programming is done in machine language or when objects are handled in a file. When a high-level language, such as C++, manages the data area automatically, users may not be aware of where the data are being stored or of which type of deque is being applied.

TABLE 16.4 Summary of `Deque` Class Methods and Operations

Methods and Operations	Type	Description
`deque<DataType> name`	constructor	Creates an empty deque named `name` with compiler-dependent initial size
`deque<DataType> name(source)`	constructor	Creates a copy of the source deque
`deque<DataType> name(n)`	constructor	Creates a deque of size `n`
`deque<DataType> name(n, object)`	constructor	Creates a deque of size `n` with each object initialized as `object`
`deque<DataType> name(src.beg, src.end)`	constructor	Creates a deque initialized with objects from a source container beginning at `src.beg` and ending at `src.end`
`~deque(DataType>()`	destructor	Destroys the deque and all objects it contains
`name.at(index)`	accessor	Returns the object at the designated index, and throws an exception if the index is out of bounds
`name.front()`	accessor	Returns the first object at the front of the deque with no check for the existence of a first object
`name.pop_front()`	mutator	Removes, but does not return, the first object at the front of the deque
`name.push_front(object)`	mutator	Inserts `object` at the front of the deque
`name.back()`	accessor	Returns the object at the back of the deque with no check for the existence of a last object
`name.pop_back()`	mutator	Removes, but does not return, the last object at the back of the deque
`name.push_back(object)`	mutator	Inserts `object` at the back of the deque
`name.insert(itr, object)`	mutator	Inserts `object` at iterator position `itr`
`name.insert(itr, src.beg, src.end)`	mutator	Inserts copies of objects from a source container, beginning at `src.beg` and ending at `src.end` at iterator position `itr`
`name.insert(itr, n, object)`	mutator	Inserts `n` copies of `object` at iterator position `itr`

TABLE 16.4 *(continued)*

Methods and Operations	Type	Description
`name2.assign(n, object)`	mutator	Assigns n copies of `object`
`name2.(src.begin, src.end)`	mutator	Assigns the objects of the `src` container (need not be a deque) between the range `src.begin` and `src.end` to name2
`name.erase(pos)`	mutator	Removes the object at the specified position
`name.erase(begin, end)`	mutator	Removes the objects within the specified range
`name.resize(value)`	mutator	Resizes the deque to a larger size with new objects instantiated using the default constructor
`name.resize(value, object)`	mutator	Resizes the deque to a larger size with new objects instantiated as `object`
`name.clear()`	mutator	Removes all objects from the deque
`name.swap(nameB)`	mutator	Swaps the objects of `nameA` and `nameB` deques; can be performed using the `swap()` algorithm
`name.begin()`	accessor	Returns an iterator to the first object in the deque
`name.end()`	accessor	Returns an iterator to the position after the last object in the deque
`name.rbegin()`	accessor	Returns a reverse iterator for the first object in the deque
`name.rend()`	accessor	Returns a reverse iterator for the position after the last object in the deque
`nameA == nameB`	relational	Returns a Boolean `true` if `nameA` objects all equal `nameB` objects; otherwise, returns `false`
`nameA != nameB`	relational	Returns a Boolean `false` if `nameA` objects all equal `nameB` objects; otherwise, returns `true`; same as `!(nameA == nameB)`
`nameA < nameB`	relational	Returns a Boolean `true` if `nameA` is less than `nameB`; otherwise, returns `false`
`nameA > nameB`	relational	Returns a Boolean `true` if `nameA` is greater than `nameB`; otherwise, returns `false`; same as `nameB < nameA`
`nameA <= nameB`	relational	Returns a Boolean `true` if `nameA` is less than or equal to `nameB`
`nameA >= nameB`	relational	Returns a Boolean `true` if `nameA` is greater than or equal to `nameB`
`name.size()`	capacity	Returns the number of objects in the deque as an `int`
`name.empty()`	capacity	Returns a Boolean `true` if deque is empty; otherwise, returns `false`
`name.max_size()`	capacity	Returns the maximum possible objects as an integer
`name.capacity()`	capacity	Returns the maximum possible objects as an integer without relocation of the deque

Program 16.4 uses the `deque` class to implement a stack. The program is straightforward in that only one stack is instantiated and user-entered names are pushed to the front of the deque until the sentinel value of `x` is entered. Upon detection of this sentinel string value, the names are popped from the front of the deque as long as the deque is non-empty.

PROGRAM 16.4

```cpp
#include <iostream>
#include <deque>
#include <string>
#include <cctype>
using namespace std;

int main()
{
  string name;
  deque<string> stack;

  cout << "Enter as many names as you want, one per line" << endl;
  cout << "To stop enter a single x" << endl;
  while(true)
  {
    cout << "Enter a name (or x to stop): " ;
    getline(cin, name);
    if (tolower(name.at(0)) == 'x') break;
    stack.push_front(name);
  }

  cout << "\nThe names in the stack are:\n";

  // pop names from the stack
  while(!stack.empty())
  {
    name = stack.front();  // retrieve the name
    stack.pop_front();  // pop name from the stack
    cout << name << endl;
  }
}
```

Following is a sample run using Program 16.4:

```
Enter as many names as you want, one per line
 To stop enter a single x
Enter a name (or x to stop): Jane Jones
Enter a name (or x to stop): Bill Smith
Enter a name (or x to stop): Jim Robinson
Enter a name (or x to stop): x

The names in the stack are:
Jim Robinson
Bill Smith
Jane Jones
```

1. State whether a stack is appropriate for each of the following tasks. Indicate why or why not.

   a. A word processor must remember a line of up to 80 characters. Pressing the Backspace key deletes the previous character, and pressing CTRL and Backspace deletes the entire line. Users must be able to undo deletion operations.

   b. Customers must wait one to three months for delivery of their new automobiles. The dealer creates a list that will determine the "fair" order in which customers should get their cars; the list is to be prepared in the order in which customers placed their requests for a new car.

   c. You are required to search downward in a pile of magazines to locate the issue for last January. Each magazine was placed on the pile as soon as it was received.

   d. A programming team accepts jobs and prioritizes them on the basis of urgency.

   e. A line has formed at a bus stop.

2. Modify Program 16.4 to implement a stack of integers rather than a stack of strings.

3. Modify Program 16.4 to instantiate three stacks of digits named `digits1`, `digits2`, and `digits3`. Initialize `digits1` to contain the digits 9, 8, 5, and 2, which is the number 2589 in reverse digit order. Similarly, the `digits2` stack should be initialized to contain the digits 3, 1, 5, and 7, which is the number 7513 in reverse digit order. Calculate and place the sum of these two numbers in the `digits3` stack. This sum should be obtained by popping respective objects from `digits1` and `digits2` and adding them together with a variable named `carry`, which is initialized to 0. If the sum of the two popped objects and `carry` does not exceed 10, the sum should be pushed onto `digits3` and `carry` set to 0; otherwise, `carry` should be set to 1, and the units digit of the sum pushed onto the `digits3` stack.

4. Write a C++ program that permits a user to enter a maximum of 100 integers into a stack object. Then have the program:

   a. Reverse the stack contents into a second stack of integers.

   b. Using two additional stacks, reverse the contents in the original stack. If the original stack contains the integers 1, 2, 3, and 4, it should contain the integers 4, 3, 2, and 1 at the end of the program.

5. Write a C++ program that permits a user to enter a maximum of 50 characters into a stack object. Then have the program sort the stack contents in increasing order. If the contents of the stack are initially D, E, A, and B, the final contents of the stack will be A, B, D, and E.

16.4 QUEUES

A **queue** (pronounced *cue*) is a list in which items are added to one end of the list, called the top, and removed from the other end of the list, called the bottom. This arrangement ensures that items are removed from the list in the exact order in which they were entered. This means that the first item placed on the list is the first item to be removed, the second item placed on the list is the second item to be removed, and so on. Thus, a queue is a **first-in, first-out (FIFO)** list —a list in which the first item added to the list is the first item that can be removed.

As an example of a queue, consider a list of people waiting to purchase season tickets to a professional football team. The first person on the list should be called when the first set of tickets becomes available, the second person should be called for the second available set, and so on. The names of the people currently on the list are shown in Figure 16.10.

FIGURE 16.10 A Queue with Its Pointers

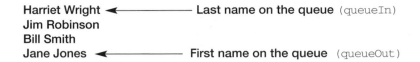

As illustrated in Figure 16.10, the names have been added in the same fashion as on a stack; that is, as new names are added to the list, they are stacked on top of the existing names. The difference in a queue relates to how the names are popped off the list. Clearly, the people on this list expect to be serviced in the order that they were placed on the list—that is, first in, first out. Thus, unlike a stack, the most recently added name to the list *is not* the first name removed. Rather, the oldest name still on the list is always the next name removed.

To keep the list in proper order, where new names are added to one end of the list and old names are removed from the other end, it is convenient to use two link variables: one that locates the front of the list for the next person to be serviced and one that locates the end of the list where new people will be added. The link variable that locates the front of the list where the next name is to be removed is referred to as the tail pointer, or tail, for short. The second link variable, which locates the last person in the list and indicates where the next person entering the list is to be placed, is called the head pointer, or head, for short. Thus, for the list shown in Figure 16.10, the tail points to Jane Jones and the head points to Harriet Wright. If Jane Jones were now removed from the list and Lou Hazlet and Teresa Filer were added, the queue and its associated position indicators would appear as in Figure 16.11.

FIGURE 16.11 The Updated Queue Pointers

Deque Class Implementation

A queue is easily derived using the STL `deque` container. The operation of placing a new item on the queue is formally referred to as **enqueuing** and more causally referred to as a **push** operation, whereas removing an item from a queue is formally referred to as **serving** and casually as a **pop** operation. Operationally, enqueuing is an operation similar to pushing on one end of a stack, and serving from a queue is an operation similar to popping from the other end of a stack. How each of these operations is implemented depends on the list used to represent a queue.

Because you will use the `deque` class as the base class, you can easily create the push and pop operations using the `deque` class's `push_front()` and `pop_back()` methods (see Table 16.4). Program 16.5 illustrates using the `deque` class to construct a queue within the context of a complete program, where names are pushed onto the front of the deque and popped from the back. This creates the FIFO ordering that characterizes a queue.

PROGRAM 16.5

```cpp
#include <iostream>
#include <deque>
#include <string>
#include <cctype>
using namespace std;

int main()
{
    string name;
    deque<string> queue;

    cout << "Enter as many names as you want, one per line" << endl;
    cout << " To stop enter a single x" << endl;

    // push names on the queue
    while(true)
    {
        cout << "Enter a name (or x to stop): " ;
        getline(cin, name);
        if (tolower(name.at(0)) == 'x') break;
        queue.push_front(name);
    }

    cout << "\nThe names in the queue are:\n";

    // pop names from the queue
    while(!queue.empty())
    {
        name = queue.back();   // retrieve the name
        queue.pop_back();   // pop a name from the queue
        cout << name << endl;
    }
}
```

A sample run using Program 16.5 produced the following:

```
Enter as many names as you want, one per line
 To stop enter a single x
Enter a name (or x to stop): Jane Jones
Enter a name (or x to stop): Bill Smith
Enter a name (or x to stop): Jim Robinson
Enter a name (or x to stop): x

The names in the queue are:
Jane Jones
Bill Smith
Jim Robinson
```

A BIT OF BACKGROUND

Artificial Intelligence

One of the major steps toward creating programs that "learn" as they work is the development of dynamic data objects.

In 1950, Alan Turing proposed a test in which an expert enters questions at an isolated terminal. Presumably, artificial intelligence (AI) is achieved when the expert cannot discern whether the answers returned to the screen have been produced by a human or by a machine. Although there are problems with the Turing test, its concepts have spawned numerous research efforts.

By the mid-1960s, many AI researchers believed the efforts to create "thinking machines" were futile. Today, however, much lively research and development focus on topics such as dynamic problem solving, computer vision, parallel processing, natural language processing, and speech and pattern recognition—all of which are encompassed within the field of AI.

The development of techniques that allow machines to emulate humans have proliferated in recent years with the development of computers that are smaller, faster, more powerful, and less expensive. Most people agree that computers could never replace all human decision making. There is also general agreement that society must remain alert and in control of important decisions that require human compassion, ethics, and understanding.

Exercises 16.4

1. State whether a queue, a stack, or neither object would be appropriate for each of the following tasks. Indicate why or why not.

   a. A list of customers waiting to be seated in a restaurant

   b. A group of student tests waiting to be graded

   c. An address book listing names and telephone numbers in alphabetical order

   d. Patients waiting for examinations in a doctor's office

2. Modify Program 16.5 to use a queue of integers rather than a queue of strings.

3. Write a C++ program that permits a user to enter a maximum of 20 character values into a queue. Then have the program sort the queue contents in increasing order. If the contents of the queue are initially D, E, A, and B, the final contents of the queue will be A, B, D, and E.

4. Write a queue program that accepts an object consisting of an integer identification number and a floating-point hourly pay rate.

5. Add a menu method to Program 16.5 that gives the user a choice of adding a name to the queue, removing a name from the queue, or listing the contents of the queue without removing any objects from it.

6. A group of people have arrived at a bus stop and are lined up in this order:

1. Chaplin	4. Laurel	7. Oliver	10. Garland
2. West	5. Smith	8. Hardy	11. Wayne
3. Taylor	6. Grisby	9. Burton	12. Stewart

   Read the names from an input file into a queue and display the order in which the passengers board the bus.

16.5 COMMON PROGRAMMING ERRORS

Two common programming errors related to using the STL's `list` and `deque` classes are:

1. Inserting objects instantiated from different classes into the same list.
2. Attempting to use indices rather than iterators when using STL class methods and algorithms.

The five most common programming errors related to linked lists, stacks, and queues, which occur when programmers attempt to construct their own lists, are:

1. Not checking the pointer provided by the `new` operator when constructing a non-STL list. If this operator returns a `NULL` value, the user should be notified that the allocation did not take place and the normal program operation must be altered in an appropriate way. You simply cannot assume that all calls to `new` will result in the requested allocation of memory space being successful.
2. Not correctly updating all relevant pointer addresses when adding or removing records from dynamically created stacks and queues. Unless extreme care is taken in updating all addresses, each of these dynamic data structures can quickly become corrupted.
3. Forgetting to free previously allocated memory space when the space is no longer needed. This is typically only a problem in a large application program that is expected to run continuously and can make many requests for allocated space based on user demand.
4. Not preserving the integrity of the addresses contained in the top-of-stack pointer when dealing with a stack and the queue-in and queue-out pointers when dealing with a queue. As each of these pointers locates a starting position in their respective data structures, the complete list will be lost if the starting addresses are incorrect.
5. Not correctly updating internal record pointers when inserting and removing records from a stack or queue. Once an internal pointer within these lists contains an incorrect address, it is almost impossible to locate and reestablish the missing set of objects.

16.6 CHAPTER REVIEW

Key Terms

associative list	pointer variable
collection	pop
container	push
deque (double-ended queue)	queue
enqueuing	serving
FIFO	sequence list
LILO	stack
link variable	STL
linked list	

Summary

1. An object permits individual data items to be stored under a common variable name. These objects can then be stored together in a list.

2. A linked list is a list of objects in which each object contains a pointer variable that locates the next object in the list. Each linked list must have a pointer to locate the first object in the list. The last object's pointer variable is set to NULL to indicate the end of the list.

3. Linked lists can be automatically constructed using the STL's list class.

4. A stack is a list consisting of objects that can only be added and removed from the top of the list. Such an object is a LIFO (last-in, first-out) list, which means the last object added to the list is the first object removed. Stacks can be implemented using the STL's deque class.

5. A queue is a list consisting of objects that are added to the top of the list and removed from the bottom of the list. Such an object is a FIFO (first-in, first-out) list, which means objects are removed in the order in which they were added. Queues can be implemented using the STL's deque class.

Exercises

1. Modify Program 16.2 to list the names and phone numbers in reverse order.

2. Stacks can be used to efficiently determine whether the parentheses in an expression are correctly balanced. This means that each left-facing parenthesis is matched by a right-facing parenthesis. For example, consider the string:

$$(a + b) / ((x + y) * z)$$

Using a stack, each character in this string, starting from the left, is examined. If the character is a left-facing parenthesis, it is pushed onto the stack. Whenever a right-facing parenthesis is encountered, the top stack object is popped. An unbalanced expression results if a right-facing parenthesis is encountered and the stack is empty or if the stack is not empty when the end of the string is encountered. Using this information, write a C++ program that permits the user to type a string and determines if the string contains a balanced set of parentheses.

3. The program written for Exercise 2 can be expanded to include braces, {} , and brackets, [] , as well as parentheses. For example, consider the string:

$$\{ (a + b) / [(x + y) * z] \}$$

To use a stack to determine if such string contains balanced pairs of braces, brackets, and parentheses, each left-facing delimiter is pushed onto a stack of characters starting from the leftmost character. Whenever a right-facing delimiter is encountered, the top stack object is popped. An unbalanced expression results if a right-facing delimiter is encountered and the popped object is not its matching left-facing delimiter or if the stack is not empty when the end of the string is encountered. Using this information, write a C++ program that permits the user to type a string and determines if the string contains balanced sets of braces, brackets, or parentheses.

4. A group of people have arrived at a bus stop and are lined up in the order indicated:

1. Chaplin	4. Laurel	7. Oliver	10. Garland
2. West	5. Smith	8. Hardy	11. Wayne
3. Taylor	6. Grisby	9. Burton	12. Stewart

Read the names from an input file into a stack and display the order in which they board the bus.

5. Write a single-line word processor. As characters are typed, they are to be pushed onto a stack. Some characters have special meanings:

#	Erase the previous character (pop it from the stack).
@	Delete the entire line (empty the stack).
?, !, ., or Enter	Terminate line entry. Move the characters to an array and write the contents of the array to the screen.

6. In recursive methods, the parameters are usually stored on a stack. For example, when the method

```
int factorial(int n)
{
  int fact;

  if (n = 0)
    fact = 1;
  else
    fact = n * factorial(n - 1);
  return (fact);
}
```

is called, the successive values of the parameter n are stored on a stack. For example, if the initial call were `value = factorial(5)`, then 5 would be pushed onto the stack for n. The next call to `factorial` would push 4, then 3, and so on, until the last parameter value of 0. Then the values would be popped one at a time and multiplied by the previous product until the stack is empty.

Using this information, write a C++ program that performs the same operation as the `factorial` procedure for a given value of n, entered by the user. After each push, the contents of the stack should be displayed. After each pop, the contents of the stack and the value of factorial should be displayed. Once the display indicates that your method works properly, stop the display and have the method return the correct factorial value.

7. Write a queue handling program that asks customers for their names as they place orders at a fast-food restaurant. Each object in the queue should consist of a name field with a maximum of 20 characters and an integer field that keeps track of the total number of customers served. The value in the integer field should be automatically provided by the program each time a name is entered. Orders are processed in the same sequence as they are placed. The order taker examines the queue and calls the names when the order is ready. When the queue is empty, a message prints telling the staff to take a break.

8. Descriptions of jobs waiting in a computer for the printer are generally kept in a queue. Write a C++ program that keeps track of printing jobs, recoreded by user name and anticipated printer time (in seconds) for the job. Add jobs to the queue as printouts are requested, and remove them from the queue as they are serviced. When a user adds a job to the queue, display a message giving an estimate of how long it will be before the job is printed. The estimate should consist of the sum of all the prior jobs in the queue. (*Hint:* Store the accumulated times in a separate variable.)

9. a. On your electronic mail terminal, you receive notes to call people. Each message contains the name and phone number of the caller as well as a date (in the form month/day/year) and a 24-hour integer clock (in the form hours:minutes) that records the time that the message was received. A latest attempt field is initially set to 0, indicating that no attempt has yet been made to return the call. For example, a particular object may appear as
   Jan Williamson (555)666-7777 8/14/05 17:05 0

   Write a C++ program to store these objects in a queue as they arrive and to feed them to you, one at a time, upon request. If you cannot reach a person when you try to call, place that object at the end of the queue and fill the latest attempt field with the time you tried to return the call, in the form days later/hours:minutes. Thus, if your last unsuccessful attempt to return Jan Williamson's call was on 8/16/05 at 4:20, the new enqueued object would be
   Jan Williamson (555)666–7777 8/14/05 17:05 2/16:20

   b. Modify the program written for Exercise 9a so that the time and date fields are automatically filled in using system calls to time and date methods provided by your compiler.

17 | Additional Capabilities

Previous chapters have presented C++'s basic structure, statements, and capabilities. This chapter presents additional C++ capabilities, which you may require or find useful as you progress in your understanding and use of C++. Except for using binary files, none of these are advanced features, but their usage is typically restricted. The features described in Sections 17.1 and 17.2 are almost never used to the extent of the topics presented in the prior chapters. Unlike the other topics, command line arguments, the topic of Section 17.3, are used extensively by some programmers in commercial applications. With the exception of the material on binary files presented in Section 17.4, the remaining topics included in this chapter can be introduced almost at any point within your study of C++.

17.1 ADDITIONAL C++ FEATURES

This section presents a number of additional C++ statements and features. The first feature presented permits creating an alternate name, referred to as an alias, for existing C++ data types. The next feature permits defining a list of symbolic integer constants, which is sometimes convenient for creating case labels for a `switch` statement. The last feature presents the conditional operator, which is an alternate way of writing a short `if-else` statement. In practice, this feature is seldom, if ever used.

858

The `typedef` Declaration Statement

The `typedef` declaration statement allows you to create alternate names for any C++ data type name. For example, the statement

```
typedef double REAL;
```

makes the name `REAL` a synonym for `double`. The name `REAL` can now be used in place of the data type name `double` anywhere in the program after the synonym has been declared. For example, the definition

```
REAL val;
```

is equivalent to the definition:

```
double val;
```

The `typedef` statement does not create a new data type; it creates a new name for an existing data type. Typically, uppercase names are used in `typedef` statements to alert the programmer to a user-specified name, similar to the uppercase names used as symbolic constants. The statement

```
typedef double REAL;
```

actually specifies that `REAL` is a placeholder that will be replaced with another variable name. A subsequent declaration such as

```
REAL val;
```

has the effect of substituting the variable named `val` for the placeholder named `REAL` in the terms following the word `typedef`. Substituting `val` for `REAL` in the `typedef` statement and retaining all terms after the reserved word `typedef` results in the equivalent declaration `double val;`.

Once the mechanics of the replacement are understood, more useful equivalences can be constructed. Consider the statement:

```
typedef int ARRAY[100];
```

In this statement, the name `ARRAY` is actually a placeholder for any subsequently defined variables. Thus, a statement such as `ARRAY first, second;` is equivalent to the two definitions:

```
int first[100];
int second[100];
```

Each of these definitions is obtained by replacing the name `ARRAY` with the variable names `first` and `second` in the terms following the reserved word `typedef`.

As another example, consider the following statement:

```
typedef struct
{
  string name;
  int idNum;
} EmpRecord;
```

In this example, `EmpRecord` is a convenient placeholder for any subsequent variable. For example, the declaration `EmpRecord employee[75];` is equivalent to the declaration:

```
struct
{
    string name;
    int idNum;
} employee[75];
```

This last declaration is obtained by directly substituting the term `employee[75]` in place of the word `EmpRecord` in the terms following the word `typedef` in the original `typedef` statement.

The `enum` Keyword

The `enum` keyword creates an enumerated data type, which is simply a user-defined list of values that is given its own data type name. Such data types are identified by the reserved word `enum` followed by an optional, user-selected name for the data type and a listing of acceptable values for the data type. Consider the following user-specified data types:

```
enum flag {true, false};
enum time {am, pm};
enum day {mon, tue, wed, thr, fri, sat, sun};
enum color {red, green, yellow};
```

In the first statement, the user-specified data type is named `flag`. Any variable subsequently declared to be of this data type can take on only a value of `true` or `false`. The second statement creates a data type named `time`. Any variable subsequently declared to be of type `time` can take on only a value of am or pm. Similarly, the third and fourth statements create the data types `day` and `color`, respectively, and list the valid values for variables of these two types. For example, the statement

```
enum day a, b, c;
```

declares the variables a, b, and c to be of type `day` and is consistent with the declaration of variables using standard C++ data types such as `char`, `int`, `float`, or `double`. Once variables have been declared as enumerated types, they may be assigned values or compared to variables or values appropriate to their type. This again is consistent with standard variable operations. For example, for the variables a, b, and c declared above, the following statements are valid:

```
a = red;
b = a;
if (c == yellow)
    cout << "The color is yellow" << endl;
```

Internally, the acceptable values for each enumerated data type are ordered and assigned sequential integer values beginning with 0. For example, for the values of the user-defined type `color`, the correspondences created by the C++ compiler are that `red` is equivalent to 0, `green` is equivalent to 1, and `yellow` is equivalent to 2. Program 17.1 illustrates a user-defined data type.

PROGRAM 17.1

```cpp
#include <iostream>
using namespace std;

int main()
{
  enum color {red, green, yellow};
  color crayon = red;   // crayon is declared to be of type
                        // color and initialized to red
  cout << "\nThe color is " << crayon << endl;
  if (crayon == red)
    cout << "The crayon is red." << endl;
  else if (crayon == green)
    cout << "The crayon is green." << endl;
  else if (crayon == yellow)
    cout << "The crayon is yellow.' << endl;
  else
    cout << "The color is not defined.\n" << endl;

  return 0;
}
```

A sample run of Program 17.1 produced the following output:

```
The color is 0
The crayon is red.
```

As illustrated in Program 17.1, expressions containing variables declared as user-defined data types must be consistent with the values specifically listed for the type. Although a `switch` statement would be more appropriate in Program 17.1, the expressions in the `if-else` statement better highlight the use of enumerated values. Program 17.1 also shows that the initialization of a user-specified data type variable is identical to the initialization of standard data type variables. In order to assign equivalent integers to each user-specified value, the C++ compiler retains the order of the values as they are listed in the enumeration. A side effect of this ordering is that expressions can be constructed using relational and logical operators. For example, for the data type color created in Program 17.1, expressions such as `crayon < yellow` and `red < green` are both valid.

The numerical value assigned by the compiler to enumerated values can be altered by direct assignment when a data type is created. For example, the definition

```cpp
enum color {red, green = 7, yellow};
```

causes the compiler to associate the value `red` with the integer 0 and the value `green` with the integer 7. Altering the integer associated with the value `green` causes all subsequent integer assignments to be altered too; thus, the value `yellow` is associated with the integer 8. If any other values were listed after `yellow`, they would be associated with the integers 9, 10, 11, and so on, unless another alteration was made.

The name of an enumerated user-defined data type can be omitted in its definition. For example, the declaration

```
enum {red, green, yellow} crayon;
```

defines `crayon` to be a variable of an unnamed data type with the valid values of `red`, `green`, and `yellow`.

Scope rules applicable to the standard C++ data types also apply to enumerated data types. For example, placing the statement `enum color {red, green, yellow};` before the `main()` function in Program 17.1 would make the data type named `color` global and available for any other function in the file.

Finally, because there is a one-to-one correspondence between integers and user-defined data types, the cast operator can either coerce integers into a user-specified data value or coerce a user-specified value into its equivalent integer. Assuming that `val` is an integer variable with a value of 1, and `color` has been declared as in Program 17.1, the expression `(enum color) val` has a value of `green` and the expression `int(yellow)` has a value of 2. The compiler will not warn you, however, if a cast to a nonexistent value is attempted.

Conditional Expressions

In addition to expressions formed with the arithmetic, relational, logical, and bit operators, C++ provides a conditional expression. A **conditional expression** uses the conditional operator `?:` and provides an alternate way of expressing a simple `if-else` statement. The general form of a conditional expression is:

```
expression1 ? expression2 : expression3
```

If the value of `expression1` is nonzero (true), then `expression2` is evaluated; otherwise, `expression3` is evaluated. The value for the complete conditional expression is the value of either `expression2` or `expression3`, depending on which expression was evaluated. As always, the value of the expression may be assigned to a variable.

Conditional expressions are most useful in replacing simple `if-else` statements. For example, the `if-else` statement

```
if ( hours > 40)
    rate = .045;
else
    rate = .02;
```

can be replaced with the one-line conditional statement:

```
rate = (hours > 40) ? .045 : .02;
```

Here, the complete conditional expression

```
(hours > 40) ? .045 : .02
```

is evaluated before any assignment is made to `rate`, because the conditional operator has a higher precedence than the assignment operator. Within the conditional expression, the expression `hours > 40` is evaluated first. If this expression has a nonzero value, which is equivalent to a logical `true` value, the value of the complete conditional expression is set to .045; otherwise the conditional expression has a value of .02. Finally, the value of the conditional expression, either .045 or .02, is assigned to the variable rate.

The conditional operator is unique in C++ in that it is a ternary operator. A **ternary operator** connects three operands. The first operand is always evaluated first. It is usually a conditional expression that uses the logical operators. The next two operands are any other valid expressions, which can be single constants, variables, or more general expressions. The complete conditional expression consists of all three operands connected by the conditional operator symbols ? and :.

Conditional expressions are only useful in replacing `if-else` statements when the expressions in the equivalent `if-else` statement are not long or complicated. For example, the statement

```
maxVal = a > b ? a : b;
```

is a one-line statement that assigns the maximum value of the variables a and b to `maxVal`. A longer, equivalent form of this statement is:

```
if (a > b)
    maxVal = a;
else
    maxVal = b;
```

Because of the length of the expressions involved, a conditional expression would not be useful in replacing the following `if-else` statement:

```
if (amount > 20000)
    taxes = .025(amount - 20000) + 400;
else
    taxes = .02 * amount;
```

Exercises 17.1

1. Rewrite each of the following `if-else` statements using a conditional expression:

   a. ```
   if (a < b);
       minimumValue - a;
   else
       minimumValue = b;
   ```

   b. ```
   if (num < 0)
       sign - B1;
   else
       sign = 1;
   ```

   c. ```
   if (flag == 1)
       value = num;
   else
       value = num * num;
   ```

   d. ```
   if (credit == plus)
       rate = prime;
   else
       rate = prime + delta;
   ```

   e. ```
   if (!bond)
       coupon = .075;
   else
       coupon = 1.1;
   ```
   ```

17.2 BIT OPERATORS

C++ operates with data entities that are stored as one or more bytes, such as character, integer, and double-precision constants and variables. In addition, C++ provides for the manipulation of individual bits of character and integer constants and variables. Generally these bit manipulations are used in engineering and computer science programs and are not required in commercial applications.

The operators that are used to perform bit manipulations are called **bit operators**. They are listed in Table 17.1.

TABLE 17.1   Bit Operators

Operator	Description
&	Bit-by-bit AND
|	Bit-by-bit inclusive OR
^	Bit-by-bit exclusive OR
~	Bit-by-bit one's complement
<<	Bit-by-bit left shift
>>	Bit-by-bit right shift

All the operators listed in Table 17.1, except ~, are binary operators that require two operands. Each operand is treated as a binary number consisting of a series of individual 1s and 0s. The respective bits in each operand are then compared on a bit-by-bit basis, and the result is determined based on the selected operation.

The first three bit operations listed in Table 17.1 can also be used in logical expressions. When used in a logical expression, the & and | operators perform the same function as the Boolean operators && and || operators, but the bit operators always evaluate both operands. That is, they do not use the short-circuited evaluation performed by the Boolean operators && and || (see Section 5.1). For this reason you should use the && and || operators for Boolean operations unless a specific result is required or you must logically compare two integer operands.

The AND Operator

The AND operator & causes a bit-by-bit AND comparison between its two operands. The result of each bit-by-bit comparison is 1 only when both bits being compared are 1s; otherwise, the result of the AND operation is 0. For example, assume that the following two eight-bit numbers are to be ANDed:

```
1 0 1 1 0 0 1 1
1 1 0 1 0 1 0 1
---------------
```

To perform an AND operation, each bit in one operand is compared to the bit occupying the same position in the other operand. Figure 17.1 illustrates the correspondence between bits for these two operands. Bitwise AND comparisons are determined by the following rule: *The result of an AND comparison is 1 when both bits being compared are 1s; otherwise, the result is 0.* The result of each comparison is, of course, independent of any other bit comparison.

FIGURE 17.1 A Sample AND Operation

```
      1 0 1 1 0 0 1 1
  &   1 1 0 1 0 1 0 1
      ----------------
      1 0 0 1 0 0 0 1
```

AND operations are extremely useful in masking, or eliminating, selected bits from an operand. This is a direct result of the fact that ANDing any bit (1 or 0) with a 0 forces the resulting bit to be 0, whereas ANDing any bit (1 or 0) with a 1 leaves the original bit unchanged. For example, assume that the variable op1 has the arbitrary bit pattern x x x x x x x x, where each x can be either 1 or 0, independent of any other x in the number. The result of ANDing this binary number with the binary number 00001111 is

```
   op1 =    x x x x x x x x
   op2 =    0 0 0 0 1 1 1 1
            ---------------
Result =    0 0 0 0 x x x x
```

As shown in this example, the 0s in op2 effectively mask, or eliminate, the respective bits in op1, and the 1s in op2 filter, or pass, the respective bits in op1 through with no change in their values. In this example, the variable op2 is called a **mask**. By choosing the mask appropriately, any individual bit in an operand can be selected, or filtered, out of an operand for inspection. For example, ANDing the variable op1 with the mask 00000100 forces all the bits of the result to be 0, except for the third bit. The third bit of the result will be a copy of the third bit of op1. Thus, if the result of the AND is 0, the third bit of op1 must have been 0, and if the result of the AND is a nonzero number, the third bit must have been 1.

The Inclusive OR Operator

The inclusive OR operator | performs a bit-by-bit comparison of its two operands in a similar fashion to the bit-by-bit AND. The result of the inclusive OR comparison, however, is determined by the following rule: *The result of the comparison is 1 if either bit being compared is 1; otherwise, the result is 0.*

Figure 17.2 illustrates an OR operation. As shown in the figure, when either of the two bits being compared is 1, the result is 1; otherwise, the result is 0. As with all bit operations, the result of each comparison is, of course, independent of any other comparison.

FIGURE 17.2 A Sample Inclusive OR Operation

```
      1 0 1 1 0 0 1 1
  |   1 1 0 1 0 1 0 1
      ----------------
      1 1 1 1 0 1 1 1
```

Inclusive OR operations are extremely useful in forcing selected bits to take on a 1 value or for passing through other bit values unchanged. This is a direct result of the fact that ORing any bit (1 or 0) with a 1 forces the resulting bit to be 1, and ORing any bit (1 or 0) with a 0 leaves the original bit unchanged. For example, assume that the variable op1 has the arbitrary bit pattern x x x x x x x x, where each x can be either 1 or 0, independent of any other x in the number. The result of ORing this binary number with the binary number 11110000 is:

```
       op1 =   x x x x x x x x
       op2 =   1 1 1 1 0 0 0 0
               ---------------
    Result =   1 1 1 1 x x x x
```

As shown in this example, the 1s in op2 force the resulting bits to 1, and the 0s in op2 filter, or pass, the respective bits in op1 through with no change in their values. Thus, using an OR operation a similar masking operation can be produced as with an AND operation, except the masked bits are set to 1s rather than cleared to 0s. Another way of looking at this is to say that ORing with a 0 has the same effect as ANDing with a 1.

The Exclusive OR Operator

The exclusive OR operator, ^, performs a bit-by-bit comparison of its two operands. The result of the comparison is determined by the following rule: *The result of the comparison is 1 if one and only one of the bits being compared is 1; otherwise, the result is 0.*

Figure 17.3 illustrates an exclusive OR operation. As shown in the figure, when both bits being compared are the same value (both 1 or both 0), the result is 0. Only when both bits have different values (one bit a 1 and the other a 0) is the result 1. Again, each pair or bit comparison is independent of any other bit comparison.

FIGURE 17.3   A Sample Exclusive OR Operation

```
      1 0 1 1 0 0 1 1
    ^ 1 1 0 1 0 1 0 1
      -----------------
      0 1 1 0 0 1 1 0
```

An exclusive OR operation can be used to create the opposite value, or complement, of any individual bit in a variable. This is a direct result of the fact that exclusive ORing any bit (1 or 0) with a 1 forces the resulting bit to be of the opposite value of its original state, and exclusive ORing any bit (1 or 0) with a 0 leaves the original bit unchanged. For example, assume that the variable op1 has the arbitrary bit pattern x x x x x x x x, where each x can be either 1 or 0, independent of any other x in the number. Using the notation that x̄ is the complement (opposite) value of x, the result of exclusive ORing this binary number with the binary number 01010101 is

```
    op1 = x x x x x x x x
    op2 = 0 1 0 1 0 1 0 1
          ---------------
 Result = x x̄ x x̄ x x̄ x x̄
```

As shown in this example, the 1s in `op2` force the resulting bits to be the complement of their original bit values, and the 0s in `op2` filter, or pass, the respective bits in `op1` through with no change in their values.

The Complement Operator

The complement operator, ~, is a unary operator that changes each 1 bit in its operand to 0 and each 0 bit to 1. For example, if the variable `op1` contains the binary number 11001010, `~op1` replaces this binary number with the number 00110101. The complement operator can be used to force any bit in an operand to 0, independent of the actual number of bits used to store the number. For example, the statement

```
op1 = op1 & ~07;    // 07 is an octal number
```

or its shorter form

```
op1 &= ~07;     // 07 is an octal number
```

sets the last three bits of `op1` to 0. Either of these two statements can, of course, be replaced by ANDing the last three bits of `op1` with 0s if the number of bits used to store `op1` is known. If `op1` is a 17-bit short integer, the appropriate AND operation is:

```
op1 = op1 & 0177770;     // in octal
```

or

```
op1 = op1 & 0xFFF8;     // in hexadecimal
```

For a 32-bit integer value, the foregoing AND sets the leftmost or higher order 16 bits to 0 also, which is an unintended result. The correct statement for a 32-bit integer is:

```
op1 = op1 & 037777777770;     // in octal
```

or

```
op1 = op1 & 0xFFFFFFF8;     // in hexadecimal
```

Using the bitwise NOT operator in this situation frees the programmer from having to consider the storage size of the operand.

Different Size Data Items

When the bit operators &, |, and ^ are used with operands of different sizes, the shorter operand is always increased in bit size to match the size of the larger operand. Figure 17.4 illustrates the extension of a 17-bit unsigned integer into a 32-bit number.

FIGURE 17.4   Extending 17-Bit Unsigned Data to 32 Bits

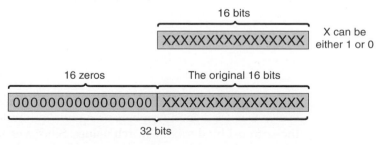

As the figure shows, the additional bits are added to the left of the original number and filled with zeros. This is the equivalent of adding leading zeros to the number, which has no effect on the number's value.

FIGURE 17.5   Extending 17-Bit Signed Data to 32 Bits

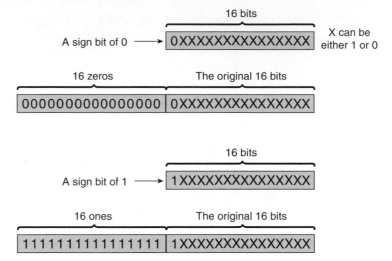

When extending signed numbers, the original leftmost bit is reproduced in the additional bits that are added to the number. As illustrated in Figure 17.5, if the original leftmost bit is 0, corresponding to a positive number, 0 is placed in each of the additional bit positions. If the leftmost bit is 1, which corresponds to a negative number, 1 is placed in the additional bit positions. In either case, the resulting binary number has the same sign and magnitude of the original number.

The Shift Operators

The left shift operator, <<, causes the bits in an operand to be shifted to the left by a given amount. For example, the statement

```
op1 = op1 << 4;
```

causes the bits in `op1` to be shifted four bits to the left, filling any vacated bits with a zero. Figure 17.6 illustrates the effect of shifting the binary number 1111100010101011 to the left by four bit positions.

FIGURE 17.6   An Example of a Left Shift

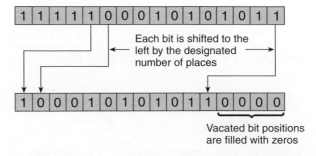

For unsigned integers, each left shift corresponds to multiplication by two. This is also true for signed numbers using two's complement representation, as long as the leftmost bit does not switch values. Since a change in the leftmost bit of a two's complement number represents a change in both the sign and magnitude represented by the bit, such a shift does not represent a simple multiplication by two.

The right shift operator, >>, causes the bits in an operand to be shifted to the right by a given amount. For example, the statement

```
op2 = op1 >> 3;
```

causes the bits in op1 to be shifted to the right by three bit positions. Figure 17.7a illustrates the right shift of the unsigned binary number 1111100010101011 by three bit positions. As illustrated, the three rightmost bits are shifted "off the end" and are lost.

For unsigned numbers, the leftmost bit is not used as a sign bit. For this type of number, the vacated leftmost bits are always filled with zeros. This is the case that is illustrated in Figure 17.7a.

For signed numbers, what is filled in the vacated bits depends on the computer. Most computers reproduce the original sign bit of the number. Figure 17.7b illustrates the right shift of a negative binary number by four bit positions, where the sign bit is reproduced in the vacated bits. Figure 17.7c illustrates the equivalent right shift of a positive signed binary number.

The type of fill illustrated in Figures 17.7b and c, where the sign bit is reproduced in vacated bit positions, is called an arithmetic right shift. In an arithmetic right shift, each single shift to the right corresponds to a division by two.

Instead of reproducing the sign bit in right-shifted signed numbers, some computers automatically fill the vacated bits with zeros. This type of shift is called a logical shift. For positive signed numbers, where the leftmost bit is zero, both arithmetic and logical right shifts produce the same result. The results of these two shifts are only different when negative numbers are involved.

FIGURE 17.7a An Unsigned Arithmetic Right Shift

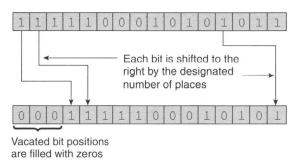

FIGURE 17.7b The Right Shift of a Negative Binary Number

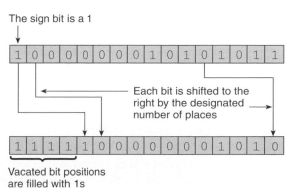

FIGURE 17.7c   The Right Shift of a Positive Binary Number

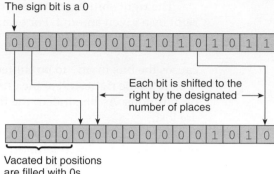

Exercises 17.2

1. Determine the results of the following operations:

   a.   11001010   b.   11001010   c.   11001010

      & 10100101 | 10100101   ^ 10100101
      ----------   ----------   ----------

2. Write the octal representations of the binary numbers given in Exercise 1.

3. Determine the octal results of the following operations, assuming unsigned numbers:

   a. The octal number 0157 shifted left by one bit position

   b. The octal number 0701 shifted left by two bit positions

   c. The octal number 0673 shifted right by two bit positions

   d. The octal number 067 shifted right by three bit positions

4. Repeat Exercise 3 assuming that the numbers are treated as signed values.

5. a. Assume that the arbitrary bit pattern xxxxxxxx, where each x can represent either 1 or 0, is stored in the integer variable flag. Determine the octal value of a mask that can be ANDed with the bit pattern to reproduce the third and fourth bits of flag and set all other bits to zero. The rightmost bit in flag is considered bit 0.

   b. Determine the octal value of a mask that can be inclusively ORed with the bit pattern in flag to reproduce the third and fourth bits of flag and set all other bits to 1. Consider the rightmost bit in flag to be bit 0.

   c. Determine the octal value of a mask that can be used to complement the values of the third and fourth bits of flag and leave all other bits unchanged. Determine the bit operation that should be used with the mask value to produce the desired result.

6 a. Write the two's complement form of the decimal number -1, using eight bits. (*Hint:* Refer to Section 1.6 for a review of two's complement numbers.)

   b. Repeat Exercise 6a using 16 bits to represent the decimal number -1 and compare your answer to your previous answer. Could the 16-bit version have been obtained by simply extending the sign bit of the 8-bit version?

17.3 COMMAND LINE ARGUMENTS

Arguments can be passed to any function in a program, including the main() function. This section discusses the procedures for passing arguments to main() when a program is initially invoked and having `main()` correctly receive and store the arguments passed to it. Both the sending and receiving sides of the transaction must be considered. Fortunately, the interface for transmitting arguments to a `main()` function has been standardized in C++, so both sending and receiving arguments can be done almost mechanically.

All the programs that have been run so far have been invoked by typing the name of the executable version of the program after the operating system prompt is displayed. The command line for these programs consists of a single word, which is the name of the program. For computers that use the UNIX operating system, the prompt is usually the `$` and the executable name of the program is `a.out`. For these systems, the simple command line

`$a.out`

begins program execution of the last compiled source program currently residing in `a.out`.

If you are using a C++ compiler on an IBM PC, the equivalent operating system prompt is typically C>, and the name of the executable program is typically the same name as the source program with an .exe extension rather than a .c extension. Assuming that you are using an IBM PC with the C> operating system prompt, the complete command line for running an executable program named `pgm17.2.exe` is `C>pgm17.2`. As illustrated in Figure 17.8, this command line causes the `pgm17.2` program to begin execution with its `main()` function, but no arguments are passed to `main()`.

FIGURE 17.8　**Invoking the Program pgm17.2.exe**

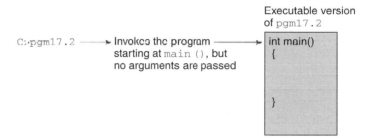

Now assume that you want to pass the three separate string arguments "three blind mice" directly into `pgm17.2`'s `main()` function. Sending arguments into a `main()` function is extremely easy. It is accomplished by including the arguments on the command line used to begin program execution. Because the arguments are typed on the command line, they are called **command line arguments**. To pass the arguments "three blind mice" directly into the `main()` function of the `pgm17.2` program, you only need to add the three-word phrase after the program name on the command line:

`C>pgm17.2 three blind mice`

Upon encountering the command line `pgm17.2 three blind mice`, the operating system stores it as a sequence of four strings. Figure 17.9 illustrates the storage of this command line, assuming that each character uses one byte of storage. As shown in the figure, each `C-string` terminates with the standard C++ `NULL` character \0.

FIGURE 17.9   The Command Line Stored in Memory

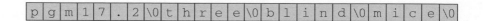

Sending command line arguments to main() is always this simple. The arguments are typed on the command line and the operating system nicely stores them as a sequence of separate strings. Now you must handle the receiving side of the transaction, and let main() know that arguments are being passed to it.

Arguments passed to main(), like all function arguments, must be declared as part of the function's definition. To standardize argument passing to a main() function, only two items are allowed: a number and an array. The number is an integer variable that must be named argc (short for argument counter), and the array is a one-dimensional list that must be named argv (short for argument values). Figure 17.10 illustrates these two arguments.

FIGURE 17.10   An Integer and an Array Are Passed to main()

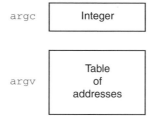

The integer passed to main() is the total number of items on the command line. In this example, the value of argc passed to main() is four, which includes the name of the program plus the three command line arguments. The one-dimensional list passed to main() is a list of pointers containing the starting storage address of each string typed on the command line, as illustrated in Figure 17.11.

FIGURE 17.11   Addresses Are Stored in the argv Array

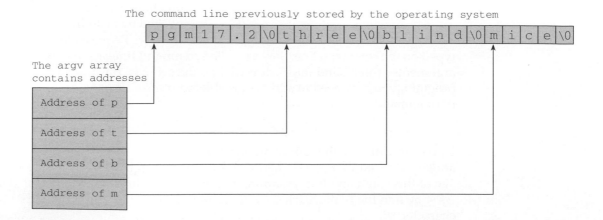

You can now write the complete function definition for `main()` to receive arguments by declaring their names and data types. For the function's two arguments, the names conventionally used are `argc` and `argv`, respectively.[1] Because `argc` will store an integer value, its declaration will be `int argc`. Because `argv` is the name of an array whose elements are addresses that point to where the actual command line arguments are stored, its proper declaration is `char *argv[]`. This is nothing more than the declaration of an array of pointers. It is read "`argv` is an array whose elements are pointers to characters." Putting all this together, the full function header for a `main()` function that will receive command line arguments is:

<code>int main(int argc, char *argv[])</code>

No matter how many arguments are typed on the command line, `main()` only needs the two standard pieces of information provided by `argc` and `argv`: the number of items on the command line and the list of starting addresses indicating where each argument is actually stored.

Program 17.2 verifies this description by printing the data actually passed to `main()`. The variable `argv[]` used in Program 17.2 contains an address. It is this address that is displayed by the first `cout` statement within the `for` loop. For ease of reading the output, this address is cast into an integer value (the default display for addresses is hexadecimal). The string notation `*argv[]` in the second `cout` statement refers to "the character pointed to" by the address in `argv[]`.

PROGRAM 17.2

```
#include <iostream>
using namespace std;

int main(int argc, char *argv[])
{
  int i;

  cout << "\nThe number of items on the command line is "
       << argc << "\n" << endl;
  for(i = 0; i < argc; i++)
  {
    cout << "The address stored in argv[" << i <<"] is "
         << int(argv [i]) << endl;
    cout << "The character pointed to is " << *argv[i] << endl;
  }

  return 0;
}
```

Assuming that the executable version of Program 17.2 is named `pgm17.2.exe`, a sample output for the command line

<code>C> pgm17.2 three blind mice</code>

is:

<code>The number of items on the command line is 4</code>

---

[1] These names are not required, and any valid C++ identifier can be used in their place.

```
The address stored in argv[0] is 3280036
The character pointed to is p
The address stored in argv[1] is 3280044
The character pointed to is t
The address stored in argv[2] is 3280050
The character pointed to is b
The address stored in argv[3] is 3280056
The character pointed to is m
```

The addresses displayed by Program 17.2 clearly depend on the computer used to run the program. Figure 17.12 illustrates the storage of the command line as displayed by the sample output. As anticipated, the addresses in the `argv` array "point" to the starting characters of each string typed on the command line.

FIGURE 17.12 The Command Line Stored in Memory

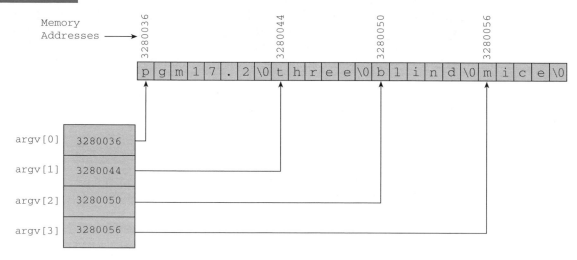

Once command line arguments are passed to a C++ program, they can be used like any other C++ strings. Program 17.3 causes its command line arguments to be displayed from within `main()`.

PROGRAM 17.3

```cpp
// A program that displays its command line arguments
#include <iostream>
using namespace std;
int main(int argc, char *argv[])
{
  int i;

  cout << "\nThe following arguments were passed to main(): ";
  for (i = 1; i < argc; i++)
    cout << argv[i] << " ";
  cout << endl;

  return 0;
}
```

Assuming that the name of the executable version of Program 17.3 is pgm17.3.exe, the output of this program for the command line

```
C> pgm17.3 three blind mice
```

is:

```
The following arguments were passed to main(): three blind mice
```

Notice that, when the addresses in argv[] are inserted into the cout stream in Program 17.3, the strings pointed to by these addresses are displayed. As mentioned previously, this occurs because cout automatically dereferences these addresses and performs the required indirection to locate the actual string that is displayed.

One final comment about command line arguments is in order. Any argument typed on a command line is considered to be a string. If you want numerical data passed to main(), you must convert the passed string into its numerical counterpart. This is seldom an issue, however, since most command line arguments are used as flags to pass appropriate processing control signals to an invoked program.

Exercises 17.3

1. Enter and execute Program 17.3 on your computer.

2. Write a program that accepts two integer values as command line arguments. The program should multiply the two values entered and display the result. (*Hint:* The command line must be accepted as string data and converted to numerical values before multiplication.)

17.4 WRITING AND READING BINARY FILES[2]

An alternative to a text file, where each character in the file is represented by a unique code, is a binary file. Although, at a basic level, all files are stored using binary numbers, files that are referred to as **binary files** store numerical values using the computer's internal numerical code. For example, assuming that your C++ compiler stores integers using 32 bits (4 bytes), the integer numbers 125 and −125 are represented as listed in Table 17.2.

TABLE 17.2   Binary and Hexadecimal Representations of Integer Numbers

Integer	Binary Representation	Hexadecimal Equivalent
125	0000 0000 0000 0000 0000 0000 0111 1101	0x00 00 00 7D
−125	1111 1111 1111 1111 1111 1111 1000 0010	0xFF FF FF 83

Because a binary file's storage codes match the computer's internal storage codes, no intermediary conversions are required for storing or retrieving the data. This means that there is no number-to-character conversion required when writing a number to a file and no character-to-number conversion required when a value is read from the file. For files consisting predominantly of numerical data, this is a

---

[2] This topic requires familiarity with the computer storage concepts presented in Section 1.6.

distinct advantage and can improve program efficiency. The resulting file frequently requires less storage space that its character-based counterpart. The disadvantage is that the file can no longer be inspected using either a word processing or text editing program, which means that the ability to see the numerical values as textual information is lost. In this section, the creation of a binary file is presented first, followed by a number of examples for reading such a file.

The specification for explicitly creating and writing to a binary file is made using the `ios::binary` mode indicator when the file is opened. Table 17.3 provides a complete list of file mode indicators.

TABLE 17.3   File Mode Indicators

Indicator	Description
ios::in	Open a text file in input mode.
ios::out	Open a text file in output mode.
ios::app	Open a text file in append mode.
ios::ate	Go to the end of the opened file.
ios::binary	Open a binary file (default is text file).
ios::trunc	Delete file contents if it exists.
ios::nocreate	If file does not exist, open fails.
ios::noreplace	If file exists, open for output fails.

For example, the following two statements can be used to open a binary file named `prices.bin` using an output stream named `outFile`:

```
ofstream outFile;
outFile.open("prices.bin", ios::binary);
```

Alternatively, these two statements can be combined into the single statement:

```
ofstream outFile("prices.bin", ios::binary);
```

As with text files, an output stream for a binary file creates a new file and makes the file available for writing. If a file exists with the same name as a file opened for output, the old file is erased. For example, assuming that `outFile` has been declared as an object of type `ofstream` using the statement

```
ofstream outFile;
```

then the statement

```
outFile.open("prices.bin", ios::binary);
```

opens the file named `prices.bin` for output.

An `ofstream` binary file object opened in `ios::app` mode means that an existing file will be made available for data to be added to the end of the file. If the file opened for appending does not exist, a new file with the designated name is created and made available to receive output from the program. For example, again assuming that `outFile` has been declared to be of type `ofstream`, the statement

```
outFile.open("prices.bin",ios::app | ios::binary);
```

opens a binary file named `prices.bin` and makes it available for data to be appended to the end of the file. Notice that the mode indicators listed in Table 17.3 are combined using the bit operator, | (see Section 17.2).

Finally, an `ifstream` object opened in input mode means that an existing external file has been connected and its data is available as input. For example, assuming that `inFile` has been declared to be of type `ifstream`, the statement

```
inFile.open("prices.bin",ios::binary);
```

attempts to open a file named `prices.bin` for input.

Once opened, the actual writing of data to a binary file takes a rather simple, but convoluted form. Program 17.4 illustrates the required procedure after the file is correctly opened as an output binary file.

In reviewing Program 17.4, first notice that the file name has been designated as a string object at the top of the `main()` function in the same manner as was done for text files. Next, notice that the open statement is also identical to that for a text file, with the addition of the mode indicator specifying that the file is to be a binary file.

Finally, concentrate on the three highlighted statements used to write data to the file. Notice that all of these statements use the syntax:

```
fileObject.write( (const char *) &variable, sizeof(variable));
```

In this syntax the first `write()` method argument is always the expression `(const char *)`, which is followed by the address operator, `&`, and a variable name. The second argument uses the `sizeof()` operator to determine the number of bytes to be written. Although this notation requires an understanding of pointers, you can still make some sense of it and use it as given. The `&` means "the address of" the following variable, and the expression in parentheses represents a cast operation. In effect, the address of each variable is cast into a pointer to a character constant. The second argument, which uses the `sizeof()` operator, specifies the number of bytes to be written to the file. Thus, starting from the first byte stored in the variable, which is provided by the first argument, the exact number of bytes in each variable is then written to the file. This places the internal binary code for each variable, byte-by-byte, into the file.

FIGURE 17.13   The Stored Binary Data in the `prices.bin` File and Their Decimal Equivalents

```
                        |00 00 00 7D| <--- corresponds to   125
                        |FF FF FF 83| <--- corresponds to  -125
            |3F F1 47 AE 14 7A E1 48| <--- corresponds to   1.08
```

The binary file created by Program 17.4 is illustrated in Figure 17.13, which uses hexadecimal values to indicate the equivalent binary values. The specific bit patterns for the two integers can be converted to decimal notation using a hexadecimal to decimal conversion. This can be accomplished by first converting each

PROGRAM 17.4

```cpp
#include <iostream>
#include <fstream>
#include <cstdlib>   // needed for exit()
#include <string>
#include <cctype>
using namespace std;

int main()
{
  string filename = "prices.bin";  // put the filename up front
  ofstream outFile;
  ifstream inFile;

  int num1 = 125;
  long num2 = -125;
  double num3 = 1.08;

  char response;

  // check that a file by the given name does not already exist
  inFile.open(filename.c_str());
  if (!inFile.fail())
  {
    cout << "A file by the name " << filename <<  " exists.\n"
         << "Do you want to overwrite it with the new data (y or n): ";
      cin >> response;
      if (tolower(response) == 'n')
      {
        cout << "The existing file will not be overwritten." << endl;
        exit(1);  //terminate program execution
      }
      inFile.close();
  }

  // okay to proceed
  outFile.open(filename.c_str(), ios::binary);;
  if (outFile.fail())
  {
    cout << "The file was not successfully opened" << endl;
    exit(1);
  }

  // send data to the file
   outFile.write((const char *) &num1, sizeof(num1));
   outFile.write((const char *) &num2, sizeof(num2));
   outFile.write((const char *) &num3, sizeof(num3));

  outFile.close();
  cout << "The file " << filename
       << "has been successfully written." << endl;

  return 0;
}
```

hexadecimal digit to its binary form using the conversions provided in Table 17.4, and then using the two's complement value box presented in Section 1.6 to convert from binary to decimal (direct conversion from hexadecimal to decimal can also be used).

TABLE 17.4 Hexadecimal Digits to Binary Conversions

Hexadecimal Digit	Binary Equivalent
0	0000
1	0001
2	0010
3	0011
4	0100
5	0101
6	0110
7	0111
8	1000
9	1001
A	1010
B	1011
C	1100
D	1101
F	1110
F	1111

Converting a floating-point number requires using the real number storage specification presented in Appendix D. Although the figure separates the file's data into three individual lines, with bars, |, used to distinguish individual items, in actuality the file is stored as a consecutive sequence of bytes. As indicated in the figure, each integer value consists of 4 bytes, and the double-precision number is 8 bytes. Reading a binary file, similar to the one illustrated in Figure 17.13, requires constructing an input binary stream and then using appropriate input methods.

Program 17.5 illustrates the opening of a binary input stream object, the input of the data stored in the file created in Program 17.4, and the display of this data. Because the construction of the input stream objects should be familiar, you have used the single file declaration syntax for creating and opening the input stream object named `inFile`. In reviewing the actual input of the data, notice that the individual data items are read in almost the identical manner in which they were written. Again, although cryptic, the usage is direct. Although the input values are displayed directly, the input values, in a more typical application, would be assigned to double-precision variables for further numerical processing.

PROGRAM 17.5

```cpp
#include <iostream>
#include <fstream>
#include <cstdlib>    // needed for exit()
#include <string>
using namespace std;

int main()
{
  string filename = "prices.bin";  // put the filename up front

  int num1;
  long num2;
  double num3;

  ifstream inFile(filename.c_str(), ios::binary);
  if (inFile.fail())
  {
    cout << "The file was not successfully opened" << endl;
    exit(1);
  }

  // read data from the file
  inFile.read((char *) &num1, sizeof(num1));
  inFile.read((char *) &num2, sizeof(num2));
  inFile.read((char *) &num3, sizeof(num3));

  inFile.close();
  cout << "The data input from the " << filename << " file is:  "
       << num1 << "   " << num2 << "   " << num3 << endl;

  return 0;
}
```

The output produced by Program 17.5 is:

```
The data input from the prices.bin file is: 125 -125 1.08
```

Exercises 17.4

1. Enter and execute Program 17.4. Once the `prices.bin` file has been written, execute Program 17.4 a second time to verify that it does not overwrite the existing file without your permission.

2. Enter and execute Program 17.5 on your computer.

3. Write, compile, and run a C++ program that writes the numbers 92.65, 88.72, 77.46, and 82.93 as double-precision values to a binary file named `results.dat`. After writing the data to the file, the program should read the data from the file, determine the average of the four numbers read, and display the average. Verify the output produced by the program by manually calculating the average of the four input numbers.

4. a. Write, compile, and execute a C++ program that creates a binary file named `points` and writes the following numbers to the file:

```
6.3   8.2  18.25  24.32
4.0   4.0  10.0   -5.0
-2.0  5.0   4.0    5.0
```

   b. Using the data in the `points` file created in Exercise 4a, write, compile, and run a C++ program that reads four numbers using a `for` loop and interprets the first and second numbers in each record as the coordinates of one point and the third and fourth numbers as the coordinates of a second point. Have the program compute and display the slope and midpoint of each pair of entered points.

5. a. Write, compile, and run a C++ program that creates a binary file named `grades.bin` and writes the following five lines of data to the file:

```
90.3   92.7   90.3   99.8

85.3   90.5   87.3   90.8

93.2   88.4   93.8   75.6

82.4   95.6   78.2   90.0

93.5   80.2   92.9   94.4
```

   b. Using the data in the `grades.bin` file created in Exercise 5a, write, compile, and run a C++ program that reads, computes, and displays the average of each group of four grades.

17.5 COMMON PROGRAMMING ERRORS

The common programming errors associated with the topics covered in this chapter are:

1. Using the bit operators `&` and `|` in place of the logical operators `&&` and `||`. Although using the bit operators will work, their appearance forces evaluation of all operands; whereas the logical operators use a short-circuited evaluation that stops at the first operand that either satisfies the OR operation or disqualifies the AND operation from being true.

2. Attempting to use the command line arguments as members of the `string` class rather than C-strings.

3. Not using the `(const char *)` cast and specifying the number of bytes to be written when writing a binary file.

4. Not using the `(char *)` cast and specifying the number of bytes to be read when reading a binary file.

17.6 CHAPTER REVIEW

Key Terms

AND operator (`&`)	exclusive OR operator (`^`)
binary file	inclusive OR operator (`|`)
bit-by-bit operators	left shift operator (`<`)
command line	mask
command line argument	right shift operator (`>`)
conditional expression	ternary operator
conditional operator (`?:`)	typedef
enum	

Summary

1. A `typedef` declaration statement allows you to construct alternate names for an existing C++ data type name.

2. An `enum` (enumerated) data type is a user-defined data type consisting of a list of constants. Each constant corresponds, by default, to an integer value.

3. A conditional expression provides an alternate way of expressing a simple `if-else` statement. The general form of a conditional expression is:

```
condition ? expression1 : expression2
```

The equivalent `if-else` statement for this is:

```
if (condition)
    expression1;
else
    expression2;
```

4. Individual bits of character and integer variables and constants can be manipulated using C++'s bit operators. Bit operators include the AND, inclusive OR, exclusive OR, one's complement, left shift, and right shift operators.

5. The bit operators AND and inclusive OR operators are useful in creating masks. These masks can be used to pass or eliminate individual bits from the selected operand. The exclusive OR operator is useful in complementing an operand's bits.

6. When the bit operators AND and OR operators are used with operands of different sizes, the shorter operand is always increased in bit size to match the size of the larger operand.

7. The shift operators produce different results depending on whether the operand is a signed or an unsigned value.

8. The `main()` function can accept arguments. The arguments supplied to the `main()` function are referred to as command line arguments.

9. A binary file is a file that stores numerical values using the computer's internal numerical code.

Exercises

1. Write a C++ program that displays the first eight bits of each character value input into a variable named `ch`. (*Hint:* Assuming each character is stored using eight bits, start by using the hexadecimal mask 80, which corresponds to the binary number 10000000. If the result of the masking operation is a zero, display a zero; else display a one. Then shift the mask one place to the right to examine the next bit, and so on until all bits in the variable `ch` have been processed.)

2. Write a C++ program that reverses the bits in an integer variable named `okay` and stores the reversed bits in the variable named `reversed`. For example, if the bit pattern 11100101, corresponding to the octal number 0345, is assigned to `okay`, the bit pattern 10100111, corresponding to the octal number 0247, should be produced and stored in `reversed`.

3. Write a program that accepts the name of a data file as a command line argument. Have the program open the data file and display its contents, line by line, on the screen.

4. Would the program written for Exercise 3 work correctly for a program file?

5. Modify the program written for Exercise 3 so that each line displayed is preceded by a line number.

6. a. Create a binary file containing the following car numbers, number of miles driven, and number of gallons of gas used by each car (do not include the headings):

Car No.	Miles Driven	Gallons Used
54	250	19
62	525	38
71	123	6
85	1,322	86
97	235	14

   b. Write a C++ program that reads the data in the file created in Exercise 6a and displays the car number, miles driven, gallons used, and the miles per gallon for each car. The output should also contain the total miles driven, total gallons used, and average miles per gallon for all the cars. These totals should be displayed at the end of the output report.

7. a. A binary file named `polar.dat` contains the polar coordinates needed in a graphics program. Currently, this file contains the following data:

DISTANCE (INCHES)	ANGLE (DEGREES)
2.0	45.0
6.0	30.0
10.0	45.0
4.0	60.0
13.0	55.0
8.0	15.0

   Write a C++ program to create the data in this file (do not store the headings) on your computer system (without the header lines).

   b. Using the `polar.dat` file created in Exercise 7a, write a C++ program that reads this file and creates a second binary file named `xycord.dat`. The entries in the new file should contain the rectangular coordinates corresponding to the polar coordinates in the `polar.dat` file. Polar coordinates can be converted to rectangular coordinates using the equations

$$x = r \cos\theta$$

$$y = r \sin\theta$$

   where r is the distance coordinate and θ is the radian equivalent of the angle coordinate in the `polar.dat` file.

8. Write and test a C++ function named `getyn()` that returns either the character value 'y' or 'n' depending on the user's input. If the user enters either 'n', 'N', or any upper or lowercase version of no, including leading and trailing blanks, the function should return 'n'. Similarly, if the user enters 'y', 'Y', or any upper or lowercase version of yes, including leading and trailing blanks, the function should return a 'y'. The function should also continuously request input until it can return either 'n' or 'y'.

P A R T

IV

Appendices

A Operator Precedence Table

Table A.1 presents the symbols, precedence, descriptions, and associativity of C++'s operators. Operators toward the top of the table have a higher precedence than those toward the bottom. Operators within the same box have the same precedence and associativity.

TABLE A.1 Summary of C++ Operators

Operator	Description	Associativity
`()`	Function call	Left to right
`[]`	Array element	
`->`	Structure member pointer reference	
`.`	Structure member reference	
`++`	Increment	Right to left
`--`	Decrement	
`-`	Unary minus	
`!`	Logical negation	
`~`	One's complement	
`(type)`	Type conversion (cast)	
`size of`	Storage size	
`&`	Address of	
`*`	Indirection	
`*`	Multiplication	Left to right
`/`	Division	
`%`	Modulus (remainder)	
`+`	Addition	Left to right
`-`	Subtraction	
`<<`	Left shift	Left to right
`>>`	Right shift	
`<`	Less than	Left to right
`<=`	Less than or equal to	
`>`	Greater than	
`>=`	Greater than or equal to	
`==`	Equal to	Left to right
`!=`	Not equal to	
`&`	a Command Prompt Window	Left to right
`^`	Bitwise exclusive OR	Left to right
`|`	Bitwise inclusive OR	Left to right
`&&`	Logical AND	Left to right
`||`	Logical OR	Left to right
`?:`	Conditional expression	Right to left
`=`	Assignment	Right to left
`+=` `-=` `*=`	Assignment	
`/=` `%=` `&=`	Assignment	
`^=` `|=`	Assignment	
`<<=` `>>=`	Assignment	
`,`	Comma	Left to right

B ASCII Character Codes

Key(s)	Dec	Oct	Hex	Key	Dec	Oct	Hex	Key	Dec	Oct	Hex
Ctrl 1	0	0	0	+	43	53	2B	V	86	126	56
Ctrl A	1	1	1	,	44	54	2C	W	87	127	57
Ctrl B	2	2	2	-	45	55	2D	X	88	130	58
Ctrl C	3	3	3	.	46	56	2E	Y	89	131	59
Ctrl D	4	4	4	/	47	57	2F	Z	90	132	5A
Ctrl E	5	5	5	0	48	60	30	[	91	133	5B
Ctrl F	6	6	6	1	49	61	31	\	92	134	5C
Ctrl G	7	7	7	2	50	62	32	]	93	135	5D
Ctrl H	8	10	8	3	51	63	33	^	94	136	5E
Ctrl I	9	11	9	4	52	64	34	_	95	137	5F
Ctrl J	10	12	A	5	53	65	35	`	96	140	60
Ctrl K	11	13	B	6	54	66	36	a	97	141	61
Ctrl L	12	14	C	7	55	67	37	b	98	142	62
Return	13	15	D	8	56	70	38	c	99	143	63
Ctrl N	14	16	E	9	57	71	39	d	100	144	64
Ctrl O	15	17	F	:	58	72	3A	e	101	145	65
Ctrl P	16	20	10	;	59	73	3B	f	102	146	66
Ctrl Q	17	21	11	<	60	74	3C	g	103	147	67
Ctrl R	18	22	12	=	61	75	3D	h	104	150	68
Ctrl S	19	23	13	>	62	76	3E	i	105	151	69
Ctrl T	20	24	14	?	63	77	3F	j	106	152	6A
Ctrl U	21	25	15	@	64	100	40	k	107	153	6B
Ctrl V	22	26	16	A	65	101	41	l	108	154	6C
Ctrl W	23	27	17	B	66	102	42	m	109	155	6D
Ctrl X	24	30	18	C	67	103	43	n	110	156	6E
Ctrl Y	25	31	19	D	68	104	44	o	111	157	6F
Ctrl Z	26	32	1A	E	69	105	45	p	112	160	70
Esc	27	33	1B	F	70	106	46	q	113	161	71
Ctrl <	28	34	1C	G	71	107	47	r	114	162	72
Ctrl /	29	35	1D	H	72	110	48	s	115	163	73
Ctrl =	30	36	1E	I	73	111	49	t	116	164	74
Ctrl -	31	37	1F	J	74	112	4A	u	117	165	75
Space	32	40	20	K	75	113	4B	v	118	166	76
!	33	41	21	L	76	114	4C	w	119	167	77
"	34	42	22	M	77	115	4D	x	120	170	78
#	35	43	23	N	78	116	4E	y	121	171	79
$	36	44	24	O	79	117	4F	z	122	172	7A
%	37	45	25	P	80	120	50	{	123	173	7B
&	38	46	26	Q	81	121	51			124	174	7C
'	39	47	27	R	82	122	52	}	125	175	7D
(	40	50	28	S	83	123	53	~	126	176	7E
)	41	51	29	T	84	124	54	del	127	177	7F
*	42	52	2A	U	85	125	55				

C Input, Output, and Standard Error Redirection

The display produced by the cout object is normally sent to the terminal where you are working. This terminal is called the standard output device because it is where the display is automatically directed, in a standard fashion, by the interface between your C++ program and your computer's operating system.

On most systems it is possible to redirect the output produced by cout to some other device, or to a file, using the output redirection symbol, >, at the time the program is invoked. In addition to the symbol, you must specify where you want the displayed results to be sent.

For purposes of illustration, assume that the command to execute a compiled program named salestax, without redirection, is:

```
salestax
```

This command is entered after your computer's system prompt is displayed on your terminal. When the salestax program is run, any cout object activated within it automatically causes the appropriate display to be sent to your terminal. Suppose we would like to have the display produced by the program sent to a file named results. To do this requires the command:

```
salestax > results
```

The redirection symbol, >, tells the operating system to send any display produced by cout directly to a file named results rather than to the standard output device used by the system. The display sent to results can then be examined by either using an editor program or issuing another operating system command. For example, under the UNIX operating system, the command

```
cat results
```

causes the contents of the file results to be displayed on your terminal. The equivalent command under a Command Prompt window is:

```
type results
```

In redirecting an output display to a file, the following rules apply:

1. If the file does not exist, it will be created.
2. If the file exists, it will be overwritten with the new display.

In addition to the output redirection symbol, the output append symbol, >>, can also be used. The append symbol is used in the same manner as the redirection symbol, but causes any new output to be added to the end of a file. For example, the command

```
salestax >> results
```

causes any output produced by `salestax` to be added to the end of the `results` file. If the `results` file does not exist, it will be created.

In addition to having the display produced by `cout` redirected to a file, using the > or >> symbols, the display can also be sent to a physical device connected to your computer, such as a printer. You must, however, know the name used by your computer for accessing the desired device. For example, on an IBM PC or compatible computer, the name of the printer connected to the terminal is designated as `prn` and on a UNIX system it is typically `lpr`. Thus, if you are working on an IBM or compatible machine, the command

```
salestax > prn
```

causes the display produced in the `salestax` program to be sent directly to the printer connected to the terminal.

Corresponding to output redirection, it is also possible to redesignate the standard input device for an individual program run using the input redirection symbol, <. Again, the new source for input must be specified immediately after the input redirection symbol.

Input redirection works in a similar fashion to output redirection, but affects the source of input for the `cin` stream. For example, the command

```
salestax < dataIn
```

causes any input functions within `salestax` that normally receive their input from the keyboard to receive it from the `dataIn` file instead. This input redirection, like its output counterpart, is only in effect for the current execution of the program. As you might expect, the same run can have both an input and output redirection. For example, the command

```
salestax < dataIn > results
```

causes an input redirection from the file `dataIn` and an output redirection to the file `results`.

In addition to standard input and output redirection, the device to which all error messages are sent can also be redirected. On many systems this file is given an operating system designation as device file 2. Thus, the redirection

```
2> err
```

causes any error messages that would normally be displayed on the standard error device, which is usually your terminal, to be redirected to a file named `err`. As with standard input and output redirection, standard error redirection can be included on the same command line used to invoke a program. For example, the command

```
salestax < dataIn > show 2> err
```

causes the compiled program named `salestax` to receive its standard input from a file named `dataIn`, write its results to a file named `show`, and send any error messages to a file named `err`.

Because the redirection of input, output, and error messages is generally a feature of the operating system used by your computer and not typically part of your C++ compiler, you must check the manuals for your particular operating system to ensure that these features are available.

D Floating-Point Number Storage

The two's complement binary code used to store integer values was presented in Section 1.6. In this appendix we present the binary storage format typically used in C++ to store single-precision and double-precision numbers, which are stored as floats and doubles, respectively. Collectively, both single- and double-precision values are commonly referred to as floating-point values.

Like their decimal number counterparts that use a decimal point to separate the integer and fractional parts of a number, floating-point numbers are represented in a conventional binary format with a binary point. For example, consider the binary number 1011.11. The digits to the left of the binary point (1011) represent the integer part of the number, and the digits to the right of the binary point (11) represent the fractional part.

To store a floating-point binary number, a code similar to decimal scientific notation is used. To obtain this code the conventional binary number format is separated into a mantissa and an exponent. The following examples illustrate floating-point numbers expressed in this scientific notation.

Conventional Binary Notation	Binary Scientific Notation
1010.0	1.01 exp 011
−10001.0	−1.0001 exp 100
0.001101	1.101 exp −011
−0.000101	−1.01 exp −100

In binary scientific notation, the term "exp" stands for "exponent." The binary number in front of the exp term is the mantissa and the binary number following the exp term is the exponent value. Except for the number zero, the mantissa always has a single leading 1 followed immediately by a binary point. The exponent represents a power of 2 and indicates the number of places the binary point should be moved in the mantissa to obtain the conventional binary notation. If the exponent is positive, the binary point is moved to the right. If the exponent is negative, the binary point is moved to the left. For example, the exponent 011 in the number

$$1.01 \text{ exp } 011$$

means move the binary point three places to the right, so that the number becomes 1010. The −011 exponent in the number

$$1.101 \text{ exp } -011$$

means move the binary point three places to the left, so that the number becomes:

$$.001101$$

TABLE D.1 IEEE Standard 754-1985 Floating-Point Specification

data format	sign bits	mantissa bits	exponent bits
Single-precision	1	23	8
Double-precision	1	52	11
Extended-precision	1	64	15

In storing floating-point numbers, the sign, mantissa, and exponent are stored individually within separate fields. The number of bits used for each field determines the precision of the number. Single-precision (32 bit), double-precision (64 bit), and extended-precision (80 bit) floating-point data formats are defined by the Institute of Electrical and Electronics Engineers (IEEE) Standard 754-1985 to have the characteristics given in Table D.1. The format for a single-precision, floating-point number is illustrated in Figure D.1.

FIGURE D.1 Single-Precision Floating-Point Number Storage Format

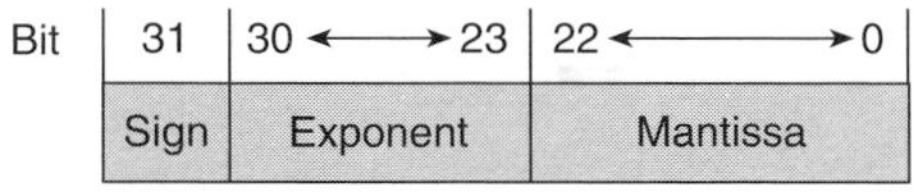

The sign bit shown in Figure D.1 refers to the sign of the mantissa. A sign bit of 1 represents a negative number, and a 0 sign bit represents a positive value. Since all mantissas, except for the number zero, have a leading 1 followed by their binary points, these two items are never stored explicitly. The binary point implicitly resides immediately to the left of mantissa bit 22, and a leading 1 is always assumed. The binary number zero is specified by setting all mantissa and exponent bits to 0. For this case only, the implied leading mantissa bit is also 0.

The exponent field contains an exponent that is biased by 127. For example, an exponent of 5 would be stored using the binary equivalent of the number 132 (127 + 5). Using eight exponent bits, this is coded as 100000100. The addition of 127 to each exponent allows negative exponents to be coded within the exponent field without the need for an explicit sign bit. For example, the exponent −011, which corresponds to −3, would be stored using the binary equivalent of +124 (127 − 3).

Figure D.2 illustrates the encoding and storage of the decimal number 59.75 as a 64-bit single-precision binary number.

FIGURE D.2 The Encoding and Storage of the Decimal Number 59.75

The sign, exponent, and mantissa are determined as follows. The conventional binary equivalent of

$$-59.75$$

is:

$$-111011.11$$

Expressed in binary scientific notation this becomes:

$$-1.1101111 \text{ exp } 101$$

The minus sign is signified by setting the sign bit to 1. The mantissa's leading 1 and binary point are omitted, and the 23-bit mantissa field is encoded as:

$$11011110000000000000000$$

The exponent field encoding is obtained by adding the exponent value of 101 to 1111111, which is the binary equivalent of the 127_{10} bias value:

$$1\,1\,1\,1\,1\,1\,1 \;=\; 127_{10}$$

$$+\;1\,0\,1 \;=\; 5_{10}$$

$$1\,0\,0\,0\,0\,1\,0\,0 \;=\; 132_{10}$$

Index